The Long
Nineteenth Century

The Long Nineteenth Century

A History of Germany, 1780–1918

DAVID BLACKBOURN

New York   Oxford
OXFORD UNIVERSITY PRESS
1998

WINGATE UNIVERSITY LIBRARY

Oxford University Press

Oxford   New York

Athens   Auckland   Bangkok   Bogota   Bombay
Buenos Aires   Calcutta   Cape Town   Dar es Salaam
Delhi   Florence   Hong Kong   Istanbul   Karachi
Kuala Lumpur   Madras   Madrid   Melbourne
Mexico City   Nairobi   Paris   Singapore
Taipei   Tokyo   Toronto   Warsaw

and associated companies in
Berlin   Ibadan

Copyright © 1997 by David Blackbourn

Maps by Leslie Robinson

Originally published in Great Britain in 1997 by Fontana Press,
an imprint of HarperCollins Publishers

First published in the United States in 1998 by Oxford University Press, Inc.
198 Madison Avenue, New York, New York 10016

Oxford is a registered trademark of Oxford University Press

All rights reserved. No part of this publication may be reproduced,
stored in a retrieval system, or transmitted, in any form or by any means,
electronic, mechanical, photocopying, recording, or otherwise,
without the prior permission of Oxford University Press.

Library of Congress Cataloging-in-Publication Data
Blackbourn, David, 1949–
[Fontana history of Germany, 1780–1918]
The long nineteenth century: a history of Germany, 1780–1918/
David Blackbourn.
p.   cm.
Originally published in Great Britain in 1997 by Fontana Press
under the title: Fontana history of Germany, 1780–1918.
ISBN 0-19-507671-0 (alk. paper)—
ISBN 0-19-507672-9 (pbk.: alk. paper)
1. Germany—History—1789–1900.
2. Germany—History—1871–1918.
3. Germany—Intellectual life—19th century.
4. Germany—Social conditions—19th century.
5. Germany—Social conditions—1871–1918.   I. Title.
DD203.B59   1998   943'.07—dc21   97-29535

1 3 5 7 9 10 8 6 4 2

Printed in the United States of America
on acid-free paper

For Jack Plumb

CONTENTS

MAPS

TABLES AND FIGURES

LIST OF PLATES

PREFACE

In 1807 the great theorist of modern war, Carl von Clausewitz, wrote an article called 'The Germans and the French' in which he compared the two nations. One was militaristic, and the subject-mentality of its people doomed them to political 'obedience'; the other had a more literary bent, and its hypercritical inhabitants would be unlikely to submit to tyranny.[1] The obedient militarists were, of course, the French, the critically minded literary types the Germans. So much for 'national character'. Clausewitz's judgment was no doubt affected by his recent experiences as a French prisoner of war. But his was not an exceptional contemporary view, or a peculiarly German one. For another sixty years, many in Britain still saw France as the archetype of a bureaucratic police society and militarist power. Germany, on the other hand, long enjoyed a reputation as a quaint, half-timbered land – and a country whose industrial goods were still regarded, even in the 1870s, as cheap and nasty. Times change, and so do clichés. The book that follows will try to show why new political, cultural and economic stereotypes of the Germans arose in the course of the nineteenth century. It will also suggest that some of those stereotypes need to be viewed with scepticism.

This is a book about Germany in the 'long nineteenth century'. The term is widely used by European historians to describe the period between the 'double revolution' of the late eighteenth century (the French Revolution of 1789, the Industrial Revolution in Britain) and the First World War. The French Revolution and the armies it spawned destroyed the centuries-old Holy Roman Empire of the German Nation. German-speaking Central Europe was reshaped, on the map and internally. True, Germany was no political backwater in the late eighteenth century: modern research has demonstrated that. But the ideas and institutions of the French Revolution – revolution itself, citizenship, the sovereign state, nationalism – did create a new grammar of politics. In Germany, as in other parts of Europe, the nineteenth century was a period of coming to terms with that legacy – accepting, adapting, or rejecting it.

The case for the Industrial Revolution as a starting point raises more questions. Historians are generally less willing now than they once were to accept a big-bang theory of industrialization, and more likely to propose a later date for the emergence of industrial economies. But there are still at least two good reasons to begin this account in the late eighteenth century. That was when the forces driving the process of economic change in Germany first made themselves felt: a sharp population increase, more commercialized agriculture, expanded manufacturing for the market. Furthermore, even if we drop the 'revolution' tag, industrial transformation must be a major theme in any history of nineteenth-century Germany; and Germans themselves were very aware even in the 1780s that Britain was the pioneer, hence the efforts to attract inventors and copy machinery. In the early chapters of this book we find Germans seeking to emulate and catch up; by the end of the nineteenth century Germany had overtaken Britain in key areas of industry, with consequences that were not just economic.

There is a final reason to begin this account in the late eighteenth century. It concerns not politics or economics, but culture. The Enlightenment and its critics offered a dress-rehearsal of arguments that would run through the nineteenth century: about the past, about nature, about religion, about progress. The late eighteenth century also saw the beginning of one of the most important developments described in this book. Growing numbers of books, newspapers and clubs began to stitch together a reading public, even something that could be described as public opinion. The self-conscious literary and philosophical debates of these years did something else. They sounded the idea that Germany was the 'land of poets and thinkers'. A major strand in the cultural history of the nineteenth century consisted of the debate between Germans who wanted to throw off this reputation, and those who insisted that it described a special

German virtue. When the German intelligentsia went to war in 1914, it was the supposedly superior depth of German culture that it brandished against the enemy.

If there are grounds for argument about where a history of nineteenth-century Germany should begin, few are likely to disagree that it should end with the First World War. There were certainly continuities even across the great divide of 1914–18, but there is a powerful case for seeing these years as a watershed. More than one and a half million Germans were among the 10 million killed in the conflict, not counting the millions more who died of malnutrition and the influenza epidemic that arrived with the end of hostilities. Total war magnified every strain and tension in prewar Germany: social, generational, political. It led to revolution, and left its mark on everything from painting and literature to the subsequent era of mechanized human destruction in which Germany played such a large part. The Great War ripped the fabric of society for those who lived through it. Eighty years later it continues to stand out as a turning point in modern history, the first great catastrophe of our century, from which so much else flowed.

That is the 'When' – the long nineteenth century of the title. The 'Where' – Germany – may seem more obvious, but is not. In 1797 the writers Goethe and Schiller posed a famous question: 'Germany? But where is it? I don't know how to find such a country.'[2] The difficulty begins at the most basic level, with lines drawn in the ground, or borders. The Holy Roman Empire, still in existence when Goethe and Schiller wrote (but only just), was not a territorial state in the modern sense. It consisted of hundreds of separate entities, whose inhabitants owed loyalty to an even larger number of people – not just local rulers, but church, guild and feudal lord. In so far as there were clear territorial boundaries in the Empire, they divided it internally as much as they defined it externally. That is the point at which this book begins.

The nineteenth century gave a series of answers to the question asked by Goethe and Schiller. Napoleon's success on the battlefield simplified German geography. It turned hundreds of

separate states into mere dozens, and gave those states a stronger
sense of their own borders. Two of them, Austria and Prussia,
already rivals in the eighteenth century, now pursued their interests within the German Confederation that replaced the Holy
Roman Empire. What contemporaries increasingly called the
German Question was posed again in 1848–9 against a background of revolution and nationalist demands. But the revolution produced no German nation-state, and its defeat restored
the loose Confederation. It was Bismarck and the Prussian army
which provided the decisive nineteenth-century answer to the
question 'where is Germany?', by defeating Austria in 1866 and
paving the way for the German Empire established in 1871.
Nationalist historians writing at the time not only lionized Bismarck and his achievement. They projected Prussia's 'German
mission' back into the past, making the form taken by German
unification seem natural and inevitable. It was neither. Austria
remained a major actor in German history until 1866. Together
with other states like Saxony and Bavaria, Austria was proposing
alternative arrangements right up to the moment when the German Question was answered on the battlefield – an engagement
that was no foregone conclusion, and one which pitted Prussia
against every other major German state. What we call the unification of Germany was actually a partition. Austrian history is
therefore treated in this book as a part of German history until
1866.

Unification meant that there was now a Germany on the map
as well as a Germany in the head. This had paradoxical results.
On the one hand, the characteristic nineteenth-century process
of state-building worked after 1871 to create Germans, rather
than Prussians, or Bavarians, or Saxons. A common flag, anthem
and currency fostered German identity within the boundaries
of the new nation-state, even if other identities – religious,
regional, dynastic – did not disappear. On the other hand, German national sentiment could not be neatly contained within the
particular form of 'Lesser Germany' established under Bismarck.
Before that time, many nationalists had found it hard to envisage
a future German nation that would not include Austrians who

spoke the same tongue. Afterwards, the rise of hypernationalism in the late nineteenth century threatened to spill over the boundaries of 1871. If Germany was defined in terms of language, culture or even race, how could it end at the borders created by Bismarck? Should it not include Germans in Austria, in White Russia, in the Americas and the African colonies? Arguments of this kind extended beyond the lunatic fringe of the Pan-German League. A new nationality law in 1913 emphasized the importance of ethnic German bloodlines over place of birth. There were enormous implications in all this for the twentieth century. For the purposes of the present book, it means that any history of Germany in the age of mass migration and imperialist thinking has to include some consideration of 'Germany abroad', from Marienbad to Milwaukee.

So much for the chronological and geographical bearings of the book. But what *kind* of history can readers expect? History is an intrinsically wide-ranging subject: every aspect of human life is potentially grist to its mill. It is also a generous discipline, in the sense that almost no approach is ever 'falsified' or completely discarded. (Even work done by conformist historians in the Third Reich – on peasant society and on settlement patterns, for example – turned out to have permanent value independent of the racialist nonsense that originally brought it into being.) History, then, is capacious, and becoming more so as newer approaches demand attention. Its practitioners, invoking the muse of history, sometimes refer rather pompously to 'Clio's many mansions'. Perhaps we should imagine instead a large hotel, where new guests constantly check in but old residents are never asked to leave. This particular hotel is in Germany – but it might be anywhere. The diplomatic and military historians are among the oldest residents, although they have recently been joined by some young bloods. Mostly they ignore the other guests, although they have been known to mutter when they overhear the words social science. Experts on the press and historians of elections, on the other hand, get on well together. So do the many subspecies of social historians, although the transport specialists sometimes gather among themselves to talk about counterfactual conditional analysis, and the historians of housing have an irritating habit of tapping the walls and flourishing their damp-meters. It is hard to know who is more disturbed by this – the historians of ideas gathered in the reading room, or the psychohistorians interrupted at their habit of peering through keyholes at the other guests. Not all the residents are what you might expect. The historians of crime and violence are always genial; and the same applies to those who devote themselves entirely to the history of army barracks. But you would be unlikely to confuse either group with the cultural history set, who are younger, more brightly dressed, and can often be found standing around the lobby talking about webs of signification. It is worth adding that none of these, or the scores of other subgroups who inhabit the Hotel History, ever have cause to complain about the standards of catering – the historians of food and drink see to that.

The Hotel History, it should be clear, is a stimulating place to visit. The problem is that no one can get the residents to agree on what they are doing: they seem to speak different languages. And the problem with writing a general history of Germany – or anywhere else – is the same. Fragmentation and subspecialisms have eroded any common understanding of what history is, or ought to be. On the one hand, the experts go their own way and some historians influenced by postmodernism argue that there can be no more 'grand narratives'. On the other hand, there is a trend among those who *have* written general histories to try to put everything in, with predictable effects on the size of their offerings. Two rightly heralded recent histories of nineteenth-century Germany both take three volumes and several thousand pages to complete the task.[3] The book that follows is more modest in scale. It is concerned with historical developments at three levels: politics, economy and society, and culture. I want to say a few words about what I understand by each, then indicate the sort of connections between the three that this book tries to establish.

Modern professional history originated in nineteenth-century Germany, where its practitioners placed great-power relations and high politics at the centre of their accounts. That remained true, in Germany more than most countries, well into our own century. My book is concerned with politics in the broader idiom of what might be called mainstream modern political history. War and diplomacy receive the consideration they demand; but the rise of the modern state, with its legal, fiscal, police and welfare functions, is also a central theme; so are revolution and counter-revolution, parties and popular politics. This emphasis does not mean, as is sometimes believed, substituting the history of 'ordinary people' for the history of 'kings and battles'. The old staples of high political history themselves acquire an extra dimension if we look at, say, the domestic impact of conscript armies, or at the ways in which ruling élites tried (and sometimes failed) to establish their legitimacy. Court society and the decision-making of aristocratic politicians become more interesting, not less, when we stop treating them as events that occurred in a self-contained world.

This book is therefore about power and how it was exercised and distributed in the realm that we call politics. It is also about the great brute facts of material and social life: birth rates and death rates, production and consumption. Economic and social history took longer to establish themselves in Germany than in Britain, America or France. Within the narrow 'guild' of German historians, the subject was often looked down upon even through the 1950s. That changed in the following two decades, when the contours of modern German history were redrawn. A generation of scholars, reacting against a narrowly conceived political history and often drawing on the social sciences, put economy and society at the centre of their accounts. Their efforts and those of German historians in other countries drove research forward into previously neglected fields: social mobility, migration, urbanization, housing, diet, crime, medicine. Central to most of this work was a belief in the importance of class as a tool of historical analysis. These subjects have a large place in my book, which also – unapologetically – takes class as a major theme in the great social transformation of nineteenth-century Germany. In order to avoid misunderstanding: I do not believe that transformation can simply be reduced to the shorthand of 'industrialization' or 'urbanization'. The German material world and its social relations were being fundamentally changed before the railway and iron rolling mill arrived, and before the great movement into the cities during the second half of the nineteenth century. Land reclamation projects and rural manufacturing were among the developments already reshaping the German landscape in the eighteenth century. Even after the advent of the factory and big city, agriculture and small business, countryside and market town, continued to have an importance that is often overlooked. But their relative position had changed. The latter part of this book describes the emergence of a modern, urban-industrial class society. It is a society whose outlines are now all the more clear in retrospect because we have watched them blur and dissolve in Germany, as in other parts of the postindustrial world.

What has also dissolved over the same period is the once confident belief that social-science history with its hard facts could (any more than political history) tell the whole story. We have witnessed a move away from 'quantification', and a larger dissatisfaction with structural, socioeconomic history. These gave us new ways of understanding the past, but also left a lot out: the human dimension, for one thing, local variation, for another, the fact that societies consist of women as well as men, for a third. In Germany, as elsewhere, there has been a shift in historical interest from structures to experiences, from the abstract to the specific. Nowadays we are more likely to read about riots, or poaching, or the policing of a particular locality, than about aggregate crime statistics. The trend can be seen in almost every area of historical enquiry. One sign of change is the use that many historians now make of concepts drawn from anthropology or the humanities, rather than the social sciences. The common denominator here is culture – the magic word that is nowadays dropped like a good-luck charm into so much historical writing. Culture, in this context, means not so much literacy and education, subjects that social historians have long written about, but culture in the anthropological sense: the symbols and practices that inform everyday life. Like earlier shifts of perspective, this one opens up new ways of looking at history. It has brought us closer to how those we write about understood their own lives, and made us more alert to the existence of multiple, overlapping identities in society: not just whether someone was a worker or a bourgeois, say, but whether they were Westphalian or Bavarian, Protestant or Catholic, young or old, male or female, and why these things mattered. From the rediscovery of religion to the discovery of gender, both largely absent from general histories of Germany written a generation ago, the new cultural history has shaken the kaleidoscope and let the past settle into new patterns. There has been a price to pay. Attention to the local and immediate can become an end in itself, and modern cultural historians sometimes seem to celebrate the fragment at the expense of the larger whole. Distrust of overarching generalizations has led some German historians of *Alltagsgeschichte*, or everyday life, to reject the 'cold abstraction' of theory altogether. This retreat into rapt contemplation or sentimentality is an abdication of the historian's job, which involves explaining as well as describing. We should offer something better than the showman's refrain of the heritage industry, which invites its customers to 'step into the past'.

Politics, economy and society, culture – these are three slices through the German long nineteenth century. Since total history is desirable but impossible to write, we need some broad analytical or descriptive categories of this kind – and I know of none better. As a confirmed lumper rather than splitter, I none the less hope my book shows why it is essential not to treat these spheres of life in isolation from each another. Politics has a powerful symbolic and ritual dimension – we refer, after all, to political *culture*. That is one thread running through the following chapters, from the cockades and festivities of democrats to the efforts made by monarchs to find – or manufacture – usable 'traditions'. But wielding or seeking power is also about resources, and the question 'who benefits?' should always be asked. The economic transformation of Germany, in turn, can be properly understood only in the context of political decisions over matters like tariffs and taxes, while the symbols of that transformation – the steam engine, the factory chimney, electricity – had a profound effect on the imagination of German society. Finally, by any definition, culture is anything but self-contained. That will be obvious enough when readers encounter, say, 'the culture of progress' (see Chapter Six); but even culture in the narrower, formal sense cannot usefully be separated from the forces that shaped it – education and literacy, patrons and markets. The three categories that figure in the headings and subheadings of this book should not be regarded as fixed, like triangulation points. They are a way of giving shape to a potentially overwhelming mass of material. I am aware, none the less, that many topics have had to be covered with almost indecent brevity. The decision not to have separate chapters dealing with 'the arts' and 'science' brings the advantage that these subjects are not left dangling in limbo, separated from the 'real' history, but the disadvantage that less attention can be given to internal developments within painting, or music, or physics. The same applies to the history of ideas: Kant, Hegel, Marx, Nietzsche and Weber have their place in this book, the last especially, but readers will not find a detailed account of their thinking. Finally, in a book that necessarily has a lot to say about wars, there is relatively little on military strategy or individual battles. In making these and other decisions, I have tried to console myself with a useful German phrase: that one must have *die Mut zur Lücke* – the courage to leave things out.

* * *

The debts incurred in writing a general book are more numerous and widespread than they are with a more specialized study. This book is based on twenty-five years of working on modern German history. It draws on research and reading in many archives and libraries, German, British and American. I have thanked these institutions individually in previous books, and hope that on this occasion they will accept a collective acknowledgement. I want to express my particular gratitude to an institution that was my mainstay in writing this book, the Widener

Library at Harvard. I am also grateful to the Dean of the Faculty of Arts and Sciences at Harvard for granting me a year of leave, part of which was used to complete this book, and to colleagues in the History Department and the Center for European Studies, for the support and encouragement they have invariably shown.

This book owes a great deal to friends and colleagues too numerous to list individually who have provided encouragement and criticism. Over the years I have benefited repeatedly from acts of intellectual generosity that contrast sharply with popular stereotypes of the academic world. I should like to thank those who read parts of the book in draft and offered valuable assistance: Dirk Bönker, John Czaplicka (who also gave helpful advice over the choice of illustrations), Charles Ingrao, Jennifer Jenkins and Susan Pedersen. Special thanks go to John Breuilly, who commented on the entire manuscript. It would be hard to exaggerate how much a general book like this rests on the prior labours of others, and I want to acknowledge my debt to all those whose work I have used with profit. The customary disclaimer applies: I alone am responsible for any errors of fact or wrong-headed interpretations the book may contain.

I want to thank Annette Schlagenhauff and Gina Fried-Miller, my staff assistants during the period when the book was being written. My editors at Fontana Press and HarperCollins proved patient in waiting for the manuscript and exemplary in editing it. I should also like to thank my agents Maggie Hanbury and Robin Straus for their continuing support. My wife, Debbie, and our children, Ellen and Matthew, sustained me with their love and placed everything else in life into true perspective.

There are two final debts of gratitude it is a pleasure to discharge. The first is owed to the undergraduates of four universities – Cambridge, London, Stanford and Harvard – who have taken my courses on German history over the last twenty years. Academics learn as much by teaching as they impart. By thinking about what we want to say, we define our own views. Finally, I want to express my thanks to Jack Plumb, who first opened the door that led to my becoming a historian. I shall always be grateful. He believes strongly in professional scholars writing books for a wider public. I hope he will be pleased with this one, which is dedicated to him.

DAVID BLACKBOURN
Lexington, Massachusetts, January 1996.

ACKNOWLEDGEMENTS

I am very grateful to the following for permission to use illustrations: Archiv Gerstenberg, Wietze (1, 7), Stadtmuseum Berlin (3), Krauss Maffei, Munich (8), Mary Evans Picture Library, London (9), Bayerisches Nationalmuseum, Munich (10), Landesbildstelle, Berlin (11, 12), Archiv für Kunst und Geschichte, London (13), AEG Firmenarchiv, Frankfurt (14), Museum für Post und Kommunikation, Frankfurt (17), Imperial War Museum, London (18), Historisches Archiv Krupp, Essen (19).

The Long
Nineteenth Century

Germany in
the Late Eighteenth Century

Small Worlds

Many who have read little German history will know the folk tales collected by the brothers Grimm, the first two volumes of which were published in 1812 and 1815. Their stories are set in a landscape of dense woods where wolves are never far away. They depict a world shaped by bereavement, peopled with orphans, stepmothers and widowed women believed to be witches. Beggars are commonplace and most people are hungry, except for princes or a fortunate miller. Life is hard and filled with toil: children are valuable for the work they perform but a potential burden when they eat more than they produce. The stepmother of the folk tale often cruelly exploits the step-children; sometimes she and her husband abandon them altogether.

These tales, recorded and reworked by two middle-class academics, are infused with elements of violence and the supernatural typical of German Romanticism in the early nineteenth century. They cannot be seen as a simple reflection of everyday life in German-speaking Europe under the old regime.[1] Even passed through the filter of their collectors, however, the subjects and attitudes depicted in these stories offer some insight into the world that contemporaries experienced, and how they tried to make sense of their lot. It was a world in which wolves did frequent the forests that the following century would idealize, and women were executed for witchcraft into the 1780s. Life was, by our standards, short and precarious. It was threatened by inadequate diet, poor hygiene, and disease. The twin spectres were epidemic disease (dysentery, measles, smallpox, typhus), and harvest failure that created widespread starvation, such as occurred in Saxony, Bohemia, Berlin and southern Germany in 1771–4. Between a quarter and a third of all infants failed to survive their first year; half would die by the age of ten. At a time of plague, even more children would be culled. Small wonder that fatalism was so common. It is true that we have to be careful here not to take at face value everything educated contemporaries said about parental 'indifference' among the rural lower classes. The rare instances of direct diary testimony suggest that peasants did mourn dead infants. But there is also evidence that when times were especially hard, 'superfluous' children were the victims of infanticide, or of that semideliberate neglect known in Bavaria as *himmeln lassen* – letting children be taken up to heaven.[2]

To survive childhood was an achievement, and life expectancy remained low even for those who survived. At a time when men typically married at twenty-eight, and women at twenty-five, less than half of a given generation would normally reach marriage age. In Koblenz during the 1770s and 1780s it was 45 per cent. The average marriage around 1800 lasted just twenty years, and was ended by death, not divorce. This grim statistic explains why step-parents were so common – stepmothers especially, for a new wife was essential on the land, and widowers remarried more often than widows. The centrality of remarriage in peasant life is nicely brought out in a land transaction conducted by one Hans Michael Dalm in the Württemberg village of Neckarhausen, with his brother's wife's previous husband's previous wife's father's brother's son's wife's previous husband.[3] It was normal for a working child of fourteen to have lost one or both natural parents, and it would have been unusual if more than one grandparent was still alive. The supposedly 'traditional' three-generation family was actually rather rare. Less than one German in ten lived beyond the age of sixty, and those over sixty-five made up just 4–5 per cent of the population (the proportion is more than three times as great in present-day

Germany). Attitudes towards age reveal as much as the brute numbers. The old enjoyed greater respect in the eighteenth century than they did in the periods before or after, and this was in many ways a gerontocratic society run by old men – but these 'old men' were in their 40s and 50s.[4]

The prospect of illness or early death faced all Germans of the period, but it did not face all equally. Where you lived and who you were made a huge difference. We might expect that town-dwellers would fare best. Doctors were concentrated in urban centres – there were twice as many per head in Berlin around 1800 as there were in the surrounding Mark Brandenburg – and enlightened circles in the towns despaired of the 'backward' rural areas where three-quarters of Germans lived. In his *Health-Catechism for the Rural Population and the Common Man* (1781), the doctor Adam Senfft describes a day labourer who failed to follow his instructions, concluding bitterly that 'he died, as was fitting'.[5] But towns were more deadly, and maintained their populations only by a regular influx of migrants. In Bremen deaths exceeded live births in every decade from 1740 to 1799. Urban centres were filthy and noxious: the botanist Linnaeus likened Hamburg to an open sewer. Doctors served the nobility, officials and merchants, and might be called in by a better-off tradesman; they would not be consulted by members of the underclass who made up a third to a half of the typical urban population. In Prussia, a doctor's visit would cost twenty days' wages for a labourer or cook, twice as much if an infectious disease was involved. It should be said that in this period consulting the doctor was not necessarily beneficial. Contemporary handbooks on dealing with patients were revealing in more ways than one when they emphasized attributes such as mastery of French, dancing and the avoidance of swearing, rather than diagnostic skills. Doctors seldom examined their patients physically. As for the various classes of surgeon who dealt with 'external' ailments or injuries, they were rightly regarded with fear and suspicion. The shepherd bonesetter or 'old maid' herbalist to whom the peasantry resorted may have done less harm, perhaps even more good, than many doctors. In the end, differences in the demands made by work, in diet, housing conditions and hygiene had a greater impact on sickness and mortality rates than differences in medical provision. There is certainly no doubt about the inequalities in basic matters of life and death, as studies from urban Giessen to rural Bavaria have shown.[6]

Inequalities of this kind were not specific to late eighteenth-century society. As we shall see, ill-health and susceptibility to epidemic diseases were strongly linked in the nineteenth century to social position. But medical provision in the eighteenth century gives a pointer to the fact that we are dealing with something other than a modern class society. The most obvious feature of this provision was its highly segmented character, which matched the many subgroups of medical practitioners (doctors, surgeons, barber-surgeons) to the social groups they were expected to serve. There was more to this than simply the length of one's purse. As Claudia Huerkamp has argued, such segmentation was characteristic of eighteenth-century corporate society, a society of 'orders' or 'estates' rather than classes.[7] What this meant is even more obvious if we turn our attention from medicine to law. In class societies, such as Germany became in the course of the nineteenth century, it is a commonplace that formal equality before the law exists alongside actual inequality: in practice, not everyone has equal access to the law. The point about the German states of the eighteenth century is that their inhabitants were not equal before the law in the first place. There was no single law, but instead a complex patchwork of legal jurisdictions exercised by rulers, the church, the nobility, guilds, municipalities, and others. Nobles, clergy, burghers, craftsmen, peasants: all enjoyed different rights (rights that were limited and highly specific) and were subject to different jurisdictions, according to the 'estate' to which they belonged. Again, it is the segmented quality of this society that we need to grasp.

German corporate society worked on the principle of 'a place for everyone, and everyone in his (and her) place'. Take the relationship of lord and peasant. Under the prevailing seigneurial system, the majority of peasants were personally subject to one or more lords. Details varied, but one of the most firmly established generalizations of modern German history is the difference between east and west. In Prussia east of the river Elbe (and the Habsburg lands east of the Bohemian forest), under the so-called *Gutsherrschaft* system, the lord enjoyed direct control over the peasant. In exchange for the land they worked, peasants provided labour services and made other payments in cash or kind: the lord could prescribe where they milled their grain or sold their own produce; they were not free to move without his permission. The East Elbian lord had other powers, including police authority and rights of 'patrimonial' justice over the peasants on his estate, control over local government, and often the right to nominate to church livings. In the regions to the west and south the prevailing *Grundherrschaft* system was less stifling. Labour services had often been commuted over time into cash payments, so that peasants were in effect tenants. In some cases tenant rights had even become hereditary. This distinction was first established in the late nineteenth century by the liberal G. F. Knapp and his students, who believed their scholarship showed the gulf between vigorous 'western' and servile 'eastern' peasants. It has remained as a powerful argument ever since, buttressing claims that developments in East Elbian Prussia helped to set the catastrophic course of twentieth-century German history. The east-west distinction is not false, but recent research suggests that it needs some qualification. As far as western *Grundherrschaft* is concerned, everyone agrees that, while the peasantry was not personally dependent to the same degree, noble and clerical lords not only remained legal owners of the land but retained some seigneurial privileges, typically involving hunting. The real question is whether seigneurialism in the east amounted (or still amounted) to fully fledged serfdom. Before the population rise of the mid eighteenth century peasants had exploited labour shortages to improve their conditions; and as the rural social structure became more differentiated they hired others to perform labour services on their behalf. By 1800 the East Elbian countryside contained a complicated pecking order of domination and subordination, not a straightforward clash between powerful lords and servile peasants. The peasantry also had two other weapons, in addition to becoming runaways: revolt, and resort to law. Both were frequently used, as they were in western regions. Lawsuits became so common in the eighteenth century that historians refer to a 'juridification' of peasant protest. It was fostered in Prussia by the state, which established arbitration registers of peasant rents and obligations. As a result there was, at least in some places, a 'breakdown of serfdom'.[8] Of course, seugneurial powers remained formidable, even if stronger in some provinces (Mecklenburg, Pomerania) than others (Brandenburg, East Prussia). Nor does the revisionist historiography give us any reason to accept the idealized picture of lord-peasant relations promoted during the wave of nostalgia for 'Old Prussia' that has washed over Germany in recent years. A few landowners lived up to the 'father' image; most did not. When King Frederick William III was told about a genuinely paternalist seigneur, he was 'heartily cheered by it, the more so as it is so rare'.[9]

What of social relations in urban centres? 'City air makes free' was a phrase that went back to an earlier period of German feudalism, and in the late eighteenth century there were still many privileges that expressed the distinction between country and town. Town walls, the right to hold markets, the monopoly of craft guilds: all were jealously maintained by urban dwellers against potential challenges from outsiders, whether territorial rulers or non-guild producers in the countryside. The defence of urban rights was common to cities and towns alike. It found its apotheosis in what Mack Walker has dubbed Germany's 'home towns', the small towns with up to 10,000 inhabitants that were prevalent in the central, western and southwestern areas between Westphalia and the Danube, the Rhine and Upper Saxony.[10] However, preserving town or city prerogatives did not have the same meaning for all. These privileges would have meant more to master craftsmen than to the journeymen whose riots punctuated the eighteenth century, and they would have meant nothing at all to the labourers, servants and poor who were often recent arrivals from the countryside. Once again, these social divisions went beyond class – or, rather, they were *pre*-class divisions. Towns also had a corporate structure anchored in legal distinctions. At the top was a 'patriciate' whose composition was based on birth and rank. Urban dwellers were further divided into full citizens, who exercised all the rights possessed by the community, residents such as *Schutzbürger* ('denizens'), who enjoyed some rights, and the rest, who had no rights. These divisions partly overlapped with, partly cut across, other divisions such as those enforced by the craft guild. The guild was a classic institution of corporate society. It was based on a specific privilege (the monopoly production of certain goods within a particular area); it made highly elaborate distinctions between masters, journeymen and apprentices; and to preserve this internal order and the standing of the guild it aimed to regulate how its members should behave beyond the workshop. Just as the guilds tried to maintain control over prices and quality, and to guarantee each master a suitable pool of customers (neither too few, nor too many), so it prescribed the conduct appropriate to masters, journeymen and apprentices in matters ranging from sleeping hours to marriage.

When we look at seigneurialism, urban corporations or guilds, we see institutions that regulated many different spheres of existence. Their prescriptions and proscriptions transcended what we (and nineteenth-century Germans) would be inclined to view as separate areas of life: economic, social, legal, moral. Their role was also political, where matters such as citizenship or the composition of a patrician élite were concerned. The same point could be made about the churches, especially the Catholic church, which was richer and more laden with privileges than any of the Protestant denominations or sects (Lutherans, Calvinists, Pietists). The Catholic church of the late eighteenth century was at once seigneurial lord, employer, purveyor of charity and wielder of spiritual authority, while prelates were political rulers in the ecclesiastical principalities. There were two sides to these corporations, therefore. While their authority cut across many divisions we take for granted, they also maintained distinctions and asserted prerogatives that seem as alien to us as they increasingly did to nineteenth-century Germans. The 'home town' defended guild monopolies and citizenship restrictions, Prussian nobles their tax exemptions and exclusive right to entail property, nobles everywhere their hunting rights, the clergy their seigneurial claims and the privileges that had accrued to cathedral chapters and religious foundations, university professors their rights to firewood and food from land owned by the university corporation, or their licences to maintain beer and wine cellars for public sales.

It was this patchwork of rights, privileges, exemptions and prerogatives – to display a coat of arms or put servants in livery, to make and sell furniture, to be free from certain taxes or dues, even to operate a monopoly postal service (like the Thurn und Taxis family) – that underpinned, at least in theory, the corporate social order. Similar distinctions applied to aspects of everyday life like forms of address, or apparel. The fine gradations between *Wohlgeboren* and *Hochwohlgeboren*, *Frau* and *gnädige Frau* were as well understood by contemporaries as the more obvious distinctions between citizen and denizen, master and apprentice. When it came to dress, some privileges had clearly become a dead letter (like the exclusive right of nobles to wear a sword), but nobles and commoners reportedly fought duels over the wearing of plumed hats. Nor are we dealing just with residues of an earlier age: the eighteenth century was rich in new sumptuary codes (regulations on dress). In Braunschweig servant girls were forbidden to use silk dress materials or to wear shoes made of anything other than plain black leather. In the Prussian province of Posen burghers' wives were not permitted to wear their hair loose down their backs.[11] When we add to all of these distinctions the numerous internal markers that divided the 50,000 noble families, for example, into 'imperial', 'territorial', 'court', 'country', 'patent', it is not surprising that foreign visitors like Lady Mary Montagu and Madame de Staël referred to the German 'caste' system. Perhaps the most famous satire on this was Voltaire's *Candide*, depicting the Baron von Thunder-ten-Tronckh, who had supposedly rejected one of his sister's suitors because the man could demonstrate only 71 quarterings. *Candide* was caricature, of course – and written by an effortlessly superior Frenchman, at that. As we shall see below, the success of men like educated officials tells a different story. Formally, however, this remained a society in which birth and inherited privilege were crucially important.

Was it also a geographically immobile society? One would certainly expect so, given the abject state of contemporary communications. German-speaking Europe was richly endowed with rivers that were only partly navigable. True, these arteries had long been important for moving many goods around, from the salt dug out of the Bavarian state mines to the wood that was rafted down the Rhine and Elbe. There was also canalization in the eighteenth century, especially in Prussia. But it was not until the 1820s and 1830s that the course of major rivers, including the Rhine, Neckar, Mosel and Danube, was straightened to make season-round river traffic easier (and to reduce flooding). Travel by water remained hazardous and slow. Overland routes were hardly preferable. They may have been a little better in the south than the north, but properly constructed highways were a rarity everywhere: Prussian travellers routinely complained about sandy roads that turned to churning mud when it rained, creating ruts that swallowed carriages up to the axles. That was why Prussian regulations insisted on so many horses per passenger – four horses for three people, as many as eight for a vehicle containing four passengers and heavy luggage. These obstacles made progress painfully slow. It took at least nine days to travel from Frankfurt to Berlin; even the modest distance from the garrison town of Potsdam to Berlin required six hours on the coach that made the journey just once a day. Travel was also dangerous, on four wheels as well as two legs. The late eighteenth century was a last golden age of banditry and highway robbery. Brazen and well-organized gangs like that of Matthäus Klostermaier, the notorious 'Bavarian *Hiasl*', preyed on the mobile in the Rhineland and Bavaria, Hessen and Thuringia.[12]

Given these problems, it is striking how many Germans were on the move in the second half of the eighteenth century. Young nobles made the grand tour, studying local conditions, making notes and sketches, perhaps bringing back ideas for an ornamental garden. England, the Netherlands, France and Italy were favoured destinations. Men of good birth might take a man-servant, perhaps a tutor; young princes, of which the Holy Roman Empire had so many, would travel with a larger retinue. On the first of his two grand tours, Frederick III of Gotha took a steward, two gentlemen-in-waiting, a secretary, a chaplain, a treasurer, a doctor, two pages, a groom, a lackey, a cook and two other servants. Travel became something of a mania in this period among the upper ranks of society and the educated, and I want to return later to the importance of this. But they made up a small proportion of eighteenth-century travellers. Much more important numerically were those such as emigrants, trav-elling on foot or in rudimentary wagons. Many came from areas of partible inheritance in the south and west where holdings became too small to support a family – Baden, Württemberg, the Palatinate, the Westerwald and the Hunsrück. Up to 300,000 migrated to Prussia in the course of the century, many being settled on reclaimed land at the mouths of the Oder and Vistula. Others made the longer journey to areas where the Habsburgs were encouraging settlement in the east, such as the Banat, Galicia and Bukowina, adding a potentially explosive element to the history of modern 'Germany'. The numbers involved were large. In 1789 it was estimated that in the Rhenish administrative districts of Bad Kreuznach, Stromberg and Bacharach (which included the Hunsrück) a twelfth of the total population had departed for Hungary or Poland in the previous decade. Just to the west, the area around Tholey and Lebach was known as 'Turkey' because so many of its inhabitants had left to settle there, moving from the western to the southeastern margin of central Europe.[13] Similar areas provided most of what was already a considerable transatlantic emigration. Others went to America for a different purpose: over 30,000 German soldiers served with the British forces during the American revolution.

Migrants and soldiers were joined on Germany's suspect but crowded roads by the many other travellers of the late eighteenth century. As much as 10 per cent of the German population was itinerant at this time. Shepherds all over the southwest took their flocks down from the high meadows to winter over in the Danube, Rhine and Main valleys, then made the return journey to the Swabian or Franconian Alps in March. These routes could be hundreds of miles long; some Franconian flocks were driven north to Thuringia, occasionally even to the mouth of the Weser and the Dutch border.[14] Journeymen went 'on the tramp' in search of work after serving their apprenticeships, typically for two years. Pilgrims journeyed to shrines and other devotional sites, despite the best efforts of the Catholic Enlightenment to discourage them. Pedlars, hawkers, gypsies, knackers, charcoal-burners, knife-grinders, prostitutes, troupes of players and musicians travelled around purveying their goods and services. Some of these groups merged imperceptibly into the ranks of the beggars and thieves who made such a powerful, hostile impression on the nonitinerant majority.

That, of course, is the central point about Germany's moving or floating population. It confirmed the immobility of the larger society, of those whose lives were bound to one place. Some forms of mobility were strictly temporary, journeys between two fixed points. Peasants might leave Swabia or the Eifel, but they remained peasants when they reached the Vistula or the Banat. Journeymen wandered, but normally returned to their workshop for two further years before seeking a mastership, just as young aristocrats went back from the grand tour to their estates. Here, mobility was generation-specific, a part of the life cycle. Corporate society as a whole was defined by opposition to the itinerant. Gypsies and hawkers aroused dislike and suspicion, beggars outright fear and hostility among peasants and hometownsmen; shepherds and knackers belonged to what were deemed 'dishonourable' occupations. It is true that the legal statutes on dishonourable status were removed during the seventeenth and eighteenth centuries, but communities were slow to accept the change. Jurists were still concerned in the late eighteenth century with the case of a young man denied admission to a tailors' guild because his maternal grandfather had been a shepherd.[15] The activities of these 'outcasts' served to establish the boundaries of the corporate social order to which they were marginal. Like the upside-down world of the annual carnival, itinerant Germany was the exception that proved the rule. For most inhabitants of the old regime were neither geographically nor socially mobile. They lived and died where they had been born, locked into a series of small worlds. It is worth recalling that there was not even a standard time in German lands to unify these separate worlds: that would come only with the railway.

A similar patchwork of small worlds provided the framework for production, consumption and trade. Perhaps 80 per cent of Germans were engaged in agriculture, and most of what they produced was geared to subsistence and consumed locally. That was why famines such as those in the 1770s struck so hard – because food could not be transported easily from area to area. The markets for most manufactured goods were equally limited. Almost all of those engaged in manufacturing were craftsmen serving local needs: shoemakers, tailors, carpenters, masons, coopers. Even in towns where trade was more diversified and sophisticated, the gold-beater, hatter, bookbinder and skilled furniture-maker would generally be working for bespoke customers, servicing members of court, patriciate or some other corporation. This was the pattern of old-regime production. The relative isolation of these self-sufficient worlds was reinforced by a luxuriant structure of tariffs and excises both between and within the individual German territories. This made moving goods frustrating, and helps to explain why smuggling – the black economy of the period – was so extensive. The smuggler had much in common with the hawker and other itinerants. All were revealingly characteristic figures of the old regime, for they crossed the boundaries that divided Germany's small worlds, yet remained outside a bounded, corporate society.

Political Fragmentation and the Territorial State

The countless borders on which smugglers operated were a product of Germany's political fragmentation. There was, in fact, no 'Germany' at the end of the eighteenth century, although there was something that sounded as if it might be: the Holy Roman Empire of the German Nation. But this ramshackle, invertebrate entity neither was, nor aspired to be, a German nation-state. It excluded many German-speakers (in Switzerland, Greater Hungary and East Prussia), while including non-Germans within its boundaries (Czechs, Poles, Slovenes, Italians, Walloons and Flemings). This is not so extraordinary in itself, given the fluid linguistic boundaries and countless 'language islands', German and non-German, to be found in central Europe. The united Germany created in the nineteenth century also excluded Germans and included non-Germans. What is more striking in the Holy Roman Empire is that, because German princes ruled in countries such as Denmark, Sweden and Britain, 'foreign' sovereigns had a role in the Empire's affairs. Thus the British monarch, as a Hanoverian, helped to elect the emperor. The Empire was neither a nation-state, nor indeed a modern, territorial state of any kind. It was a product of historical accretion, loosely draped over an array of independent, highly diverse territories. Some of the dynastic states within the Empire were, had been, or aspired to become major players on the European stage. They included Prussia, Austria, Saxony, Bavaria, Hanover, and Württemberg. Others, such as Lippe or Lichtenberg, were tiny statelets, mere specks on the map. These motley principalities existed alongside ecclesiastical territories that were equally varied in size and influence, from the important prince-bishoprics of Mainz or Cologne, through relatively substantial abbeys such as St Blasien or Weingarten, to tiny entities numbering a few hundred souls. The fifty-one imperial cities were no less diverse. Some were economic powerhouses like Hamburg and Frankfurt; others, like Nuremberg, had seen better days but still possessed territory more extensive than that of many nominal states; most were small communities like Weißenburg or Leutkirch with populations in the thousands. These last, the classic 'home towns', were especially prevalent in the southwestern regions of Swabia and Franconia. The same was true of a final category, the imperial nobility, more than a thousand knights and counts whose family estates were theoretically sovereign territories, and who jealously guarded the legal status that made them subject to no ruler other than the emperor.[16]

Look at a map of late eighteenth-century Germany, and the most striking feature is the very large number of very small political units. The reason for this, and the central issue to grasp, is that sovereignty did not go together with compact blocs of territory in the way that we take for granted. This can be seen by looking from the bottom up, or the top down. If we start at ground level, we find that an area like the Palatinate contained 37 different jurisdictions in 127 different parcels of land. The lords included the Archduke of Austria and the King of France as well as local princes, church foundations and imperial knights. One village of 50 families had 4 different lords. If we turn the telescope around and ask what a given political sovereignty consisted of, the answer is predictable – a jumble of rights and privileges all over the map, very much like an estate with land here, woods in the next valley, and rental property in a distant town. These were more like estates than states in the modern sense. Prussia was physically divided between east and west; the Electorate of Mainz consisted (simplifying a little) of seven separate pockets of lands. The old-regime state was not a territorial unity, but an archipelago of jurisdictions.

The institutions of the Empire were as complex and, to modern eyes, as disconcerting as its constituent parts. Thus, the emperor himself was the feudal overlord of the Empire, and represented executive authority within it; but he was also one of the leading territorial princes, as ruler of the Austrian Habsburg lands. These two roles often came into conflict. The powers and revenues of the emperor as emperor had been reduced over the centuries by the electors. We get an idea of the difficulties

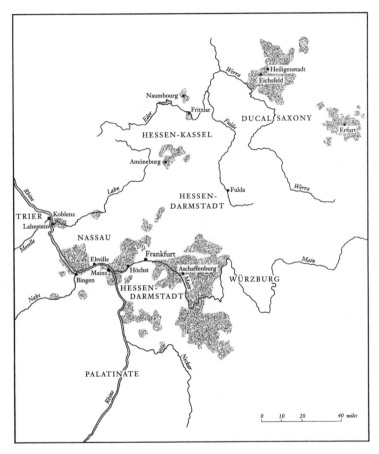

The Electorate of Mainz in the Eighteenth Century

this created by looking at the classic problem facing eighteenth-century rulers: raising and equipping an army. For administrative purposes the Empire was divided into ten circles, units that excluded important areas like Silesia and Bohemia, and cut across the boundaries of individual territories. A law of 1681 obliged these circles to recruit and provision troops for the imperial army on request. This produced a fighting force stronger on paper than in the field. When the system worked, the result was a disjointed army, officered by men chosen by quota from the different imperial estates. But the system rarely worked, because the more powerful rulers provided soldiers, or failed to provide them, according to their own interests. The shortcomings of the imperial army were harshly revealed in the Seven Years War (1756–63), fought significantly enough against Prussia, a nominal member of the Empire.

The imperial legislature, or Reichstag, was equally ineffectual. It met in Regensburg, an assembly of ambassadors from the 150-plus territories, institutions and families possessing the right to representation. In practice, the number of ambassadors present was smaller than this, sometimes no more than two dozen: some failed to attend, others were delegated to speak for several different interests. The parliament itself was divided into three houses or councils representing the imperial electors, princes, and cities. Although the Reichstag was in permanent session from 1663 to 1806, its legislative accomplishments were few. The procedural sloth of the parliament was not a result of its creaking machinery. That was symptom, not cause. The composition of the Reichstag faithfully mirrored the many divisions within and between the diverse constituent parts of the Empire. One of the most important fault lines continued to divide Catholic and Protestant rulers, a legacy of the Reformation that also played itself out within individual territories. In the imperial city of Augsburg, for example, an 'invisible border' separated the two communities.[17] Further divisions arose from the princes' territorial ambitions. The checks and balances of the Reichstag only reflected mutual rivalries and suspicions.

Finally, the Empire had two separate superior courts. The so-called Aulic Council in Vienna functioned relatively well. The same could not be said of the Imperial Cameral Tribunal in Wetzlar, which had a backlog of 60,000 cases pending by the 1770s. Its inefficiency owed much to nepotism (a characteristic vice of eighteenth-century institutions), as jobs went to a tightening circle of 'Cameral families'.[18] Appellants therefore found themselves ground between the wheels of a slow-moving justice.

At the same time, individual states also claimed ultimate jurisdiction, and the imperial courts often found it difficult to enforce their judgments. Parties to a decision had the right of appeal to the Reichstag; sometimes they simply ignored judgments they disliked. Like the Law on Military Organization, court decisions were most likely to be flouted by powerful territorial rulers.

In Goethe's *Faust*, Part I, Frosch begins his drinking song with an often-quoted couplet: 'Das liebe heil'ge röm'sche Reich, Wie hält's nur noch zusammen?' (The dear old Holy Roman Empire, How *does* it hold together?) Brander, one of his companions in Auerbach's cellar, responds:

> . . . A nasty song! Thank God in constant prayer
> The Roman Empire isn't your affair.
> I thank my stars, and think myself the wiser,
> That no one calls me Chancellor or Kaiser.

The Empire certainly did not lack contemporary critics, and nineteenth-century historians were even more caustic in their judgments. They were contemptuous of its convoluted and seemingly haphazard institutions, scorned its overlapping jurisdictions and weak notion of sovereignty; above all they deplored the role that it allowed to the rulers of England, Denmark and Sweden in German affairs. Hence they saw its collapse not only as welcome, but as inevitable. Many modern historians have conveyed a similar impression through their language, peppering their texts with adjectives like 'ridiculous' and (a favourite) 'anachronistic'. Recent revisionist accounts have resisted the temptation to judge by later standards. They have noted that the administrative circles had real achievements to their name in Swabia and Franconia, and rightly underlined the point that the Empire was not a centralized state that failed, but a loosely articulated institution that allowed its members a large degree of sovereignty and held the ring between them.[19] Its importance lay in its symbolic and legal functions. The emperor played the role of broker, as when he eased the resettlement in Prussia of 20,000 Protestants expelled from the Archbishopric of Salzburg.[20] Weak members of the Empire looked to institutions like the Aulic Council for protection against ambitious and more powerful neighbours. The existence of the court as a forum for conciliation prevented the principality of Anhalt from being absorbed into Prussia, kept the imperial counties of Isenburg and Solms from falling into the hands of Hesse-Darmstadt, and offered some protection to the knights and free cities of the southwest against the electors of Bavaria and the dukes of Württemberg. Contemporaries understood this well enough, which explains why there were so many attempts to reform the Empire as an institution capable of containing aggression. After the Seven Years War there was an almost millenarian temper to the dream of 'German renewal'. The election and pomp-laden coronation of Emperor Joseph II symbolized these hopes. The literature on the Empire written after 1763 was affectionately critical and virtually unanimous that the institution should be preserved, albeit in modernized form.

The point is well taken. The institutional virtues of the Empire were largely negative – they were the virtues of procrastination, obstruction, and the lesser evil. Historians are agreed that imperial enthusiasm among constituent members was inversely related to their size and strength. The Empire protected the particular in the name of the universal. It succeeded, up to a point, in acting as a counterbalance to ambitious princes. The guilds, a thorn in the side of those princes, looked to the Empire for redress – and guild issues were among the few that could stir the Reichstag to legislate in the eighteenth century. Under the imperial umbrella minuscule territories jealously defended their rights, especially to administer justice. Thanks to the Empire, imperial counts or cities continued to assert their sovereignty even when physically surrounded by much larger states. The Empire was an 'incubator' (Mack Walker), keeping alive what might otherwise have died. It is not difficult to see why modern historians, less enamoured of power and progress than many of their nineteenth-century predecessors, have been less quick to dismiss these attributes.

Yet the Empire failed, in the end, to maintain a balance between weak and strong. It could not hold back the growing power of larger member-states whose policies threatened the basis on which the Empire rested. The institutional dynamism in Germany was to be found in the rising territorial states. Profound changes were taking place within the political shell of the Empire. They can be summarized in the phrase state-building. This had two meanings. It applied, first, to the physical expansion of a given territory through peaceful or nonpeaceful methods. Thus the Protestant Margrave of Baden-Durlach doubled his lands at a stroke in 1771 when he inherited Baden-Baden from the extinguished Catholic branch of the family. Secondly, it meant attempts by individual rulers to construct more centralized, rationalized states within their territorial borders. These efforts, part of a European-wide phenomenon of absolutism, involved the enlargement of state bureaucracies and were directed against intermediate institutions that stood between ruler and subject: nobility, churches, guilds, parliamentary estates. Princes asserted their authority in areas ranging from material production to expressions of piety, but their principal concerns were taxation, policing, the dispensing of justice, and conscription. In states with large standing armies (a development dating from the mid seventeenth century), conscription was potentially the greatest challenge to the Empire, for it threatened the status quo the latter existed to preserve. As the Thirty Years War, the 'potato war' and other late eighteenth-century hostilities showed, this challenge was by no means abstract. Assaults on guild autonomy and the promulgation of state legal codes were hardly less subversive of what the Empire stood for. The same was true, at a symbolic level, of the growing princely courts that were such a feature of the eighteenth century. Often, it is true, they were designed to corral and domesticate the local nobility, but these burgeoning mini-Versailles in Mannheim, Berlin, Dresden, Munich, Hanover, Dresden and elsewhere also amounted to an assertion of power and prestige that challenged the authority of the emperor.

Even this abbreviated list of courts suggests how widely princely power was asserted across the German lands. A similar list could be compiled of universities founded, in large part, to

train the growing ranks of state officials in useful skills such as
the law and cameralism, the German version of political economy which emphasized the importance of economic management in the interest of state treasuries. It would include Halle
(1694), Göttingen (1737), Erlangen (1743), Münster (1780) and
Bonn (1786), not counting existing institutions that were
reformed in the eighteenth century. In Bavaria and Württemberg, Hesse and Saxony, standing armies grew, officials multiplied, and rulers tried to regulate and tax their subjects more
effectively, against the inevitable opposition of estates and corporations. The phenomenon was not confined to secular rulers.
Similar developments can be seen in the ecclesiastical territories.
To take a prominent example, from the 1740s onwards a series of
electors in Mainz pursued administrative, economic, educational
and ecclesiastical reforms that challenged the prerogatives of
cathedral canons, monasteries and imperial knights.[21]

The most important cases of state-building occurred in the
two largest German states, Austria and Prussia. In Austria –
strictly speaking, the agglomeration of lands belonging to the
Habsburg dynasty – efforts to create a new, more centralized
basis for rule were underway from the mid eighteenth century.
They came in a series of waves, driven by military imperatives.
After the shock of defeat in war and territorial losses during the
1740s, the young Empress Maria Theresa instituted a series of
reforms in 1748–55. The main objective was a better-trained
standing army of 100,000 men. Achieving this required Vienna
to exploit the resources of its far-flung realm more effectively,
and led not only to restrictions on guild powers and the encouragement of efficient enterprises, but to more centralized administration and tax-gathering. This policy entered a new phase
after the Seven Years War, a conflict that recent German historians have emphasized as a turning point in stimulating internal
political reforms.[22] To finance the army, the new chief minister,
Kaunitz, tried to extend the fiscal reach of the state still further,
against the vested interests of feudal landlords, provincial estates
and a Catholic church that enjoyed widespread tax exemptions.
Central administration was reorganized in 1760–62 and a state

council created whose competence extended throughout the monarchy. Educational reforms that cut across clerical privileges and a newly codified civil law in 1766 were steering in the same direction.

Under Maria Theresa's impatient and austerely rational son, who ruled as Joseph II from 1780–90, this policy was pursued more single-mindedly. 'Josephinism' was a frontal assault against seigneurialism, guild restrictions, urban patriciates, ecclesiastical privilege and provincial rights. These corporate prerogatives offended the tidy-minded emperor; they were also obstacles to the raising of revenues sufficient to support the standing army of 300,000 men which Joseph deemed necessary. The drive for administrative uniformity embraced administrative, fiscal, ecclesiastical and legal reform, as well as more efficient mechanisms of policing under Interior Minister Pergen. Its chief instrument was a centralizing bureaucracy which, after 1784, was required to use German as a common official language. That should not be confused with any ambition on Joseph's part to infuse new meaning into his role as head of the Holy Roman Empire of the German Nation. When he called the German states 'provinces' of the Empire he was speaking as a Habsburg. Joseph toyed with the idea of renouncing the imperial title altogether, and his ambitions to strengthen the Austrian position in German affairs (notably his designs on Bavaria in 1777) were those of a predatory territorial ruler.

Austrian aspirations were resented by many other German princes, but they were challenged by one other German power in particular – the power that seized Silesia from Austria, fought against her in the Seven Years War, frustrated her in the War of Bavarian Succession, and blocked her further German ambitions in the 1780s by leading the League of Princes. That power was Prussia. Historians rightly consider Prussia the classic example of the new type of state. From the mid seventeenth century through to the death of Frederick II ('the Great') in 1786, a series of energetic rulers turned a modest margraviate in Brandenburg-Prussia into an extensive kingdom that became the major power of northern Germany. Territorial expansion came about by means of judicious marriages, strategic land purchases, and – above all in the Frederician period – military conquest. Prussia grew phenomenally during the eighteenth century: the Polish partitions alone almost doubled its size and population. This was a constantly changing, protean state, and its growth posed novel administrative problems (the same problems faced by the Margrave of Baden-Durlach, but on a much larger scale). The new territories, especially New East Prussia, became something of a laboratory for Prussian administration, as royal power at the centre looked for ways to digest new land and subjects. We should remember this need to integrate diverse, often recently acquired provinces when we consider the state-building drive that was one of the two great hallmarks of the Hohenzollern state.

The other hallmark was militarism. 'Prussia was hatched from a cannon ball,' said Napoleon, something of an expert on the subject.[23] The rise of the Prussian army is, in fact, hard to separate from the larger process of bureaucratic state-building. The administrative machinery built up by the Hohenzollerns blended the management of military and civil affairs. Under successive rulers who steadily expanded the standing army, in a society where military drill reached down into the villages and officers enjoyed a high status, ways had to be found to pay for and provision the soldiers. That meant maximizing the flow of royal revenue, against opposition from privileged estates and corporations. The institutions designed to achieve this included the General Directory in Berlin and the provincial War and Domains Chambers, the centrepieces of a growing apparatus of career officials or 'dynastic servants' who concerned themselves with military, judicial and fiscal affairs. These officials were trained and examined (after 1770 all applicants underwent written and oral examinations); they were expected to devote themselves exclusively to their jobs; and they began to develop a marked *esprit de corps*. The permanent hunger for revenue explains efforts to exploit Prussia's human and economic resources fully and promote self-sufficiency, through colonization, subsidies to manufacturers, and measures to control trade.

State treasury income doubled during Frederick's reign, while state foresters, mining officials and excise agents proliferated, alongside regional administrators and tax commissars. The needs of the army drove this activity. As Friedrich von Schrötter mordantly observed a few years later: 'Prussia was not a country with an army, but an army with a country'.[24]

The urge to maintain a strong army, to centralize, codify and remove barriers between ruler and subjects, provides the context of what historians call Enlightened Absolutism (once known as Enlightened Despotism).[25] The term is not self-contradictory, nor does it indicate bad faith or hypocrisy on the part of rulers. Take Frederick the Great, the Philosopher of Sans-Souci, as an example. A celebrated correspondent of Voltaire and author of philosophy, poetry and music, he advocated religious toleration and employed enlightened jurists. In both cases there was a genuine commitment to the dictates of reason, but it is hard to unscramble from 'reason of state'. As Frederician Prussia acquired new Catholic subjects in Silesia and elsewhere, toleration served the interests of state-building. With similar flexibility, earlier Hohenzollerns had sponsored the Pietist movement as a Trojan horse inside the Lutheran church, to weaken the nobility's powers of patronage and to encourage the creation of a more productive citizenry. Pietism called for Protestant spiritual renewal, emphasizing the importance of direct religious experience, rebirth, and meetings in small groups for Bible reading and prayer. Its spread through Prussia's scattered provinces, carried by men with relatively uniform cultural backgrounds, helped to break down provincial isolation and fostered centralization. Like religious toleration, legal reform was a central concern of Enlightenment rationality; but the great weapon of legal reform, codification, also had another side to it. The Prussian Civil Code initiated by Frederick and promulgated in 1794 promised to increase efficiency and uniformity while asserting the king's justice over rival jurisdictions. Similar points could be made about economic policy, educational improvements or the development of 'health police' in the broad eighteenth-century sense of police. All conduced to the well-being of the prince's subjects; all were understood by contemporaries as a rational investment in valuable resources. Even the care of orphans had its place in a larger scheme. The Berlin military orphanage claimed that its task was 'to deliver to the army and the country the greatest number of healthy and well-schooled, soldierly, i.e. patriotic-minded recruits who have been accustomed to hard work and subordination'.[26]

There are family resemblances between enlightened rulers, but also differences of emphasis. In Prussia the military motif was everywhere; in ecclesistical principalities like Mainz and Trier clerical privilege was a special target of reformers. Fiscal concerns went together with genuine distaste for 'obscurantism' (symbolized by the Jesuits and monastic orders) and a belief that the church should inculcate rationality, not pious superstitions, in the ruler's subjects. When the Elector of Trier curtailed or suppressed pilgrimages, he was trying to prune away pious 'excess' and limit the number of lost working days. His counterparts in Fulda, Würzburg and Mainz were equally keen to prevent what the Elector Emmerich Joseph of Mainz called 'sinful idleness'.[27] Beyond this distinctive element, Enlightened Absolutism in these states bore familiar features, as rulers wielded bureaucratic power, economic initiatives and legal codification as weapons against vested interests.

We can clearly see the contours of more centralized territorial states in eighteenth-century Germany. But how far had this process gone by the late eighteenth century? Consider for a moment the titles by which the Habsburgs and Hohenzollerns claimed to rule. Among the dozens of appellations of the Habsburg monarch, he was Archduke of Austria, King of Hungary, Bohemia, Dalmatia, Croatia, Slavonia, Lodomeria and Illyria, Duke of Styria, Salzburg, Carinthia, Carniola and Bukowina, Grand Prince of Transylvania, Margrave of Moravia, Princely Count of Habsburg and Tyrol, Count of Hohenembs, Leldkirch, Bregenz, Sonnenberg, Great Voyvod of Voyvodina, and many other things besides. The Hohenzollerns could boast a similar, if shorter list of titles attached to possessions stretching from Poland to the Netherlands. In the mid eighteenth century,

'Prussia' was still routinely referred to as 'His Royal Majesty's States and Provinces'. What's in a name? In this case, a good deal, for the proliferation of titles alerts us to an enduring reality. Territorial princes – even the most powerful – still ruled over a loose collection of diverse lands. Contemporaries liked the metaphor of the machine, the finely balanced mechanism, and often wrote about the absolutist state in these terms. The tone could be critical, especially of armies: soldiers were 'automata that have no thought but only physical movements' in the words of one Prussian commentator.[28] It was more difficult to drill historic lands or privileged estates into uniformity, however. Absolutist state-building was an arduous, uncertain process: local or corporate rights were not easily expropriated. Joseph II's last frantic bout of centralizing zeal met with such resistance in the Habsburg lands that much of what he achieved had to be conceded by his successor, Leopold II. Centrifugal forces were also powerful in Prussia, perhaps more powerful at the end of the eighteenth century than fifty years earlier. New acquisitions put strains on the machinery of state. Further tensions arose as the bureaucracy developed a will of its own, to which Frederick II responded with a policy of divide-and-rule.[29] Add the jealous independence of local estates, and the result was absolutism considerably tempered in practice. The compromises and qualifications in the 19,000 paragraphs of the Civil Code provide a good example. As the smugglers and bandits showed, there were limits even to basic policing of the 'well-ordered police state' (Marc Raeff).[30]

Beneath the absolutist machinery the territorial prince was still a *Landesvater*, a personal ruler. Like any imperial knight, but on a greater scale, he remained dependent on patrimonial resources to fulfil his ambitions. The royal domains of the Hohenzollerns continued to provide a significant part of Prussian state income into the nineteenth century. Old-regime princes were always strapped for cash. Hesse-Darmstadt lived permanently on the edge of bankruptcy thanks to the spending of Ludwig VII (castles and theatres), Ludwig VIII (hunting) and Ludwig IX (soldiers). Not every state could sell its soldiers as mercenaries to make ends meet, like neighbouring Hesse-Kassel.[31] Loans from 'court Jews' and expedients like a state lottery were both responses to this problem. And so was the unceasing attempt to squeeze more of the surplus from production, especially on the land. Because of their need for revenue, territorial rulers were dependent on some kind of power-sharing with privileged groups.

Even where the towns, guilds and clerical corporations had been cut down to size, aristocratic power remained. In major territorial states, there was usually a triangular distribution of power between prince, bureaucracy and aristocracy. Prussia represented one variant: the aristocracy was coopted into the state service, especially the officer corps, while retaining many local rights over the peasantry – a kind of military-agrarian complex.[32] Württemberg, where there was no equivalent of the Junkers but the estates could check the power of the ruling duke through representative institutions, was another. Württemberg was unusual: its parliament was described by the English Whig Charles James Fox as the only one in Europe that deserved comparison with Westminster.[33] But nobles everywhere exploited corporate institutions and estates to thwart princely authority. Rulers faced a tug of forces. Where state-building had gone furthest, bureaucracies began to acquire independent political weight. Yet a corporatist reaction was always possible, especially from the aristocracy, if the central power pressed too hard on its privileges. The fate of Joseph II's ambitious programme was only the most spectacular example.

The Forces of Social and Cultural Change

Territorial state-building represented a dynamic element in German-speaking Europe of the eighteenth century, but not the only one. Change was also occurring at other levels. Perhaps most basic, because of its many implications, was the rise in population that took place in Germany from around 1750. The statistics are treacherous, but historians agree that these years marked the beginning of a period of rapid and sustained growth in population. Within the borders of the future German nation-state the number of inhabitants rose from around 16–18 million in 1750 to some 24 million in 1800, with German-speaking Austrian provinces adding another 8 million by the latter date. There were, predictably, great regional variations. Population growth was higher in Austria and Württemberg than in Bavaria or Saxony, and greater in the eastern provinces of Prussia than in the western ones. There were special reasons for some of the changed distribution of population in these years. Fast-growing Prussian provinces like Pomerania, for example, reflected aggressive colonization policies. But we still have to explain the fact that the total German population rose by between a third and a half in fifty years. Why? It is generally agreed that the increase had less to do with a lower age of marriage, increased marriage rates, or increased fertility, than with changes in the mortality rate as a result of small improvements in diet and hygiene, and the relatively lower incidence of epidemics (especially the disappearance of the plague). These developments were uneven. As we have seen, famine and epidemic did not disappear, and changes in the mortality rate were at best fairly marginal. But even a small downward movement could make a difference to the demographic balance and hence to future population growth. Like other parts of western Europe, Germany in this period was experiencing the 'end of the biological old regime'.[34]

Population increase was intimately connected with productive resources and their use. This was a two-way relationship, as the example of agriculture shows. Improved diet lowered mortality rates and led to a growing population: a larger population placed increasing demands on the food supply, stimulating changes in agricultural production.[35] This was a period of agrarian revolution. It was signalled by state encouragement for new agricultural techniques, a developing agronomic literature, and the emergence of 'improving landlords' who modelled themselves on English or Dutch originals. More efficient rotations and new crops began to make inroads throughout Germany – fruit, peas, beans, maize, lentils, and that great boon to humankind, the potato. Manure was more widely used and yields rose. Stocks of cattle grew (by 50 per cent in Prussia from the 1750s to the end of the century), stall feeding became more common with the rising production of fodder crops, breeds improved. Finally, and closely connected with these developments, a growing commercialization of agriculture was evident on the back of steadily rising prices for agricultural produce – particularly for grain, which accounted for a comfortable majority of all the land given over to arable. The value of land itself floated up with prices. Around 1801, it was claimed in Wetzlar that farms that could have been bought a century before for 10,000 Gulden were hardly to be had for ten times as much.

The best-known beneficiaries of this process were large estate owners, the classic example being the Junker landlords of eastern Prussia who intensified their demands on peasant labour services to take advantage of rising prices (that was one reason for peasant protests and lawsuits). The manorial estates of East Elbia became major grain-exporters in the last decades of the century, especially to Britain. This had important social consequences, for the market and investment opportunities of land attracted new commercial, bourgeois elements and prompted a faster turnover of properties. The Silesian estate of Comorno, which increased in value nearly six-fold from 1761 to 1797, experienced twelve changes of owner in fifty years. But estate owners were not the only ones to benefit from the bounty of rising prices. Some peasant farmers also took advantage. From areas with substantial peasant farms (Westphalia, Bavaria) to southern and western regions of small holdings (Württemberg, the Rhineland), change was underway. Marginal heathland, marsh, fen and scrub was brought into cultivation, holdings were consolidated and new crops introduced, agreements were made with shepherds to protect newly planted fallows. Much, perhaps most, of this was happening independently of German princes who drained marshes and encouraged model husbandry.

These changes need to be kept in perspective. We should not forget the resistance to new crops like the potato (some blamed it for epidemics), the primitive implements that were still the general rule, the continuing subdivision of strip holdings in the southwest, or the fact that yields remained pitifully low even by nineteenth-century standards. Above all, we should remember the harsh labour required to winnow even a modest existence from the land that supported most Germans, efforts that could be suddenly undone by harvest failure, family illness, fire, or some other natural catastrophe. The agrarian change that occurred under the pressure of population growth and increased demand was no modern fairy tale of challenge-and-response. It also created new privations and insecurities. We do not need to (and should not) idealize earlier periods to recognize that agricultural commercialization led to a sharper differentiation of rural society. It was most obvious on large manorial estates, but it also occurred outside the Prussian east, as the lines that separated large, medium and small peasants, 'dwarf-holders', cottagers and day labourers became more well-defined. The erosion of the form of agrarian cooperation (the *Gehöferschaft*) practised in the Hunsrück and elsewhere symbolized the change. At the top of the emerging rural hierarchy stood a class of large farmers who had done well from cattle, corn or other cash crops, and increasingly separated themselves out as local 'notables' from the rest of the village population – the 80 per cent who were most vulnerable to seasonal, climatic or family mischance. At the bottom stood a growing rural underclass, its ranks swollen by population growth. The late eighteenth century was a bad time for them, as common land disappeared and prices rose. Some of the enlarged pool of the landless and land-poor was mopped up because agricultural innovation, such as projects to clear or reclaim land, was labour-intensive. Others migrated or went permanently on the road as itinerants and beggars, a symptom of contemporary social crisis.

There was another option for the small peasantry and rural underclass, however, one that introduced a further dynamic element into old-regime society. That was the putting-out system, or protoindustrialization as it is often called.[36] Through their agents or 'factors', merchants provided raw materials that poor rural households worked up into finished goods. This had gone on since the late middle ages, but the practice became much more widespread in the second half of the eighteenth century. It was found in many branches of production, including metals, but especially in the spinning and weaving of textiles. The advantages to the merchant were obvious: minimal fixed costs, flexibility, and the cheap labour of a poor, often desperate part of rural society. For those who worked in this sort of dispersed rural production, in the Rhineland, Silesia or Bohemia, the income it provided was essential. In regions of partible inheritance, where population growth put exceptional pressure on the land, the putting-out system was often the only alternative to starvation or migration. There is some evidence that migration rates were lower where cottage industry was most intensive. In other words, the additional income helped to anchor the rural population.[37] Just as commercialized agriculture and rising population were linked both ways, so rural industrialization was cause as well as effect of population increase. It encouraged the landless and small peasantry to increase their family size, because children as well as women played a major part in this form of household production. And the children, in turn, could marry and have families earlier, without waiting for an inheritance. This made short-term sense, but it exacted a high price in the long term. Insecurity and family self-exploitation were endemic in the putting-out system, which permitted dangerous levels of rural over-population to persist. Both problems became major crises in the nineteenth century.

Before 1800, protoindustrialization was another sign of the economic and social change taking place within the institutional shell of the old order. Most obviously, it challenged the guild system. The growth of cottage industry marked a clash of cultures as well as productive systems. It pitted the untrained rural labour of peasant families, in which female and child labour was decisive and the end-product destined for an anonymous market, against the bespoke products of the urban master-craftsman who was proud of his training, wedded to hierarchy, and conscious of his role as a paterfamilias. This was not the only competition

faced by guilds in the 'autumn of the old crafts'.[38] Many craftsmen worked outside guilds, often as one-man concerns, in both
countryside and town. The German ratio of two masters to one
journeyman was a symptom of how guild dominance had been
eaten away. Hence the constant complaints about 'cowboys'
('ground-rabbits' in contemporary parlance) and the fruitless
efforts by the guilds to seek redress from an unsympathetic state.

The putting-out system and the rise of the village craftsman
posed more of a threat to guild privilege than competition from
state-run concerns or other large enterprises. Rulers were mainly
concerned with two things, the sinews of war and the manufacture of luxury goods that would eliminate or reduce costly
imports. Despite some notable exceptions (such as the large state
salt-mining operations in Bavaria), their efforts were concentrated on the production of weapons and uniforms, or on the
obligatory state porcelain factory that no self-respecting ruler
wanted to be without. State-run concerns or concessions
accounted for only a modest share of total manufacturing output.
The same was still true of large-scale production in general.
Around 1800 there were probably no more than a thousand
concerns throughout the German lands employing more than
ten men, with Saxony, Brandenburg, Bohemia, Bavaria and
Lower Austria leading the way. Large concerns remained
insecure, often one-generation affairs, and suffered from shortages of raw materials, trained labour and capital. The putting-
out system employed perhaps six times as many as the early
'manufactories'. One prominent Augsburg producer of cotton
prints employed 350 people in his 'manufactory' during the
1770s, compared with 3500 who worked outside.[39] 'Factories'
in the nineteenth-century sense were almost unknown. The
localized, limited production that was the hallmark of the craft
guilds predominated everywhere.

Yet anyone surveying non-agricultural activity around 1800
must be struck by the sense of change. Rural industry was growing, alongside other crafts – the construction trades, for example.
In some parts of Germany, large-scale glassworks, breweries and
mines dotted the countryside, often run by members of the

nobility who had recognized the possibilities of industrial investment. An example would be Silesia, sometimes called the 'Prussian Peru' because of its mineral riches. Of the 243 mines
operating there in 1785, 191 were owned by nobles (and another
20 by the King of Prussia). In the towns, businessmen and merchants were growing in numbers and wealth, men like Bolon-
garo, the Frankfurt tobacco merchant, Schüle, the Augsburg
cotton king, and the von der Leyen family which controlled 90
per cent of Krefeld silk production in the 1760s. As in England
and France, a significant proportion of entrepreneurs were 'outsiders' – members of religious minorities, or foreigners, such
as the Huguenots, Jews and English so prominent among the
manufacturers of Königsberg.

Demand, fed by a rising population, stimulated the growth
in output. The debates that took place over 'luxury' goods and
new sumptuary codes were a sign that patterns of consumption
were changing. There was another dimension to this: the growth
of German foreign trade. Once again, this was not entirely novel.
From their position in the centre of Europe, Germans had
enjoyed long-distance trade links for centuries: north to the
Baltic, west to France, east to an area of Europe where German
merchants and craftsmen had long played a role, and south to
the Mediterranean, where the commerce of an earlier period
left its mark in the Italianate architecture of Augsburg and the
'German' inns of Venice. The established trade fairs of Frankfurt
and Leipzig were also a residue of these trade patterns – although
their survival can be seen as a symbol of relative backwardness,
for these typically medieval institutions had disappeared from
the economically more advanced Britain and France. Nevertheless, in the last decades of the eighteenth century Germany
became more actively involved in international trade, exporting
linens, silks, woollens and metal goods, importing timber, fish
and iron from Scandinavia, coal and manufactured goods from
Britain, furs from Russia, luxury goods from France, fruit, oil
and wine from the Iberian peninsula, and cotton from the
Americas. The total value of German foreign trade grew by
75 per cent between 1780 and 1800. Imports still comfortably

exceeded exports, and Britain and France (Germany's two major trade partners) had a much greater share in the burgeoning Atlantic trade. But, even here, things were changing. The last decades of the eighteenth century saw a relative decline of Baltic ports like Rostock and Lübeck, where maritime commerce and shipbuilding had once been concentrated, in favour of North Sea ports like Emden, Bremen and – above all – Hamburg, which provided an opening on to the Atlantic.

Like the officials who manned the growing state apparatuses, entrepreneurs, merchants and factors belonged to the 'movers and doers'.[40] Their activities and interests ran counter to the established structures of the old social order. To say that they represented an urban middle class is true, although it needs some qualification. Urban was not always synonymous with dynamic. Up to a quarter of the Empire's population lived in its 4000 towns, but many of these remained small and inward-looking. Their citizens, or *Stadtbürger*, should be thought of less as 'bourgeois' than as figures best described by the archaic English term 'burgher': hostile to those producing for larger markets, defensive about any challenge to their legal privileges, wedded to the local worlds in which their power was rooted. This picture should not be overdrawn, as it sometimes is. Change and conflict were already being felt within these towns. In a sizable town like Aachen (26,000 inhabitants in 1800), guildsmen and other defenders of the status quo tried desperately, with the help of imperial institutions, to keep more expansionist, mercantile elements at bay. The old middle classes of Wetzlar, the court town, were caught 'between persistence and change'.[41] Nevertheless, the real urban dynamism was to be found in the princely residential cities, with their concentrations of officials, merchants and retailers, and in growing commercial centres. The six largest cities in the Empire fulfilled one or both of these functions: Vienna (207,000), Berlin (173,000), Hamburg (100,000), Prague (76,000), Breslau (57,000) and Dresden (53,000). Neither in these cities, nor in their smaller counterparts, was the caste spirit absent – the truckling of court suppliers, the defence of patrician prerogatives, the attachment to the good old ways.[42] But it was here that we are most likely to find the practitioners of new economic forms, the advocates of legal and institutional change – and those who believed in the lively traffic of ideas, especially 'enlightened' ideas.

The Enlightenment had common European features. It was rooted in the belief that men could understand the workings of the universe through the exercise of reason, by observing, measuring and classifying natural phenomena. Hence the great eighteenth-century interest in botany, mineralogy, optics and colour theory. Enlightenment also meant, as the name suggests, illuminating the dark corners of human nature and making it more transparent. It insisted on the possibility of ordering institutions in such a way that society would become imbued with reason and moral sense, creating the conditions for self-fulfilment and the realization of human happiness. Thus law, administration, economics, education, health and welfare all belonged to the enlightened project. These concerns were not wide-ranging by accident: belief in the unity of knowledge and the inter-connections between different kinds of improvement was a given. That was why a key figure in the early German Enlightenment, Christian Wolff, was able to write a book with the apparently immodest title *On God, the World, the Human Soul and all Things in General.*[43] The German 'Aufklärung' belonged to a pan-European movement, but was heavily coloured by local conditions. It had no single centre, for example. Berlin, Hamburg and Leipzig were important; but we also find Lessing in Wolfenbüttel, Wieland in Weimar and Kant in Königsberg. More than in France or Britain, it also developed within established institutions: universities, state academies of science, churches. We have already seen the practical impact of Catholic Enlightenment, a backlash among theologians, academics and clergy against the Baroque piety associated with the Jesuits. For the German Enlightenment generally, the role of Protestantism (and especially Pietism) was central: the movement could almost be described as a branch of progressive Protestant theology. Deists of the French or British kind were rare in Germany, and unbelievers virtually unknown. It is striking how many German Enlightenment writers were Protestant clergymen, or their sons and protégés. The institutions of state and church placed their stamp on the German movement, even when the late Enlightenment outgrew its original institutional base after the 1760s.

In the following two decades enlightened thinking spread through a host of new channels. One was the expansion of the reading public. This was evident in the greatly increased output of German books, pamphlets and periodicals. Other unmistakable signs were the rising numbers of bookshops, reading clubs and masonic lodges, together with the spread of cafés and coffee gardens where newspapers were available. Another measure of the same process was the flourishing of salons like the celebrated one presided over by Rahel Varnhagen in Berlin.[44] Newly popular spa towns like Bad Pyrmont – taking the waters became a fashion in the late eighteenth century – were a seasonal extension of urban gatherings in the reading club, where cultivated officials and professional men gathered with like-minded aristocrats to talk.[45] The reading public expanded in tandem with the rise of publishers, promoters and literary entrepreneurs like Friedrich Nicolai, enabling more writers to earn a living. Württemberg had 120 authors in 1774, 285 in 1790.[46] If the second quarter of the eighteenth century saw the development of German as a literary language, the last quarter saw the tentative emergence of the professional writer – although the greatest revolution in writing was the 'craze for letter-writing' (*Briefwut*) that swept over Germany in the decades before 1800. These deepening channels of communication provide the context against which we must view the extraordinary flowering of talent that produced the philosopher Immanuel Kant and other prominent writers of the Enlightenment, and the German literary renaissance of Lessing, Goethe and Schiller, whose reputations were already established by the end of the century. Travel also helped to create an enlightened public, expanding knowledge in developing disciplines like philology, geography and ethnology (in which German scholars were prominent) and stimulating comparisons. At Göttingen University, Professors Schlözer,

Heyne, Wrisberg and Beckmann taught courses in the art of travelling.[47] Their lectures were designed to educate and discipline the instinct that sent Carsten Niebuhr to Arabia, Alexander von Humboldt up the Orinoco, and Georg Forster around the world with Captain Cook. These were obviously exceptional cases, but thousands more read about travel in works like Forster's *A Journey Around the World*, published in 1778 to enormous acclaim. Recent German scholarship has shown how travel literature became a contemporary cult.[48] It was matched by an apparently insatiable appetite for French and English works, and interest in the mores and manners of Germany's western neighbours.

We can map the enlightened public by the keywords it employed. These were many – virtue, utility, harmony, humanity, patriotism – but the most characteristic was reason. In his famous answer to the question posed by the *Berlinische Monatsschrift* in 1783 ('What is Enlightenment?'), Kant argued that it meant the liberation of the individual from self-imposed tutelage through the use of reason.[49] Five years later the manager of the *Berlin Journal for Enlightenment* saw the task of the movement as 'an effort of the human spirit fully to illuminate, in accordance with the principles of pure reason and with a view to the advancement of the useful, every object in the world of ideas, every human opinion and its consequences, everything which has any effect upon man'.[50] This was a typically ambitious and optimistic programme. But reason had its limits, and I want to end this chapter by exploring these – and the boundaries of the Enlightenment more generally – at three levels: intellectual, social and political.

Intellectually, a frontal reaction against Enlightenment rationalism was visible by the 1770s. Its representative figures are Justus Möser, whose history of Osnabrück praised the value of traditional, seasoned institutions and warned against abstract, mechanical 'levelling', and Johann Georg Hamann ('The Magus of the North'), a publicist from a Pietist background who turned against the dry moral calculus of the Enlightenment, preferring instead intuition, the heart over the head. Both emphases – on tradition and history in collective community life, mystery rather than transparency in individual human affairs – anticipated the Romantic revolt at the turn of the century. More complex perhaps, certainly more central within the intellectual landscape of the 1770s and 1780s, were two other challenges to the supremacy of cold, dry reason, particularly the kind of reason taken over from early French Enlightenment figures like Voltaire. Johann Gottfried Herder, together with many unsung mini-Herders among local writers and clergymen, questioned the abstractly rational notion of a timeless, universal 'human nature'. He insisted instead on the importance of attending to what was local, specific, of this place and time, not any place and time – language, law, custom. The importance of Herder for the future of German history as a discipline and for German nationalism is enormous. Herder was demonstrably influenced by Hamann, and we might view his insights as another anticipation of Romanticism. Alternatively, and more accurately, we could say that he and other eighteenth-century writers discovered (or invented) the German 'Volk' and the genius of local culture some time before the Grimm brothers and Romantic poets.[51]

Herder remained within an Enlightenment framework, both in his cosmopolitan outlook and his eighteenth-century passion to classify. We must be equally careful in placing the larger group of *Sturm und Drang* ('Storm and Stress') writers who emerged in the 1770s, to which both Goethe and Schiller initially belonged. They embodied what is often called 'Romantic idealism', and looked to break through the confines of desiccated, well-tempered reasonableness (they called it mediocrity) in the name of individual genius, inspiration and feeling. This meant following the spontaneity of the heart, but it also had a model that was both literary and French – not the dry Voltaire, but the wet Rousseau, with his (artful) emphasis on simplicity, self-revelation and sensibility. For these writers, as for Herder, the vital qualities of 'popular culture' also proved a stimulus, even if (like writers for the next 200 years) they were always chasing something that had been commercialized just before they caught it. Goethe, at least, made no bones about his child-

hood fascination with the sensational literature of popular alma-
nacs, with their miracles, demons and executions. *Storm and
Stress* literature was a further challenge to the reign of reason,
but again it was not necessarily incompatible with the project
of Enlightenment. Indeed, the later German Enlightenment was
preoccupied with coming to terms with the claims of the heart,
never entirely absent given the Pietist legacy. This applies most
obviously to the three great Critiques written by Kant in the
1780s. Kant had a portrait of Rousseau in his study. Not coinci-
dentally, his first great book was called *A Critique of Pure Reason*
(1781), and emphasized the necessity of feeling for perceiving
the good.

The Enlightenment could accommodate 'enemies' like these;
it was its rational friends who proved most problematic. Scholars
of the Enlightenment have often presented the movement as
the antithesis of everything 'irrational': it was detached, cool,
scientific, reasonable. This misses its ambiguity. The cranky fads
and byways of German enlightened thought have been less well
explored than their French counterparts. It is surely significant,
though, that the pseudomedieval charlatanry of Rosicrucianism
developed out of the masonic lodge, that self-proclaimed temple
of reason; and that early museums were known as *Wunderkam-
mern*, or storehouses of marvels. Long before Romanticism,
there was a strain in the Enlightenment that was drawn towards
Begaffen – gaping or staring at the extraordinary. It was first
cousin to a taste for the exotic, to which an opera like Mozart's
Seraglio (1772), with its pantalooned pasha, appealed. Above all,
contemporary science and fashion often combined to produce
movements that were anything but cool or rational. Scientific
discoveries like electricity, magnetism and oxygen bred their
own pseudoscientific fads. They included 'animal magnetism'
(brainchild of the Frenchman Mesmer, but a great German
enthusiasm), 'oxidation' and 'deoxidation', 'Plutonism' and
'Neptunism', and the numerous other cults of an age given
to what Georg Forster called a 'mania for innovation'. The
well-heeled who made the pilgrimage to Johann Lavater, Swiss
founder of 'physiognomy' (and the 'Lutheran pope'), were as

wide-eyed as any peasant seeking miracles from the bones of a saint.[52] What should perhaps strike us as most familiar and 'modern' about the Enlightenment is not reason, or even the highly instrumental view of nature, but the taste for the exotic and the relentless pursuit of the latest fashion. We are mesmerized by 'being digital'; they were simply mesmerized.

The second limitation of the Enlightenment is more obvious and familiar. The number of new journals may have been large, but the new public remained small. Even the best-known weeklies – Nicolai's *Allgemeine deutsche Bibliothek*, Wieland's *Der Teutsche Merkur* – sold no more than 2000 copies. Regional journals had circulations in the low hundreds. The German reading public of the 1780s probably made up no more than 5 per cent of the population, and Nicolai put the number of the highly educated in Prussia at just 20,000, out of a population of 5.5 million.[53] The social base of the Enlightenment was thin, a narrow stratum of nobles, clerics, officers and the educated middle classes. This is not surprising, given the scarcity and manifold shortcomings of contemporary primary and secondary education, even in more advanced states like Prussia – despite eighteenth-century advances designed to 'civilize' the population through school attendance.[54] That is the background to Kant's observation that this was an age of enlightenment, but not an enlightened age. We should not overstate the extent to which a new cultural market, or national public, had taken shape. Rahel Varnhagen's salon, for example, was certainly an important new form of cultural conduit, as well as notable because (like other salons) it was presided over by a Jewish woman, at a time when the position of both Jews and women in old-regime society was strictly circumscribed. Yet the essence of the salon is to display artists or writers to potential well-born patrons, and personal patronage remained the dominant mode of cultural support in late eighteenth-century Germany. Even writers still depended on the largesse provided by a court or noble patron, working as secretaries, private tutors or (as in the most famous case, Goethe in Weimar) ministers. A position at court or commissions from a patron were essential for artists, architects and musicians. Sometimes the relationship was a success: Haydn valued the freedom to 'be original' during his thirty-year tenure at the Esterhazy court south of Vienna. Not all wanted that freedom, of course. On the other hand, not all who wanted it, had it. Those we call classical composers were actually employed on the same basis as chief pastry cooks or huntsmen. That was why music ran in families (the Bachs, the Mozarts), the craft handed down from father to son. What lifted Wolfgang Amadeus above Leopold Mozart was the imponderable of genius, schooled by a father who retained a courtier's anxiety while hoping his prodigy would burst the suffocating confines of the Salzburg court. As things turned out, the genius was ground between the court, where he chafed and clowned, and a conventional, noble-dominated Viennese public that refused to follow his formal innovations or accept the implicitly subversive message of his mature operas.[55]

A final set of questions must be raised about the flowering of German culture in the later eighteenth century. It has often been difficult for historians to contemplate it without a sense of the discrepancy between the achievement and its larger social and political context. Rolf Engelsing once observed that in the late eighteenth century Britain had an industrial revolution, France a political revolution, Germany a mere 'reading revolution'.[56] The idea that Germans lived life at second hand sounds intuitively plausible. As readers they devoured British and French writings; and while men from those countries physically penetrated India and the Levant, the two most celebrated German works on the 'Orient' – Goethe's *Westöstlicher Diwan* (*The West – Eastern Divan*) and Schlegel's *Über die Sprache und Weisheit der Inder* (*On the Language and Wisdom of the Indians*) – were based respectively on a Rhine journey and research in Parisian libraries. As Karl Marx later put it, the Germans had merely thought what other peoples had done.[57] The notion that Germany suffered from 'underdevelopment' was to enjoy a long career. But there is plenty to quarrel with in such a baldly stated proposition, including the assumptions being made about the historical development of Britain and (especially) France. Let us grant that Germans played a smaller role than the French or British in eighteenth-century voyages of discovery; let us also accept that German merchants were less 'entrepreneurial' than the most commercially aggressive businessmen of the day, in Britain and the United Provinces. When these points have been conceded, questions still remain. Were German merchants really more 'backward' than most in contemporary Europe, including France, or more hemmed in by tolls and other restrictions? The answer is surely no. And if we turn to Germany's educated middle classes, did they have fewer opportunities to gain an education and rise on their merits, or suffer more frustrations at the hands of the corporate society of estates, than their counterparts did in the French *société d'ordres*? Again, surely not. True, they lived and wrote 'in the shadow of the courts', as one historian has put it.[58] Some were undoubtedly frustrated by the stifling, airless quality of the Empire. But this should not blind us to the overwhelming evidence of general optimism about the possibilities for change within the German social and political system.

At the heart of all the arguments about backwardness is the alleged political passivity of the German public. Hence Friedrich Hölderlin's old jibe that the Germans were 'poor in deeds but rich in thoughts'.[59] This, too, is misleading. Can we really dismiss the German 'reading revolution' so summarily, on the eve of what became the century of the word? Education and culture, after all, were to be central aspects of nineteenth-century claims to social authority. We should be especially wary about accepting the argument that enlightened bourgeois (or noble) Germans retreated into 'inwardness', the apolitical cultivation of thought and sensibility. Quite the contrary: if we look at the works that were popular in the masonic lodges and reading clubs, or at the writings of the late German Enlightenment, we see criticism of princely arbitrariness and censorship, alongside attacks on serfdom, advancement based on birth, and other aspects of corporate society. To put it another way, a public concerned with moral philosophy, pedagogy and jurisprudence not surprisingly emphasized the virtues of education, toleration, civil rights, public opinion – and property rights untrammelled by accidents of birth or the 'dead hand' of clerical privilege. This added up to a fairly coherent set of values that looked forward to the construction of an emancipated civil society, or society of citizens. Nor was the celebrated canon of 'bourgeois virtues' (*bürgerliche Tugenden*) as limited or private in scope as it might appear. In this ubiquitous eighteenth-century genre the repeated emphasis on honesty, uprightness, reliability, industry, thrift and order was not simply a listing of desirable domestic attributes, but a representation of private virtues that ought to inform public affairs as well.

None of this amounted to a programme for revolutionary change. From the standpoint of enlightened contemporaries, there was no reason why it should. German governments, after all, employed and promoted men who had advanced by merit and academic achievement. That was a basic element in German cameralism, the science of good government, with its emphasis on efficiency and honesty. Enlightened critics inside and outside the machinery of government naturally wanted their princes to go further in creating the conditions for improving the citizenry and fostering the 'common good'. But most were fearful of risking social disorder by going too far, and sympathetic to what they saw as the obstacles to improvement – such as peasants who were 'brutish', only 'half-human'. Overall, there was a high degree of satisfaction with the direction in which German rulers were going. The critique of arbitrariness, censorship, sinecures and the rest was supposed to keep those rulers up to the mark, and warn them against slipping (or slipping back) into the bad old absolutist habits of 'tyrannical' France. Enlightened officials and writers were, of course, liable to criticism from within the established order, from courtiers and unreconstructed old-regime aristocrats. That was especially true of men with middle-class origins. They might have acquired an education, worked hard and led blameless lives, so it was said, but they lacked birth or title. These sneers from the caste-conscious rankled – but not too much. They could be construed as a sort of backhanded compliment paid by vice to virtue. After all, members of the university-educated middle classes were themselves becoming ennobled; and a significant proportion of the established nobility itself identified with the cause of good government based on enlightened precepts.

The enlightened German public of the late eighteenth century was not wrapped up in its own, apolitical world. While merchants and shippers tended to criticize very specific aspects of the absolutist state (typically, tolls and duties), enlightened ideas had larger political implications. And if the public nevertheless devoted more attention to conduct than to constitutions, or concerned itself more with pedagogy than with power, that was because reformers operated within a system they ultimately believed open to meliorative, incremental change. Nor were they necessarily self-deluding. In Austria, Prussia and many smaller states the impact of Enlightenment ideas was obvious. It is true that reforms depended ultimately on the prince concerned continuing to back them, and the doubts on that score grew among the reformers when, for example, Frederick William II of Prussia succeeded Frederick the Great in 1786. One could also argue that reform amounted to a series of half-victories – growing extension of the 'toleration' principle to Jews, for example, but no hint of the full civic equality or 'Jewish emancipation' that Moses Mendelssohn and others began to call for in the 1780s. Yet in the end, there was general satisfaction with the pace as well as the direction of late eighteenth-century reform from above, which was occurring in a similar way and at a similar tempo across many parts of Europe, from Spain to Scandinavia.

In the 1770s and 1780s there was widespread awareness of what was happening beyond the borders of the Holy Roman Empire. German opinion showed a strong interest in the American revolt and followed the war of independence closely despite the problems involved in acquiring accurate information. The colonists' struggle struck a chord in Germany: Benjamin Franklin was already a well-regarded figure and 'liberty' had become something of a modish term by the 1780s. There was also a strong identification with the goal of equality, interpreted as the ending of stifling restrictions and the precondition for creating a society of citizens. Even the republican form of state gained a surprising degree of support in Germany, although it is hard to be sure exactly what this meant. Public opinion read events in America through a German optic, and the German understanding of American concepts like republicanism or popular sovereignty was often cloudy.[60] German interest in events across the Atlantic had diminished anyway by the time of the 1787 American constitution. The former English colonies were too far away: it was very hard to follow detailed debates, and their direct impact on Germans was minimal. Neither held true of what occurred in France in 1789. This was a neighbour whose actions bore directly on German lives, as well as a country to whom the educated had long been accustomed to look for moral and intellectual instruction – although not for models of good government. In Germany, as elsewhere, the French Revolution proved to be a convulsive and defining experience.

PART ONE

*The Age
of Revolutions,
1789–1848*

CHAPTER ONE

In the Shadow of France

The French Revolution in Germany

Asked what the effect of the French Revolution had been, the Chinese Communist leader Chou En-lai supposedly replied: 'It's too soon to say.' Perhaps it is also too soon to answer the question with reference to Germany: there are no final balance sheets in history. But there are interim judgments. I shall be concerned below with the 'shadow' cast by France on Germany in the short term, between 1789 and 1815. There was no revolution of the French type in Germany – nor was there anywhere in Europe.[1] What we find in Germany, as elsewhere, is a wide range of reactions to a French upheaval that itself passed through many stages, from moderate revolution, through regicide and terror, to conservative stabilization under the Directory, and finally to Napoleon's appropriation of the revolutionary legacy. German responses ran the gamut of possible positions: would-be imitation, selective borrowing, efforts to head off radical threats from below by timely reforms from above, and outright condemnation. These reactions were formulated over a period dominated by European war, when Germany was transformed. The Holy Roman Empire disappeared, the German states of 1815 were barely recognizable versions of their earlier selves, and the vocabulary of politics was permanently changed. One interim judgment on the French Revolution was passed by a prominent German nationalist in 1814. It would be a sign of ingratitude and hypocrisy, said Ernst Moritz Arndt, not to acknowledge 'that we owe an enormous amount to this wild and raging revolution, that it ignited a great sea of fire in the mind . . . It accelerated that process of intellectual ferment through which we had to go, as through our purgatory, if we wished to reach the heavenly gates of our new conditions.'[2] Arndt, as always, was both vivid and opaque. This chapter will try to make his meaning clearer.

Among those concerned with public affairs, initial German reactions to the French Revolution were welcoming. Nowhere was this more obvious than among writers and intellectuals. 'The tremendous interest aroused by the French Revolution crowds out all other concerns', noted one literary editor.[3] The most committed became 'pilgrims of revolution', travelling to Paris to see for themselves.[4] Others contented themselves with poems and pamphlets. Klopstock, former bard of the American revolt, found a new subject for his odes to liberty, and the roll call of German poets who welcomed the revolution is as impressive as its British counterpart. Wieland, Tieck, Hölderlin and Wackenroder voiced their support as strongly as Wordsworth, Southey, Coleridge and Blake. They were joined by the philosophers, the established Kant and Herder as much as the youthful Hegel and Fichte, and by Enlightenment publicists like Nicolai. There were exceptions – Goethe kept a measured distance from all this rapture – but enthusiasm was uppermost in the lodges and reading clubs. It was natural to see France leading humanity towards a new future, and frustrated dwellers in the crabbed and cramped little worlds of the late Empire greeted events across the Rhine as an embodiment of the reason, justice, liberty and human happiness that had so often been talked about. Reading club libraries were flooded with new revolutionary texts. More translations of French political works appeared in these years than in the whole of the previous eighteenth century. From Lübeck to Nuremberg, the left bank of the Rhine to Saxony, revolutionary pamphlets and newspaper articles kept a radical Grub Street of writers and editors busy. Some popular texts circulated in as many as six different versions. Distinctive themes can be found in this literary outpouring. The revolution was a 'dawn' or 'sunrise': the large French literature on the fall of the Bastille was eagerly reproduced, with its demonization of tyranny and quasi-mythic drama of emancipation.[5] It was a motif that also had its place in contemporary German high culture. The sixteen-year-old Tieck, later a central figure in German Romanticism, wrote a youthful dramatic fragment on the fall of the Bastille, entitled 'The Prisoner'.[6] And Beethoven's *Fidelio*, an opera driven by an allegro of progress, ends with the victims of tyranny finally released from the dungeons into the light of freedom.

This aspect of the revolution tapped the twin German currents of Enlightenment and cosmopolitanism. What had happened was believed to have universal significance. 'It was not just a French, but a European revolution', one of its admirers later wrote. If the revolution faltered in France, the cause of progress would be damaged everywhere. 'Were France to fail, I should despise the whole world', as Tieck rather extravagantly put it, for the Germans were 'barbarians' compared with the French.[7] The stimulus from France was therefore believed necessary to bring change to backward parts of Europe: the rising tide of revolution would lift all boats. There was, however, another reaction that placed the French Revolution firmly within a German context. One obvious point of reference was the Reformation. Herder made the comparison of the two great world-historical events. Franz Josias von Hendrich and Johannes Weitzel drew more specific parallels, arguing that the French Revolution had completed the freeing of human energies that the Reformation began.[8] Here was the germ of an idea with antirevolutionary implications. But in 1789–92 French events were more often viewed through another German optic, that of Enlightened Absolutism, as a more dramatic increment of rational reform, or philosophy made flesh. This reading of events found wide support among many who served the old regime as ministers, senior officials or army officers, especially the younger ones. It was the stance even of prominent figures, such as Prussia's foreign minister, Count Hertzberg, and its ambassador to the Reichstag, Count Görtz. Indeed, what did enlightened rulers themselves have to fear from a revolution that (before regicide and terror) identified noble, clerical and guild privilege as its enemies and preached equality before the law? Were these not their own enemies, their own aspirations? Hence the initial sympathy of the Duke of Braunschweig, the Duke of Gotha, Prince Heinrich of Prussia, and – most prominently – Joseph II of Austria and his short-lived successor, Leopold. Joseph, confident to the end, believed that the French were merely borrowing his own ideas.

This view was not universal among the German princes. Frederick William II of Prussia was sympathetic neither to the French Revolution nor to enlightened ideas. A reactionary mystic with a penchant for alchemy, astrology and women, he believed that God addressed him through the medium of a hunchback with the healing touch, and surrounded himself with fellow-members of the Rosicrucian order who encouraged his ambition to roll back the enlightened aspects of his father's achievements. Frederick William hoped to replace reason and toleration with piety and orthodoxy. Not surprisingly, he failed to welcome revolutionary events that religious conservatives attributed to enlightened ideas and masonic machinations. On the other hand, the Prussian king saw no particular danger emanating from France during the early stages of the revolution. In this he was typical of other 'unenlightened' German princes who were unsympathetic but not counter-revolutionary by instinct. In 1790, most princes in the Empire, including the rulers of Austria and Prussia, were more concerned about Habsburg-Hohenzollern rivalry than they were about events in Paris. They took comfort – false comfort, as it turned out – from the likelihood that revolution would preoccupy the French with their own domestic problems.

However, even before the radicalization of 1792 and the export of revolution at bayonet point that followed, popular revolts in Germany faced rulers with a major domestic problem. Unrest began in the western parts of the Empire closest to France. There were riots in 1789–90 in the Rhenish towns of Boppard, Trier, Koblenz, Aachen, Mainz and Cologne. Widespread rural disturbances occurred simultaneously in the Rhineland, the Mosel valley, the Saarland and the Palatinate, often in villages long noted for peasant *jacqueries*. There were similar events in the east. Rural discontent in Mecklenburg over feudal exactions was overshadowed by revolts against Junker landlords in Silesia. Military force was deployed and martial law declared. Then, in 1793, a journeymen's revolt broke out in Breslau and a weavers' rebellion took place in the Erzgebirge involving an estimated 20,000 people. Perhaps the most serious challenge to authority came in Saxony. Following successive harvest failures and harsh winters, peasants angry over seigneurial rents, labour services and hunting privileges began to protest in the spring of 1790. By August a large-scale insurrection of 10,000 peasants was underway. Landlords fled to Dresden, agents and officials were threatened, documents were burned, and peasants armed with stolen guns and pitchforks took physical control of central Saxony. The Elector Frederick August used armed force to crush the rising, but it was not entirely quelled until October. Further peasant disturbances broke out in 1793 and 1794. The second half of the 1790s saw new outbursts of rural and urban discontent over taxes and prices, against a backdrop of the war by then being fought against France. Unrest was now widespread across southern Germany, in Munich, Nuremberg, Augsburg, Stuttgart and Ulm, where journeymen who had picked up French ideas on their travels often led these movements. There were similar outbursts in Breslau, Greifswald, and the northern coastal towns of Hamburg, Bremen, Lübeck and Rostock.[9]

In addition to uprisings, German states faced the formation of 'Jacobin clubs' and revolutionary propaganda flooding in from border towns like Strasbourg, Basel and Altona. There was no unified response from imperial institutions. The Reichstag ambassadors' deliberations in the second half of 1789 set the tone. They disagreed about everything: whether the situation should be formally debated in Regensburg; whether an approach should be made to the emperor, and if so, whether formal or informal; whether Vienna should issue an imperial proclamation; and whether it was better to clamp down on unrest, or try to strengthen the imperial courts and channel discontent into the legal system. Predictably, territorial rulers went their own way, most opting for repression. The Saxon Decree Against Tumult and Insurrection in 1791 was directed against defiance of government decrees or refusal to perform traditional obligations, and declared illegal any gathering or written text that could be construed as hostile to the existing order. In Prussia, the pursuit of pious orthodoxy took on an increasingly antirevolutionary colouring. The theological faculty and students of Halle were denounced as 'spiritual and temporal Jacobins': censorship became harsher; the minister for Silesia ordered the arrest of anyone who even mentioned the French Revolution.[10] In Austria, the young and uncertain Francis II acceded to the throne in 1792 and came under strong pressure to adopt a similar policy. After the uncovering of the so-called 'Jacobin Conspiracy' in Vienna in 1794, he yielded to the entreaties of the hardliners.[11]

Did these and other German princes overreact? Was Germany close to revolution in the 1790s? Modern historians have mainly insisted that it was not, arguing that revolution was the pious dream of a few isolated zealots – when it was not a figment of some frightened ruler's imagination. It is hard to quarrel with this verdict, although the case is less open-and-shut than it might appear. The revolution in France was a singular occurrence, the product of a particular combination of social stress, fiscal crisis, noble intransigence, mounting opposition, and loss of confidence in the political system. Some of those elements were present in all parts of Germany, and all of them in some. Take the social question, for example. Rural overpopulation, pauperism and vagabondage had contributed to the perception of social crisis. Merchant capitalism had created angry craftsmen in Germany as it had in France. And German peasants revolted over grievances often very similar to those of the French peasantry in 1789: feudal privileges, of course (labour services, taxes, game laws), but also the pressure of increased landlord demands resulting from the common trend towards commercialized agriculture and rising prices. There has been a tendency among historians to write off German popular risings as localized and 'backward-looking' – the settling of old scores between families, Protestants and Catholics, craftsmen and patricians, peasants and lords. That is invariably the effect of looking at the micro-level: examination of the French Revolution at local level has shown how it was fed by similar conflicts. Thus, the common argument that German urban revolts featured masters and journeymen who looked 'backwards' makes a falsely absolute distinction. In France too, militant craftsmen fed politically on ideas of the just price, the dignity of labour, and an intense moralism that owed much to long-standing corporate forms of organization and identity. There was common ground between the sansculotte tailor in Paris and his German counterpart, in language as well as experience. Conversely, we should not ignore evidence that in Germany, as in France, old quarrels could be expressed in new ways. Thus, the peasants of Dentingen appropriated the new language of rights to continue a longstanding battle against their lords.[12]

All this is true, yet there remained crucial differences between France and the German lands. The Saxon ambassador at Regensburg rightly observed in December 1789 that there had been no such angry popular gatherings in Germany for over a century.[13] More clearly than some later writers he recognized that there were limits to the restraining power of that perennial historical favourite, Lutheran obedience. Yet revolt in the Empire still did not occur on the same scale or with the same intensity as it did in France. There was nothing in Germany, even in Saxony, to compare with the wholesale rural unrest in France, an essential component of revolution. There were structural reasons for this. The pressure of feudal exactions weighed more heavily in old-regime France, and commercial exploitation of the land had gone further. Conversely, German peasants enjoyed greater access to legal means of redress. In the towns, a less advanced capitalism and the effects of the guild mentality worked against a widespread revolutionary movement in Germany. But so did the political fragmentation of the Empire, which kept revolts local. The 'failure' of social revolution was as much effect as cause of German revolutionary politics.[14]

A differentiated answer is also required if we address the question of potential revolutionary leadership, or the German lack of it. A familiar line of argument emphasizes Germany's 'apolitical' bourgeoisie, drawn to philosophy rather than politics. That is hard to accept without major qualification. As we have seen, Germany did not lack a critical middle-class public: the lawyers, officials, writers and like-minded nobles who discussed the events of the day in coffee houses and reading circles were hardly unpolitical, as reactions in 1789 made clear. Entrepreneurs and merchants may have been thinly represented in their ranks – but that was also true in France, and no serious historian would argue anyway that self-conscious capitalists provided the political energy for the revolution in France (even if many eventually benefited from it). More obviously relevant here is the vexed question of the 'German Jacobins'.[15] For decades, postwar historians in both Germanys created a sizable research industry on this subject. In the process they exaggerated the importance of the 'German Jacobins': in particular, they attached a misleading label to heterogeneous groups of republicans, constitutional monarchists, members of the 'Illuminati' (a secret society of 'enlightened' zealots), and a few authentic Francophile Jacobins. However, sceptical revisionists may have overreacted. In puncturing Jacobin legends, they have given too little weight to the wide incidence of radical groups, or to the serious attempts many of them made to reach down to a broader public through ballads, broadsheets, simple revolutionary catechisms, graphics and innovative political theatre. Total daily press circulation in the 1790s was around 300,000, with perhaps 3 million readers. This revolutionary underground is still being uncovered.[16]

The preceding comparisons between France and Germany have been concerned with political ideology and leadership. In the last resort, however, the entirely different political contexts were probably decisive. It was not the absence of a German Robespierre (or Mirabeau) that made the difference, but the circumstances in which all German would-be revolutionaries found themselves. As shrewd contemporaries like Knigge pointed out and historians have emphasized ever since, even the most pungent German critics of the 1790s were more closely tied to the existing order than their French counterparts, through patronage or employment. Progressive public opinion had always looked to reforms from above for solutions, and in that sense Enlightened Absolutism acted as a form of 'immunization' against revolution. It is true that in the critical period of the late 1780s and early 1790s the tradition of reform from above seemed to be at risk in several major states, notably Prussia, Bavaria and Austria. But the continuing attachment to the idea only showed how much critics had come to depend on enlightened princes. The Viennese 'Jacobins' of the 1794 conspiracy and many of their Bavarian counterparts were really old-style Josephinist or 'Illuminati' reformers with a change of dress, looking for a return to enlightened rule.[17] Until the radicalization of the French Revolution in 1792 there was some overlap between French constitutional monarchism and German hopes for reform from above – although even in its moderate phase the French Revolution cut deeper in establishing equality before the law, abolishing the nobility as a class and emancipating the peasantry.

With the execution of Louis XVI and the terror, German revolutionary sympathizers peeled away. Enthusiasm gave way to revulsion. As the Romantic writer Caroline Schlegel put it: 'They have betrayed our ideals and dragged them in the mud, these evil, stupid and base people who no longer know what they are doing.'[18] Disillusion flowed into at least two channels. One was a strengthened German attachment to the moderate, Girondin version of the French Revolution, reflected in a preference for translated texts from figures like Mirabeau, Brissot, the Abbé Sièyes and General Dumouriez, rather than Jacobins, let alone social radicals like Marat or Hébert. The other was an enhanced appreciation for the virtues, real or imagined, of the Empire. What had formerly seemed cramped now looked reassuring. Like their British counterparts, many young Romantic writers began the journey that would take them full circle, jettisoning their belief in the dawn of universal humanity and instead embracing everything that was 'traditional' or 'organic' in Germany. By the end of the 1790s Klopstock had stopped

writing liberty odes and given pride of place in his study to a
bust of Charlotte Corday, Marat's aristocratic assassin.[19] Gentz
and Görres followed the same path. For German Girondins,
Romantics turning towards reaction, and others in between, the
common denominator was a heightened respect for German
'moderation' and avoidance of domestic terror.

That is an important chapter in German intellectual history,
with long-term consequences. It also gets to the heart of the
difference between Bourbon France and the Holy Roman
Empire: the former collapsed under the weight of structural
crisis, the latter did not. The German princes faced fiscal problems, often for the same reason as the French crown – military
expenditure. But there was no equivalent of the crisis brought
about in France by tax-farming, the system that allowed individuals to collect and keep tax revenues in return for a fixed
sum. Nor, despite some examples of aristocratic opposition to
absolutist pretensions, as in Austria, did German territorial
rulers face anything like the same degree of noble intransigence
as Louis XVI. The imperial nobility was fragmented and impotent. The nobles of the major German states, on the other hand,
lacked the grievances of the French *Frondeurs*: they were too
secure in their exercise of local power, too well established in
armies, bureaucracies and courts. Finally, there was the question
of physical force. In 1789 the French army was 'disloyal, disaf-
fected – and in the wrong place'.[20] None of these things applied
to the armies of the German territorial states, which proved
very effective in crushing revolts. That applied to small and
medium-sized states (Nassau-Usingen, Hesse-Darmstadt) as
much as to Prussia or Saxony.

Revolution 'from below' is, historically, unusual. A complete
revolutionary break with the old order comes about when the old
order itself has been undermined from within and lost control of
the situation. It is the overall dynamics of revolution we should
look at. There was no radical revolution in Germany – no 1792–4
– because there was no 1789. The necessary preconditions were
neither so developed as they were in France, nor did they exist
in the same explosive combination. There were peasant and

urban lower-class social grievances, but they had not reached the same level of intensity. Bourgeois and noble critics were prepared to bite the hand that fed them, but not to bite it off. And discontent of all kinds was contained by the fragmentation of the German polity and the fact that princely authority remained intact, despite occasional scares. The greatest impact of the French Revolution was to be felt only after war had swept away the Holy Roman Empire and recast German politics. Institutional transformation in Germany was a product of French arms: directly, in the annexed lands of the west and the French satellite states, indirectly, through a renewed wave of reforms from above in states that had been humiliated by French armies, and looked to shore up their regimes.

The Impact of War

Warfare was a familiar feature of eighteenth-century Germany – hence Enlightenment arguments that it represented a waste of human and material resources, and attempts to refine the 'rules' of war. The hostilities of 1792–1815 did not drop out of a cloudless sky. But war against the French revolutionary, later Napoleonic, armies lasted much longer than eighteenth-century conflicts. A whole generation grew up in its shadow; it affected everything from levels of consumption to religious observance. The war also had an ideological component absent from earlier dynastic struggles, and this left its mark on the reshaped German state-system. 'In the beginning was Napoleon', runs the first sentence of Thomas Nipperdey's now-classic book.[21] His exaggeration is forgivable.

The war that broke out in 1792 was never a simple revolutionary or counter-revolutionary crusade. It resulted from a series of intertwined conflicts. First, there was the problem created by the August 1789 decree of the French Assembly, abolishing the feudal dues that German princes exacted from their lordships in Alsace and Lorraine. The princes refused to accept the decree, and their claims remained unresolved three years later. Here the principle of the modern territorial state collided with the very different principles that held the Empire together. It symbolized what Volker Press has called 'the clash of two worlds'.[22] Second, there was an obvious ideological conflict between revolution and old regime. This had European dimensions (like the response to Bolshevism after 1917), with Germany placed on the front line by virtue of geography. The Empire was also a favourite bolt hole of aristocratic émigrés from France, who turned Koblenz into a miniature Versailles. Many were content to frequent salons and watering holes, drawing criticism for their free spending and lax morals. But in a string of courts, from Trier to Vienna, émigrés led by the Count of Artois badgered German rulers to act against France. The Elector of Trier even allowed Prince Condé's army to train in Koblenz. These counter-revolutionary intrigues on foreign soil antagonized the revolutionaries and reinforced their belief that the Empire was effete and decadent. Finally, great-power calculations entered the picture. German policy in Paris, while certainly infused with the new nationalism central to the revolution, also had elements of longer-standing French concerns going back to Louis XIV. On the other side, the imagined domestic chaos of France was seen as an opportunity, especially by Prussia.

None of these considerations made conflict inevitable. It would probably have been possible to negotiate some compromise over the German princes' claims. No one was going to risk war over the Prince of Leiningen's lost feudal dues from Dürkheim – especially as the new regime in France, in placing state sovereignty over historic privileges, only did what larger German territorial rulers had themselves been doing, or trying to do, for decades. As for the émigrés, they were not universally popular among German princes. Leopold of Austria and the Elector Max Franz of Cologne rejected their overtures even though both were brothers of the French Queen Marie Antoinette. The liberal-minded Leopold resisted even the blandishments of Madame de Cassis, brought to Vienna by émigrés to work on the notoriously libidinous emperor. Prudence also played a part: the estates in Trier disliked émigrés because their presence might provoke France, and the Elector agreed – under French pressure – to disband the force gathered in Koblenz. Nor was it true, whatever some in Paris believed, that the chancelleries of monarchical Europe were permanently obsessed with France. It was certainly not true of the two main German powers. Austria was facing revolts in the Netherlands and Hungary, a campaign against Turkey, and a major conflict with Prussia over Poland, for these were the years of the crisis that would lead to the final Polish partitions of 1793 and 1795. In 1790 Prussia and Austria nearly went to war. For both, France was just one issue, and not necessarily the most pressing. The smaller states and territories did not count in power terms. The imperial knights might be an affront to reason, but they hardly threatened the revolution.

The political dynamics in France and Germany raised the temperature during 1791. Prussia and Austria had settled their differences in 1790, and the two rulers met in August 1791 to reaffirm their support for the monarchical principle. The Declaration of Pillnitz immediately followed the abortive flight to Varennes of Louis XVI: it sounded fierce, but was still carefully hedged around with conditions. However, with their hands freed, Austria and Prussia began to think more seriously about French policy – the former sabre-rattling to try to influence politics in Paris, the latter pondering the territorial gains to be made from a short, sweet campaign. The radicalization of the revolution encouraged their ambitions. And on the French side, a similar parallelogram of forces brought conflict closer. The court party, believing that war would serve its interests, played into the hands of the war campaign being conducted by Brissot and his faction in the Assembly. Austrian miscalculation, Prussian greed and French revolutionary *élan* combined to bring about the war declared by France on 20 April 1792.[23]

The opening engagements of 1792, pitting the French against the Prussians at Valmy and the Austrians at Jemappes, were not decisive. But they were psychologically important victories for the French at a turning point of the revolution, and began a string of French successes. These certainly owed something to the fact that Prussian troops were engaged elsewhere in Polish aggression. But military conflict also exposed the institutional frailties of old-regime German states, which had easily withstood domestic disturbances but crumbled before the new kind of warfare represented by French armies. These successes can be briskly catalogued. After being temporarily driven back, the revolutionary armies made territorial gains in the Low Countries and western Germany, destroying the so-called First Coalition against France and detaching Prussia from its ranks. Under the Treaty of Basel in 1795, Prussia signed a separate peace. Stealing a march on Austria in the east with its land-grab in the third Polish partition, it accepted French occupation of the Rhineland, granted France a wide sphere of influence in northwest Germany, and entered a decade of neutrality. Austria, in the same ten years, was the most committed Continental opponent of French armies. But three waves of military defeats led to the enforced peace treaties of Campo Formio (1797), Lunéville (1801) and Pressburg (1805). Prussia finally re-entered the lists in 1806, only to suffer catastrophic defeats at Jena and Auerstädt.

The campaigns of 1792–1806 brought irreversible changes to Germany. The manner of French success was significant in itself. As the Prussian military strategist Clausewitz noted in 1793: 'A force appeared that beggared all imagination ... The people became a participant in war; instead of governments and armies as heretofore, the full weight of the nation was thrown into the balance.'[24] The French were able to mobilize the population on an unprecedented scale, provide openings for the talented of all classes, and live off the land as they fought. As a result they put larger, faster, more effective armies into the field. Desertion rates remained high, it is true, and the novelty of French armies should not be exaggerated: some of their chief characteristics were anticipated in the War of American Independence, and the importance of skirmishing light infantry was already starting to be appreciated among old-regime strategists. But there remains an obvious contrast with the smaller, yet more ponderous and often poorly commanded fighting forces of Austria and Prussia. The difference was plain in the Austrian disasters of Marengo, Hohenlinden, Ulm and Austerlitz; it was even more evident in the 1806 humiliations of a Prussian army that had been the envy of Europe only fifty years earlier. Defeat was not just the product of complacency, rustiness and an aged officer corps, although all played a role. By comparison with French forces based on conscription, that travelled light and struck quickly, the Prussian army was rigid and immobile, tied to its chain of food depots and reluctant to march at night or slip through wooded terrain for fear of even more desertions from the ranks of ferociously disciplined but poorly motivated soldiers. The unequal match-up between this over-drilled, 'clockwork' army (to borrow the term used by the military critic Boyen) and the mobile, skirmishing French was a clash of more than just armies.

Austrian and Prussian defeat led to a completely new map of Germany. Borders were redrawn, populations changed hands, old forms of sovereignty disappeared, new states emerged. On the back of its military dominance, and exploiting internal weaknesses and rivalries within the Holy Roman Empire, France took the driving seat in Germany: it disposed of territories, imposed indemnities, controlled or enforced alliances, made and unmade kings. The Rhineland, occupied in 1792 and reoccupied in the mid-1790s, became a part of France in 1802, contrary to the 'no wars of conquest' policy adopted by the French National Assembly in 1790. Apart from that, initial French military successes affected the shape of Germany only indirectly, through Austrian losses in the Low Countries and Italy, and the pushing eastwards of Prussia. But what happened in the Rhineland represented the writing on the wall for the Empire. Prussia (in the Treaty of Basel) and Austria (at Campo Formio) were forced to acquiesce, in both cases signing secret clauses that showed how little importance they attached to the integrity of the Empire compared with their own territorial ambitions. And many medium-sized German states, caught between impotence and opportunism, followed the same line, signing treaties with France in which they sanctioned French annexations and gained compensation for themselves from former ecclesiastical territories. It was a foretaste of what would happen on a larger scale a few years later.

Campo Formio had made the future of the Empire subject to negotiations between imperial representatives and France. These gatherings of unequals became even more unbalanced after Lunéville, and in 1803 a report of the 'imperial deputation' was presented, passed by the Reichstag and approved by the emperor, under the terms of which the Empire disappeared in all but name. Just six of the larger imperial cities survived along with three of the ecclesiastical territories, the remainder of which were 'secularized'. These lands passed into the hands of large and medium-sized territorial states: Prussia, Hanover, Oldenburg and a phalanx of southern states (Bavaria, Baden, Württemberg, Hesse-Darmstadt) which did well in a part of Germany where imperial cities and monasteries had been profuse. The map of central Europe was radically simplified in a process that was partly a capitulation to French power and rationalizing zeal, partly a result of the German states' own healthy appetites for smaller neighbours.

The overwhelming French victories of 1805–6 brought the second instalment of the territorial consolidation that began in 1803, as the patchwork of dwarf territories in old-regime Germany gave way to some three dozen larger, more compact states. The Holy Roman Empire finally disappeared with the enforced abdication of the emperor in August 1806, although not before Francis II had already jumped ship by proclaiming himself – in line with the new spirit of the age – the Emperor of Austria. The imperial knights went the same way as the free cities and ecclesiastical territories three years earlier. Through 'mediatization', their land – where it had not already been seized – was absorbed into the middle-sized territorial states of the south. The rulers of these states were among the sixteen (eventually over thirty) German princes who joined the Confederation of the Rhine established by Napoleon in July 1806. A combination of military alliance and French-sponsored 'third Germany' designed as a counterweight to Prussia and Austria, the Confederation stretched from Mecklenburg to the Tyrol. Among the member-states of the Confederation were also two that marked the belated application to Germany of the French urge to experiment in political forms already seen elsewhere in Europe. But instead of the French-created republics of the 1790s (Batavian, Cisalpine, Ligurian, Parthenopean), Napoleon set up new non-republican states on German soil. The Grand Duchy of Berg and the Kingdom of Westphalia were strategic buffer states, gave employment to members of the large Bonaparte family, and served as laboratories for French political institutions.

While the political geography of middle Germany was thus rearranged, the position of the two largest German powers was also radically altered by 1805–6. Vienna was occupied and Austria excluded from southern Germany, losing the Tyrol, the Vorarlberg, and its territories on the Upper Rhine and in Upper Swabia to the south German states. It was then forced to acknowledge the royal credentials of those same predators, rulers such as the newly minted kings of Bavaria and Württemberg who owed their titles to Napoleon. Berlin was also occupied in 1806, and Prussia suffered crushing territorial losses. It was pushed out of Germany west of the Elbe, and saw its eastern provinces and Polish possessions stripped away to form the Grand Duchy of Warsaw under the control of its historic rival, Saxony. What remained was a sorry rump of four provinces as Prussia was reduced by the Treaty of Tilsit to about half its former size and population. Nor was that all. While the dynastically minded Habsburgs were humiliated by marriage into the upstart Bonaparte family, the parsimonious Hohenzollerns were also hit where they were most sensitive by an indemnity of 140 million francs (Austria had negotiated its indemnity down to 85 million). Prussia was further hurt in 1810 when France annexed the Hanseatic ports of Bremen, Lübeck, and Hamburg, along with the Duchy of Oldenburg, to provide access to major commercial centres and strategic control of the coast. In short, 1806 and the following years displayed Napoleon's full repertoire of methods to create buffer zones and loyal allies: direct annexations, old states that were built up as French satellites, new model states that were created as French puppets, and major states that were cut down to size.

What impact did war and French dominance have on the German people? This was a time of chronic uncertainty and insecurity. More than half of all Germans acquired new rulers during this period, and there were places that experienced five or six changes in a generation. Some regions remained relatively untouched in territorial terms – Saxony for example – but Saxony, the cockpit of Europe, was a major battleground of the period. From the Baltic to the Alps, from the left bank of the Rhine to the Vistula, local areas changed hands as armies marched and counter-marched. The unfortunate Rhenish town of Oppenheim shuttled backwards and forwards between the French and Austrians in the years 1792–8, exploited in turn by each side. Even in the modest Vorarlberg campaign of 1809, much of Lindau was destroyed and Upper Swabian towns like Wangen, Waldsee and Biberach repeatedly found themselves on the route of march. The devastation was less than that caused by warfare in the twentieth century (or by the Thirty Years War in the seventeenth century). But Germany was the scene of intermittent hostilities for twenty years, its population subject to the rape, looting, billeting and casual destruction of French, Prussian, Austrian, Bavarian, Polish, Russian, Swedish, British and Portuguese soldiers. Even more dangerous were the numerous deserters – the French Grand Army had 10 per cent desertion rates. They terrorized communities and swelled the ranks of bandit gangs, who enjoyed a final Indian Summer in central Europe during the early nineteenth century, the period of the most celebrated of all German bandits, Schinderhannes. Like epidemics, these were familiar side effects of war, but the duration of hostilities and the size of armies magnified their impact. The fact that the French abandoned the cumbersome baggage-train to live off the land was also bad news for civilians. Even more than most armies, they were locusts. And, as Clausewitz pointed out, for every three or four soldiers who needed provisioning there was a horse that ate ten times as much – a horse that would have been seized from the occupied community. *On*

War, his celebrated posthumous work, was a cold-eyed analysis of the new kind of conflict and its social impact.

There were three major aspects of French exactions: provisions, money and men. All were most directly felt in occupied areas. The Rhineland armies in the 1790s were up to 190,000 strong, to which another third can be added for ancillary personnel, not including the ragtag army of camp followers. So we are probably talking about over a quarter of a million people who needed to be provisioned. The result was procurement that was often no more than plunder. It applied, of course, to horses, forage, cattle, grain and other foodstuffs, sometimes causing local famines. But this was just the beginning. The French acquired everything they needed from their reluctant hosts: wine, coffee, cocoa, clothing, boots, shoes, hats, mattresses, blankets, linen, soap, medicine, household utensils, iron, tin, leather, paper, firewood, weapons, ammunition. Small wonder that General Beurnonville reported gloomily to his superiors in 1796 that one region near the Sieg was 'a hideous desert'.[25] In the matter of money, French armies were also left to fend for themselves by a permanently indebted government. They responded by demanding levies and 'loans' from the local population, demands that were unrealistic, arbitrary and repeated. The sanctions used to coerce payment included punitive billeting, threats to property and hostage-taking. After provisions and cash, the third French requirement was manpower: to construct fortifications, build roads, make army uniforms. This was forced labour, a civilian counterpart to the conscription of soldiers into the French army. The numbers of foreigners in the Napoleonic army increased sharply after 1800. By then the Rhenish recruits had become officially 'French', but that was probably little consolation to those sent to die in the Russian snows, or to the Napoleonic widows they left behind. (Although the long-lasting traces of a 'cult of Napoleon' among some veterans of these campaigns should also be noted.) All of these depredations in the Rhineland were later repeated in the occupied Hanseatic towns, whose problems were compounded by the impact of the French sieges mounted against Danzig (1812–

13) and Hamburg (1813–14). Finally, the occupied areas provided rich cultural pickings, although they were not ransacked on the scale practised in Italy. Experts were sent into the Rhenish provinces to assess the most valuable art works, and great quantities of books were shipped back to the Bibliothèque National, along with altar pieces, historic weapons, and scientific instruments. Stendhal was one of those responsible for selecting books from the valuable Wolfenbüttel collection.[26]

French pressure was greatest in occupied areas, but was felt in some way by almost all Germans. After their military defeats in 1805–6, Austria and Prussia faced large indemnities in addition to the costs of maintaining French armies of occupation. Prussia was especially hard-hit. In the two years following Jena, gross French receipts in cash and kind from Prussia, her German allies and the sequestered goods, ships and bank deposits of British nationals were reportedly 600 million francs. Allowing for campaign costs, the net profit to France was some 350 million francs, equivalent to half the total income of the French state in 1807. Looking at the sums involved from the opposite end, the exactions over a two-year period were equivalent to about sixteen times the Prussian government's annual revenue before the invasion.[27] As in the permanently occupied territories there were repeated levies of provisions and cash, so that Prussian and Austrian officials were forced to collaborate in extracting a surplus from the local populations that was then siphoned off by the French. The grimmest exaction, once again, was human, as losses and the mounting numbers of Frenchmen who voted with their feet led to the increased use of non-French soldiers in the Grand Army. Austria and Prussia provided a total of 50,000 men in 1812. The southern allies of Napoleon fared proportionately worse, Bavaria alone being forced to raise 40,000 troops by 1809. In Württemberg, all men between the ages of eighteen and forty were subject to conscription. The memoirs of Jakob Walter, the only extant account by a German common soldier, tell us vividly what this meant in practice. A stonemason from Ellwangen, Walter fought in the campaigns of 1806–7 and 1809, before taking part in the invasion of Russia, the retreat from which he barely survived.[28] Most savagely stripped of young (and not-so-young) men were the satellite states, the Grand Duchy of Berg and the Kingdom of Westphalia.

In the economic sphere, as in others, the French screw tightened after 1806. Germany was the pivot of Napoleon's Continental Blockade, pronounced in the Berlin Decree of that year, an attempt to move beyond protectionist measures against British manufactures to a system of controls that would force Britain's surrender by cutting off the lifeline of trade with Continental Europe. The annexed Rhenish areas suffered least from the new policy. They were already part of France, not foreign lands being coerced into compliance. Elsewhere, the Berlin Decree did not formally apply in the Confederation of the Rhine states, only in areas administered or militarily occupied by the French, and the blockade was anyway enforced with varying degrees of severity. Saxony was probably least affected, for political and geographical reasons, while Bavaria continued to provide a back door through which goods could be moved up from Trieste or Italy via southern Germany. In more obviously sensitive areas – the northern coast, the right bank of the Rhine – the policy was enforced with strict, even draconian measures. But even where the official line was tough, the sticky fingers of bribe-taking French officials could make life a little easier. Hamburg was the classic example. As a rule of thumb, French customs officials were always most interventionist where the occupying forces were most numerous. The picture was therefore mixed, but the net effect was a sharp decline in German trade with Britain, both exports of grain and imports of cloth, ironware, sugar, coffee and tobacco. Trades dependent on these goods suffered badly. Cologne, where tobacco working and the trade in colonial goods were both important, was a major victim.

One way around these restrictions was smuggling. It became so widespread that in some branches illegal trade may have exceeded the legal variety. Contraband goods were carried in both directions, for Germany was also a favoured base from which to smuggle goods into France. As French controls tightened, smuggling routes changed: Amsterdam-Rotterdam-Cologne was eclipsed by Bremen-Hamburg-Frankfurt and Stettin-Danzig-Leipzig. Behind the countless ordinary people engaged in smuggling were large concerns which underwrote the operations, demanding at least 25 per cent of their value as an insurance premium. Fortunes were made in this way: the Cologne banker Schaaffhausen was able to pay an excise fine of 100,000 francs without difficulty. But smuggling was risky, and fines were not the only penalty. After the Trianon and Fontainebleau decrees of 1810, warehouses were stormed and English goods seized or burned in every major German port and commercial centre affected by the blockade, including Hamburg, Cuxhaven, Rostock, Lübeck, Bremen, Berlin, Frankfurt, Cologne, Hanover, Mannheim, Jena and Leipzig.[29] Greater efforts were also made to police the movement of goods in the Confederation, forcing states like Baden and Bavaria to tread a difficult line between compliance, which was unpopular, and tacit toleration of smuggling, which exposed them to French ire.

In theory Napoleonic economic imperialism was supposed to make Europe serve France as a source of raw materials and a market for manufactured goods. Did it? What was the overall effect on the German economy of the blockade and so-called Continental System? The answers depend greatly on the branch or region being considered. In the case of agriculture, for example, the parts of northern Germany dependent on grain exports to England were hard hit compared with the south and west – although the long-term agricultural cycle after 1800, which saw prices turn down, eventually caught up with the south and west too. The textile industry of the Rhineland experienced similarly mixed fortunes, as the left-bank districts incorporated in France flourished at the expense of the right-bank area of Berg, although this only accelerated a process that had been going on anyway before the French arrived.[30] The textile branches show how difficult it is to generalize. The linen industry lost export markets in South America and the Caribbean, and linen manufacturing areas like Silesia were badly hurt; but the removal of English competition was a boon to the cotton industry in Saxony, where the number of cotton jennies increased twentyfold in the years 1806–18. The wool industry prospered on balance, mainly because its leading centres became part of France. And the damage done to silk producers in Barmen and Berlin has to be set against the new market opportunities for manufacturers in Krefeld. The picture is just as varied in the metal branches, where iron production stagnated, engineering grew.[31]

Some broad conclusions are possible. Germany was certainly not reduced to an agricultural producer or raw materials supplier to France. Some parts of Germany (like Silesia) did become more agricultural, but others (like Saxony) became more industrial. That was a matter of growing regional specialization, reinforced but not caused by the effects of French policy. In general, ports and shipping centres dependent on overseas trade suffered much more than inland commercial towns under a system that emphasized overland trade. Economic activity shifted to the interior, in Germany as elsewhere. Neither on the coast nor in the interior, however, was there a major break with long-term economic developments. Both Baltic and North Sea ports suffered under the French, but the latter recovered quickly while the former went into long-term decline, just as one would have expected from the late eighteenth-century trend. Similarly, the temporary shift in patterns of commercial activity benefited cities that were primed to take advantage, such as Frankfurt and Leipzig, but did nothing to revive the fortunes of former imperial cities where long-term decline was irreversible. The consensus among historians is that the years of French domination did more to stimulate than to depress the German economy, short-term spoliations notwithstanding. War gave a boost to German weapons manufacturers. Protection from British competition helped infant industries. And, in some cases, necessity proved the mother of invention. The shutting off of cane sugar imports stimulated sugar-beet cultivation, an important long-term development that was also an early example of what became something of a German speciality: import substitutions stimulated by war.

The balance sheet is as hard to draw up as it always is at times of revolutionary discontinuity. We have to set short-term pain against long-term gain. Some of the most important positive aspects of French domination were long-term. They include the benefits of an improved transportation network, despite the short-term problems caused by war. More fundamentally, social forces were freed by the emancipation of the peasantry, the diminution of guild privileges and other attacks on the corporate order, although all of these changes brought immediate hardship. In some parts of central Europe the changes were brought about by the French or their proxies, in others by states reacting to the French challenge. In both cases they represented an institutional transformation that was decisive for the development of nineteenth-century Germany, but a transformation that was far from painless.

Reform from Above

In 1799 the Prussian minister von Struensee told the French chargé d'affaires that the revolution the French had made 'from below' would be completed 'gradually, from above' in Prussia.[32] The distinction is familiar in all standard accounts of the period, and is not without point. It might nevertheless be more accurate to view *all* the institutional changes of this period as reforms from above. There were marked variations from state to state, particularly between east and west, but there are grounds for arguing that the reformers were performing variations on the same theme. Everywhere the dominance of France was decisive, whether it was imposing French-style liberation on annexed territories, using its satellite states as administrative laboratories, providing the stimulus for change in the Confederation, or provoking pre-emptive reforms in Austria and Prussia. Everywhere reform was driven by the financial burdens of war, French exactions, and the fiscal crises they created. Everywhere there were common elements to reform: corporate privilege was attacked, the power of the sovereign state and modern bureaucracy grew. And everywhere (although for different reasons) the reformers formed a relatively narrow group and encountered resistance to their measures. For all the differences between the French Rhineland and Prussia, the Kingdom of Westphalia and Austria, their developments in this period belong on the same continuum.

French rule in the Rhineland was always more than plunder cloaked by ideology. The hardships imposed by the revolutionary and Napoleonic armies were real enough, as we have seen, but (as in France itself) they were offset by substantial achievements. The occupiers broke with the old social and political order, the sharpest break that occurred anywhere on German soil. The French overthrew the existing secular and ecclesiastical princes, abolished the tithe, ended seigneurialism, eliminated guilds, overturned monopolies, nullified privileges, emancipated the Jews, introduced religious toleration, and secularized church lands. Changes in the legal system affected every aspect of life, from marriage and divorce to property rights. These and other changes transformed economy, society and political rule. They amounted to a crash course in modernization that removed the institutions of the old regime, separated church and state, rebuilt the administrative bureaucracy on a new basis, and made possible the relatively untramelled accumulation and disposition of property that is one hallmark of modern civil society. Was this not, therefore, the very acme of the French Revolution in action? Why should we call it reform from above? Most obviously, the reforms were imposed from above by Frenchmen on Germans. 'No one likes armed missionaries', as Robespierre had warned in April 1792.[33] The French armies did not lack German supporters in the early days, although these were always a small minority. But the French were understandably sceptical of the German Jacobins in the Rhineland, and reluctant to establish a Rhenish Republic as some of their German admirers urged. The experience of the short-lived 'Mainz Republic' in 1792–3 spoke against taking such a risk; so did arguments based on security. It was therefore inevitable that the wave of French reforms would be tainted by their provenance, especially once the full force of requisitions and levies was felt.

The substance of reform also created a backlash. The reforms were not, it is true, uniformly unpopular. Peasants predictably welcomed the abolition of seigneurial dues and tithe, often taking advantage of the French military presence to settle accounts with a church they associated with worldliness and privilege. When the revolutionary army reached Tholey, dominated by its abbey, peasants from the surrounding districts made a bonfire of the records of debt owed to their former tithe-lord. Such actions were common in the Zweibrücken and Saarbrücken areas, a reminder (if one were needed) that peasants can be anticlerical – even in Germany. Journeymen were freed from the crushing discipline of guild masters, merchants from the depressing multiplicity of tolls, monopolies and staples. Pragmatic Rhenish businessmen quickly adapted to the new rules. The propertied middle class were among the obvious beneficiaries of institutional change, whether from the fillip given to cottonmasters in Krefeld and ironmasters in the Eifel, or the opportunities provided by the sale of church lands – like the coal merchant in Trier who moved into a former nunnery. Yet these examples indicate one of the problems with the changes brought by the French: they were likely, at least in the short term, to be advantageous only to a minority. Even if we take into account the nobles and better-off peasants who also bought church lands, the surprising number of former officials who continued to serve the French, and the lawyers who found posts in the new judicial system, the fact remains that the French Rhineland was short of obvious beneficiaries among the mass of the population, and correspondingly short of popular support. Peasants found themselves paying the tithe under a new name, as well as a generally higher level of overall taxation; journeymen and masters suffered from the demise of the guilds, even though a few may have prospered; those servants of old-regime courts and noble establishments who had not fled with their masters were left without jobs; the poor, whose numbers almost certainly increased during the chaotic decade of 1792–1801, were deprived of the employment, alms and other forms of assistance once provided, however imperfectly, by religious foundations and orders. And those who dared to voice complaints on any of these points were likely to find the new state bureaucracy a more rigorous foe than the arbitrary but often indolent old regime.

The French reformers were isolated, therefore, and not just because of their war-related depredations. They had some German allies, but the local Jacobins were a wasting asset. For the most part the occupiers faced a population at best sullenly indifferent, at worst actively hostile. Popular resistance underlined the narrow base for French reformers. Emigration to the right bank, banditry, smuggling, tax evasion, refusal to accept French paper money, defiance by guildsmen, administrative sabotage by German local officials, defiling the tricolour, demolishing liberty trees, boycotting or disrupting official festivities, shouting counter-revolutionary slogans, intimidating pro-French locals – the repertoire of passive resistance was extensive. Sometimes it was not so passive: rioting guildsmen had to be put down by cavalry in Pirmasens, French officials were killed in Bingen, peasants engaged in sporadic partisan activity. Passive and active resistance are actually hard to separate cleanly. Take the issue of religion, and especially Catholicism. This was a major source of friction between French occupiers and Rhinelanders, because of the strategic position the church had occupied in old-regime society, and because of the innovations, proscriptions and mockery of faith that issued from the French. The response was powerful. The 1790s witnessed a wave of distress signals in the form of prophecies, apparitions and other supposedly supernatural phenomena, as well as a stubborn persistence in holding banned pilgrimages and processions. This activity appears innocuous enough, but it could easily tip over into physical confrontation with the authorities. Apparitions bore anti-French messages; processions became the scene of violent clashes. As in Italy and Spain (or, indeed, France), outraged piety easily fused with other resentments, providing the rallying-cry or justification for resistance. There was no Vendée and no Sanfedist movement in the Rhineland, but the extent of violence should not be underestimated. In the longer term, the effects of French institutional changes were decisive for Catholicism and the church. That was true in the Rhineland, as in other French-occupied parts of Europe. The French inadvertently strengthened papal authority by weakening the national churches, and made the church more 'popular' by removing aristocratic sinecures. Revolution discredited reformers of the Catholic Enlightenment variety and brought the church closer to popular piety. In the short term, the conflict over religion symbolized the problems created by revolution from above. 'Outrages' like revolutionary, anticlerical soldiers defecating in tabernacles were no doubt exceptional, but the boundless French contempt for 'superstitious', 'backward' Rhinelanders was altogether typical, and it did not apply only to religion. To the occupiers, the manifold shortcomings of the occupied was sufficient to justify forcing them to be free. But as General Hoche candidly noted in a report to the Directory: 'Those who have had to pay such a high price for liberty rarely love it'.[34]

Things became easier in the period of incorporation into metropolitan France. Napoleon's Concordat with the Catholic church in 1802 signalled an end to the era of disruption in one sphere. An improving economy took the edge off discontent, new institutions bedded down, and something like a new élite emerged from the debris of the 1790s – a mélange of businessmen, landowners and officials that resembled the 'notables' of Napoleonic France. Nevertheless, the idea that the Rhinelanders were being educated into the superior virtues of Frenchness remained. There were parallels in the new model states, the Kingdom of Westphalia and the Grand Duchy of Berg. The former, in particular, was intended to be a 'moral conquest', a blank slate on which French institutions were to be written. The Kingdom of Westphalia received a constitution (the first in German history), and efforts to achieve legal equality by abolishing traditional privileges were supposed to illustrate the benefits of the *Code Napoléon*. There were, indeed, reforms:

serfdom was ended, church lands auctioned off, religious toleration decreed, transportation projects inaugurated, weights and measures unified, administration rationalized and centralized, the power of intermediate authorities reduced. Two things should be noted about these reforms. First, they were imposed in a spirit of authoritarian confidence in the wisdom of imperial government. As the emperor wrote to Jérome Bonaparte: 'It is ridiculous that you should quote against me the opinions of the people of Westphalia. If you listen to popular opinion, you will achieve nothing. If the people refuses its own happiness, the people is guilty of anarchy and deserves to be punished.'[35] This was not so different from Napoleonic rule in France, and largely explains why the legislature promised in the constitution met just twice. Secondly, a major reason for all this rationalizing symmetry was to make French exploitation of local resources and manpower easier. These considerations combined to undermine much of the reform thrust. As Helmut Berding has shown, the granting of confiscated land as *dotations* to prominent French soldiers and Bonaparte family members (Bernadotte, Ney, Pauline Bonaparte), and ultimately to hundreds of carpetbaggers, had a decisive effect. In order to protect the value of these grants and the flow of French revenue from the imperial domain lands, landlords' rights were perpetuated in practice, whatever the constitution said. This effectively nullified legal equality and put a brake on rural social reform, just as the administration of the French domains and *dotations* by French officials as a state within a state made a mockery of bureaucratic or legal uniformity.[36] Similar circumstances limited the reach of reforms in the Grand Duchy of Berg.

What of the Napoleonic reform era in the nonsatellite states of the Confederation of the Rhine? The tendency of recent research has been to emphasize the diversity and limitations of reform measures here, as in Westphalia and Berg. Secularization did not proceed evenly according to one model, and the adoption of the *Code Napoléon* was extremely patchy (even Baden, the most enthusiastic collaborator, adopted only a diluted version). The response to French military dominance and ideas ranged from the wholesale adoption of the French system in tiny Anhalt-Köthen (population: 29,000), to minor institutional adjustments in the Mecklenburgs, Saxony and Thuringia. The greatest French impact occurred in the southern states of Baden, Württemberg, Bavaria and Hesse-Darmstadt, where Napoleonic success provided both opportunity and motive for far-reaching reforms. The opportunity was presented by the territorial revolution that accompanied the break-up of the Empire and benefited these states most. The motive came from the need to become master of their extensive new territories, while satisfying French military and political demands. The southern states gorged on the remnants of the Empire, swallowing up lands in Swabia, Franconia and the Rhineland that had formerly belonged to ecclesiastical principalities, imperial knights and free cities. Württemberg more than doubled in size between 1796 and 1812, absorbing some of the foremost families of the south German imperial nobility. Baden increased fourfold in land and sixfold in population. Digesting their acquisitions posed major problems. The new lands were diverse, with a colourful patchwork of legal and administrative traditions. They also changed the denominational balance in each state, adding Protestants to Bavaria, Catholics to Baden and Württemberg. Major questions of legitimacy were raised by the fact that rulers faced their new subjects with new titles that they owed to France, as the Elector of Bavaria and the Duke of Württemberg became kings, the Margrave of Baden a grand duke. Finally, the financial costs of integrating new territory while still meeting French demands had somehow to be met by these upstart princes. The public debt increased from 15 to 22 million Gulden in Württemberg between 1806 and 1819, from 8 to 18 million Gulden in Baden over the same period.

The result was a series of reforms that transformed the south German states. The central issue everywhere was asserting the sovereignty of the state within its new borders. Measures designed to achieve this were pushed through by a generation of officials (Montgelas in Bavaria, Reitzenstein in Baden, Gagern in Hesse-Darmstadt) who pursued the German tradition of

Enlightened Absolutism with a new urgency under changed conditions. The fundament of reform everywhere was the administrative structure itself. Centralization, functional division by departments and the hierarchical chain of command replaced local or provincial autonomy and collegial decision-making. An expanded corps of officials was built up, loyal to the new system, who enjoyed better training, pay and pensions, greater security and enhanced prestige (in Bavaria the laws of *lèse-majesté* were extended to bureaucrats), but were subject to stricter discipline. This process probably went furthest in Bavaria, but the retooled machinery of government was one of the more successful aspects of reform everywhere. It made possible the growing penetration of the state into many spheres of life: improving communications, fostering industry, building up educational institutions at all levels (primary, secondary, tertiary), collecting statistics and information that would make conscription and tax-collecting run more smoothly. From the attack on guild restrictions to the enunciation of religious tolerance, the aim was to encourage greater mobility, enhance social integration and promote efficient use of resources, while strengthening the state as guardian of the 'general interest' of society. Moves towards constitutionalism and representative institutions should be seen in the same light: as an instrument of integration, a means of legitimizing new revenue, a platform for defending reforms, and a device to check the ruler while neutralizing aristocratic discontent.[37]

These measures threatened long-held privileges and asserted one sovereignty in place of another. They were not uncontested. Mack Walker's 'home towns' predictably failed to go quietly, and the guilds managed to salvage at least some of their rights. Catholics in the 'new' Württemberg south of the Danube showed their resentment at being pitchforked into a historically Protestant state; so did their coreligionists in southern Baden. Where religious hostility towards enlightened officials combined with resentment over taxes, conscription or the destruction of the 'good old laws', the resistance could be violent. That was what happened in the new Bavarian lands of the Tyrol, where the rising led by Andreas Hofer in 1809 was the closest Germany came to an uprising on Spanish or Italian lines – pious, regionalist, militant. Mostly, however, the limits of reform were less spectacular. Guild reform was partial, Jewish emancipation was incomplete, new legal codes had exceptions built into them. Wherever we look, we find that the nobility was the most obvious beneficiary of incomplete reform. Again, only in Bavaria was there full-scale resistance to the 'levelling' measures of state bureaucracy. Elsewhere, open confrontation was avoided because governments were prepared to make concessions. Tax exemptions, the retention of police powers at local level, the right to nominate to church benefices, legal privileges – these were the areas in which south German nobles hung on to power and influence. The nobility was also to the fore in blocking constitutions and representative institutions, although in Württemberg the crown itself was at odds with reforming officials over this. Finally, rural social relations were less touched by reform than much else. Peasant emancipation remained a halfway house, and important elements of seigneurialism (admittedly less burdensome in the south than in the northeast) survived the reform era. Deference to noble sentiment was one reason. Another was the fact that secularization had turned the states themselves into major landlords, reluctant to resolve the agrarian question in a way that reduced their revenue.

It is always easy – as well as necessary – to point out the limitations of reform. A strong British historiographical tradition has always relished the argument that nothing really changes, except perhaps by accident. But the emphasis here should be on change rather than continuity. If the internal changes in the south German states were less definitive than the territorial revolution that made them possible, if they had more impact on government than on society, a transformation nevertheless took place. The fractured status quo in the Napoleonic era gave enlightened bureaucrats the chance to reprise the cause of Enlightened Absolutism and redraw the balance of power between the prince and his subjects, with the bureaucracy itself increasingly holding the ring as a force in its own right. That applies even to Württemberg, where the tradition of reform absolutism was least developed and the king took greater personal charge. Whereas the changes wrought by the French on the left bank of the Rhine and in the satellite states were soon interrupted by the withdrawal of the occupier, the legacy of the south German reformers from above was more continuous. This period established the state as the motor of modernization.

That was not true in Austria. 'Obviously not', we are inclined to say, but that makes the course of events there seem too much like a foregone conclusion. There was, after all, the precedent of Joseph II, most uncompromising of all the enlightened rulers and the man whose policies served as a lodestar for south German reformers like Montgelas. Austria also faced many of the same problems after 1805–6 that led other German states to implement internal reforms. It was placed in a position of humiliating dependence on French goodwill, watched its territories being rearranged, and was forced to pay large sums of money to France that further burdened the shaky state finances. After 1806, like other German states, Austria had to come to terms with a changed world in which the Empire no longer existed – a position that Francis II, more attached to Habsburg interest than imperial sentiment, had already anticipated by declaring himself Emperor of Austria in 1804. The Emperor Francis was as much a new monarch in a world created by Napoleon as the new kings of Bavaria and Württemberg. The disturbing facts of life in Austria, compounded of external weakness and internal incoherence, were not lost on powerful figures in Vienna. Ministers such as Sinzendorff, Saurau and Philipp Stadion urged administrative reforms, joined by Archdukes Rainer and Charles, the emperor's brothers.

Why, then, was there no sustained programme of reform from above in Vienna to match what was attempted in Munich or Karlsruhe? Francis himself provides an important part of the answer, a conservative stand-pat emperor who reacted strongly against the reforming fever of his uncle Joseph II, equated reform with revolution, and believed that streamlining the Byzantine machinery of government would weaken his own authority. Around him, everyone urged change, but the advice was contradictory: to centralize and to decentralize, to be a loyal French ally and to resume the fight against Napoleon, to construct a Danubian monarchy and to resurrect the Holy Roman Empire. This self-cancelling counsel was manna to Francis, justifying his preferred policy of doing nothing. Beyond the dynamics of courtly and ministerial faction, there were structural considerations that muffled the urge to reform. Unlike Prussia after Jena and Auerstädt, Austria after Austerlitz was not dismembered and fighting for its existence. On the other hand, unlike the south German states, forced to come to terms with complicated new acquisitions, Austria could thank Napoleon for simplifying life by removing its possessions in the Netherlands, Italy, south Germany, the Adriatic and West Galicia. Domestically, the years of counter-revolutionary policy under Francis had entrenched the power and boosted the confidence of the nobility, making it a major obstacle to anything smacking of Josephinism. It was more than a match for the reformers among the younger officers and officials, whose ranks were thinner than in south Germany or Prussia.

Some changes were made. Legal reforms begun earlier were completed with the publication of the Civil Code in 1811, although this made major concessions to noble interests. Justice and administration were separated in the middle tiers of the bureaucracy, the primary school system was expanded, and there was some increase in state control over theological training. But this added up to little more than a thin trickle of diluted Josephinist measures: church, nobility and other interests retained essential corporate privileges. Economic and fiscal reform was negligible, the peasantry was not emancipated, and – the greatest contrast with south German states – there was no reform of the slow, often chaotic administrative system. The years 1805–8 saw the most intensive burst of activity – intensive, anyway, by Austrian standards – which focused on military reform. Under Philipp Stadion and Archduke Charles, the organization of the regular army was improved and a militia established on the French principle that all citizens were potential soldiers. This was an important change, achieved against the inclinations of Francis and Archduke Rainer, for whom any form of universal conscription meant that 'we should be conducting ourselves as though in the stone age'.[38] But military reform failed when put to the test, and brought the reformers down with it. When Austria challenged the French again in 1809, hoping – another break with dynastic caution – to place itself at the head of a larger German rebellion against Napoleon, the gamble failed. Austrian troops were successful at Essling; but the French won a (close-run) victory at Wagram. Under the new chief minister Clemens von Metternich, Austria bowed to French superiority, but did not embark on any further attempts to strengthen the institutions of state by 'French' reforms.

Neither the Austrian nor the south German reformers have received the attention from historians granted to the Prussian era of reform in the period 1807–19. Well into the twentieth century, the Stein-Hardenberg reforms were celebrated by nationalist historians not only as the basis for the 'war of liberation' against Napoleon, but as a specifically German example of renewal without upheaval – 'revolution in the good sense', to use Hardenberg's own phrase.[39] Modern historians have pointed to the limitations of Prussian reform and been more critical about the future significance of this 'defensive modernization'.[40] Perhaps enthusiasts and critics alike have tended to exaggerate the importance of what occurred in Prussia compared with the Confederation of the Rhine states. If so, this is understandable. In many respects the Prussian reforms had a greater impact on society than those enacted elsewhere; and while we should resist the temptation to write history backwards, it is certainly true that the Stein-Hardenberg era left its impress not just on Prussia but ultimately on nineteenth-century Germany as a whole.

There were already reform initiatives between the accession of Frederick William III in 1797 and 1806. It was then, in what is often called the 'prereform' period, that Struensee made his celebrated observation about Prussian reform from above. Men like Scharnhorst, Clausewitz and Boyen urged changes in army organization; zealous counsellors such as Beyme and Mencken pressed for overhaul of the way government was carried on. Some measures were enacted – the emancipation of the serfs in the royal domains, intended to set an example to the nobility, modest administrative and fiscal changes – but the reformers lacked strong royal backing and faced powerful opponents at court, among the nobility, and within the bureaucracy itself. It took military disaster and the punitive French peace to give the reform movement its opportunity. Against that desperate background, a great burst of reforms took place. The Prussian administration was reshaped, the peasantry was emancipated and other restrictions on economic activity lifted, corporate distinctions and privileges were removed, the municipalities were granted a form of self-government, education was reformed at every level, and military organization was transformed.

The first goal of reformers was to strengthen the machinery of government and administration. This was common ground between Stein and Hardenberg, despite differences of policy and emphasis between the former, with his greater sympathy for corporate representation, and the latter, a more thorough-going advocate of Enlightened Absolutism in the Montgelas mould. Both men shared a belief with other reformers that the structure of government itself needed to be more unified, starting at the top. In place of the inefficient, overlapping jurisdictions of the so-called cabinet system that marked the last years of Frederick the Great and the rule of his two successors, more clearly defined ministerial responsibilities were established, not least to try to short-circuit the role played by royal favourites. As a result, bureaucratic absolutism became more real than it had ever been in the eighteenth century. Administration was also streamlined, as the uniform structure familiar to students of nineteenth-century Prussia came into being, stretching down through the district level of 'Regierungsbezirke' to the local 'Kreise'. Significantly, the areas covered by the districts were chosen for reasons of geographical and practical convenience and cut across traditional loyalties and lines of authority. They shared the geometrical qualities of the Napoleonic department. In fact, governmental and administrative reforms in Prussia had many features in common with the more directly French-inspired state-building in southern Germany. The separation of administration and justice was a further parallel, although it did not go as far in Prussia as Bavaria. Where the Prussian reforms cut deeper than those enacted elsewhere was in their impact on the larger society. The October Edict of 1807 emancipating the peasantry marked a real caesura, and it was just one of a series of measures that dismantled barriers to the ownership and free disposability of property, replacing custom by contract. The market in land that had already developed was legitimized and given a boost. Other reforms pointed in the same direction: they represented the same double thrust towards releasing social energies and reducing corporate distinctions. The introduction of freedom of enterprise severely cut back guild restrictions, and was accompanied by the removal of internal tariffs and tolls. Efforts to replace the network of fiscal privileges and exemptions with a more uniform tax burden, and the removal of some of the civil disabilities of Jews, fell within the same framework. So did extensive reforms to the content and organization of education.

A combination of motives therefore lay behind the reform measures. The interest of the state, as defined by the reformist senior bureaucracy, was paramount. Extending the reach and efficiency of government was what linked changes in the administrative structure to other reforms. Revenue was to be collected more effectively. Intermediate bodies like guilds were to be stripped of their powers. The role of the state was to be asserted in education, replacing that of local consistories or other patrons, in the training and appointment of teachers and the supervision of elementary schools, classical grammar schools and universities. The celebrated new University of Berlin, founded in 1810, was a product of this thinking (and an intended symbol of the enlightened Prussian state). A remodelled educational system was to produce good citizens, as well as officials to man the administrative machine. But that was not all. The educational reforms also sought to reward merit rather than birth, through the system of examinations, and embodied a humanistic commitment to the ideal of cultivation or self-realization. This larger moral imperative is hard to separate from the belief in education as a 'practical need of the state' (Wilhelm von Humboldt). The same intertwined motives – efficiency, social mobilization, emancipation – applied to other reforms. While the Protestant pastor Wilhelm Harnisch spoke of awakening the 'slumbering power' of the people through elementary schooling, Hardenberg wanted to arouse 'all sleeping forces' in Prussian society more generally.[41] Similar thoughts animated all the reformers. Stein wrote to Hardenberg that 'we must train the nation to manage its own affairs and to grow out of this condition of childhood'; Scharnhorst suggested to Clausewitz that it was necessary to 'kindle a sense of independence in the nation'.[42] The pronounced element of Kantian idealism in this, the emphasis on freeing individual energies and encouraging responsible citizens, was what made the Stein-Hardenberg reform era more than just another dose of Enlightened Absolutism, although it was that as well. Finally, the dismantling of serfdom, guilds and tariffs brought together the motives already discussed with another element that was different from earlier cameralist thinking. The desire to free economic activity also reflected the ideas of Adam Smith, which were widely discussed, especially in East Prussian reformist circles of officials, exporting landlords and merchants, and were channelled into the reform movement through officials like Schoen and Schrötter.

Prussian reform from above was ambitious and wide-ranging. It also had limits. There were disagreements and internecine struggles among the reformers. Stein and Hardenberg had different ideas about the direction of government at the top and the principle of representation. The disciples of Adam Smith sought to free economic forces; the apostles of cultivation who shaped educational reform created institutions that elevated the humanistically trained official over the vulgar practitioner of trade. Reforms stopped halfway (like Jewish emancipation), or were seriously diluted (like equal taxation), or ran into the sand through lack of funding and local resources (elementary school reform). If we look beyond the detailed cases, there were three general obstacles to reform. The first was the social isolation of the reformers, something they shared with their counterparts in other states. The free market and compulsory schooling were not automatically popular, and understandably so. To speak of emancipation, as the reformers did, was to accept that the 'slumbering' populace would need a good deal of awakening. That brings us to the second problem: the self-limiting aspect of reform from above. The liberal noblemen who carried the reform movement were agreed that to do nothing after 1806 would endanger the state and the social order. But might it not also be dangerous to do too much? That was why municipal self-government was really self-administration under state control, and why the larger issues of representation and constitutionalism caused so many problems.

This was by no means only, or even perhaps mainly, a question of enlightened bureaucrats fearing the populace. The real difficulty, and the third great obstacle to reform, lay elsewhere: with the vested interests of the aristocracy. When we consider that they were acting against a backdrop of popular indifference, French hostility, monarchical unpredictability and bureaucratic conservatism, it is probably unrealistic to expect from reformers who were themselves virtually all nobles that they would challenge the nobility head-on. Nor did they. On issue after issue, measures were withdrawn or tailored to noble interests. Take the question of taxes. Although distinctions between town and country and from province to province were ended, equality of the fiscal burden remained a dead letter; crucially, a uniform land tax was dropped. Again, Hardenberg's Gendarmerie Edict of 1812 posed a potentially radical threat to aristocratic control of local administration and patrimonial police powers; but the edict could not be enforced, so that below the level of the district administration the Landrat continued to embody the interests of local landowners. This was just one example of the general rule that the power of the state leached away in the sandy provinces. Even Hardenberg himself had serious reservations about ending patrimonial police powers, an illustration of how noble resistance and reformist self-limitation came together. Most obviously, the emancipation of the peasantry was carried out in

such a way that it was – as so many historians have demonstrated
– more an emancipation of the Junker nobility. They were hand-
somely compensated for their lost serfs and became the chief
beneficiaries of the free market in land. The peasantry bore the
main burden of reform, as the land they had cultivated was
swallowed up by the large estates and they became the victims
of exploitation twice over – a reserve army of labour for agrarian
capitalists, simultaneously shackled to their landlords through
'feudal' institutions such as patrimonial justice. Many Prussian
aristocrats, like their south German counterparts, howled at the
'levelling' tendencies of the reformers. But reform from above
stopped short of challenging the powers of the Prussian landowning nobility. Formal serfdom was abolished, the mingling
of old Junker and new bourgeois estate-owners was accelerated,
the principles of merit and achievement made noble sinecures
harder to find. These were important changes, but they left the
Junkers secure in their local power and did not impede the
continuing movement of talented nobles into key positions of
state service. The Stein-Hardenberg era reaffirmed the triangle
of power that bound together monarchy, bureaucracy and aristocracy.

One crucial element of the Prussian reform era remains to
be discussed: military reorganization. The disasters of 1806–7
were also disasters in strictly military terms, a sorry catalogue
of incompetence, panic, and flight. Any renewal or hope of
resisting Napoleon in the future clearly had to consider the
composition, training and organization of the army. Leading
military reformers – Scharnhorst, Gneisenau, Boyen, Grolmann
– were unusually agreed in approach, and they addressed all of
these issues. In 1807, a Military Reorganization Commission
was set up and began its activities with a purge. Of the 6600
serving officers who survived Jena and Auerstädt, over 5000
were cashiered, pensioned off or placed on half-pay. Structural
reforms followed. A decree of 1808 formally removed all privileges of birth or estate as a means of obtaining a commission:
professional competence was henceforth to be the sole criterion.
In an echo of the civilian reformers, Gneisenau sought to

'awaken' the forces that were 'asleep in the bosom of the nation'. By 1819, the aristocratic component of the officer corps had fallen from over 90 to little more than 50 per cent. New training schools were established, using instruction manuals that underlined the importance of light infantry, skirmishing, versatility and other elements of French success (they also drew on the guerrilla war in Spain, about which the reformers kept themselves well informed). The organization of military affairs was likewise improved. In an effort to prevent conflicting counsel and intrigue around the king, who remained commander-in-chief, a war ministry was established in 1809; and it was in this period that careful grooming of the most promising officers led to the creation of the modern Prussian general staff.

There were also limits to what these reforms achieved. The old caste spirit of the officer corps was not broken. The new tactics exhorted by figures like General Yorck were often ignored by the old guard. There was no permanent war minister until 1814; and by the time Boyen arrived in the post he faced the potential competition of a recast military cabinet established the same year. Above all, conscription was blocked. First advocated in a Scharnhorst draft of 1808, it was central to the reformers' ambition to forge a nation in arms. But Frederick William and Hardenberg were both sceptical, and the nobility – already discontented over changes in the officer corps – was predictably hostile to the idea of arming peasants in order to fight a Jacobin-sounding 'war of national liberation'. In the event, if French success had given the reformers their first chance, French failure gave them a second one. In 1812, a cautious Frederick William reaffirmed Prussian loyalty to France: by consigning Prussian troops to the Russian campaign he disgusted the reformers. But the horrors of the retreat from Moscow gave Prussia the opportunity to change sides and join the British and Russians against Napoleon in early 1813 – a decision to which General Yorck provided an 1812 overture by doing the same thing on his own initiative the previous December at the celebrated Convention of Tauroggen. From February 1813

Prussia was effectively on a war footing with France (Austria joined the alliance in June), and the reformers' plans were implemented. Conscription was decreed and a reserve established: Prussia, earlier restricted by France to an army of 42,000, was able to mobilize twice that number by April and put 280,000 men into the field by the time the decisive Battle of Leipzig was fought in October. Conscription and the reserve were permanently established by the Obligatory Service Law of 1814, providing Frederick William with a large army to back up Prussian claims in the peacemaking process.

Hohenzollern (and Habsburg) calculations in the period 1813–14 are a reminder that the 'war of national liberation' described by later nationalists was largely a legend. Frederick William's belated appeal to 'my people' met with widespread indifference, which can be measured by resistance to conscription and high levels of desertion. The methods used to mobilize and discipline the soldiers were not so very different from the methods used in earlier decades; they were just used more effectively. Many of the extra officers drafted in to the army were fished out of the pool of men dismissed after 1806. It was a war of princes that led to the so-called Battle of Nations at Leipzig. There was no spontaneous Prussian uprising in 1813, let alone a German-wide movement, nothing to be compared with the guerrilla war in Spain or even the 1809 revolt in the Tyrol. The role of the volunteer detachments was exaggerated by nationalist historiography, like the part played by students within them. Nevertheless, there were nationalist feelings at work that had been absent twenty years earlier. Reformist leanings among officials and younger army officers overlapped with a 'patriotic' spirit. This fuelled the contempt towards the German princes displayed by some reformers; it also explains why Stein and Clausewitz went to Russia and Gneisenau to England when Prussia capitulated to Napoleon in 1812, and why many officers resigned. Particularly among members of the educated middle class we can see a heightened patriotic sentiment. It was conditioned by the disappearance of the Holy Roman Empire, sharpened by French occupation, and fed by the growing interest in German language, history and folkways shown by intellectuals like Herder and Schlegel. This early nationalism had different inflections, from idealistic patriotism rooted in an older cosmopolitan spirit (as in the Königsberg League of Virtue), to a more mystical enthusiasm for German virtues that stemmed from turn-of-the-century Romanticism and sometimes extended to belief in a German mission. Familiar examples of this second kind of nationalism, in which bathos mingled with anti-French xenophobia, include the egregious belligerence of the gymnastic instructor 'Turnvater Jahn', the war songs of Körner and Eichendorff, the 'Speeches to the German Nation' of philosopher Johann Gottlieb Fichte, and the Francophobe literary vitriol of Heinrich von Kleist. The trope of the French 'archenemy' was expressed with particular violence in the 'catechism' of the publicist Ernst Moritz Arndt: 'I hate all the French without exception in the name of God and my people.'[43]

This kind of visceral hostility to the 'archenemy' naturally had its mirror image on the French side.[44] And we need to place sentiments of this kind in context. They were not the only currents that flowed into later German nationalism, nor did they enjoy widespread support at the time. Against the roster of nationalist intellectuals we have to set not only the continuing admirers of Napoleon (they included Goethe, Hegel and Heine), but the much greater numbers of those who felt themselves to be Saxons, or Bavarians, not Germans. The apostles of liberation and regeneration were largely confined to Prussia, and many who referred to the Fatherland still meant Prussia. That is important. It is sometimes said that the educated middle class found a new source of identity in the nation at a time of crisis. No doubt: but we should not forget the continuing hold of state, dynastic, local and religious loyalties. Lower down the social scale these loyalties were of primary importance. When Jakob Walter later described returning from the Russian campaign, he expressed his relief at finding himself back where 'German life began again'.[45] But it is clear that he felt himself to be truly home only when he reached Swabia, and more specifically the area around his own village, just as it is clear that during the years away from home he felt more comfortable as a Catholic in the company of Polish peasants than with Saxon fellow-Germans.

CHAPTER TWO

Germany in Transition

Rulers, States, Identities

Two terms have come into use to describe the years from 1815 to 1848, both coined later. The first is 'Restoration Germany'. It is usually applied to the period between 1815 and 1830, a year when revolutionary unrest occurred in many German states. The term usefully denotes the break that came after the end of the French-dominated upheaval, although it gives a misleading impression about what exactly had been 'restored'. Historians also refer to the *Vormärz*, or 'pre-March' period, with the emphasis here on the two decades preceding the outbreak of a more general revolution in March 1848. This tells us something about a time when many certainly anticipated revolution, especially in the 1840s, although it highlights one aspect of these years at the expense of others. The entire period was actually one of transition, marked by ambiguous, conflicting elements. Heinrich Heine summed it up best in his great satirical poem, *Germany: A Winter's Fairy Tale*. Germany had become a *Zwitterwesen*, a 'hybrid creature', symbolized by its knights in gaiters who were a disagreeable mixture of 'Gothic madness and the modern lie,/ That is neither flesh nor fowl'.[1]

· The Germany that so disappointed the exile Heine was established at the Congress of Vienna, where the victorious powers concluded their peacemaking in 1815. The ordering of German-speaking Europe was finally agreed in June, just as allied troops were about to hand a last defeat to Napoleon following his escape from Elba. The reshaping of Germany was crucial, for it would anchor the entire postwar settlement. It was also problematic. The outcome was obviously predetermined in part by

the defeat of France. The satellite states would disappear, along
with the Confederation of the Rhine, and there would be German redoubts on the left bank to contain future French aggression. Prussia, even before Blücher's contribution to the victory
at Waterloo, would clearly be a winner; Saxony, Napoleon's
unrepentant ally, would be a loser; and Austria would demand
a major say. But the precise territorial dispositions, and the issue
of how relations between the German states should be governed,
were the subject of intense negotiation among the major allied
powers – Britain and Russia, as well as Austria and Prussia.
Medium-sized German states like Bavaria, Württemberg and
Hanover had a subsidiary role in these discussions.

The result can be summarized under two heads: territory and
organization (the 'German question' in effect, although not yet
by name). Napoleon's territorial revolution was consolidated.
Some adjustments were made, but the southern states largely
retained their gains and the fate of the free cities, imperial
knights and ecclesiastical principalities was confirmed. The Congress recognized just 38 German states. It is true that 20 of
those 38 states had fewer than 100,000 inhabitants, and some
were tiny – Birkenfeld, Waldeck, Lippe. The solid blocks of
territory on the map were also dotted with enclaves and exclaves,
some dating back to the Empire, others newly created. But this
was anything but a restoration, as the claims of legitimacy were
overridden in favour of rewarding allies, preserving the balance
of power, or creating more viable, geographically rational, states.
Only a few small states, such as Saxe-Weimar and Braunschweig,
were strictly restorations. The territorial settlement also created
entirely new dynamics between the two leading German powers.
Austria gave up its vestigial presence in southern Germany to
concentrate on its power base in northern Italy: henceforth Austrian influence on the rest of Germany would be based on diplomacy and ties of sentiment, not on a physical presence. Prussia,
conversely, became a more obviously 'German' power. As compensation for losing eastern territory to Russia and failing to
gain the whole of Saxony (it received two-fifths of that truncated
kingdom), Prussia was granted the Rhineland and Westphalia.

The centre of gravity of the former Brandenburg-Prussia, having been shifted to the east by Napoleon, now tilted even more sharply to the west. Prussia was established as the dominant power right across northern Germany, from Trier on the Mosel to Thorn on the Vistula.

What kind of association between the German states should be created in place of the Holy Roman Empire? A German Committee considered this question even before the Congress of Vienna convened, but it proved difficult to reach agreement. The other great powers were unwilling to see too close a union, but the major obstacle was the jealously guarded sovereignty of the individual German states, and especially suspicion of Austria and Prussia among the small and middle-sized states. The German Confederation that emerged in 1815 provided for an extremely loose form of association, looser in some ways than the former Empire (there was no superior court, for example, and no head of state). On the other hand, like the Empire, the Confederation continued to exclude Germans and include non-Germans among its member-states. Some states still had foreign sovereigns, most notably Hanover. Arrangements for mutual military assistance hardly advanced on those of the Empire, and the Confederation diet had little importance: member-states exchanged ambassadors and went their own way. In practice Austria and Prussia were the two states that inevitably played a role on the European stage, while the others tried to prevent either one of them from gaining a dominant position or (even worse, if you were Bavaria) the two together establishing a joint hegemony. Austrian and Prussian concerns were not identical. Austria, still the senior partner despite declining resources, was particularly concerned with events in Italy and southeastern Europe, while keen to preserve both legitimacy and the balance of power everywhere (the so-called 'Metternich system', after the figure who made himself synonymous with defence of the European status quo between 1815 and 1848). Prussia was more alert to the threats on its own borders presented by Belgian and Polish revolts in 1830. It did not follow the counter-revolutionary Austrian lead without question, and struck a

The German Confederation of 1815

middle position in the 1820s between the 'liberal' western powers (Britain, France) and the 'reactionary' eastern powers (Austria, Russia), before drifting towards the latter after 1830.[2] Nevertheless, when it came to the most serious external challenge of the period – the French threat to the Rhine in 1840 – Prussia and Austria agreed to military cooperation if necessary. Despite latent tension, Habsburg-Hohenzollern rivalry was more muted in these years than it had been in the eighteenth century. There was to be peace between the sovereign members of the Confederation until 1866. The only warfare was psychological – and economic. Beginning on a modest scale in 1818, Prussia constructed the celebrated organization that became the German Customs Union (*Zollverein*) in 1834, and embraced more than half the members of the Confederation by 1842. Rival customs unions were broken along the way. This was certainly a major power flexing its muscles, but it is important to recognize that the customs union was a product of Prussian geographical division and fiscal interests, not part of a long-term 'German' programme.

On what basis did these sovereign states rest? All but four of them (the three Hanseatic cities, plus Frankfurt) were dynastic states. Five were monarchies (Austria, Prussia, Bavaria, Württemberg, Hanover), the rest consisting of duchies, grand duchies and other principalities. We should not pass too lightly over this array of princes. Rulers aimed to rule. 'I am the emperor, and I want dumplings', in the words of the feeble-minded Austrian emperor Ferdinand, who succeeded Francis I in 1835.[3] Most of his fellow princes demanded more than dumplings: they wanted to choose their own foreign policies and ministers. And most did not grant constitutions – not in 1815, anyway, or immediately afterwards. They maintained their courts, demanded personal oaths of fealty from their officers, and emphasized their legitimacy. These hereditary rulers expected deference, and often found it. Buttressed by the message of obedience to the ruler propagated by the churches, certainly in the early Restoration years, the prince still presented himself as a 'father of his people'. Carl Spitzweg's painting of *The Visit of His Highness* to a small principality in the 1830s is a sentimentalized but not inaccurate representation of this relationship. In Prussia, popular woodcuts and lithographs featuring royal portraits, coronations and funerals were mass-produced in Neuruppin, north of Berlin. Deference and sentimental attachment to the ruling house were strongest in smaller states and those least affected by the twenty-five-year territorial carousel. But what about the states that were quite new and artificial, like the Principality of Lichtenberg carved out for the Duke of Saxe-Coburg-Gotha around St Wendel – an area seized from the Duke of Zweibrücken by France, held in trust by Bavaria in 1815, gifted by Prussia to Saxe-Coburg as a reward for military cooperation, then bought back by Prussia?[4] And what of the old states with major new territorial acquisitions: 'new Bavaria', 'new Württemberg', the Prussian Rhine Province? After all, well over half the population in 'Restoration' Germany had new rulers. Here, historic loyalties were likely to present more of a problem.

Where tradition did not exist, rulers tried to manufacture it. They were helped in this by the cult of monarchy among Romantic artists and intellectuals, with its emphasis on the 'historic' and its fondness for an (imaginary) stable past. An example would be the painters of the Nazarene School. The impulses within Romanticism, it is true, did not always sit comfortably with power. Celebrating ruins, losing oneself in Nature, or praising 'sincerity' above everything – all lent themselves to a variety of political conclusions. Thomas Mann's Lotte Kestner (*Lotte in Weimar*) captures the ambiguity in her comment about the 'pious painters and impious writers' of the post-1815 period – although some of the painters were impious too.[5] But rulers had their own ways of making the past work for them. One was to project monarchical authority through ceremonial, display, statuary, and public buildings. Ludwig I of Bavaria was an adept: the extensive new buildings in Munich designed by Leo von Klenze, and monuments like the 'Hall of Fame' for Bavarian heroes, were intended to glorify the Wittelsbachs and establish the dynasty in the affections of the people. The great architect Friedrich Schinkel followed a similar programme in the Prussian capital – Theodor Fontane compared the harmony of Schinkel's Berlin to Wren's London.[6] Here, as in Semper's Dresden and Weinbrenner's Karlsruhe, the squares and octagons of neo-Classicism were intended to reflect royal majesty. The rather later obsession with medievalism and the neo-Gothic was also pressed into service. To celebrate the marriage of Württemberg's Crown Prince Karl to a Russian princess in 1846, local aristocrats dressed up as crusading knights and Saracens and staged a tourney in Stuttgart using original weapons, against a backdrop of palms and lemon trees specially imported for the occasion.[7] If this was madness, there was method in it. No ruler better exemplified the trend than Frederick William IV of Prussia. Often dismissed as a medievalist crank, he actually had a shrewd idea of the need for loyalties to be constructed. At the 1842 inauguration of the newly completed neo-Gothic Cologne cathedral, which Frederick William claimed as a Hohenzollern deed, the king told Metternich that Prussia had no real historical basis. It was, he said, just a random collection of territories: a Prussian tradition would have to be created.

Personal-monarchical authority only went so far, however, and Metternich's response alerts us to one of its limitations. Frederick William, he complained, was 'interfering with all the gears of the machine'.[8] This was a dry, eighteenth-century reaction, typical of Metternich, but it also expressed a nineteenth-century truth. The states of Restoration Germany rested on the machinery of administration, and on the loyalty of subjects to the state as much as the ruler. The buildings and monuments commissioned by Ludwig reflected not only Wittelsbach dynastic vanity, but the desire to establish a sense of Bavarian identity. So did similar efforts elsewhere. In some cases the symbols of state edged out those of the ruling house. The Saxon government issued a White Book in 1815 that tried to explain the disasters of the war ('how did it all happen?'), and urged 'loyalty to our dynasty'; but the old dynastic colours of black and gold, associated with failure, were dropped in favour of the new state colours of green and white.[9] Personal-monarchical rule did not disappear: it was merged into the authority of the impersonal, bureaucratic state. More than in the eighteenth century, bureaucrats truly became servants of states, not servants of princes – and princes themselves became organs of state.

None of this can be separated from the continuing process of state-building. Sometimes this happened for the same reason that it happened in Frederician Prussia or the southern states after 1806 – because new territory needed to be digested. Prussia doubled its size in 1815, and areas such as the Rhineland and Westphalia had to be integrated. That meant creating and staffing administrative offices at provincial, district and local level, establishing courts and appeal courts, setting up military commands, stationing gendarmes and customs officials, reorganizing education, making sure that the machinery existed for overseeing the appointment of Protestant and Catholic clergy, paying their salaries, building new churches and (often enough) adjudicating their disputes. Something similar was occurring in the Bavarian Palatinate and 'new Württemberg' south of the Danube. Even this cursory survey of activities indicates the extensive reach of the state. The areas in which the state claimed sovereignty may sound familiar enough – security of borders, public order, taxes, conscription, compulsory schooling, justice – but the claim was now asserted more authoritatively. This amounted to an attempt, not the first but the most general and sustained, to forge subject-citizens out of former nobles, serfs, guildsmen, townsmen and all the other subdivided categories of corporate society.

There were also spheres in which many German states became more active, either directly or through specially created agencies. One was the exploitation of the state's own resources, particularly the woodlands that had once been princely domains. Just as the painters and writers embarked on their love affair with the German forest, officials began to insist on the scientific management of a valuable resource that had been ravaged by overcutting in the war years. The pine forest of the late Romantic imagination was a creation of nineteenth-century forestry officials, who liked the quick growth of foreign imports like Douglas firs.[10] Mineral deposits also attracted greater interest.

The coal mines in the new Prussian territory of the Saarland were state-owned. In addition to exploiting its own resources, the post-1815 state stimulated the economy in other ways. It built roads, canalized waterways, and – from the late 1830s – began to construct railways. Business activity was actively fostered by establishing semigovernmental agencies like chambers of commerce and societies to promote industry, by mounting exhibitions and setting up model workshops. This process was at work from relatively *laissez-faire* Prussia to the more statist encouragement of industry practised in Baden.[11] Attempts to establish uniform legal codes and criteria for citizenship pointed in the same direction, for they were designed to increase the movement of goods and mobility of labour. Educational provision went hand-in-hand with the new attention paid to the exploitation of public and private economic resources. It is true that German states took pride in their nonutilitarian classical grammar schools and model universities like Berlin or Heidelberg, and these were well-funded (and outstanding) by European standards. But many states also set contemporary standards for technical education and training. New institutions that taught engineering or agronomy were widely established in these years.

State officials placed their stamp on this period as they had on the reform era. Bureaucracies were largely recruited on the basis of competitive examinations – in Bavaria, marks were scrutinized down to two decimal places. Edicts and decrees regularized responsibilities, promotions, disciplinary procedures and pensions. Systems varied from state to state between the hierarchical and the collegial (the latter based on collective responsibility at a given administrative level), but the emphasis everywhere was placed on uniformity of approach and working within fixed guidelines. The bureaucracy also embodied the ethos of competence, order, duty and hard work. If this sounds obvious to modern ears, we should remember that it was less so at the time: few of these attributes were apparent among those who passed for officials in, say, contemporary England or the Papal States. For historical reasons already noted, Germany was a classic land of the modern bureaucratic spirit and it is no coincidence that it produced, in Max Weber, the most celebrated modern analyst of the phenomenon. The collective identity within German bureaucracies included a lofty sense of responsibility, even arrogance. Administration was, so officials believed, disinterested: it transcended the divisions and conflicting egoisms in society; it stood for the 'general interest'. This claim enjoyed a good measure of support beyond the ranks of the bureaucracy, especially among the university-educated who shared the same background as senior officials. The philosopher Hegel, who believed that the world spirit had found true expression in the Prussian state, is only the most celebrated example. As a professor at the University of Berlin, he was himself an employee of that state.

Bureaucratic claims were not accepted everywhere at face value. There was criticism of official waste and parasitism. In Württemberg, where hostility towards bureaucratic 'scribbling' (*Vielschreiberei*) was widespread, the economist Friedrich List observed in 1821: 'Everywhere one looks there are nothing but advisors, bureaucrats, aides, chancelleries, clerks, registries, cases of documents, official uniforms; good living and luxury, from the officials down to their servants'.[12] Then there was the question of tone: senior officials were resented for their Olympian condescension, lesser officials because they were brusque and peremptory, a result of the fact that so many gendarmes and postmen had once been noncommissioned officers. Discontent was reinforced because the state was perceived as an interfering, disturbing force. It wanted to take children out of the fields and workshops and fill their heads with book-learning, prevent peasants from collecting wood in the forest, and tell municipalities who should be a citizen. In Hamburg the police reported people who cleared snow off their roofs after the permitted hour, or failed to sweep their chimneys when ordered to; in Prussia the authorities tried to forbid smoking on the streets (without notable success). When it came to religion, the tentacles of the state reached into consistories, cathedral chapters, even into the pulpit. The Stuttgart government prescribed the length of sermons and when confessions could be heard. In these and other areas, friction was usually greater in newly absorbed territories where the state was most likely to be viewed as an 'outsider', although it is a myth that either the Bavarian Palatinate or the Prussian Rhine Province was ruled by alien officials from the east. Even where state activities might have been expected to gain a warm reception, this was not always so. Businessmen welcomed the promotion of commerce and communications, but chafed at bureaucratic regulation. The more class-conscious merchants and entrepreneurs wondered why, if economic restrictions could be loosened, political controls could not also be relaxed. Among the educated middle classes, general approval for the 'improving' role of the state was offset by dislike of its restrictive activities. But the official mind was convinced that true liberty was founded on administration, not constitutions, even if there were some liberal officials who felt differently. Part revolutionary, part policeman, the bureaucratic state of Restoration Germany had many critics, although they did not always criticize the same things.

The aristocracy was predictably hostile. Its denunciations echoed those directed at Hardenberg and Montgelas during the reform era: the state was condemned for threatening historic rights and privileges; officials were salaried meddlers. Noble critics grumbled on their estates or snubbed a hapless district judge; the literary-minded went into print. A Bavarian author denounced 'the curse of this caste of bureaucrats', with their 'levelling of all social relations, their eradication of all social institutions'.[13] Support came from a growing body of conservative intellectuals such as Friedrich Julius Stahl and Friedrich Karl von Savigny, who praised everything that was corporate, historical and customary against the homogenizing, modernizing activities of state officials. We should not conclude from these cries of outrage that the aristocracy was being displaced. In states that had been little touched by the reform era, like Saxony, Anhalt and the Mecklenburgs, aristocratic privilege remained largely intact and the close prince-noble bond left little room for an independent bureaucracy. The same applied in smaller principalities where personal rule had more meaning and the legal position of the bureaucracy was less secure. There, too, the nobility had little to complain about, while the vulnerable official was trapped halfway (or less than halfway) along the evolutionary path from servant-of-the-prince to servant of state. Even in larger, more regularized administrative states, rulers had ways of intervening in the interests of the nobility: through the choice of ministers, or by limiting the number of ennoblements, which consolidated the position of the old nobility and froze out ambitious officials. Both occurred in Restoration Prussia. Everywhere, aristocrats still had institutions where they enjoyed power and influence: at court, in provincial estates, in the officer corps, and especially in local administration, for central bureaucratic rule always faded towards the edges. In short, the triangular power-relationship between ruler, bureaucracy and nobility still held. There was aristocratic persistence, even aristocratic reaction in some places, although officialdom was more entrenched in 1848 than it had been fifty years earlier.

It should come as no surprise that there was a major aristocratic presence within bureaucracies. Its extent varied. The Prussian pattern was fairly common, with nobles prominent at the top and the bottom: in the most senior positions, but even more in the local field administration – especially in the east where Junker nobles virtually monopolized the crucial post of Landrat. The middle to upper ranks of the central, provincial and district administration contained more officials of bourgeois origin, who also dominated the judicial and technical branches. The same profile can be found in Austria. Southern states had a higher proportion of officials from middle-class backgrounds. In Prussia and in some small states a modest antibourgeois shift in the composition of the bureaucracy began during the reactionary 1820s, although the numbers are hardly startling. The nobility increased its share of Prussian district posts from 18 to 27 per cent between 1820 and 1851.[14] Some of these were ennobled commoners; more would have had social ties and even intermarried with the families of officials and other educated men of bourgeois origin; and most would have been touched by the ethos of bureaucratic service. These men sat around the same green baize tables and shared the same caste spirit. No doubt some noble officials allied themselves with the broader aristocratic resistance to the bureaucratic state, especially locally, where they were more vulnerable to peer pressure. But conflicts within officialdom should not be reduced to class origin: after all, Hardenberg, Montgelas, Reitzenstein and Gagern had been nobles to a man.

The real lines of division within the bureaucracy were different, but they were important and growing. There was, first, the conflict between those who felt that it was undesirable or impossible to go back on interventionist state policies, and those who preferred to retreat. In Prussia there were debates of this kind over economic policy in every branch of the bureaucracy concerned – finance ministry, Royal Mining Corps, Overseas Trading Corporation. A parallel debate was played out over issues ranging from guilds to citizenship rights: it became more acute as social tension rose in the 1840s, when positions hardened. This conflict generally divided the bureaucracy in southern states like Baden and Württemberg more than it did in Prussia. The converse was true of questions touching on political rights or constitutionalism. When it came to church-state relations, every bureaucracy had its hawks and doves. These political fault lines were crisscrossed by others. There was, for example, a generational divide, which was partly a matter of differences in intellectual formation, partly a question of the less established resenting the established. This may sound simply like the natural order of things; but in Restoration Germany it reflected special tensions. Salaries in junior positions were low to begin with; governments allowed official incomes to stagnate at a time of inflation, cut back on hirings, tried to limit pensionable posts, and increasingly forced officials to contribute to their own pensions. Insecure younger aspirants were forced to wait ten years or more for a permanent post after completing their studies. They were denied progress through the ranks by promotion bottlenecks, and subject to superiors wielding stricter disciplinary codes. No doubt those at a lower level, the true 'official underclass' of postmen, customs officials, clerks and elementary school teachers, had more reason to complain, given their miserable pay and conditions. And they did complain, especially the schoolteachers. But the sense of hurt and frustration may have been even greater among academically trained men who came, not from the peasantry or petty bourgeoisie, but from official or professional backgrounds. This sense of resentment within the bureaucracy was growing in the 1840s.[15]

Why did the German states risk alienating their officials in this way? The most important reason was money, or lack of it. Perpetually near-bankrupt Austria was just the most spectacular instance of a general problem. The states were starved of income, given the difficulty of taxing the wealthiest (especially nobles) and the view of many rulers that parliaments were too high a price to pay for raising revenue. As a result, public spending accounted for no more than 5 per cent of gross domestic product and expenditure on official posts was skimped. The academically trained bureaucracy, the core of the administrative machine, was astoundingly small in these years, just a few thousand men. In Prussia, but not only there, it was actually smaller in 1848 than in 1820. No wonder the central bureaucracy was often, as Reinhart Koselleck has shown, simply overtaxed by the demands on it.[16] The rule of the state may not have been the exercise in bluff represented by the 'thin red line' in British India, but the comparison is not entirely out of place. That was especially true in parsimonious, cash-strapped Prussia, where its effects were felt at the most basic level: the claim of the sovereign state to maintain a monopoly of violence within its own borders (Max Weber's celebrated definition of the state). When the French Department of the Rhine-Mosel became Prussian, the number of gendarmes per head of population fell to a third of its previous level, and the situation did not change in the next thirty years. Like other German states, Prussia could man its frontiers and was able to drive the bandits and smugglers out of business in these years, but public order posed major problems. Even the number of soldiers fell. Nevertheless, the army absorbed around 40 per cent of the Prussian budget, and its presence was felt everywhere. In 1840, more than half of the state's 3.8 million urban inhabitants lived in garrison towns; there were two soldiers to every five civilians in Saarlouis.[17] Policing, in a society with few and inadequate police, often became a matter of military intervention, especially at a time of growing social unrest. The examples are legion. Like popular resentment of officials and internal divisions within the bureaucracy, this brittle public order was a prime source of vulnerability in the decades before 1848.

A Changing Society

At first glance, it is the unchanging nature of German society in these years that strikes us. Life expectancy remained desperately short, and a quarter of all children died before reaching the age of one. The rate was lower in the western regions of Prussia, higher in the eastern regions, in Saxony and in Bavaria, but was rising almost everywhere. Epidemics such as influenza, cholera (in 1830–1) and typhus (in the 1840s) continued to strike. So did harvest failures, the two most general and serious of which (1816–17 and 1845–7) bracket this period. In Germany, as elsewhere in Continental Europe, the economic old regime of periodic dearth and famine proved hard to shake off. The demographic explosion that had begun in the eighteenth century continued through the 1840s, increasing the number of those living within the boundaries of the later unified Germany from 24 to 35 million. But although it shifted the centre of gravity of the German population away from the south towards the Rhineland and the Prussian east, the increase had only a marginal effect on the urban-rural balance. Three-quarters of the population remained rural, as the growth of towns barely kept up with the overall rise in population – or failed to keep up in some prominent cases (Danzig, Frankfurt, Hamburg). At least until the 1840s, often beyond, those towns would also have seemed familiar to an eighteenth-century visitor. They remained physically small, bounded by walls and gates that were locked at night.

Over nine-tenths of the policemen on duty in Hamburg in 1844 belonged to the night watch. Even in Berlin, with a population of 400,000 by mid-century, the walls still stood, much scrawled upon by young men out – literally – to make their mark. (In town and country alike, 'rowdy' young men provided constant background music to this period, with the equally constant lamentations of magistrates and clergy as counterpoint.) Within the walls, the wide, straight thoroughfares constructed by princes in capital cities – the Kurfürstendamm (Berlin), Maximilianstrasse (Munich) – remained very much the exception. Towns consisted mostly of narrow, twisting streets and alleys, highly vulnerable to fires like the one that devastated Hamburg in 1842. Pavements were rare and lighting was poor; messengers were still more common than post boxes, shops had not yet replaced street-sellers and hawkers. Large numbers of livestock and poultry continued to share these cramped urban spaces with the human population, while the absence of central water or sewerage installations meant that water carriers and human waste were both familiar sights in the street. Despite the efforts of the ubiquitous 'health police', German towns still killed their inhabitants in such numbers that they depended on a continuing flow of migration from surrounding areas.

While the outlines of the old regime remained, German society was nevertheless shaken up and rearranged in the decades before 1848. Change began in the countryside. To understand it we need to trace the effects of peasant emancipation, which provided the legal and institutional underpinning of rural production and social relations. The working out of emancipation varied greatly across the German territories. Peasant labour services were rarely commuted at the same time that personal servitude was abolished; state, church and noble serfs were often placed in separate categories and treated differently; emancipation decrees left countless loose ends everywhere and led to many legal proceedings, not all of them initiated by former lords. But three general points can be made about the process. First, residual feudal privileges, especially hunting rights, remained in place almost everywhere. Secondly, only in French-ruled areas, Prussia and a few other places like Schleswig-Holstein was the process completed at a stroke, or even within a relatively brief time span in the early nineteenth century. Elsewhere, the main provisions of emancipation came in the 1830s (Saxony, Hanover, Württemberg), and some feudal restrictions continued until the 1848 revolutions in southern states. That was true in Austria even of personal labour services (*Robot*). Thirdly, nowhere did reform 'give' peasants the land they worked: it had to be paid for, or 'redeemed'. The ways in which this was arranged varied by region, but two broad zones of emancipation can be distinguished. The first corresponded to the areas where *Gutsherrschaft* predominated (see Prologue p. 5), including East Elbian Prussia and Mecklenburg. Here, large landowners benefited at the expense of the 'free' peasantry through the mechanism of compensation for feudal services and dues. Peasants lost somewhere between 6 and 11.5 per cent (1.25 to 2.35 million acres) of their land. Many small peasants, forbidden by an 1816 decree from becoming owners of the land they cultivated if they had no draught animals, were forced into dependence on the large estates and effectively proletarianized. Where the *Grundherrschaft* system was in operation, emancipation generally came later and the outcome was more favourable to the peasantry. It retained its land to a greater extent, either because the former lords were on the defensive due to the timing of emancipation, or because they were willing to accept cash as compensation.

These differences have become a familiar part of historians' generalizations, for they point to the important east-west division between a Junker and non-Junker Germany. On the one side stood the dominance of large estates, on the other the dominance of peasant proprietorship. The Junkers directly farmed their estates, the nobility elsewhere drew rents. The grain (especially rye) monoculture of the east was very different from the more differentiated peasant cultivation in the west. The remaining police and jurisdictional powers of the Junkers, where local administration and estate management still overlapped, had no equivalent elsewhere. And so on. We should nevertheless be careful not to attribute all of this to the divergent paths taken by reform. East-west differences owed something to historic settlement patterns and the imprint of feudalism, something to soil and climate – if the terms of French and Prussian emancipation had been reversed, it would not have created a class of peasant vintners in Pomerania, or produced rye-growing estates on the slopes of the Rhine and Mosel. East-west differences also owed something to the market. But – an important point – the workings of that market in turn created many common trends in rural German society that cut across the differences between east and west. Among the most fundamental of these were the changing shape of the land and increased output. Neither was entirely new; both were driven by rising population, and made easier by the new institutional framework that agrarian reform created. The amount of land under arable grew at an unprecedented rate in the first half of the nineteenth century: by at least 50 per cent in Germany as a whole, as much as threefold in parts of eastern Prussia. Pasture, marsh and heath were turned over to the plough, to potatoes, sugar beet, vegetables, and above all to grain (rye in the east, wheat, oats and barley in the south and west). As in the eighteenth century, only more so, the increase in cultivated land was matched by growing animal stocks. These years saw widespread application of more productive rotations, although agricultural implements changed little and increased investment usually meant employing more labour, not more machinery. The big estates of the east were increasingly commercial concerns, run by estate managers. On peasant holdings, except for the largest, most output was still dedicated to subsistence and local exchange; but here, too, production became more geared to the market, and more specialized. This went beyond obvious categories like vintners and dairy farmers. Württemberg had one village that specialized in flax, another nearby that raised snails for the Bavarian market, and a third that concentrated on producing cherry juice and dried fruit for export.[18]

All this might suggest an optimistic view of rural society, but there was another, darker side. Commercialization created winners and losers; it reinforced class stratification on the land and eventually led to severe social crisis. This was true to some degree right across Germany, a result of the fact that land was now more obviously a commodity. It was not only that, of course. Agriculture was the axis on which village work and recreation turned; it marked out the seasons and provided the basis for village nicknames. Among cultivators and would-be cultivators of the soil, and beyond them in the ranks of officials, priests and writers, the land continued to have other meanings. It was a token of permanence and stability, part of the divine order – Wilhelm von Schütz defended the three-field system on the grounds that it was based on the Holy Trinity.[19] And yet: daily life as well as the law taught that land was real estate. The Romantic conservative Adam Müller complained that God's bounty was being 'degraded into a business'.[20] Here is the thread that connects the dividing of common land, enclosures, consolidated holdings, reclamation and 'improvements'. Rising land prices (except for a downturn in the 1820s) encouraged a lively market in rural property. The extraordinary turnover of large estates in East Elbian Prussia has rightly been emphasized by historians. But something similar was going on with peasant farms: almost a quarter of Prussian farms were sold in this period, mainly to other farmers. A more active land market can also be found in Saxony and Bavaria. The notary became a more frequent village visitor and rural taverns did well out of 'sales-tippling' as the landowning peasantry now pursued its family marriage strategies with Balzacian relish.

There are two ways of looking at these transactions. Land was bought as an investment, or for a family member. But it was also sold, or auctioned, when the debts that encumbered property (rents, mortgages, redemption payments, commuted labour services) could no longer be serviced or rising levels of communal taxation met. One might expect the Junkers to have been prime beneficiaries here. Although they lost up to 20 per cent of their feudal income, they had cash in hand, received fiscal privileges, and found it easier than other classes to raise cheap credit from the state. Despite these advantages, for a variety of reasons that included overextending themselves, the vicissitudes of the market, improvident levels of consumption and sheer fecklessness, there were major transfers of land away from the nobility. Around 40 per cent of 'knightly estates' had bourgeois owners by the 1850s, a process that was to continue in later decades.[21] The figure was lower for the largest estates, but the fact remains that while the estate economy was a winner in these years, a significant slice of the old Junker class was not. Those who were had learned to play by the rules of agrarian capitalism, even while they continued to assert their remaining patrimonial rights and, often, to snub bourgeois newcomers. The large peasants, by contrast, consolidated their position almost everywhere. Like the East Elbian estate owners, they had generally done well from the division of common land, and they could mobilize family and kinship networks to raise capital for land or farm buildings. In these years, the larger peasantry – 'cattle peasants', 'lower villagers', or whatever local name was used for this local élite – cemented their position as village notables. They employed farm servants, hired agricultural labourers and poor peasants, acted as village foremen, took the lead when the local schoolteacher had to be kept in line, and served as sextons, church book-keepers or members of parochial church councils (another source of cheap credit for the insider). Land ownership, and the family reputations inextricably bound up with it, formed the basis of this village influence. The middle peasantry found it harder to maintain its landholdings, for it was more vulnerable to the cycle of debt, borrowing and eventual foreclosure, but it kept going through intensified exploitation of family labour.

Large and middle peasants formed a minority, and a declining one, even within the ranks of nominal peasant proprietors, let alone within rural society as a whole. In Saxony, where agrarian reform had been relatively favourable to the peasantry, only an estimated 22 per cent of peasant households were able to support themselves from their holdings in 1843 (it had been 39 per cent in 1750). This was fairly typical. In Brandenburg, Hanover, Bavaria and Upper Swabia, large and middle peasants made up somewhere between a fifth and a quarter of those engaged in agriculture. In Westphalia the proportion was higher; but in southern and western areas of partible inheritance it was much smaller. Throughout Germany, however, not just in classic 'dwarf-holder' regions like Baden and Württemberg, the ranks of struggling small peasants were swelling. Leaving aside the minority who could turn a profit (in good times) on a few acres, such as vintners or flax-producers, most were effectively dependent. Their land was insufficient for subsistence, and – the negative side of agricultural improvements – they were deprived of the former commons where they once gleaned, grazed a pig or goat, and gathered wood. The small peasant family with its 'parcellized' holding, forced to hire its labour out to Junker or cattle peasant, was often hard to distinguish from the families of landless or almost landless cottagers, farm and estate servants, agricultural labourers, or East Elbian *Instleute*, labourers who were tied to long-term work on estates through bonds that were part-feudal, part-contractual.

In the years before 1848 the small peasantry and landless underclass grew fast. For it was here that the population increase was concentrated, as former seigneurial or church restrictions on the right of the dependent poor to marry were abolished by reform. Some Restoration states reimposed controls in an effort to curb the growth of the 'dangerous classes'. This had some effect in Bavaria (at the price of soaring illegitimacy rates) and elsewhere in the south; it proved less successful in Hanover. Generally, however, officials and nobles denounced 'unhealthy' early marriage and the loosening of moral bonds, but did nothing. By the 1840s the underclass made up half the rural population almost everywhere; in some regions they accounted for as much as 80 per cent. Lacking self-sufficiency or the safety valve of common land, they depended on more or less regular labouring jobs. Many migrated seasonally in search of work, a roving life that was viewed by the propertied (including peasants) as something akin to the vagabondage of the late eighteenth century. Others emigrated, to Brazil, Algeria and (above all) the USA, especially small peasants from areas of subdivided holdings, who had at least some resources they could mobilize. Those they left behind, trapped between the harsh new dictates of agrarian capitalism and the old cycles of harvest failure and dearth, lived close to the edge of starvation. Of course, it can be argued that improvements in agricultural output enabled this underclass to survive in the first place. The calorific value of food production probably doubled during the first half of the century, outstripping the population increase. But that tells us nothing about how the increased output was distributed. Plenty of evidence suggests that agrarian crisis grew more severe. The emigration rate increased sharply, and reports of starvation and crime mounted in the 'hungry forties'. The classic symptom of distress was wood theft. Dirk Blasius has shown how property crimes in Prussia were closely correlated with the price of food, peaking in 1837–8, 1840–1 and 1845–7 (see Figure 1).[22]

The other classic symptom of social distress in that troubled decade was the revolt of desperate Silesian weavers in 1844, a reminder that protoindustrialization continued to employ and exploit the rural poor. The number of textile outworkers was still growing, but they found their incomes squeezed below subsistence level as the putters-out reduced costs in response to cheap, mechanized English competition. Rural weavers, spinners and hosiers faced painful, lingering decline in the face of industrialization.[23] It used to be argued that the same was true of the craft sector as a whole, or *Handwerk*, as disappearing guild controls exposed 'traditional' artisans to factory competition. Not so. The erosion of guilds had begun long before 1800. Neither then, nor in the years before 1850, was large-scale industrialization much of a threat. Numbers of craftsmen still increased, from 1.23 million in 1800 to 2 million in 1850. Their share of the gainfully employed rose from 12 to 15 per cent, and they continued to support the lion's share of the nonagricultural population (perhaps a fifth of all Germans in mid-century).

The real problems of *Handwerk* were more complex.[24] Take rural craftsmen, who made up around half the total. Many were engaged in branches concerned with consumption, such as food, clothing, and footwear. Others, like wheelwrights, blacksmiths

FIGURE 1   *Food Prices and Crime in Prussia, 1836–50*

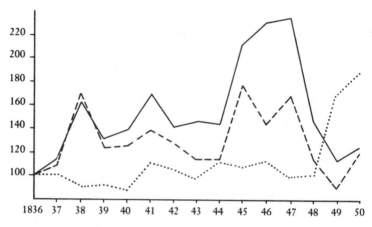

KEY
————   Rye Prices
– – – – –   Petty Theft
············   Insubordination and Defamation

1836 = 100
SOURCE: D. Blasius, *Bürgerliche Gesellschaft und Kriminalität* (Göttingen, 1976), p. 35.

and saddlers, served peasant needs. A third group, including masons, stone-cutters, joiners and plasterers, expanded because of rural improvements – the building of stalls, barns and sheds, new highway and canal projects. The fortunes of all of these craftsmen were tied to a still fragile agrarian economy, subject to periodic crisis. The shoemaker or blacksmith was indirectly affected by peasant prosperity. *Hat der Bauer Geld, hat's die ganze Welt*, as the phrase went: 'If the peasant has money, everyone has money' – and if not, not. The joiner or mason with a small-holding was more directly exposed, for teams of craftsmen in construction branches often had to post performance bonds with their land as security. Not all rural craftsmen were in 'traditional' branches, and none was threatened by the factory. They were a group in transition, tied to a rural economy itself undergoing change, threatened by old problems of the agricultural cycle and new problems generated by early, largely nonindustrial capitalism.

Even for urban craftsmen, industry was a distant enemy. True, nostalgia for the guild system might well include condemnation of the 'soulless', mechanized factory as an affront to craft dignity. But it was just as likely to include complaints about more immediate forms of 'unfair competition', from prisons or the sweatshops that employed 'inferior' female labour, a case in which hostility was bound up with the cult of masculinity that helped to define an 'honourable' craft. Here is a reminder that a major source of artisan discontent remained the putting-out system. The numbers are striking. Those engaged in putting-out grew from 1 to 1.5 million between 1800 and 1850, when they made up almost 40 per cent of the total manufacturing workforce.[25] Some were rural outworkers, but others included journeyman tailors and struggling small masters forced (like the seamstresses) into a despised piece work, and craftsmen in trades like furniture and bottle making who worked to contract under the direction of merchant capitalists. They were symptomatic of the real crisis in the crafts – the 'overcrowding' that led to underemployment and insecurity. A good half of all masters worked alone, more in overstocked branches like tailoring, carpentry and shoemaking. They lived on the margins of subsistence. In the 1840s, a meagre 400 out of 2800 shoemakers in Berlin earned enough to pay any trade tax; in Elberfeld-Barmen only half of the 1100 shoemakers were employed at a given time. The increase of more than a quarter of a million in the number of masters between 1800 and 1850 shows that journeymen could and did set up on their own account, especially in trades that required little initial capital. But this was often a flight from unemployment and mostly held out little prospect of true independence. It was a crisis-symptom, like the tendency among journeymen to extend their years 'on the tramp' indefinitely, as they became effective nomads in Germany or abroad. There were 20,000 journeymen in Paris in the late 1830s, another 10,000 in London. The abolition of guilds, where it occurred, exacerbated but did not cause the structural crisis in the crafts, which had two main elements. On the one hand, the market economy brought new degradations (merchant capitalism) and insecurities (the business cycle). On the other hand, craftsmen faced sluggish demand and a lack of alternative employment – not too much industrialization, but too little. While it is true that journeymen resisted factory employment, it is more important that there were still few factories anyway to provide work. Manufacturing continued to be driven by the broken, syncopated rhythms of craft production.

We should not discount early German industrialization. Plenty of statistics can be assembled to show that change was taking place: raw cotton consumption in the German Customs Union increased eightfold in the years 1830–50, Austrian output of iron doubled between the 1820s and 1840s, coal production within the borders of the later Germany more than doubled over a slightly shorter period, and so on. Beyond the raw cotton and the raw statistics, we can point to advances in mechanization and the use of new kinds of energy (steam, gas), the development of important industrial branches (engineering, chemicals and sugar, as well as textiles, coal and iron), the appearance on the scene of familiar entrepreneurial names (Krupp, Stumm, Borsig, Maffei, Siemens). Industrialization was more apparent from the 1830s, and in particular regions (the Rhineland and Westphalia, Silesia, Saxony, Bohemia) and subregions (the Neckar valley within largely agricultural Württemberg). Yet the limited extent of industrial change should be recognized. Growth in scale and organization of production generally ran ahead of capital investment and technological innovation, most obviously in the textile sector. The number of weavers grew from 315,000 to 570,000 between 1800 and 1850, but over 90 per cent of looms were hand-operated. Within the overall economy, industry proper continued to be eclipsed by outworking and craft production, and even more by agriculture. By the middle of the century, factory workers and miners made up around 11 or 12 per cent of all those engaged in manufacture and mineral extraction, no more than 2.5 per cent (5 per cent in relatively advanced Prussia) of the economically active population. Domestic servants comfortably outnumbered industrial workers. A glance at the international context is even more revealing. While the horse-power applied in German manufacturing rose from the low base of 60,000 to 360,000 during the 1840s, it was little more than a quarter of the British figure. Coal and iron output were no more than 6 or 7 per cent of the British. Under two-fifths of German exports consisted of finished goods, a sure sign of industrial immaturity.

Friedrich List argued that the system of international free trade could only benefit Britain, reducing others to the suppliers of food, raw materials or – in the German case – toys, wooden clocks and philological writing. (The choice of examples was surely influenced by his native Württemberg, which produced all three.) He advocated a customs union and a high tariff barrier behind which German industry could be nurtured.[26] But the Prussian and later German *Zollverein* was only mildly protection-ist, more concerned with developing the internal market than excluding foreign goods. Austria was actually more protectionist. List could take greater satisfaction from the development of the economic infrastructure, which he also urged, although this was pursued largely by the private sector or by officials dedicated to economic liberalism (especially in Prussia). In many respects transport and communications was the most dynamic part of the German economy in this period; certainly it was the darling of investors, for investment here grew faster than in any other sector. The result was that decent roads at last became more general, the canal network expanded seven-fold, coastal and inland harbour facilities grew quickly, and steamships plied all the major German rivers. Then there was, of course, the railway. The first line was constructed in 1834, between Nuremberg and Fürth in Bavaria. During the 1840s the total length of track (if Austria is included) grew from 600 to 4000 miles. But the great days still lay ahead. Before the middle of the century the econ-omic impact of the railway remained uneven. Railway construc-tion mobilized capital in unprecedented volumes, accounting for almost a third of all net investment in the 1840s. However,

German producers were not yet in a position to supply more than a quarter of the necessary track and other equipment.

Germany in these years was a bundle of contradictions. August Borsig built locomotives in his Berlin factory near the Oranienburg Gate, not far away from fields of beet growing in Luisenstadt. Improved transportation tied German towns and cities closer together, yet men and women still starved when the local harvest failed. Social mobility increased, but this continued to be a segmented society. Local attachments, like regional dialects, remained strong. For all the weight of persistence, it is nevertheless necessary to emphasize the elements of change. A residually corporate order of estates was giving way to a more individualist, class-based society. The philosopher Hegel described the emergence of civil society, a sphere of economic and social activity separate from the state, and defined as a 'system of wants'.[27] Contract was replacing custom, property becoming more important than privilege. Birth and traditional status were on the defensive against merit and achievement. These changes were not absolute, and rarely present themselves to the historian in cut-and-dried form. Thus, the sanctity of contract did not produce a brand new world of possessive individualism in the countryside, but worked with the grain of older kin and village loyalties. And when contemporaries looked for a way to describe what was happening in the towns, they adapted old and familiar terms. Rich businessmen were a 'financial aristocracy', workers made up a 'fourth estate'. But change infused most social relations in one way or another. Take the aristocracy: it clung to its remaining privileges, but also showed its staying power by adapting to change – entering the bureaucracy and professions, making money from farming, rural industry and investments. Here was testimony to a society that had become more bourgeois.

What, then, of the bourgeoisie? The German middle classes had grown in size and self-awareness by mid-century, but the most typical expression of bourgeois values was still the plain, comfortable domestic world of the Biedermeier home, with its sewing and reading corners, and gentle family pleasures. Antiaristocratic sentiment certainly existed: 'the locomotive is the hearse which will carry absolutism and feudalism to the graveyard', boasted entrepreneur Friedrich Harkort.[28] But the triumphalist captain of industry was rare, and industrialists were still the object of negative stereotypes in contemporary German literature. At the margin, the businessman of this kind was hard to separate from the successful tradesman. In fact, the term Mittelstand continued to apply to both. German towns had many energetic small and middle-sized businessmen. But capitalist wealth still meant, above all, wealth from mercantile and financial activities. That was not only true in Frankfurt or the Hanseatic cities, among great patrician families like the Amsincks, Mönckebergs and Schröders in Hamburg. A study of Düsseldorf shows that the few manufacturers in liqueurs, straw hats, umbrellas and the like were easily outnumbered by merchants and rentiers.[29] Here, as in many German towns, the educated middle class was also more weighty than the business class, and there remained important divisions between the two. They used the educational system differently, for example, the sons of businessmen being removed from school earlier to learn the ropes in the commercial world, those of the educated middle class staying on at the grammar school to acquire the *Abitur*, or entry ticket to university. Within the educated middle class, in turn, we must be careful not to exaggerate bourgeois substance or dynamism. Many occupational groups – doctors, for example – were only just starting to see themselves as 'professionals'. There was a large penumbra of insecure officials, untenured academics, would-be professional men, and marginal figures like journalists, a sign of what has been called the 'excess of educated men' in the *Vormärz* period – the exact counterparts of those known in Russia as 'superfluous persons'.[30] Their position generated frustration and resentment as much as a sense of bourgeois buoyancy. All in all, it is probably best to refer, as contemporaries often did, to the 'middle classes' or 'middle strata', within which a bourgeoisie proper existed only in embryonic form.

The same point can be made about the bottom end of society. Contemporaries began to use the term 'proletariat' from the

1830s, but they meant something different from the class of industrial factory workers in Karl Marx's celebrated *Communist Manifesto* (1848), a work that was more prophetic than descriptive in the German case. There were workers of this kind, in railway workshops and in the industrial suburbs beyond the walls of many German towns. There were also increasing numbers of journeymen in the construction, metallurgical and other trades who had become simply wage-earners. But we cannot really refer to the formation of a German working class at this time.[31] The term proletariat in the 1840s meant something less clear-cut. It referred to the urban equivalent of the rural underclass, those gathered together in towns and cities who lacked not only the means of production, but property, regular employment or security. The term embraced casual workers, labourers, servants, apprentices, unemployed journeymen and impoverished masters, as well as the floating urban population of knife-grinders, messengers, hawkers and the dangerous classes of beggars, vagrants, prostitutes and criminals. In its taxonomy and its moralism, this sounds like a description of the old-regime poor. But contemporaries used the term proletariat to indicate something they rightly believed was new, even if those who placed all the blame on industrialism were wrong. The urban underclass was growing. Typically, more than half the population lived at or below subsistence levels, and increasing numbers depended on public relief, charity or criminality to make ends meet. They were a product of structural social change. Their numbers swollen by population increase, cut adrift from the securities of the corporate world but not yet absorbed by an industrial world-in-the-making, they were victims of a crisis period of transition.

The Development of Political Life

German politics in these years was also marked by a striking juxtaposition of old and new. More than geography separated unreconstructed, old-regime Mecklenburg from more liberal southern states like Baden and Württemberg. Even within a given state, however, there were dissonant elements: embryonic versions of modern parliaments and public opinion existed alongside princely arbitrariness that would not have been out of place a century earlier. Naturally, any period contains a mixture of elements – residues of what has gone before, intimations of what is to come. But this seems especially true of the period 1815–48. One way of dividing these years is to draw a line in 1830. The revolutions that occurred then marked an obvious break. But it may be better to see the whole period from 1815 to 1848 in terms of a series of cycles, in which political expectations rose to a high pitch, only to give way to repression. The build-up to the 1848 revolution and the reaction that followed it was the third, and most intense, of these cycles.

The immediate postwar seemed (as so often) a promising time for those who wanted change. 'Patriots', flushed with the victory over France, looked for the creation of a more unitary Germany. The most ardent exponents of this position were the members of the student *Burschenschaften* (societies or fraternities) that began in 1815 at Jena, and first established the idea of the red-black-gold German tricolour. Some five hundred of them gathered at the Thuringian castle of Wartburg in 1817 in a 'national festival' to celebrate the anniversary of the Battle of Leipzig and the tercentenary of Luther's German translation of the Bible – an early pointer to the enduring relationship between Protestantism and nationalism in Germany. Liberal reformers were also optimistic. The lead in repulsing France had been taken by reformist Prussia, not conservative Austria, and reformers were still in the saddle there under chancellor Hardenberg, just as reforming ministers were still in power elsewhere (Montgelas, for example, until 1817). Frederick William III had promised a constitution in 1815, albeit in ambiguous language, a project warmly approved by Hardenberg, and details were under consideration. In fact, the years 1814–19 saw new constitutions granted in eleven German states, including the southern trio of Baden, Württemberg and Bavaria. Karl Rotteck

called the constitution in the first of these 'the birth certificate
of the Badenese people'.[32] But constitutionalism and reform had
powerful enemies: rulers looking to flex their muscles after the
Napoleonic years, nobles who wanted familiar corporate forms
of representation, conservative ministers and officials. The Austrian chief minister, Metternich, personified this resistance and
the antipathy to nationalism. The German settlement he had
brokered at the Vienna Congress was already a disappointment
to reformist and nationalist opinion. With the possibility that
constitutional government might establish itself in Prussia as
well as the south, Metternich exploited the 1819 murder of a
reactionary playwright and part-time Tsarist agent by a radical
student to persuade Frederick William III a crackdown was
necessary. Prussian reform came to an end. Hopes of a constitution disappeared, and in 1823 the king set up corporate provincial estates that underlined monarchical reliance on the landed
nobility, not a representative, state-wide parliament. Under Austrian and Prussian leadership, the Confederation passed the
harsh Karlsbad Decrees of 1819 aimed at wiping out the alleged
threat to the social order. The next year the basis of the German
Confederation agreed at Vienna was revised in a reactionary
direction.

The shift of 1819–20 led to a renewed emphasis on hereditary
rulers ruling without dangerous modern constitutions, and sanctioned the suppression of 'subversive' ideas. The 1820s were a
reactionary decade. *Burschenschaftler* were arrested, universities
monitored and professors dismissed, suspect organizations
closed down, newspapers and books censored. Heine and many
others emigrated. This repressive wave – the 'hunting down of
demagogues' – swept over much of Germany. Older accounts
tended to emphasize its 'police-state' character – post offices
with mail-opening departments, or the army of waiters and
doormen supposedly mobilized to report on political activities
in Austria. Metternich certainly liked to boast that he was 'the
chief Minister of Police in Europe'.[33] But centrally directed
police activity and censorship commissions were probably not
the most important elements in the campaign against 'subver-

sion'. States with limited police forces and small central bureau-cracies often delegated this task to local notables, such as clergymen, bailiffs, magistrates and university rectors.[34] What-ever the precise local form taken by the political reaction, it brought with it arbitrariness and the victimization of individuals. Constitutions and parliaments offered only a flimsy defence. Austria and Prussia possessed neither. Württemberg, Bavaria and Saxe-Weimar tried to temper the impact of the Karlsbad Decrees, arguing that these were inconsistent with their existing constitutions, but they were the exceptions. Many states had constitutions of some kind, but few spelt out the rights of citi-zens; and most assemblies were designed to build in the rep-resentation of particular estates or interests, not to facilitate broader deliberative activities, let alone criticism. That was to be expected, perhaps, in Prussia or Braunschweig – or in the Hanseatic cities, which remained thoroughly oligarchical. But it was also true in more liberal states. Baden was unique in having a lower house based exclusively on the representation of individuals, just as its constitution was singular in making no mention of 'communities'.[35] Elsewhere parliaments not only had upper houses with entrenched aristocratic powers, but lower houses that typically contained seats reserved for corporate interests. A quarter of the seats in the Bavarian lower house were set aside for unelected representatives of the nobility and churches. A similar bloc of seats was reserved in Württemberg for representatives of the 'privileged' – the former imperial nobility, churches, the University of Tübingen. That was not all. Elections were managed and indirect: they were also based on a stiflingly limited suffrage. Few could vote, and even fewer were eligible to stand. Property qualifications were so high in Nassau that only seventy men in the entire state met the test: in 1815 no eligible candidate could be found in eight out of the twenty electoral districts. In Bavaria just 1 per cent of the adult male population was qualified to stand (this amounted to one person in Pirmasens, not even that in Amorbach), about 6 per cent to vote.[36] If we add together censorship and surveillance, weak constitutional safeguards, and the narrow bridgehead established by parliamentarism, we see the limitations of political life in the German Confederation during the 1820s. Only in a few southern legislatures, where parliament enjoyed powers to approve laws and question ministers, did the language of 'rights' have much meaning.

This gloomy picture needs to be qualified in several respects. First, we need to remember contemporary standards of political life. Not only was the German variety more advanced than anything to be found in eastern or southern Europe; it was also little different in principle from what existed in post-1815 western Europe. Comparison can be made with the narrowly based Chamber of Deputies and rigged elections in Restoration France, or with Britain in the repressive age of 'Peterloo' (1819), when the (pre-1832) unreformed House of Commons was replete with 'rotten boroughs' and seats reserved for the universities of Oxford and Cambridge (they were abolished in 1947). The comparison also holds good at municipal level. In 1830 only one in 500 inhabitants of Cologne had a local vote – exactly the same proportion as in Portsmouth.[37] Secondly, the Confederation – unlike the former Empire – recognized the sovereignty of individual member-states, and removed the possibility of appeals to a higher authority by groups within the state. It had a stabilizing effect, allowing states to work out their own constitutional futures, and this was ultimately more important than the arm-twisting of 1819. Perhaps it is not a paradox that the one state which explicitly declared itself a member of the Confederation, Baden, was also the most liberal. The other effect of autonomy was to create islands of relative freedom even during the most reactionary periods, because legal codes and censors varied widely. Political émigrés did not always have to go abroad.

That leads to a third point. We should not equate politics with parliaments, constitutions and formal political debate. Public life in the broad sense was not frozen in this period. The printed word, to take an obvious example, could not be fully policed as numbers of books and periodicals continued to grow. Even 'subversive' thoughts found their way into print, especially in larger, more expensive and scholarly books (volumes with more than 320 pages were exempt from prepublication censorship). Apart from the sheer incompetence and haphazardness of censorship, writers found ways of smuggling in political messages. They used the old device of disguising critical comment about Germany as travellers' tales from other countries, or they dressed politics up as literary criticism. Heine's contributions to the *Augsburger Allgemeine Zeitung* were a notable example. What was happening here raises an important question about how we define the political. There was an apparent retreat during the 1820s into the apolitical, into those Biedermeier living rooms or into the harmless sociability of clubs. Yet many seemingly innocuous activities actually had a political content. Carnival festivities expressed veiled criticism of the status quo; choral and gymnastic societies (where they had not been closed down) often had a strongly liberal-nationalist complexion. In a more general sense, the growth of associations was important because it signified the extension of a 'public sphere', between private life and the state, where men (although not women) gathered together and public opinion could take shape. Formal politics may have been driven underground, but it was displaced, not destroyed. A further point follows. Given the allergic reactions of most Restoration states to criticism, even apparently neutral issues acquired political undertones: an association to fund a monument, honour a literary figure or assist the poor could easily arouse suspicion. The breadth of the state's interests only multiplied the points of potential friction with groups of its citizens – businessmen, religious communities, universities. Associational life provided a kind of safety valve for public opinion, but frustration was still rife. The restrictions on free speech and assembly made for a brittle political order. Those who argued that civil liberties, the rule of law and representative institutions would integrate citizens seemed to be vindicated by events in 1830, when Germany experienced revolutionary upheaval.

The July revolution in France was the trigger, prompting convulsions in many parts of Europe – Belgium, Poland, Italy. In Germany the storm centres of revolt were the most rigid and arbitrary Restoration regimes in Braunschweig, Saxony, and Hesse-Darmstadt, but there was also serious unrest in Hanover and on the Upper and Middle Rhine. Beyond the major areas of disturbance there were revolts in some of Germany's major cities, including Hamburg, Berlin, Frankfurt, Munich and Vienna, while university towns everywhere proved prone to disorder. Paris, revolutionary capital of Europe, may have shown the way, but revolution and unrest fed off indigenous grievances. Poor harvests in 1830 and high bread prices, the adverse effects of customs wars between the states, the specific grievances of journeymen, outworkers and (especially in Saxony) factory workers, peasant discontent over debts and remaining feudal privileges – these, with regional variations, provided the combustible material of popular anger. There was a pattern to insurrectionary violence. It was directed against economic targets, such as merchants, the homes of the rich, records of indebtedness and Jews, who were branded as 'usurers'; some incidents of machine-breaking occurred. But there were also attacks on customs posts, police stations, town halls and other symbols of political power. In Braunschweig the ducal palace was stormed and burnt down. Pressure from the streets and villages, almost always working across the grain of moderate liberal demands, brought about several changes of ruler and helped to extract a flurry of new constitutions. The southern states experienced nothing of this kind, but the political mood of 1830 manifested itself in a stronger showing of opposition forces at elections and successful pressure on rulers to expand the boundaries of political expression. The most striking example came in the Bavarian Palatinate, where local political and economic grievances against Munich led to widespread mobilization of opinion through clubs, meetings, pamphlets and petitions, helped by the more liberal French legal system that remained in force. At the centre of this activity stood the Press and Fatherland Association. In May 1832 the Association organized a gathering at the ruined castle of Hambach attended by more than 20,000 supporters from throughout the southwest, a festival dedicated to political liberty that was allowed to proceed by a nervous Bavarian government and provided a stage for nationalist, liberal, even democratic and republican rhetoric.

The revolutionary successes of 1830–2 proved short-lived. The authorities in Hesse-Darmstadt, Prussia and Saxony had already shown that they were prepared to crush disturbances by military force, and in the wake of Hambach a further cycle of repression began. Bavarian troops occupied the Palatinate, constitutional concessions were retracted, and under the orchestration of Metternich the Confederation approved a series of measures in 1832 (the Six Acts and Ten Articles) that laid the basis for a renewed crackdown. As in 1819, a piece of student adventurism – this time, a feeble coup attempt in Frankfurt in 1833 – provided the pretext for intensified police activity. Political gatherings and associations were outlawed, along with the wearing of political colours, flying political flags and planting liberty trees. Censorship extended in Bavaria even to sporting that badge of radicalism, the moustache. University professors lost their posts, the most celebrated victims being the 'Göttingen Seven' (they included the brothers Grimm and the historians Gervinus and Dahlmann), dismissed by the King of Hanover, who rejected protests with the surly observation that 'professors and whores can always be had for money'.[38] Ernst August was an exceptionally unappealing prince – it was said that he had committed every crime except suicide – but the purge was general. It extended from Prussian Bonn and Breslau to the southern universities of Tübingen and Heidelberg. The liberal Carl Welcker was actually dismissed twice from Heidelberg, in 1832 and 1841. Efforts were made to suppress the entire literary school known as Young Germany ('an antisocial conspiracy'), and Austria banned 5000 books, including works by Spinoza, Rousseau, Goethe and Schiller. Censors even monitored inscriptions on gravestones, cuff links and tobacco boxes – not as foolish as it might sound, given the way that all were used to convey political loyalties. The political and literary emigration spilled out once again, to France, England, Switzerland and the USA. At home, political freedom retreated into parliaments, where they existed. From his Parisian exile, Ludwig Börne wrote bitterly about 'prisons of freedom': 'To prevent liberty running freely around in the land, it is locked up in parliament'.[39]

But history did not simply repeat itself: the ratchet effect of events in 1830–2 meant that public life did not return to what it had been in the Restoration period. The renewed censorship was a back-handed compliment to the quickening growth of the reading public. The number of books published in Prussia increased by 150 per cent between 1821 and 1840. By the 1830s Bavaria had 100 bookshops, Prussia 300; Berlin alone had 60. Reading clubs and lending libraries expanded. These institutions grew even faster in the 1840s, and so did the press: the *Vossische Zeitung* doubled its circulation to 20,000 during the decade. This was still predominantly a middle-class and aristocratic reading public. Even in advanced Prussia 15 per cent of the population was illiterate; working hours made reading a luxury for most people; books, newspapers and library subscriptions were expensive. When the writer Friedrich Hebbel left the Swabian parish of Wesselburen in 1838, he noted that every book which chance brought to the community was a great event.[40] Nevertheless hawkers carried broadsheets into the countryside, and the family Bible could (as we shall see) be as potent a source of subversive ideas as the works of Young Germany, the 'left Hegelians' or liberal encylopaedists like Rotteck and Welcker. Through the 1830s political opposition was still often forced to express itself obliquely. 'Public life stormed and raged in the theatre and concert hall because there was nowhere else it was allowed to storm and rage', as Wilhelm Heinrich Riehl rather tartly observed.[41] Many still practised the discretion that had governed meetings of the professorial Moderation Club in Göttingen: no talk about religion or politics, no slights on 'good morals', and nobody allowed in who might breach these conventions, even if they were good friends. There is evidence that in universities much informal negotiation went on between liberal-minded professors and their colleagues charged with exercising censorship.[42] The policing (and self-policing) of society did not end in the following decade, but political life grew in intensity during the 1840s, as controls were gradually relaxed, even in Austria.

Public debate became more vigorous, new clubs and societies sprang up, parliaments were more active. In Prussia, where no state parliament existed, provincial assemblies and municipal bodies became livelier. Within parliamentary and other assemblies, parties developed and – especially in the south – party labels started to matter more at elections.

What was the content of *Vormärz* political debate: what did contemporaries argue about? Historians rightly refer to the role played by nationalism in these years, but we must keep this in perspective. The intensity of 'patriotic' sentiment was probably greater in 1806–13 than in later decades, although the French threat to the Rhine in 1840 did stimulate national feeling. Nationalism was a product of the print and communications revolution and a cause of the educated middle class, who defined (even created) the idea of a German nation with their grammars, dictionaries and collections of folk tales. In this period, writing on German law, customs and – not least – history helped to establish the idea of a linguistic and cultural nation. There was an element of assertiveness and hubris to this: in music, litera-ture, even in fashion, the belief in German distinctness shaded into a sense of German superiority and greater 'profundity', especially by contrast with the supposedly frivolous French. These ideas represented a further development of the anti-French feeling that had surfaced during the early nineteenth-century 'liberation' struggle. The Rhine issue in 1840 even gave such sentiments something of the same visceral quality, at least in the short term. Nevertheless, the France of the Revolution still provided a positive model of national self-realization, 'uni-versal' and thus capable of imitation. Most contemporary Ger-man nationalists owed some debt to French ideas, especially more radical elements like Young Germany, and were sympath-etic to the parallel and similarly inspired nationalist aspirations of others like the Greeks and Poles. Where the latter struggled against foreign oppressors, German nationalists saw their enemies in the discredited German Confederation and the nar-row, selfish dynasticism of the German princes. What they saw around them (notwithstanding Ludwig I's construction of

Walhalla as a 'national' monument) was *Kleinstaaterei* – a petty, stultifying preoccupation with local concerns, or 'particularism'. In short, the nationalist cause and the liberal cause, unity and liberty, went together.

Liberalism was an umbrella movement of oppositional tendencies, clearly gaining strength in the *Vormärz* period. It is frequently associated with a 'rising middle class', and referred to as 'bourgeois liberalism'. That is a little too simple. Right up to 1848 and beyond, sympathetic state officials played an important part in liberal movements and parties. Nor should we forget the aristocratic liberalism of areas like East and West Prussia, a phenomenon similar to the Whig liberalism of British and Hungarian landowners, although less powerful. It is true, however, that liberalism was generally strongest among the still amorphous middle strata of German society, especially among the educated and the professionals, stretching down to notaries, schoolteachers, journalists and other members of the academic proletariat. In a few advanced commercial areas like the Rhineland we find wealthy merchants and steamship magnates as leading liberals. Almost everywhere, the movement rested on the local efforts of modest businessmen, innkeepers, tradesmen and shopkeepers.

What did liberals stand for? There was little common ground on economic policy, except perhaps support for cheap credit. The liberal movement included both free-traders and champions of protection for the 'small man'. Liberals were more united on the issues to which they attached most importance, and these were political and legal. They wanted an end to remaining feudal privileges, although not to the monarchical system. They argued for constitutionalism and a division of powers, for representative parliamentary bodies whose members would be freely elected, have some control over legislation, and be able to hold ministers accountable. Predictably, then, there was widespread admiration for Britain. Carl Welcker described the British state as 'the most glorious creation of God and nature and simultaneously humanity's most admirable work of art'.[43] Above all, liberals believed in the rule of law: the basic rights of free speech, assembly and association, and an end to 'arbitrariness' (a key concept of the period). For some this included jury trials; for virtually all it meant the separation of justice from administration, with the establishment of autonomous public prosecutors' departments on the French model.

Liberals were not democrats. True, they criticized the arbitrary state in the name of the 'people', organized petitions, and held liberal banquets and other politically based festivities. But liberals were alarmed by the poorest and most ignorant, critical of those they thought of as the 'masses'. They rejected universal manhood suffrage, as they rejected female suffrage, because the poor (like women) were thought to be dependent and suggestible. Independence, based on maturity (of years and judgment), together with a certain level of property and education, was regarded by almost all liberals as a prerequisite of responsible citizenship. The Rhenish liberal Peter Merkens attacked the privileges of the local provincial nobility, but also objected to any broadening of the franchise to the Cologne Chamber of Commerce that would admit poor fruit pedlars. His colleague David Hansemann denounced popular sovereignty as a 'pernicious theory'.[44] Views like this may have been voiced with unusual firmness by liberal Rhineland merchants, but they were not exceptional. The ideal of pre-1848 liberalism was a society of (male) citizens who were active, industrious, and self-reliant.

In the years before 1848 a more radical strain of political opposition emerged. It was present at Hambach, became stronger in the 1830s, and acquired distinct organizations in the 1840s. Radicalism is hard to pin down because it was so diverse. Sometimes it grew out of liberalism, pursuing the same goals, only more firmly; in other places it developed a distinctive programme. One favourite argument has painted radicalism as a generational affair, carried by a group of younger leaders such as Johann Jacoby (East Prussia), Robert Blum (Saxony) and Friedrich Hecker (Baden). But moderate liberalism also had a new generation of leaders in the last ten years before the revolution, while some of the radicals – like the septuagenarian Christian Winter in Baden – were veterans of the opposition movement. Another familiar distinction is that radicalism had a more academic-philosophical slant in the north, associated with footloose journalists and iconoclastic intellectuals like the Young Hegelians (including Marx and Engels), whereas southern radicals were closer to the people. There is something in this, although the divide may be as much east-west as north-south. In the Rhineland and the southwest, closest to France and Switzerland both geographically and socially, radical opposition often took a populist form. This might have Jacobin features, emphasizing popular sovereignty, progressive taxation, citizens' militias, even republicanism. Alternatively, in states such as Baden and Württemberg, many radicals went with the grain of local, communal resentment against the centralizing, bureaucratic state. 'Tradition' or the 'good old laws' could be an effective rallying cry against authority, with a strong appeal to craftsmen and small tradesmen. Radicalism came in many forms, some openly democratic, others not. One common feature, often overlooked, is the importance of the personal. A local merchant might receive popular trust as a leader because he was known, but Hecker (a lawyer) and Blum (a journalist) also inspired great personal followings as 'tribunes of the people'.

Radical-democratic ideas such as universal manhood suffrage were sometimes labelled 'socialist' – the terms were not clearly distinct in this period. That is just one reason why it is important not to misunderstand what socialism meant – and did not mean – prior to 1848. Marxist 'scientific' socialism would later have strong support in Germany; in these years Marx and Engels had a modest influence, mainly within the radical milieu of émigré journeymen and intellectuals. Even there, Marx's very specific views on class conflict and the role of the proletariat had to compete with other socialist ideas, which used words like class and exploitation but offered cooperation or mutuality as the solution. Hence the differences between Marx and a figure like Wilhelm Weitling, a radical journeyman tailor who settled in Paris and become a member of the underground League of the Just. Weitling stood, above all, for a small-man artisanal socialism which Marx condemned as 'utopian'. Yet, at a time when the factory-based working class was very small, that was the kind of socialism most common both abroad and at home, for it addressed the moral universe of the craftsman. To the extent that a German 'workers' movement' existed beyond the ranks of the émigrés, it was largely to be found in the self-help organizations, cooperative ventures and educational associations of journeymen tailors, cabinet-makers and other artisans. They fed off ideas of craft honour; and the emphasis that so many organizations placed on education as well as economic justice – bread and knowledge, as their English contemporary William Lovett put it – further underlines how much this embryonic movement was still operating within a larger framework of politically radical ideas.

When we think about politics in this period, it is natural to think first of oppositional currents – nationalism, liberalism, radicalism, socialism. But we should not forget the development of another important 'ism'. Political conservatism also took shape in these years as a force of resistance against the forces of change. It emerged in response to two threats. The first was the 'levelling' role of the bureaucratic state. This prompted an argued justification for the corporate, traditional, privileged social order that owed much, but not everything, to aristocratic self-interest. Secondly, a postrevolutionary conservatism developed in opposition to the ideas of 1789 and to the German movements discussed above. Against the 'revolutionary' insistence on reform, rights and freedoms, it urged the importance of legitimacy, obedience and authority. Like their counterparts elsewhere, such as Burke in England and de Maistre in France, German conservatives of this stamp emphasized the power and wisdom of the past, the superiority of experience over abstract speculation, and the threat to stability posed by mechanical meddling with the fabric of an 'organic' society. The point is that conservatism now began to organize and justify itself intellectually, in the bureaucracies, in parliaments, and in public debate through press organs such as the *Berliner Politisches Wochenblatt*, founded in 1831 by the Gerlach brothers. Many conservatives rested their arguments on religion, presenting the 'natural order' as a divine order and offering religious justifications for authority and hierarchy. Hengstenberg's *Evangelische Kirchenzeitung*, for example, represented an important strain of Lutheran-conservative thinking in Prussia. A similar note was struck by many Catholics.

Religion, we should not forget, was still a vital force in *Vormärz* Germany. But it did not always serve the conservative cause: religion could and did provide weapons of moral resistance against the established order. Carl Welcker invoked God and the resurrection when writing about the liberal hopes of the 1840s; Friedrich von Sallet's *Lay Gospels* reworked the message of the Sermon on the Mount into a progressive programme.[45] As with liberalism, so with the social movement. Artisanal socialism was suffused with religious imagery, as we see in the case of Wilhelm Weitling. Works such as *The Gospel of the Poor Sinner* were written in the idiom of Christ-the-carpenter so familiar in contemporary French socialism. Protesting outworkers and peasants found similar biblical justifications for revolt, just as they reworked the Lord's Prayer in numerous satirical variations as a moral weapon against lordship and authority.[46] Most striking of all, and almost entirely neglected by mainstream historians, were the characteristic millenarian movements and cults of the period like those around Ludwig Proeli in Bavaria and the maverick Father Ambros Oschwald in the Odenwald. In all of these cases religion was as much a symptom of contemporary conflict as a panacea against it.

That is also true of what was happening inside the established churches. Liberal Protestant theologians cast down the gauntlet against orthodoxy, while the 'Friends of the Light' and 'free communities' mounted an explicitly political, liberal challenge to Christian conservatism. For supporters of the status quo, Catholicism was equally problematic. The success of Daniel O'Connell ('The Liberator') in Ireland and events in Poland and Belgium inspired a new level of Catholic political activity in the 1830s, especially in the Rhineland. In Germany, as elsewhere in Europe, this was the short-lived heyday of liberal Catholicism. The Catholic clergy also became more assertive in its dealings with the state, a stance that drew strength from, and in turn helped to shape, the revival of Catholic popular piety that occurred from the late 1830s. In 1837, mass demonstrations took place after Prussian authorities arrested the Archbishop of Cologne following a dispute over mixed marriages. Then, in 1844, half a million pilgrims went to see the supposed 'Holy Coat' of Jesus displayed in Trier, easily the largest incidence of mass mobilization in this period. It served notice of the popular energy Catholicism could harness. And the internal quarrels it created underlined the fact that the Catholic church was divided no less than the Protestant between an orthodox (in this case 'ultramontane') and a 'liberal' wing. The breakaway 'German Catholic' movement provided a political schooling for several important liberal figures, among them Robert Blum.

Division ran through the institutions of state and society in the 1840s: churches, universities, bureaucracies. It was a restless decade, when the pace of political debate picked up and public opinion grew bolder. Formal political opposition mounted. Both the radicals (at Offenburg) and moderate liberals (at Heppenheim) announced party programmes. Opposition leaders forged closer links across state lines, and other institutions broadened the political nation. The gatherings and festivities of gymnastic and choral societies played a particularly important role because of the numbers involved. German choral societies had at least 100,000 members by the end of the 1840s; the gymnasts boasted slightly fewer, but they did have strong support among journeymen and in the lower middle class, providing a reservoir of support for the radical-democratic cause. A genuinely national public started to become a reality. Not least, the expansion of press and telegraph, together with the arrival of news agencies like Reuters and Wolf, meant that an incident in one part of Germany was quickly taken up elsewhere. Many issues provided a focus of discontent – railway financing, the repression of a religious festival, a disputed election. But the issue that came to overshadow all the others was the social question, or the 'social crisis' as it increasingly appeared to contemporaries. The word 'pauperism' became a familiar part of political discourse as left and right tried to come to terms with the growing problem of an underclass whose desperate situation was signalled by criminality and periodic revolt. Thus the Silesian weavers' rising of 1844, the Galician peasants' revolt of 1846, and the Berlin 'potato revolution' of 1847, all put down by force, acquired prime political significance. It should be emphasized that liberal politics and social protest ran on separate tracks. From the point of view of opposition political leaders, social unrest had a symptomatic importance: it was evidence of governments' failure to feed their own subjects, or address the roots of disorder. During the economic crisis of 1845–7, as prices and unemployment rose and larger numbers of town-dwellers became dependent on charitable relief, the feeling grew that there was something fundamentally wrong with the established order.

The social crisis reinforced public disillusion with the *Vormärz* regimes. The expectations of those who wanted change had been aroused in Prussia by the accession of the supposedly liberal crown prince Frederick William in 1840. Relaxation of censorship had the same effect in other parts of Germany. But Frederick William turned out to be a deep disappointment: in Prussia, as elsewhere, political appetites were fed rather than satisfied. While princes, ministers and officials gave the appearance of division and paralysis, public discontent expressed itself in the growing attention paid to 'scandal' – not least in the princely houses themselves. In Protestant Saxony there was anger at the religious 'provocations' of the Catholic ruling dynasty. In Bavaria, Ludwig I's relationship with the exotic dancer Lola Montez was the object of dislike among the Catholic establishment, hard opposition questions about misuse of the civil list, and pornographic popular woodcuts. In Prussia, one Berlin official was shocked in 1845 to find, scrawled on the city wall between the Neues Königstor and the Prenzlauer Tor, the words 'death to the king!'[47] This was no doubt an exceptional case; but the reputation of Frederick William was certainly very low in these years. The king's brother Karl was embroiled in a series of financial scandals; the wife of another brother, Albrecht, had conducted an affair with a huntsman that led to a messy separation and divorce. Frederick William himself was widely known as the red-nosed king because of his drinking habits. Religion, sex, money and alcohol – these were the usual royal suspects. All had featured in broadsheets and political gossip before the 1840s, of course; in fact, the princes of *Vormärz* Germany were probably more continent than their predecessors fifty or seventy-five years earlier. But the scandalous stories spoke to a public mood of bitterness and disillusion. There was political ferment across much of Germany and a palpable sense of crisis. The attacks on Lola Montez are reminiscent of the pornographic broadsheet offensive against Marie Antoinette at a comparable period of the French old regime. And when Frederick William summoned the provincial estates in 1847, contemporaries drew plausible parallels with the summoning of the French Estates General in 1788, on the eve of revolution.

CHAPTER THREE

The Revolutions of 1848–9

From Spring to Autumn

European revolution was widespread in 1848, but not universal. Revolution did not break out in the backward east, in Russia and the Ottoman Empire, nor in the most advanced western areas of Britain, Belgium and the Netherlands. Its effects were mainly felt in the areas that were, in more than just a geographical sense, in between: by regimes that were neither liberal nor simply repressive, in societies that were no longer predominantly agrarian but in which industry had not yet established itself. In other words, it was the parts of Europe most obviously in transition, politically and socially, which proved the most explosive. Looking back on events three years later, the democrat Victor von Unruh put his finger on this point: 'We live in transitional times. The old has not yet been overcome, the new is still being born.'[1] Outside France, where 1789 and 1830 had bequeathed a powerful revolutionary tradition, the events of 1848–9 had their greatest impact in the states of the German Confederation and the non-German lands of the Habsburgs, including Italy, Bohemia and Hungary. The uneven development in this part of Europe gave the revolution its force, but also created the fault lines along which it spent itself.

Revolution in Germany was the result of several superimposed crises. At the economic level, an old-style crisis of harvest failure in 1845–7, more serious than those of 1816–17 or 1830–1, had important and cumulative effects throughout society. Peasants could not pay their rents, mortgages and other debts, which led to increased levels of foreclosure and hurt rural crafts that depended on agricultural prosperity. Crop failure also doubled the price of basic foodstuffs like rye and potatoes, causing widespread distress among those living on the edge of subsistence. Even in normal times, food accounted for 80 per cent of spending by poor families. Parts of the rural population were now reduced to eating grass, clover and potato peelings. The cost of food rose even more steeply in the towns, and this had an important secondary effect. It further reduced the purchasing power available for other produce, driving many businesses into bankruptcy. Textile towns like Krefeld were devastated.

In urban Germany, and in areas where outworking or rural industry was extensive, this last old-style crisis of dearth coincided with a crisis of a different kind: a downturn of the business cycle in 1847, imported from England, which hit the textile and engineering branches especially hard. Small businesses failed as markets collapsed and creditors called in their loans. Bankruptcies caused severe pressure on the banks, some of which suspended activities early in 1848, placing hundreds of firms and tens of thousands of workers at risk. Larger concerns, including Borsig and Krupp, laid off men. Yet another problem was therefore added to the crisis of food shortages and rising prices, as the normally high levels of underemployment in German towns now became, in many cases, chronic unemployment. In Pforzheim (Baden) three-quarters of the labour force was idle. The double aspect of the crisis made it all the more potent. So did the weight of accumulated social grievances – peasants angry at feudal privileges and their exclusion from former common woodlands, craftsmen chafing over their loss of security, the urban underclass barely subsisting at the best of times. The second half of the 1840s saw growing social unrest. Peasants in Galicia rose in protest in 1846. The following year there were bread riots and other forms of violent collective action across Germany, from Hamburg, Braunschweig and the eastern provinces of Prussia in the north, to Baden and Württemberg in the south.

Bread riots peaked in the summer of 1847, and it has often been pointed out that the harvest that year was good. But the improved crop could not help peasants who had consumed their seed corn or been foreclosed, just as it meant little to those who remained unemployed or had already fallen victim to bankruptcy. Nor should we expect some automatic relationship between hunger and revolution. Often it was not the most debilitated who rioted, but the small peasant, journeyman or struggling master. The psychological impact of the economic double crisis was immense. It further eroded trust in 'complacent' governments, placing a question mark against their competence and their very legitimacy, not least among the propertied, the relatively well off and members of the political opposition. So an event like the Silesian 'hunger-typhus' of 1847 became a political as well as an economic fact. The Prussian government initially tried to conceal the extent of a tragedy that cost thousands of lives; then it belatedly sent Rudolf Virchow to the scene, a liberal doctor who bitterly criticized the incompetence of the authorities for allowing loss of life on the scale of 'a small war'.[2] Official responses to the food crisis varied. Southern governments were the most active, buying up grain and effectively suspending the rules of the free market. But Prussia would not even suspend grain exports. When it finally got around to distributing food from military stores and purchasing from grain-dealers in 1847, the result was to drive up prices and hamper the relief efforts of municipalities and charities, especially in the west. This was typical of the stumbling uncertainty with which many governments responded to the crisis. Sometimes popular protest was harshly repressed, as in Galicia in 1846 and during the Berlin 'potato revolution' of 1847. Other protesters were left on a looser rein. It was a divided response which, with hindsight, both angered and emboldened the population.

Material and nonmaterial grievances reinforced each other to create a crisis mentality. This mood was fostered by events elsewhere, for what happened in Germany belonged to a larger European ferment. In 1847, unrest in northern Italy prompted Austrian military intervention and raised the political temperature in the German Confederation. The social and political struggles that led to civil war in Switzerland at the end of the year also had an impact on German opinion, especially in the southwest. Revolution broke out in Palermo in January 1848; and when news reached Germany of the February revolution in France that overturned the regime of Louis-Philippe, it seemed to signal that the old order was ripe for collapse everywhere in Metternich's Europe. Trains bringing newspapers and letters with the latest news from Paris were met by excited throngs of people. Efforts by the censors to play down events only provided grist for the rumour mills. The result was an eruption of pent-up feelings. Even in isolated, politically backward Oldenburg, a gathering in Delmenhorst on 28 February toasted the 'world-shaking news from Paris'.[3] Crowds formed in the German cities, bringing together members of the professions, especially the more marginal, shopkeepers, journeymen and labourers. They were swollen by thousands, sometimes tens of thousands, from outlying districts who descended on the local seat of government when they heard the news. Monster meetings were held, petitions drawn up and crowds gathered outside parliaments, palaces and town halls, calling for an end to censorship, the establishment of citizens' militias or civil guards, liberal ministers, a national parliament and the removal of remaining feudal privileges. There was a striking uniformity to these demands, but it was a product of the general politicization of the 1840s, not of any organized leadership. The crowds were spontaneous, animated by a heady belief that abuses would now be corrected and the old world made over. That diffuse and generous enthusiasm, the motif of springtime, was an important part of the German revolutionary mood in March 1848.

What had happened in 1830 in Braunschweig and a few other states now occurred throughout the Confederation, although not simultaneously. The popular movement began in Baden in the more radical southwest, and spread north and east through the states of the 'Third Germany': Württemberg, Bavaria, Nassau, the two Hessens, Saxony, Hanover. Revolutionary demands were also raised in the Prussian provinces, especially the Rhineland and Silesia. Faced with crowds that only the most conspiratorially-minded (like Prince William of Prussia) could blame on revolutionary agitators, against a background of parallel outbreaks of rural violence that showed contempt for established authority, the German regimes were torn by indecision. To the two classic preconditions of revolution – economic crisis and revolutionary demands – was added a third: a divided and vacillating ruling élite. There were clashes between government troops and insurgents in several capital cities where rulers acceded slowly or incompletely to popular wishes. In Berlin, where antimilitary feeling ran especially high, there was sporadic skirmishing from 13 March onwards, accompanying the daily mass meetings and hail of petitions. This culminated in the building of barricades out of carts, beams and woolsacks on 18 March after military provocation, and 300 died in the subsequent fighting, mainly journeymen and workers. A similar sequence of events in Vienna led to 50 deaths. But no ruler in March 1848 proved willing to commit the degree of armed force that might have crushed the revolutionary crowds. Instead, a collective loss of nerve gripped rulers, courts and nobility. The Prussian landed élite was, in the words of one of them, Adolf von Thadden-Trieglaff, 'paralysed by icy fear'.[4] Only one German ruler lost his throne, Ludwig I of Bavaria making way for his brother Maximilian, but everywhere the structure of ruling authority collapsed relatively quickly. Demands were conceded, elections promised. Metternich, reactionary symbol of the *Vormärz*, fled to London after his hardline advice had been rejected. Following the bloody clashes in Berlin on 18 March, a disorientated Frederick William IV withdrew his troops, performed a characteristically moist-eyed act of penance before the revolutionary martyrs, and issued an address to 'my people and the German nation'.[5] His hated reactionary brother, Prince William, decamped to England, and members of the shrinking royal entourage struggled to get out of uniform and into civilian clothes. 'Is there still a Prussia?' asked the elder statesman Hans von Gagern on 23 March.[6] In 1848, unlike 1830, the revolution did not stop short of Austria and Prussia, the two great powers in Germany.

Three general points deserve emphasis. First, one of the most striking aspects of these events was the speed with which they occurred, underlining the importance of new means of communication. This was the first European revolution of which news spread by steamer and telegraph, the first in which the train carried rural inhabitants to the urban centres of political power. Secondly, without trivializing the deaths on the barricades or the seriousness of local rural disturbances, the March revolutions can be described as relatively bloodless. As in other parts of Europe, the most violent revolutionary and counter-revolutionary episodes would come later. In March, contemporaries of varied political persuasions were struck by the sheer theatricality of events: the posturing of Frederick William, the dandyism of the Viennese students and German poet-revolutionaries, with their flowing locks, feathered hats and loosely-tied scarves, the way in which dramatic symbols of fire and light were used to celebrate the revolution. In countless small towns windows were illuminated and torchlit processions held. Viennese workers destroyed the gas lamps between the old city and its surrounding industrial suburbs, so that the flames flared into the sky.[7] We should not underestimate these gestural aspects of the revolution: they were potent symbols of release from the restrictive *Vormärz* order. But the drama of the March events, like their suddenness, also disguised something important. There was a gulf between the rhetoric of March and the reality of what had happened. The revolutionaries were less powerful than they appeared, the forces of the old order less weak. That was to be crucial in what followed.

Thirdly, and finally, the focus of revolutionary energy was fairly clear in March: it was the capital cities, where nervous rulers fell over themselves to make concessions. The capitulation of authority created a temporary power vacuum which new political institutions and movements filled. From that point onwards it is more difficult to determine where the revolution had its centre. The problem is not simply geographical, although the fact that the revolution proceeded unevenly from state to state is also of prime significance. Just as important, while many different elements combined to make the revolution possible, its outbreak released forces of still greater diversity. The collapse of authority produced an intoxicated sense of new possibilities that spurred some Germans to further actions, but filled others with fear. Between March 1848 and June 1849 the revolution proceeded, or stalled, at many different levels: within the reconstructed political institutions of the states, in the national parliament established at Frankfurt, and in the multitude of new extra-parliamentary organizations. Events during these fifteen months would repeatedly underline the importance of the complex interaction between these different levels.

Among their very first concessions, the German princes named new men to head the so-called 'March ministries': Römer in Württemberg, Bekk in Baden, Hergenhahn in Nassau, Stüve in Hanover, Braun in Saxony, Camphausen in Prussia. Most were prominent opposition figures in parliament, bourgeois or noblemen with moderate liberal views. This marked a first step to try to tame the revolution by directing it into narrowly constitutional channels. Also in March, a self-selecting group of similar liberal notables met in Heidelberg to organize the convening of an assembly that would discuss elections to a German national parliament. This body, the 'preparliament', met in Frankfurt on 31 March. Its deliberations immediately exposed the difference that was already becoming clear in the individual states between moderates and radicals, the former keen to work with the princes and the still-existing Confederation, the latter impatient to deepen the revolution. In Frankfurt, the Badenese radical Struve called for the preparliament to turn itself into a permanent, Jacobin-type convention. When this was decisively rejected, and the moderate March ministry in Baden acted to curb local radicalism in the name of order, Struve and Hecker proclaimed a republic in south Baden, the scene of exceptional agrarian unrest. Here, a poorly led ragtag army of journeymen, labourers, peasants and students was quickly crushed by 30,000 Confederation troops. It was the first example of the reserve power still available to authority, and it served to harden the lines of political division inside and outside parliaments.

What happened in Baden also made something else very clear:

the sheer vigour of popular activity. As so often in revolutionary situations, the initial revolution was only the starting point. Once it had occurred, it made new things thinkable and unleashed fresh demands. The summer of 1848 provided ample evidence of this radicalization effect. Peasants, rural labourers, journeymen and industrial workers demanded redress of their grievances and engaged in direct action – burning records, machine-breaking, attacking grain stores. Actions like these were usually triggered by particular local circumstances, and historians have often portrayed the disturbances as narrowly materialist and inchoate. Belly-issues were understandably prominent, but we should not overlook the powerful moral categories that underlay popular anger: the right to the fruits of one's labour and a fair wage, hostility to hoarding and 'usury', emphasis on the 'just price' and the journeyman's 'honour'. It is also true that protesters often posed their demands in terms of a return to some imagined golden age – masters calling for a restored guild system are an obvious example. But these aspirations were accompanied by calls for the abolition of feudal privileges, the guaranteed right of association and fairer taxation. The fifteen thousand or so workers and journeymen who belonged to the Workers' Brotherhood organized by the printer Stephan Born demanded employment and security in a way that looked backwards and forwards, using a familiar vocabulary to assert the rights of labour in a new world. And while popular demands often ran at an oblique angle to political debate, it is also striking that social protest often shaped itself along 'modern' political lines. The Workers' Brotherhood offers a good example, for it was much less antipolitical than its French equivalents. Masters and journeymen more generally organized themselves as interest groups, held congresses, sent petitions. They formed part of a larger political awakening, made possible by the revolution, that local studies are increasingly uncovering.[8] Businessmen, workers, lawyers, primary school teachers, academics – the impulse to organize existed throughout German society. Among those for whom the revolution offered new possibilities were two groups who had in common their lack of emancipation: Jews and women. While, on the one hand, widespread anti-Semitism accompanied peasant unrest in many areas, the revolution also brought Jews into German parliaments for the first time, including influential figures such as Johann Jacoby and Adolf Fischhof. Women were excluded from the electoral and parliamentary arenas, but played a significant role at demonstrations and meetings. The revolution opened up new opportunities at every level. An organization of female domestic servants was formed in Leipzig in April 1848, which aimed 'to assert with appropriate modesty our just demands for humane treatment on the part of our masters, and to protect ourselves against incursions and illegalities'.[9] This was also a decisive moment in the creation of separate women's organizations, of an embryonic women's 'movement'. Kathinka Zitz-Halein's Mainz women's association, *Humania*, had 1700 members; Louise Otto's newspaper, the *Frauen-Zeitung*, was a product of the revolutionary years. There was support for the political rights of women from the left wing of the revolutionary movement. Ludwig Bamberger called for women's entry into public life, demanding their emancipation from 'perfumed slavery'.[10] It should be said, however, that the revolution also bred misogynist militants. Ladies of the court remained prime targets of caricaturists' vulgarity, and the satirical press abounded in heavy-handed jokes about the 'marriage constitution' and the 'republic of women'.

Associations, or *Vereine*, hitherto largely the preserve of notables, became a vehicle for much wider participation during the revolution. The most obvious sign of this political flowering was the enormous growth in the number of clubs that identified themselves with a particular ideological position or party. They included democratic, liberal and conservative associations, the Communist League, and the Pius Associations (named after Pope Pius IX) that were the principal focus of a formidable Catholic political mobilization. The extent of popular political involvement was extraordinary by prerevolutionary standards. An idea of what this meant in practice can be gained by considering just two examples. Democratic associations not only flourished in radical areas like the Rhineland and Württemberg:

by August 1848 200,000 members were enrolled in 200 local branches of Ludwig Schlinke's Silesian *Hauptrustikalverein*. And the Pius Associations were able, with considerable clerical assistance, to collect well over a quarter of a million Catholic signatures on petitions. The press was also revolutionized: new papers appeared (more than 300 in Austria alone), alongside pamphlets and satirical broadsheets – 'a flood of street literature'.[11] 'March verses' were sold by hawkers and 'March songs' sung; unpopular figures were serenaded with charivaris or 'rough music' outside their windows, when they were not hanged in effigy.

Popular political life had its own dynamic, but also fed off the many elections that took place in 1848. May was the crucial month, when elections were held for the Prussian and other state parliaments, and for the German national parliament in Frankfurt. These were unprecedented political events in German history, given the publicity that surrounded them and the wide suffrage. All 'independent' adult males could vote in elections to the national parliament. This was differently interpreted in the individual states, but it has been calculated that as many as three-quarters of adult males were eligible to vote and the turnout varied regionally between 40 and 75 per cent. The body that met in the Frankfurt Paulskirche on 18 May was nevertheless heavily weighted towards the social élite. There are several explanations for this – the widespread use of indirect voting as a filter, the desire of voters to send figures of stature to the national parliament, simple deference towards 'popular' notables. The result, anyway, was striking. No fewer than 436 of the 812 members who sat during the lifetime of the parliament were employed by the state, led by administrative and judicial officials. (Professors, contrary to legend, numbered a fairly modest 49, although their influence was disproportionately great.) A total of 100 businessmen and landowners were outnumbered by about 150 members of the free professions, two-thirds of them lawyers. Another 50 were clergymen. Craftsmen and peasants numbered just seven in total.[12] It was a parliament of university-educated officials and lawyers. Not surprisingly, its members thought in constitutional and legal terms. They emphasized the lines of continuity between themselves and the Confederation, and were mindful of the power wielded by the states so many of them served.

Starting with contemporaries, the Frankfurt parliament has been the object of harsh criticisms: that it was a mere talking shop obsessed with the fastidious discussion of fine ideas; that it ignored or postponed grappling with the central issues of the revolution while it still had the chance; that – in the scornful words of Engels – it was 'nothing but a stage where old and worn-out political characters exhibited their involuntary ludicrousness and their impotence of thought, as well as action'.[13] These charges are hard to accept as they stand. The discursive style at Frankfurt was no more florid than that of other contemporary parliaments, and in many ways the assembly turned itself with impressive speed into a modern legislature. Procedural rules were drawn up from nothing, and a system of parties (*Fraktionen*) emerged that was more developed than anything seen in even the most advanced pre-1848 parliaments. The achievement of the Constitutional Committee in preparing a draft on basic rights in less than six weeks hardly suggests pedantic procrastination – it took the parliament of the later North German Confederation three years to come up with the citizenship laws of 1870. The committee's recommendations concerned fundamental issues: the rights of free speech and assembly, religious equality, the abolition of the aristocracy as a privileged class, national citizenship for all Germans. And it needs to be emphasized that the parliament's preoccupation with basic rights between July and October accurately reflected the central concern of all *Vormärz* oppositional currents, moderate and radical, with this subject. Indeed, nearly a fifth of the 17,000 petitions received by the Frankfurt parliament concerned basic rights, and another fifth the question of church-state relations that fell under the same rubric. On the crucial question of executive power, the parliament proved almost bold in exceeding its formal mandate. After stalemate between the right (who insisted on recognizing the princes' powers) and the left (who wanted parliamentary sovereignty), there was overwhelming support for a compromise proposed by the president of the assembly, Heinrich von Gagern, whereby the parliament established a 'provisional executive' on its own authority, without reference to the states or the Confederation – but with the Habsburg Archduke Johann as its nominal head. Four days later, on June 28, a German government was formed.

Yet the fact remains that the national parliament failed to seize the summer. The social question offers a prime example. For the most part the assembly maintained an Olympian detachment from pressing popular needs, believing that large political questions had to take precedence. Its Economic Committee, faced with a torrent of contradictory petitions and demands, torn between protectionists and free-traders, proved divided and inconsequential. The Württemberg representatives at Frankfurt, probably more attuned than most to popular impatience, found that their urbane reassurances fell on deaf ears. It was reported from Ulm that there was 'little trust for the learned men of the Paulskirche, who are viewed as too theoretical and moderate'.[14] The criticism applied equally to the treatment of constitutional and national questions, discussion of which was postponed during the crucial summer months. But what was the use of basic rights if the issue of sovereignty remained unresolved? What did it mean to declare national citizenship if the borders of Germany remained unclear and there was open conflict between Danes and Germans in Schleswig and Holstein? The underlying issue in both cases was the relationship of national assembly to the Confederation and individual states, especially Prussia and Austria. And this issue was ducked. Political practice at Frankfurt was based on consensus, within an assembly where the parliamentary arithmetic heavily favoured the centre, and especially the centre-right. This was reflected in the composition of the first provisional executive, headed by a prince and numbering four nobles (one a Prussian general) and two Hanseatic merchants as its six ministers. The caution and moderation displayed at Frankfurt were not risible in themselves, but they had disastrous effects as social and political polarization eroded the middle ground.

The parliament, like the March ministries in the individual states, was left behind by the dynamic of the revolution. On the one side, democratic and radical elements mobilized popular support – in the southwest and west, in Saxony, even in rural areas of eastern Prussia like Silesia. Popular impatience led to a series of uprisings, put down by Confederation troops ordered in by the provisional executive: in Wiesbaden and Frankfurt-Sachsenhausen in July; in Frankfurt again and in Baden in September, an insurrection that brought together social discontent, radical impatience and nationalist anger over the Schleswig-Holstein crisis; in central Germany, where salt miners and toy-makers rose in October. By these actions, the provisional executive acquired a reputation among the radical and socially discontented as being no better than the repressive *Vormärz* regimes. At the same time, its attempts to maintain 'order' played into the hands of reactionaries and revealed its own fundamental impotence. Recognized diplomatically only by the USA and small European powers like Greece, Belgium and Sweden, the provisional executive also possessed little real power at home. It had a minister of the interior without police, a minister of finance without revenue. The one area in which it acted decisively – deploying Confederation troops to suppress disorder – was dependent on the goodwill of the German states. And here the counter-revolution was growing in strength through the summer and into the autumn.

Counter-Revolution and 'Second Revolution'

Outside Austria and Prussia, in the 'third Germany', this process was mostly unspectacular and incremental. Princes, courts and bureaucrats started to recover their confidence. Their resolve was strengthened by the obvious ability of Confederation troops to crush further uprisings. Events elsewhere in Europe, like the repression of the June days in Paris, about which ambassadors kept their masters well-informed, also raised morale in ruling circles. So did the growth of conservative law-and-order sentiment within the bourgeoisie and lower middle class – master craftsmen, shopkeepers, small businessmen. In this critical swing group, fear of the urban mob and the 'proletariat' started to replace the anger of March. The shift found expression in those symbols of March, the civil guard detachments: some swung over very quickly to the side of 'order' (Hanover, Munich, Augsburg), in others a conservative wing vied with radical elements (Dresden), or a separate conservative formation was established (Hamburg). There was also counter-revolutionary potential in the countryside, especially where rulers were shrewd enough to make quick concessions over remaining feudal privileges. Where they did so, it was possible to drive a wedge between property-owning peasants and rural underclass. The former were happy to tolerate, even to participate in destroying seigneurial records or attacking an unpopular bailiff; they reacted very differently when the spectre of rural 'communism' among the landless seemed to threaten their own dominance.

With international and local indicators apparently moving in their favour, the German princes began to play for time. They delayed elections until the end of the year, as in Saxony, Bavaria and Hanover; or they held elections on the pre-1848 suffrage, then delayed the subsequent meeting of parliament, as in Württemberg; or they exploited moderate fears of radicalism to delay holding elections at all in 1848, as in Baden. None of this means that regimes in the 'third Germany' were inactive. One notable development was a new willingness to make credit available to bail out banks and businesses, thereby creating work that would take the edge off social discontent. This policy was actively pursued in Saxony. Large sums were funnelled into the industrial towns, identified as the most dangerous centres of unrest. The growth of the state paper money supply in Germany between 1847 and 1850, from 30 million to 53 million Thaler, shows the extent of the intervention.[15] But these measures did not automatically assuage popular discontent; they might even exacerbate it. While financiers and businessmen welcomed policies that aided work-creation, many members of the lower middle class were outraged. 'The humanity shown to the workers exceeds the limits of common sense, only the artisan, the productive *Mittelstand*, has been deserted', complained one petition to Frankfurt.[16] Yet the radicalization among journeymen and workers meant that what might have been welcomed before the revolution was now seen as too little, too late.

Exactly the same problem arose when it came to political and constitutional issues. Baden provides a good, if somewhat atypical, illustration. No new elections had been called; but the existing parliament, the new Bekk ministry and the Karlsruhe bureaucracy did enact substantial political reforms. A revised structure of local administration was officially gazetteered in the spring of 1849; and a new constitution that included an elected upper house and other concessions to radical demands was ready in draft in April 1849, before being overtaken by national events. But this was no longer enough for the growing body of republican sentiment. One can understand why regime and moderates found it irksome that their willingness to undertake reforms, even after two republican risings in Baden, earned them so little credit. Radicals, on the other hand, were frustrated at what was happening nationally, angered at the Badenese state regime's refusal to recognize locally elected republican mayors, and convinced that concessions would only be wrung out of Karlsruhe by maintaining their political pressure. In short, what would almost certainly have been acceptable in February 1848 was no longer so a year later, thanks to the radicalizing effect of revolution.[17] Baden was unusual in the relative willingness of moderate ministry, civil service and ruling prince to make concessions, but the tug of political forces there was characteristic. Across the 'third Germany' the reluctant revolutionaries of the March ministries, or their successors, faced difficulties caused by the different time-scale of events taking place at Frankfurt. Meanwhile, they were caught locally between radicalized (but often conflicting) popular demands on the one side, moderate fears and the foot-dragging of the princes on the other. Their instincts usually favoured law and order. In Hesse-Darmstadt, for example, legislation 'Concerning the Maintenance of the Legal Order' in July 1848 was followed three months later by measures against 'Abuse of the Press and Popular Assemblies'. In most of the smaller states it was creeping political reaction that threatened the clubs, newspapers and other popular political institutions that had been formed in the wake of the revolution.

The counter-revolution was more open as well as more decisive in the two largest states, the weather vanes of the German revolution. In the summer of 1848 the very existence of Austria appeared to be at stake. The Hungarians, Czechs and Italians had rebelled, and threatened to pull apart the whole multi-national Habsburg empire. Vienna itself was the most radical of all German capital cities. When a restrictive franchise for the promised parliamentary elections was announced by the new government in May, dissatisfaction brought thousands back on to the streets and attempts to disperse them led to a further uprising. The court fled to Innsbruck, prompting one of many satirically reworked Lord's Prayers: 'Our Father, which art in Innsbruck, hallowed be thy name, but our will be done, for we are the sovereign people.'[18] From late May, for fully three months, a revolutionary coalition of democratic associations, radical workers' clubs, municipal politicians, Civil Guard and the students' Academic Legion shared control in Vienna with a nervous government and (after July) the newly elected Austrian parliament. Its main political creation was the Jacobin-sounding Committee of Public Safety. Against this background the army, successful in suppressing a Galician uprising in April, assumed critical importance as the embodiment of Habsburg authority, and it proved more loyal to the exiled court than to the moderate government in Vienna. The rolling back of the revolution began with military operations against the rebellious nationalities. Windischgrätz crushed the Czech revolution in June, the fall of Prague marking the first military defeat of a revolutionary capital. Martial law, mass arrests and military dictatorship followed. In a strategically more important campaign during late July, Radetzky enjoyed similar success in northern Italy, and Milan was reoccupied. The Hungarians offered stiffer resistance to

General Jellačić, and it was the attempt to mobilize troops in Vienna to reinforce his campaign that sparked a final, bloody clash in the capital city in October 1848. Mutinous soldiers, joined by workers, democrats, students and a newly formed radical militia made up a revolutionary body of perhaps 100,000, armed with weapons stolen from the armoury. But they were overmatched against the regular army. The retaking of Vienna by Windischgrätz at the end of October cost more than 2000 lives; parliament was dismissed and a reactionary government installed under Prince Schwarzenberg.

The victory of the Austrian counter-revolution was significant at many levels. In the first place, it underlined the military superiority of regular soldiers. Almost as important, the loyalty of Habsburg troops from the smaller 'subject nations' (Jellačić himself was a Croat) showed how the conflict of nationalities could work against the revolution – a point with larger significance for the German revolutions as a whole. What happened in Vienna also demonstrates how social divisions undermined the revolution. By October, 'red' Vienna was surrounded by a countryside that was now pacific: early in September, the Austrian parliament decreed the end of all remaining feudal privileges, and further peasant interest in the revolution ceased abruptly. In Vienna itself, the arrival of soldiers was greeted with relief by most members of the middle and lower middle class. Their growing anxiety through the summer had already been signalled by the severity with which the Civil Guard, dominated by property owners, put down workers' protests in August over wage cuts for public works. It was then that the Civil Guard left the coalition of March revolutionaries, and the Committee of Public Safety collapsed. Social divisions had fractured and undermined the revolution in Vienna two months before Windischgrätz arrived with his 60,000 men. Finally, the recapture of Vienna was important in strategic and symbolic terms. One celebrated victim of the repression that followed was Robert Blum, a leading member of the left in the Frankfurt parliament, who travelled to Vienna in October and was executed the following month for his part in the revolution. Blum saw the events there as a turning point, and so they were. The revolution had suffered a major defeat, and counter-revolutionaries everywhere were emboldened.

Prussia is a case in point. The counter-revolution there proceeded along distinct but parallel lines. One obvious difference was the role played by the Prussian constituent assembly elected in May. Like the multinational Austrian parliament that finally convened in July, the Prussian parliament contained more members of the lower classes than the national parliament – peasants and craftsmen together made up about a sixth of all Prussian deputies. Unlike the Vienna or Frankfurt assemblies, the parliament in Berlin had a political centre of gravity on the left and centre-left, and it pressed hard over questions of political power. During the summer and early autumn of 1848 it passed resolutions that called for parliamentary rule and an army bound by the constitution; it demanded the abolition of hunting rights without compensation, and denied the monarch's claim to rule 'by the grace of God'. All of this was clearly provocative, and criticized as such by moderates, but it must be seen as part of a power struggle waged against an increasingly obdurate king and the growing threat of counter-revolution. Once again, as in the 'third Germany', the king's ministers were prepared (especially in the early months of revolution) to provide state credits to aid work-creation; but they became progressively less willing to make political concessions. Quite the reverse: a reactionary tendency can be clearly read off from the fact that a series of ministerial changes shifted the government step by step to the right. There were other pointers to a determination on the right to roll back the revolution. Immediately after the March events a reactionary 'Camarilla' had formed at court; the founding of the conservative *Kreuzzeitung* newspaper followed in July, and the so-called Junker parliament convened in August. The right was outraged by what it saw as parliamentary presumption; it was also – as in Vienna – appalled by what was happening in the streets. There may have been no Committee of Public Safety in the Prussian capital, but there was another attempted uprising in June, democratic associations were very active, and 'flying

units' of intellectuals, workers and craftsmen organized themselves alongside the Civil Guard. Young journeymen and construction workers appropriated the streets, mocking gendarmes,
demanding money from the well-dressed, and forcing tribute
from shopkeepers in the form of food, cigars and clothing.

A further parallel with Austria was the hope for order that
court, nobility and bureaucracy vested in the army. 'The army,
that is now our fatherland', observed Albrecht von Roon.[19] Prussian troops had withdrawn in March, angry and frustrated: they
had not been defeated or disarmed. Just as the Habsburg army
first fought back in Cracow, so the Prussian army first measured
its strength by crushing a Polish revolt in Posen in early May.
The following month it put down the attempted rising in Berlin;
in July a clash with the Civil Guard in a Silesian town left
fourteen civilians dead. Through the summer the shadow of
the army fell over Prussian politics. Soldiers pressed Frederick
William in September to draw up plans to overturn the constitution, and the naming of the hawkish General Wrangel as
supreme commander in Berlin served virtually as advance
notice of a coup. Following the interim ministry of General
Pfuel, the coup arrived when the reactionary general Count
Brandenburg was named prime minister on November 1 and
parliament prorogued. Nine days later General Wrangel entered
Berlin with 80,000 men; martial law was declared and political
rights were suspended. Attempts by the left to organize the
withholding of taxes proved unsuccessful, despite substantial
support in the Rhineland, Westphalia and Silesia.

Not only did the timetable of counter-revolution in Berlin
shadow events in Vienna: there were also structural similarities.
In Prussia, as in Austria, the spearhead of counter-revolution
was the army, but there was a broader basis of popular support.
Military rule in Berlin was greeted with relief by many bourgeois
and shopkeepers, the backbone of the Civil Guard which had
often clashed with workers and 'flying units'. In rural and small-
town Prussia there were popular 'church and king' riots during
1848–9. Some occurred in areas where there had been food
riots in 1847, a reminder that the fund of deference to the 'just

ruler' and the 'father of his country' was not exhausted, and that the antagonism of March 1848 towards individual officials or landlords – but not to the system as a whole – could also direct itself against liberals, democrats and Jews.[20] Sentiments of this kind were mobilized by conservatives, especially in the core provinces of Brandenburg and Pomerania, through the Association for King and Fatherland, patriotic and Prussian leagues, ex-servicemen's and peasant associations. By early July 1848 conservative organizations had 20,000 members, by the summer of 1849 numbers had risen to 60,000, most of them peasants, master craftsmen and shopkeepers.

The Austrian and Prussian counter-revolutions in autumn 1848 marked a turning point, but they did not put an end to the revolution. The balance of forces had altered, but the political situation remained fluid. Even in the two most powerful states the military crackdown did not mean a return to *Vormärz* conditions. The new Austrian chief minister, Schwarzenberg, was no simple-minded reactionary. Disinclined to stick back together what had been cracked in March, he unsentimentally insisted that the Emperor Ferdinand abdicate in favour of his eighteen-year-old nephew Francis Joseph. Key liberal ministers were retained; and the parliament disbanded by Windischgrätz in Vienna reconvened in the Moravian town of Kremsier. In Prussia, too, Count Brandenburg dissuaded Frederick William from following a course of outright military dictatorship. The Prussian parliament was dissolved, but a new constitution was proclaimed in December, designed to isolate the radical left. It provided for a democratically elected lower house, even as it guaranteed the monarch generous executive and emergency powers. Elections to a new parliament were held early in 1849. In other words, in both Austria and Prussia the real power of the army existed in conjunction with a flexible postrevolutionary conservatism. Equally, the contempt displayed towards the Frankfurt parliament in autumn by Berlin and Vienna, most brazenly in the execution of Robert Blum despite his parliamentary immunity, was balanced by the recognition in both states that the 'German question' remained open until the national parliament finished its work.

It would also be wrong to think that the events of October and November put an end to popular politics. On the contrary: as in France, counter-revolution in the capital was the prelude to more furious political mobilization in the provinces. Some of this was undertaken by conservatives, as we have seen. Moderate liberal organizations also grew in number, under the loose direction of the National Association, established at Kassel in November, with around 160 affiliated groups by April 1849. But mobilization took place, above all, on the left. When the second Democratic Congress met in Berlin in late October, its delegates represented 260 associations in 140 towns. Following the November events in Prussia, left-wing members of the Frankfurt parliament established the Central March Association to coordinate the activity of these organizations. By the spring of 1849 the Association had at least 950 affiliated branches and half a million members. Democratic organizations were greater in number, larger in size and generally better coordinated from the centre than those of their rivals. Their support also reached down impressively into the popular classes. While the leadership was mainly drawn from the professions, especially the minor professions (elementary school teachers, pharmacists, notaries, editors), journeymen, masters and small businessmen predominated among ordinary members, and in some places (Dresden, for example) there were significant numbers of workers among the rank and file.

The Frankfurt parliament therefore found itself placed within a still-changing political landscape as it turned in October 1848 from the discussion of basic rights to the question of the form the future Germany should take. There were really three interrelated issues here: territory, squaring the new German nation with the existing states-system, and sovereignty. The territorial question arose most obviously over disputed borders – Schleswig, Posen, the Tyrol. But that, in turn, raised the decisive issue of relations with Austria and Prussia, whose independent actions did much to determine where the outer borders were drawn.

On October 27, the parliament voted overwhelmingly for the so-called 'greater German' solution, that would include the German parts of the Habsburg empire but not the non-German lands (Hungary, Galicia, Croatia, Northern Italy). However, this ran up against Austrian determination to maintain its empire intact. That, after all, was what Windischgrätz, Radetzky and Jellačić had been fighting for. In late November, Schwarzenberg declared Austria's continued existence as a state to be 'a German and a European necessity'.[21] This decisively shifted the terms of debate at Frankfurt. The outward sign of this was the resignation of Schmerling, who had been prime minister of the provisional executive since September, and his replacement by the pro-Prussian Gagern. More profoundly, the political groups in the national assembly realigned themselves around 'greater German' and 'lesser German' positions. The former brought together Catholics, conservatives, Austrians and southern Germans, with members of the left who wanted a unitary greater Germany. It was a negative coalition in a double sense: held together only by common hostility to a Prussian-dominated Germany, it had no idea how to achieve its goal in the face of Vienna's obstructionist policy. The 'lesser German' party, with its strength among north Germans, Protestants and moderate liberals, looked to Prussia as the more progressive of the two major powers in spheres such as economics, communications and education. The Württemberger Otto Abel typically praised Prussia for 'the liveliest traffic in goods and ideas'.[22] But advocates of a lesser Germany also faced problems. They, too, were only loosely united in their aims, and regarded Prussia with varying degrees of enthusiasm or resignation. On top of that, all Lesser Germans – whether more or less enthusiastic – had to overlook Frederick William's stated refusal to become German emperor without the approval of the other German princes. Instead, they seized upon his more 'national' rhetoric in March, and comforted themselves with the sympathy displayed by Prussian prime minister Brandenburg for a hereditary Prussian emperor of Germany.

It would be easy to argue that both sides built on illusions, but we have to remember the position of an assembly whose principal authority was moral, forced to react to the tactical gambits and mixed signals coming from Vienna and Berlin. Austria still insisted on acting as a member of the Confederation; Frederick William revealed the true extent of his contempt for the assembly only in correspondence with ambassadors and fellow monarchs. Against this uncertain background Gagern, the great architect of compromise, put together a plan that would combine a Prussian-led Germany with a form of looser Austrian association. Historians disagree on whether this was an absurdity, or a realistic proposal that prefigured the German-Austrian alliance of 1879. But the question is moot: the fragile majority for the plan failed to hold, and Vienna slammed the door on greater German hopes when Schwarzenberg issued the Kremsier constitution in early March, re-emphasizing the unity of the Habsburg empire. This step gave notice that Austria would accept no German state-form more advanced than the loose pre-1848 Confederation, and was simultaneously designed to block Prussia. Yet it left the Frankfurt parliament with nothing but the Prussian option, unless members of the assembly were prepared to pack their bags and go home. Tactical considerations now shaped the final form of constitution approved by the assembly. First, in order to win over members of the formerly greater German left, the moderates of the lesser German party made two major concessions. They accepted a more limited monarchical power of veto, and a German national parliament elected by universal manhood suffrage. Secondly, disappointed greater German conservatives deliberately voted for these more radical provisions in order to make the ensuing constitution unacceptable – in short, they engaged in the same kind of sabotage practised by Vienna itself. Thus, at the end of March the assembly voted to establish a genuine constitutional monarchy, a federal system that preserved the existence of the individual states but included several unitary features, among them central responsibility for matters of war and peace, a uniform currency and post, and a single tariff and trade policy. A somewhat larger majority also voted to offer the hereditary imperial crown to Frederick William.

But would the Prussian monarch accept? It was not entirely ridiculous to believe so. He had reacted positively to Gagern's earlier compromise and formally encouraged other German princes to help bring the work at Frankfurt to a fruitful conclusion. Prussia, along with eighteen other individual states (although not Austria, Bavaria, Württemberg, Saxony or Hanover), had approved the first draft of the constitution, despite its unitary and 'democratic' aspects. Both houses of parliament and substantial parts of the Prussian military and civilian establishment urged the king to accept – or, at least, to accept conditional on changes to the veto power and suffrage that the Frankfurt parliament would be forced to swallow. But Frederick William refused, politely in public, contemptuously in private: he wished to remain a sovereign by the grace of God, unsullied by a crown that was really a 'dog-collar'. Given his views, it is difficult to believe that he would have accepted any constitution emanating from the national assembly, even a more 'moderate' one.

Frederick William's refusal radically simplified the political terrain. Although twenty-nine German states accepted the constitution, they did not include the most important ones: Austria, Prussia, Bavaria, Hanover and Saxony. On the other side, a popular movement sprang up in support of the constitution. Members of the Frankfurt assembly had no more room for compromise: they faced the choice of capitulating, or encouraging popular efforts. On 4 May a narrow majority took the second course. They emphasized the legality of their handiwork and called on state governments, elected bodies at all levels and 'the whole German people' to recognize the constitution and bring it into effect.[23] Further motions in the same defiant spirit continued to be passed throughout the month, but the national parliament became increasingly irrelevant. Its last weeks resembled 'the slow death of a sick person who is beyond saving'.[24] At odds with Archduke Johann and the new right-wing cabinet he constructed after Gagern's resignation, the assembly shrank as moderates drifted away and other members were (illegally) ordered home by their governments. To escape the growing threat of military intervention, the radical rump adjourned to Stuttgart where the parliament was eventually dissolved by Prussian troops in June. By then, the polarization always implicit in the revolution had become complete.

The last act pitted a radicalized popular movement against counter-revolutionary soldiers. This may have been an epilogue to the revolution, but it was a long and bloody one that deserves to be called a 'second revolution'.[25] For fully three months, from the third week of April to the third week of July, some of the leading German states became the scene of demonstrations, revolts and uprisings. The gravity of what occurred needs to be recognized. Ruling princes fled from their capitals in Württemberg, Baden and Saxony. Revolutionary governments were established briefly in Dresden, and for longer periods in the Bavarian Palatinate and Baden. Even in Prussia, barricades went up in Silesian towns, armouries were stormed on the Mosel, a revolutionary committee of public safety was established in Elberfeld. Soldiers of the reserve went over to the revolutionaries in parts of Prussia, regular units did the same in Bavaria and Baden.

How to explain the radicalism of these last, violent revolutionary episodes? Their ostensible cause was support of the constitution produced by the Frankfurt national assembly. The events of April to July were concentrated on the states that had rejected it – the two exceptions being Baden, revolutionary despite prudently accepting the constitution, and Austria, quiet as the grave despite rejecting it. The 'lawful' constitution provided the insurgents with legitimacy. But the last wave of revolutions clearly went beyond support for the document issued at Frankfurt.[26] It contained, in the first place, an important social-revolutionary strand. Journeymen and workers played a prominent part, especially in the Prussian Rhineland and Saxony: Stephan Born of the Workers' Brotherhood fought on the barricades in Dresden. Thwarted lower-class aspirations found expression in the campaign for the constitution, infusing these final stages of the revolution with a strong whiff of class war. The repressive role played by many bourgeois Civil Guard detachments provides negative confirmation of the same point. Yet this aspect should not be overemphasized. The insurgents certainly represented a kind of distillate of what was most radical in the 1848-9 revolutions, but theirs was above all a political radicalism with an appeal beyond the ranks of journeymen and workers. Its bearers included radical Civil Guards in towns such as Mainz, Hanau, Düsseldorf, Heilbronn and Breslau, left-wing deputies from parliaments and municipalities, and democratic associations under the direction of the Central March Association. Its slogans were democracy, the rights of the citizen, the republic and the people in arms – in short, the watchwords of Jacobin radicalism. This characteristic was, not surprisingly, most obvious in the western redoubts of the revolution: the Rhineland, the Palatinate and Baden.

These last insurrectionary movements were crushed by military force, above all Prussian force. In the first three weeks of May, order was restored in Breslau and the rebellious western provinces, where antagonism towards the mainly Catholic inhabitants lent an extra edge to the army's settling of accounts. A hundred died in the town of Iserlohn. During the same period, Prussian soldiers were instrumental in helping the Saxon army, which remained loyal, to put down the Dresden uprising, with 250 casualties among the revolutionaries. Prussian troops under the command of Crown Prince William then marched south. The Palatinate was captured and the provisional government forced to flee on 14 June. On the following day Mannheim was taken, and the defeat of the Badenese revolution was sealed at the battle of Waghäusel on 21 June. The final success of the counter-revolution had to wait another month, until the surrender of the insurgent soldiers and other revolutionaries in the garrison of Rastatt. Reprisals were harsh. In Baden, a tenth of those who surrendered in Rastatt were shot; court-martials and special courts handed down death sentences. Across Germany, not only in states that rose in 1849, charges of treason and sedition were now taken out of bottom drawers. Often they applied to speeches or actions going back to the very beginnings of the revolution in spring 1848 – retroactive justice with a vengeance. And from Baden, Saxony, the Palatinate and elsewhere the defeated forty-eighters escaped by emigration, to the USA, Switzerland or some other safe haven, an estimated 80,000 from Baden alone.

The Causes of Failure

Two overriding facts explain the defeat of the revolutions: divisions among the revolutionaries, and the unbroken powers retained by German princes. Both were disguised by the swift initial successes of March 1848. The very suddenness of events caused German rulers to lose their nerve and capitulate – but only in the short term. The divergent aspirations vested in the revolution were also temporarily obscured by the spontaneous enthusiasm of spring – but not for long. There were multiple divisions among the revolutionaries. They can be ordered for convenience into conflicts over the national question, issues of power and sovereignty, and the social problem, although we need to remember that these questions were often interlinked, and were in turn overlaid by religious, regional and other divisions.

The undoubted centrality of the national question in 1848 was as much effect as cause of the revolution. It was the revolution itself that brought the existence of the Confederation into question and placed the German nation-state squarely on the agenda. That was especially true because in 1848, unlike 1830, Prussia and Austria were rocked by events. It was nevertheless a measure of how much German nationalist sentiment had grown in the 1840s that moderates and radicals alike thought immediately of establishing a national assembly. The presence of German flags and slogans even at the earliest popular demonstrations tells the same story. In these respects, the national question served as a lowest common denominator of the political (although not the social) revolution. Every grievance, however locally specific, could be attributed to the stifling rule of petty tyrants, sustained by a discredited Confederation. Nor did the clash between German and other national aspirations in 1848 necessarily prove divisive in Germany itself. Certainly there were differences of emphasis over how to reconcile German claims with those of, say, Danes (in Schleswig-Holstein) or Poles (in Posen). Despite notable exceptions, the left was more inclined to stress the 'progressive' character of German nationalism (one thinks of Marx), something that was reinforced when 'backward' Slavs fought on the side of the counter-revolution in the Habsburg empire. On the whole, however, a shared conviction of German cultural superiority united at least as much as it divided. The local differences between democrats and moderate liberals in Holstein were relatively muted in the face of what was perceived as the common Danish foe. Yet the Schleswig-Holstein question played a major part in the September crisis of 1848, in many ways a decisive moment in the revolution. And that episode, when the argument turned on whether Prussia would or could fulfil its 'German mission', points up why the national issue was seriously divisive – because it interlocked with questions of power, and the relationship of the revolution to the individual states. Those were the issues on which all three prime ministers of the provisional executive in Frankfurt resigned: Prince Leinen over his government's acceptance of Prussian actions during the Schleswig-Holstein crisis; Schmerling in December 1848, after Schwarzenberg's statements had undermined his 'greater German' position; and the 'lesser German' Gagern in May 1849, following Frederick William's refusal of the German crown. Of course, the division between greater and lesser Germans was important in its own right; it highlighted differences between south and north, Catholics and Protestants, democrats and moderates. But beyond the particular issues at stake between pro-Austrian and pro-Prussian advocates lurked the decisive question: what should be the relationship of the national assembly to the existing structures of Confederation and state sovereignty?

Fundamental issues of power obviously divided the political inheritors of the revolution. Even calling them all 'revolutionaries' would be misleading, for the March ministers and a majority in the national assembly were reluctant revolutionaries, keen to divorce themselves as quickly as possible from the violent and radical aspects of the March events. The Saxon Karl Biedermann, a prominent centre-right figure at Frankfurt and a member of the deputation that offered the crown to Frederick William, actually referred in his memoirs to 'the catastrophe of 1848'.[27] For the left, on the other hand, March was just the beginning. The difference became immediately apparent in the preparliament, viewed by some as a Jabobin-type national convention, by others as the means of establishing a body to work with the German princes. That stark gulf could be found at Frankfurt and in the state parliaments. These conflicting ideological positions had, of course, preceded March 1848. But the events of the following fifteen months magnified them and the dynamism of the revolution itself deepened them. Moderates emphasized cooperation with the German princes, were nervous of popular forces, supported constitutional monarchy but not parliamentary government, and opposed universal manhood suffrage. The left wanted to use popular pressure as a lever against the German rulers, emphasized the powers of parliament, and advocated a broad suffrage. Similar disagreement existed over taxation, education and the role of civilian militias. These differences can be traced through the speeches and pamphlets of 1848–9. They emerge with particular clarity when the two sides used a common body of material to reach opposite conclusions. Thus, the American constitutional experiment was frequently invoked during the German revolution, but to very different ends. Radicals emphasized the democratic, republican and unitary features of the United States, just as they placed Washington the military leader in their pantheon of heroes. Moderate liberals were attracted to the 'English' aspects of the American system, especially the balance of powers, arguing that press freedom, religious liberty and legal accountability could be achieved within a constitutional monarchy, where an emperor would play the role of president.[28] Conflicting views on a wide range of issues were institutionalized at the extraparliamentary level in the rival organizations grouped respectively under the National Association and Central March Association. Here the ideological divide had a sociological counterpart. We need only contrast the officials, judges and academics who led the moderates with the minor professionals and lower middle-class figures who predominated among democratic leaders.

A further point can hardly be overemphasized. The repeated insurrections that occurred after March 1848 hardened the lines of division. To radicals, the April uprising in Baden was a legitimate response to the betrayal of the revolution, to moderates an irresponsible putsch that jeopardized the constructive work of constitution-making. The uprising of September 1848 bred similar mutual recrimination. These were not abstract differences of opinion: one side manned the barricades, the other supported the soldiers who dismantled them. There was no common ground between the constitutional moderate Bassermann and the radical Struve – each argued in September 1848 that his opponents should be arrested for treason. We should not forget that leading actors in the revolutionary events lost their lives during insurrections. Heinrich von Gagern's elder brother Friedrich was killed commanding Confederation troops against the Baden uprising of April 1848. Two members of the national assembly were killed by crowds during the September rising. And Robert Blum, whose execution was mourned by democrats with an almost religious intensity, became the martyr of the left, the great lost leader. He had spilled his 'precious blood', and democrats pointed the finger at Heinrich von Gagern as the man who was ultimately responsible.[29]

All of this has to be recognized before we pose the question: what if? Could it have altered the course of the revolution if liberals and radicals had managed to bridge their differences? It is a legitimate counter-factual question to which there is no simple answer. On the one hand, we can point out that the two sides not only differed in emphasis, but actually wanted different things and mourned different martyrs. Yet there is another perspective. In the national assembly and the state parliaments there were fluctuating divisions and political crosscurrents: everyday contact and the discipline of working together produced possibilities for compromise as well as discord. At Frankfurt the moderate Gagern and the democrat Blum, both widely respected beyond their own parliamentary groups, provide good examples of this. Broad consensus was in fact achieved by the national assembly on basic rights, and the final constitution showed a striking willingness to compromise even on fundamental issues like the veto and suffrage. In the Prussian parliament, left and centre-left managed to sustain a broad measure of agreement through the summer and autumn of 1848. In the end, however, such cooperation availed them little: it was force that neutered both assemblies – even if there were plenty of moderates who greeted 'strong measures' with relief.

Every account of failure in 1848 mentions a further division: the one between the political and the social revolutions. And rightly so. Many parliamentarians of the revolution were aloof and clubbable, poorly attuned to popular aspirations. Even on the left, they were often more concerned with political and legal questions, not social issues like the journeyman's demand for work or the master's fear of free trade. Expressions of popular anger such as machine-breaking or anti-Semitism frightened and appalled them; the peasants who wanted a German republic composed of individual monarchies made them despair. The political and social strands of the revolution were undeniably hard to reconcile. Given all this, we should perhaps be more impressed by the extent to which the political left, in particular, was able to mobilize popular sentiment in the course of the revolution. The crucial point here is that the lower classes were not simply 'materialist', however pressing their immediate concerns. In the cities, journeymen came into contact with political ideas through democratic clubs, ballads and street theatre, as well as through their own organizations like the Workers' Brotherhood. In the countryside and small towns, democrats were able to build on existing relationships – trust for a familiar 'peasant advocate', respect for a well-known local schoolteacher or doctor – to extend their organization. Alongside the paraphernalia of political mobilization, the pamphlets and cockades, we should not forget the importance of the personal in forging political identification. Hecker was a genuinely charismatic popular leader in the southwest (Struve less so). His picture hung in peasant cottages; 'Hecker hats' were worn, 'Hecker songs' sung.[30] In short, the minor professionals and middling sorts so prominent among the democratic leadership were often very successful in harnessing the social discontents of journeymen and 'small men', those who saw themselves as the 'productive' elements of society, behind an advanced political programme. The basic unit of mobilization may have been the village or commune, but the discussions there ranged widely over national and indeed international issues. There are parallels here to the process described by Maurice Agulhon in contemporary France, and Friedrich Engels was wrong as well as arrogant when he wrote off these 'petty-bourgeois democrats' and 'brave shopkeepers'.[31] The proof of their success can be seen in the half-million members grouped under the Central March Association, and the strength of the campaign for the constitution.

Some scepticism is also called for when we consider a final division in the revolution often noted by historians: its regional diversity, the absence of a single revolutionary capital like Paris. The fact itself is not in dispute. The former Confederation contained at least two major capitals, and contemporaries sometimes distinguished between Berlin as the head of the revolution, Vienna as its heart. At the national assembly in Frankfurt, a variety of other cities were proposed as possible capitals of the future Germany – Leipzig, Dresden, Erfurt, Hanover. Nor is it difficult to argue that this polycentrism was a source of weakness. We have seen that the reality of a revolution without a centre was one of the problems facing the politicians of 1848, as they struggled to keep up with events occurring in Berlin, Vienna, Frankfurt, the individual state capitals, and numerous other, constantly shifting flashpoints – Baden, Posen, Schleswig. Then, with the revolution crushed in Vienna and Berlin during the autumn of 1848, the areas of revolutionary resistance in the summer of 1849 – the Rhineland and Silesia, Saxony, the Palatinate, finally Baden – could be picked off one by one.

There is another way of looking at this sequence, however. It is best understood from a wider European perspective. In Italy, Milan was recaptured by the Austrians in August 1848, but unrest broke out again during 1849 and had to be put down finally not in the centre but at the periphery, especially in the Veneto. In France, the June days of 1848 marked a counter-revolutionary turning point – for the capital. But the strength of the left-wing *démocs-socs* continued to grow in the provinces: that was the base from which serious resistance was mounted when Napoleon III capped the counter-revolution with his coup d'état in 1851. So in Germany, while the success of the reaction in Vienna and Berlin was undoubtedly a grievous blow to the revolution, it did not stop the work of the Frankfurt assembly, nor did it close off the possibility of provincial political mobilization behind the constitution in 1849. The local focus of that final resistance can be seen as a weakness, but it was also a strength. It built on the communalism that was such a prominent feature of the revolution, and it went with the grain of powerful local sentiment, whether Rhenish dislike of Protestant core-Prussia, Badenese dislike of Prussian northerners, or Palatine dislike of Munich.[32]

There is obvious truth in the cliché that divisions among the revolutionaries helped to undermine the revolution, but we should not exaggerate these divisions or their effect. Conversely, we should not underestimate the importance of the powers of recovery showed by the German regimes. In many ways, of course, these are two sides of the same coin. As various elements of the March coalition peeled off from the revolution, so they became potential supporters of reaction. This was obviously true of the peasantry, who clambered off the revolution when their demands for the abolition of feudal privileges had been met, first in the south, then in Bohemia and Austria, finally in Silesia and Saxony, the earlier hotbeds of rural radicalism. The process was not universal – the west and southwest were important

TABLE 1:   *Forms of Protest in Germany, 1848-9*

	March-April 1848		May-June 1849	
	CASES		CASES	
	Number	as %	Number	as %
Peasant actions	85	17.4	11	2.3
Agrarian under-classes	88	18.0	14	5.1
Urban under-classes	94	19.2	34	7.2
Artisan actions	6	1.2	8	1.7
Labour conflicts	49	10.0	47	9.9
Political actions	150	30.7	335	70.6
Miscellaneous	17	3.5	15	3.2
TOTALS	489	100	474	100

SOURCE: M. Gailus, 'Soziale Protestbewegungen in Deutschland 1847–1849', in H. Volkmann and J. Bergmann (eds), *Sozialer Protest* (Opladen, 1984), p. 98.

exceptions – but the large-scale defection of the peasantry granted German princes the great boon of rural quiescence. In parts of core-Prussia, the rural population was more actively recruited into conservative king-and-fatherland organizations. Many bourgeois and petty-bourgeois Germans also turned against the revolution, fearing disorder and social upheaval. While craftsmen and shopkeepers continued, as we have seen, to provide an important component of the democratic left, others swung over behind law and order, especially perhaps in the larger towns. That was important for the behaviour of many Civil Guards.

The resources of the German regimes went beyond this actual or potential layer of popular support. After a short period when they kept their heads down, court advisors, diplomats, nobles and bureaucrats recovered their confidence and re-emerged.

Most important of all, the armed forces of the German princes remained intact. It is striking how rarely troops went over to the revolution in 1848–9 – by contrast with Russia in 1917, say, or Germany itself in November 1918. Throughout the revolution, Confederation troops drawn from the individual states were garrisoned close to strategically sensitive areas, in Mainz and Ulm, for example, and were easily able to quell further revolutionary uprisings like those of April and September 1848. Every military engagement of 1848–9 showed the superiority of well-equipped conventional troops over the revolutionaries, even when the latter were reinforced by volunteer 'legions' of Hungarians, French and Swiss. That was true of the Austrian and Prussian armies, and of those belonging to Saxony and the smaller states. We should not be surprised by this, given that Habsburg troops eventually defeated even the 170,000 men mobilized by the Hungarian rebels, with little help from the Russian army that Vienna had reluctantly asked for assistance. Generals such as Windischgrätz and Wrangel did as much to determine the outcome of the German revolution as Cavaignac did in France.

Was the revolution a complete failure? Clearly not: it removed Metternich, symbol of the pre-1848 era; more fundamentally, it removed the last formal traces of feudalism from the country-side. The clock was not turned back. Almost all of the German states had some kind of parliament and constitution after 1850. If nothing else, rulers and élites had learned the benefits to be gained from appealing over the heads of liberal parliamentarians to the peasantry, although they had also learned that a reliable army was the surest guarantee of survival. The importance of military power was not lost on moderate nationalists, and this placed its imprint on the 'realistic' politics of the following decades. One of the most important legacies of the revolution was in heightening national feeling. 1840 had turned the Rhine into a German issue; 1848 did the same for Schleswig-Holstein. As early as 3 March, Heinrich von Gagern wrote to his brother Friedrich: 'The lightning has struck, and Germany will not allow itself to be lulled back to sleep.'[33] It was a dramatic utterance in keeping with the period, but it was also true, for the apparent political slumber of the 1850s was deceptive. The most obvious casualty of revolutionary defeat and reaction was the exuberant mass mobilization and popular politics of 1848–9. When German political life revived again at the end of the 1850s, that aspect of it was less prominent than it had been a decade earlier – although more prominent than historians were, until a few years ago, willing to accept. The revolution provided a wealth of political experience, parliamentary and participatory. Ultimately, however, neither the barricades, clubs, festivities and petitions of 1848–9, nor the efforts of the Frankfurt notables, achieved their purposes. When a united Germany and a permanent national parliament came into being, they did so by sterner means, from above, not from below.

PART TWO

The Age
of Progress,
1849–80

CHAPTER FOUR

Economy and Society Transformed

Industrialization

Historians are more reluctant than they once were to talk about an industrial 'revolution', in Germany or anywhere else. The long gestation of protoindustrialization, the continuing importance of agriculture, the persistence of preindustrial forms of production – all make it more difficult to sustain a 'big bang' theory of industrial revolution. But we should not overwork this argument. Changes in technology or industrial processes could occur very quickly. The use of coke in iron smelting was virtually unknown in the 1830s, and in 1850 it still accounted for only 25 per cent of iron output. By 1853 – in just three years – the figure had risen to 63 per cent. This example, one of many that could be cited, also serves as a pointer to the timing of German industrialization. A number of studies identify the 1840s as the period when a first industrial breakthrough occurred, spearheaded by the railways and supported by the growing Saxon textile industry.[1] Yet industrialization remained partial and patchy in this decade. Germany had to import raw iron and steel track for the railways, just as it remained dependent on superior foreign technology in many branches from metals to textiles. Joint-stock companies were few in number, and governments followed a restrictive credit policy. Even the cyclical boom of 1845–7 was shorter and less intense than the ones that followed in 1850–6, 1860–5 and 1867–73, as Reinhard Spree has shown.[2] The 1840s marked an important beginning, true enough, but there is a strong case for regarding the following decades as the decisive period of economic development in Germany, whether we look at growth rates, capital formation, manufacturing output or technology. By the 1870s, Germany possessed an unmistakably capitalist market economy with a major industrial sector.

Rates of economic growth are notoriously difficult to calculate, but there is general agreement that the German economy grew at something like 2.5 per cent a year in the period 1850–73, higher than in the decades before mid-century or the years 1873–96. Industry was mainly responsible for setting this new tempo. There, the annual growth of production was around 4.8 per cent, in railways an astounding 14 per cent.[3] Changes in the rate of capital formation tell a similar story. Investment in the thirty years after 1850 ran at about four times the level of the thirty years before, and – once again – industry led the way. When it comes to output, the numbers are even more striking. In Prussia, coal production increased eightfold between 1849 and 1875, raw iron output fourteenfold, steel output fifty-fourfold. Over the same period, the number of steam-powered machines in Rhineland-Westphalia grew from 650, with a total of under 19,000 HP, to nearly 12,000 with a combined HP of 380,000. The statistics on investment, output and new forms of technology all point to another important feature of these years: the growing size of factory plant and mines. The aptly named Phoenix iron foundry was established in 1851; within twenty years it had a workforce of 4400. Or, to take perhaps the best-known case of all: Alfred Krupp employed just 60 men in 1836; by 1858 the figure was over 1000, 8,000 by 1865, and by 1873 16,000.[4] A comparative study of the Ruhr and South Wales coalfields has shown that, although the former developed later, the collieries were larger and more capital-intensive from the outset. This had something to do with geology, more to do with the fact that German industrial concerns were generally larger and more technologically advanced than British ones.[5] Here was one of the advantages enjoyed by the 'latecomer' over the industrial 'pioneer'.

It is appropriate that the examples above are drawn from coal, iron and steel, for they clearly formed the leading sector in this explosive stage of industrialization. Coal produced the heady new energy source of the era, steam. Its coke derivative finally

FIGURE 2 *Miners and Coal Production in the Saarland, 1849–78*

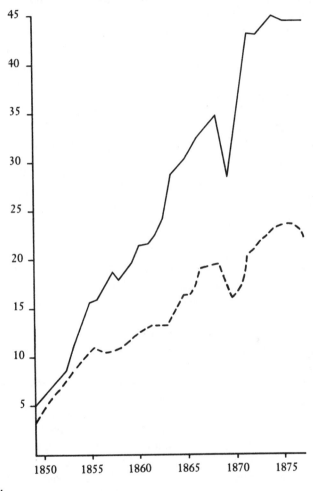

KEY

------ Miners (in Thousands)

———— Coal Production (in Hundreds of Thousands of Tons)

SOURCE: H. Horch, *Der Wandel der Gesellschafts- und Herrschaftsstrukturen in der Saarregion während der Industrialisierung* (St Ingbert, 1985), p. 209.

replaced charcoal in the smelting plants and powered the burgeoning gas industry (the number of gasworks multiplied tenfold in these years). Iron and steel made possible the rapid growth of the metallurgical and engineering sectors, and they in turn provided the heavy goods that were characteristic of this phase of industrialization: pressed steel and metal pipes, boilers and factory machines. At the centre of everything was the railway, an insatiable consumer of coal, steel track and the locomotives now turned out in their thousands by manufacturers like Borsig in Berlin. These heavy-industrial sectors were closely interlocked. In the Ruhr during the 1860s and 1870s the railways consumed about half the output of the iron industry and the iron industry about a third of local coal production, while coal provided a half of railway freight. The great expansion of the German rail network, from 4000 miles in 1852 to 24,000 in 1873, drove demand throughout the industrializing economy.[6] Not only coal, steel and engineering, but other branches that ranged from carriage-making, wood and upholstery to quarrying and glass, were beneficiaries. The leading role played by the railways illustrates two points. The first is what economic historians call backward linkages – the stimulus it gave to the producers of capital goods. The chemical industry provides another example of the same thing. The 1860s saw the founding of great firms such as Hoechst, Bayer and BASF, which received a fillip from the demand for dyestuffs and similar treatments required by a more sophisticated textile industry. Indeed, growing mechanization across the board stimulated the metallurgical and engineering sectors: deepening German industrialization now increasingly led to the production of machines to make machines. The second point that railways illustrate is the crucial importance of construction. The rail network required not just track, locomotives and rolling stock, but stations and signal boxes, bridges and viaducts. This was one, but only one, of the reasons for the construction boom in the third quarter of the nineteenth century. Over a million new buildings went up in Prussia alone during the years 1852–67, the fastest growth coming in factory plant and public buildings. In Germany as a whole, total investment in nonagricultural buildings rose four-fold between the 1850s and the 1870s, from 280 million to 1077 million marks. The mushroom-like growth of factories, gasworks, waterworks and railway workshops (like the one in Bad Cannstatt that transformed the spa town once visited by Balzac), new urban dwellings built for renting, the reshaping of German cities as old walls were knocked down and new public buildings erected – add all of these together, and it is clear what the construction sector contributed to economic growth.

The great industrial spurt in this period was therefore marked by the primacy of capital goods. Cyclical ups and downs were governed by the demand for these goods, and by the expectation of profits among those who produced them, or their financial backers, not by consumer demand. In fact, one of the things that benefited businessmen – a labour surplus that kept wages down and boosted profits – tended to depress demand for consumer goods. Nevertheless, a growing urban population severed from the means of self-sufficiency and real wages that edged slowly upwards meant that consumer demand also rose, stimulating the production of cheap, standardized products. Textiles are the classic example, but not the only one. The woodworking, leather, glass and ceramics branches all benefited from the new demand for furniture, kitchenware, household utensils, and the like. Two consumer sectors stand out. Almost a quarter of all those employed in manufacturing in the 1850s were engaged in the production of apparel – shoes, hosiery, clothes, hats. Another 14 per cent were involved in food and drink production, which now became notably more large-scale in organization. Food processing was a major business in towns throughout Germany, giant mills were established in ports like Mannheim to grind shipments of foreign corn, beer production started to become concentrated among larger breweries. Sugar was the greatest success story among these branches, as well as acquiring something of the same political influence that brewing had in Britain. While German-born businessmen provided America with its two great nineteenth-century sugar magnates, Havemeyer and Spreckels (the inventor of the sugar cube), the domestic sugar

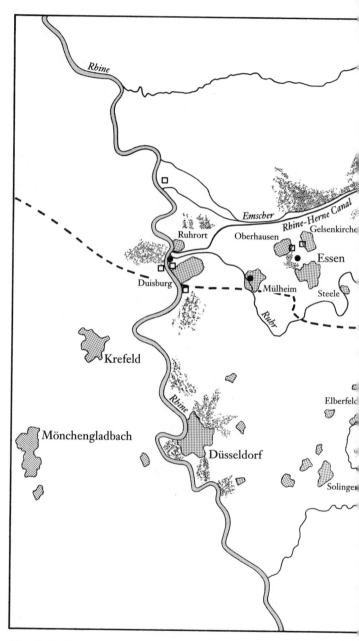

The Ruhr Industrial Region, 1850–70

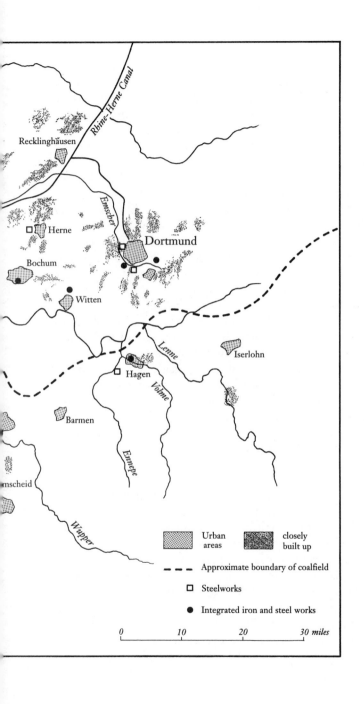

Recklinghausen

Rhine-Herne Canal

Emscher

Herne

Dortmund

Bochum

Witten

Lenne

Iserlohn

Hagen

Volme

Barmen

Ennepe

mscheid

Wupper

	Urban areas		closely built up

– – – Approximate boundary of coalfield

□ Steelworks

● Integrated iron and steel works

0   10   20   30 miles

industry was already beginning the ascent that made it one of Germany's best-organized, most capital-intensive branches by the end of the century, when the value of sugar exports comfortably exceeded those of coal or machinery.

A regular supply of raw materials and a means of distributing the finished goods to the consumer were essential to the new economic system. Once again, the railway was at the centre of things. In the first place, it had a dramatic effect on costs: the mature railway network reduced the costs of bulk transport by 80 per cent. Improved distribution also reduced the amounts of capital tied up in stock. But the railway did not just lead to cost-savings within an existing market. It widened the circle of consumers, helping to spread the market culture into previously virgin land, and it even had an impact on the formation of a new labour force. The construction of track, embankments and bridges required hundreds of thousands of men, many of whom were first tempted off the land by the prospects of higher pay as 'navigators'. The rail network then made labour more mobile, as workers sought the higher wages available in towns. In the years 1850–75 around 25 per cent of all investment went into railways, and it is generally agreed that railways played a decisive role in Germany, where there was no early 'canal era' comparable to those in England or the United States.[7] Railways were particularly important in Prussia, a state that extended a vast distance from east to west, but whose major rivers flowed from south to north. Nevertheless, railways should be viewed alongside waterways and roads as part of a larger transportation revolution, with its origins in the decades before 1850, that was a decisive element in permitting economic growth. Indeed, we are probably justified in referring in the period after 1850 – although not before – to a revolution in communications, as institutions like the telegraph, improved postal services and a growing insurance sector provided for greater speed and security in market transactions.

These were crucial enabling elements. So were other kinds of infrastructure investment, or overhead capital – education, research, technical training, the promotion of manufacturing through industrial exhibitions and model workshops. This raises the question of the role played by the state in German industrialization. Nationalist historians typically exaggerated this, just as they ascribed too great a role to the *Zollverein*. A residue of their approach remains in the fact that the German term for political economy is 'national economy'. Modern historians have been more sceptical, noting the relatively small amounts that even advanced states like Prussia actually put into fostering economic growth. We should also remember that, while the state built canals and highways, over half the German rail network was in private hands until the 1870s. The south German railways were state-owned, however. And in Prussia there was substantial state investment in railways, even if much of it was indirect – the assumption of planning costs, guarantees, subsidies. This was a major reason why the Prussian state debt more than doubled between 1848 and 1865, eloquent testimony to the continuation of the more liberal fiscal policy first introduced during the revolution. The mines of the Saar and parts of Silesia were also state-run.

All this was typical of a Continental rather than an Anglo-Saxon road to industrialization, one marked by closer links between private capitalism and the state. Take chambers of commerce as an example. To the British or American reader, these automatically conjure up a picture of businessmen banding together: German chambers of commerce were semipublic, semiprivate institutions, fostered by the state. These were years in which the German states pursued policies that favoured industrial and commercial development: taxation systems that fell most heavily on land and consumption, measures of economic liberalization such as new company law and freedom of movement that allowed greater mobility of capital and labour. Nor should we underestimate the stimulus provided by the *Zollverein*, a growing and dynamic free trade area that was successful enough to persuade businesses from neighbouring Belgium and Switzerland to establish themselves in Germany. It can be argued that the *Zollverein* acquired a new significance from the early 1850s, after Hanover joined and the organization took on responsibility for international tariff negotiations. From the 1860s the larger political background then exerted its own effect on economic developments, as the prospect of unification promised to deliver the prized goals of a uniform currency, weights and measures and patents, and a common legal framework for commercial operations. These developments fostered a climate of confidence and a willingness to invest that reached its apogee in the heady 'founders' boom' that followed the creation of a united Germany in 1871.

Enhanced confidence among investors was part cause, part effect of industrial growth. It is now well established that rates of capital accumulation were already considerable in Germany during the 1830s and 1840s. Money flowed into agriculture, state paper, railway stock and early urban construction schemes. But, for the most part, it did not flow into industry. Potential investors were nervous about the high levels of risk in industrial concerns; conversely many family firms remained suspicious of 'outside' capital. Few conduits had developed to channel available capital into industry. This changed after mid-century. It needed to, because the capital requirements became much greater. Sinking a deep mining shaft in the Ruhr cost around half a million Thaler over four years. Some of the profits from large-scale agriculture found their way into industry (and in areas like Upper Silesia there were landowners who financed the extraction of the mineral deposits beneath their own estates). Private banks in Cologne, Leipzig, Dresden, Augsburg and Berlin lent money to promote industry, although mainly to local entrepreneurs whom they knew personally. And the prominence of former or active merchants among early industrialists meant that they could put up their own working capital, augmented by money raised through long-standing mercantile networks. The mine-owner Matthias Stinnes and the iron and steel magnate Franz Haniel both began as coal traders; Ludolf Camphausen moved from an oil and corn business and private banking into industry and transport. Industry was therefore financed from a variety of sources. Profits were increasingly reinvested, and older sources of finance were diverted to new ends. But we should also recognize the importance of novel institutions. Two deserve special mention: the joint-stock company that raised public capital, and the joint-stock bank geared to industrial investment, such as the celebrated 'D-banks' founded between the early 1850s and the early 1870s (the Darmstädter, the Discontogesellschaft, the Deutsche and the Dresdner). Together, they constituted a powerful new engine of industrial investment. The contribution of joint-stock banks to German industrialization may have been exaggerated in some of the literature, especially for the period before the 1870s, but they played a key strategic role and represented the shape of the future. Although one of their models was French, they channelled more savings into domestic industry and less into overseas investment or foreign bonds than the French (or British) financial sectors. From the 1870s, close ties and interlocked directorships between banks and industry became a hallmark of German industrial capitalism. The closest parallel is with Japan.

The giant smelting works supported by the joint-stock bank: that is the convenient symbol of German economic growth after 1850, and with some reason. Large units of production remained highly atypical in this period, however. The workshop, not the factory, was the main site of industrialization. In the middle of the 1870s, almost two-thirds of those engaged in manufacturing still worked for firms employing five people or fewer. Here, as in many larger concerns, working capital still primarily meant credit raised from family members, not from a bank. This was true even in some technologically advanced sectors, like paper. Nor should we overlook the extent to which old technology coexisted alongside the new. The steamships that plied the Rhine and the railways that ran along both banks still passed floating mills that had been there for centuries. In the late 1870s there were still seventeen of them at Ginsheim on the Middle Rhine. At the same date, 55 per cent of the mechanically generated power for manufacturing in Württemberg came from water wheels, only a minority from steam. Even in advanced Saxony, water-power produced a third of all energy.[8] After a quarter of a century of heady industrialization, one in five of the manufacturing labour force was still employed in the putting-out system. True, the figure had been two in five during the 1840s, and the absolute numbers fell (from 1.5 to 1.1 million) at a time when the total labour force was growing.[9] But putting-out was dominant in some textile branches (cotton, silk weaving), and in the garment trade, where it actually grew thanks to the sewing machine that was introduced into the sweatshops of Berlin, Breslau and Bielefeld from the 1850s. Here is a reminder that new technology does not always mean mass production in a centralized factory location – or a more humane working environment.

We should also remember how important agriculture still was. More than half of those one million buildings erected in Prussia between 1852 and 1867 were farm buildings. Agriculture's share of the labour force remained 49 per cent in 1880 (down from 55 per cent in 1852, while industry's share rose from 25 to 30 per cent), and agriculture provided the largest part of German domestic product throughout this period. The progress of agriculture in the third quarter of the nineteenth century contributed crucially to industrial growth. It was arguably the subsistence crises of the 1840s that had choked off potential industrial take-off a decade before it finally came. Certainly the shortfalls in urban food supply, the hoarding of inefficient rural labour, and the lack of investors' confidence caused by periodic crisis add up to one of the key variables that distinguish the 1840s from later years. The period from 1850 to the 1870s was something of a golden age for agriculture, between the old crises of dearth and the new problems caused by cheap foreign imports. The process of bringing new land into cultivation was largely completed in the 1850s and 1860s. Productivity rose. The growing urban population enjoyed a more regular and diversified food supply, as improved transportation and the emerging commodity exchanges made for better distribution. Dairy produce became more widely available; meat consumption increased from under twenty to around thirty kilos per head in the years 1850–70. Primary producers benefited from buoyant markets, and in the case of the large east Prussian estate-owners from a strong export market for grain. For parts of the peasantry, savings and loan banks like those established by Friedrich Wilhelm Raiffeisen after 1848, and the cheaper rates for everything from seedcorn to hail insurance provided by organizations such as the early Catholic peasant associations, offered an extra margin of security.

Agriculture and industry, countryside and town started to become more distinct in these years. That was the logic of growing economic specialization, a sign of declining self-sufficiency. The separation was not clear-cut. We shall see later in this chapter how migrants formed a link between the worlds of agricultural and industrial employment. In the towns, animals were still kept in considerable numbers and the goat (the 'miner's cow') was ubiquitous in the coalfields. Conversely, the country-side continued to be home to crafts that served the peasantry and to many thriving rural industries – quarrying, brickworks, distilleries, sawmills. The growing economic division of labour is nevertheless unmistakable. In Baden, for example, the indus-trializing north diverged from the rural south, which assumed an increasingly 'provincial' character. In Prussia, a similar process favoured the west over once advanced eastern areas like Silesia, now relatively left behind by economic development. This was starting to happen on a German-wide scale, as changes in trans-portation and technology redrew the regional map, bringing industrialization to some regions and deindustrialization to others. With the demise of water-power and charcoal as energy sources, ironworks moved from dispersed upland sites like the Eifel, the Siegerland, the Thuringian Forest and the Harz mountains to areas such as the Saar and Ruhr. The starkly uneven regional character of German industrialization has deservedly become a central theme of research in the last fifteen years.[10]

Industrialization removed some problems, only to create new ones. It broke the cycles of dearth and starvation, boosted output and demand, and provided employment for the underemployed of *Vormärz* Germany. But it also disrupted old patterns of pro-duction, accentuated the uneven development between regions, and subjected men and women to new insecurities. After 1850, it was clear that newfangled capitalism was there to stay. That was a source of stability, and investors' confidence grew. But the population was exposed to the vicissitudes of the trade cycle, the ups and downs of what was now becoming a world market. As we have seen, the agricultural crisis of the late 1840s was exacerbated by a simultaneous slump in trade. The boom years of the 1850s and 1860s were seriously interrupted only once, by the worldwide commercial and financial crisis of 1857. Then, beginning in 1873, came an unprecedented jolt to the new economic order in Germany. It was triggered by the collapse of an investment boom that began in 1869 and continued on the back of the indemnity paid by the French after the Franco-Prussian war in 1871. More was invested in new limited companies in three years than during the entire period 1851–70. The bubble burst when German and Austrian markets collapsed in May 1873, with effects that were felt through western Europe, Russia and the United States. Businesses failed and the serious excess capacity created by overinvestment led to a sharp fall in the share index and dividends, followed by falling prices, wage-cuts and lay-offs in mining, iron, steel and other industries. In the Saarland, a booming region in the previous two decades, dividends at the Burbach iron works were halved and the numbers employed fell from over 2000 to under 1300 between 1873 and 1877.[11] The position in Germany was made worse by the fact that other industrialized nations faced problems of overproduction. At the same time, German agriculture was faced with a crisis that sprang more directly from the operation of a world market. Prices for primary produce fell as new land was opened up, and lower transportation costs brought an influx of cheap grain, meat and other produce from Europe and overseas.

Industrial recession and sliding agricultural prices marked the beginning of what is commonly labelled a 'Great Depression', lasting from 1873 to 1896. This is a controversial subject among historians, some of whom reject the term altogether.[12] Certainly there were upswings and downswings within this twenty-five-year cycle, some sectors were affected more than others (heavy industry more than textiles, for example), and we are talking about a period in which growth continued, although at a lower rate. The overall decline in prices gives grounds for referring to a 'great deflation' rather than a great depression. That said, there is no doubting the shock and gloom of contemporaries whose confidence was rudely interrupted. The recession of the 1870s was especially serious, its impact measured by the sharp drop in investment levels. Unlike the blip of 1857, the years 1873–80 left permanent changes in the German economic landscape. Primary producers, like their counterparts elsewhere, faced long-term structural changes in the world market. The beginnings of an organized response could already be seen in the 1870s. Industrialists also moved towards what would become a characteristic feature of the German economy, namely the attempt to control markets through concentration and the formation of cartels, or agreements between producers. Finally, both industrial and agricultural interests pressed for tariff protection, with heavy industry and the large grain-growing estate owners of Prussia Eastern Elbia especially prominent (the so-called marriage of iron and rye). In 1879, two decades of movement towards liberalized free trade was reversed when Germany reintroduced tariffs on selected commodities, a step with significance beyond the economy.

Emigration, Migration, Urbanization

If goods and capital moved increasingly within a national and international market, so did people. Migration of one sort or another is a hallmark of these years. It was not entirely novel, of course. We have seen how many people were on the move in old-regime Germany, and the contrast sometimes drawn between a static rural society and a mobile industrial society is a false one. Whether we look at emigration beyond German borders, internal migration or movement into the towns, there are elements of continuity between industrializing Germany and earlier decades. Nevertheless, we cannot mistake the fact that migration assumed new patterns in the third quarter of the nineteenth century.

The rising number of emigrants was the most dramatic novelty of this period. Emigration was not unknown in earlier years, Germans having settled for centuries in eastern and southeastern Europe, and on the eastern seaboard of America. It was the volume that was unprecedented. The numbers began to rise in the 1840s, and the first great wave of emigration saw 1.3 million people leave the German states between 1845 and 1858. In the peak year of 1854 the total reached nearly a quarter of a million. Numbers then declined, before a second great wave in 1864–73 carried another million from Germany. The final, most intense wave began in 1880, with 860,000 leaving in the years 1880–5, 220,000 in 1881 alone. Emigration remained high until the beginning of the 1890s, after which it slowed to a trickle of no more than 20,000 to 30,000 a year.

That is the chronological outline, the 'when'. But who were the emigrants, why did they leave, and where did they go? Some had religious or political motives. Earlier nineteenth-century religious emigrants – Swabian Pietists to Russia, Prussian old-Lutherans to America or Australia – had their counterpart after 1848 in the movement of millenarian religious communities to the New World. The followers of Ludwig Proeli left Bavaria for Pennsylvania; the maverick Catholic priest Ambros Oschwald took his mainly female supporters from the Odenwald to Nebraska. After the defeat of the revolution a sizeable number of forty-eighters settled permanently in the United States, some of them (like Carl Schurz) achieving fame in their adoptive land. Socialist and Catholic victims of political persecution followed after 1870. But all of these together made up only a small minority of emigrants. Most went for material reasons, the emigration statistics providing a yardstick of economic distress in the German regions. The first wave was made up disproportionately of small peasants and craftsmen from the overpopulated rural areas of partible inheritance in the southwest: Baden, Württemberg, the Palatinate. Many districts in Württemberg

lost a sixth of their total population during the 1850s, including
Marbach, Welzheim, Nürtingen, Backnang, Waiblingen and
Balingen. Rural overpopulation also drove the second wave of
emigrants, although agricultural areas in the west were now the
storm-centres, districts like the Eifel, the Hunsrück and the
Mosel valley in the Prussian Rhine Province. From the 1860s,
however, emigrants came increasingly from the east and northeast, from regions where large-estate agriculture and outworking
were prominent such as Mecklenburg, Saxony and the eastern
provinces of Prussia. Between 1855 and 1869 their numbers
grew to make up a sixth of the total; thereafter it was a good
third. This signalled a major change, reflected in the occupations
of those who left. The earlier emigrants were predominantly
peasant or artisan families, would-be settlers. Families still provided the largest numbers in the later waves, children making
up a quarter of the total; but the proportion of independent
small peasant and artisan families fell as the share of single
agricultural labourers, outworkers and factory workers rose.
Workers accounted for 30 per cent of emigrants in the early
1880s, compared with only 18 per cent a decade earlier. Three-
quarters of those who departed Mecklenburg were agricultural
labourers or servants; a majority of those from Saxony described
themselves as outworkers or workers.

To use the mechanical metaphor favoured by contemporaries,
emigration was the 'safety-valve' of rural overpopulation. It followed the rhythm of rural distress, with a certain time-lag. Particularly in the first two waves, when peasant and artisan families
predominated, the greatest volume of emigration occurred during relative upturns, after the opportunity had been taken to
pay off debt and land could be sold on a more buoyant market.
Hence the peaks in the 'good' years of 1854 and 1867, and the
fall-off in numbers after the onset of crisis in 1873. Whereas
1410 people left the administrative district of Trier in 1871–2,
only 568 did so during 1873–4. Here, as elsewhere, the numbers
picked up again in 1880, when the first phase of the Great
Depression (1873–9) had come to an end.

Where were emigrants bound for? An established pattern of

Continental emigration persisted into the nineteenth century. Germans still travelled in large numbers to settle in areas like southern Russia. Other emigrants, or semipermanent migrants, sought employment in economically advanced neighbouring states like Belgium or the Netherlands. There was a large German community in Paris, drawn disproportionately from the rural poor of areas such as Hessen and the Palatinate and concentrated in proletarian occupations like construction, street-cleaning, factory work and domestic service. This 'Little Germany' contained an officially registered 86,000 people by the middle of the century, but some estimates put it at over 100,000, which would have made Paris the sixth largest 'German' city of the time. The German community in the French capital remained substantial even through the Franco-Prussian war. Only when the adverse economic situation of the 1880s caused Frenchmen to take over their 'dirty jobs' did large numbers return home. By then, the main stream of German emigration had, for fifty years, been directed overseas. The destinations were numerous, including Canada, Australia, Brazil, Argentina, Chile and Venezuela. Algeria enjoyed brief popularity, as the French tried to settle their new colony with Europeans. (A particularly desperate class of German emigrants also provided the French Foreign Legion with most of its NCOs.) Towering statistically above all other destinations, however, was the United States. It accounted for 85 per cent of all overseas emigrants in the first great wave, a share that later rose to 90 per cent. Of the roughly 4.5 million Germans who left their homeland between 1847 and the First World War, almost 4 million went to the United States. Brazil was a distant second with 86,000.

A movement of population on this scale would have been impossible without the new means of transportation. The railway made it easier for would-be emigrants to reach the ports of departure, even if we still read in the 1860s of families making the journey from the interior to the coast in covered wagons. Even more important were the growing capacity and falling cost of transatlantic passenger transportation. In the earlier stages,

FIGURE 3 *Overseas Emigration from Nineteenth-Century Germany*

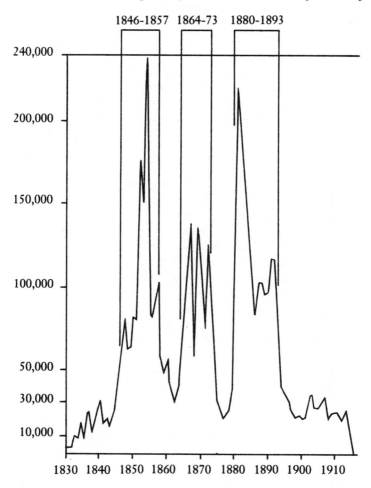

SOURCE
K. J. Bade, *Vom Auswanderungsland zum Einwanderungsland?* (Berlin, 1983), p. 18.

when the America-bound came from the southwest or west, Antwerp and Rotterdam handled much of the traffic. Later, as emigrants came increasingly from the north, Hamburg and Bremen became the great entrepôts of this human cargo. Emigration agencies and associations worked their market (the advertisements of some as misleading as those of any speculative construction company), and the shipping companies competed for custom. As the numbers grew, organizations to advise emigrants were established by state agencies and the churches, such as the St Raphael Association to aid Catholic emigrants run by the Limburg merchant Peter Paul Cahensly. The communications revolution fostered emigration in another way. It made possible the letters home and the financial remissions of those who had already gone. The letters encouraged others to follow by painting an idealized picture of a land of opportunity; the prepaid ticket brought the opportunity within reach. By the 1880s the 'uncle in America' was a familiar figure. The theme of the frontier also played a part in best-selling novels like Gustav Freytag's *Soll und Haben* (*Debit and Credit*), and a popular literature arose to trumpet the virtues of American opportunity, like Friedrich Gerstaecker's *Nach Amerika!* (*To America!*).

Germans had a central place in the great nineteenth-century mass movement across the Atlantic. In the third quarter of the century they were rivalled only by the Irish in their contribution to the peopling of America. The peak period of German mass emigration coincided with that of other north Europeans (British, Irish, Scandinavians), overlapping at the end with the beginnings of growing emigration from southern and eastern Europe. The timing of their arrival, during a phase of dramatic westward expansion and white settlement in the United States, meant that a significant proportion of those in the first waves of German emigrants could exchange the land-hunger of home for a farm in Wisconsin or Indiana. Around a third of the German-born population in America was engaged in agriculture in 1880. But we need to beware of myth. A growing majority of immigrants worked in manufacturing industry or (a German speciality) in transport, trade and services. New and solidly German farming communities were indeed established, in south-western states like Texas as well as the Middle West, but the typical German experience in America was urban. German-born immigrants and their children made up a steady 25–30 per cent of the population in Chicago during its phenomenal growth after 1850. From New York and New Jersey through the industrial towns of Pennsylvania and Ohio to the 'German triangle' in the Middle West around Milwaukee, Cincinnati and St Louis, Germans played a huge part in American urbanization. In these cities and towns they formed German neighbourhoods and cultivated a specifically German culture, establishing their own press, choirs, theatres, gymnastic and shooting clubs, philanthropic organizations – and beer gardens. This was more a transplanting than an uprooting, a purposive 'inventing of ethnicity' (Conzen) that was strengthened by the effects of 'chain-migration', which forged links between particular areas in Germany and particular parts of the United States.[13] The dreams of those who wanted to establish solidly German colonies came to nothing, but the German diaspora remained strikingly unassimilated through the great period of mass emigration up to the 1880s. Only in the following decades, and quite slowly, did the ethnic networks of countless Little Germanys lose their hold.

While German emigrants filled American cities, internal migration began to have the same effect at home. Urbanization is the second great symbol of population movement in this period. Like emigration, it needs to be grasped as a complex process that contained many different experiences. First of all, urbanization did not mean the sudden disruption of a previously stable rural population. Other kinds of internal migration were still extensive, like the seasonal journeys of agricultural labourers. The so-called *Sachsengänger* of East Silesia are the best-known example. Nor was the movement into the towns always a one-way journey, a once-for-all decision. Urban employment also attracted seasonal migrant labourers from the land, men (for it was mainly men) who retained a base in the countryside. Thus workers from the Eifel found jobs in the Westphalian industrial belt, returning to their villages just twice a year. Something similar, marrying older forms of migration with the new industrial world, developed in the Saarland, where the labour shortage in the Prussian state mines led to a workforce that drew heavily on surrounding rural areas. In 1875 a third of Saar miners were weekly commuters, who typically walked to work at dawn Monday morning along 'miners' paths' and returned on Saturday evening. A variant on the same pattern emerged in Württemberg. At least through the 1870s, when most internal migration was still short-distance, many people kept a foot in both camps, moving backwards and forwards between town and country. The sharply seasonal nature of large urban trades like construction, catering and transport made this perfectly logical. Indeed, it is hardly surprising that the umbilical cord between countryside and town was not cut within German regions, given the close links that were sustained between Hessian and Saxon villagers and their kin in Milwaukee or Chicago.

The miner-peasants of the Saarland and the worker-peasants of Swabia were idealized by many contemporary conservatives because of a supposed rustic sturdiness deriving from the soil that still clung to their workboots. This view has little to recommend it. There is more truth in the argument that the blurred edges of the geographical and occupational divide between town and country qualify overemphatic claims about traumatic upheaval. Yet migration of this kind still exacted a heavy price. Clara Viebig wrote a famous novel, *Das Weiberdorf* (*The Village of Women*), about a village in the Eifel that lost its men of working age for most of the year.[14] Here, as among the worker-peasantries of the Saarland and elsewhere, extra burdens fell on the men who left and on the women, the children and the old who stayed behind. The men lived in two worlds but were at home in neither, poorly housed and scorned as rate-busting bumpkins where they worked, semi-strangers in their own villages. Those who remained in the village, especially women, had extra work and responsibilities to shoulder.

Important though it is to recognize these diverse patterns of human movement, there is no mistaking the rapid growth of the permanent urban population in Germany. The tides of migration flowed unevenly, depositing larger numbers in the towns than they carried back into the countryside. Some examples will illustrate this. In 1850 there were six German cities with a population of 100,000 or more; twenty years later there were eleven. If we exclude Vienna, Prague and Trieste, which fell outside the borders of the German state established in 1871, the number of cities with a population of 100,000 or more doubled in this period from four to eight, Cologne, Dresden, Königsberg and Leipzig joining Berlin, Breslau, Hamburg and Munich (see Table 2). A number of other German cities, including Frankfurt, Hanover and Stuttgart, crossed this threshhold of 'big-city' status during the 1870s. Between 1850 and 1870 alone, the population of Dresden grew from 97,000 to 177,000, that of Hamburg from 175,000 to 290,000. In other established cities the population grew even faster, doubling in Berlin and Stuttgart, tripling in Hanover. In the Ruhr, the population of Dortmund, Bochum and Essen increased four-, five- and even sixfold in a generation.

The curve of urbanization was rising in the 1870s, and the period of fastest, pell-mell growth still lay ahead. But it was in the decades after 1850 that urbanization became established and irreversible. Expanding towns, along with emigration, drained off the 'surplus' rural population, and now – by contrast with the *Vormärz* period – the growth in urban population ran ahead of the overall increase. While the net German population grew at 0.75 per cent a year, the rate was around twice that in industrializing Saxony and Westphalia. The proportion of town-dwellers rose in Prussia from 28.1 to 32.5 per cent in these years, a figure that rises to 37.2 per cent if we define a 'town' as a community of more than 2000, rather than using a historical or legal definition. In Saxony the urban population was 40 per cent by 1871, 50 per cent using this statistical definition. The gap that opened up between these different criteria of a town was itself a sign of urbanization; so was the adoption of the modern, head-counting definition by the new Reich Statistical Office.

The question of definition alerts us to a problem. Any account

TABLE 2: *Germany's Largest Cities, 1850, 1870/71, 1910*
(hundreds of thousands)

	1850	1870/71	1910
Berlin	412	826	2071
Hamburg	175	290	931
Leipzig	63	107	679
Munich	107	169	596
Dresden	97	177	548
Cologne	97	129	517
Breslau	111	208	512
Frankfurt am Main	65	91	415
Düsseldorf	27	69	359
Nuremberg	54	83	333
Charlottenburg*	9	20	306
Hanover	28	88	302
Essen	9	52	295
Chemnitz	34	68	288
Stuttgart	47	92	286
Magdeburg	52	84	280
Bremen	53	83	247
Königsberg	73	112	246
Rixdorf (after 1912 Neukölln)*	3	8	237
Stettin	47	76	236
Duisburg	9	32	229
Dortmund	11	44	214
Kiel	16	32	212

* Both later incorporated into Greater Berlin

SOURCE: J. Reulecke, *Geschichte der Urbanisierung in Deutschland* (Frankfurt, 1985), p. 203.

of urbanization which includes overgrown villages of 2000 souls and a metropolis like Berlin with almost a million inhabitants clearly needs to be broken down further. The first point to make is that a clear majority of town-dwelling Germans still lived in modestly sized communities. In 1871, 14.8 million inhabitants of the newly unified country were classified as urban. Of these, 5.1 million lived in towns of between 2000 and 5000 inhabitants, another 4.6 million in towns of between 5000 and 20,000. These two groups, nearly 10 million people, made up two-thirds of German town-dwellers. Many of their towns were growing, some of them rapidly, as they became attached to the modern economy. Vohwinkel in the Wuppertal grew from 58 to 5000 between 1850 and the 1880s, first as a railway junction, then as the site of repair shops. Perhaps half of the towns with fewer than 5000 inhabitants were industrial, especially where textiles persisted or mining put out its tentacles. However, some towns were declining as rural deindustrialization occurred. Others remained relatively stable market towns, fattened up by the favourable agriculture of the period but fundamentally unaltered, the sort of small town in which so many novels and magazine serials of the period were set. The only generalization that can safely be made about this middle Germany in which one out of four Germans lived is that few of its urban settlements resembled the bustling industrial or commercial city we usually associate with urbanization.

Among the larger German towns, urban growth was also diverse in character. Capital cities that had long been administrative centres and regional metropolises now developed a major industrial sector. Berlin, Vienna, Stuttgart and Dresden were among the most important. The same thing took place in other large cities previously noted mainly for their commercial importance, such as Cologne, Düsseldorf, Breslau and Leipzig. All were urban centres that performed mixed roles within an increasingly complex economy. However, a feature of urban growth was specialization of function. Cities like Frankfurt, Hamburg and Bremen grew as centres of commerce, banking and insurance; others became identified with the provision of particular services, whether administrative and military (Koblenz, Kiel), or educational (Bonn, Königsberg). A different kind of service centre was the spa town with a heavy concentration of retired people, such as Wiesbaden. From the island of Sylt in the north to the shores of Lake Constance in the south, this period witnessed the development of towns dependent on tourism and recreation. More obviously characteristic of the new economic era were towns that became identified with a single industry, their reputations based on textiles (Krefeld, Barmen, Chemnitz, Plauen), iron (Dortmund), engineering (Nuremberg, Magdeburg), or cutlery (Solingen). Other urban centres – Braunschweig, Halle, the towns on the middle Neckar near Stuttgart – had a more diversified industrial structure. Finally, and most spectacular because of the dizzy speed with which they grew, were the new urban agglomerations based on coal, iron and steel. Here, in the Ruhr, the Saarland, Upper Silesia and parts of Saxony, it was not a question of established towns expanding, but of virtual villages that grew into towns and into each other, so that the traveller through the valleys of the Saar or the Wupper found it impossible to tell where one community ended and the next began. Beuthen and Gleiwitz in Upper Silesia, Bochum and Duisburg in the Ruhrgebiet, Neunkirchen and Dudweiler in the Saar basin, were classic boom towns of the new industrial conurbations.

While areas like this grew in a sprawl across the countryside, the spatial development of older towns followed a different pattern. Physical expansion was impeded by city walls and gates, and their removal became a symbol of urban growth in the decades after mid-century. To take just one example, the town walls were pulled down in Trier during the 1870s, apart from a small section near the Mosel, and those arriving after 10 p.m. no longer had to ring a bell for admission or pay a fee to be allowed in. The *glacis* immediately beyond the old walls typically became the site of the first industrial suburbs. With time, towns spilled over into the surrounding rural areas, acquiring new contours that followed the lines of major radial routes. New mass transit systems accelerated the process in larger towns.

Surrounding villages, swallowed up by this expansion, became effectively annexed to the town in economic and social terms before they were formally brought within the municipality by incorporation, a process that was beginning in this period. All of these developments marked a final break with the town-country divide of the old regime, a parallel to the change from legal to statistical definitions of the town itself.

Towns not only grew outwards; the physical shape of urban centres was also transformed. The arrival of the railway required land for track, marshalling yards and stations; it created station districts, which often served as the focus of a 'new town' that grew alongside the old centre. The area between the two frequently became the new axis of urban life. The building boom from the 1840s to the 1870s reshaped German towns in other ways. Pockets of grazing or waste land were developed, roads were widened and pavements plastered, new city streets were cut through the dense networks of alleyways or constructed where fortifications had once stood. Handsome new public buildings and parks sprang up along them – although not yet banks, business houses and department stores in the same numbers that were to be found in the contemporaneous reshaping of Paris or London. The imposing Ringstrasse construction in Vienna and the rebuilding around the Alster in Hamburg are among the best-known examples. In postunification Berlin, the Post Office alone built major new central facilities in the Jägerstrasse, Leipziger Strasse, Oranienburger Strasse and Spandauer Strasse during the 1870s. As land values rose, the poorer inhabitants of the old central areas such as craftsmen and labourers were crowded into the remaining 'undeveloped' districts, or squeezed out to the new industrial suburbs on the outskirts of town.

The growth of German towns took place in a society from which the last remaining restrictions on freedom of movement were being removed, as they were on freedom of occupation. These changes had a double-edged character. On the one hand, they meant that urban notables could not keep (or push) the lower classes out of towns by denying them poor relief. Under the revised Prussian Poor Law of 1855, those who became a burden on the public purse during their first year in a new place could be returned to their 'original place of support', but not those who had established one year of residence. The basic tenet of free movement was established in most states during the 1860s, and the principle was enshrined in the newly unified Germany. The other side of the coin, however, was the freedom allowed to urban developers to proceed as they saw fit. Towns grew in this period with little of the overall design so characteristic of the absolutist era or the princely projects of the early nineteenth century. True, there were some moves towards town planning in the 1860s and 1870s, anticipated by architects like James Hobrecht in Berlin. On the ground, however – in the literal sense – building usually went on piecemeal and with little regard for the mass of inhabitants. Vienna serves as the classic example. The immense care taken over the layout of the Ringstrasse contrasted starkly with the indifference shown towards the outer suburbs against which it stood as a form of insulation. The growing city of the lower class was expressly exempted from the controls of the City Expansion Commission.

Under these circumstances, the influx into the towns brought predictable problems. Housing was in short supply and often appallingly bad, something that is not denied by recent 'revisionist' historians.[15] Conditions were probably worst in the raw new urban agglomerations like the Ruhr and Saarland. Some mine owners and heavy industrialists constructed workers' housing or 'colonies' in an attempt to recruit, retain and discipline the labour force. The Eisenheim colony attached to the Gutehoffnungshütte in Oberhausen was the first of its kind. The state mine authorities pursued a similar policy in the Saarland. But this accommodation was often unsalubrious (in the Saarland it was 'overcrowded and leaves much to be desired hygienically', according to one official[16]); it imposed quasi-military restrictions on behaviour, and anyway met only a small part of the demand. Most workers lived in the tenements thrown up by speculative builders, where rents were so high that multiple occupation or taking in lodgers became the norm. Conditions were almost as bad in established cities, where rising rents created similar cramped existences in so-called 'rental barracks'. In Berlin, half of all dwellings had just one heatable room in 1875, another quarter just two. At that time, 20 per cent of the city's inhabitants lived five-to-a-room; 10 per cent lived in cellars. The figures were slightly worse in Dresden, Breslau and Chemnitz. Overcrowding was exacerbated by the conditions to which the occupants of attics, cellars and tenements were exposed – damp, lack of natural light, poorly constructed stoves that claimed poison-fume victims every winter, primitive sanitary arrangements that made the perfect breeding ground for infectious diseases. Periodic outbreaks of cholera and typhus were the most vivid symbol of dangerous, degraded living conditions, but we should remember that a heavier toll was taken, year in and year out, simply by the fact that those conditions weakened people so much that they were unable to withstand the great killers of the age like tuberculosis, pleurisy, pneumonia and other infectious diseases including influenza, diphtheria and scarlet fever. The very young were especially vulnerable. At a time when infant mortality was still rising (it began to turn down at the beginning of the 1880s), the evidence shows that – in Saxony and Prussia at least – it was riskier to be born in the town than the country, and riskiest of all in the large town. In Saxon Zwickau and Prussian Berlin during the late 1870s, almost a third of all infants died before the age of one. Among illegitimate children, the figure for Berlin was nearly one in two.

There is no reason to idealize the conditions of life in the German countryside. After all, infant mortality was higher in the Bavarian Forest and in Upper Swabia than it was in Berlin. But the speed with which towns grew, and the lack of planning – or, rather, the very selective planning – that accompanied growth meant deteriorating conditions for many first-generation urban dwellers. Things got worse before they got better. Inhabitants of the newest industrial agglomerations, once again, faced the most acute problems. Mines and factories sprang up in Silesia and the Ruhr without an infrastructure to match – roads, water supply, social amenities. Communities developed overnight, with all the charm of gold-rush towns and levels of drunkenness and violence to match. The Saarland was actually dubbed 'black California' (the black denoted coal, of course). But this was only the extreme version of a general problem. At a time when most expanding towns still bore a raw look, when shanty-towns developed on the outskirts of many, the provision of basic services simply did not grow at the same pace. The network of municipal utilities that became familiar in later decades started to take shape in these years, but provision was still very patchy. Local transportation developed fast, sometimes ahead of the suburbs it was intended to serve. Gas supply, divided roughly half-and-half between private and municipally owned companies, also made headway. Piped water arrived more haltingly, and the prominence of profit-orientated private companies in the early years made for a less than comprehensive supply. Public waterworks designed to serve the whole citizenry were rare before the 1870s. Only twelve Prussian towns had one in 1870; eighteen more were established in the next five years. As reservoirs were created in surrounding areas and water filtration technology advanced, the supply of fresh water began to improve, but 60 per cent of the Prussian population still acquired its water from wells, cisterns or natural sources even at the end of the century. The local authorities in Trier, showing little of the hydrological verve possessed by the city's Roman founders, made seven or eight attempts to improve the inadequate water supply, beginning in the early 1850s. Not until the early twentieth century did a municipal waterworks replace these unsuccessful, piecemeal efforts.[17] Finally, the high-cost, unrewarding business of sewage and waste disposal made it the Cinderella of urban utilities. Large cities like Berlin, Hamburg, Frankfurt and Munich began to lay down new systems in the early 1850s, but they were often unsatisfactory and still utilized open gutters. Municipal councils dominated by property-owners through a weighted franchise jibbed at the expense of underground sewerage systems, and their installation proceeded very slowly.

The Hamburg cholera outbreak of 1892 was the most dramatic instance of the price paid for urban squalor. A recent comprehensive study of the episode has shown how the poor were the principal victims of the epidemic, as they were of overcrowded and insanitary housing conditions.[18] It is true that special factors operated in Hamburg, but a similar social divide could be found throughout urban Germany. The lines along which towns were physically reshaped, variations in housing density, the pattern of water and sewerage provision, the urban geography of morbidity and mortality rates – all show that a key indicator of where, how and even if a person lived was class.

A New Class Structure

Class is a set of relationships, not a thing, and changes in class structure are even more difficult to pin down than a process like industrialization. Nevertheless, by analogy with the way in which we can observe water freeze or molten metals harden under changed conditions, so it is possible to identify periods when class relations seem to set in a new form. That is true of Germany in the quarter-century after 1850. We see it in the growing division between masters and men under the new economic dispensation. We see it in the residential segregation that separated the middle-class suburbs of Wilmersdorf and Schöneberg from the working-class districts of Rixdorf and Lichtenberg in Berlin. We see it, not least, in the spheres of reproduction and sociability, dress and cuisine, the everyday realm where class values and mores were expressed. Words did not just reflect but helped to fix the lines of a new social structure, as political commentators, fashion writers and the authors of etiquette manuals all began to elaborate the language of class.

Wilhelm Heinrich Riehl published a book in 1851 called *Die bürgerliche Gesellschaft* (*Bourgeois Society*). In it he observed that 'our entire era has a bourgeois character', something that the socially conservative Riehl registered with regret.[19] For a long time, German historians slighted or played down the emergence of the German bourgeoisie, partly for reasons of interpretation taken up later in this book (see Chapter Eight), partly because social historians tended to direct their attention to the lower classes, not businessmen or professionals. This situation has changed with a vengeance in the last fifteen years, thanks to a series of research projects and monographs. We now have a more detailed and differentiated picture of the German propertied and educated middle class. What does it tell us?

No one would want to resurrect old clichés about a 'rising middle class', but there are good grounds for arguing that the third quarter of the nineteenth century saw the real formation of a powerful German bourgeoisie. The most obvious sign of this was the growth of a wealthier and more confident group of merchants, bankers, manufacturers and entrepreneurs. They included the clans of textile manufacturers in Westphalia, the Upper Rhine and Central Germany, iron and steel magnates like Stumm on the Saar and Krupp in the Ruhr, the steamship and mercantile notables of Cologne and Hamburg, and the great locomotive builders to be found in almost every industrial city. But a dynamic, diversifying economy created opportunities for investment and profit in every area of life. Men made their fortunes from the construction and property boom of the period, from furniture and food, from gas lamps and the electric telegraph. Several general points can be made about this entrepreneurial group. Its emergence as a major force was relatively rapid compared with England or France, a function of the belated but then explosive character of German industrialization. This, in turn, probably increased the element of homogeneity at one level by minimizing the divisions between long-established and newcomer concerns. It almost certainly explains the resourcefulness and lack of sentimentality with which German businesses organized themselves, especially under the impact of recession during the 1870s, in matters such as price-fixing, cartels, and the formation of interest organizations on a branch or sectional basis.

Much more easily overlooked is something else: the growing wealth and confidence of Germany's provincial and small-town middle class. Although the lines between countryside and towns, agriculture and industry, had started to become more clearly drawn, this was not yet a period when the term 'provincial' had acquired the meanings of 'sleepy' and 'backward' that it later did. On the contrary: these were buoyant, successful years for small-town businessmen – corn and timber merchants, auctioneers, land agents, brewers, booksellers, local newspaper proprietors, hoteliers. The countryside had never been so wealthy and stable; peasants had more purchasing power, and people from the large towns were starting to make recreational visits in larger numbers (much to the disgust of Riehl, and the early defenders of the 'unspoiled' German *Heimat*). Local capitalists reaped the benefits. Indeed, commercialized agriculture generated its own entrepreneurs. Take the wine trade as an example. The local notables in the Palatine town of Deidesheim prospered from bottling wine, hence their nickname the 'bottle barons'; the family of the playwright Carl Zuckmayer owed their position in the Mainz bourgeoisie to the manufacture of crown corks.[20] None of this was very dramatic; but it was an important chapter in growing bourgeois wealth and confidence.

Alongside businessmen, merchants and entrepreneurs of diverse kinds, Germany's educated middle classes also became more conscious of what they believed to be their importance in society. State officials still made up a major segment of the educated: regional and provincial administrators, judges and legal officials, professors and grammar school teachers, senior foresters and medical health officers. University-trained officials recruited on the basis of merit had been at the heart of German state-building before 1850 (see Chapter Two). But they remained a relatively small group. Now their numbers increased, and their social standing, already high, rose further. The importance of educated officials, and the prestige they enjoyed vis-à-vis businessmen, was reflected in much contemporary literature. Here we have a Continental European pattern very different from the one to be found in Anglo-Saxon countries where the state was weaker. That said, the phenomenon was probably even more pronounced in Germany than elsewhere, and it spilled over into the way in which the educated middle classes as a whole thought about themselves. There was, for example, nothing uniquely German about the fact that the state had a greater role in the training, recruitment patterns and regulation of professions like law and medicine than it did in, say, England. But even in France or Italy the state did not enjoy the monopoly over the training of lawyers that existed in Germany. All German lawyers were in some sense state officials until national legislation in 1878 established freedom of access to the profession, and the desire for emancipation from state tutelage and greater self-regulation was offset by the value lawyers placed on the enjoyment of an official's status. Similar points could be made about the medical profession.[21]

The buoyancy of the professions after mid-century also had features familiar from other parts of the capitalist world. Like their counterparts elsewhere, German doctors, lawyers, surveyors, architects and engineers stepped up their claims to possess specialized knowledge and appropriate qualifications. They developed their own codes of ethics, created professional bodies like the Association of German Engineers (1856) and the German Lawyers' Congress (1860), and tried hard to outlaw those who challenged their monopoly service – 'quacks' and herbal healers in the case of doctors, so-called *Winkeladvokaten* in the case of lawyers. Historians, in the country that pioneered modern professional history, took a similarly dim view of lay practitioners. This, the thinly veiled professional version of market control, was common enough elsewhere. The insistence of German professionals on their disinterested service for the common good was also a familiar offshoot of professionalization everywhere. Nevertheless, there was a closer overlap in Germany than elsewhere between rhetoric of this kind and the bureaucracy's claim to represent a 'general interest'. The difficulty of making a clean distinction between officials and members of the 'free' professions explains why the single word *Bildungsbürger* was later coined to describe both. The term, with its suggestion of the almost caste-like sense of status that coloured the identity of all professionals, is distinctively German (and Austrian). Not for nothing did German professors of history come to be seen as a *Zunft*, or 'guild'.

Members of the propertied and educated middle classes, with their dependants, made up some 5 per cent of the German population in these years. Whether or not we also count those whose claim to inclusion is less clear-cut – members of marginal professions such as pharmacists and veterinary surgeons, journalists, or the managerial and technical staff of large firms – it is obvious that the German bourgeoisie had many internal divisions. There were sectional differences, such as those between heavy and light industry, and there were manifest variations of income and social origin within every constituent group. Most important of all, there were underlying differences between the two main wings of the propertied and educated middle class: in their relationship to the market, the degree of economic security they enjoyed, and the divergent patterns of education and recruitment to their respective occupations. The sons of the educated middle class typically attended the classical grammar school, while the offspring of businessmen were more likely to go to the nonclassical secondary school, with its emphasis on science and modern languages. As we saw earlier (see Chapter Two), even where both groups used the classical grammar school, they withdrew their sons at different stages, commercial men preferring them to get early experience in business, the educated regarding university attendance as the norm. As late as 1879, the Rhineland entrepreneur Gustav Mevissen complained that his business colleagues had rarely attended university themselves and prevented their sons from going, out of fear that academic learning would seduce them away from business practicalities.[22] There is also evidence that the propertied and the educated intermarried with their own kind. The marriage strategies used by entrepreneurs to forge links with other businesses had their counterparts in the heavily interrelated clans among the educated (and especially academic) middle classes. The Mommsens and Baumgartens were the German equivalents of England's celebrated Darwins and Huxleys.

These differences should not be overdrawn. There was also

much that united bourgeois Germany; indeed there were signs of convergence between the two groups after mid-century. Take education, for example. The nonclassical secondary school became more humanistic, the grammar school taught more maths and natural science. And the increasingly scientific basis of industry, from the extractive branches to chemicals, meant that higher education became more of a necessity for businessmen. These changes reduced the distance between propertied and educated. The same thing was happening at another level. Both business and professions were, to a significant degree, 'self-recruiting', a sign of the modest levels of contemporary social mobility. But there were signs in this period of occupational movement across the educated/propertied line. There was a growing tendency for the sons of medium-sized businessmen to enter professions like medicine, law and architecture, with a slightly later movement into academic and official careers. A long-term study of history professors from the 1840s to the end of the First World War has shown that a fifth of them had fathers who were industrialists, businessmen or bankers.[23] The evidence on intermarriage points in the same direction. This had always been a feature of great mercantile and service centres like Hamburg or Frankfurt; now it became more general, especially in the form of academics and officials marrying the daughters of businessmen. There were other ties of sociability that bound the bourgeoisie together in city and small town alike – common membership of middle-class clubs (Wednesday Club, Museum Society), dining together at the Ratskeller. In fact, it was in the realm of cultural and social identity that the propertied and educated were probably most united. This bourgeois identity included a shared belief in property, hard work, competition, achievement, and the rewards and recognition that were expected to flow from them; in rationality, the rule of law, and the importance of living life by rules. Correct table manners, sartorial codes, the emphasis placed on cleanliness and hygiene, the importance attached to timetables, whether in the school, on the railway or at mealtimes – all are instances of the way in which these bourgeois values informed everyday life. Underlying many of these aspects of bourgeois self-understanding was a shared idea of independence that rested on economic security, the possession of sufficient time and money to plan ahead, and certain standards of education and literacy.[24] A general respect for literary, artistic and musical culture – for the *idea* of it, anyway – was a further common denominator.

The institution that epitomized shared bourgeois values was the family. At the heart of it was the separation of workplace from home, now much clearer than it had been, and the possession of material resources sufficient for the employment of servants to run the household. Domestic servants still made up one of the largest occupational categories in most German towns, and no one who reads the classified columns of contemporary newspapers can fail to notice their importance to the middle classes. The family became a sphere of private, domestic compensation for the hard-working and 'public' male, while his wife was expected to devote herself to the cultivation of domesticity and the transmission of proper cultural values and norms to the next generation. The family was the institution which displayed the wealth and cultural capital of the bourgeoisie, provided the means by which dynastic ambitions were realized, and offered the man a haven from the rigours of the male world of business or professional affairs. This was the distribution of roles ascribed in Meyer's *Grosse Conversations-Lexicon* of 1848 ('while the woman in the main lays the foundations for the ties that bind the family, the man is the link with the external world') and endlessly reiterated in contemporary tracts like Rudolf Virchow's *On the Education of the Woman for her Occupation* (1865).[25] Within the emotional economy of the bourgeois family, men and women were held to possess distinctive, complementary qualities: strength/sensibility, cold reason/warm heart, ambition/humility. The man was prey to the temptations of the flesh; the woman tamed and civilized these instincts. Women, in short, represented the 'better half' – and therefore the 'weaker sex'. This amounted to the full flowering of a tendency to 'feminize' women and sentimentalize the family, already apparent in the Biedermeier period before mid-century. It can be regarded as another example of functional specialization within German society, as the line was more clearly drawn between male earners and female nurturers, between the spheres of production and reproduction. The differences between man and wife were anchored in law and frequently underlined by a difference in age, as men delayed marriage until they were established in business or profession. Of course, none of this excluded bourgeois women from roles outside the home, such as philanthropic activity or the public consumption of culture. Daughters, after all, were taught to sketch and play the piano so that they could appreciate art and music in a befitting manner. Claims by women to exercise a special role as conduits of culture won wider acceptance in these years, especially in educated circles; but that confirmed rather than challenged the idea of separate spheres.[26] The subordinate position of women (and children) was built into the structure of the bourgeois family, and in this period the doors of educational and career opportunities remained firmly closed to women.

So far we have been considering the internal values, structures and institutions that held the bourgeoisie together. But there is something else that united it: a sense of itself vis-à-vis other classes. In the first half of the nineteenth century, a developing bourgeois identity was most likely to define itself against the aristocracy, with its positions of influence within the corporate state, its legal privileges, and the disdain that some of its members expressed for values like hard work and achievement. Middle-class attitudes may not have amounted to an antiaristocratic front, but among the more class-conscious there was a sharp edge of dislike. This did not disappear after mid-century, but it became more muted. The removal of most formal aristocratic legal privileges, either in 1848 or in the course of the 1860s, contributed to the change. So did the growing sense of bourgeois self-importance. It was signified at one level by businessmen who sought a title such as Commercial Councillor or Privy Commercial Councillor, the numbers of whom more

A seigneur inflicts
corporal punishment,
late eighteenth century.

The passion for phrenology. 'Cranioscopical Manipulations', a Daniel Hess
caricature of 1795.

The comfortable age of Biedermeier: a middle-class nursery around 1840.

Censorship before 1848: gagged intellectuals in 'The Thinkers' Club' discuss the question of how much longer they will still be allowed to think.

Off to the Political Club: a sardonic view of women's emancipation in the revolution of 1848.

Counter-Revolution, 1848: the Prussian General Wrangel's 'Street-Cleaning Machine'.

Counter-Revolution, 1848: the Execution of Robert Blum in the Brigittenau near Vienna, 9 November.

Overleaf Early industrialization: the construction of a railway engine at the Maffei engineering works in Hirschau near Munich, 1849.

A shanty-town on the outskirts of Berlin, 1871.

Votive offering of the 1880s (tempera on wood), in which a Bavarian peasant family displays its four-legged assets.

than doubled in Prussian Rhineland-Westphalia between the 1850s and the 1870s.[27] It found expression at a different level in the shift from the plain middle-class domestic interiors of the Biedermeier period to the more cluttered, plush and pretentious style that came into favour after 1850, and especially in the 1870s. As better-off businessmen and professionals became more sure of themselves and their place in society, so tilting at the nobility became less common. The bourgeoisie was buoyant, not combative, and the language recorded in contemporary political encyclopaedias and dictionaries shows that the *Bürger* was defined less often vis-à-vis the old social élite. Some writers have gone further, referring to middle-class traits like attraction to the reserve officer corps and the habit of duelling as a 'feudalization' of the bourgeoisie. This is an altogether more dubious argument. It is taken up in detail in Chapter Eight, for almost everyone would accept that the pattern of behaviour in question – however widespread, and however we interpret it – started to become significant only from the 1870s.

What was already clear in the third quarter of the nineteenth century was the tendency of the German bourgeoisie to separate itself off from the lower social classes. This may have been least true in the case of the peasantry, with which urban, bourgeois Germany had enjoyed little contact anyway. In fact, the growing 'urbanization' of the German countryside (the spread of new forms of consumption, the greater employment of notaries by better-off peasants) may have multiplied the points of contact. What occurred gradually, after a revolution that demonstrated apparent peasant loyalty and at a time of agricultural boom, was a relaxation of bourgeois attitudes, so that contempt and fear towards the 'uncivilized' peasant gave way after mid-century to a more idealized view. The pages of middle-class family journals like *Die Gartenlaube* contained comforting depictions of yodelling rustics and cherry-picking maids; so did sentimental works in the *Heimat* genre. This was a bourgeois appropriation of a prettified rural way of life, running parallel to the spreading interest in nature as a source of edification and a place for recreation. It did not bring middle class and peasantry closer together: even the richest peasant was set apart from the clergy-man or resident local official by manual work, lack of education and style of life. Social intercourse between the classes remained minimal.

A more obvious separation of the bourgeoisie from the classes below it can be seen in the case of the petty bourgeoisie. Earlier in the century the term 'burgher' (*Stadtbürger*) had denoted the citizen of a town, and included the master craftsman as well as the merchant. But restricted citizenship disappeared after mid-century, and with it the shared privilege that united bour-geoisie and petty bourgeoisie against the rest. The term Mittel-stand (literally: middle estate) underwent a similar change of meaning. Before 1850 it included substantial businessmen as well as shopkeepers and craftsmen: now it increasingly applied to the petty bourgeoisie alone. This shift of meaning was not absolute, and it applied to a far greater extent in cities than in small towns, where the social distance between merchants and tradesmen remained smaller. Still, the new and narrower mean-ing of Mittelstand flagged the fact that a distinctive lower middle class was taking shape. Its most important component consisted of those who ran small, independent concerns – master crafts-men, small businessmen, publicans, shopkeepers. Together they accounted for perhaps 8 per cent of the gainfully employed in the early 1870s. The most significant growth came among shopkeepers, as itinerant traders and hawkers gave way to fixed retail outlets. Of course, there had long been shopkeepers in large mercantile centres, trading imported commodities like tobacco and coffee, but changing popular consumption now established the retailer as a familiar urban figure. Even as popu-lation rose, the ratio of customers to traders fell from 83:1 to 54:1 between 1861 and 1882. By the latter date there were some 450,000 German shopkeepers.[28]

The petty bourgeoisie stretched from the margins of the working class, from which some had come and among whom others lived, to the borders with the bourgeoisie proper, where the more established regarded their businesses in bourgeois dyn-astic terms (bakers almost always handed over to their sons), and might aspire to the gentility of the middle-class family – the piano in the drawing room. There were fundamental differences between the cobbler eking out a living from repairs or the widow who ran a precarious greengrocery store, and the master butcher or haberdasher who carried a substantial inventory and boasted a prosperous clientele. These extremes defined the limits of a new, ambiguous class that possessed some capital or its own means of production, yet depended on family labour, a class that was fluid and transitional, contained some who were rising and others who were falling, and represented a kind of social buffer zone. Much the same can be said of the new lower middle class of white-collar employees (contemporaries referred to them as 'black-coated'), the clerks, cashiers, procurists, book-keepers and overseers who first emerged in significant numbers during this period. In the private sector alone they numbered 400,000 by the beginning of the 1880s, or 3.4 per cent of the labour force. The new lower middle class, like the independent petty bourgeoisie, was situated between the class fronts. Its members prided themselves on the badges of status that lifted them above manual workers, like distinctive forms of remuneration and conditions of work, yet there was a gap separating even the most 'trusted' and best-paid (such as procurists) from the established bourgeoisie.[29]

Finally, these years saw the emergence of a new urban working class. The most compelling image of this, counterpointing the rise of the entrepreneurial bourgeoisie, is provided by the workers who sold their labour power to the factory or mine owner. This was the period when a true factory proletariat came into being, working to the rhythm of machines, subject to the division of labour, disciplined by factory clock and works regulations, supervised by foremen, remunerated by fixed wages or piece rates and not by the contracts to deliver entered into by craftsmen or outworkers. That is the ideal type of the new, more uniform proletariat; it does not describe the life of most workers. By the 1870s, factory workers and miners still made up no more than 10 per cent of the whole labour force. Nevertheless, this was a marked increase compared with mid-century, and the underlying trend was towards the formation of such a workforce. Just as important, we can see the same tendency towards a dependent, anonymous class of 'hands' in the far more numerous small workshops. This was a watershed period in the separation of masters and men, symbolized by the decline of journeymen living in. In fact, smaller concerns in trades like construction, woodworking, leatherworking, and cigar-making often had the most militant workforces and were especially strike-prone. The wave of strikes among small-shop journeymen in Bremen during 1865–74 is one example of many.[30] This had a lot to do with the greater bargaining power of journeymen against small employers, but it also signalled the growing class-divide in the artisan world.

The concept of a well-drilled proletariat needs to be modified in another way. Few employers tried to dragoon their workers with the energy of a hard-faced ironmaster like Baron Stumm in the Saarland. In transportation and construction the rhythm of work remained more broken and irregular. Many first-generation factories were neither efficient nor minutely regimented: production often stopped because supplies failed to arrive or machinery broke down; parts of the production process were subcontracted out to quasi-independent groups of skilled craftsmen working under the same roof. Commonly, a core of permanent skilled workers – those whom employers strove to keep – was surrounded by a larger, floating labour force, so that industrial turnover rates of 50 per cent a year were normal and 100 per cent not uncommon, movement in and out peaking in spring and early summer. Unskilled younger workers were more vulnerable to dismissal, but they also voted with their feet in search of 'better' employment. The eighteen-year-old Carl Dingler, a second-generation factory worker, wrote a letter home in August 1864 describing his peregrinations over the two previous years – from Esslingen in Württemberg to Eltville, near Mainz, then on to Berlin after a short stopover near Magdeburg when he 'ran short of money', before moving to Dresden (where 'payment was miserable') and finally on to Chemnitz.[31] His story was not unusual.[32] The work-experience of the early industrial labour force was as diverse as the sources from which it was recruited – former masters and journeymen, refugees from cottage industry, day labourers, the rural poor (especially in the mines). What it meant to be a worker varied from branch to branch, according to age, whether you came from a rural or urban background, and across a wide spectrum of skill-levels – with high wage-differentials to match. In the factory, skilled workers were self-consciously superior to their unskilled fellows. In the mine, no one would confuse the collier with the haulier or pony-boy, certainly not the collier.

A 'making' of the German working class, then? Certainly there were signs that it was taking place. First, these years saw some blurring of skill differences and a rise in the number of those in the intermediate category of the semi-skilled – this on top of the fact that, because of the speed of industrialization and the rural origins of many workers, skill demarcation lines had never been quite so minutely observed or calibrated as they were in Britain. Secondly, this was also the period when the money wage became the dominant form of remuneration for workers of all kinds, another common bond. Thirdly, however much early factories might fall short of entrepreneurial dreams, there was a clear movement towards greater control of the labour force, such as efforts to wipe out the absenteeism associated with 'Blue Mondays' following Sunday festivities, and this caused collective resentment. Workers generally did not dislike their machines – there is evidence that when these functioned well they could develop real attachment to them – but there was widespread resistance to foremen, who enjoyed extensive powers to hire and fire (sometimes used to look after a neighbourhood or kinship clan), to levy fines and sometimes to fix wage levels. Disputes with foremen were a common cause of dismissal or resignation. Like miners' resentments towards colliery over-seers, they fostered solidarity. How far all of this created a common identity as workers is more open to question. A genera-tion of broadly shared experience undoubtedly produced a more homogeneous group than the mélange of the urban underclass as it existed in 1840. It is significant that growing numbers of journeymen designated themselves as workers. And some sense of belonging to a class rather than a specific trade can be inferred from the movement of the children of first-generation factory workers (especially those in textiles) into other branches, as occurred in industrially diversified areas like Saxony. But it may overstate the case to refer, as some have done, to the existence of a born proletariat by the end of this period. There is evidence that – in some places at least – the tradition of following one's father into the factory was very weak. In Düsseldorf, only one factory worker's son in seven was himself a factory worker in 1875.[33]

As the working and nonworking parts of the day became more distinct, daily life outside the workplace may have done more to forge a sense of collective identity. Residential segregation created solidly proletarian suburbs where workers rented living space that was similar in being cramped and inadequate. Here, there would be no resident bourgeoisie – at most, a few shop-keepers and publicans who took their values from the proletarian milieu, extending credit during strikes and lay-offs, for example. Inside their homes, the modest household possessions workers now began to accumulate were also likely to be fairly uniform. Young, single male workers would aim to buy a certain number of distinctive 'prestige' possessions, a best suit and a silver watch (objects that could later be pawned if necessary), and there is both systematic and anecdotal evidence that efforts were made to save before marriage, so that even a poor couple might start their married life with special linen and a bespoke bed. But much of what they owned – which was more than their equivalents a generation earlier, but incomparably less than middle-class households – would be mass-produced for the lower end of the market. Marriage partners themselves usually came from within the working class.[34] And when children were born, so the evidence from a detailed study of Leipzig suggests, it became increasingly common for working-class parents to choose other workers (and not just fellow-workers in their own trade) as god-parents, rather than, say, a guild master or manufacturer.[35] Out-side the home, daily life and recreational pursuits in the neighbourhood bound inhabitants together. The new industrial suburbs were raw, but they were not entirely the barren, rootless places sometimes depicted, even if official and clerical observers agreed in deploring many features of working-class sociability – children who played in the streets, the centrality of alcohol in the lives of many male workers, the garishness and casual violence that went with popular fairs, often former parish festivals now transplanted into new urban surroundings. A distinctive working-class culture was starting to take shape.

It did not include the expectations for oneself and one's children that were characteristic of the bourgeoisie, or the hopes that animated the better-off lower middle class. Insecurity hung over the workers' world. True, there was more work to find than there had been in *Vormärz* Germany, and there was less grinding poverty among those fit to do it. Real wages rose modestly from the late 1850s, even if they did not keep pace with the profits made during the long boom period. But it was normal for two-thirds of income to be spent on food, with most of the rest going towards housing, heating and light, and all members of the working class – even the families of skilled engineers or compositors, the labour élite – lived with the realistic fear that a change in their circumstances could drag them below the level of subsistence. Permanent or seasonal lay-offs were most likely to affect the unskilled, but the arrival of recession in 1873 showed that even long-serving 'core' workers could find themselves out in the cold, like the miners in the Ruhr and Saarland who had once enjoyed protected status as members of the semicorporate Prussian state *Knappschaft*. The following years saw higher levels of unemployment. An accident, injury, illness, or the death of an adult or working child could suddenly alter any family's position for the worse. Labour itself sapped the worker's energy: the average working week of six days remained constant at around seventy-five hours in the period 1850–70, before starting to shorten. It was generally longer in textiles – although not as long as the hours worked in agriculture. Heat, dust, fumes, noise and dangerous machinery were common work hazards, while the sheer physical demands of toil left many workers in a state of permanent exhaustion that exposed them to illness. Life expectancy edged upwards in the third quarter of the century, but for a man born in the 1870s it was still only 36.5, for a woman 38.5. There was little leisure for women under this grim regimen, and what stands out again is the difference between middle-class and working-class families. Women, it is true, did not figure prominently in manufacturing employment. Half of all women in the (officially) registered labour force were engaged in agriculture, another third in paid household or domestic service, and no more than a sixth in manufacturing, trade, commerce and transport – 1.4 million of the total female labour force of 8.2 million in 1882. But while bourgeois moralists preached the virtues of domestic economy to proletarian women, working-class wives were actually working much more than the statistics suggest. In addition to household labour performed, of course, without servants, they made an essential contribution to family budgets by sewing at home on piece rates, cleaning, taking in laundry and ironing, delivering milk and bread, or taking in lodgers. This work remained largely invisible to statisticians. The working-class family differed from the families of peasants or outworkers because it was not a unit of production; but it differed from the bourgeois family even more because of the demands made on all of its members as a result of material shortages, insecurity and lack of leisure.

A distinctive working-class life cycle can be discerned in this period. The working life began at around age fifteen (child labour was insignificant after mid-century except, unpaid, in agriculture), and earnings reached their maximum in the second half of a worker's twenties, coinciding with marriage and beginning a family; they then stayed on a plateau before declining from the age of forty. There were some variations – the earnings of the unskilled began to decline earlier, those of skilled workers like turners and locksmiths later. Household income was also boosted during the years when working children still lived at home, before leaving to begin their own families. But for all, the poverty of old age was the great problem, and old age began very early by our standards, or even measured against the standards of the decades before the First World War. Workers were often physically broken by their forties; widows made up the largest single group of the very poor. Sickness and health were significantly determined by class position. Even relations with doctors were different. Medical men were more likely to be curt in manner towards working-class patients, with whom they seldom enjoyed a family-doctor relationship. The growing insistence of the nineteenth-century medical profession on the authority of the doctor – he issued the 'orders', the patient was expected to 'obey' – had a clear class dimension that translated into didactic, even hectoring attitudes towards the lower classes. Bourgeois families might receive advice about the virtues of a holiday in the mountains; workers, when they saw a doctor at all, were more likely to hear a lecture about their insanitary living conditions or diet.[36] Once again, working-class perceptions of the world, as well as the brute facts of everyday life, created a consciousness of belonging to us, not them.

Contacts with the state had the same effect, helping to forge a working-class identity. Trade unions, like other forms of labour organization, were viewed with hostility by the authorities and widely suppressed in the 1850s. The right to combine was generally ceded during the liberal 1860s and established in the North German Confederation in 1869 (in Austria a year later). But there was heavy, one-sided state intervention in the many strikes of the 1860s and early 1870s, and official suspicion was always latent.[37] It was directed at unions, friendly societies and educational associations, even those that formally eschewed politics, as well as the two working-class parties founded in the 1860s – Ferdinand Lassalle's General Union of German Workers (1863), and the Social Democratic Workers' Party of August Bebel and Wilhelm Liebknecht. Just three years after these had combined to form the Social Democratic Party of Germany (SPD), the antisocialist law of 1878 outlawed the new party. Trade unions and other labour organizations were caught up in the repression. All of this created an understandable sense among workers that they were being persecuted simply for seeking what was fair, or even for pursuing self-improvement. Beyond instances of obvious political persecution, this perception was reinforced by a frequently one-eyed system of justice and the heavy-handedness with which working-class popular recreations were policed, in the name of safety, hygiene or a cause like animal welfare.

The tendency towards a separating out of classes is clear enough in this period, but classes are never neatly demarcated. It is characteristic that workers' education associations often recruited a mixture of workers, small independent artisans and sympathetic professionals. As we have seen, there were divisions within all classes relating to market position, different levels of skill or status, age and life cycle. And there were other cleavages and identities that could cut across those of class: regional, urban-rural, religious denomination, gender. One of the most important lessons from the shift in historical perspectives during the last decade or so is the recognition that classes cannot and should not be taken for granted. They are constructs, not flesh-and-blood realities waiting to become aware of themselves. And the consciousness of being a bourgeois, or a worker, was not necessarily prior to, or superior to, the consciousness of being a woman, or a Catholic, or a Bavarian. When that has been said, however, it remains the case that class, as a matter both of objective criteria and of self-labelling, was a more powerful binding – and dividing – element in German society by the end of the 1870s than it had been a generation earlier. And the many other identities through which Germans of the period defined themselves could, and did, reinforce the structures of class. The gender-divide in bourgeois life was fundamental: the roles assigned to men and women helped to constitute the bourgeoisie as a class. Religious loyalties could equally strengthen working-class solidarity if the employer was of a different denomination, usually where Catholic workers faced Protestant bosses. These and other forms of self-identification, including political affiliations, were frequently intertwined with class identity. They were a part of, not apart from, the more class-based society that was now emerging.

CHAPTER FIVE

From Reaction to Unification

The Age of Reaction and the New Era

A period of reaction began in autumn 1848 that lasted for ten years. It stamped German politics during the 1850s. In August 1851 the reconstituted German Confederation issued its Reactionary Resolution, but even before then the course had been set in many states. The 1848 constitutions were withdrawn or unilaterally revised by rulers, liberal ministers dismissed and conservatives installed, parliaments limited in their powers and electoral systems restricted, bureaucracies purged. Where former revolutionaries had not already fled to Brussels, Basel or America, they were – like other suspected oppositional elements – subjected to surveillance. Outweighing the element of revenge in all this was the fear that revolution would break out again unless political life was rigidly controlled. Here, on the face of it, was another cycle of repression like the period following the Carlsbad Decrees and the revolutionary unrest of 1830–2. The parallels were certainly not lost on contemporaries. But rulers and ministers in the 1850s were even less able than their predecessors to turn the clock back. In many cases they were also less willing. The 1850s remain less well studied than most decades, but the evidence suggests that the forces of order had learnt lessons from the revolution, that they were starting to adopt a different and more modern idiom. This had already been signalled by the attitudes of conservatives like Brandenburg in Prussia and Schwarzenberg in Austria during the latter stages of the revolution. The repression of the 1850s could be harsh, but this was no rerun of the age of Metternich. That is one reason why the period of reaction gave way relatively soon, in the late 1850s, to the political thaw known as the New Era.

The timing of the reaction was not uniform. In most German states, including Prussia and Austria, the decisive changes came in 1849–51, although in Prussia the constitutional revisions extended through to 1854. In other states, among them Bavaria and Hanover, the real shift did not come until the middle of the 1850s. The clampdown also varied in intensity. It was more severe in Austria than in Prussia, most severe in several of the medium-sized and small states: Saxony, Hanover, Thuringia, Hesse-Darmstadt, Hesse-Nassau. That was where the swings between revolution and reaction had also been most violent before 1848. In the historically less authoritarian south, Baden generally remained more liberal than Bavaria or Württemberg; but if there was a geographical pattern to reaction, it was more east-west than north-south, with authority being reasserted more strenuously in eastern areas. Predictably, constitutional forms and political life were most frozen in the two Mecklen-burgs. But there were exceptions to this rule of thumb: few states in the Confederation were more completely stifled by reaction than Hesse-Darmstadt, under its ruler Ludwig III and his long-serving chief minister Dalwigk.

On what institutions did the reaction rest, what principles did it espouse? After the ignominies of 1848, there was a clear reassertion of princely authority, varying in tone from the impatience of King William with the Württemberg parliament to the flights of fantasy about God-given monarchy indulged in by the increasingly unstable Frederick William IV of Prussia. Hanover's George V ruled without a constitution after 1855; so did the new young emperor Francis Joseph of Austria after issuing his New Year's Eve Patent in December 1851, which withdrew the (imposed) constitution of 1849. Even before that the principle of ministerial responsibility had been disavowed, and the ministers' political influence replaced by a circle of reactionary advisors around the emperor. Thereafter the conscientious but rigid Francis Joseph sought to rule personally under a system of so-called neoabsolutism. Despite this important exception, most German princes in the 1850s ruled constitutionally, including Frederick William IV – even if he advised his younger brother, the later régent and King William I, not to manacle himself by swearing allegiance to the Prussian constitution of 1850. However much Frederick William might have dreamed of it, encouraged by reactionary courtiers like Leopold von Gerlach, the unbridled exercise of the monarchical will was a nonstarter in Prussia and most other Confederation states.

The same was true of the parallel ambition harboured by men like Gerlach and the Prussian ultras, to return to a corporatist system and restore substantial noble privileges. In many ways, Prussia provides the benchmark of how far it was possible to go in this direction – and where the limits lay. There is no doubt that the Prussian nobility did claw back real privileges. The district and provincial estates, symbols of everything the *Vormärz* opposition hated, were restored in 1851, in violation of the constitution. In the following years legislation was passed on several issues dear to the hearts and pocketbooks of Junker nobles, including the right to entail their estates and to continue administering local justice as a kind of estate management. And when a Prussian upper house of parliament with powers of veto was created in 1854, it lived up to its name as a House of Lords for its composition was, and remained, overwhelmingly aristocratic. Yet the process of recasting noble privilege had definite limits. There was no going back on the legal disappearance of the nobility as an 'estate', that is, on equality before the law; nor was there any question of undoing peasant emancipation. One important symbol of this was the survival of the hunting laws passed during the revolution, which abolished seigneurial privilege by prohibiting hunting on the property of third parties. Hence the aristocratic mutterings about the 'black year' of 1848, and the horror stories that spread in their circles about hunts in which every Tom, Dick and Harry took part and 'the dogs of the dilettantes' ripped open young and pregnant animals for the approval of their vulgar masters.[1] The hyperbole of such accounts signified a real sense of loss. Finally, there were limits to the restoration of noble influence at the political level. The aristocratic Camarilla associated with the Gerlach brothers and the *Kreuzzeitung* newspaper was just one group among others in a faction-ridden court and its overtures were mostly snubbed by Manteuffel, Prussian prime minister from 1850–8 (nicknamed 'Fra Diavolo' by his conservative opponents). The restored provincial estates were more marginal now that a state-wide parliament existed, and that parliament in turn was far from being an instrument of the nobility. The upper house was an aristocratic bastion: the lower house was not.

This issue is so important for our understanding not just of the era of reaction, but of the future shape of German politics, that some detail is necessary. The notorious Prussian three-class franchise of 1849, which survived down to 1918, divided the population into three groups according to wealth and gave equal electoral weight to each. This meant that electors of the minority classes I and II had twice as much influence on the composition of the lower house as all the rest – the three-quarters or more of the population relegated to the third class. It was grotesquely inequitable, but it was a suffrage based on tax returns and the reactionary bugbear of 'head-counting', not on the corporate principles the aristocratic ultras favoured. Contrary to what is often assumed, the three-class suffrage was modelled on the local franchise arrangements in the more advanced western provinces of Prussia, not on something dreamed up by the east Elbian squirearchy.[2] Its shortcomings owed as much to Rhenish merchants as it did to diehard Junkers, although the system of open voting certainly favoured noble landowners in the east. For all the benefits gained by Prussian nobles during the 1850s, the system of reaction was not synonymous with their corporate interests. And what was true of Prussia was true elsewhere. The personal-feudal style of Francis Joseph in Austria should not divert attention from the fact that the centralizing tendency of neoabsolutism ran counter to the interests of the nobility.

The churches were also ambiguous allies of the reaction. In the Protestant church, riven by internal differences in the 1840s, the more conservative, orthodox voices were favoured by reactionary regimes in the following decade. This applied to Mecklenburg, Bavaria and Hesse-Kassel as much as Prussia. Rulers saw the church as a bulwark against sinful revolution; high churchmen were happy to accept an alliance of throne and altar that gave them the opportunity to settle accounts with liberal theologians and the advocates of synodal government. The church-state partnership came about on different terms in the Catholic case. Reactionary regimes aimed to win the support of the church in the fight against revolution by allowing it more latitude in matters like education, the training and appointment of clergy, and internal church affairs. The most obvious example was in Austria, where Josephinist ideas of state control over the church gave way to greater autonomy and favoured status, marked by the concordat with Rome in 1855. Several south German states also signed concordats and followed a similar policy. In Hesse-Darmstadt there was particularly close cooperation between the reactionary Dalwigk government and the clerical establishment in Mainz, headed by Bishop Ketteler. In Protestant states with a significant Catholic minority, like Württemberg and Prussia, relations between state and Catholic church also improved in the 1850s. The church enjoyed a greater degree of independence under the Prussian constitution of 1850, more funds were released for Catholic church building, and teaching orders like the Jesuits and Redemptorists were now permitted to hold popular missions on Prussian soil, something that would have been unthinkable before the revolution.[3] For their part, Catholic bishops warned their flocks against the immorality of social upheaval. The common front of church and state against revolution was a key element of the age of reaction. But it was not without difficulties. On the Protestant side, conservative high-church orthodoxy could be counter-productive as liberal churchmen refused to be intimidated out of existence. Concordats with the Catholic church also antagonized non-Catholic opinion, while closer state-church relations were never more than a tactical accommodation. Many sources of friction remained, especially at local level, and the apparent identity of interests disguised genuinely different aims. Even reactionary ministers wanted the bishop to be a prefect in purple: the tradition of what was known in Bavaria as the 'royal priest' and in Nassau as the 'ducal deacon' died hard. But when Christoph Moufang, regent of the powerful seminary in Mainz, observed that 'the priest can do more than the police', he was actually staking a claim to church autonomy that sat uneasily with the interests of the state.[4]

The chief instrument of the reaction, setting the tone of the 1850s everywhere, was the state's own bureaucracy. We have already seen how powerfully the idea of the state developed before 1848: now the administrative machinery started to match the idea. Austria's centralizing officials became known as the 'Bach hussars', after minister of the interior Alexander Bach. The Prussian regime of the 1850s was bureaucratic-statist under Manteuffel, himself a former minister of the interior. Bureaucracies expanded and became more efficient; liberal elements were purged from field administrations, judiciary and teaching institutions. From Saxony to Baden, university professors were once again sacked on political grounds. Even railway and postal officials came under political pressure. Local officials were expected to manage elections (gerrymandered boundaries helped them), and reliable officials themselves formed a major bloc in many pliant state parliaments. They accounted for 61 per cent of all deputies in the so-called Prussian 'Landrat chamber' of 1855. Police and security forces became more formidable. Revamped, quasi-military gendarmeries operated in both the major German states, and improved systems of surveillance were established. The Police Association of the More Important German States was a more successful agency for cooperation among state security forces than anything that existed before 1848. Regular meetings, weekly reports and telegraphic communications allowed the coordinated surveillance of press and opposition. This was counter-insurgency with a modern face: when the Italian revolutionary Mazzini was suspected of being on German soil in 1858, a large-scale search was mounted in Württemberg which included the mass dissemination of 'wanted' photographs.[5] In Prussia, even the Koblenz court of Crown Prince William was subject to surveillance. Prime Minister Manteuffel himself was caught up in a scandal after trying to acquire the papers of an ultra opponent by bribing the man's servant through a shady intermediary. Exemplifying all this was Carl von Hinckeldey, Berlin police chief from 1848 until his death in an 1856 duel, whose spy system, identity checks, press seizures and deportations became notorious.[6]

Armies, the saviours of order in the revolution, had a special place in the reaction. Martial law continued in parts of the Austrian empire until 1854, and the Prussian constitution of 1850 contained detailed plans to divide the country into districts under military jurisdiction in the event of serious civic unrest. When the Vienna Ringstrasse was being planned, the army urged that the *glacis* beyond the old walls be retained as a bulwark against the proletarian menace beyond: its views were accommodated in the convenient siting of barracks in the eventual plan. Armies were the reserve instrument for the preservation of order, and enjoyed favoured status. The Austrian Supreme Army Command asserted its independence from civilian control; the Prussian army was not bound by the constitution or subject to parliamentary scrutiny. In both cases, senior soldiers had the ear of the monarch.

This was the uncomplicated, repressive side of reaction. But there was another side: bureaucracy wielded a carrot as well as a stick. An example is the way in which, during the 1850s, German states established press offices under their ministers of the interior, designed to promote favourable news reporting. Here we see the more flexible, modern side of German conservatism, as it tried to apply the lessons of the revolution by building consent. Take the peasantry, which now became the darling of conservatives, from the writer Wilhelm Heinrich Riehl to the ambitious young diplomat Otto von Bismarck, as a 'loyal' class. Rural land banks and other state agencies were set up to bolster these supposedly conservative instincts. Similar efforts were made to woo craftsmen with cheap credit. This approach extended to the lower orders in the towns, as the factory legislation of the period indicates. In Prussia, Hinckeldey used his wide powers as Berlin chief of police to establish a fire department, open public baths, plant trees, improve municipal street-cleaning and press for a better water supply. There are obvious parallels here with Hinckeldey's opposite number in France, Baron Haussmann, the Emperor Napoleon III's Prefect of the Seine, who was responsible both for public order in Paris and for the large-scale rebuilding of the city.[7] But the chief beneficiaries of recast cities – Berlin and Vienna as much as Paris – were the middle classes, and it was they whose political grievances were most likely to be blunted by economic prosperity. Governments certainly acted on that basis, for the political purging of bureaucracies by no means purged them of officials committed to economically progressive measures. It is striking how reactionary regimes of the 1850s fostered industry and sought to modernize the infrastructure, all in the name of social stability. Even in Austria, neoabsolutism was accompanied by liberal commercial policies, enthusiastic railway building and a new industrial code in 1859. Conversely, there is no doubt that bourgeois energies were channelled into activities other than politics, such as the railway committee or chamber of commerce.

Some have seen this as a middle-class willingness to take the money and run, the classic by-product of a depoliticized decade. There is some truth in this. Businessmen took care of business; professional organizations flourished while political life stagnated. But the argument should not be overdone. The material changes that gathered pace in the 1850s could not be so easily compartmentalized. The railway, for example, carried a heavy symbolic weight as a symbol of 'progress' and 'improvement' (see the following chapter). It was not devoid of political implications, and these were broadly liberal. The demand of lawyers for legal codification on a German-wide basis was also implicitly political. As in the *Vormärz* period, organizations like choral societies and shooting clubs were tinged with liberal-nationalist sentiment. German workers' mobility also made it practically impossible to clamp down on all their organizations, such as friendly societies; and these were the basis on which a more openly political labour movement was built in the 1860s. In these and other ways, more was going on politically during the era of reaction than meets the eye. Even at the formal, institutional level, political life was not snuffed out as it had been during earlier bouts of repression. Despite an authoritarian executive, managed elections, a cramped debating chamber and poorly reported deliberations, the Prussian parliament did meet and the habits of constitutional politics started to form.[8] The new era at the end of the 1850s did not drop out of a blue sky.

Nevertheless, the tempo of German political life quickened perceptibly after 1858. William I finally became regent in Prussia, carrying with him the weight of liberal hopes so often invested in a crown prince (Frederick William IV had shouldered a similar burden of expectation in 1840). The new ruler broke with the overt supporters of reaction, appointed moderate conservative ministers and loosened the authoritarian grip on public life. With electoral manipulation relaxed, liberals flooded into parliament at the 1858 election on an increased turn-out. This was a time of liberal revival across the Confederation, marked by a resurgent press, meetings and great electoral victories from Saxony to the southern states. In Austria, military and financial reverses led to the winding up of neoabsolutism, the granting of a constitution, and the introduction of a parliament with limited powers. This parliament, like the Vienna city council, promptly became a liberal bulwark.

Who were the German liberals ten years after the revolution, and what did they stand for? In many ways they resembled their predecessors in 1848–9. Often they were the same men, coming out of political cold storage or, in some cases, returning cautiously from exile. This was largely a movement of the propertied and educated middle classes, lawyers, academics, officials and businessmen, although it included a significant sprinkling of liberal nobles, and its activists stretched down into the ranks of primary school teachers and tradesmen. As a broad oppositional current of the late 1850s and early 1860s, liberalism enjoyed cross-class support. In Berlin the movement had overwhelming backing from entrepreneurs, but was also supported by the most politically conscious workers, including printers and engineering workers. And there were many constituencies in states across the Confederation where liberal candidates could count on the

votes of craftsmen and peasants, despite conservative efforts to
woo these groups. Liberal attitudes to its potential popular base
varied. The right wing, heirs to the moderate constitutionalists
of the revolution, believed that public life should be the preserve
of those with property and education. They welcomed the
indirect voting and other franchise restrictions that served as
buffers between the political class and the people. Theirs was
a 'politics of notables' (*Honoratiorenpolitik*): they were deeply
suspicious of the masses, considering them lacking in independence (a key liberal concept) and therefore too easily led by
demagogues of left or right. As in 1848–9, however, there was
a more radical strain of liberalism. Many called themselves
democrats, and their rhetoric was very different – they were the
'friends of the people' and claimed to do 'everything for the
people and with the people'. Here we find a greater willingness
to hold popular meetings, set up associations and organize petitions. But there were still limits on this appeal to the masses.
The radical slogans of left liberalism were diffuse; they did not
necessarily imply a commitment to popular sovereignty, or even
the abolition of class-franchises like the one that elected the
Prussian lower house.[9] Even those who advocated universal manhood suffrage were wary. One of them, the left-liberal
cooperative organizer Hermann Schulze-Delitzsch, warned
about popular 'passions': the 'unbound beast', once aroused,
would 'tear everything apart with its lion claws'.[10]

Liberal views on voting rights are illuminated by their attitudes towards female suffrage. Women such as Louise Otto and
Hedwig Dohm were calling for the vote, although the women's
associations that emerged in the 1860s did not make this a
central concern. Only in the labour movement was there support
for female suffrage, and even it fudged the issue to hide internal
disagreements. Liberals opposed any such demands. Sometimes
their views resembled those of conservatives: enfranchising
women would subvert the family. At other times they betrayed
distinctively liberal concerns: that women would be the
cat's-paws of priests, for example. All their arguments reveal how
liberals conceived of citizenship: women were too emotional and

incapable of 'logical reasoning' (Sybel); they did not perform military service, or possess adequate education, or create taxable wealth. In short, women did not qualify for the vote because this right (or privilege, as right-wing liberals thought of it) had to be earned by particular activities and achievements. Liberal attitudes towards the female half of humanity therefore tell us much about their difficulties with male suffrage, too. As conservatives gleefully chided left-wing liberals: how could they accept the case for excluding all women from the vote, yet agree to enfranchise ignorant or impoverished men?[11]

Liberals believed in individual effort and accomplishment, in progress and enlightenment. They wanted a society of citizens, liberalized economic institutions, the rule of law, freedom of association and assembly, parliaments with real powers, and some measure of ministerial responsiveness to the legislature, although not necessarily a fully-blown system of parliamentary government. There were very few republicans, fewer than in 1848–9. These were the demands of mid-century, educated by the experience of the 1850s. Economic advance sharpened the demand for the final removal of old constraints on trade, while generating calls for policies on credit, cooperatives and education that would tame the 'raw instincts of the masses' (Hermann Baumgarten) and produce a more harmonious society.[12] The police scandals, censorship and electoral chicanery of the 1850s reinforced a long-standing concern with the rule of law. These were familiar liberal issues. Another important element in the liberal revival was novel to the 1850s. Religious reaction created a backlash. In the New Era liberals enunciated their own brand of Protestantism by founding the German Protestant Association in the early 1860s. There was an even more vigorous liberal response to the cooperation of reactionary regimes with the Catholic church: concordats in Austria and the south German states helped to fuse liberal opposition in the second half of the 1850s. The situation was complicated by the fact that many Catholics themselves, from the Prussian Rhineland to Württemberg, still gave their votes to liberal oppositional movements. Nevertheless, German liberalism was starting to become more closely identified with Protestantism and anticlericalism. It was an association that fed off the reactionary policy being pursued in Rome by Pope Pius IX, and it became closer in 1864, when the pope (in the Syllabus of Errors) hurled his anathemas against 'progress, liberalism and modern civilization'.[13] Liberal hostility to the Catholic church was coloured by events in Italy, where the Vatican stood out against the creation of a nation-state. Closer to home, the association of liberalism with Protestantism and dislike of the Catholic church was fuelled by the re-emergence of the 'German question', for liberalism and nationalism were closely intertwined.

The revolutions of 1848–9 had brought the question of German unity to the forefront. Thereafter, dynastic conflict within the Confederation could no longer ignore the nationalist agenda. Frederick William IV's refusal of the German crown in 1849 dashed nationalist hopes in the short term, however, and the two major German powers worked in parallel to crush the revolution. Freed from the interference of upstart revolutionaries, Prussia and Austria continued their great-power rivalry by more traditional means – diplomacy, alliances, and threats of war. During 1849–50, under the leadership of prime minister Radowitz, Berlin tried to organize a German Union headed by Prussia. It attracted moderate liberal support, but antagonized Prussian conservatives and failed to sustain the initial support of the other German monarchies (Bavaria, Württemberg, Saxony, Hanover), who backed away one by one. Austria, confident after finally defeating the Hungarian insurgents, played on the anti-Prussian fears of the 'third Germany' and called the Prussian bluff by adopting a belligerent posture. Faced with the prospect of war, very real in autumn 1850, Prussia backed down as conservatives won the upper hand in Berlin and Radowitz was forced from office. In November 1850 Prussia and Austria signed an agreement at Olmütz which restored the looser German Confederation of 1815. Deplored by later German nationalist historians as a betrayal of Prussia's 'German mission', Olmütz was no more than a truce in the conflict between the two major German states.

That conflict was played out during the 1850s at three levels. First, at a time when everyone recognized the growing importance of economics for great-power status, Austria tried to establish a Central European Customs Union that would merge with the Prussian-dominated *Zollverein* and dilute Prussian leadership within the German trade area. Here it could play on the independence and resentments of the third Germany. But Prussia blocked Austrian entry into the *Zollverein* and used its economic muscle to hold the smaller states in line. Secondly, Austria and Prussia crossed swords in the German Confederation over matters both substantive and symbolic. Austria sought to strengthen the Confederation, assert its own hegemony within it, and stifle Prussian ambitions; Prussia insisted on the equality of the two German powers and blocked any move to strengthen the Confederation at its own expense. The states of 'middle Germany' were pawns in this game, too. Finally, the Confederation was not only a forum within which German domestic arrangements were haggled over, but a body whose members pledged nominal assistance to each other in European affairs. The outbreak of hostilities in any European trouble spot was therefore likely to have an impact on German concerns, confronting Austria and Prussia with difficult decisions, but also providing the opportunity to score political points over one's rival. At each of these levels – economics, domestic politics, foreign policy – nationalist opinion was a presence German rulers could not ignore, and to which they might potentially appeal.

The first major European conflict of the postrevolutionary period, the Crimean War of 1854–6, broke open the German question. It was then, not in 1848–9, that the international order established in 1815 broke down, with major implications for the future shape of Germany. When France and Britain went to war to block Russian ambitions in the declining Ottoman empire, the two German powers were internally divided over how to respond, torn between neutrality and intervention. Austria engaged itself more actively, but was more damaged by the outcome. By supporting the western powers belatedly and haltingly to try and control the war, Austria antagonized Russia without gaining the gratitude of France or Britain. Even writers sympathetic to the Austrian position recognize that this was Vienna's last, unavailing attempt to perform the role of 'stage manager' in a concert of Europe that now disappeared.[14] Prussia remained neutral and strengthened its position with the smaller German states, painting Austria disingenuously as a warmonger trying to force Confederation members into a conflict on the side of 'anti-German' France. The aftermath of the Crimean war threatened Austria with diplomatic isolation, and began to stir greater public interest in the German question.

Events in Italy in 1859 had a more direct impact. The Kingdom of Piedmont, backed by France, went to war over the Habsburg possessions in northern Italy and forced Austria, after defeats at Magenta and Solferino, to cede the province of Lombardy. This was not just an Austrian military disaster, but widely viewed as a German humiliation. It reinforced the view of those German nationalists who argued that the Habsburg power was rotten within, and that German unification – like Italian unification – would only be brought about by the exclusion of Austria. The same year, 1859, saw the founding of the National Association, an organization primarily of the German middle classes, loosely modelled on the Italian National Society, and committed to fostering a lesser-German, Prussian-led solution to the problem of unity. The National Association never had more than 25,000 members, but they were influential men in the universities and professions, the liberal movement and the burgeoning big-city press. The widespread centenary celebrations of Schiller's birth in 1859 reflected the views of this important segment of opinion – nationalist, sympathetic to Prussia as the trustee of 'German culture', and strongly tinged with Protestantism. Had not Schiller himself written in 1804 that Berlin was destined to become 'the capital of Protestantism'?[15]

It would be easy to see this as the writing on the wall for Austria – but wrong. We should not assume that Prussian leadership was inevitable, as nationalist historians like Sybel, Droysen and Treitschke did. Austria was still considered a natural part of Germany by most Germans who thought about the question. Not only did high conservatives want to preserve the status quo, and Catholics to prevent a Protestant-dominated lesser Germany: family-feeling for Austria extended to many liberal and democratic nationalists. The German question remained an open question, and the turbulent events of 1859 cut two ways. Austria not only escaped with limited losses, but could point a finger at the Prussian failure to support its German ally, for Berlin had hung back in the hope of gaining a decisive advantage from the Italian imbroglio, only to find the fighting over before it could intervene. This could be plausibly painted by Vienna as unheroic and self-serving. While some on the left like Bamberger and Lassalle were certainly pushed towards Prussia by events in 1859, others refused to see the diplomatic and military triumph of Napoleon III in Italy as a cause for German rejoicing. On the contrary, it was – in the words of Friedrich Engels – necessary 'to defend the Rhine on the Po'.[16] This, Prussia had conspicuously failed to do. Finally, as always, the states of the third Germany were nervous of any tilt of the balance of power within the Confederation that would send them sliding towards Prussia.

At the beginning of the 1860s domestic and international politics within the German Confederation were delicately poised, and the two were closely interconnected. Internally, regimes faced with revived liberal demands took their cue from the new course set in Prussia after 1858. Conservatism was moderated in Saxony, as it was in Austria. The Bavarian king dismissed the chief minister of the reactionary era and chose cooperation rather than confrontation with the liberal majority in parliament. In Württemberg there was a similar move towards conciliation, although not yet towards the major reforms of justice and administration that would be passed later in the decade. Neighbouring Baden, on the other hand, now acquired the reputation it would retain until 1918 as the major German laboratory for constitutional experimentation. The grand duke brought moderate liberals into government, one of them even heading the sensitive ministry of the interior. Liberalism became the 'governing party' (Lothar Gall) in alliance with an enlightened state bureaucracy, even if this arrangement fell short of full parliamentary government and was eventually undermined by divisions between liberals and regime.[17] Taking the Confederation as a whole, we find an impressive number of openings towards a more liberal, or at least more conciliatory course. But the most important development of these years – for contemporaries as well as historians equipped with hindsight – occurred in Prussia. This was where the New Era had begun; but crown and parliament soon found themselves engaged in a conflict that would have decisive consequences for German as well as Prussian history.

William I did not share his brother's taste for extravagant pronouncements about divine kingship, but he was stubbornly conservative when it came to preserving Hohenzollern authority. In spring 1848 he had been the most hard-line member of the family, the advocate of a military solution, and in 1849 he had led the Prussian army into Baden. Neither his brief sojourn in England nor his experiences in the 1850s turned him into a liberal. He still saw the Prussian army as the bedrock of the monarchical state, and looked to strengthen it. In 1860 his new Minister of War, Albrecht von Roon, a comrade-at-arms from 1849, introduced a bill into parliament that would expand the standing army, increase the period of service from two to three years, and reduce the role played by the reserve, or militia. This proved understandably provocative to a liberal opposition that had, until then, fought shy of pressing its programme too hard, for fear of frightening William back into the reactionary camp. While there was general agreement about the need for military reform, Roon's bill touched a number of sensitive nerves. It raised questions of cost, but that was not the major sticking point. The extended period of service aroused fears of an army that would become even more a state within a state, a sore point in view of the military role in domestic repression. And the attack on the militia, a favourite liberal offspring of the early nineteenth-century reform era, met with an outraged response. There was certainly room for compromise on the detail, but both sides believed that principles were at stake. William was determined that army matters be kept above parliamentary approval. The liberals, alienated by the violent language of the regime (the army would 'irretrievably rot in the sewer of doctrinaire liberalism', said Roon), stiffened their position and refused to vote a regular budget.[18] In January 1861 a new, more resolute liberal group, the Progressive Party, was created. Following elections in December 1861 it formed the spearhead of a large liberal majority. When the deadlock continued, William appointed a reactionary ministry and dissolved parliament in March 1862, but the liberal opposition emerged from the ensuing May elections with three-quarters of the seats.

We know how the 'constitutional conflict' ended: the liberals lost, and the unification of Germany transformed domestic politics. The temptation of hindsight is to play down the contemporary seriousness of the crisis, a tendency already apparent in the liberal politicians whose later respectability led them to suppress their fire-eating days. Unruh and Miquel ordered their correspondence to be destroyed; Reyscher's memoirs stopped in 1862 and picked up again in 1866; others wrote a sanitized version of events. But this was a major power struggle, and the liberal opposition was hardly timid. Official receptions and communal politics were boycotted in a campaign of passive resistance. Electoral committees were formed, political banquets held, processions and meetings arranged. This was reminiscent of 1848–9. So were the demonstrative steamship journeys on the Rhine organized by the Rhenish and Westphalian Progressive deputies, which were greeted by flags, saluting guns and waving crowds on both banks.[19] As in spring 1848, the authorities were nervous and half-heartedly repressive. It was no doubt an exaggeration to proclaim, as a liberal newspaper in Frankfurt did, that Prussia would soon be 'ripe for revolution'.[20] The Progressive leadership tried to avoid provocation, and was ultimately more concerned to keep the right and left wings of the liberal opposition together by blurring its programme than it was to mobilize craftsmen and workers for a frontal assault on the Prussian state. Yet the political atmosphere was uncertain and highly charged.

While William faced a prolonged constitutional crisis at home, Prussia found itself facing a renewed challenge over the German question from Austria and the smaller German states. By 1862, under the new political course set in Vienna, constitutionalism was clearly operating better in Austria than in Prussia. The point was not lost on men like Austrian interior minister Schmerling, who looked to bolster Vienna's reputation within the Confederation and retake the initiative in German affairs. The early 1860s provided two major opportunities to do so. When Saxony proposed a plan for a stronger Confederation, the hard-line Prussian response allowed Austria to play on the fears of the third Germany and line up almost all of the smaller states behind its own version of a reformed Confederation. This conflict came to a head in August 1862, when Prussia was isolated in the diet. The Prussian position in German affairs was simultaneously threatened by renewed conflict over trade policy. In March 1862, Prussia concluded negotiations with France over a trade treaty, designed to prevent any future Austrian efforts to join the *Zollverein*. But the strategy backfired as Austria encouraged the opposition to the treaty of the smaller states in the Customs Union. This conflict also came to a head in August 1862, as Bavaria and Württemberg rejected the French trade treaty and Austria looked to gather support from other states for its old idea of a central European customs union.

With the *Zollverein* apparently in jeopardy, against the background of a two-pronged Austrian counteroffensive over the German question, Prussia appeared to be boxed in. Domestically, too, William I had little room for manoeuvre. Ruling out capitulation to the liberal opposition, or a coup, he thought seriously about abdicating, but was dissuaded by Crown Prince Frederick. It was in these circumstances that, in September 1862, Otto von Bismarck was appointed Prussian prime minister.

The Making of a United Germany

Nine years and three wars later, the German Confederation was dead, Austria had been excluded from German affairs, and a united Germany established under Prussian auspices. William I became Emperor of Germany, Bismarck Imperial Chancellor. The European balance of power and German domestic politics were transformed as Germany was unified 'from above'. How and why had this sea-change occurred?

The sequence of events can be briefly recounted. While constitutional deadlock continued in Prussia, a crisis arose over the duchies of Schleswig and Holstein, disputed between Denmark and the Confederation, and already a hot issue for Danish and German nationalist movements. When the Danish king died in 1863, a succession dispute led the following year to intervention by Prussian and Austrian troops, who defeated Danish forces and arranged to administer the duchies jointly. Bismarck then applied pressure on Austria. The smaller German states were forced by Prussia to renew the *Zollverein*, thus excluding Austria economically from Germany, and the Gastein Convention of 1865 divided the administration of Schleswig-Holstein between the two powers, creating new points of friction that Prussia could exploit. After intricate negotiations designed to weaken Vienna's position, Bismarck proposed a radical reshaping of the Confederation that would exclude Austria and make Prussia the undisputed master of northern Germany. This provoked war with Austria, which was backed by most of the 'third Germany' and all the other German monarchies (Saxony, Hanover, Bavaria, Württemberg) in defence of the Confederation. Prussian victory at Königgrätz in July 1866 led to the Prussian annexation of substantial north German territory and the creation of a North German Confederation the following year, with a parliament elected by universal manhood suffrage but essential elements of Prussian monarchical power still intact.

This was the decisive moment in what we call German unification: a German civil war that led to the partition of Germany and the expulsion of Austria. It was also decisive in domestic political terms. Two months to the day after Königgrätz the Prussian constitutional conflict was resolved when the lower house agreed to 'indemnify' the regime for its four-year breach of the constitution, and the Progressive Party split, as supporters of Bismarck broke away to form the National Liberal Party. The construction of a Prussian-led lesser Germany was completed four years later. The establishment of the North German Confederation left the south German states in limbo. Historically and sentimentally they still looked to Austria; practically, after Königgrätz, they were bound to Prussia by military alliances as well as commercial ties. Bismarck attempted to tighten these links, but when elections were held to a newly established 'Customs' Parliament' in 1868, a southern backlash returned predominantly anti-Prussian deputies, stalling the Berlin initiative and causing political turmoil in Bavaria and Württemberg. The situation was resolved when conflict broke out between Prussia and France, now the major great-power obstacle to the southern states being swallowed up into Lesser Germany. Its immediate cause was another disputed succession. When a Hohenzollern, Prince Leopold, was offered the vacant Spanish throne, France objected and the candidature was withdrawn. But the French overplayed their hand and sought a pledge that the candidature would never be renewed. When Prussia failed to capitulate, France declared war. The southern states honoured their alliances with Berlin in the Franco-Prussian war of 1870–1, and German national sentiment was strongly aroused. Prussian victory was followed by the proclamation of a German Empire at Versailles in January 1871.

Where to begin analysing this cascade of events? I want to start with the larger picture, then turn to the many arguments about the nature of Bismarckian unification. It is worth noting, first, some striking contemporary parallels. The decade of German unification, the 1860s, also saw decisive episodes of nation-building (or rebuilding) elsewhere. In Japan, the Meiji Restoration of 1868 laid the basis of a modern state, against a background of growing national sentiment, argument over sovereignty, and civil war. The Tokugawa regime was not the

German Confederation and the samurai reformers produced no Bismarck, but there are obvious similarities in the pattern of 'revolution from above' and the interplay of domestic and foreign politics. In the USA, during the same years, a civil war was also fought between north and south over the location of sovereignty within a federal system. In America, as in Germany, it was the more economically dynamic north that won – with the major difference that in Germany the north, Prussia, was the secessionist. Finally, and most obviously, the unification of Italy not only occurred at the same time, but was interwoven with developments in Germany. The war of 1859 weakened Austria and brought the German question to a new pitch. Piedmont was a Prussian ally in 1866, opening a second front against Austria in Italy. It proved a military failure, but a political success after Prussia's victory: 1866 excluded Austria from Italy as well as Germany. Prussian defeat of France in 1870–1 then gave Italy the great prize of Rome, previously occupied by French troops. In military and diplomatic terms, therefore, events in Germany and Italy shadowed each other closely. There were also structural similarities, with Piedmont as an Italian Prussia, Cavour as an Italian Bismarck. The latter himself noted this in typically brutal fashion when (in 1869) he likened the 'stubborn, heavy, backward race' of south Germans to the southern Italians, concluding: 'We do not want to have attached to us another Calabria'.[21] The Italian parallel suggests many of the same issues that must be central to any explanation of German unification as an international and domestic phenomenon. It is those issues I turn to now.

Germany was unified as a result of three wars that created a new power in the centre of Europe. Why did the other great powers allow this to come about? An important part of the answer is obviously the success of Prussian arms when put to the test. It cannot be emphasized too much that unification was, in the last resort, achieved on the battlefield. But other elements smoothed the Prussian path to success. Russia had suffered military humiliation in the Crimean war, and was absorbed during the 1860s in a bout of internal reforms. Early Russian indus-

Unified Germany

SWEDEN

Baltic Sea

KLENBURG
:LITZ

West
Prussia

East
Prussia

Posen

Oder

Vistula

RUSSIAN

POLAND

0   50   100   200

miles

Prussia

North German
Confederation and
German Empire

Austria-Hungary

Area incorporated in
North German
Confederation in 1871
to form German Empire

Vienna

Budapest

AUSTRIA - HUNGARY

Danube

trialization also depended on Russo-German trade, and placed a premium on good relations with the emerging German power. Prussian non-participation in the Crimean war had already strengthened its hand in St Petersburg, a favourable disposition that Bismarck cultivated with the Alvensleben Convention of 1863, expressing support for Russia after the Polish uprising that year. All of this outweighed Russian Pan-Slav criticism of the Prusso-German menace. Britain had pressing colonial problems; it was primarily suspicious of French ambitions on the Continent, and viewed the emerging Germany as a power that neither threatened fundamental British interests nor possessed a significant navy. Add to this the general British approval of national self-determination (as in Italy), the high regard for German culture, and Gladstone's concern with domestic issues, and it is clear why British sympathizers comfortably outnumbered those suspicious of Prussian 'militarism'. If we turn to the two powers directly defeated by Prussia on the road to unification, it is their weakness rather than their benevolent neutrality that requires emphasis. Austria was desperately isolated in this period. Vienna had failed to repair the alliance with Russia, broken by the Crimean war; and the great irony of the Austrian position, as well as the central weakness, was the fact that its principal ally, Prussia, was also its archrival in German affairs. Compounding these problems were the perpetual difficulties created by the subject nationalities of the far-flung Habsburg monarchy, Hungarians, Italians and Slavs. This was an important part of the background to 1866; then, during the Franco-Prussian war, the restlessness of the Czechs and Poles pushed Vienna into a more pro-'German' stance. Last, but not least, France under Napoleon III was the loose cannon in European affairs, an adventurist power that excited universal suspicion and found none to mourn its fate in 1870.

This combination of factors favouring German unification was no series of happy accidents. The vulnerability of the European system to Prussian aggrandizement was structural, or systemic. Prussia (like Piedmont) was able to benefit from a period of uncertainty in international relations, a diplomatic interregnum between the breakdown of one system and the advent of another. The equilibrium of the Concert of Europe, based on dynastic legitimacy and the status quo, had disappeared in the Crimea. A new system based on the legitimacy of nation-states, Germany and Italy among them, had yet to emerge. The successes enjoyed by Prussia and Piedmont were simultaneously effect and cause of these shifting ground rules in the great game of European power politics.

Prussia subverted the status quo within Germany as it subverted the international order. The loose Confederation patched back together in 1850 was destroyed: a federal state was established in its place. Generations of Lesser-German historians not only celebrated this achievement but made it seem inevitable. We should resist the temptation to do the same. Recent scholarship has rightly emphasized the open-endedness of the situation, the alternative possibilities.[22] There were other Germanys, just as there were non-'Borussian' historians whose voices became marginalized when they ended on the losing side. The Confederation, precisely because it blurred the issue of ultimate sovereignty, offered many attractions – to the sense of legitimacy and dynastic solidarity among German princes, to the adherents of particularism (and not just in the south), to the 'third Germany' that feared Prussian or Austrian dominance and tried to keep alive the idea of a German 'trias' that would give the smaller states a voice alongside the major powers. Right up to the end the Confederation, like the Holy Roman Empire, attracted plans to reform it. Austria, the advocate of shared sovereignty, presented some of these plans and seized on plans devised by others like the Saxons, just as it played on the fears of the smaller states. It remained a serious player in German affairs. Austria wielded commercial policy as a political weapon, just as Prussia did, and possessed an army that – backed by every major non-Prussian army in the Confederation – was widely expected to prevail in 1866. Had it done so (and it came very close), the Confederation would have been restored.

All this is true. And yet: if the Lesser Germany that came about was not inevitable, it was certainly the least surprising outcome. Even if the Confederation did not lack legitimacy, there was a widespread contemporary sense that it was living on borrowed time after the Olmütz agreement of 1850. The smaller states lacked real independence, as the history of the *Zollverein* showed and the position of the south German states after 1866 confirmed. Their paralysing weaknesses have been noted even by historians who take the 'third Germany' seriously. They quarrelled among themselves and were snubbed over every major issue of the 1850s and 1860s – the Crimea, Schleswig-Holstein, customs, military reform of the Confederation.[23] In the end, the struggle was between Prussian attempts to resume the union policy of 1849–50, which would establish Prussian hegemony in the northern part of a partitioned Germany, and Austrian efforts to block them. In this *pas-de-deux*, the roles were clear: Prussia led and Austria followed. Viewed in terms of resources and circumstances, Prussia was always likely to come out on top. Austria not only had chronic financial problems and non-German distractions; it also lagged well behind Prussia in economic development and institutional modernization, obvious enough in any comparison of the two bureaucracies. Prussian national income increased at twice the rate of Austria's between the 1780s and 1850, and their paths continued to diverge in the following decades. In 1865, Prussia possessed 15,000 steam engines with a total horsepower of 800,000, Austria just 3400 engines with a horsepower of 100,000. This was important for several reasons. It made access to Prussian markets essential for the smaller states, whatever their political sympathies, and gave Prussia a decisive advantage over Austria in the battle of the customs unions. If the 1873 recession had occurred earlier, it might have reduced the advantage that Prussia gained from the weapon of free trade. As things stood, Prussian economic strength translated into monetary dominance, and monetary dominance foreshadowed political union. At a time when material resources increasingly defined great-power status, Berlin clearly had the edge on Vienna. The economist John Maynard Keynes, varying one of Bismarck's most celebrated phrases, once remarked that Prussian success was based, not on blood and iron, but on coal and iron. This had important military consequences, too, demonstrated by Prussia's superior *matériel* and logistical use of the railway.

Just as important, Prussia's economic and social dynamism built up a powerful head of steam behind demands for a German nation, among businessmen, bureaucrats, professors and professionals. These were the men, organized in a handful of interlocked bodies created in 1858-62 – the National Association, the League of German Economists, the National Organization of Chambers of Commerce, the Congress of German Jurists, the German Parliamentarians' Organization – who made up the bourgeois political élite of Germany.[24] By degrees, and often with mixed feelings, these influential sections of opinion came to place their hopes in Prussia as the realistic alternative to what Theodor Mommsen called the 'bankruptcy of particularism'.[25] Austrian statesmen had no such winds at their backs. Compare the 25,000 members of the National Association with the 1500 members of its pro-Austrian counterpart. It is true that, right up to 1866, many German nationalists were reluctant to exclude Austria. Articles in liberal-nationalist encyclopaedias of the early 1860s still looked for reform within the Confederation; those self-proclaimed guardians of Germandom, the choral, gymnastic and shooting societies, still invited Austrians (and Swiss-Germans) to their gatherings.[26] In practice, however, greater-Germany advocates received the cold shoulder from Vienna. Of the two major German powers, only Prussia was seriously bidding for support from organized nationalists, and they increasingly drew the obvious conclusion. Otto Elben, a leading figure in the choral movement, was still speaking in the 1850s about an indivisible Germandom; by the 1860s he was a Bismarck-enthusiast.

Volatile great-power relations, Prussian-Austrian struggle for mastery in Germany, new economic forces and nationalist sentiment – these, together with the constitutional conflict in Prussia, made up the parallelogram of forces within which Bismarck operated after September 1862. That is the context necessary to judge Bismarck's achievements, which were immense but not superhuman. Contemporary historians and countless biographers created the legend of the infallible statesman of genius, far-sighted and resolute, a giant among pygmies. More critical commentators often perpetuated this larger-than-life picture, simply reversing all the moral signs, so that the genius now became the ruthless archmanipulator. Recent works on Bismarck have tended to strike a better balance between the man and his times. To echo Karl Marx, he made history, but not in circumstances of his own choosing. That, emphatically, was Bismarck's own view. One of his favourites among the Latin tags so beloved of contemporaries was *fert unda nec regitur*, which Bismarck rendered as: 'Man cannot create or control the tide of time, he can only move in the same direction and try to direct it.'[27] Again and again, he referred to the stream of history that carries men along with it. This view of life and politics had a strong religious dimension. After a restless, fretful youth, marked by a broken-off career as an official and unhappy love affairs, marriage to the pious Johanna von Puttkamer converted Bismarck to a new and lasting religious faith. He carried devotional books around with him, key passages dutifully underlined, and insisted that mortals could only 'leap in and catch hold of [God's] coat-tail and be dragged along as far as may be'. *That* was 'political wisdom'.[28]

Formulations of this kind can be taken at face value with greater confidence than much of what Bismarck said, especially in the highly unreliable memoirs composed at the end of his life. Yet they reflect only one side of the man and his motives. Just as Bismarck's unusual sensitivity was mixed with coarseness, his classically pure rhetoric punctuated by violent sarcasm, so his genuine piety combined humility and arrogance. The fatalistic strain in his thinking became uppermost only in later years. At the height of his powers, in the 1860s, Bismarck was more inclined to see himself cast by the Almighty as a man of destiny. A failed assassination attempt in 1866 apparently strengthened his belief that he was 'God's chosen instrument'.[29] Immoderate in his appetite for food, drink and tobacco, he was also a man of huge ambition, convinced that he was destined for a great political role.

What background did Bismarck bring to the Prussian prime ministership in 1862, and where did he stand on the great issues of the day? He came from a classic upper-class Prussian family, landowning nobility on one side, bureaucratic service on the other, and first came to prominence at the meeting of the united provincial estates in 1847. After acquiring a name as a violently antirevolutionary spokesman in 1848, Bismarck cemented his reputation as the darling of the right when he supported the Olmütz compromise in a speech widely distributed by conservatives. Through these connections he obtained the post of Prussian envoy to the Confederation diet in Frankfurt. This sounds conventional enough. Nor is there any doubt that Bismarck was fundamentally committed to the untrammelled authority of the Prussian monarchy and army. That was a constant. Yet Bismarck was an unusual and heterodox Junker. An economically successful landowner with conventional prejudices about the superiority of rural life, he was nevertheless easily bored by the company of his fellow-squires and their pursuits. He wrote to his future brother-in-law sarcastically about Pomerania as 'the focal point of European civilization'.[30] Living in Frankfurt for much of the 1850s, Bismarck became familiar with the new economic and social forces at work in Germany, and recognized the need to come to terms with what he once called the era of 'double-entry book-keeping and chemical studies'. In addition to that, his appointment as Prussian envoy came, not after years spent at court or being schooled in state service, but because he had leapt into the spotlight during a revolution. Bismarck was, if not quite a 'professional politician', an almost wholly political animal, lacking the caution or baggage of conventional opinions possessed by most Prussian conservatives.

Already, in the 1850s, he was moving away from orthodox conservative views in two respects. First, he quickly came to the conclusion that Prussia and Austria were set on a collision course. They were breathing the air out of each other's mouths; the Confederation was 'too small for the two of us'; Prussia, in pursuing its interests, should exploit whatever circumstances arose to establish hegemony in Germany.[31] Elements of this view were bound to figure in the thinking of any Prussian policy-maker, but Bismarck expressed his scornful reflections on the Confederation, the smaller states and Austrian diplomats in characteristically unbuttoned terms. His many letters and memoranda were harsh and vivid. This alienated him from former backers among archconservatives, made him an uncomfortable figure for the Prussian government, and led in 1859 to his 'promotion' to the ambassadorship in St Petersburg, away from the centre of things. Secondly, by 1858 at the latest, Bismarck was showing an interest in harnessing the national movement and the more moderately liberal middle classes. Again, this kind of flexibility was not entirely novel. As we have seen, Manteuffel's government in the 1850s was prepared to try to use some of the new forces in post-1848 Prussia. Once again, though, Bismarck put his views with unusual boldness and cynicism. He not only appalled archconservatives like the Gerlachs – they were also appalled by the 'realist' Manteuffel – but caused suspicion throughout Prussian ruling circles. In 1862, when crisis brought him to power, Bismarck was still widely regarded as something of a wild man, outspoken, Machiavellian and reckless.

How he put his ideas into practice after 1862, and the structures within which he worked, have already been described. There was no Bismarckian 'master-plan', only the firm determination to secure Prussia's position in north Germany and maintain the substance of the military monarchy. At the great-power level, Bismarck pressed for advantage when he saw it, but the chief characteristics of his policy were flexibility and the skilful exploitation of opportunities. He always tried to keep alternative strategies in play – in his own metaphor, to use every square on the chessboard. Within that broad framework, Bismarck's policy towards Austria, for all its tactical twists and turns, was more single-mindedly bent on a particular outcome than his policy towards France or the southern states. Nothing is inevitable, but it is hard to see the Gastein Convention as anything other than a truce before the willed conflict of 1866. This was the

Radowitz policy of 1850, except that this time Prussia had a strengthened army and did not draw back from the brink. After the North German Confederation was established, on the other hand, alternative outcomes can be plausibly imagined. France might have accepted some form of territorial 'compensation', rather than lurching into war. For it is now well-established that France bore a large share of responsibility for the 1870–1 hostilities (as virtually all contemporaries believed): it was Bismarck's later boasting about his own cleverness that fed legends to the contrary.[32] Similarly, with Bismarck keen not to press the southern states, and time now on his side, the issue of closer links between the southern states and the North German Confederation might have been deferred until the *Zollverein* came up for renewal in 1877.

For some years, it is the domestic calculations and effects of Bismarck's policy that have dominated historical debate. Neutralizing the liberal opposition, ending the constitutional conflict, preserving the substance of the Prussian political system – these have been seen as crucial to the course of unification. The strong version of this argument presents Bismarck as a Bonapartist. That means, he was willing to break with monarchical legitimacy, balance himself above the social classes, wield the weapon of mass suffrage on behalf of conservative authority, and use foreign policy for domestic purposes.[33] There is some evidence for this view. Like other intelligent conservatives of the period – Constantin Frantz, Hermann Wagener – Bismarck paid close attention to the form of regime developed by Napoleon III in France. He argued against archconservative Ludwig von Gerlach that French Bonapartism put revolutionary principles at the service of the social order. Wagener became a close political ally. Bismarck breached monarchical solidarity in the war with Austria, to nationalist applause, and followed this by introducing universal manhood suffrage over the heads of the liberal opposition. Like Napoleon III, he believed that enfranchising the lower classes would swamp liberalism, as the liberals themselves feared when they accused him of Caesarism, or (in Karl Twesten's words) of 'stirring up the poorer classes against the propertied middle class'.[34] Bismarck also pursued power politics with an eye to public opinion. The war of 1864 was stage-managed for domestic consumption. The occasion in the new Reichstag when the German crown was offered to William I was deliberately dramatized, and when the episode fell flat, Bismarck remarked impatiently that the event 'needed a more skilful stage-manager, there should have been an effective *mise-en-scène*'.[35]

There are, however, serious objections to this argument. The classic Bonapartism thesis, as applied to Napoleon III's France, assumes a 'stalemate' between the social classes and hardly fits the German case. Bismarck's French-style flirtations with public opinion were also interspersed with conventionally conservative actions. He was more fatalistic, more traditionalist, more of a sheer opportunist than the French emperor, seizing whatever weapons came to hand. And, in the end, Bismarck was of course no emperor, but a servant of his prince, William I, even if the relationship between chancellor and king was often different from the one laid down in the constitution. There was a Bonapartist strain in Bismarck's style of politics during the 1860s, but it was one that became most apparent only in later years. In the era of unification, Bismarck was an intelligent and flexible conservative, very aware of liberal-nationalist demands and prepared to play with fire to preserve the essentials of the Prussian military monarchy. It was 'better for Prussia to incur any risks from a foreign enemy than from revolutionary movements in Germany', he told the British ambassador in 1864. Or, again: 'If there is to be a revolution, we want to make it rather than suffer it'.[36] He can perhaps best be summed up, in Lothar Gall's phrase, as a 'white revolutionary'.

What was preserved in this 'revolution from above'? Lesser Germany was, in many respects, a Greater Prussia. Prussia accounted for some 60 per cent of the territory and population of the new Germany. The king of Prussia became German emperor, the prime minister of Prussia became German chancellor, the Prussian army effectively became the German army (despite some concessions to the sensibilities of southern states like Bavaria). Under the constitution of the North German Confederation, the provisions of which were largely carried over into the imperial constitution of 1871, the elected parliament (Reichstag) was subordinate to a Federal Council (*Bundesrat*) of representatives from the individual states, in which Prussia had an effective veto power. Government business was introduced in the Federal Council, not the parliament, and all measures had to have the approval of the Council. The powers of parliament were limited, and the absence of ministerial responsibility was expressly underlined by a clause in the constitution preventing any member of parliament from becoming a minister without first resigning his seat. Following a compromise, members of parliament had the right to approve an annual budget, but this was restricted in the case of military appropriations, which were fixed for several years at a time and linked to the size of the army. There was no compromise over the all-important 'power of command' exercised by the king-emperor over the army. This was left untouched. Other characteristic institutions remained intact within Prussia, the dominant state, including the three-class franchise used to elect the parliament. These arrangements were the fruits of Bismarck's double success in unifying Germany from above and ending the constitutional conflict on his own terms.

Conversely, the liberal opposition suffered key defeats. Unified Germany had a political and institutional shape different from what they would have liked. Partly, as historians have never tired of pointing out, the achievement of 1866 dazzled those who went on to form the National Liberal Party. Before the defeat of Austria, Rudolf von Ihering was 'revolted' by Bismarck's policy: he would prefer to 'cut off my hand than to use it in such a disgusting operation as Prussian policy is now launching against Austria'. Just four months later, after Königgrätz, it was a different story: 'I bow before the genius of Bismarck. . . . He is one of the greatest men of the century'.[37] Similar contortions were performed by other prominent liberals – Baumgarten, Droysen, Sybel – and the cartoons of the liberal press hero-worshipped Bismarck by depicting him as Hercules,

Jupiter, Prometheus, Samson and Atlas. In fact, Karl Twesten proved remarkably prescient when he noted in 1862 that if a Prussian Cavour stepped forward to create unity by violating international law and tearing up treaties, he would not be condemned, but have monuments erected in his honour.[38] Even the less star-struck liberals were forced to recognize that Bismarck's achievements reduced their own room for manoeuvre and threatened to marginalize them. 'Realism', that political keyword of the period, dictated that what could not be changed had to be accepted. As Eduard Lasker said of the indemnity bill, if the liberals rejected it they would be excluding themselves from the unfolding political development in Germany. The alternative to realism, at least in the short term, was the impotence to which the remaining anti-Bismarck liberals were consigned. Worse, in Lasker's view, intransigence towards Bismarck would amount to a 'frivolous continuation' of the constitutional conflict, and threaten to set Germany on the 'road to dictatorship'.[39]

Unification, then, has often been presented as a more or less willing liberal capitulation. But that is one-sided, and ignores those aspects of the process that liberals could welcome. After all, anything that was disliked by conservative ultras, particularists and Catholics was bound to have positive features in liberal eyes. Unification finally answered the question of where Germany was located, a question that the Confederation fudged. It created a sovereign, territorially defined national state, with a constitution, a parliament and a German chancellor. Nor did liberal nationalists simply sacrifice 'liberal' values to the 'national' cause. The new Germany embodied much that was central to contemporary liberal programmes: the rule of law and the legal accountability of ministers, freedom of movement, a liberal commercial code, the harmonizing of currency and patents. These were not trivial matters to liberals, but an institutional foundation on which they hoped to build a genuinely liberal state. They did not choose unity over freedom, but looked to extend freedom through unity. True, the centralizing North German Confederation was rather closer to liberal conceptions of the modern state than the Empire of 1871, with its greater concessions to states' rights and generally looser, federal features. But the National Liberals were the most powerful political party in Germany by the end of the unification process. There was good reason to believe that they would place their own imprint on the state-building process that began in earnest after the inauguration ceremonies at Versailles.

Divisions and Consolidation

Accounts of German unification generally take 1871 as the end point; actually it was just the beginning. When a notably unenthusiastic William accepted the imperial crown, Germany existed on paper, but it lacked widespread legitimacy as well as seasoned institutions. This should come as no surprise. At a comparable stage in Italian unification, the nationalist Massimo d'Azeglio observed plaintively: 'We have made Italy, now we have to make the Italians.'[40] Prussian-dominated Germany did not face quite the problems of Piedmont-dominated Italy. Most (although not all) inhabitants of the new Empire spoke and wrote German. Prussians and Bavarians, for all their mutual dislike, could still insult each other in a common language; indeed, language standardization picked up pace in the last decades of the century. No sectional division within Germany could be compared to the north-south divide that undermined the unity of Italy. And there was no major group in Germany which followed the example of those Italian Catholics who, encouraged by the pope, simply boycotted national politics. Yet the creation of internal, as opposed to external or formal unification in Germany was beset with difficulties. Consider for a moment the problems that have so often faced new nations in our own century, inside and outside Europe: disputed boundaries, disgruntled neighbouring powers and internal minorities, the threat of authoritarianism from a political 'strong man' at the helm, the opportunities for corruption during the development of a national infrastructure. Every one of these elements was present in the fledgling German Empire. When we further bear in mind the background of European political uncertainty and economic crisis in the 1870s, perhaps we should be less surprised that this was a period of internal division in Germany, and more impressed that there were also signs of consolidation in the new Empire.

A convenient way to begin drawing up the balance sheet of 'divisions' and 'consolidation' is to consider those who were actively hostile to the new state. The obvious starting point here is the national minorities. The German Empire was not multinational like its Habsburg counterpart, but it did contain three significant groups of non-Germans within its borders. The largest was the minority of longest standing: the Poles. Two other groups became involuntarily German as a consequence of unification: the Danes of Schleswig-Holstein, and the inhabitants of Alsace-Lorraine, annexed by Germany after the Franco-Prussian war. Danes and Alsace-Lorrainers were understandably aggrieved to find themselves members of the Empire (200,000 Alsace-Lorrainers left the provinces for metropolitan France in 1871–2), and restrictions on the use of their own language were a source of friction for all three minorities. French-speaking Alsace-Lorrainers received the most conciliatory treatment on this score; but they had their own peculiar problems as inhabitants of a sensitive border region (especially during the 1870s, with its 'war in sight' crisis), treated brusquely by German soldiers who referred to them with the derogatory expression 'Wackes'. Alsace-Lorraine was also administered, for almost the whole period of the Empire, as a special territory with its own governor, rather like a colonial dependency. The Poles, for their part, were the butt of historic German feelings of superiority and subject to periodic bouts of a Prussian 'Germanization' policy that aimed (with little success) to plant German settlers on Polish border land. Poles, Danes and Alsace-Lorrainers were all, in one way or another, treated as actual or potential 'enemies of the Empire' and all established nationalist or separatist parties to fight Reichstag elections. Between them, these parties garnered slightly more than 10 per cent of the vote in 1874. Yet the minorities' alienation from the Empire became less raw over the years, as new generations began to be quietly Germanized through schools, conscription and everyday experience. We should certainly not exaggerate how far this process had gone; the Polish school strikes at the beginning of the twentieth century, and the notorious Zabern incident of 1913, when German soldiers ran amok in an Alsatian garrison town, demonstrated the limits to peaceful assimilation. But the total vote of the separatist parties declined after 1874 (it had almost halved by the 1890s) and the number of seats they won peaked in 1881. Alsace-Lorrainers and Poles came increasingly to vote for a German-based party, the Catholic Centre.

German Catholics themselves made up another, altogether larger minority within the Empire. By excluding Austria, unification created a Lesser Germany that was roughly two-thirds Protestant, one-third Catholic. It is often assumed that this sizable minority was located mainly in the south. In fact, there were twice as many Catholics in Prussia as there were in Bavaria, and Catholics were to be found in the west and east as well as the south, forming the German equivalent of a 'Celtic fringe' around the Protestant heartland of the Empire. This was another unhappy minority. Austrian defeat by Prussia in 1866 had sparked off Catholic riots.[41] Catholics felt themselves beleaguered within a Protestant-dominated Germany, understandably so, given the persecution they faced during the so-called Kulturkampf in the 1870s. This – literally a 'struggle of civilizations' – was a serious church-state conflict, principally in Prussia but spilling over into other parts of the Empire. Like similar episodes elsewhere in Europe, it had complex origins. It was partly a domestic preventive war against the Catholic minority, depicted as an enemy within by Bismarck, who was genuinely alarmed about 'disloyalty' among the eastern Poles (this was an old shibboleth), while also spotting a tactical opportunity to draw liberals behind him in a fight against the Catholic church. Liberals were, with few exceptions, happy to follow. In the wake of the pope's pronouncement of infallibility (1870), they regarded the conflict as one that pitted German 'progress' against papal pretensions and Catholic 'backwardness' (see the following chapter). The conflict was much more serious than the rather anodyne squabble between church and state often depicted in textbooks. After the expulsion of the Jesuits from the Empire in 1872, the Prussian May Laws of the following year sought to establish state control over the education and appointment of clergy. The failure of these measures led to a second wave of punitive legislation that authorized the seizure of church property, the expulsion of 'illegally' appointed clergy and the removal of financial support from priests who refused to declare support for government measures (the 'bread-basket law'). During its most repressive phase in the mid-1870s, the Kulturkampf led to the imprisonment of clergy, wanted notices being issued for bishops, and violent episodes when the army was called in against Catholic crowds who resisted the arrest of their priests or the confiscation of church property by state commissioners. By the end of the conflict, 1800 priests had been gaoled or exiled and 16 million marks of property seized. The Catholic lawyer and publicist Julius Bachem drew a parallel with the early Christians when he talked about a period of 'Diocletian persecution'.[42]

The persecution failed in its objective, however, and by the late 1870s the Kulturkampf was effectively over. The death of Pope Pius IX in 1878 eased this process. More important, the winding-up of the struggle and the Centre Party's subsequent support for many government measures formed just one part of a major realignment of German politics at the end of the 1870s, which included Bismarck's ditching of the liberals (on whom he did not want to become too dependent in parliament) and the reintroduction of tariffs. The Kulturkampf left a powerful legacy among German Catholics, a sense of being branded as pariahs that reinforced the existence of a separate Catholic subculture. Yet, just as the Centre Party came in from the cold, so Catholics also came slowly to accept the new Germany, led by the professional and business classes, even if a more vigorous Catholic initiative to move 'out of the ghetto' had to await the end of the century. For all the continuing strength of local loyalties on the one hand and supranational allegiance to Rome on the other, Catholics in the Empire came to feel more German with the years.

The end of the Kulturkampf coincided with the beginning of an attack on the organized German working class: the anti-socialist law of 1878. Here was another outsider group in Bismarckian Germany. Most parts of the early labour movement had greeted unification from above with lack of enthusiasm. Against a background of the bloody Paris Commune of 1871, union militancy in the early Empire, and German anarchist 'outrages' during the 1870s, the Social Democratic Party formed in 1875 was an object of fear and suspicion among the ruling élite. Two assassination attempts on William I provided a pretext for outlawing the party organization and press, still in fact rather small in this period, and certainly no threat to public order. What followed was a campaign of repression that included many well-documented dirty tricks (such as children being plied with alcohol and tobacco by criminal policemen seeking information on their 'subversive' fathers).[43] By the time the antisocialist law lapsed in 1890, 1500 people had been imprisoned and others driven into exile, while the trade union movement had also felt the force of state power. In the end, the law proved as counterproductive as the Kulturkampf. Social Democrats could still stand legally for parliament, and they provided a focus of loyalty. SPD members organized themselves clandestinely, and the party press survived underground thanks to an impressive network of couriers. Under the 'red postmaster' Julius Motteler, 10,000 copies of *Der Sozialdemokrat* were smuggled into Germany every week. As in the case of Catholics, repression reinforced the subculture of the workers' movement. In another parallel with Catholics, the experience of being outlawed left an ambiguous legacy. It created bitterness and alienation. But compared with the more vicious and continuing repression meted out to the left in, say, Italy, German socialists' experiences did not prevent a certain domestication. The fact that parliamentary candidates were permitted to stand even during the period of the antisocialist law enhanced the centrality of electoral politics, and with it the importance of the parliamentary arena as one in which redress of grievances could be sought. More generally, organized German workers wrestled with their desires to be good socialists and good Germans – what historians refer to as the problem of 'double loyalty'. As the later history of the SPD within the Second International showed, the 'German' part of this identity included a certain national hubris.

In a sense, all inhabitants of the newly unified Germany were learning to acquire new loyalties. This was not just an issue that faced non-German minorities, or those singled out for persecution in the first decades of the Empire's existence. There is little doubt that, if we add to the groups already discussed those sections of the population that had their own reasons to dislike the Bismarckian creation, or were at best lukewarm – Junker traditionalists, the 'Guelphs' who remained attached to the Hanoverian state dismembered in 1866, Protestant south Germans, much of the peasantry everywhere – they make up a clear majority. Perhaps, after all, there was a need (paraphrasing d'Azeglio) to 'make Germans'. In reality, the situation was not as bleak as it might appear. Among propertied and educated middle-class Protestants who, together with landowners, made up a substantial proportion of the effective political nation, there was widespread support for the Empire. This was true not just in Prussia, but perhaps even more in non-Prussian states like Hanover. And just as middle-class nationalists there looked to Berlin as a counterbalance against local particularism, so other regional populations had reason to welcome the new German nation-state. For inhabitants of the Rhineland or Palatinate, reluctant citizens of Prussia and Bavaria respectively, adopting a German identity was a means of escaping, or relativizing, their subordination at state level – much as an early-modern peasant might regard the king as a distant court of appeal against a local lord.

From the beginning, then, the Empire could draw on important sources of support. Others found their way, more or less reluctantly, to acceptance of the new Germany. As we have seen, this happened gradually with national minorities, Catholics and the labour movement. In the south, local politics were initially introspective, but gradually orientated themselves more towards Berlin. The Centre Party did much to further this process in Bavaria and Baden. Similarly, the landowners who welcomed the Empire straight away (roughly, those who supported the well-named 'Reich Party)' were joined in the 1870s by traditionalist Junkers who came to terms with the newfangled Bismarckian creation. The title of their main political vehicle, the German Conservative Party (founded 1876), told the story of this accommodation. How to explain this process of coming to terms with the Empire? In part, we are dealing with brute reality. As it became increasingly obvious that the Empire was there to stay, initial resignation turned into habituation. Then there was the fact that the Empire offered economic opportunities and jobs – to reject the first meant denying oneself the second. Beyond these factors, the German Empire acquired a creeping legitimacy through its institutions, from banknotes and postage stamps to parliamentary elections and the national flag. There were limits to this. The early Catholic boycotts of national Sedan Day celebrations had their counterparts among national minorities and socialists. By its very nature, the process of habituation did not happen overnight: it was more obvious by the 1880s than in the 1870s. It is nevertheless important that the new state met with growing acceptance as it became more familiar. And central to this was the process of institutional consolidation – the construction of a state that existed only on paper in 1871.

How this occurred can be followed through at a number of levels. The most basic level of all was the relationship between the Empire and its constituent parts. In strict constitutional terms, 'unification' was no more than a series of treaties in international law, a compact between sovereign states that ceded certain powers to the centre but retained their own rulers, representative institutions and rights over matters like taxation. The largest states still exchanged ambassadors with each other. In all of these respects, the federal Empire resembled more closely the present-day European Union than it did contemporary federal (but republican) states such as the USA or Switzerland. None of this was magically transformed after 1871: the Empire remained distinctively federal down to its disappearance in 1918. But it did, clearly, become more unitary. Unification had laid down that the emperor could proclaim imperial law, which took precedence over that of the individual states. This became increasingly important as a result of the raft of new legislation (legal, fiscal, commercial, social) that was passed in the Reichstag during the 1870s – in such quantities, in fact, that it threatened to overwhelm the parliament.[44] A single currency, common weights and measures, the harmonization of laws (although codification of the civil law was not complete until the 1890s) – these inexorably made the Empire more centralized. So did the *de facto* unification of separate railways, the establishment of an imperial civil service, the creation of an effectively German army, and much else. In the space of just a few years the following imperial institutions were established: the Audit Office (1871), the Statistical Office (1872), the Railway Office (1873), the National Debt Administration (1874), the Health Department and the Post Office (1876), the Patent Office, the Justice Department and the Supreme Court (1877). Those who prefer to read (or for that matter, write) about history as a tableau of dramatic, colourful incidents will probably find this terribly humdrum. But it was important. In 1871 the Empire could still have been mistaken for a reworked version of the old German Confederation, minus Austria. That was no longer true by the 1880s. The uneasy 'diplomatic phase' of the Empire was over, just as fears about its very existence raised by incidents like the French 'war in sight' crisis had been dispelled.

This tacit move towards a more unitary, or at least more centralized, structure had implications for the constitutional organs of the Empire. In particular, it tilted the balance between the Federal Council on the one hand, embodiment of the centrifugal, states-rights elements of the constitution, and the imperial executive and Reichstag on the other. By deliberate Bismarckian design, the Federal Council was supposed to function as the real executive. The Empire had no true ministers, only a series of 'state secretaries', glorified clerks who worked under the chancellor (Bismarck himself); and the Reichstag was

just as deliberately deprived of power. However, as a result of
the sheer volume of legislation passing through the Reichstag,
and the tendency of new laws to increase the functions performed by the Empire, political reality began to diverge from
constitutional precept. The state secretaries became, in effect,
ministers; and the Reichstag acquired an institutional momentum and influence not originally envisaged. In both cases the
Federal Council was the loser.

There is more that needs to be said about the Reichstag. In
the first place, it was dominated in the 1870s by liberals, who
had a major hand in the 'national' consolidating legislation of
that decade. Without the efforts of figures like Bennigsen,
Lasker and Twesten, especially in legal matters, the Empire
would have looked very different. They did not achieve everything they wanted, and some of what they prized as liberal (like
the expulsion of the Jesuits) looks illiberal to our eyes; but their
prominence and achievements give the lie to any simple idea
that unification represented a defeat for liberalism. The 1870s
represented, in many ways, a liberal high-point in nineteenth-
century Germany. Secondly, it mattered that the Reichstag –
unlike the Prussian parliament or many other state parliaments
– was elected by a franchise that was universal, direct and equal
for males over the age of twenty-five. Add to this the fact that
elections were almost entirely free of interference or chicanery,
and it is not surprising that the national parliament acquired a
genuine popular legitimacy. There is a striking contrast here
with Italy. The Reichstag became a focal point for those
(national minorities, Catholics, socialists) who were treated as
pariahs in the early years of the Empire. Outsider groups in
Imperial Germany availed themselves of the ballot, rather than
turning to the bullet, the boycott, or banditry. The importance
of that should not be underestimated. Thirdly, it is hard not to
be impressed by the speed with which a party system emerged
in these years. The division of liberalism into National Liberal
and left-liberal wings had occurred in the aftermath of 1866,
and the moderate conservative Reich Party dated from the same
period. With the formation of the Catholic Centre Party and

the national minority parties in 1870–1, the SPD in 1875 and the German Conservative Party in 1876, the Empire saw the quite sudden crystallization of a party system that was to persist through to 1918, and in some respects until the 1930s.

The 1870s was a crucial decade. What has been presented above, under the broad heading of 'consolidation', adds up to a picture different from the one often drawn, in which the early Empire was marked by abiding Prusso-German authoritarianism and deep internal fissures accentuated by the deliberate playing up of 'friend-foe' distinctions.[45] My own interpretation is certainly less negative. But we should also acknowledge the limits to the integration and political evolution of the Empire. There was, in the first place, what might be called the Bismarck-problem. As the celebrated architect of unification, the imperial chancellor and Prussian prime minister was a dominant figure at the height of his powers, determined not to yield the political initiative, least of all to parliamentarians whom he publicly scorned. The numerous contemporaries who called him dictatorial, or accused him of tolerating only an 'unmanned' parliament, captured the sense in which he still set the terms – and the tone – of German politics. There is equally no doubt that a major weapon in his armoury was to rally support by pointing to the 'threat' posed by one or another supposed 'enemy of the Empire', whether the French, the Poles, the Catholics or the socialists. The constitutional machinery of the Empire also operated in many respects as Bismarck had intended, despite the authority the national parliament began to acquire. The Federal Council may not have been able to function as a true executive, and the 1870s already saw its powers begin to drain away. But it had great negative importance, simply by existing. It could block measures inimical to Prussian interests (as Bismarck defined them), stop any wholesale move towards a unitary Empire, and prevent – as it was intended to – liberal initiatives in the direction of greater parliamentarization. The Federal Council allowed Bismarck to mobilize the princes and particularists against the threat of centralization, and to counter any idea that either the chancellor or the imperial state secretaries were 'responsible' to parliament.

Bismarck's ability to dominate and manipulate the hybrid constitutional system he had invented was evident in the political sea change that occurred in the years 1878–9. The historians who refer to this as a 'refounding of the Empire' tend to neglect the underlying political and constitutional evolution of the Empire discussed above.[46] Nevertheless, the ending of the Kulturkampf, the passage of the antisocialist law and the reintroduction of protective tariffs, taken together, marked an important change. And there were smaller, but symptomatic, signs of this. The death penalty had not been applied during the 1870s; now the executions began. After a decade when liberalism was electorally dominant in Germany, and the liberal parties in the Empire (and many individual states) placed their imprint on legislation, Bismarck was determined to free himself from liberal majorities. Their electoral support had shown signs of decline in the Prussian elections of 1876 and the Reichstag elections of 1877, although National Liberals and left liberals together still held the largest bloc of seats in the national parliament. In April 1877, Bismarck initiated discussions with party leader Rudolf von Bennigsen over the entry of National Liberals into the government. But the talks broke down: Bennigsen wanted to push further in the direction of parliamentary responsibility, Bismarck to isolate and domesticate liberal leaders. Instead of agreement with the liberals, what occurred was a series of measures and policy changes designed to embarrass and compromise them.[47] By the time Bismarck exploited the demands that arose from the Great Depression to reintroduce tariffs in 1879, he had succeeded in splitting the liberals and putting together a new progovernmental alignment. The Iron Chancellor was still, for the moment, master of the political system he had devised.

CHAPTER SIX

Progress and its Discontents

The Culture of Progress

During the first half of the nineteenth century, visitors from economically more advanced countries like Britain and France tended to single out particular features of Germany for comment. They predictably dwelt on its political divisions, the numerous small courts with their liveried officials. In similar vein, foreign travellers often wrote about German provincialism, the widespread differences in dress and dialect, the persistence of half-timbered villages and cosy, inward-looking small towns. Germany had no single pulsating capital city like London or Paris. It was comparatively cheap to live in, and it seemed less driven by materialism than its neighbours. German riches, it was often said, were more spiritual or cultural than worldly: this was the land of 'poets and thinkers'. Judgments of this kind, already clichés by the middle of the nineteenth century, were both affectionate and patronizing. They also echoed a widespread German self-image. Take the German Michel, that universal symbol of national character so different from the British John Bull – a gentle, simple, nightcap-wearing figure, honest and frequently taken advantage of. He might have been invented by scoffing foreigners: in fact the German Michel was a figure in whom contemporary Germans recognized themselves. In the same way, German writers on fashion like Friedrich Vischer and Max von Boehn praised German naturalness and simplicity, contrasting these qualities with French artificiality and refinement.[1] Foreign stereotypes of the unworldly, metaphysical German also corresponded to a widespread native view that contrasted German 'inwardness' and idealism with the crass materialism of others – such as the British, the nation of shop-keepers.

There is no doubt that such attitudes were widely voiced or reported by contemporaries, German and non-German, in the period between the Enlightenment and the middle of the nine-teenth century. An influential body of work on German cultural and intellectual history has built on this evidence and tried to establish how the 'German mind' diverged from 'western' patterns of thinking – how it was different from what we find in Britain or France.[2] Thus, the Germans were antimaterialist rather than materialist, celebrated the natural and organic over the mechanical, favoured 'culture' (which was deep) over 'civiliz-ation' (which was shallow). Whereas the money-grubbing Eng-lish and the cynical French developed the realist novel, the Germans had music and lyric poetry. It would be easy to quote other examples of the argument. The case is plausible; it is also partial and one-sided. Even before the middle of the nineteenth century it is not difficult to find intellectual countercurrents. This was not the way that early industrialists or steamship mag-nates looked at the world, and it was precisely such patterns of thought that angered Germans as different as Friedrich List and Karl Marx, who viewed them as the mental reflex of German 'backwardness'. (Both men, it is true, became exiles.) The homely figure of the German Michel prompted impatience as well as self-satisfaction. For the period after the middle of the nineteenth century, arguments about antimaterialist German 'inwardness' seem increasingly implausible. In fact, during the years when Germany was transformed economically by indus-trialization and politically by unification, it is hard not to be struck by the rampant celebration of technology and material improvements that accompanied these changes. This is what I call the culture of progress.

The third quarter of the century was a great age of statistics, and contemporaries wielded them ceaselessly to show how everything was becoming larger, better or quicker. A classic instance is the obsession with the spread of steam-power – steam engines, steam ploughs, steam boats, steam locomotives. It was the sense that this new form of energy was remaking the world that inspired so many contemporary flights of enthusiasm. The essayist Otto Gildemeister wrote in 1873: 'It is no exaggeration to say that, when it comes to trade and communications and industry, the gulf that separates the years 1873 and 1773 is greater than the gulf separating 1773 and the Phoenicians.'[3] It *was* an exaggeration, of course, but one that perfectly captures the spirit of the time. The best example of the welcome given to the new mechanical civilization is provided by the railway. In Germany, no less (perhaps even more) than in Britain or France, the railway became the symbol of a progress that was seen as moral as well as material. The 'iron steed' was a source of emancipation, a demonstration of the human capacity to transcend nature. A vast body of doggerel verse expressed this tremulous enthusiasm, works like Karl Beck's 'The Railway' or Anastasius Grün's 'Poetry of Steam'.[4] Max Maria von Weber, eldest son of the composer and an engineer who had worked on the Saxon railways, was proclaimed by his publisher as the inventor of the 'technological novella'. He had, said a friendly critic, 'discovered the poetry of rails'. A passage from one of his essays suggests what it was these contemporaries admired: 'Mightier beyond compare than steed or chariot, than oar or sail, it is the new and powerful motor of our day: steam, which, with aquiline speed, guides ocean castles and rolling towns.'[5] In short, steam became a metaphor of progress.

The advent of steam and the values associated with it had an impact throughout German society. When the *Adler* left Nuremberg on 7 December 1835, pulling the first train ever to travel between two German towns, there was amazement among the crowd. By the 1860s the experience had become routine, but remained a cause for celebration. No local history of a German town in this period lacks its description of the railway opening, complete with local dignitaries, ribbons, bands, toasts and the hurrahs of the crowd. A whole section of the popular Leipzig *Illustrierte Zeitung* was set aside to describe these festivities. The opening of new bridges, such as the Rhine Bridge at Kehl or the Ravenna viaduct in the Black Forest, also captured the popular imagination and drew large crowds, just like the opening of Brunel bridges on Britain's Great Western Railway. The railway altered German everyday life in numerous ways. It made possible journeys that could not have been undertaken before. To take just one example, the growing popularity of seaside and lakeside holidays, and the increasing numbers who took the waters at spa towns, depended on the new means of transportation. But the railway also had its effect on those who used a new means to achieve an old purpose. Pilgrims availed themselves enthusiastically of the iron steed; artisan autobiographies reveal the fascination that the new mode of transportation exerted on the former 'tramping' journeymen. The railway inspired its own popular songs ('Wir fahren auf der Eisenbahn, so lang es uns gefällt'), and like other technical marvels of the age it was rapidly miniaturized as that classic possession of the middle-class boy, the model railway. The railway cast a spell on contemporaries that went beyond its immediate usefulness. The evidence of letters as well as public accounts suggests that a major reason for this was the fact that it allowed the world to be apprehended in new ways. Like other instruments now starting to become familiar in the bourgeois home – the camera, the telescope, the child's 'bioscope' – it altered the sense of time and space, offering a new panorama of sights and sensations.

Towns and cities also presented new spectacles during the third quarter of the century. They provided a home for the showcase exhibitions of the period (the London Great Exhibition of 1851 at the Crystal Palace was the prototype). Vienna hosted an international exhibition of this sort in 1873, but smaller versions were regularly mounted in Germany. The Karlsruhe exhibition of 1861 attracted 100,000 visitors, equivalent to 10 per cent of the Badenese population over the age of fourteen. Among the crowds that flocked to exhibitions were people from the countryside, a reminder that when historians speak of urbanization (as distinct from the growth of towns) they are referring to a spreading familiarity with urban material goods, consumption patterns and mores even in rural areas – a process accelerated by the railway.[6] At a time when German cities were being completely reshaped, they offered other new sights and sources of recreation for their inhabitants and visitors. There was the modern iron and glass architecture most conspicuously displayed in the new railway stations, then the parks and promenades characteristic of the new city layout. Novel forms of lighting added to the effect after dusk, for this was the classic age of the 'gaslit city' – a further symbol of human triumph over the natural order. Another innovation of the period conveyed the same message: the zoological garden, whose walkways led visitors to viewing areas where they could observe nature tamed. The Berlin zoo, built on the site of the old royal pheasantry, was completed in 1844; Frankfurt zoo opened to the public in 1858, and there were zoos in Cologne, Dresden and Hamburg by the early 1860s. They aimed to provide both recreation and edification. In the words of David Friedrich Weinland of the Frankfurt zoo, they were created by and for 'citizens' who wanted institutions 'for their own instruction and the beautification of their daily life'.[7] This was the civic gospel of moral improvement. It went hand in hand with contemporary efforts (not entirely successful) to banish more unruly, less instructive forms of popular entertainment such as performing animals and displays of 'freaks' from the city streets.

The visitor to almost any German city in the 1870s was bound to notice how much had changed over the previous thirty years. The new structures reflected bourgeois civic pride and optimism. Laid out along Vienna's new Ringstrasse, in addition to parliament, stock exchange and law courts, were the emblems of cultural progress: opera house, university, museum, library, botanical and zoological gardens. The pattern was repeated with variations across Germany. Of course, older landmarks remained, sometimes dominated: churches, princely palaces, town halls, and other examples of vernacular architecture. But even these began to be appreciated in new ways. Baedeker in hand (for this was also the age of the guide book), the visitor was encouraged to appreciate past cultural glories. For their part, municipal history or preservation societies looked after buildings and monuments more systematically.

The historical preservationist, the museum curator and the botanical garden director had at least two things in common. First, they saw themselves engaged in a process of classifying, ordering, and passing on the fruits of new-found knowledge. Most would have described this activity, without embarrassment, as a contribution to human progress. Secondly, these and similar cultural spheres were increasingly suffused in this period with a sense that they were part of a national endeavour. This is not surprising. Behind both cultural and national optimism lay pride in German education and scholarship. At the time of unification, Lesser Germany had nineteen universities (fifteen more than England), plus numerous technical high schools, mining schools and the like. This was the period when German higher education confirmed its world-class reputation. Germany was not only the home of modern, archival, 'scientific' history, but an international leader in philosophy, philology and law. When art history established itself as a modern discipline towards the end of this period, German scholars were predictably in the van. Even more striking, perhaps, were the achievements of German scholars in the fields of medicine, physiology, biology, chemistry and physics. During the years 1860–79, the seventy major discoveries by German medical researchers compare with fifty-five by all others. The German lead in physiology was even more overwhelming.[8] This was something that went beyond a few leading figures (Robert Koch, Rudolf Virchow, Max von Pettenkofer) and reflected the depth of German scientific scholarship. In the natural sciences, as in the humanities, German success was based on well-funded and competitive universities, a high degree of professional specialization, and a strong emphasis on research. As foreign students were drawn to German institutions in growing numbers, the domestic prestige of the university and the high status of the professor indicated how both were regarded as important national assets.

The metropolitan culture of the university and museum had its local, provincial pendants. Take the case of archaeology. Alongside the development of the academic discipline and the founding of institutions such as the Archaeological Museum of

Berlin, archaeology became a great amateur passion of the period. The most spectacular example of this was the retired millionaire businessman, Heinrich Schliemann, who located the site of Homeric Troy at Hissarlik in Asia Minor and donated the fruits of the subsequent excavation to the Berlin Museum. The city of Berlin made him an honorary citizen, only the third person (after Bismarck and Moltke) to be recognized in this way. But the real mania for popular archaeology began earlier and its main sites were German. In 1856, 'Neanderthal Man' was discovered in a chalk quarry east of Düsseldorf, stimulating countless nonprofessionals to try their hand at weekend digs. They were further encouraged by books on prehistoric Germany, such as Weinland's best-selling novel *Rulaman*. Roman remains were also unearthed in large quantities during this period, especially in the Rhineland. Sometimes there were tensions between amateurs and professionals, a sign of growing professionalization, but we should also recognize the ties that bound the scholarly world and the activity of local enthusiasts. The latter could subscribe to learned journals, read reports on the latest findings in serious newspapers, and join the local archaeological association. The same was true of the official, professional man or merchant with an interest in, say, history or public hygiene. Alongside an expanding specialist literature in these fields there were popular articles, and societies, that addressed a broader public.

The press and associational life were two of the principal bearers of the culture of progress, vehicles for the mobilization of civic and moral energies. The press grew enormously in these years. Berlin had no fewer than thirty-two newspapers in 1862, together with fifty-eight weeklies. Germany boasted 2400 papers by the end of the 1870s. The press reflected the fact that the country had many important regional centres: the leading newspapers included not only the *Vossische Zeitung* of Berlin, but the *Kölnische Zeitung*, the *Frankfurter Zeitung* and the *Augsburger Allgemeine Zeitung*, for many years the closest Germans came to having a 'national' organ. Newspapers became more widespread, appeared more frequently, and delivered the news more quickly.

In 1862, the Berlin correspondent of the *Kölnische Zeitung* was the first German journalist to telegraph the outcome of a trial to his paper (it was the trial of the socialist Lassalle on charges of 'inciting to hatred and contempt').[9] These changes meant that the press did more to form public opinion than had been the case before 1848. Politically, it was still subject to governmental interference – one liberal Königsberg paper was taken to court more than a hundred times during the Prussian constitutional conflict – at least until the imperial press law of 1874. Even then, papers remained very susceptible to 'inspired' stories. This, like the common habit of taking news from the wire services or simply lifting stories from their rivals, was not unconnected with the fact that most newspapers still had few full-time correspondents. On the other hand, they devoted growing space to economics and culture, gave detailed attention to museum exhibitions and scientific discoveries, and reported respectfully on scholarly congresses (and even on professors' inaugural lectures). The major big-city newspapers, mainly liberal in tendency, conveyed the general message that Germany was going through a period in which material, intellectual and moral improvement were proceeding hand-in-hand.

That was also what readers would find in the pages of the weekly illustrated magazines: the *Leipziger Illustrierte, Über Land und Meer, Daheim*, and – the most important of them all – the *Gartenlaube*. Founded by Ernst Keil in 1853, the last named already had a circulation of 100,000 by 1860 and nearly 400,000 by 1880, giving perhaps 2 million readers per issue.[10] With its articles on steam and magnetism, on the workings of the mechanical plough and the physiology of the screech owl, the *Gartenlaube* perfectly encapsulates the heady contemporary belief in both science and popular education. The same applies to cheap popular imprints like Joseph Mayer's 'Penny Library' (motto: 'knowledge is freedom, freedom is power'), and to the well-filled ranks of scientific popularizers: Hermann Helmholtz, Ludwig Büchner, Rudolf Virchow, Ernst Haeckel. The former two belong squarely to the world of what Thomas Love Peacock satirically labelled 'steam intellect'. Helmholtz described the body as a steam engine; Büchner argued that the human brain generated thought just as a steam-engine produced motion. Virchow and Haeckel also spoke the language of science and progress, but used the biological idiom that was becoming increasingly familiar in these years. Haeckel was one of the leading contemporary popularizers (and vulgarizers) of Charles Darwin's ideas, which became a major cult in Germany.

Like the press and popular publications, the voluntary association helped to form opinion and played an important part in disseminating the gospel of progress. As we have already seen, associations had existed for decades – among gymnasts and singers, for example. From the 1840s and through the middle decades of the century, however, contemporaries noted a growing 'passion for association', a 'hypertrophic growth' in their numbers. It has been calculated that by 1870 one German citizen in two belonged to an association.[11] Some of these were concerned purely with sociability, others with narrow business or professional concerns. But we can hardly miss the many associations dedicated to social or moral improvement, the fostering of culture, and public edification. Consider the activities supported by the Saarland ceramics manufacturer, Eugen-Anton von Boch. In addition to business concerns, Boch's causes included civil engineering projects, public health, education and archaeology.[12] He was not untypical of the substantial provincial bourgeoisie in this period. What his example shows is the range of public issues. There were the ubiquitous railway committees and other associations designed to foster the local economy. Then we find an array of groups concerned with the 'social question': philanthropic societies like the Berlin Central Association for the Welfare of the Working Classes, bodies concerned with hygiene, such as the German Association for Public Health Care, and numerous other associations with specific purposes – to discourage the drinking of spirits, encourage school attendance by the children of the poor, provide support for a hospital or orphanage. These organizations were usually local in scope and high-minded in tone: they sought to harness civic energy in the name of the common good or public welfare. This civilizing mission informed other voluntary groups bent on 'improvement', such as the associations for the protection of animals that emerged in towns across Germany, especially from the 1860s, and tried to outlaw customs that were 'superstitious' or 'barbaric'.[13] Finally, the same earnest, moralizing rhetoric pervaded associations dedicated to cultural or educational goals, from the local antiquarian society to a nationally organized body with nationalist perspectives such as the Schiller Association. Of all the organizations that preached the cause of moral improvement through useful knowledge, perhaps the most typical in this period were the workers' education associations. The 1850s and 1860s saw the high point of their extent and influence.

Optimism about the new mechanical civilization, pride in German culture, the importance of mobilizing civic energies, a belief in social and moral 'improvement' – these values ring out clearly from press, associations, private letters and diaries. They were also the values that men of affairs (and we are talking largely about men) lived out in their business and professional lives, whether as entrepreneurs, doctors, engineers or teachers. It was a part of their growing professional self-confidence. Even dentists felt the winds of change. When, in 1846, the Förster publishing house of Berlin produced a new journal, *Der Zahnarzt* (The Dentist), a triumphalist 'note to the reader' managed within a few lines to introduce all the key words that would reverberate through the following quarter-century: education, progress, science.[14] We are talking here about a largely bourgeois phenomenon. Men from this background were numerically preponderant in the spheres of education, science, art, music, medicine, and the press, as well as business. Members of the propertied and educated middle classes also dominated voluntary associations, as many studies have shown.[15] They had the time and money, the access to meeting places and the experience to draft formal rules of procedure. It is possible to argue, as Ludwig Beutin has done, that the twin ideas of material and moral progress provided a glue that bound together the different parts of the German middle classes in these years.[16] On the one hand, progress meant the victory of modernity over 'feudality', nowhere more optimistically fêted than in support for the railway. 'With each new iron steed that travels the rails, a piece of feudalism falls into the abyss of an irrecoverable past', argued the historian Johannes Scherr in 1858.[17] Realist novelists like Karl Gutzkow and Friedrich Spielhagen provided self-satisfied descriptions of outmoded aristocrats unable to come to terms with the age of steam. Voluntary organizations dedicated to moral improvement often had a similarly antiaristocratic edge: the German Association Against the Misuse of Alcoholic Spirits criticized self-interested Junkers who grew the grain from which liquor was distilled.[18] In a more general sense, civic institutions like theatres and concert halls, philanthropic societies that raised public money, even the emergence of a large reading public, all represented something at odds with the model of aristocratic or courtly patronage. They were an alternative, more 'modern' means of supporting culture or morally worthy causes. Of course, the highborn patron did not disappear (as the career of composer Richard Wagner demonstrates). Many aristocrats also joined associations. But they did so as individuals, coming to terms with the spirit of the times, like the improving landlord investing in a steam plough, or Bismarck accepting that it was an age of 'chemical studies and double-entry book-keeping'.

To what extent did these values have an impact further down the social scale? Certainly they were intended to. That was the point of popular edifying literature, workers' education associations, and campaigns against animal abuse: to turn the lower classes into respectable and self-respecting citizens. The rules of many organizations that dealt directly with workers had a clearly disciplinary element, in matters of hygiene or alcohol, for example. This was most obviously so in the philanthropic sphere. The widely copied Elberfeld poor relief system allocated unpaid overseers to small groups of families in order to monitor domestic arrangements, moral conduct and willingness to accept work. This was an internal civilizing mission, in which the disciplines of the railway timetable and the more sober civic amenities of the period also had their part to play. We should not be too quick to criticize such efforts – the doctrine of improvement and self-help was generally preached in (subjective) good faith and fuelled more by zeal than hypocrisy, even if it meshed well with (objective) self-interest. Nor should we assume that it always fell on deaf ears, or met with resistance. Particularly among the petty bourgeoisie, these values were frequently internalized to a high degree, just as the bourgeois family model found willing imitators among more substantial parts of this intermediate class. In fact, the solid shopkeeper or better-off master craftsman (the butcher or bookbinder, rather than the cobbler) often played a subaltern role in a local association, acting as secretary or minute-taker. Within the more skilled, 'respectable' parts of the working class there was also significant support for organizations like education associations, reflecting a desire for personal realization and cultural enrichment that – at least in the earlier part of this period – often outweighed suspicion of bourgeois tutelage. But we should not exaggerate how far this went. However considerable the cumulative everyday effects of the new mechanical civilization, and they are impossible to measure, most outworkers, casual labourers and migrant workers were probably little touched by the culture of progress. And that is likely to have been more true in the countryside, beyond a relatively narrow stratum. Even among wealthier peasants, the idea of progress – as it was understood by the bourgeois notables of the urban Museum Society – spread more slowly than the railway or the pocket-watch.

To the extent that this was changing, the principal agency of change was the state. It had a prominent role in the social and cultural arenas described above. The state operated or underwrote the new means of communication, funded universities and museums, fostered the new emphasis on hygiene through the regime of local medical health officers (and, in Prussia, state mine doctors). In the countryside, peripatetic teachers and schools of husbandry addressed the peasantry. Above all, the states were trying hard in these years to make compulsory elementary schooling a reality – and in Prussia, to enforce a higher school-leaving age as well. German professionals were, of course, often themselves officials. Even businessmen had links with the machinery of state through half-private, half-public institutions like chambers of commerce. All of this underlines the large degree of common purpose that united the typical 'improvement'-minded association and the state. As we have seen, the commitment of the German states to economic and institutional modernity continued even through the political reaction of the 1850s. During the 1860s, the aims of state bureaucracy and the aspirations being voiced in civil society overlapped still more. In 1865 an enthusiastic forestry official in the Trier district observed that compulsory schooling was needed until the people understood that 'knowledge is power and time is money'.[19] The point could not have been better put by a Rhenish professor or shipping magnate. And that was one important reason (the maintenance of law and order was another) why most entrepreneurs and educated bourgeois saw the state as a natural ally in its domestic civilizing mission. With the advent of the German nation-state in 1871, this sense of identification acquired an extra dimension. Now social and cultural advance became a testimony to German progress, proof that the age of the German Michel was finally over. This sense of pride, sometimes hubris, merged seamlessly with the celebration of science and discovery in the pages of the *Gartenlaube* and *Daheim*. Politically, it represented a powerful element of consensus among the National Liberal, left liberal and moderate Conservative parties in the 1870s.

Anticlericalism was a touchstone of these views. The Roman Catholic Church was, in the first place, a supranational institution, an alternative source of allegiance to the nation-state. It also stood for everything the advocates of progress detested: 'backwardness', 'superstition', 'medievalism'. Through the third quarter of the nineteenth century the cause of improvement was projected as something that would be achieved by breaking the power of the church. Modern civilization and education would begin to emancipate men (and perhaps even women) from 'clerical tutelage'. This was the old message of the Enlightenment, with its Manichaean categories of darkness and light, recast in the newer idiom of science. Scientific language permeated anticlericalism. Catholicism was a 'brake on civilization', a 'swamp', a symbol of 'stagnation', a form of 'pathology'.[20] One author described religious orders as 'outgrowths of diseased aberrations of human social drives'; action should be taken against them as one would act against 'phylloxera, Colorado beetle, and other enemies of the Empire'.[21] Darwinism became a favourite weapon in the anticlerical armoury, a confirmation that the days of the church were numbered. 'Progress is a natural law that no human power, neither the weapons of tyrants nor the curses of priests, can ever succeed in suppressing,' exulted the Darwinist Ernst Haeckel.[22] The culmination of this verbal onslaught against the forces of clerical darkness coincided with the Kulturkampf of the 1870s, which symbolized better than anything else what it was that the supporters of progress wanted. As an anticlerical opponent of a compromise settlement put it: 'Going to Canossa will bring us no railways.'[23] The vehemence of the language used by supporters of the Kulturkampf indicates how much was at stake, and helps to explain why most left-liberals and virtually all National Liberals enlisted with so few qualms in the campaign of repression. At the same time, the vigour of anticlerical sentiment reminds us that in this period religion still remained a central issue in German society and culture. Reading the unrelenting, violent denunciations of clerical stupidity, hocus-pocus and fanaticism, one has the unmistakable sense that the advocates of progress must have harboured real doubts about the success of their own programme – that their vitriol reflected a sense of impotent frustration in the face of a still powerful enemy.

Religion

Until very recently, most general accounts of nineteenth-century German history treated religion as something of a leftover – still powerful in the countryside, no doubt, but essentially a stubborn residue whose importance was fading in an age dominated by the modern 'isms': liberalism, nationalism, socialism, materialism. Two parallel processes are normally seen as having pushed religious faith to the sidelines. One was the scholarly and scientific challenge to revealed religion. This included the biblical scholarship associated with David Friedrich Strauss and his highly influential *Life of Jesus* (1835), which questioned the historical truth of the bible; the arguments of left-Hegelian materialists like Ludwig Feuerbach, built upon in turn by Marx and Engels, who presented religion as a legitimation of existing property relations ('the opium of the people'); and the broader onslaught of 'vulgar materialist' writers, especially in the third quarter of the century, already discussed above.[24] At the same time, it is argued, surrogate religions emerged: culture, nationalism, the socialist hope of salvation in this world. The Saxon pastor's son Friedrich Nietzsche had many antecedents when he announced in 1882 that 'God is dead'.[25] Nietzsche, however, was talking about something more than intellectual debate: he was referring to a broader dechristianization of society. That is the second process usually discussed by historians charting the declining role of religion. They point to the ways in which science offered an alternative to faith in the everyday material world, so that – for instance – the veterinarian was called in instead of cattle being blessed. The examples could be multiplied, summed up in the Dutch phrase: 'artificial fertilizers make atheists'.[26] Above all, those who see declining religious affiliation as part of a broader modernization of society identify movement into the towns and the formation of a new kind of class society as major causes of dechristianization or secularization (the two terms are often used interchangeably).

All of these arguments have truth in them. Philological scholarship and the natural sciences did make belief in God and the literal truth of the Bible less self-evident among the educated by 1880 than they had been earlier in the century, and unbelief affected significant sections of the lower classes, especially in the form of vulgar materialism. Culture or politics did become an ersatz religion for some, although religious indifference characterized many more. There is no doubt that a decline in both church-going and religious faith was well underway in many German towns. This is hardly surprising given the uprooting that urbanization often caused, the wider range of institutions offering identity, succour or sociability in the town, and the problems that all the churches had in keeping up with new urban classes – problems that ranged from reorganizing pastoral care to the barriers of class and imaginative sympathy that often divided the institutional churches from workers. When all of this is conceded, however, arguments about a steady, linear decline of faith or church-going are misleading. It is often overlooked that many champions of modern biblical scholarship or the claims of science remained committed Christians. Much contemporary debate was not concerned with revealed religion *versus* science, but turned on disputes within particular communities – the arguments between broadly 'liberal' and 'conservative-orthodox' that characterized Protestantism, Catholicism and Judaism. This is a reminder that religion continued to play an absolutely central role in German public debate. If God was dead, theology certainly was not. In 1851, one sixth of all the books published in Germany was a work of theology; the figure was still one in eight twenty years later.[27] Religion continued to colour the way contemporaries thought about large areas of their lives. The Bach and Palestrina revivals testified to the importance of church music. German lyric poetry was suffused with religious images, and debates raged in architecture between advocates of Christian neo-Gothic and neo-classicists. In the political world, Bismarck invoked Divine Providence, Conservatives put a cross on the masthead of their leading newspaper, and the Catholic Centre Party likened nationalism to a 'modern Islam'. The left also continued to draw on religious imagery as a source of moral justification. The progressive Georg Jung called the voice of the people 'the voice of God'; the feminist Hedwig Dohm proclaimed that 'the day will come when the woman will force her way into the temple of the men, mount their pulpits and preach a new gospel, the glad tidings of woman become human'.[28] Charities were often organized along the lines that demarcated religious communities, whether Protestant, Catholic, or Jewish. The issue of religious conversion – of Jews to Christianity, of Catholics to Protestantism, or vice versa – was a highly charged topic for contemporaries, more so than we can readily imagine today. It is easy to be misled on this point by the utterly exceptional – Heinrich Heine arguing that his conversion to Christianity was easier than having a tooth pulled, or Richard Wagner equating Protestantism and Catholicism with the choice between tea and coffee. Religious or denominational differences, and how they were perceived, showed the powerful bonds of faith within German society.

The great fault line was the one that divided the heirs of the Reformation and the Counter-Reformation. In the early 1850s, Wilhelm Riehl observed that there was a Protestant Germany and a Catholic Germany.[29] Protestants and Catholics not only had their own brands of faith; they had their own literary canons, their own historical pantheons – their own sense of what it meant to be German. Far from being a mere residue of distant religious struggles, these separate identities were becoming more distinct again in the third quarter of the nineteenth century. As migration and urbanization made populations less homogeneous, zealous efforts were made to minister to coreligionists in the respective 'diasporas'. A Protestant organization for this purpose, the Gustavus Adolphus Association, was set up as early as 1832; its Catholic equivalent, the Boniface Association, came into being in 1849. There were other, more aggressive signs that separate identities were preserved and even reinforced as demographic change created a complicated patchwork quilt of religious observance. Denominational tension was rising from the 1840s, triggered by 'mixed' marriages and disputes about church bells and burials in areas where Protestants and Catholics had to share a single place of worship. In towns, especially in areas like the Ruhr and Saar where pell-mell industrialization had flung the two communities together in bleak surroundings, communal hostility manifested itself in turf-battles fought by youths with name-calling and physical violence. Mutual animosity of this kind was also found in the countryside, between neighbouring villages of different denominations. It would therefore be wrong to attach the simple label of secularization to this period (or to the century as a whole). The great debates over science and revealed truth, like interdenominational wrangling among Christians, were a sign that religion remained vital despite novel intellectual challenges. Urbanization and the culture of progress were not synonymous with dechristianization, even if they sometimes worked in that direction. Indeed, secularization had a counterpoint in the religious revival that was such a conspicuous feature of Catholic Germany in the third quarter of the century, although much more muted among Protestants and Jews. The overall picture is complex and ambiguous. It is best understood by considering in somewhat more detail what happened in the different religious communities, where we find highly distinctive experiences as well as developments in common.

Let us start with a small but important minority. In 1850 there were around 400,000 Jews living within the boundaries of the later unified Germany, a figure that had risen to just over half a million in 1871, or 1.25 per cent of the population. Another 200,000 lived in Habsburg lands within the German Confederation, mainly in Austria and Bohemia, where they made up 1.5 per cent of the population. In most general accounts of Germany in this period, the history of the Jews has been written without much reference to Judaism. Instead, it is the twin movements of emancipation and assimilation that receive most attention. This emphasis is understandable. Both processes were decisively important for German Jews, and both proceeded at a new tempo in the third quarter of the century. 1848 was an important landmark in the slow, stage-by-stage movement towards emancipation; the 1860s finally brought complete Jewish legal and civil equality in most German states, confirmed in the North German Confederation in 1869. The assimilation of Jews in these years was even more striking. Its conventional symbols are the large-scale entry of Jews into banking, trade and the professions, amounting to a virtual occupational revolution, Jewish overrepresentation in institutions of secondary and higher education, and the great movement of Jews to the towns and cities from the 1870s. In short, Jews embodied the developments taking place within an emerging bourgeois society, only in heightened form. It is a commonplace that the Jewish community identified to an unusual degree with the currents of modernity and 'progress'. Jews were disproportionately represented in the propertied and educated middle class where the doctrine of progress was most strongly developed, and a majority warmly embraced the liberal-nationalist version of German culture that became so powerful in the 1860s and 1870s. That is no surprise. Jewish emancipation was closely linked to this particular form of liberalism during its nineteenth-century high point.

Emancipation necessarily meant some kind of break with Jewish religious tradition. For the movement of Jews out of the ghetto was simultaneously a movement away from a corporate community that had been centrally defined by Judaism – by religious practices and rituals such as the Sabbath, dietary laws and the injunction to cover the head, by the Hebrew language (alongside the Yiddish vernacular), by the rabbinical 'walls around the Torah'. This break can be described as the price of emancipation. It was, in the first place, a means of trying to neutralize traditional, Christian anti-Jewish prejudice, which was centred on the 'otherness' of the 'unassimilable' Jew, symbolized by caftan and ringlets. The offer of emancipation by the German states was also conditional on the denial of certain traditional features of Jewish religious identity. How, it was asked, could Jews serve as soldiers on an equal basis if they remained bound to observance of the Jewish Sabbath and dietary rituals? Questions of this kind were central to the emancipation debate from the late eighteenth century. For both Jewish and Gentile supporters of civic and legal equality, this process meant emancipation *from* the weight of suffocating tradition (not least religious tradition), as well as emancipation *within* the larger German society. These were two sides of the same coin. This view found its most radical development in the writings of Karl Marx and others on the left, for whom the expunging of 'Jewishness' represented emancipation of the individual Jew into full humanity; but the idea of assimilation through the casting off of tradition drove the emancipation process more generally. What did this mean in practice, however? There were obvious limits to everyday assimilation. Christian prejudices remained. Even in a large city like Frankfurt, coffee-house concerts were advertised for 'Christian citizens'. The generally optimistic Ludwig Philippson noted in 1867 that anti-Jewish antipathies were still fostered by 'pulpit, school, literature'.[30] Jews were boycotted, snubbed, and excluded. Social relations between Jews and non-Jews became more extensive in the third quarter of the century, but they typically lacked intimacy. At spa resorts, for example, the two groups kept their distance. On the Jewish side there was an element of defensiveness to this, but also a positive desire not to give up every aspect of Jewish identity. This was what David Sorkin has called the emergence of the 'voluntary Jew'.[31] We see the phenomenon most clearly in the continuing low levels of marriage outside the Jewish community. It is even more obvious in the infrequency of conversions to Christianity: no more than 22,000 in the entire nineteenth century, mainly Jews seeking advancement in an official or academic career, for which a baptismal certificate was virtually required. The point is that, even among the most assimilated, embracing German culture rarely meant a willingness to jettison Jewish identity entirely, rather a desire to strip away the more 'backward' or 'traditional' markers of the former ghetto community. Religion remained central to Jewish identity – the favoured self-description of acculturated Jews was 'German citizen of the Jewish faith' – but a religion shorn of its external, 'Oriental' characteristics.

Reform Judaism, not secularization or the complete rejection of belief, was the main channel into which these aspirations flowed. The reform movement dated back to the late eighteenth century, gathering pace in the nineteenth, especially after 1848. It paralleled Jewish educational reform initiatives and the broad trajectory of emancipation. Buttressed by the growing scholarship on Judaism and the proliferation of Jewish periodicals after mid-century, it also found many powerful rabbinical advocates. Reform Judaism was the creed of those who wanted to be German and 'modern' – but Jewish. It sought to reconcile theology and science, to adapt the faith, to make it more a matter of individual conscience than a collective, community concern. Reformers addressed Jews, not Jewry. They drew a line between moral and 'ritual' commandments, and favoured the moral law over ceremonial law. The Reform Rabbi Samuel Holdheim distinguished between eternally valid religious elements in the Torah, and those that reflected ancient Israelite theocracy – concluding, for example, that the binding day of rest, although Saturday in ancient Israel, could well be Sunday in nineteenth-century Prussia. There were close parallels here with American Reform Judaism of the 1885 'Pittsburgh Programme', which rejected ceremonies 'not adapted to the views and habits of modern civilization'.[32] German Reform Judaism meant that dietary proscriptions were tacitly ignored, heads went uncovered, and the talented young man now went to the classical grammar school and university, not to the Talmudic academy, or *yeshiva*. When an Orthodox rabbi left a liberal congregation, organ music might be imported into the synagogue. The Reform movement made enormous advances during the middle decades of the nineteenth century. When the painter Moritz Oppenheim began his series of 'Pictures of Traditional Jewish Family Life' in the 1850s (several of them later reproduced in the *Gartenlaube*), they were already an exercise in nostalgia for a disappearing world.[33]

Yet Orthodox Judaism persisted, with its emphasis on the essential rather than voluntary character of the ceremonial laws and its vigorous rejection of what was seen as the opportunism of Reformers. Paradoxically, the process of emancipation, by dissolving the old Jewish corporate collectivity, offered the Orthodox the possibility of seceding from Reform-minded communities. This began to happen in 1848, and the emergence of rival Orthodox and Reform synagogues became the norm in larger cities in following decades, once state legislation made it possible (after 1875 in Prussia, earlier in the Hanseatic cities).

Orthodoxy often made the running. Reform Judaism also stimulated the emergence of so-called neo-Orthodoxy, which
accepted some of the implications of 'adaptation' but differed
from the Reformers in what should be retained from Jewish
tradition and what discarded. Orthodoxy, old and new, did not
lack support from Jewish historical and theological scholarship.
The leading figure in the 'Science of Judaism' school, Leopold
Zunz, began as a radical Reformer but later adopted a more
conservative stance. Another prominent figure of the historical
school, Zacharias Frankel, argued for retaining the bulk of ritual
and religious laws (*Halakah*). The traditional identity between
Jewish religion and Jewish people was not easily broken. Within
individual Jewish communities there were battles between
Reformers and Orthodox, in which rabbis of both persuasions
found themselves at odds with their congregations. The lines
of division did not follow any simple rural-urban pattern. While
Reform enjoyed strong early support in small towns of 5–
20,000, as Steven Lowenstein has shown, Orthodoxy not only
enjoyed an edge in the countryside and villages but held its own
in the cities, at least until the great wave of Jewish urbanization
from the 1870s.[34] Before then Orthodoxy seems not only to have
enjoyed particular success among Jewish women, but to have
benefited from the tendency among nontraditional urban Jews
to lose interest entirely in religious services, leaving the way
open for conservatives to keep control of their communities.
Only in the 1880s and after did the cities become identified with
the Reform cause (and with outright secularization), while rural
and small-town Jewish communities became the bastions of
Orthodoxy.[35]

The Protestant church was also broadly divided into orthodox
and liberal wings, although the situation was complicated by the
different historical traditions (Lutheran, Calvinist, Pietist) that
went into the making of German Protestantism. By the middle
of the century, the orthodox consisted of conservative elements
from the combined Lutheran-Calvinist church, with their insistence on inherited faith and church dogma, joined by Pietists
who brought their own particular brand of personal religion,

rooted in the centrality of the bible, the 'pious heart' and inner faith. Liberal Protestantism flowed out of the Enlightenment and the encounter with nineteenth-century historical and scientific scholarship. It aimed to mediate between the claims of reason and revelation, emphasizing morality over dogma, and seeking to adapt Christianity to the modern age. In that sense it had much in common with Reform Judaism – which, in fact, received strong support in its early years from the great theologian of liberal Protestantism, Friedrich Schleiermacher. Orthodox and liberal Protestantism were at loggerheads over everything from theology to synodal government, differences made all the more bitter because – as we have seen – they were closely bound up with politics in Germany's state churches. The defining characteristics of each wing of the church also had implications for the broad hold of the faith in a country that was (after unification) two-thirds Protestant. Liberal Protestantism tended towards an accommodation with the this-worldly that could readily turn the profession of faith into little more than a formality: it also had an under-developed sense of social mission. It was from among the ranks of the orthodox that anxiety over dechristianization produced a social programme of missions, rescue homes and poor-schools; and it was the Pietist wing of conservative Protestantism that produced the closest German equivalent to British or Scandinavian revivalism, in the form of the 'awakenings' in parts of Westphalia and the Lower Rhine, with their violent emotionalism and emphasis on salvation through 'rebirth'. That said, there were serious limits to the popular hold of orthodoxy, in whatever form. Pietism was socially as well as geographically limited in its appeal. Conservative Protestantism in general suffered from the incubus of paternalism, and its identification with throne, altar and established order.

Taken as a whole, Protestant Germany was especially affected by secularization, which was already underway by mid-century and accelerating. It was a complex process, however, with wide variations according to class, region and gender. There is general agreement that the urban bourgeoisie fell away notably from the faith. Writing in the 1880s, Nietzsche referred to the religious indifference 'of the great majority of German Protestants in the middle classes', including in this category both businessmen and the educated.[36] Many pastors came gloomily to the same conclusion, and the evidence seems to bear them out. The middle-class movement away from the church was underway in Berlin before mid-century; in the growing industrial town of Barmen it can be traced through the 1850s and 1860s, as it can in Württemberg and Saxony. Alienation took different forms: lukewarm or token observance, playing a smaller part in parochial affairs, leaving the church altogether, or attending only for the great rites of baptism, marriage and burial. The last was common by the end of the century. There were several reasons for this progressive abandonment – liberal middle-class dislike of orthodox church dominance after 1848, new forms of sociability and the claims of Mammon among successful businessmen, the intellectual inroads made by historical and scientific culture among the educated middle class.

It is important to recognize, however, that a form of secularized Protestantism persisted even when regular observance and the dictates of spirituality had disappeared. What historians call 'cultural Protestantism' was an extraordinarily powerful force among the middle classes.[37] It was eminently compatible with the culture of progress – indeed, progress was largely equated with Protestantism – and a sublimated Protestant pathos left its traces on bourgeois enthusiasm for everything from German unification to the German literary canon. Most middle-class Protestants would have applauded Schiller's comment about Berlin's destiny as the capital of Protestantism, even though few of them went to church in Berlin by the 1880s. That was not the point: German culture *was* Protestant. The Reformation was never far below the surface of educated discourse. Even for those who saw themselves (in Max Weber's later phrase) as 'religiously unmusical', pride in German culture had an unspoken Protestant undertow. It became unmistakable when that culture was defended against the Catholic 'threat'. As middle-class Protestants deserted the pews, their spiritual values reappeared in semisecularized guise in episodes like the Kulturkampf.

The alienation of Protestant workers from the church was more wholesale, and more bitter. The evidence here is overwhelming. As early as 1869 a survey showed that only 1 per cent of nominal church members attended Sunday morning services in the working-class parishes of Berlin. Overall figures were around 3 per cent in Bremen during this period, but lower in proletarian districts. Investigations in Saxony at the end of the century produced similar results, with working-class attendance even lower in solidly working-class small industrial towns than it was in cities like Leipzig.[38] The examples could be multiplied across Germany. Why? One practical problem was pastoral provision, as cities grew and church-building failed to keep pace. Berlin developed gigantic parishes of 50,000 or more. But this was a symptom of deeper changes, as migration and new work-patterns loosened clerical control and disrupted the devotional settings in which faith had been rooted, such as family prayers or bible readings. The changes that took place in one Swabian village indicate what this meant in everyday terms. Berkheim was transformed after 1850 from a village of peasants and craftsmen into a dormitory suburb of industrial Esslingen. Growing numbers of young men broke away from pious fathers, spent their earnings on new urban diversions, and preferred to relax on Sunday – their only full day of the week in the village – before joining their fellows at the inn. Church attendance dropped sharply.[39] The question that arises is why demographic and economic changes of this kind, or urbanization in general, should have led to more widespread dechristianization among Protestant workers than it did among their Catholic counterparts. Here we need to take into account the special problems the Protestant church faced when dealing with workers – its identification with state authority, and the social divide that branded the pastor one of 'them' rather than 'us', because Protestant clergy came from higher up the social scale than Catholic priests. Many apostate workers were actively hostile to Protestant clergy and the institution of the church: ridicule of those who still attended church became a common part of working-class subculture. Such attitudes fed, and fed off, the developing labour movement. Within the predominantly Protestant SPD, militant irreligion was widespread, part of an ideological materialism that owed as much to vulgar Darwinism as to Marx.

At first sight, popular adherence to Protestantism follows a predictable pattern, urbanization and secularization going hand-in-hand. Religious observance was definitely higher in the countryside than the towns, but it was also far from uniform. One variable may have been the extent to which a local pastor was prepared to accommodate popular peasant superstitions and animistic forms of faith; for belief in witchcraft, magic and talismans remained powerful through to the end of the century, although less well studied than its Catholic counterpart.[40] A more demonstrable correlation exists between intact, solidly peasant communities, where religious observance was relatively high, and areas of large farms and estates, where it was lower. Agricultural labourers were much more likely to drift away from the church. This distinction shows up in the broad north-south divide (rural church attendance being generally higher in the south); it can also be seen in states such as Saxony where different forms of agriculture coexisted. Wherever local industrialization drew rural labour off the land, it was also likely to reduce religious observance, for the resulting labour shortage meant that middle peasants spent many more Sundays in their fields.

Protestant church-going was most solid, therefore, in communities of substantial peasant farming, such as Bavarian Franconia. There were other bastions of faith. One was the aristocracy. Despite the occasional 'freethinker', and those commercially minded landowners of whom it was said that 'their temple is the brewery or distillery', the aristocracy in Prussia, Saxony and elsewhere generally provided the backbone of their Protestant communities.[41] Within the towns, observance was usually strong among craftsmen and small traders, perhaps because of their greater social deference and more rigid, old-fashioned values, and because religion underwrote the paternalism, industriousness and fragile sense of respectability involved in maintaining small family businesses. Clerks and minor officials also remained more attached to the church than workers, no doubt for some of the same reasons that applied to independent 'little men' – and because the church provided security and access to urban social networks (and potential marriage partners) for respectable young men making their way in the world. Where an area was denominationally divided, Protestant observance also tended to be higher. We see this in the Bavarian Palatinate, among the Protestant working class of the Ruhr, and in pious Stuttgart, where the predominantly Protestant population faced a growing Catholic minority. The importance of a final consideration can hardly be overestimated: the gender imbalance. Religious observance was consistently higher among women than men. Rainer Marbach's study of the areas around Göttingen shows that by the later nineteenth century women made up two-thirds of congregations.[42] In working-class communities, including solidly Social-Democratic ones, it was mostly women who went to church. 'Feminization' of religion was not confined to Protestantism (or to Germany). In a society marked by separate male and female spheres, the church and its associated activities – philanthropy and 'visiting', mothers' meetings, bible study – were an acceptable realm of activity for women. They also provided a focus of sociability, more readily available to men in secular forms, whether clubs or drinking-places. For women living in straitened circumstances, such as young mothers and widows (the poorest of the poor), the church was a source of charity, affirmation and consolation. In such a setting, the gospel of piety, humility, frugality and – not least – sobriety struck chords.

Turning to Catholic Germany, we find both comparisons and contrasts with developments in Judaism and Protestantism. Catholicism too was divided between orthodoxy and liberalism. The difference was that, in the Catholic case, orthodoxy won a resounding victory in the third quarter of the nineteenth century. The residual doctrines of the Catholic Enlightenment, the liberal Catholicism associated with figures like Hermes, the modern theological views of academics like Ignaz Döllinger and

Franz-Xaver Kraus – all were suppressed. Hermesianism was condemned as heresy; Döllinger, Lord Acton's friend and Germany's most internationally celebrated theologian, was excommunicated for refusing to accept papal infallibility; Kraus became a marginal figure, filling his diary with bitter diatribes about the false direction taken by the church. The triumph of orthodoxy meant a Catholic theology dominated by neoscholasticism and the rejection of attempts to adapt the teachings of the church to a changed world. This standpoint was summed up by the notorious denunciation of 'modern civilization' in the *Syllabus of Errors*. The reactionary position of the church was also a victory for ultramontanism, the doctrine of papal supremacy, and its allies like the Jesuits. Both the *Syllabus* and papal infallibility had Catholic opponents, not least in Germany, but Rome enforced its will and few were willing to resist. The German 'Old Catholics', who broke with the church over infallibility, remained a small, predominantly middle-class sect.

Ultramontane success was partly a matter of organization and church bureaucracy: the promotion, in Germany as elsewhere, of Roman rites and liturgy, the more regular summoning of bishops to Rome, the growing intervention in diocesan disputes. By the 1870s this had acquired a powerful momentum, as the products of the more independent and ultramontane seminaries of the postrevolutionary decades moved into positions of power within the church. Ultramontanism also benefited from the emotions unleashed by political events. After Italian unification, the pathos of the self-styled 'prisoner in the Vatican' led German (like other) Catholics to demonstrate their solidarity – collecting Peter's pence, showering the pontiff with expressions of goodwill, celebrating papal anniversaries with new fervour. Conversely, the fact that Catholics were a very self-conscious minority within the newly unified Germany strengthened the tendency to look towards Rome as a source of identity and solace. This phenomenon reached a high point during the Kulturkampf. Many, mystical and militant in equal parts, saw Rome, quite literally, as a source of deliverance. Bishop Ketteler, the most politically prominent Catholic clergyman of the century (and a pragmatist on unification), expressed his disapproval of 'a certain bragging and boasting about the power of the pope, as if he were in a position to cast down his enemies and muster the whole world against them with a single word'.[43] Papal iconography was also prominent in many highly disciplined demonstrations of Catholic defiance. Flying the papal flag or displaying flowers in the papal colours of yellow and white, often in the face of legal penalties, formed an important symbolic component of Catholic resistance to the Kulturkampf.

Catholic solidarity resulted partly from the tendency to close ranks at a time of external attack and widespread contempt on the part of non-Catholics. 'As ultramontanes we are more or less unclean,' observed the art historian August Reichensperger.[44] In that sense, the Kulturkampf turned out to be a self-fulfilling prophecy. At a deeper level, popular piety and the loyalty to their clergy shown by Catholics in the 1870s rested on changes that had taken place over the previous three decades. Anticlericals were wrong when they referred with distaste to 'traditional' fanaticism and clerical tutelage. Much of what they disliked was the product of a religious revival that began in the 1840s. It took many forms. Large-scale pilgrimages were organized, new sodalities and brotherhoods founded, popular missions mounted by Jesuits, Redemptorists and other orders. The motif that ran through all these activities was the reassertion of clerical discipline over the faithful. Like the larger process of Romanization, these changes testified to more efficient church bureaucracy at diocesan and decanal levels, reaching down to the individual parish. Seminary education was overhauled and the clergy more rigorously prepared for their pastoral roles. The priest became subject to greater control, and in turn demanded a greater degree of obedience from parishioners. The 'machinery' of the church (Max Weber) showed how Catholicism adapted the forms, if not the content, of the age of progress.[45] In the railway era, the new model pilgrimages to Kevelaer or Aachen were more disciplined than their often ragged predecessors: they were expected to run to timetable. And the church learnt from the great exhibitions of the period how to use electric lighting effectively in displaying bones and other holy objects.[46]

The renewed popular piety of these years was connected to organizational changes, for the devotional forms of the church also underwent a kind of centralization. The key element here was the growing emphasis placed on the figure of the Virgin Mary. The lead came, once again, from Rome, where Pius IX enunciated the doctrine of Mary's Immaculate Conception in 1854 and missed no opportunity to foster the cult of the Blessed Virgin. In Germany, as elsewhere, Mary became the symbol of more uniform devotions. Marian sodalities replaced parish organizations that had become too worldly. Pilgrimages to approved Marian sites were substituted for visits to the shrines of local saints credited with dubious powers. The practice of celebrating May as 'Mary's month' spread to Germany from Italy and France after mid-century, placing a Marian imprint on festivities that previously bore a pagan character. The liturgy, diocesan hymnals, statuary – all reflected the Marianization of Catholicism. Of course, many local cults persisted; and other, non-Marian cults that were clerically approved, like the Sacred Heart, also grew. But Mary Immaculate was the central figure in the cloying, emotionally laden, frequently sentimentalized popular piety that took shape in the third quarter of the century. In an age of mass production, this devotional renewal was accompanied by the spread of religious artefacts of every kind: pictures, postcards, statuettes, rosaries, medallions, candles and representations of the Virgin Mary in materials ranging from soap to gingerbread.

We can trace these changes and gauge their impact by examining the experience of one village. Marpingen, in the Saarland, was a pastoral nightmare in the first half of the nineteenth century. There were disputes over drinking, dancing, gambling and irregular church book-keeping; a shrine to the Virgin Mary was knocked over by a cart and not replaced; successive parish priests faced unruly congregations and even physical threats. The situation was transformed from the late 1840s. Church attendance and behaviour improved, the shrine was restored and a Marian sodality successfully established. The sea change symbolized the religious revival in the Trier diocese to which Marpingen belonged, and owed much to the arrival of an intensely Mariolatrous parish priest. It was against this background that the village achieved celebrity (and notoriety) in 1876, when three young girls claimed they had seen apparitions of the Virgin Mary. Within a week, 20,000 pilgrims were gathered at the spot, singing Marian hymns and praying on their rosaries. They took water from a 'miraculous' spring, ate earth and stripped bark from surrounding trees as talismans. Hundreds of miraculous cures were claimed and celestial omens reported. The alleged apparitions continued for fourteen months, engaging the attention of Prussian civilian, military and legal authorities. Like the many other minor incidents of this kind during the 1870s, the 'German Lourdes' (as it was soon dubbed) suggests the desperation of Catholics during the Kulturkampf, as they looked for a sign of deliverance. The episode also shows the impact of the Catholic religious revival, and – not to be overlooked – the ways in which popular piety could, from the clerical point of view, get out of hand.[47]

The Marpingen pilgrimage also gives us an accurate snapshot of Catholic Germany in the second half of the nineteenth century. Consider the sociological profile of the apparition supporters. The most conspicuous absence was the Catholic bourgeoisie. This reflected the general underrepresentation of Catholics among businessmen, managers and the educated middle class in Germany; it also indicated the relative coolness of bourgeois Catholics towards ultramontanism and extravagant forms of piety. It was from these strata that support for Reform Catholicism would come at the end of the century. By contrast, the Catholic aristocracy was well represented at Marpingen, again an accurate reflection of the renewal of piety in these circles. Heinz Reif has given us a compelling account of this process among the Westphalian Catholic nobility.[48] Among the lower social classes, the most striking aspect of popular support for the apparition movement was its inclusive, wide-ranging character. In addition to peasants, farm servants and tradespeople, the pilgrims included large numbers of workers, particularly miners from the Saarland coalfield. Once again, the close-up shot of Marpingen fairly represents the larger picture. Catholic workers deserted the church in much smaller numbers than their Protestant counterparts. The fact that Catholic workers so often faced Protestant bosses was undoubtedly one reason; another was the more 'popular' character of the Catholic church, whose priests came from humbler backgrounds than the Protestant clergy and typically displayed more pastoral zeal. A third reason follows on from this, and can be summed up in the word organization. Whether we look at the journeymen's associations pioneered by Father Adolf Kolping, the St Barbara Brotherhoods joined by miners, or Catholic workers' associations more generally, we see evidence of a practical social Catholicism that addressed the everyday needs of wage-earners. It was paternalist and often heavy-handed, but it worked. There were parallel initiatives for other classes, like the Christian peasant associations whose leaders were mostly aristocrats or priests. As the century went on, almost no Catholic subgroup lacked its own organization – craftsmen, servants, steamship clerks. Alongside clerical-led organizations, Catholic Germany boasted an array of lay associations without equal in Europe (except possibly in the Low Countries). Whether dedicated to spiritual concerns, charity, church music, politics (as in the case of the Centre Party), or simply to sociability, they institutionalized the comforts of the faith and nurtured allegiance to the church. The continued adherence of so many Catholics to the faith meant that the gender-gap was less significant than it was among Protestants (and less marked than it was in Catholic France or Spain). Nevertheless, it existed. Just as women played a disproportionate role in events at Marpingen, so they generally went to mass more regularly and on pilgrimages more often. The 'feminization' of Catholic devotions, particularly the emphasis on the Virgin Mary, was matched by a feminization of the faithful. Prurient and sexist though they often were, liberal anticlericals had reason to emphasize the relationship between priests and women.

There are clearly several reasons why the Catholic church

proved more successful than its Protestant counterpart, and why the balance between liberalism and orthodoxy was so different within Catholicism and Judaism. As a minority, Catholics were frequently derided and discriminated against by Protestants, especially Protestants in positions of power. They responded by holding to the faith, closing ranks and wearing their religion as a badge of identity. For all the vigour of the religious revival, this was essentially a defensive reaction. The Kulturkampf sealed the emergence of what has sometimes been called 'ghetto Catholicism'.[49] Here was a striking contrast with German Jews, who moved rapidly out of the ghetto, leaving the more traditional baggage of Judaism behind. In sociological terms, Reform Judaism appealed to Jews whose movement into business, finance and the professions gathered pace in these years. Conversely, liberal and 'reform' beliefs became marginalized within Catholicism, just as the educated middle classes (including the university theologians) who espoused such views remained underrepresented within Catholic Germany. This was the phenomenon variously described as the Catholic 'educational deficit' or (more brutally) as 'Catholic backwardness'.[50] In a reversal of the trend that dominated at the beginning of the nineteenth century, Catholicism traded on its closeness to the 'people' and 'popular' beliefs. The new attention paid to children, now confirmed at an earlier age and even accepted as potential visionaries, was one sign of this emphasis on simplicity rather than learning, the heart rather than the head. The figure of the coldly rationalist professor – whether a liberal-Protestant Kulturkampf supporter, or a Catholic black sheep like Döllinger – was prominent in the clerical demonology.

Doubts and Anxieties

Ultramontane Catholicism was one obvious position from which the culture of progress came under attack. Similar criticism came from Protestant conservatives and Orthodox Jews. The declining respect for tradition, the atomization of society, the exaggerated faith in science and technology, the vulgarity of the press, the cult of novelty for its own sake – these belonged to a familiar litany of complaints from religious conservatives. But the critique of progress or modernity did not come only from these quarters. While religious conservatives deplored the worship of mammon, critics like Friedrich Nietzsche, Paul de Lagarde and the Swiss cultural historian Jacob Burckhardt derided the empty materialism and self-satisfaction of the new Germany. Pompous display and tasteless consumption are always inviting targets. The German Empire was rich in examples, as new public buildings proliferated and the once plain interior of the middle-class home became plush and cluttered. In text and line-drawings, Wilhelm Busch satirized the smug, domesticated life of the comfortable German, symbolized by the top hat, the umbrella and the paterfamilias at table. Nor did the much-vaunted German culture lack critics. Take those temples of culture so characteristic of the era. The Catholic August Reichensperger viewed the 'excessive accumulation' of objects in grand new museums as a 'calamity'; Nietzsche condemned 'the madness of art galleries' that ripped artefacts from their original contexts. Even the *Frankfurter Zeitung*, in many ways the embodiment of the values under attack, issued a sardonic commentary on 'the ballyhoo about beating the cultural drum'.[51]

Worries like this troubled many beyond the ranks of full-time culture critics and prophets of despair. While belief in education and *Bildung* was central to the culture of progress, it also raised questions. One concerned the price exacted by the conveyor belt of classical grammar school and university. Did these institutions not deaden the spirit and encourage mere rote-learning? The term that summed up this concern was *Paukerei*, or 'cramming'. It was, of course, possible to see the singing and carousing of German student life as a happy antidote to this stifling regime. But Nietzsche was not the only contemporary who saw the tawdry excesses of the student prince ('the alcoholism of scholarly youth') as a further symptom of the same disease, just another sign of coarseness and mental torpor.[52] Concern on this score applied not only to academic institutions, but to the lives later led by those who had passed through them. Again, contemporary tropes signal the concern. Pedantry was one, most famously depicted in the figure of Beckmesser in Wagner's *Mastersingers of Nuremberg*, who was modelled (rather unfairly) on the music critic Eduard Hanslick. Probably more familiar to contemporaries was the episode in Joseph Viktor von Scheffel's best-selling historical novel about the Middle Ages, *Ekkehard*, in which a well-meaning monk is humiliated when he uses the accusative rather than the ablative form of a word.[53] Even more ubiquitous than the pedant was the philistine. The word had a long history: Goethe and Novalis deployed it, Eichendorff declared 'war on the philistines' in 1823, Marx used it widely in the 1840s as an all-purpose term of abuse. In the third quarter of the nineteenth century the term came to describe the cultural consumer who *thought* himself educated. August Reichensperger satirized the 'newspaper philistine' (he awakes 'only half-human' but 'as he reads one light after another goes on').[54] Again, it was Nietzsche who pinned down the type with his devastating criticism of the 'educated philistine' in *Thoughts out of Season* (1873). Behind some of these concerns was the question of the half-educated, as Burckhardt called them. What if the nostrums of the progress-mongers produced only a uniform mediocrity? Worse, what if the attempts to spread culture and education succeeded only in laying a thin veneer of civility on the brutish masses? At this point, doubt turned easily into fear.

Some of the central symbols of progress generated anxiety as well as pride. The two reactions are often hard to separate: one was the shadow-side of the other. The railway, for example, was not perceived as an unmixed blessing. It was not only reactionary monarchs who worried about the impact of the new means of transportation. As in other European countries, many doctors initially predicted dire effects on the human body. The Bavarian medical authorities warned that travellers would succumb to brain damage; a Dr Lips of Marburg claimed that the human respiratory system would be unable to withstand the high speeds. Physiological catastrophes of this kind were quickly disproved, together with Dr Lips' calculation that wagon-axles would melt and convert entire trains into glowing beams of fire.[55] Concerns about the alleged psychological effects on the passenger who became a mere 'projectile' were more persistent, and difficult to disprove. Many lamented the loss of experience of the areas travelled through, as familiar landmarks became a blur. And the railway created novel dangers. After all, boilers did explode and viaducts collapse, accidents that were widely reported in the press. Then, in the 1860s, there was a series of 'panics' following a spate of murders, assaults and robberies in isolated first-class compartments. As one commentator rather luridly put it in the 1870s: 'the passenger is pleased when he finds a vacant compartment; but he is not so fortunate when he acquires a fellow passenger who robs him in his sleep, or perhaps even murders him, and then ejects his body from the compartment piece-meal'.[56] The genre of railway-murder detective stories that flourished in Germany (as in England) no doubt reinforced fearful imaginations. Finally, the impact of the railway on the urban landscape created further anxieties. There were complaints about the noise and constant shaking of nearby buildings: a cartoon in the *Fliegende Blätter* depicted a line being constructed through the middle of a bourgeois bedroom. The areas around railway terminals often became associated with crime and prostitution.

Towns, especially large towns, were perhaps the most ambiguous of all the symbols of progress. The shadow-side of urban life was palpable to many contemporaries. In the early 1850s Wilhelm Heinrich Riehl laid out what was to become a widespread view, contrasting the healthy countryside with the ills of the city.[57] For Riehl and other critics such as Hermann Wagener these ills were legion: the breakdown of the family, illegitimacy, prostitution, alcoholism, pornography, the housing misery, rootlessness and fragmentation, the threat of social unrest. The point, for antiurban writers, was not the existence of this or that 'problem' (many of the issues they identified were, after all, well-documented), but the malaise of a whole way of life. The city, in short, was a source of moral corruption. It was from a deliberate rejection of this supposedly poisoned atmosphere that many town-dwellers used the opportunity to escape periodically into the countryside, extolling the 'unspoiled' lakes, forests and mountains. Others began to pay more flattering attention to rural costume and folk ways, although what they praised was often (as Hermann Bausinger has noted) a fantasy constructed out of the 'peasant past and bourgeois longings'.[58] German literature, including the 'realist' novels of the period, also preferred to dwell on the small town. A specific genre of rural *Heimat* works became popular, with their idyllic portrayals of the peasantry. Conversely, there was no German equivalent of the Balzacian novel in which the gifted young provincial hero makes his way in the capital. When Berlin was fictionalized, it was invariably as the 'big and loathsome city' described by Lagarde.[59] Thus Wilhelm Raabe's *Der Hungerpastor* (*The Star-vation Pastor*) (1864) concerns a poor provincial who eventually becomes a contented local pastor in rural obscurity – but not before a period spent as a tutor in Berlin, where he is horrified by the materialism and spiritual degradation.

One aspect of expanding cities that offended critics was their rectilinear quality – the broad, straight new streets that signified a dreadful uniformity compared with the twisting alleyways that were swept away. A one-eyed nostalgia was clearly at work here, which we have come to think of as 'antimodern'. So it was. But the critics were also concerned with conservation (a word used by contemporaries), anxious to save as much of the historical built environment as possible from urban development. Across Germany, there were arguments over churches and city walls. In Cologne a partly successful battle was fought to preserve the ancient town gates. Here was another ambiguity of progress. The extraordinary prestige of German historical scholarship, and of history as a discipline, made the broader German public much more sensitive to the claims of the past. This saturated whole areas of life. Accurate detail came to be expected from the painters of historical scenes, whose popularity grew; the same applied to the authors of historical novels, who also won a larger audience. 'We are *historical* through and through,' wrote

Nietzsche in 1878.[60] Yet this made it more difficult to tear down what was 'historic' (an increasingly capacious category) in the name of progress or culture. More accurately, perhaps, it did not prevent such acts from taking place, but it bred a sense of discomfort characteristic of the age, even among some of the most apparently serene advocates of the brave new world.

Building or rebuilding the city had another shadow-side to it: scandal. In the heady early years of the new Empire government contracts for public buildings were awarded on a huge scale. The process was punctuated by periodic scandals, usually concerned with overspeculative ventures rather than outright corruption. Whatever the degree of illegality involved, Germany experienced some spectacular building scandals, especially after the crash of 1873, which burned the fingers of large, small and institutional investors. There were parallels in other sectors, where the prospectuses of numerous railway, steamship and mining promoters were now exposed as hopelessly optimistic. The bust that followed the 'founders' boom' led, as we have seen, to a fall in rates of profits and (initially at least) to falling real wages as well as lay-offs. But this was far more than just an economic or financial event: it had the impact of a psychological shock that eroded confidence in progress and was widely perceived in moral terms. The effect was probably greatest on two groups. One was the craftsmen and tradespeople, often predisposed anyway to dislike the anonymous forces of the market. Many saw the crash as the product of straightforward 'swindle'. The other group consisted of more conservative educated Germans already hostile to the culture of progress – or torn between pride and anxiety. For them, the crash was also a confirmation of existing doubts, the sign of a deeper moral malaise. For both groups, the Jew became the scapegoat for everything that was wrong with the world.

During the 1870s formerly scattered references to 'Semites' and 'Semitism' started to become more frequent and systematic. The 'Semite', emancipated and overrepresented in business, professions, press and progressive politics, became the perfect symbol of the disturbingly modern. He was associated with liberal capitalism or 'Manchesterism', with finance or 'mobile' capital and its fraudulent speculation, with money-power and materialism divorced from a sense of moral responsibility. As the historian Treitschke put it: 'Indisputably the Semites have had a large share in the lies and falsehoods, the brazen greed of the promoters' evil practices, a heavy responsibility for the vile materialism of our times.'[61] Jewish lawyers came under similar attack (several, such as Eduard Lasker, were prominent legal draftsmen for the liberal parties); so did writers and critics who allegedly mocked tradition and fostered the dissolution of social ties. Anti-Semitism – the word itself was coined by the writer Wilhelm Marr in 1879 – grew out of the uncertainties of Germany after the crash. It was a postemancipatory concept. The charge was no longer (as antiemancipationists had once argued) that the Jew was poor and unassimilable, but that he was rich and all-too-well assimilated. The Jew could no longer be distinguished by dress, appearance and outward religious signs; therefore new racial criteria were deemed necessary to identify the Jew who had 'hidden' himself within German society. Hence the 'Semitic' cranium, haunch-formation and all the other nonsense that characterized the new, pseudoscientific anti-Semitism.[62]

This clearly was something novel. Anti-Semitic writers like Marr and Eugen Dühring spoke a different language from older, anti-Jewish sentiment (which was not racially based, and accepted the baptized Jew). But we should not exaggerate the break.[63] Traditional Christian-conservative prejudice also found newly virulent expression in the 1870s, from court chaplain Adolf Stöcker and the *Kreuzzeitung* newspaper on the Protestant side, from prominent political figures (Peter Reichensperger, Julius Bachem) and publicists on the Catholic side. Catholic resentment was fuelled by the Jewish presence among National Liberal and progressive supporters of the Kulturkampf. Like Protestant prejudice, it also drew on long-standing stereotypes of 'Jewish' usury and moral contamination, now applied to Germany in the wake of the 1873 crash. Both timing and specific character of the Christian-conservative backlash therefore had elements in common with the new racial anti-Semitism. There was no sharp break; the two overlapped. Marr's coinage provided a term under which new and old prejudices were grouped, and during 1879–80 it quickly achieved general currency. In those same years an Anti-Semitic League was established; Treitschke (who combined elements of both approaches) lent the movement respectability with his prestige; and an anti-Semitic petition circulated in 1880–1 acquired a quarter of a million signatures. The history of anti-Semitism, old and new, was to be convulsive and irregular in the following decades. It would be wrong to see the 1870s as the beginning of an inexorable growth in anti-Semitic sentiment. Yet this ugly episode, shocking to a liberal like Theodor Mommsen, showed how easily Jews could become the scapegoats of social anxieties. The anti-Semitic spasm of these years testified to the discomforts of modernity. With its pseudoscientific jargon, it also revealed the shadow-side of the culture of progress.

Cultural historians have often referred to a particular German penchant for 'inwardness', an antimaterialism that rejected arid mechanical civilization and took pride in greater German spiritual depth. The reality is rather different. Certainly in the third quarter of the nineteenth century, attitudes towards material progress were more often jubilant, sometimes absurdly so. The evidence on this score is overwhelming. These 'modern' strains of thought carried their own sinister shadow-side: both the Kulturkampf and the anti-Semitic outburst of the 1870s showed how pseudoscientific language could be used to dehumanize an entire group within society. At the same time, the bombastic culture of progress was open to attack from various directions – from the left in the name of the working class and the future, from the religiously orthodox (Protestant, Catholic and Jewish) in the name of tradition and authority, from cultural conservatives in the name of civilized values. There could be significant degrees of overlap between the positions. The Catholic August Reichensperger and the anticlerical Nietzsche agreed in abusing museums and 'educated philistines', although Nietzsche's advocacy of 'Dionysian' passion sat uneasily with Reichensperger's desire to sweep nudes and other neoclassical 'obscenities' out of Germany. Conservatives and socialists cited similar evidence of urban social problems and even used a shared idiom of denunciation, although their solutions differed. Not all of this was wholesale, kneejerk antimodernism. Much more common was ambiguity: pride in German material and cultural achievements, tempered by doubts about some of the implications. Anxiety was growing by the 1870s, but a general belief in progress continued to be widespread throughout these years – and beyond. In so far as it was seriously challenged, this would come only in the decades before the First World War, in the true age of modernity.

PART THREE

The Age of Modernity, 1880–1914

CHAPTER SEVEN

'Made in Germany': A New Economic Order

Agriculture, Industry, Small Business

By the 1870s Germany had become a respectable European industrial nation; on the eve of the First World War it was a major world economic power. The transformation can best be appreciated by looking at Germany alongside the industrial pioneer. In 1880 Britain produced twice as much steel as Germany; by 1913 the position was reversed. Something similar occurred in other branches: in none did Germany fail at least to narrow the gap appreciably. The strides Germany had taken were most obvious when it came to finished, manufactured goods designed for the export market. Many German exhibits at the centennial exposition at Philadelphia in 1876 were denounced by critics at home as cheap and nasty. But within two decades the trademark 'Made in Germany' became an international symbol of high quality, discussed by anxious editorial writers on *The Times* and other British commentators.[1] In a generation, Germany passed from being Britain's favourite market to Britain's major industrial competitor. How this came about, and the specific shape assumed by the dynamic German economy, form the subject of the present chapter.

Rapid and successful industrialization did not mean that the agricultural sector disappeared. Far from it. Almost ten million Germans were registered in the census of 1907 as working in agriculture, forestry or fishing. That was 35 per cent of the economically active population, almost four times the British level. When we think of German rural society the Junker land-

TABLE 3: *The Structure of Landholding in Imperial Germany*

The Percentage of Agricultural Land in Holdings of	1882	1895	1907
Under 5 acres	5.7	5.6	5.4
5–12.5 acres	10.0	10.1	10.4
12.5–25 acres	12.3	13.0	14.5
25–50 acres	16.5	16.9	18.2
50–250 acres	31.1	31.3	29.3
over 250 acres	24.4	24.1	22.2
TOTAL	100	100	100

Note: The German unit of land is the hectare. In this table the hectare is taken as equivalent to two and a half acres. It actually equals 2.4711 acres.

SOURCE: S. Dillwitz, 'Die Struktur der Bauernschaft von 1871 bis 1914', *Jahrbuch für Geschichte*, 9 (East Berlin, 1973), p. 101.

owners of the east probably come to mind first, with their large, directly farmed estates dedicated to rye, beet and their derivatives (sugar, distilled alcohol). The Junkers certainly had a role and influence disproportionate to their numbers. But the agriculture of the Empire was notable for a diverse peasant economy that included all the main grains, fodder crops, fruit and market gardening, animal raising, dairy farming, wine-growing and even – in the warm, humid southwest – tobacco. The distribution of land mirrored this diversity (see Table 3).

Those owning more than 250 acres (they were not all Junkers, of course) accounted for just over a fifth of agricultural land in 1907, a slight decline since 1895. At the other extreme, those with less than 5 acres – some 3.25 million of them – owned just over 5 per cent of the total cultivated area. Almost three-quarters of all land, in other words, was in the hands of large, medium and small peasants, who numbered well over 2 million in total, although only about 280,000 fell into the category of 'large peasants', i.e. those who owned between 50 and 250 acres.[2] Peasant proprietors (there were very few sharecroppers, or tenant farmers of the English type) therefore dominated the landscape west of the river Elbe, and landholding in Germany as a whole.

On the face of it, agricultural production in this period was an unbroken success story. As in earlier decades, more new land was devoted to the main food crops: another 4 million acres. Yields and output rose steadily. By the early twentieth century the Empire produced 40 million tons of potatoes a year, a ton for every adult German. Stocks of horses, cattle, pigs and poultry also rose, although not of sheep. Various changes helped to drive these improvements. There was rising demand from a rapidly urbanizing society, and branch-line construction made it easier to market produce. On the supply side mechanization advanced, mainly on larger holdings, with the spread of the steam threshing machine and use of the electric motor for sawing and pumping. Scientific methods were increasingly applied to choosing grains, drilling methods and stockbreeding, while the prominence of the German chemical industry made possible the growing use of artificial fertilizer. (Chemicals were not yet helping German wine producers in the way that became notorious later in the twentieth century.) Agricultural colleges, winter schools and state agricultural chambers played an important pedagogical or advisory role. A network of rural purchasing cooperatives helped to bring the fruits of technology within reach of peasant proprietors.

These achievements were real, but there was more to Imperial German agriculture than phosphates or pedigree pigs, and gains in productivity were not achieved without major assistance. Throughout this period, primary producers operated behind a protectionist wall designed to limit cheaper foreign imports from

Europe and overseas, at a time when world production was rising and freight rates were tumbling. Introduced in 1879 at fairly modest levels, agricultural tariffs were raised substantially in the 1880s. They were lowered under a series of controversial trade treaties negotiated under Chancellor Caprivi in the 1890s, the most important of which opened up Germany to larger imports of Russian grain. But the tariffs were increased again under Chancellor Bülow in 1902 and remained in force down to the war. Producer interests and their 'agrarian' academic friends argued that Germany had to maintain the ability to feed itself, especially in the event of war.[3]

German agricultural tariffs have been widely criticized, starting with contemporary liberal critics, continuing through Alexander Gerschenkron's brilliant polemic of 1943, *Bread and Democracy in Germany*, down to the historiography of the last twenty-five years.[4] Consumers certainly paid more than they would have done given a free market in agricultural produce, for protectionism kept German food prices above world levels. It is less clear that the Junkers were, as so often claimed, the predominant beneficiaries. True, the East Elbian staple, rye, received favourable treatment; protection raised the price of fodder for peasants practising animal husbandry; and the higher cost of rye bread left consumers with less to spend on peasant dairy produce and the like. But tariff duties were also levied on peasant-produced grains (wheat, oats, barley, as well as rye), and research suggests that middle and large peasants benefited substantially. Protection was similarly extended to almost everything in which peasants had an interest, including horses, cattle, fruit, vegetables, wine, and wood. Other measures were also designed to help the peasantry. Hygiene regulations were often abused in order to block meat imports. The consumer interest served as an equally spurious pretext for protecting dairy farmers from the competition of cheaper margarine – by requiring the latter to be dyed an obnoxious colour, for example.[5] All in all, agricultural protectionism was neither a Junker ramp, nor did it completely distort the pattern of German primary production by preventing diversification away from grain-growing, even if it is true that the Empire produced more rye than it would have done in the absence of tariffs. The most important acts of favouritism to the Junkers lay in other areas: tax privileges, the ability to entail their estates, preferential freight rates for their produce on the state railways, and what amounted to export premiums through manipulation of import-export 'identity certificates'.

The tariffs prompt two further questions. First, how exceptional were they? Helmut Böhme refers, like many, to Germany's 'tariff isolation', but it would actually be more accurate to talk of Britain's 'free trade isolation'.[6] Agricultural protectionism was the norm rather than the exception in these years – note the Méline tariffs in France, or the McKinley tariffs in the USA. German tariffs were not particularly high by international standards. Secondly, just how effective were they? The recovery of world prices in the early twentieth century probably did more for German agriculture than the Bülow tariffs. At the same time, neither import duties nor other concessions to agrarian interests could disguise the fact that farmers faced major structural problems. These were many, and went well beyond price levels. One was, quite simply, the growing subordination of primary producers to developments beyond their own control. The chemical industry may have provided phosphates and nitrates for the cultivator: it also produced the hated margarine, and allowed brewers to reduce their dependence on hops by partial use of surrogates like rice. Refrigeration freed the buyers of primary produce from seasonally high prices, and created the spectre of transatlantic meat imports. To resist these trends was to swim against the current. Then there was the question of debt. The revised Prussian land law of 1872 treated land like any other form of property when it came to indebtedness and distraint. Rural debts became negotiable on the capital markets like any other paper. Despite entailment, rural debt rose in this period – in fact, indebtedness was most severe on large estates.

Finally, there was the problem of rising costs. Phosphates and the rest were expensive, and agrarian communities had some reason to denounce 'fertilizer rings'. That was one reason why purchasing cooperatives spread. Local taxes were also rising, despite Junker fiscal privileges. Above all, labour costs rose as the supply diminished. The Junker estates illustrate the problem. While farm workers remained under contract, their conditions were dreadful. They were subject to the harsh Prussian master-and-servant law, and excluded from new welfare legislation. Naturally enough, they took every opportunity to vote with their feet. Recruits failed to return to their villages after serving in the army, and there was a vast movement of labourers to the growing industrial areas – Berlin, central Germany, the Ruhr. Hence the increasing resort of estate owners to cheap foreign seasonal labour, mainly Poles from across the Russian and Austrian borders, to try to fill the holes and hold down costs. The so-called flight from the land was felt beyond the estates, despite the high levels of self-exploitation among peasant families. Bavarian and Westphalian peasant proprietors also had to recruit foreign labour – Italian or Swiss in the south, Dutch in the north. There were around half a million foreign agricultural labourers in Germany on the eve of war, not counting illegal workers.[7]

Germany had changed from being a net exporter to a net importer of grain in the 1870s. Now German agricultural labour had to be imported as well, for almost all of the natural increase in rural population was drained off into the towns. Both trends indicated that the German Empire had become primarily an urban-industrial state. The distribution of the labour force is the most obvious sign of change. Between 1882 and 1907, the agricultural sector fell from 42 to 35 per cent of the economically active, while industry rose from 36 to 40 per cent. The turn-around is more obvious if we look at the respective shares of the total population, where that of agriculture fell from 42 to 28 per cent while those dependent on industry rose from 35 to 42 per cent. (The discrepancy reflects the fact that so many 'dependants' in agriculture were already counted as economically active.) But even this second set of figures understates the real shift. After all, German forestry employed more people in the early twentieth century than the chemical industry, but

FIGURE 4 *Index of German Industrial Production, 1870–1913*

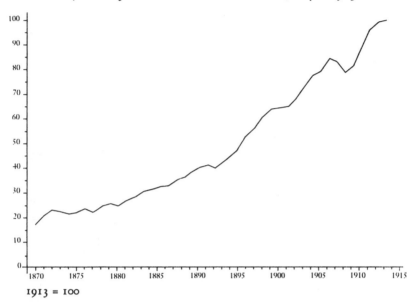

1913 = 100

SOURCE:
G. Hohorst, J. Kocka and G. A. Ritter (eds), *Sozialgeschichtliches Arbeitsbuch II: Materialien zur Statistik des Kaiserreichs 1870–1914* (Munich, 1978), p. 78.

that says nothing about their relative importance for the national economy. The share of gross national product tells a starker story. While the total value of German agricultural output almost doubled between 1870 and 1913, its share of GNP declined from 41 to 23 per cent. By the latter date, industry, mining and transport together accounted for 52 per cent.[8]

The German industrial economy expanded and diversified in the decades before the war. The bedrock remained extractive and heavy-metal branches: coalmining, iron, steel, engineering. All grew fast, especially after the 'Great Depression' finally gave way to sustained boom in the mid-1890s. In the years 1896–1913, the number of miners in the Ruhr increased from 100,000 to 400,000. Total coal output tripled between the 1880s and the eve of war, by which time Germany was raising a quarter of all the world's coal. The Silesian coalfield alone, very much secondary to the Ruhr, had an output exceeding that of the whole of France. In the same period, raw iron output quadrupled, steel output increased thirteen-fold. These branches benefited from the industrial tariffs also introduced in 1879, although that is not the major reason for their dynamism. Construction remained a leading sector as urbanization proceeded even faster and the municipal infrastructure became more comprehensive, including new features like urban tram systems. The numbers employed in construction rose from half a million to 1.7 million between 1875 and 1907, up from 10 to 16 per cent of the labour force. The most significant novelty of this period, and a marker for the rest of the twentieth century, was the advent of the 'second industrial revolution', associated with branches like chemicals, electrics, precision instruments and optics. Blue-chip firms such as Bayer, BASF, Hoechst, Siemens, Bosch and Zeiss indicate German quality and world leadership in these fields. There is symbolic significance in the fact that, while Britain had pioneered the gas industry, the first overhead electrical transmission line became operational in Germany. Carl Benz and Gottfried Daimler also built the first car in 1885–6, although the French first exploited the invention and it was not until the turn of the century that the German automobile industry really started to develop. There was still no volume car-production. Before 1914 the steam train and the electric tram were still seeing off the horse, without yet facing a major challenge from the internal combustion engine. Finally, the expansion of the consumer branches was now more important than it had been in the earliest phase of industrialization. Food and drink are classic instances. Sugar consumption increased threefold between 1873 and 1912, and this was also the period when milling and bread-making became widely industrialized. As for drink, we can point to the large rise in both milk and beer consumption, the latter stimulated by the development of new bottling technology (the subject of later foreign minister Gustav Stresemann's PhD) and by the arrival in the 1880s of 'beer palaces' run by the large breweries.

At the beginning of the twentieth century, Germany's 425 joint-stock breweries had a total of more than a billion marks of capital invested. Beer was big business.

Consumer branches like these illustrate one of the major trends of the period: the movement towards concentration. The number of firms declined, the average size increased. Sugar, for example, had always been a relatively large-scale, capital-intensive industry, but between 1895 and 1912 the number of factories fell by a quarter while the average workforce grew from 200 to 300. The number of large cotton spinning businesses halved between 1882 and 1895, the average number of employees doubled. Whether we look at the number of large (50-plus) and giant (1000-plus) concerns, or at their share of the labour force, or at the fixed capital invested by the biggest businesses, or at the proportion of total production accounted for by the leading 50 firms in a given branch – by all of these criteria, the process of concentration was proceeding relentlessly throughout the economy. Contemporaries referred to businesses being 'soaked up' (*Aufsaugungsprozess*), and many were struck by the way that this was happening in branches hitherto characterized by small-scale production: spinning, weaving, shoemaking. But the greatest levels of concentration were to be found in mining, heavy industry and the new, technologically sophisticated sectors. The ten largest coal concerns in 1913 accounted for 59 per cent of all production, the five largest dyestuff manufacturers shared 90 per cent of output, and just two electrical companies (Siemens and AEG) with their subsidiaries controlled more than half of everything produced.

Concentration of industry was an international phenomenon, but it was accompanied in Germany by a distinctive development: the construction of powerful cartels, or market agréements between firms. Cartels sought to minimize competition, to maintain price levels and prevent their fluctuation. Their aim was stability and the capacity to plan investment on a long-term basis – at the expense, naturally, of consumers, whether these were individuals or other businesses.[9] Historians usually distinguish between two different kinds of cartel: the 'horizontal' which linked firms in the same branch, and the 'vertical', which brought together branches concerned with consecutive stages of a production process, such as coal-iron-steel. The building of cartels is often linked to the 'Great Depression' although this is only partly true. There were isolated attempts earlier to come to market agreements, among rail producers and in the alkali industry for example. The real advance then came in the 1880s, followed by another burst of agreements in the early twentieth century. In other words, cartels were created in bad times and good: they were a response to the falling profit rates and sense of anxiety in the depression years, but also to growing demands for capital investment and the costs of technical innovation. They were aggressive as well as defensive. By 1905, there were more than 350 cartels. The most important were, predictably, in the most concentrated branches where this kind of market control was easiest: coal, iron, steel, electrochemicals. One of the best-known and strongest was the Rhineland-Westphalia Coal Syndicate formed in 1893. But there were effective agreements in most major industries, including sugar, cement, paper and glass. Even the producers of skates and perambulators formed cartels. The simplest form of cartel was content to fix prices; others concerned themselves with the common acquisition of raw materials, production levels and marketing. The more elaborate the agreements, the more ground there was for friction. Cartels were inherently volatile, the product of bargaining, threats and bluffs – a replication in the business world of high diplomacy. Some collapsed; others were weakened by the strategic advantage enjoyed by 'mixed' concerns that straddled agreements. Recent writers have tended to question the power of the cartels. The overall verdict is probably that their influence on the market varied from minor to very substantial, depending on branch, although none exercised complete control.

The resources of the cartel, like the tendency towards concentration, potentially freed industrial concerns from reliance on the banks as a source of funds. Very large concerns could generate their own capital. But this was much more true of some branches than others – it applied to electrics and chemicals, for example, more than mining or metals. In general, reinvested profits, reserves and share issues hardly covered the high investment requirements of German industry. The role of the banks was therefore decisive, much more so than it had been in the first phase of industrialization up to the 1870s. Above all, the banks offered long-term financing. Like cartel arrangements, this gave entrepreneurs the security of long-term planning. From the 1880s, industrial and financial capital became increasingly interlocked. It is sometimes said that the banks directed industry, even that they provided the impetus towards trusts and mergers. Certainly the banks had a crucial say in industrial strategy by placing their own representatives on the boards of firms in which they had an interest. In some well-documented cases – like the relationship between the Deutsche Bank and Mannesmann – the bank clearly called the tune. But the industry-finance relationship was not all one-way. Large concerns also placed their men on the boards of banks, and successful businesses could exploit the competition and pick their bank. In a different sense, the large amounts of long-term capital invested in an industry committed bankers to continue their support, even – or particularly – during bad times. By tying up their capital, they tied their own hands. This was a potent weapon in the hands of the industrial concern. The bank could threaten to turn off the life-support system; the concern could threaten to die.

The businesses that set the tone of German industry in this period were not just larger than their predecessors. Their character also changed as they grew. By the beginning of the twentieth century, a recognizably modern corporate structure had established itself in industry. The largest firms were controlled by managers, not individual entrepreneurs. From the boardroom, through the department heads, technicians and office workers, down to the shopfloor, where some efforts were made to introduce American-type 'scientific management' techniques, the watchwords were: division of labour, planning, rationalization.[10] The degree to which corporate organization had been instituted varied from branch to branch, with electrics in the van and textiles probably the least affected of the major sectors. But the trend was general. The composition of the labour force was the most obvious indicator of change, as the numbers of managers, draftsmen, scientific personnel, accountants and book-keepers grew disproportionately. Above all, these years saw the emergence of the modern office, complete with filing cabinets, pneumatic tubes for internal communication, typewriter, telephone, and a growing staff of salaried clerks to operate them. The expansion of the white-collar labour force was dramatic. In a sophisticated firm like Siemens, it grew from around fifty in the 1870s to 12,500 in 1912. This was much faster than the growth of the manual workforce. In 1872 the ratio of manual to white-collar workers had been 10.6:1; forty years later it was just 3.5:1.[11] While the number of blue-collar workers in Germany as a whole increased by 38 per cent between 1882 and 1907, the number of white-collar workers nearly tripled, from 1.2 to 3.3 million. The growth was boosted by the great expansion of tertiary sector branches like banking, shipping and insurance, where the proportion of managerial and office workers was especially high. The retail equivalent of the large corporate concern was the department store, slower to develop in Germany than in France, but now making a powerful impression on contemporaries with its often strikingly modern, American-influenced design and grandiose interior.[12] Like the industrial corporation, the department store was based on organization and planning, in this case concerning matters like the inventory, the selection of loss leaders and the rationalization of space on the main floor area. Then, as now, the customer could expect to find the perfume or haberdashery counter in exactly the same location in any Tietz or Wertheim store. The department store also depended on a hierarchical structure of salaried employees, from purchasers and advertising experts to window-dressers, floor supervisors and the modern army of salesgirls.

This was what big business increasingly looked like. But what about small business? Here we broach one of the most controversial issues in modern German economic history: what happened to the 'little man'? To answer this question, it makes sense to deal separately with the two groups of craftsmen and shopkeepers. Contemporary observers on both right and left had few doubts about what was happening to the craftsman or small producer: he was disappearing, squeezed out by the large concern. Conservatives deplored the demise of the 'independent' man; socialists saw confirmation of the Marxist prognosis that capitalist development was dividing society into capital-owners and proletariat. Then, as later, those who argued this way pointed to the inexorable rise of factory competition, the effects on small producers of concentration and cartels, the unwillingness or inability of craftsmen to adapt to new tastes or techniques of production, and their disadvantages when competing for labour and capital in a market dominated by the big battalions. All of this seems intuitively obvious. But the 'pessimist' case has been subjected to some telling revisions. The deepening process of industrialization – so the argument runs – increased purchasing power and offered the small man opportunities to sell specialist goods. It also widened the possibilities for auxiliary and service roles (plumbing, for example). At the same time, cooperatives and savings banks made cheaper credit available, and the advent of the electric motor brought something of a renaissance to the small workshop. If the depression period had taken its toll on small producers, then this had in fact worked beneficially to clean out weak, one-man concerns, leaving healthier small businesses better placed to succeed.[13] In short, rather than the degraded craftsman we are offered the embryonic small businessman, bristling with entrepreneurial initiative and busily adapting to change. Some of these arguments can be traced back to contemporary liberals, others were formulated in the course of attempts in the 1960s to quantify the contribution of small concerns to German industrialization. The 1980s love affair with small business added another dimension to the case, as academic enthusiasts for contemporary 'flexible specialization' in small firms identified precursors even in the classic era of mass production.[14] A favourite example of these authors is the cutlery industry based on Solingen, where dispersed workshops produced high-quality ware in small batches, a system in which it was possible to adapt quickly to changing demand.

There is much of value in this optimist case. It clears away a lot of misleading nostalgia about the 'good old days' of the traditional craftsmen, in which there was (as we have seen) a large element of myth. Arguments like these also remind us that small producers played a genuinely important role even in the age of Krupp and Siemens. The optimist case is nevertheless an oversimplification. In many ways it presents a mirror image of pessimist accounts. One approach sees industrialization as a juggernaut destroying the old craft world; the other presents it as a vehicle for advancement. The reality is that many structural problems persisted among small producers. A third of all craftsmen in 1895 were tailors, shoemakers or carpenters, the majority of them one-man concerns. These were clearly not the budding entrepreneurs the optimists have in mind. Yet they somehow survived the 'healthy' shake out of the depression years, symbolized by the rising average number of employees in small businesses. How to explain this apparent discrepancy? The aggregate statistics on growing small business probably mask a double process, of concentration on the one hand and semiproletarianization on the other. All branches had their success stories – the masters who expanded their concerns, and so often decided the fate of cooperatives by refusing to join them. But a much larger number of precarious little men struggled on with family labour and maybe one assistant, while below them was a proletarianized mass of one-man concerns eking out a living in rented back rooms and cellars. One 1890 survey showed that as many as 87 per cent of craftsmen in the clothing trade worked alone. The figure was more than 50 per cent in all trades; in Berlin it was almost 60 per cent.[15]

These businesses possessed little capital and their 'independence' was a mere courtesy title. They included the tailors who worked in the sweated trades, the shoemakers who sewed on the soles of factory shoes, the carpenters who worked on contract for the furniture store. *De facto* dependence of this kind was not so different from what had existed in the middle of the century, but fifty years later it was more widespread. Small producers had lost ground relative to large concerns. In 1875 businesses employing up to five people still accounted for two-thirds of those engaged in manufacturing. By 1907 the figure was just one-third. Small workshops' share of the capital stock also fell, although the evidence suggests it may have stabilized in the 1890s at around 10 per cent.[16] Growing numbers of small men became locked into processes of production and distribution over which they had little control. This applied not just to proletarianized tailors, a true reserve army of labour that could be hired or fired as demand dictated, but to coopers who worked for large breweries, or smiths and wheelwrights employed by coach-builders. Imperial statistics always underestimated the extent of this and thus exaggerated the number of nominally independent producers, for they counted technical units, not plant units. The Solingen cutlers were an unusually well-paid, high-skilled example of the phenomenon: their contracts were effectively wages, their individual workshops integrated into a larger system. The whole of Solingen can be thought of as a factory without a roof.[17]

Shopkeepers were in a different position from small producers, ostensibly at least. Urbanization, declining self-sufficiency and rising purchasing power all helped the growth of retailing. The number of shops relative to population doubled in the thirty years up to the 1890s, then in the boom years 1895–1907 it increased by a further 42 per cent, five times faster than the population. By the latter date there were almost 800,000 retail concerns employing up to five people.[18] Nor did most shopkeepers face serious competition from large concerns, although that did not stop them complaining about the 'Jewish' department store. There were more than 200 such stores in Germany by the early twentieth century, but they accounted for little more than 2 per cent of total turnover. Consumer cooperatives, despite their nearly two million members in 1914, had an even smaller share. The same was true of officials' consumer unions, a very German phenomenon. Consumer organizations competed seriously only with the sellers of certain goods, above all bread and shoes. Like other novelties of the period – the mail-order catalogue, automatic vending machines on railway stations – they were hardly a major threat to the small shopkeeper. The real problems lay elsewhere. The independent retailers counted in the statistics covered a broad spectrum of businesses. A minority, located in prime city-centre sites and better-off suburbs, or long established in market towns, enjoyed wealth and security. Jewellers, drapers, the sellers of leatherware and furniture – these belonged to the shopkeeping élite, with substantial capital invested in their stock. The same was usually true of butchers and bakers, officially counted as 'craftsmen' in government statistics. The solid middling ranks of retailing were made up of haberdashers, ironmongers and colonial goods traders, the last-named an indicator of how imperialism was affecting domestic consumption. A buoyant market offered many shopkeepers in these categories an opportunity to better themselves. In his autobiography, Karl Scheffler describes an ambitious grocer who expanded an old family firm, rented out rooms above the shop to raise capital, undercut his competitors, advertised and installed plate-glass windows, until he had turned his corner shop into a substantial store.[19] But there was a very different kind of small shopkeeping: overcrowded, insecure, undercapitalized. In Bremen a third of all retail concerns listed in trade directories had disappeared within six years. These were typically dealers in cheap items like greengroceries, milk and other perishables, second-hand clothes, 'mixed goods', or tobacco. We are dealing here with an activity that merged into stallholding or itinerant selling, often in poor, working-class districts. These were the retailing equivalents of the impoverished tailor or shoemaker. More than half of all businesses were one-man operations, often undertaken by a craftsman squeezed out of production or a worker who was the victim of unemployment, blacklisting or sheer physical decline. For example, a collier, whose loss of strength in middle years often meant, at best, a transfer to overground work at lower pay, might sink his savings into a modest local shop or cigarette stall. Small publicans in proletarian districts often had a similar background. Many 'one-man' operations of this kind were actually run by women, the wife or widow of a factory worker looking to supplement the precarious family income. In Bremen, once again, a third of all shops were part-time in 1907, and a third were run by women. Concerns like this were growing in numbers before the war, but not in capital stock or commercial expertise. They were invariably insecure, with low levels of income and high rates of bankruptcy.[20] It is difficult to imagine anything more removed from the jeweller on Berlin's Kurfürstendamm or the shop selling fashionable hats on Stuttgart's Königstrasse.

Despite the differences between small producers and retailers, we therefore find similarities as well: a wide gap separating the secure from the insecure, with a mass of precarious, one-man concerns at the bottom of the pile. There was a further similarity. All shopkeepers faced problems that jeopardized their independence. As rents, insurance and other costs rose, shortage of capital could affect even the most solid business. Shopkeeper cooperatives developed too slowly to have any impact on this (the figures on cooperatives suggest that shopkeeper individualism was greater than the much-vaunted peasant individualism), and special banks geared to the needs of the small concern also proved inadequate to the need. As a result, many retailers fell into dependence on wholesalers or deliverers for credit. This threatened to turn the shopkeeper into a mere agent of large-scale commercial capital. An exact parallel existed in the relationship that developed between the big breweries and those they supplied. Innkeepers and publicans were positively encouraged to borrow, with loans of up to 40,000 marks advanced against a turnover of 130 gallons a day. Some loans were secured on third or even fourth mortgages at rates of interest that provided cash for the breweries as well as tying the publican to one supplier. Contemporaries spoke of 'debt bondage' or 'servitude'.[21] In the early twentieth century, small business in Germany was caught between a rock and a hard place. Craftsmen, shopkeepers and publicans were faced by the tendency towards incorporation by large capital on the one side, proletarianization on the other.

For all the differences between them, their problems tended to converge as the pace of economic development quickened.

Germany and the International Economy

A true world economy developed in this period, tied together by shipping and the technology of undersea cables, marked by intensified trade and the economic annexation of previously undeveloped parts of the globe. The volume of world trade increased phenomenally, especially at the beginning of the new century. It doubled in the years 1900–10. Germany took an increasing share. In relative terms, the growing German presence in the world economy was matched only by the inexorable rise of the USA.

The most obvious measure of this is the development of German trade. The value of imports increased from 2.8 to 10.8 billion Marks between 1880 and 1913, with the curve rising in the last ten years. Significantly, food and raw material imports grew faster than finished and semifinished goods, a sign of Germany's arrival as an industrial giant. Exports followed a similar trajectory, rising from 2.9 to 10.1 billion Marks over the same period, with an even more striking spurt in the decade before the war. The value of exports doubled in the years 1903–13. In a mirror image of what happened to imports, exports of food and raw materials became less significant. Despite the importance of sugar and (subsidized) rye, food exports contributed only half as much to the total value of exports in 1913 as they had done in 1880, while raw material exports like coal held steady. The real growth came in finished and semifinished goods, which accounted for three-quarters of the value of all exports by the war, up from 63 per cent in 1880.[22] Iron and steel were an important part of this, frequently 'dumped' in world markets at low prices while the depression lasted, thanks to tariffs that maintained a high domestic price level. Among finished goods, textiles lost ground to what became the single most lucrative category of German exports: the products of the metallurgical and engineering sectors. These ranged from the arms of Krupp with their world-wide markets (China, Turkey) to the turbines installed at Niagara Falls. Finally, the last prewar years saw an impressive increase in exports from the branches that now symbolized the 'Made in Germany' slogan – precision optical and surgical instruments, chemicals and dyestuffs, electrics. By 1914 Germany was the European front runner in chemicals, the world leader in electrical goods. It was especially in sophisticated products like these that Germany overtook Britain in European and non-European markets.

The negative trade balance that opened up between German imports and exports alarmed conservatives and featured in the great debate between 'agrarians' and 'industrializers' in the 1890s. It arose during the transition to an industrial state, and continued in the early twentieth century because of the recovery in world prices for food products on which Germany depended. The trade gap was filled by 'invisible earnings'. These included repatriated profits earned by German businesses that established plants outside the country, to take advantage of cheaper labour or circumvent the effects of local tariffs. There were also earnings from services, such as the large German contribution to international construction projects like the Gotthard pass and Baghdad railway. German engineers and architects acquired a higher profile in the world during these decades: the celebrated architect Hermann Muthesius worked during the late 1880s in the Japanese office of the architects Ende & Bockmann, where he was construction supervisor. These were all signs of growing German capital investment outside the country. True, Germany continued to invest more of its surplus capital in domestic industry than did Britain or France, and to export less. In 1914 foreign investments were still lower than the French and less than half the level of the British. Nevertheless, Germany had become the world's third largest creditor nation and German banks were established world wide, from South America and the Far East to western Europe and the Balkans.

Finally, what of those classic areas of invisible earnings, shipping and insurance? Germany remained insignificant in the sphere of international underwriting, in which the City of London continued to be the undisputed world leader. Shipping was a different story. The building of the German battle fleet is fairly familiar, but the remarkable rise of the German merchant marine is more often overlooked. In 1880 the Empire possessed less steam tonnage than Spain. Thirty years later, German steam tonnage was three times greater than the French, four times greater than the American. Only the British merchant marine was larger. The former Hanseatic cities of Hamburg and Bremen, fully integrated into the Empire by the 1880s, were the spearhead of this advance. Shipbuilders received state subsidies, which enabled them to increase the German share of global shipbuilding to 11 per cent – although this was achieved in yards that were slower, costlier and more top-heavy with administrators than those of their British counterparts. New harbour facilities were added at a dizzying tempo. By 1914 the value of trade passing through the port of Hamburg was exceeded only by New York and Antwerp. Shipping lines like the Hamburg-Amerika and the Nord-Deutscher Lloyd, also subsidized, extended their activities beyond the Atlantic and enjoyed a world-wide presence. A global network of German shipping agents and coaling stations accompanied their expansion.

How important were German colonies in all of this? The last quarter of the nineteenth century witnessed a new imperialism that led to a large part of the world being carved up between the leading industrialized powers. The area of Africa under direct European control rose from 11 to 90 per cent. Germany was a major player on this stage, especially during the 1880s, acquiring colonies or protectorates in Africa and the Pacific, and establishing a presence in China. This overseas empire encompassed some 900,000 square miles, four times the territory of unified Germany. Non-economic motives provide part of the explanation for this burst of imperialist activity. Colonial possessions became a contemporary status symbol, and enthusiasts organized in pressure groups like the German Colonial Association of 1882 argued that Germany could not afford to be outdone by neighbours like France – or Belgium. Missionaries had their own interests to push, and there was strong support for colonies among the nationalist-minded, academically educated middle class. (Support in the universities acquired its own momentum, for colonial acquisitions spawned new academic subdisciplines in fields like oceanography, geography and botany.) For all that, 'non-economic' causes should not be exaggerated, as they sometimes are. Imperialism can be seen as the outcrop of a broad mood of assertiveness, often expressed as the belief in a German 'mission', that would hardly have existed without Germany's economic dynamism. At the same time, and a more specific product of the depression years, colonies were viewed as the great antidote to short-term economic difficulties.[23] German imperial possessions, so it was argued, would provide raw materials and a market for German goods and capital, as well as sustaining settlers who would otherwise be 'lost' to Germany. Lastly, we need to consider the dynamics of colonial acquisitions. German protectorates were the outcome of economic calculations being made at different levels, and the way they interacted with each other. Africa is the classic case. At one level we have the buccaneering capitalist adventurer, who carved out a mercantile empire at the price of creating local unrest or antagonizing other European powers in the area. Examples include Carl Peters (Zanzibar), Friedrich Fabri (Angola) and F. Lüderitz (Southwest Africa). But behind these often dubious characters stood more sober interests such as chambers of commerce, manufacturers' associations or the 'D-Banks'. It should not be forgotten that the membership of the Colonial Association read like a 'Who's Who' of prominent figures in the German business world: Siemens, Hansemann, Krupp, Kirdorf, Haniel, Stumm, Henckel von Donnersmarck.[24] It was the combined effect of the adventurers' activities, the lobbyists' hopes and the depression's uncertainties that persuaded an initially reluctant German government to declare protectorates. Political calculation provided the final element, as Bismarck saw an opportunity to counteract the social dangers of the depression while embarrassing the anticolonial left.[25]

German possessions in Africa, Samoa and New Guinea turned out to have embarrassingly little economic significance. They attracted almost no settlers, for the colonies were established just at the time when emigration from Germany declined sharply, and those who did leave the country preferred the USA. The overseas empire also provided fewer raw materials than the optimists had predicted, especially minerals, although some sectors benefited. Palm oil, peanuts, ivory and rubber all turned a profit for firms who dealt in those commodities, with Hamburg mercantile interests very much to the fore. German East Africa was also a source of raw cotton for the domestic textile industry, at a time when world supplies and prices were uncertain. Cotton was produced under a system of forced labour until the Maji-Maji rebellion in 1905–7 led to the introduction of a more incentive-based regime.[26] As for exports, there were always opportunities for the sale of capital goods (railway track, electrical equipment, dynamite for mining), even in colonies that possessed no consumer market. Germany began building colonial railways in the mid-1890s; after 1904 the pace of construction quickened, especially in Africa.[27] And those twin symbols of the German civilizing mission, guns and schnapps, both sold well in the colonies. Ultimately, however, colonial possessions made a feeble contribution to German trade, accounting for a fraction of 1 per cent of imports and exports. It is striking that in Africa, German economic success was greatest in territories where it did not enjoy political control. The Congo is one example. The Transvaal is an even better one, where the Deutsche Bank was active alongside major industrial concerns such as Krupp and Siemens. German firms exported steel, machinery, chemicals and household utensils, supplied the water, and held local monopolies for dynamite and (naturally) whisky. Perhaps it should come as no surprise that German capital investment in Africa – as much as 2 billion Marks in 1914 – was largely in non-German colonies.

There is a larger point here. German imports of food and raw materials from non-European parts of the world grew spectacularly in this period, nearly doubling from 24 to 45 per cent between 1890 and the last prewar years. But Samoa and the Cameroons do not provide the explanation: the produce of Australasia, North and South America was incomparably more important. The same applies to German export of capital, around half of which was invested outside Europe, but in the Americas, not the colonies.[28] In short, Germany was an imperialist power, but its formal colonial possessions were of almost no economic significance – less so than in the case of the British or even the French empire. German informal imperialism was the real success story: the achievement of economic penetration without political annexation or control. Latin America is the textbook example. It was a part of the world where, despite sizable German settlements, the dominant political influences were Anglo-Saxon. But South America served Germany as a source of food, a place where 3.8 billion Marks were invested by 1914, and a major market for manufactured goods.

Europe continued to be by far the most important market for German goods, absorbing three-quarters of all exports on the eve of war. That was why – to cite one telling example – industrialists warned about antagonizing Spain during a dispute over the Caroline Islands, for Germany would lose far more from a breach of trade with metropolitan Spain than it could ever gain in the Pacific.[29] German economic expansion can be seen at its most formidable on the European Continent. German business spilled over the western border, in the form of common transportation projects and coproduction ventures with firms in France, Belgium and Luxemburg. German exports penetrated Scandinavia, and made major inroads into the British market. The commercial treaties negotiated by Caprivi in the 1890s, a symbol of the German transition to an industrial state, were all bilateral agreements with European trading partners.

Even within Europe, however, we can see a kind of German informal imperialism at work, in areas to the east and southeast. This was, in economic terms, the soft underbelly of the Continent. Not for nothing did Lenin describe Russia as the 'weakest link in the chain of imperialism'. The Tsarist Empire, attempting to industrialize from a standing start, became a lucrative market as it borrowed French money to spend on German goods. No less important was the area between east and west that a growing number of German publicists in the early twentieth century referred to as *Mitteleuropa*. The literal English translation of this term – 'central Europe' – fails to communicate its reverberations for influential sections of business, academic and political opinion. These were, of course, areas of long-standing German migration and settlement. But the concept of *Mitteleuropa* went beyond that. It implied cultural influence, political cooperation and economic dominance – a combination that made eastern and southeastern Europe the German Continental counterpart to the overseas empires of other European powers.[30] The Lower Danube and Turkey were undoubtedly important for the German economy. They bought railway track and manufactured goods, providing foodstuffs and oil in return. In 1913, German exports to Romania were three times greater in value than exports to all the colonies combined. But *Mitteleuropa* was even more important in the German imagination than it was in the immediate balance sheet. Overheated speculation about the future of the region as a German granary, as a source of oil and untold mineral wealth, resembled colonial enthusiasm elsewhere. For many Germans, not only businessmen, the area became the equivalent of what the Raj signified for the British, Algeria for the French, or the mythic 'China market' for the Americans. While Cecil Rhodes enthused about a British railway linking 'the Cape to Cairo', his German equivalents looked to the Baghdad railway. For an important segment of German opinion on the eve of war, *Mitteleuropa* was a playground for German interests and influence. And the fact that the region lay within the shaky, multinational empires of the Habsburgs and Ottomans, next door to a sensitive Russia, was to make this German Eldorado a politically explosive element in international relations.

Organized Interests, Politics and the State

Two features became characteristic of all the advanced industrial economies in the decades before the First World War. The first was the tendency for economic interests to organize themselves as pressure groups and lobbies. The second was the interlocking between those economic interests and politics, including both political parties and the state. These trends were present to an unusual degree in Germany. That is why terms such as organized capitalism and corporatism have gained such widespread currency among historians of the period. No one doubts the importance of these phenomena. But which interests prevailed and what role the state played in mediating them remain controversial questions.[31]

Organized interests took different forms. The cartels and cooperatives already mentioned were attempts by particular groups of producers to combine in order to gain an advantage in the market. They were generally branch-specific – the wiremakers' cartel, the dairy farmers' marketing cooperative, the shoemakers' raw-materials cooperative, and so on. Many were local or regional in scope, especially when small producers were involved. On the other side stood the trade unions, whose prewar growth was phenomenal. Membership of the Free Trade Unions rose from 300,000 in 1890 to 2.5 million in 1913; 340,000 workers belonged to a Christian trade union and another 100,000 were enrolled in the liberal Hirsch-Duncker unions. But these are not the organizations historians usually have in mind when they refer to interest groups – the *Verbände*.[32] The term is normally applied to bodies that tried to influence government, parties and public opinion in decisions over economic policy, taxes or trade. Semipublic bodies like chambers of commerce and their agricultural counterparts had always tried to do this in a discreet fashion, but the 1870s brought a heightened level of activity. New organizations were established, like the Association for the Protection of Common Interests in the Rhineland and Westphalia (usually called the 'Long Name Association'), the Union of Tax and Economic Reformers (mainly agrarians), and the Central Association of German Industrialists. A number of Catholic or 'Christian' peasant associations were also founded in these years. From the 1890s, the organization of interests became still more intense. The pro-heavy industry Central Association was challenged by the Confederation of Industrialists, representing smaller firms who manufactured finished goods, and the Hansa-Bund of 1909 was conceived as a union of commercial, exporting and shipping interests against the influence of heavy industry and agriculture. By that date, agrarian interests also had a number of powerful new representatives. The largest was the Agrarian League (1893), a Junker-led organization with a third of a million members by 1914, mainly peasants; but we should not forget the simultaneous emergence of the Bavarian Peasant League and of new Christian Peasant Associations, and the later, liberal-leaning German Peasant Association. Alongside these groups there were organizations for every imaginable interest: bankers, white-collar workers, urban property-owners, craftsmen, retailers. After 1900 periodic attempts were made to unite these last-named groups of small independents into an umbrella 'Mittelstand movement', culminating in the Imperial German Mittelstand Confederation of 1911.

German historians usually refer to these organizations by their initials, an understandable decision if you are writing about a group like the white-collar *Deutsch-Nationaler Handlungsgehilfen-verband*. Hence we have pages studded with the DHV, CVdI, BdI, BdL, RDMV, an alphabet soup of the interests. What prompted this rage of pressure-group activity? Organized interests were a symptom of, and in turn reinforced, the growing importance of economic affairs in public debate and political life. This was evident at every level: in the academic enquiries and publications of the influential Association for Social Policy, in the 'materialist' platforms of the political parties, in the steadily expanding role of the state as employer and contractor, regulator and mediator, taxer and spender. Attention has usually focused on the great issues of the period – tariffs, trade treaties, finance reform – and it is true that these had a particular tendency to spawn new interest groups, or the realignment of existing ones. But economic issues increasingly provided the raw material of everyday political debate. In the period 1890–3 alone, Reichstag committees considered the following: trade treaties, patents, the telegraph, railway freight, the protection of goods and trademarks, working hours, the hire-purchase system, limited company law, the accountancy system, taxation of distilled spirits, internal trade regulations, the bankruptcy code, trade descriptions and labour statistics. In the Reichstag, as in every other German parliament, the annual budget also provided an occasion on which conflicts of interests could be rehearsed. It has been calculated that economic affairs accounted, directly or indirectly, for 90 per cent of Reichstag business by 1914.[33] Even the language of business entered political life, as contemporaries referred to the political speculator, the broker, the political mass market.

Pressure groups operated at a variety of levels. The best-organized tried to work directly on public opinion, through newspapers, pamphlets and travelling lecturers. The Agrarian League was very active in these fields; so was the Hamburg-based German National League of Commercial Employees, which was smaller in membership but had a very active press. Interest groups also sought to influence government, formally through submissions and evidence to committees, informally through lobbying and cultivating ministers or officials. Most of all, however, they worked through the parties. As early as the 1860s the liberal Karl Twesten observed gloomily that 'the landed interest calls itself conservative, the money interest liberal, the labour interest democratic'.[34] In the following two decades Bismarck encouraged the political parties to become the vehicles of economic pressure groups, as a diversion from potentially threatening political demands and as a means to divide and rule. By the 1890s the process was well advanced. The Agrarian League tail wagged the Conservative Party dog. Left liberals pressed the interests of smaller manufacturers, exporters and commerce. The SPD represented the working-class trade unions and consumer cooperatives. And the two 'middle parties' – the National

Liberals and Catholic Centre – tried to perform a balancing-act between conflicting groups, the former divided between heavy-industrial and agrarian wings, the latter between the demands of peasants and other small producers and the claims of the Catholic working class.

It is an apparent paradox that those who owned estates or industrial concerns now became less likely to take parliamentary seats themselves (although there were still many landowners sitting in the Prussian lower house). The number of businessmen in German parliaments dropped sharply from the end of the nineteenth century. They were replaced by pressure-group spokesmen, paid functionaries, and other intermediaries. This marked a decisive change in political life that was noted by Max Weber and other contemporary commentators. It symbolized both the 'bureaucratization' of politics, parallel to what was taking place in business, and the invasion of the parties by inter-est groups. The example of Gustav Stresemann helps, once again, to give this process a human face. After he had completed his dissertation on bottled beer, Stresemann's first political task was to organize the Saxon chocolate manufacturers against the sugar cartel. From this experience came his belief in the need to create a front of liberal industry, commerce and white-collar workers against the vested interests of heavy industry, a perspec-tive he carried into the National Liberal Party as its rising star in the prewar years.[35] Apart from their ability to influence public opinion independently, the interest groups wielded power over the political parties because of their importance during elections. They could, on the one hand, threaten to remove their support from a party if their needs were not taken into account in the choice of candidate or programme. This might even extend to running a rival candidate. The Centre Party was regularly embarrassed in this way by its agrarian wing. On the other hand, the interest groups had money. As elections became increasingly expensive – the cost of fighting a Reichstag seat increased twenty-five-fold between 1880 and 1912 – the resources of the interests became indispensable. The Agrarian League supported candidates in the Centre, National Liberal and Conservative parties, requiring written undertakings on how they would vote on key issues if elected. For its part, the Central Association of German Industrialists funded 120 Reichstag candidates in 1912 to the tune of more than a million Marks.[36]

What general conclusions can we come to about the significance of organized interests? Their undeniable importance was partly a sign of 'modernity', a reflection of the sophisticated, pluralist industrial society that Imperial Germany had become. The role played by the interests showed that Germany was further along the road towards a modern corporatism than most of its economic competitors. By their very existence, organized pressure groups showed that discreet lobbying was no longer enough. If the Junkers had been able to get what they wanted by bending the ear of the Kaiser or exploiting their contacts in the bureaucracy, the Agrarian League would not have been necessary. To leave it there, however, would certainly be to paint too benign a picture. The interests had the effect of furthering divisions both between and within the political parties. True, politics did not become solely a matter of bartering interests, and the role played by pressure groups was in many ways a symptom as much as a cause of weaknesses in the Imperial political system (see Chapter Ten). The interests did not 'replace' political debate, although there were certainly agrarians and heavy industrialists who dreamt of a corporatist system that would do away entirely with parliament, parties and their tiresome debates. But the activity of the interest groups did help to deform the parties, and it created a powerful public distaste for the 'system' – a reaction against the deals and horse-trading (the Germans call it 'cow-trading', or *Kuhhandel*). This would have consequences for German parliamentary democracy in the 1920s.

Finally, there is the question of who gained from this system. Plenty of evidence points to the asymmetrical weight wielded by the different interests. Just as large landowners and heavy industrialists tended to have privileged informal access to the highest levels of the political system (Fritz Krupp was a member of the Kaiser's entourage and his frequent host at Villa Hügel), so their pressure groups were disproportionately powerful. Against that, however, the liberal manufacturing and commercial interests represented in the Hansa-Bund also disposed of a wealth and influence that should not be disregarded. It can even be argued that the general openness of the political system to interest representation had a wider compensatory effect – that it provided the 'little man' with a weapon at a time when the economic big guns, especially in industry, were increasing their market control through mergers, cartels and modern means of workforce discipline ('scientific' management, company unions). Many industrial workers and small independent producers clearly did see activity in the political market place as a potential means of redressing their weaknesses in the market proper. To what extent was this illusory? There is no simple answer to the question of winners and losers. We can try to draw up a balance sheet only by examining the overall shape and direction of state economic policy in this period.

Many have seen the favouring of heavy industry and large-scale agriculture as the red thread running through economic policy. Following this interpretation, there was a pattern that can be followed from the reintroduction of tariffs in 1879 through the reconsummation of the 'marriage of iron and rye' in the period 1897–1902, when higher agrarian tariffs were traded off against the battle fleet for heavy industry.[37] No question, there were structures that systematically favoured these interests. As we have seen, the significance of agricultural tariffs and the estate-owners' share of the largesse have both been exaggerated, but primary producers did receive numerous fiscal and other concessions, with the Junkers the foremost beneficiaries. Without doubt, agriculture had political weight and was prepared to throw it around. Two of Bismarck's successors found that out when they were effectively toppled by disgruntled agrarians, Caprivi for negotiating the trade treaties, Bülow when he tried to pass a finance bill that threatened to tax estates. Heavy industry, too, had a special status. This was not just a question of the battle fleet, which gave Krupp (thanks to its monopoly) a profit of 1600 Marks on every ton of armour plate

Berlin, Building Boom: a construction gang working on the new Paul Wallot
Reichstag, opened in 1894.

Overleaf Berlin, Big City: Blücherplatz, Belle-Alliance Bridge and Hallesches
Tor, photographed by Waldemar Titzenthaler, 1901.

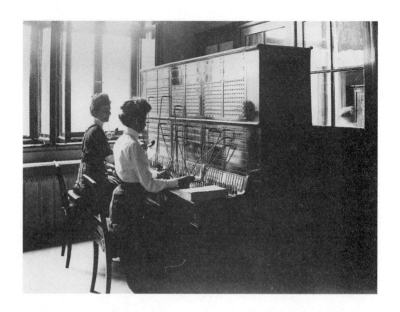

Opposite Berlin, Slums: a cellar room in the south-west of the city. 1905.

Above The 'New Woman': a telephone exchange in 1911.

Left The workers inherit the earth! Two powerful proletarians relieve an exhausted Atlas of his burden. An 1891 caricature from the Social-Democratic magazine, *Der wahre Jakob*.

'You know Dickens, of course,
Herr Rittmeister?' – 'Naturally,
terribly famous fellow, such a pity
he had to be put down' – 'What?!'
– 'That's right, broke both his
forelegs last year in the
Hoppegarten'. Cartoon, from
Eduard Thoeny's 1899 collection,
Der Leutnant.

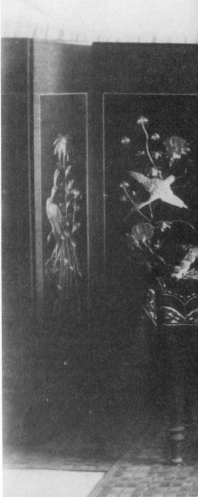

The Masterful Imperialist: the private room of a postal official in German
East Africa, 1894.

A German First World War dugout, with former occupant.

Women performing heavy manual labour in 1917.

it sold to the navy at 2300 Marks.[38] There are other examples of privileged treatment. When the Imperial government followed a suggestion by the Central Association and set up a committee in 1897 to prepare the new tariffs, the mouthpiece of heavy industry was allowed to name its own nominees – unlike the light-industrial interests. The rhetoric mouthed by powerful government figures, from Bismarck through to Johannes Miquel at the turn of the century, which emphasized the defence of 'national labour' and the 'productive estates', was very much the language used by heavy-industrial interests rather than bankers and exporters. And when nonagricultural sectors were required by government policy to make a symbolic sacrifice, either to appease the agrarians or to fill gaps in the budget left by the Junkers' unwillingness to bear their share of the fiscal burden, it was generally the financial and commercial sectors, not heavy industry, that had to pay. Examples include the ban on futures trading in the 1896 stock exchange reform, and the stamp duty controversially included in the 1909 Reich finance reform. In short, the 'national' interests of iron and rye seem to have enjoyed an inbuilt advantage over 'international' commercial and financial sectors, or the interests of the consumer concerned with lower prices.

This interpretation is pleasingly neat and symmetrical, but it raises many problems. Relations between agriculture and heavy industry periodically broke down, most obviously in the 1890s and again in the lead-up to financial reform in 1909. Even during the years 1897–1902, when tariffs and navy were supposedly brought together under the slogan of *Sammlung* ('rallying-together'), conflicts of interest were substantial and mutual recrimination was rife. As Geoff Eley has persuasively argued, the navy was actually played down by the architects of *Sammlung* because the fleet was so strongly identified with industry and commerce that to emphasize it would, in the words of one agrarian, make rallying-together 'impossible'.[39] The basis for compromise remained narrow and unstable. There are also grounds for questioning any straightforward division between protectionist heavy industry and more internationally minded exporting sectors – an exaggerated 'bad boys-good boys' distinction that has also featured in many discussions of industry and fascism. Both the chemical and electrical industries stood, in some senses, between the fronts. Finally, we must recognize that its own more wide-ranging goals made it impossible for German governments to follow a consistent iron-and-rye policy.

There were certain limits beyond which, in its own self-interest, the German state was not prepared to coddle heavy industry or large landowners – especially the latter. Consider the many noisy agrarian demands that were rejected. They include the proposal to nationalize imported grain and set a minimum price (the Kanitz bill), the call for 'bimetallism' (the panacea of agrarians everywhere, which would have taken Germany off the gold standard), and the demand for tariffs higher than the level set by the compromise of 1902. These were all matters of Imperial trade and monetary policy. The agrarians met with further reverses at state and local level. Historians have often noted the spectacular Junker resistance to the Mittelland canal project in Prussia, designed to link eastern and western regions of Prussia. Agrarians managed to get the project postponed – but not abandoned. The price they paid was that many sympathetic local officials were sacked by the government. This was, anyway, the exception, not the rule. Numerous agrarian complaints about government spending policies went unheeded. They objected to bulk postal rates that helped business – without effect. They condemned special workers' trains for supposedly fostering an industrial proletariat – unsuccessfully. They criticized changes in primary education that would tempt workers off the land by giving them ideas above their station. This, too, proved fruitless. Finally, in an important but usually neglected sphere, agriculture complained bitterly about the workings of the poor-relief system. This made support of the indigent the responsibility of the district they had left until the age of twenty-six – until, that is, they were 'adult' (defined as twenty-four), and for two further years while they acquired new residence status. Millions of Marks were transferred from rural to urban areas under this national scheme, especially from the agricultural east of Prussia to the industrial west. Agricultural districts understandably jibbed at having to pay for the support of migrants whose departure was causing their own depopulation. They persistently tried to alter the system, but were no more successful than they were in their efforts to roll back freedom of movement, the underlying principle that drove this Junker subsidy towards the formation of the urban working class.[40]

All of these cases point to the same conclusion. Governments, even when sympathetic to landowning interests, simply could not afford to concede too many agrarian demands. To do so would have strained the patience of industry beyond breaking point and provided more grist to the mill of the Social Democrats, never more successful than when they were exploiting the 'dear bread' issue. More than that, the Junkers especially were seeking to turn back the clock in a manner that flew in the face of the modern state and its needs. That was not true of heavy industry, of course, and it certainly profited from its links to the state apparatus. But what needs to be emphasized is that it was not alone in receiving favours: manufacturing and commerce also benefited from the economic imperatives of state that ministers and officials recognized. Krupp made handsome profits from the Imperial navy, but so did Siemens. Iron and steel were favoured by industrial tariffs, but shipbuilders and shipping lines also received their subsidies. And all exporters benefited from the generous levels of help provided by consular officials.

If there is a red thread that runs through state policy, it is less the favouring of iron and rye than the recognition that a modern, efficient industry was indispensable for a successful great power – the source of revenue, effective armaments and international prestige. Much of the great expansion in the activities of the prewar German state addressed the demands of a burgeoning industrial society. Between 1890 and 1913, the public sector share of GNP grew from 13 to 18 per cent.[41] Some of this was accounted for by publicly owned economic enterprises, notably railways, local transportation and utilities. The Prussian state railway was the world's largest employer in the early twentieth century, and infrastructure expenditure accounted for half the Prussian budget in 1913. Growth also reflected the establishment of new regulatory agencies, together with expanded provision of education, public health and welfare. As urban population rose new schools were built, and the number of primary school teachers doubled in the years 1882–1911, while the average class size fell from 66 to 51. Similar statistics could be cited for hospitals, doctors or nurses. In every case the numbers increased faster than the population: there were three and a half times as many nurses per 10,000 inhabitants in 1909 as there had been just twenty years earlier. The point here is not to celebrate heroic achievements, but to recognize the thickening network of social provision that aimed to create a better-educated, healthier, more satisfied citizenry and workforce.

Easily the most familiar aspect of this state provision is the social insurance system introduced by Bismarck in the 1880s: for illness (1883), accidents (1884), invalidity and old age (1889). Like most things authored by Bismarck, this was not quite what it seemed. The Chancellor had his own motives, which included trying to shift the tax-base in the Empire and split the liberals. He was also looking to bind workers to the state through the pension scheme: this was the carrot, the antisocialist law the stick. In line with other arguments about the 'backward' nature of the Imperial German state, it has often been suggested that the laws of the 1880s were paternalist in character, not really a forerunner of 'modern' social security at all. This is more dubious. The measures were attacked by agrarian interests on the grounds that they were all too modern, and strongly supported by chambers of commerce and manufacturers, including prominent heavy industrialists and the Central Association. These interests were attracted by measures that promised to create a more healthy and integrated labour force – a position that was neither paternalist nor charitable, but a rational evaluation of their needs at a time when difficulties in recruitment and retention, like high accident rates, impeded production. Considered overall, the 1880s legislation was undeniably modern, with its universal coverage and compulsory participation, income-related contributions and benefits, lack of means testing, and centralized administration. Not for nothing was the German scheme seen by contemporaries in other countries as pioneering. It was not only emulated in the French legislation of 1893–1905, but the nonmandatory element of the French system was attacked by critics on the left who demanded a universal, compulsory scheme on the German model. In Britain it was the advanced liberals of the day, Lloyd George and Winston Churchill, who were most enthusiastic about the German pattern of compulsory participation.[42]

The insurance schemes of the 1880s established themselves over the next thirty years. On the eve of war, more than 15 million Germans were covered by sickness insurance and 500 million Marks was being paid out annually. Twenty-eight million were insured against accidents and 1 million were receiving pensions every year.[43] This was not the only level at which the state was active. Alongside social insurance and poor relief came an array of regulatory, interventionist initiatives. In the world of work, factory regulations were made compulsory, the length of the working day was limited for female employees, labour exchanges were established, industrial courts were set up and arbitration procedures encouraged. After 1890, heavy industry became notably less enthusiastic about the extension of social policy, partly because public provision duplicated or cut across the in-house programmes run by a growing number of employers as part of their strategy of workforce control. But governments and officials extended these policies anyway, with support from other industrial and commercial interests (such as chambers of commerce). Again, their initiatives were not simply paternalist. Policies of this kind were driven by a conviction that they constituted an investment in the human capital of an industrial society. Of course, the desire for social stability and 'harmony' was also important, but even the conservatively inclined minister or official faced the question: Was stability now best served by traditional, paternalist nostrums, or by more modern policies geared to the new kind of society that had emerged?

A good indicator of where government priorities really lay is provided by the issue of *Mittelstandspolitik*, or the policy of protecting craftsmen and small shopkeepers. An enormous amount has been made of this in the literature of the last twenty years, partly because these social groups were later to become key supporters of the Nazis. Historians have presented *Mittelstandspolitik* as another means by which government propped up a strongly 'traditionalist' element in society, a policy parallel to its favourable treatment of the Junkers. On the face of it there is a case to be made. 'Saving' master craftsmen and retailers as the 'backbone' of society was always a conservative-agrarian cause, and German governments took up the issue with a whole battery of measures aimed at these groups: craft chambers, the partial reintroduction of guilds and certification of masters, changing the system of tendering for government contracts to help the small man, taxes on department stores to preserve the independent shopkeeper. Every measure came fully equipped with flattering references to the Mittelstand as a 'loyal', state-supporting class. But what was the reality? The craft chambers were largely window-dressing, the new guilds lacked real powers, department store taxes were ineffectual. Changes in the tender system proved equally cosmetic. The Prussian Ministry of War complained that craftsmen produced poor quality work and missed their delivery dates: tenders were placed in publications that no craftsmen read. As these and many other examples suggest, *Mittelstandspolitik* was an exercise in rhetoric, not a policy designed to succeed. The needs of a sophisticated economy, including the state's own labour and revenue requirements, gave governments as much interest in pruning as in preserving the ranks of the small independents. As I have argued elsewhere, the disillusionment with the 'system' that led artisans and shopkeepers into the arms of the Nazis began before 1914.[44]

It was in the area of social policy outside production and the workplace that hard-headed arguments based on efficiency had most impact, strongly influenced by contemporary ideas about eugenics and 'national fitness'. Welfare (*Fürsorge*) became one of the most influential concepts of the pre-1914 period. Maternity welfare, infant welfare, youth welfare, family welfare, workers' welfare – the subspecialisms sprouted as the ranks of welfare professionals multiplied, with women playing a crucial role. An enlarged housing inspectorate, mother-and-child clinics, public health campaigns against alcoholism, tuberculosis and venereal disease: all were manifestations of the drive to 'improve' the population. There were important imperial agencies in fields like public health, but much of the new welfare activism took place at local level. The municipalities played a growing role. By 1914 their share of public expenditure had risen to more than a third of the total, spending that was funded by growing yields from income tax and capital, gains taxes on urban land, as well as loans raised on the capital market. Here, in the realm of city government, we see in heightened form the forces that were shaping the state response to industrial society and the interests it spawned. A recognizable new breed of powerful big-city mayors pushed reforms in housing, labour exchanges and welfare, citing considerations of social and political harmony, but couching their measures in technocratic terms that empha-sized the importance of a productive labour force for national efficiency. Manufacturers, with more direct power and influence at this level, often supported municipal initiatives out of a belief that spending money in these areas took the edge off social conflict and counteracted urban 'degeneration'. And Social Democrats, where they were elected despite restrictive local franchises, usually went along with these initiatives because of their beneficial everyday effects. It was property-owners and small businesses, backed by traditionalist conservatives, who were most resistant to increased spending. Like the agrarians in the national parliament, and the Mittelstand movement at every level, they wanted state intervention to benefit them, the sym-bols of an older, more ordered society, not to be poured out over the social problems that accompanied industrialization. Their stance was obviously self-interested. It also reflected a mental confusion over cause and effect, so that social welfare and 'generosity' to urban workers came to be seen as a inducement to industrialization and proletarianization, not a by-product. There was a large measure of self-delusion in the conservatives' preferred approach. By the beginning of the twentieth century, the time was long past when any German government at any level was going to address the problems of industrial society by returning workers to the countryside or reclassifying them all as apprentices to guild masters.

Interest groups had an important place in German life, as they moved from informal lobbies to highly organized pressure groups. They helped to shape the political parties by their activities, and they worked directly on governments and officials. The interaction of business and politics went well beyond any particular benefits that accrued to agriculture and heavy industry. Agriculture was, along with the Mittelstand, one of the noisiest interest groups. It gained significant concessions, the Junker estates most of all, although the importance of protective tariffs in this pattern of favouritism has been exaggerated. But there were limits to what the state was prepared to concede to agrarian interests. The limits were much more tightly drawn in the case of *Mittelstandspolitik*, which was largely a sham. In both cases, these limits were set by what ministers and officials, including conservatively inclined individuals, perceived as the larger needs of society. International prestige, armaments policy, social stability, national efficiency – all required the continuing growth of industry, trade and exports. Any special privileges enjoyed by heavy industry have to be set against the larger context of government support for the industrial economy as a whole. This was the old idea of the state as representative of the 'general interest', now cast in a more modern idiom. State and bureaucracy aimed to stand above and harmonize the conflicting interests, not make concessions to any one group that would jeopardize that goal.

CHAPTER EIGHT

Society and Culture

For Better, For Worse

German society was extraordinarily dynamic in the years before 1914. The population rose to 68 million on the eve of war, 60 per cent higher than at the time of unification. It was growing at a pace that would have seen the population double in seventy years. The fastest growth came in the 1890s and the first years of the new century; then the rate fell back slightly. Nevertheless, the generally high rates gave Germans a sense of their own vigour, especially by comparison with France where the population barely grew. This demographic pattern produced a youthful Germany. The age-cohorts most important for the workforce (15–20 and 21–45) accounted for a higher proportion of the population in 1911 than at any time in the previous forty years. There were more Germans in their late teens than there would ever be again in the twentieth century, even after the post-1945 'baby-boom', and four-fifths of the population were 45 or younger. The rate of natural increase was the most important factor, but this was also the period when Germany changed from being a net exporter to a net importer of people. As we saw in the last chapter, Poles made up the largest single group of immigrants, but there were significant numbers of Italians, Dutch, and non-Polish Slavs. There were even – shades of things to come – smaller groups of Turks. In his struggling early years the husband of Lou Andreas-Salomé, the feminist writer and companion of the famous, kept going by teaching German to Turks who had settled in Berlin.[1]

Germany was also an increasingly urban society. The movement to the towns that began in the third quarter of the century continued at an even faster pace in the prewar decades. By 1910 nearly two-thirds of Germans lived in towns. More than a fifth lived in the forty-eight 'big cities' with populations exceeding 100,000. Berlin, still just under a million in 1875, crossed the 2 million threshold in 1907, of whom 60 per cent had been born outside the city. Even these figures understate the real growth, for newcomers to the capital increasingly settled in suburbs that remained formally unincorporated until the early 1920s, but already belonged to what contemporaries called Greater Berlin. Charlottenburg alone had 300,000 inhabitants in 1910, compared with just 25,000 in 1875. Berlin was the most striking example of a general trend. By the war, Hamburg had reached almost a million and a string of other cities had passed the half-million mark – Breslau, Cologne, Dresden, Leipzig, Munich. Rates of growth were even faster in the great industrial conurbations. Duisburg in the Ruhr grew sixfold in thirty-five years, to 230,000. The figures on net urbanization – giving the size of a town in a particular year – also understate the real volume of population movement, for they count only those who stayed and miss those who migrated from one town to another. Evidence from the booming Ruhr suggests that a net increase in population of, say, 10,000, was the result of 100,000 coming and 90,000 going.[2] In short, Germans were moving to town in unprecedented numbers, and continuing to move, with effects on every aspect of life.

These decades saw major changes not only in where Germans lived, but in whether and how they lived. The decisive change here was the fall in infant mortality, from around 25 per cent in the 1870s to just under 15 per cent in 1912 (see Figure 5). Improvements in hygiene and living conditions lay behind this, and the inroads that were made into infant deaths from infectious diseases. Compulsory immunization against smallpox was introduced in 1874; then a diphtheria serum became available in the early 1890s, instantly cutting the number of children who died of it from one in two to one in six. New fever-reducing pharmaceuticals also appeared. Paediatrics, long looked down on by the medical establishment, finally established a secure

FIGURE 5 *Infant Mortality in Prussia and Saxony, 1840–1920*

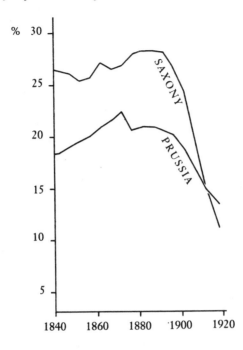

SOURCE:
P. Marschalck, *Bevölkerungsgeschichte Deutschlands im 19. und 20. Jahrhundert* (Frankfurt, 1984), p. 189.

footing as a specialism, and the German Paediatric Society was founded in 1883. The sharp drop in infant mortality raised life expectancy. As we saw earlier, a man born in the 1870s could expect to live to thirty-six, a woman to thirty-eight; for those born in the first decade of the twentieth century, the figures were forty-five and forty-eight respectively. Those who survived the first year could now expect to live into their middle fifties. Life expectancy was improving at double the rate of the period 1850–80, a genuine breakthrough. Morbidity rates also declined and life became somewhat less brutal for the sick, or at least the more fortunate among them, thanks to sharp increases in hospital beds and nurses per head of population and the impact of medical research. There were advances in diagnostic skills, surgery and – not least – the relief of pain.[3] In a period that saw the emergence of numerous things that modern industrial societies now take for granted, we should not neglect the advent of the aspirin.

Life became a little easier in other ways too. Urban tram networks, special trains and the bicycle made getting to work less exhausting for millions. In the office, the routine drudgery of the copy-clerk was eased by the arrival of the typewriter and carbon paper, while tasks that had once required a letter could now be dealt with by a telephone call – a dreadful blow to the archival historian, but an important innovation for contemporaries. Germans made 155 million phone calls in 1888, the first year for which we have figures; by 1904 the number reached a billion, and by 1913 more than two and a half billion. (Numbers of letters and telegrams also increased very fast, although not at the same precipitous rate.) This was also the age of the department and chain stores, the mail order catalogue, delivery vans and advertising. These, like colonial goods stores with their exotic tinned produce, symbolized the reality of mass consumption. They were a sign that the great increase in national wealth was benefiting more than just the well-off. Income differentials seem to have eroded somewhat in these years, most clearly documented in the narrowing gap between the pay of senior and junior state officials. Real wages rose – in the depression years before 1896 because prices were falling, afterwards because money wages increased more than prices. (In Britain, by contrast, real wages sagged in the prewar decade.) Income tax returns show the same trend. Between 1896 and 1912, the proportion of Prussian taxpayers assessed on incomes of under 900 marks a year (including those with no earnings) fell from 75 to 52 per cent of the total, while those with incomes in the range 900–3000 marks doubled, from 22 to 43 per cent.[4] The value of savings grew, including those of skilled workers. This trend helped to trigger the great debate within the SPD over 'revisionism', as Eduard Bernstein and his supporters argued that the Marxist theory of increasing proletarian 'immiseration' needed revising to take account of the fact that many workers now had more to lose than their chains. Finally, any account of the ways in which life became relatively easier must include the growth of leisure-time, at least for those in the urban occupations that were now characteristic. Working hours in mining and industry were almost a third lower on the eve of war than they had been in the middle of the nineteenth century, most of the gains coming in the last decades. The typical work day (including, still, Saturday) in the nonagricultural sector fell from about twelve to nine-and-a-half hours. This was another fundamental change, and it underlay the spread of popular leisure activities – 'mass culture' – considered in the last section of this chapter.

At the beginning of the new century, editorial writers looked ahead to continued progress on all of these fronts. Their optimistic tones resembled those heard in the third quarter of the century, although welfare measures and the spread of material benefits figured more prominently in the paeans of praise. Then came the prewar boom, further encouragement for those who wanted to accentuate the positive. However, this was still a society in which 30 per cent of the population lived at or below the poverty line: the dynamism and material improvements have to be placed alongside a darker reality. Rural society is a good place to start. On the one hand, we should certainly reject any idea that the countryside in these years remained 'traditionalist'. Even before agricultural prices picked up at the end of the century, there is evidence that many rural inhabitants were becoming better dressed and housed. For example, all-in farmhouses where people and animals lived together became less common: the separate accommodation of animals became the norm in the extensive new constructions of the period, a trend that was strongly encouraged by agricultural associations of all kinds.[5] Many middle peasants had turned themselves into successful commercial farmers – something else that Social-Democratic revisionists took note of. We should also remember that self-appointed 'agrarian' spokesmen had a vested interest in complaint, so that pessimistic portrayals cannot be taken at face value. When all that has been said, however, there *was* a darker side to rural society. Early in the new century the Bavarian 'peasant doctor' Georg Heim, referring to urban educational opportunities, noted that 'the peasant on the land does not have all these. The plough and the shovel are his pen, with which he writes his diary on the tilled earth. If the railway lines rush past the end of his fields, and the four corners of the earth meet above his head in the telephone wires, he remains tied to the soil, held within his small circle.'[6] Heim put his finger on several points. First, there was a genuine problem of rural isolation from the rest of society. For example, while Germany was exceptionally well endowed with railways, around 30 per cent of the population had no access to a railhead. Virtually all were rural dwellers, especially in upland areas. The fear of being left behind fuelled the numerous contemporary electoral battles over branch-line construction, which often turned normal political loyalties upside down. Structural disadvantage applied not just to transportation, but (as Heim noted) to education – and to medicine. During early industrialization mortality rates were higher in the town than the country; but disproportionate urban gains meant that by the early twentieth century the positions were reversed. It was now the rural child who was more likely to die before the age of one. A pattern was set that would persist through the twentieth century, whereby country people had inferior access to every kind of medical service compared with their urban counterparts. Small wonder that fatalism remained widespread or that so many peasants still turned to 'quacks' like the herbalist.

Doctors with rural practices were usually either dedicated, poor, or both. We have the letters that some of them wrote to leading figures in the profession, complaining about their stunted lives.[7] Similar sentiments were often expressed by those who passed through the village (trainee teachers, for example), or were born in the country but made careers in the town. For them, rural Germany was synonymous with inflexibility, brutalism and superstition. The energy and self-conscious modernity of urban life in these years helped to make the countryside seem more 'backward'. Recent writers have referred plausibly to the 'provincialization' of rural Germany, to the provinces as the 'stepchildren of progress'.[8] The issue here was not so much isolation, as becoming marginal. Those who stayed in the country, rather than leaving or passing through, perceived the same thing in a different way. Whether it was branch-line struggles, the 'milk wars' and 'phosphate wars' fought against urban consumers and suppliers, or the mystery of prices and interest rates fixed by distant powers, they felt the unevenness of the town-country exchange. More than anything else, the constant haemorrhage of population was at once an existential threat and a source of profound pessimism.

The so-called flight from the land was one reason why most rural lives remained very hard. Labour shortages in peasant society led to high levels of family self-exploitation, including extensive child labour. Rural schools rarely functioned normally during harvest time, and agriculture remained outside many welfare provisions. Mechanization came slowly to peasant holdings, the backbone of rural society, and work was physically punishing. It was hardest for one of the most exploited groups in Germany: the agricultural workers and short-term contract labourers employed by large farmers and estate owners. There were more than seven million of them in 1907, accounting for more than 40 per cent of those categorized as 'workers' in the occupational census, and three-quarters of all those employed in agriculture. The accounts we have of their lives make grim reading.[9] They were crudely housed, roughly treated and poorly fed: even on holdings with large herds of dairy cattle, labourers received cheap American lard to spread on their low-quality bread. Estate inventories confirm the autobiographical evidence, showing that more was spent on pigs than on hired hands. Above all, labourers were overworked to the point of exhaustion, especially during haymaking and harvesting when the working day began at three or four in the morning and went on until late at night, with minimal breaks. A 100-hour week was normal;

120 hours was not unknown. In many ways, the advent of mechanization only made things worse, for it intensified the seasonal nature of agricultural labour, heightening demand during peak seasons but reducing the work available during winter, thus creating more irregular employment and adding to the problems of migrant labourers. While work was available, the steam-powered threshing machine became a new tyrant, alongside the overseer, as workers laboured to keep up with the pace of the 'sweat-box' which howled and rumbled the whole day, spat grain into their eyes, blocked their noses and covered them with dust.

The threshing machine had its urban counterparts – mechanization that was potentially labour-saving but often had the practical effect of raising the work-tempo. The sewing machine is a good example, on which a submerged and ill-paid female labour force worked in sweatshops and at home. In Berlin, one of the main centres, there were nearly 100,000 female garment workers in 1907. Nor should we forget the 'mechanized office', a favourite subject of early sociologists. The typewriter, calculator, addressograph, pneumatic message tube, subdivided work assignments: all tended to reproduce some of the regimented conditions of the factory floor, and were often seen as such by company employees. Tibor Süle has recently shown that minor state officials experienced something similar.[10] This was the darker side of the world of clean collar and cuffs that appealed to many, especially from the declining crafts, as the salvation of their children. Manual workers also faced new forms of mechanization – coal-cutting machines, dockland cranes, the automatic lathe. These usually increased the pace of work; they also raised the spectre of deskilling, the fear that those who sold their labour were becoming more interchangeable, and thus dispensable. The skilled craftsman could thus see himself threatened, if only distantly, with the fate of the 'mass worker', another subject that fascinated contemporary social observers, including Max Weber.

If a working class was in the making during the decades after 1850, was it now 'made'? Many differences of background and skills still divided those who earned wages, and the mobile, dynamic society of late Imperial Germany created new divisions, or reinforced old ones. The female proportion of the (official) workforce rose from 13 to 18 per cent in the period 1882–1907, but this did nothing to alter the fact that women were concentrated in particular niches within the labour market. Even in industries where the sexes worked side by side, such as textiles, women were usually relegated to subordinate, 'unskilled' tasks. Men and women belonged to different shopfloor cultures: there was tension between them, and the problem of sexual harassment was real, noted by contemporaries of diverse political persuasions but then overlooked by most historians until the last ten years. If gender was an important variable, so were language and ethnicity. Polish Catholic migrants to the Ruhr created their own subculture; so did Italian workers, also concentrated in particular neighbourhoods and occupations. Altogether, the volume of internal migration calls into question the idea of a 'fixed' working class; at the very least it underlines the differences between older, more settled and younger, more mobile workers. A generation of research has added nuance to our picture of working-class lives under mature industrialization, recording the gap that separated the 'rough' from the 'respectable' and offering a differentiated account of leisure, housing, crime, sexuality, and much else.[11] The working class now familiar from monographs and scholarly articles is harder to pin down, more multi-hued than the monochrome proletariat that absorbed the attention of many earlier labour historians.

And yet, these men and women were none the less bound together by common experiences, problems and attitudes. The number of industrial workers doubled between 1882 and 1907, so that many more had now been born into a second- or even third-generation working-class family. Urban geography made it more true than it had been even a few decades earlier that 'you tell me where you live, and I'll tell you who you are'. Workers were ill more often than the better-off, died younger, and were smaller (heroic images of the muscle-bound proletarian notwithstanding). They lived in more overcrowded housing, and spent much more of their income on food – a good half in the prewar decade, despite rising real wages. The bourgeois family ideal rang hollow when most proletarian households were dependent on the earnings of women and children, multiple sharing of beds and taking in lodgers were common, and insecurity was endemic. Unemployment rose from 1.35 million in 1882 to 3.41 million in 1907, and official statistics understated the reality. Perhaps a third of the workforce experienced some unemployment in a given year. Long-term unemployment and the continuing urban housing crisis combined to produce a rising problem of homelessness. Around 4000 men slept every night in Berlin's municipal shelter for the homeless, thousands more in privately run hostels. The Berlin Homeless Shelter Association accommodated 100,000 men a year before 1900 and twice that many afterwards, plus women and children. One form of work-loss was rising sharply: the employer's lockout. In no year between 1905 and 1913 did the number of these fall below 200; in 1910 nearly a quarter of a million workers were the victims of almost 1000 separate lockouts. Strikes also became more frequent in the prewar decade, as employees used the boom conditions to exert leverage. On average, 200,000 workers struck in each of the years 1905–13; the number was twice as high in the peak year of 1912.

Being out of work for whatever reason dramatized a common proletarian plight. Other aspects of everyday life had the same effect. Working-class districts were tied together by informal exchanges of services and favours. Migration and job-switching – from the sugar refinery to the brickyard to the chemical works – widened the sense of common experience, at least among men. So did conversations in that established bastion of male sociability, the tavern (temperance was very much weaker among German workers than it was in, say, England or Sweden). Police spies eavesdropping in taverns reported conversations with a strong sense of class identity that defined itself against 'moneybags' and 'parasites'. Social investigators found the same. A Berlin mechanic who was fond of the countryside told one of them: 'I'd like to go walking all day the way the rich people do'.[12]

Attitudes like this were a product of experience, and of the increasing role played by the organized labour movement. Naturally, not all workers were class-conscious; or if they were, they often remained (like virtually all agricultural workers, and most women) unorganized; or they were enrolled in clerical or liberal organizations, not in 'the' labour movement. None the less, there were 3 million trade union members by the war, 85 per cent of them in the socialist-leaning free trade unions. The SPD had almost a million members, making it easily the largest socialist party in the world. It was successful because it went with the grain of workers' lives. The language it used – exploitation, inequality, class justice – made sense to those who heard it. As many accounts testify, encountering a Social-Democratic speaker or newspaper could come as a revelation to a worker struggling to make sense of the world. The labour movement reinforced a sense of self-respect. It insisted on the dignity and worth of the worker, and offered hope for a better world in the 'state of the future'. In the here-and-now, the labour movement sustained workers through a host of organizations that belonged to *them*: not just unions and cooperatives, but choral societies, drama groups, lending libraries, educational courses, cycling and gymnastic clubs. May Day celebrations, after 1890, became festive as well as ritual occasions for the whole working-class family. The labour movement was a fixed point in a turning world, fostering a common identity and providing – through party, press, unions, cooperatives – an opportunity for working men to exercise responsibility.

Starting with contemporaries, the argument has been made that those who rose through the ranks in this way became 'bourgeois' or 'petty bourgeois'. Like similar arguments that the value placed on respectability in the labour movement was a sign of 'embourgeoisement', it has been overworked.[13] It does, however, raise the question of social mobility. Research suggests that opportunities to rise from the manual working class were poor. As in earlier periods, no more than 2–5 per cent became self-employed. Moving into a nonmanual position of some sort was more common, especially for skilled workers and their families. In late nineteenth-century Bochum, as many as a quarter of skilled workers from some branches entered nonmanual occupations, and around one sixth of their sons (although more sons dropped into lower-skilled occupations). In iron, steel and engineering, many foremen and overseers were recruited from the ranks of skilled workers; so were mine inspectors. But the growth of specialized technical training for supervisory personnel limited some of these openings. Even where that did not happen, as in mining, the chances of a given miner becoming an inspector were remote – about one in sixty in the Ruhr. The growth of the tertiary sector in the prewar decades certainly provided greater opportunities for workers' children: a prewar investigation in Cologne and Euskirchen indicated that a quarter of workers' sons moved into either white-collar or minor official posts.[14] But there were real material and mental barriers to upward mobility. Even a skilled craftsman's family was hard-pressed to find the money needed to keep children in school (and forgo their income); it was virtually impossible for the unskilled. Many placed a higher value on the collective improvement of their occupational group than on individual advancement, while the working-class ideal was more likely to take the form of a skilled job, security, and perhaps home-ownership, not an expensive education that would remove children into an alien world. There was widespread scorn for the 'soft' life of the white-collar worker, a reminder that strength and manual dexterity continued to be a source of pride, even for the clear majority of workers who (as every survey showed) hated their jobs. This was so despite the importance the labour movement attached to self-improvement.

Nevertheless, the likely destination of the upwardly mobile worker was the new lower middle class of foremen, clerks and petty officials. Movement from proletariat to professions was rare indeed. Even as universities expanded – higher education enrolments rose from 23,000 (1875) to 72,000 (1912) – students from working-class backgrounds remained negligible. When it happened at all, joining the bourgeoisie from the ranks of manual workers was a two-generation affair, via the lower middle class, which now became the great conduit of social mobility. Like the old petty bourgeoisie of craftsmen and retailers, the new white-collar groups were often closer to the working class than they liked to believe. The mechanized office in the one case, lack of capital or true independence in the other, undercut lower middle-class claims to superiority. But that did not prevent many from emphasizing the differences – it may actually have made them more emphatic. White-collar workers took pride in what separated them from manual workers (monthly payment, a separate insurance scheme), and often sought to advance their children by limiting family size. More substantial master craftsmen and shopkeepers typically laid stress on old-fashioned morality and discipline, often to the point of rigidity, and took pride in their connections to the bourgeoisie, even if the respect and desire to emulate was often mixed with misgivings about bourgeois 'license'. At any rate, the evidence is unambiguous that both old and new lower middle class made use of the educational system to place their children in better positions. The expansion of German universities brought an invasion of students from these backgrounds, who accounted for around a half of all Prussian enrolments in the last prewar years.[15] A cautionary note is necessary. We should form a misleading impression of those born into the English lower middle class of the late 1920s if we judged it by one particular grocer's daughter who went to Oxford and became prime minister, and in late Imperial Germany, too, most lower middle-class boys (let alone girls) did not rise into the bourgeoisie. But those who did formed an important group in the class they joined and helped to replenish.

That class was, in many respects, at its apogee. The bourgeoisie was growing, increasingly wealthy, and ready to take credit for what it viewed as its own achievements – rapid economic advances, a widely admired bureaucracy, the prestige of German scholarship and culture. If the last twenty years before the war later came to be seen as a golden age for the bourgeoisie, there was some reason. It was a time of regular dividends, the Gold Standard and low income tax. More of the established bourgeoisie advertised their wealth by moving into suburban villas. Even in a city like Hamburg, where unusually large numbers of the well-off still lived in fashionable central areas like Harvestehude and Rotherbaum, families decamped to the country for the summer, when the dangers and aromas of urban pollution were at their greatest. This became the pattern everywhere. A productive economy allowed the bourgeoisie very comfortable levels of consumption. This was the period when the grand hotels and fashionable restaurants achieved unprecedented renown. Walter Benjamin, one of the great critics and essayists of the 1920s and 1930s, has given us a wonderful description of his childhood in the years around 1900, as the son of a partner in an auction house who later sold up and lived off his investments. Fifty years before Jackie Collins, and with a writer's art, Benjamin recalled the reassuring yet mysterious pleasures of shopping for brand names in prewar Berlin: suits at Arnold Müller's, shoes at Stiller's, suitcases at Mädler's, the trip rounded off by hot chocolate with whipped cream at Hillbrich's. There was a family doctor, banker, notary, wine-merchant, even a dancing-master, and each year the Benjamins took up a summer residence outside the city, in addition to occasional trips to resorts on the island of Sylt.[16]

This was, of course, a bourgeois family with very specific characteristics – Berlin-based, Jewish, artistically minded, headed by a man who worked on the borderline between commerce and professions, then became a *rentier*. We should gain different impressions from the snapshot life of a judge, a Hanseatic merchant, a provincial doctor, or an ironmaster in one of Germany's grimy Coketowns. True, many of the values and institutions that defined the bourgeoisie in its formative years remained common ground – the belief in property, achievement and the law, an attachment to rules, respectability and 'correct' conduct, the place of the family as haven and seat of dynastic ambition. Even the divide between educated and propertied bourgeoisie was muted insofar as the prestige of knowledge and culture prompted the businessman who preferred billiards to admit to owning books or reading a little history. Still, there were real differences between the industrialist and the official or professional, as there were between Protestants, Catholics and Jews. Other distinctions probably became more pronounced in these years – between 'metropolitan' and 'provincial' middle classes, for example. Above all, the generally rising level of bourgeois material comfort did not exclude, it may even have encouraged, the desire to mark oneself out as distinctive – to live in the best residential suburb, place one's son in the most prestigious student corporation, dine at the most exclusive restaurant. This was a simple game with complicated rules, and every bourgeois subgroup could play. Its most obvious winner was the emerging bourgeois plutocracy of the super-rich, businessmen and bankers who became millionaires, built themselves fabulous homes and entertained with baronial abandon. The Krupp Villa Hügel is the archetype, but the banker Carl Fürstenberg, the department store owner Oskar Tietz and the chemical industrialist Carl von Weinberg were among the many businessmen with reception and dining rooms large enough to receive 100 guests at a time.[17]

Conspicuous consumption on this scale used to be widely regarded by historians as one sign of a so-called bourgeois 'feudalization'. Like intermarriage with a Junker family, acquiring a 'von' in front of one's name, angling for honours or buying a country estate, it supposedly indicated that an important part of the bourgeoisie had jettisoned its own values and begun to ape those of the aristocracy.[18] There is certainly evidence that these things were on the increase from the 1870s. Adolf von Wilke was one of many contemporaries to comment on the 'new lords of the manor'; intermarriage and ennoblement became more common. But what did this really signify? Even where intermingling between grand bourgeoisie and aristocracy occurred, it is far from clear that it entailed the casting off of bourgeois identity. Many businessmen regarded their rural seats fairly pragmatically – as convenient places to entertain, and a badge of success. Pomp and luxury were signs of confidence, not self-abasement. The purchase of an estate, moreover, like intermarriage between successful business families and impecunious aristocrats, had two sides to it. Junkers were being forced to sell by declining income, after all, just as they often sent their sons and daughters grudgingly to the altar. Leo Poggenpuhl, son of an old Junker family in Theodor Fontane's novel, joked about the pervasive sense of social flux that alarmed and saddened his elders: 'Who today does *not* have a name? And what does a name really *mean*? Pears Soap, Blooker's Cocoa, malt extract from Johann Hoff...' There was a tendency for elements of the bourgeoisie to move closer to the aristocracy in every European country: it was not necessarily a sign of 'feudalization'. The power of the aristocratic embrace was in some respects weaker in Germany than in Britain, for the urbane, metropolitan English aristocracy assimilated newcomers more easily than the awkward, graceless, provincial Junkers. It was Max Weber, often cited very selectively on this subject, who observed that the Junkers' 'parvenu physiognomy' prevented them from offering an English-style model of the gentleman.[19] Certainly the glittering *soirées* of prewar Berlin were more likely to be hosted by Jewish bankers than by Junkers, the latter more likely to be playing cards in the country.

A growing body of evidence has undermined many assumptions of the feudalization thesis. One recent study suggests that the wealthiest businessmen of Wilhelmine Germany had broken off from the middle classes, without assimilating to the aristocracy.[20] Close examination has shown how much rarer ennoblement was among business élites in Germany than in Britain. Depending on the definition used, the percentage of entrepreneurs among the ennobled was between three and five times higher in Britain than in Prussia during the years 1870–1918, and just four cities – Berlin, Frankfurt, Cologne, Hamburg – accounted for a half of all cases. Major Ruhr industrialists – Kirdorf, the Krupps, Thyssen – did not seek and in some cases even declined ennoblement. Alfred Krupp was a notable resister. Some took a similarly dim view of honours. The Silesian industrialist Oskar Huldschinsky turned down William II's offer of the *Kronenorden* with the reported observation that, since nobody thought to honour him as one of the great industrialists in Germany, he was not going to accept an honour just because he had been sailing with the Kaiser.[21] This sort of bourgeois robustness was more common than often believed, although probably less widespread among professionals than entrepreneurs. What businessmen mostly angled for was not a noble title or the Order of the Eagle, but the title Commercial Councillor. This had nothing to do with pseudoaristocratic status, rather it placed the state seal of approval on their business activities and their position in the bourgeois social order. Hence the vigorous black market for the title. Finally, we need to revisit even that seemingly unambiguous testament to feudalization: the habit of duelling. The main point is not that many middle-class Germans abhorred duelling, including large numbers of political liberals and Catholics (more than 20,000 university-educated Catholics joined the Catholic antiduelling movement). Without doubt, duelling spread in the bourgeoisie, from academics and officials via professionals to businessmen. This was no mere imitation of feudal norms, however: the duel came to assume a place within a specifically bourgeois code of honour, centred on masculinity, and defined by the possession of property, education and reputation. Middle-class men did not ape aristocratic models, but – in the words of Ute Frevert – 'derived their own meanings from those models, meanings which directly corresponded to the bourgeois cult of individuality'.[22] The emerging consensus among historians is that the feudalization thesis has been overworked. If we are looking for distinctive features of German bourgeois thinking, it makes more sense to consider attitudes towards the state. Attachment to army and reserve officer corps, discussed in the following section, was one aspect of that. The value ascribed to the Commercial Councillor title was another. Parallel titles for nonbusinessmen, like Sanitary Councillor (doctors) and Councillor of Justice (lawyers), were equally prized. The importance of titles does not end there. State examinations or official service provided rich opportunities to distinguish oneself by title: Herr Dr, Provincial Governor, Professor, Senior District Architect (ret.) – these and countless other handles became an inseparable part of one's name. The state provided accreditation and legitimation. It was a source of prestige, the guardian of organized knowledge, and stood for values that the bourgeoisie held dear: seriousness, respect, rectitude – the 'manly' virtues.

The state was also the ultimate guarantor of domestic stability, important at a time when the 'social question' impinged powerfully on middle-class minds. Compared with the third quarter of the century, the bourgeoisie defined itself against a more organized, class-conscious proletariat. The most obvious aspect of this is seen in employer organizations, lockouts, blacklists, and other methods of domesticating labour such as company housing, welfare schemes and works celebrations. Entrepreneurs, clergy and modern social reformers, including officials, still used the language of class harmony, like their bourgeois predecessors of the 1860s who had established workers' education associations, but they did so now through clenched teeth. Few doubted that social peace would be hard to achieve, and many saw growing danger in the social depths. Pessimism on this score became a bourgeois commonplace. Fact-finders, welfare experts and those (like the clergyman Paul Göhre) who lived temporarily among workers brought back their reports from the class front, depicting a godless proletariat, cast adrift and uncivilized. Medical and pseudoscientific nostrums of hygiene produced a new buzz word in the 1890s: degeneration. The economist Werner Sombart was not unusual in lamenting the 'barbarism' of 'unrooted and uprooted proletarians'.[23]

There was another cloud on the bourgeois horizon, as the position of women began to change in Wilhelmine Germany. Some of the changes affected the bourgeoisie indirectly. The growth of female wage-labour became one explanation for the brutish proletariat, as working women supposedly 'neglected' their domestic obligations. The other side of this coin was that women who worked in the garment industry were not available in the middle-class home, as servants. Germany still had 1.25 million female domestic servants in 1907, about the same as in 1882, but they made up a declining share of the labour force. Hamburg offers an example of what this meant. There a third of all employed women were still live-in servants on the eve of war. However, only a tenth of all households now employed at least one servant, compared with a fifth in 1880. The petty bourgeoisie was the main loser, but the decline in two- or three-servant establishments and the rise in single-servant households were the first signs of an impact on the bourgeoisie proper. The 'new woman', in life as in literature, represented a more frontal challenge to male-defined bourgeois society. Women in offices symbolized a new freedom (more than we can easily imagine), although it is no coincidence that openings for women grew at the very moment when office work started to become more humdrum. The urbanely conventional could reassure themselves by taking the G. K. Chesterton view: 'A million women said "we will not be dictated to" – and became stenographers'. Women were not just becoming stenographers, however. Female teacher training expanded from the 1890s, and women were prominent in the expanding welfare professions like nursing and social work. In 1899 women were finally permitted to acquire medical qualifications, after long resistance on the grounds that they were biologically unsuitable. The pioneers often specialized in gynaecology or paediatrics, and this can be seen – like women in welfare – as another kind of gender-stereotyping. Indeed, women themselves argued for admission to teaching and medicine on the basis of their special nurturing qualities. We should avoid arrogant present-minded judgments about this, however, and recognize that women were fashioning new claims out of the materials to hand.

Male hostility to female emancipation remained deep-rooted. In 1910 Max Funke could still ask 'are women human beings?', and answer that they were in fact an evolutionary missing link between *Homo Sapiens* and less advanced species.[24] The number of women who passed through the universities continued to be tiny, and most settled for a career as an alternative to marriage, even where the latter (although frowned upon) was permitted. Women, however accomplished, remained formally inferior in law. The Civil Code introduced at the turn of the century confirmed the husband as head of the family and legal guardian of his wife; abortion was unlawful and the grounds for divorce were one-sided. A double standard persisted in sexual morality:

Fontane's *Effi Briest* shows how the adulteress could be socially and emotionally broken. Male honour was still central to bourgeois society. And yet: women were becoming more publicly active, at work, in the professions, in charities, in literary circles, even in politics. This was most obviously true of middle-class women, who had by far the greatest opportunities. Just as the bounding economy brought about a challenge to the class basis of Wilhelmine Germany, so the surpluses of money and time that accrued to bourgeois wives and daughters in the golden age helped to generate a challenge to male-dominated society.

Order and Discipline

Imperial Germany liked to see itself as an orderly, peaceable society. It is true that conservative writers often wrote about crime, blaming it – as they blamed everything – on urbanization. Elsewhere, despite concern over the effects of industrialization and debates on 'degeneration' among the urban poor, surprisingly little of this attention focused on crime or urban lawlessness. The subject had nothing like the literary resonance it had in England, nor did the press highlight it. The major exception was murder. There was national interest in the case of Grete Beier, a young middle-class woman who was executed in 1908 for killing her lover – the first woman to be executed in Saxony for fifty years. Otherwise, the reporting of transgressions became rather more extensive at the turn of the century, but remained largely prosaic in tone. Significantly, crime was often blamed on foreigners, and Germany was usually compared favourably with other countries. The belief that they lived in a fundamentally disciplined society was a part of German national hubris.

On the face of it, this might seem like self-delusion. The growing working-class districts were violent places, full of young men with few attachments. Riots took place in 1906 and 1909–10 over raised beer prices, as they had in 1873. In raw mining communities, clubs and knives were commonplace and grievous bodily harm was almost a way of life. It was said that young miners who came to the Ruhr from the Prussian east acquired first a watch, then a revolver. Certainly surprising numbers owned guns. Hamborn, about which we are well informed, had a positively wild west reputation. In the countryside, pitched battles took place when peasants drove out gypsies with rifles, pitchforks, scythes and cudgels. Farm servants revenged themselves on their former employers by setting fires. Poaching was widespread and tacitly accepted, unless commercial gangs were involved. Johann Georg Roiss, the 'Labenauer Hansgörgl', evaded capture by special police detachments in Upper Bavaria for seven years, until apprehended by chance in 1906.[25]

Is it possible to move beyond impressions and establish what was happening to crime rates over this period? Criminal statistics are notoriously difficult to use, for they are subject to the level and quality of policing, changes in what are classified as offences, and decisions on whether (and on what charges) to proceed against offenders. All of these variables operated in imperial Germany. On the one hand, crime figures were swollen by the growth of the police, and by the addition of many new offences with a political character after the lapsing of the antisocialist law in 1890. This simply reflected the pursuit of the labour movement by other means. On the other hand, in Prussia at least, fewer cases of murder were prosecuted within the criminal justice system even though the number of murders reported by coroners rose. Overall, the evidence suggests a mixed picture. Property crimes generally remained constant, with petty theft declining, but more serious offences – both robbery and white-collar crimes like embezzlement – rising after the turn of the century. When it comes to crimes against the person, simple assault rose little, but more serious cases of assault rose steadily from the 1890s; so did rape and murder. It is hard to know how far this reflected more extensive policing. What is clear is that recorded crime rose much more in urban areas and even fell in rural ones. In some cities there was an explosion of crime in the last years before the war. In 1905, 650 cases of waterfront theft were reported to Hamburg police; in both 1912 and 1913 the number of cases had grown to more than 3000. The Ruhr showed the same trend: both property and violent crime rates doubled in the city of Duisburg between 1900 and 1913.[26] None of this meant that Imperial Germany was a particularly lawless or violent society by the standards of the time, let alone of our time. On the contrary, the murder rate stood at around a twentieth of the Italian or Spanish; in the whole of Europe only the Netherlands boasted a lower rate. As Berlin became a city of 2 million, annual murders were in the range 30–40, around half of them infanticides. The number of convictions for murder was usually in single figures; for the German Empire it was mostly below 300 during this period (see Table 4). The pioneer French sociologist of crime, Emile Durkheim, was one observer who noted the significance of these statistics. Visiting Americans were, predictably, even more impressed. Ray Stannard Baker observed in 1901 that German cities enjoyed a reputation for being 'safer, perhaps, than any other in the world'.[27]

Visitors often linked this tranquillity to the great German respect for authority – perhaps, some suggested, too great a respect. The American criminologist Raymond Fosdick noted the profusion of *Verboten* signs, to which 'symbols of order the law-abiding German invariably and instinctively submits'. The Englishman Jerome K. Jerome's *Three Men on The Bummel* (1900) offered an extended satire on ubiquitous German officialdom and the absurd willingness of the natives to obey it. Contemporary German critics made the same point. 'In England, everybody is a citizen; in Germany, everybody is a subject', observed Friedrich Paulsen.[28] Heinrich Mann called his celebrated novel of bourgeois self-abasement *Der Untertan*: the subject. The theme of the German subject-mentality has retained an important place in the historical literature – and in popular attitudes towards 'the Germans'. As far as the imperial period is concerned, the argument might appear to be little more than a caricature. Abject respect for authority was scarcely evident in Spiesen during the Kulturkampf, when villagers seized gendarmes and asked their priest: 'Shall we kill them?' And Jerome K. Jerome's English clerks obviously did not visit any mining

TABLE 4: *Convictions for Murder in Germany, Prussia and Berlin,*
1882 – 1914

	Convictions for Murder		
Year	Germany	Prussia	Berlin
1882	320	199	3
1883	317	185	6
1884	269	162	2
1885	290	173	8
1886	298	166	2
1887	273	153	7
1888	212	112	4
1889	255	130	3
1890	258	130	5
1891	248	121	1
1892	316	174	10
1893	281	180	7
1894	275	156	3
1895	283	?	?
1896	270	?	?
1897	275	150	5
1898	269	126	7
1899	250	128	4
1900	251	139	2
1901	242	122	5
1902	283	154	0
1903	275	152	5
1904	273	140	3
1905	271	135	4
1906	261	150	1
1907	272	159	7
1908	290	155	6
1909	289	160	11
1910	303	174	13
1911	322	185	11
1912	323	182	6
1913	367	217	13
1914	312	179	3

NOTE: The figures include both premeditated and unpremeditated
murder. The statistics for convictions are lower than the number of reported
murders, based on coroners' reports.

SOURCE: E. Johnson, 'The Crime Rate, 1830–1930', in Richard J. Evans (ed.), *The*
German Underworld (London, 1988), p. 176.

communities, where prisoners were often forcibly released from police custody. Industrial disputes were commonly marked by violence on both sides. In the great Saarland pit strikes of 1889–93, the miners' leader Nikolaus Warken proposed solving the problem of coal stocks with 'a drop of petrol'.[29]

Yet German orderliness and obedience were not legends, even if it is misleading to talk of a uniform subject-mentality. These traits do seem to have been especially apparent in Germany. One widespread European form of disorder was entirely absent, the peasant jacqueries so common in Italy and elsewhere, and unrest expressed through physical force was probably less frequent than in most other societies at a comparable stage of development. It also occurred less often than it had in the past. Efforts to measure incidents of 'collective protest' are fraught with difficulties, but they do indicate strongly that there were fewer such incidents after 1850 than before, and that the numbers declined sharply between 1850–81 and 1882–1913.[30] This cannot be attributed solely to material improvements. Germans were not innately docile, but they lived increasingly in a world of institutions that sought to discipline them. These institutions might encounter resistance, particularly from the lower classes, but their capacity to shape society was considerable.

Foremost among them was the army. Its presence was visible everywhere – in barracks, drills and manoeuvres, regimental bands and military parades. Gymnastic clubs promoted soldierly virtues, and so did schools. In his memoirs, Karl Retzlaw described his youth in the small West Prussian garrison town of Schneidemühl, where he attended the Moltke School, sang martial songs every morning and, like each of his fellow pupils, was asked the ritual question by his class teacher 'What do you want to be?', to which the correct answer was 'Soldier, Sir!'[31] Ever since the term 'militarism' became common currency in Germany (it was first used by Catholic and democratic critics in the 1860s), it has denoted not only the external role of the army but its impact at home. This was partly a matter of the place occupied by the army in domestic politics, a subject to which I shall return in the following chapter. It also meant what is often referred to as the 'militarization' of German society. The symbol of this was the power of the uniform. Soldiers had special legal privileges, and civilians were expected to step aside to allow an officer to pass on the street. In a famous incident that occurred in 1906, a cobbler with a criminal record dressed up in a captain's uniform and led ten soldiers to the Köpenick town hall, where he arrested the mayor and stole 5000 Marks. A better demonstration of the servile mentality could hardly have been invented, and 'The Captain of Köpenick' was put on the stage by no fewer than five different playwrights.

Civilian Germany was not universally won over by the army. Peasants resented manoeuvres because they spread foot and mouth disease and interrupted harvesting, grievances repeatedly aired in agrarian publications. The army also made enemies through its brutal handling of industrial and other disputes. Three were killed and seventeen injured in 1894 when the army intervened in a conflict between squire and peasantry in rural Prussia. In the notorious Zabern case of 1913, soldiers ran amok in an Alsatian garrison town, abusing and manhandling local inhabitants. Zabern became a *cause célèbre* in press and parliament, underlining the fact that the ugly face of militarism could create outrage. It was not the only scandal. The many dramatizations of the Köpenick incident indicate that public opinion was not blind to the absurdities of military pretensions, while contemporary cartoons could be savage, not just in the socialist *Der wahre Jakob* (*The Right Way*), but in bourgeois publications like *Simplicissimus*. Military legal privileges caused resentment among the propertied and educated; so did the tendency of officers to keep themselves apart and look down on civilians. Finally, the officer corps limited its appeal as a would-be 'school of the nation' in so far as it tried to exclude unwanted elements – Jews, Catholics, members of the middle classes with progressive ideas or too close to grubby trade.

When all this has been said, however, there is no doubting the generally high prestige of the army, starting with its role as the architect of unification, celebrated each year in the 'national holiday' of Sedan Day. Many middle-class Germans were attracted by the army as an emblem of the nation's resolve. Invitations to dine in the mess were eagerly sought as a badge of insider status, and the harsh, order-giving tones of military routine seeped into civilian life. Diederich Hessling, the central character of Heinrich Mann's *Der Untertan*, remains the fictional embodiment of this, abjectly deferential to figures of authority above him, domineering towards those below. The reserve officer corps, 120,000 strong by 1914, was the principal conduit of such values. Access to it was filtered to keep out 'undesirables', even if this was not always possible – how could 'trade' be kept out in Hamburg? Members were schooled in conformism and respect for the military virtues; manoeuvres heightened the sense of commonality with regular officers. There are many examples of men who were more proud of their rank than they were of their civilian accomplishments, although sometimes the hierarchical distinctions were actually the imported snobberies of bourgeois life. One of Ed Thoeny's superb cartoons shows two reserve officers on horseback, one saying to the other: 'Does *Kamerad* not feel that the lawyers are so to speak the cavalry of civilian life – the better sort?' Fontane deplored these 'everlasting reserve officers', and contemporaries observed that they seemed to fight even more duels than regulars.[32]

The regular officer was an important role-model, deferred to in matters pertaining to 'honour'. And, on the face of it, the officer corps proper remained strikingly aristocratic, a bastion of monocled feudality. On the eve of war, 30 per cent of all officers still came from noble families. The figure was higher above the rank of colonel, and aristocrats dominated guards and cavalry regiments. This evidence is not as clear-cut as it seems, however. In the first place, it does not distinguish between the old rural nobility and recently ennobled men from commoner backgrounds. Even on the figures as they stand, the percentage of officers from bourgeois backgrounds rose steadily from 50 per cent in the 1860s to 70 per cent in 1914, giving them an important place within infantry regiments and a dominant one in expanding specialisms like artillery and engineering corps. As the regular officer corps grew from 17,000 to 30,000, it proved impossible to prevent the bourgeoisie increasing its share. And further change in the same direction was in the pipeline, for in 1914 two-thirds of students in the Royal Prussian Cadet Corps schools were from non-noble families.[33] Of course, that did not preclude middle-class entrants assimilating aristocratic values, and this certainly took place. The 'nobility of the mind' demanded of all officers by William II was a codeword for it. But are we really seeing here the 'feudal' ethos so often referred to? It could be argued that the emphasis on tradition within the officer corps was a very self-conscious phenomenon, something that was necessary to bind brother officers together at a time when the true nature of the army had become very different. The keynote here is professionalism. Moltke's army that built Germany was already celebrated for the proficiency of its staff work, the ability to transport men and use modern technology. These characteristics grew steadily in importance. The General Staff took pride in its famous railway section, its careful choice of weapons and contract-vetting, its capacity to manage and deliver manpower – and its sheer hard work. Von Einem's recollections of his years on Schlieffen's General Staff constantly brag of eighteen-hour days: they defined a self-image compounded of manly endurance and professionalism.[34] These values spread to line regiments, as the education and application required of officers became more demanding and efforts were made to curtail excessive card-playing and horse-racing. Regular officers, more concerned with function than frills, also expressed impatience with the 'uncles of the reserve' who got in the way, and deplored 'playing at soldiers' as a civilian affectation (the Kaiser's penchant for the aesthetics of military display was not immune to criticism). In short, this ethos combined honour, professionalism, hard work – and a self-conscious masculinity that viewed women as weak, subordinate creatures. It was broader than the Junkers-in-uniform caricature, and offered a more attractive model of German discipline to the propertied and educated – including Catholics and liberals. The liberal Max Weber was a keen reserve officer despite, not because of, his feelings about the Junkers, whom he viewed as a selfish caste that had outlived its usefulness.

Increasingly professional officers commanded a growing mass army of conscripts. Its peace-time strength stood at 400,000 in the 1870s, 600,000 by 1900, and 800,000 following the expansion of 1911–13. What effect did this military machine have on the men who passed through it? Two-thirds of recruits still came from rural areas in 1911, just 6 per cent from big cities. Whether this reflected a belief at the top that peasants and agricultural labourers made more pliant soldiers than industrial workers, as often argued, or whether it resulted from the real or perceived physical unfitness of urban recruits, it is impossible to be sure – the documentary evidence is not available. What is clear is that, once they had passed the barracks' gate and donned uniforms, conscripts severed any links with the outside world for at least 4–6 weeks, until they had been 'broken in' and could be trusted to mingle – sparingly – with civilians. Discipline was harsh and physical. The most eloquent testimony to that was a suicide rate of 220–40 a year (mostly, not all, in Prussia), fourteen times the level of the civilian population. But the barracks was a symbol of something more than just arbitrary maltreatment. Soldiers had once been billeted on civilians, or housed in unsuitable accommodation like former convents. The many purpose-built barracks constructed in the late nineteenth century, usually on a new, decentralized pattern, had several objectives: to confine, to discipline, but also to mould a more efficient soldiery. Space, light and washing facilities were often superior to those the recruits enjoyed in civilian life. Emphasis was placed on physical fitness and hygiene; swimming was encouraged. The historian Treitschke might sneer that the English confused soap and civilization, but the German army saw soap as a civilizing agent.

It is hard to gauge the impact of the conscript experience. Probably it went down best with the more established parts of the lower middle class, who also provided the NCO backbone of the regular army, and whose everyday moral code was built on disciplined self-abnegation and respect for hierarchy – photographs of the Kaiser's jubilee parade of 1913 show the master chimney sweeps marching in their guild uniforms, complete with top hats, shouldering their brushes like rifles. Among young peasants military service may have made them dissatisfied with rural life, as the liberal Oskar Muser hoped; it certainly showed them something beyond the parish pump.[35] The barracks' inside toilets were often their first contact with modern technology, the rifle the second. As for the proletariat, the efforts made to identify 'subversives' and ban socialist newspapers suggest a concern that workers might infect the army before the army could inoculate them. Military discipline was far from instinctive, and often resented. But all who 'got through' the period of service shared an experience that let them take pride in their toughness and bound them in a male – indeed, strongly masculine – camaraderie. Up to 3 million Germans belonged to ex-servicemen's organizations by 1914.

Soldiers were not the only men who wore uniforms in Imperial Germany; so did customs officers, postal workers, state mine officials, railwaymen and foresters. Braid and piping were as commonplace as titles. This went beyond external appearance. Former soldiers were given preference in many parts of the nonmilitary bureaucracy through the system of 'military candidates' for posts – such that disgruntled officials who had risen through the ranks (or hoped to do so) established their own organization of 'civilian candidates'. Despite their efforts, and despite the fact that the 'character' bred in the army was a poor substitute for the specialized training increasingly required within the civilian bureaucracy, former soldiers – especially NCOs – still set the tone of German officialdom in its dealings with the public. That tone was usually described as *barsch* – harsh, or brusque. It was especially apparent among the police, who were heavily recruited from among ex-servicemen and expected to conduct themselves accordingly. This was true not only of the quasi-military and mounted rural gendarmerie, but of city police forces. Thus, while rapidly expanding police forces assumed the basic public-order functions once performed by the army, their bearing – not to mention their swords and spiked helmets – made the transition less obvious than it might have been. In practice, poor pay and conditions (especially night shifts) made it hard to attract the desired manpower at lower levels, and urban forces had to make do with what they could find. Dismissals for drunkenness and dereliction of duty were common. The poor quality of beat policemen was a major reason why the regular issue of firearms became common only around the turn of the century. At the upper level, a nonuniformed detective branch developed (until the 1870s there had been virtually no detectives outside Berlin), proud of its forensic skills and keen to emulate its more advanced British and French counterparts.

The German police was subject to constant reorganization in these years; it was not highly regarded by international observers, nor did it have the domestic reputation for efficiency enjoyed by other branches of the bureaucracy (and by the army). But the police did intervene to an astonishing degree in everyday life. This was partly because so many activities were 'policed', in the broadest sense, by buildings police, trade police, mine police, health police, and so on, a legacy of absolutism. Between this and the wide terms of reference of the regular police, almost nothing was left unregulated, from the colour of automobiles to the length of hatpins. As these examples suggest, the lower classes were not the only sections of society to be affected. Evidence from such different cities as Duisburg and Stuttgart shows a rate of police infractions running at over 10 per 100 inhabitants per year – 40,000 annual police penalties for a population of around 300,000 in the latter. In Recklinghausen, where the number of infractions reached 17 per 100 inhabitants in the late 1890s, miners and workers were underrepresented and the petty bourgeoisie overrepresented, a result of the many prosecutions for trading offences such as adulteration, contravention of fire and safety regulations, failure of masters to release apprentices for continuing education, and so on.[36] Nevertheless, the police did intervene extensively in working-class life, not just in political and industrial contexts but in the regulation of everyday affairs, where they were responsible for enforcing public order in the streets and moral order in the lodging houses. Above all, the police administered the system of registration and deregistration that was intended to monitor the every move of a highly mobile population.

One police duty was to apprehend the marginal and 'workshy'. Under article 361 of the Criminal Code, anyone guilty of vagrancy, homelessness or begging could be sent to the workhouse. The latter was no relic of an earlier age, but a means of supplementing the poor-relief system with institutional confinement. Some 20,000 a year were sent to Prussian workhouses in this period, swept from urban streets and rural areas with large numbers of itinerant labourers. If Breitenau in Hessen (founded in 1874) is typical, the workhouse functioned as a cross between poorhouse and correctional facility, its inmates simultaneously subject to welfare and punishment. A forced-labour system, harsh discipline, the use of the disrespectful 'Du' form to inmates, indeterminate 'sentences' (up to two years) and the possibility of release for good behaviour – all are reminiscent of the penitentiary. And the different coloured uniforms worn by different categories of inmate make it difficult not to think ahead to the time, after 1933, when Breitenau housed a variety of groups considered 'asocial' by the Nazis.[37]

Barracks, police cell, penitentiary, workhouse: these are the obvious symbols of a society that sought to discipline through confinement. It is possible to see other, less immediately apparent examples of what Michel Foucault and others have termed the 'carceral society' – institutions such as the school, the clinic, the asylum. Consider schools. The main point here is not so much the rigidly disciplinarian grammar schools (which generated a major literature on teenage suicides), but the larger picture of a society of 200,000 schoolteachers commanding obedience and school attendance that was closely monitored. In just one year 13,500 parents were spoken to by Düsseldorf police about truancy (the total population of the city was 91,000); over 3000 were prosecuted, and more than 1000 children had a daily police escort to school.[38] In industrial cities it was normal for truancy to account for half of all police ordinance transgressions, although this declined in the early twentieth century as school-going habits became more routine. Similarly, the growing medical intervention typical of this period was partly driven by fear of 'degeneration' and belief that a 'social hygiene' campaign was necessary to protect the population (especially the young) from alcoholism, venereal disease and other dangers. Medical policing of homeless shelters was one manifestation of this; another was the attempt to regulate prostitution by confining it to certain areas, together with the powers to subject prostitutes to compulsory medical examination. In the words of one historian, prostitutes inhabited an 'invisible prison'; the workhouse was provided with a similar pseudo-medical justification, for it confined 'the worst parasites of humanity' (Dr Otto Mönkemöller).[39] Here was the punitive face of the great explosion of youth and family welfare discussed in the previous chapter. Finally, criminological reformers of the period, influenced by the Italian Cesare Lombroso, began to establish new classifications to explain why offenders offended – they were abnormal, degenerate, mentally deficient. Some reformers advocated sterilization; the main thrust was to legitimize the detention of criminals, not on the grounds of retributive justice, but as a measure of social hygiene. The insane asylum was already spreading as an institution. Psychiatric observation wards were now added to prisons, and by the early twentieth century reformers were even arguing for the preventive detention of those who were 'prone to commit crime'.

A sense of perspective is needed here. First, not every aspect of life was or could be policed. There were lower-class rookeries in older cities and parts of new industrial conurbations that were effective 'no-go' areas. Inadequate policing led to widespread evasion of the registration system in practice, and police were reluctant to be drawn into the more zealous morality campaigns, including those with official backing. Detailed regulations often remained a mere aspiration. Popular consumption of alcohol and pornography were frequently left alone; the regulation of prostitution had all but broken down by 1914. Secondly, we should acknowledge that the 'carceral society' had two sides. If historians imbued with the idea of progress once viewed the

spread of education, welfare and other forms of institutionaliz-
ation too innocently, we should not simply turn their perspective
on its head. Every silver lining may have a cloud, but every
cloud still has a silver lining. Strong measures against truancy
created an enviable literacy rate and saved many children from
the crassest forms of exploitation. Only shopkeepers objected
to the enforcement of adulteration and food hygiene regulations.
And these, like other laws, were enforced by officials with notably unsticky fingers. The policing of homeless shelters and the
obsession with hygiene had, as the virtue of its vice, that the
authorities responded quickly to incidents like the mass-
poisoning outbreak among residents of the Berlin municipal
shelter in 1911 (traced to schnapps cut with methylated spirits)
which claimed seventy-two lives. The Social Democrats praised
official actions, as they supported many kinds of state welfarism
– indeed, there was strong labour pressure for welfare measures.
Finally, the sinister implications of criminological arguments
about the 'mentally defective' offender, obvious to us, have to
be recognized in their contemporary context as a reformist
response to vengeful conservative insistence on retributive justice. The same arguments also encompassed more liberal attitudes towards first-time offences and the desire to rehabilitate
youthful offenders through special juvenile reformatories. This
meant more incarceration, of course – a special kind of insti-
tutionalization designed to 'save youth'. But we should note the
countervailing tendency: there was a sharp decline in the overall
use of custodial sentences by the criminal courts of Imperial
Germany.

If the barracks and the police station were two powerful symbols of German society, the law court was a third, and no less
important. Germany was a state based on the rule of law. Prussia
was not Russia; it was not even Italy. The great liberal ambition
from pre-1848 through the 1870s to constrain arbitrariness and
anchor legal norms was largely achieved. There were limits,
certainly. Equality before the law still stopped short of the barracks' gate, although the reforms of the 1890s made some headway. And 'class justice' was real, evident on the picket line and

in the relative failure to prosecute white-collar crime. But class justice was neither made in Germany nor notably conspicuous there: it is not easy to think of any major contemporary state, including Britain, France and the USA, that could point to a better record. The bureaucracy worked with rulebooks and was legally accountable. It was established that the police operated under the supervision of the public prosecutors' offices; individual officers could be, and often were, tried and convicted for transgressions. Many of the more notorious cases of army or civilian officiousness became notorious precisely because they were aired in court. Feeble cases were routinely thrown out as the legal bureaucracy refused to do the bidding of the field administration, and the victims of dubious charges were regularly acquitted – as the Social Democratic press enjoyed pointing out. The judiciary, historians agree, enjoyed genuine independence. The 'get-tough' spasms emanating from the Kaiser and other circles seem, if anything, to have had quite the opposite effect from the one intended in matters such as sentencing policy.

If there is a common denominator to the theme of order and discipline in Imperial Germany, it is something broader than the subject-mentality, social militarism or the carceral society. The true common element is bureaucracy. That is what linked the conscript army to the growing armies of schoolteachers, policemen, postal officials and the rest. The word that contemporaries kept using recalls critics of the Frederician army in the eighteenth century, but described something more all-embracing: the machine. The liberal Franz von Roggenbach complained that advocates of the 'perfect' state had reduced individuals 'to the level of trained machines': the Berlin police department was likened to 'a huge ponderous machine'; Max Weber's widow, Marianne, wrote of her husband's admiration for the military 'machine'.[40] Weber himself rightly saw growing bureaucracy as something that went well beyond the state. Business, political parties, even the churches were becoming bureaucratized. And his greatness as a writer on the subject lay in his double-sided perspective. The bureaucratic machine was rational, essential, a motor for good; it also threatened to confine humans in an 'iron cage'.[41] Weber's theme was universal, but it was informed by the experiences of the era. His German contemporaries felt the same ambivalence. Officials were generally held in high regard. People wanted their sons and daughters to enjoy the security and other rewards of service in the growing bureaucracies, public or private, and by 1914 their ranks included many workers, such as railwaymen. There was also an expectation that letters be delivered on time and the state provide in countless everyday ways. Yet there was another side to all this: the bureaucratic machine was also a source of resentment, whether it came in governmental or some other form – even the Social Democratic Party. It bossed, classified, interfered. The population of prewar Germany had become largely habituated to a more bureaucratic society, but this did not prevent a strong sense of suffocation.

Culture and Revolt

As the Kulturkampf showed, culture meant more than just literature, painting or music. In the prewar period the word continued to carry a heavy charge. Infused with growing nationalist sentiment, Kultur supposedly denoted superior German accomplishments in scholarship and the arts. For some it also stood, more intangibly, for a greater German seriousness and 'depth' than could be found in the mere 'civilizations' of the Anglo-Saxons or the frivolous decadence of the French (see Chapter Seven). At the same time, culture was starting to acquire its modern sense of 'way of life'. This idea of culture as something that included manners, customs and material artefacts developed from the new disciplines of ethnology and ethnography, the forerunners of anthropology, and received a powerful stimulus from the imperialist encounter with 'native cultures'. Closer to home, Karl Lamprecht caused a stir by writing a new kind of cultural history of the German people along the same lines.

Culture, then, was becoming a more capacious category than it had been a generation earlier. But even if we restrict our use of the term to the arts in a formal sense, Wilhelmine culture presents a picture of enormous diversity. It included avant-garde art and academicist painting, naturalist drama and sentimental genre literature, Richard Strauss's *Elektra* and the music of the dancehall. Culture in the narrower sense was also becoming more difficult to pin down. Historians often use the simple binary distinction between 'high' (or élite) and 'low' (or popular) culture. As we shall see, this is hardly adequate to the complexities involved here.

What has lasted and continues to be valued from these years is, by definition, what has entered the cultural canon. That includes both works done within an established idiom – the novels of Fontane and Thomas Mann, the late compositions of Brahms – and works by the avant-garde, the high priests of contemporary modernism. The literary avant-garde can be tracked through successive waves of the great 'isms' (naturalism, symbolism, expressionism), as these were manifested in the drama of Hauptmann and Wedekind, the poety of Rilke, George and Benn. In the case of music, seen by many contemporaries as the quintessential 'German' art form, the great myth-maker Wagner remained a dominant presence, even though his last opera (*Parsifal*) was produced in 1882 and the composer's death in Venice followed early the next year. After the turn of the century Strauss and Schoenberg represented a further willed break with tradition. It was art that produced the most self-conscious modernism of the period, however, with all its typical characteristics: 'secessions' by avant-garde painters from the stifling academic salon; the emergence, as in literature, of successive new 'movements' from realism through impressionism (belatedly adopted in Germany) to Jugendstil and expressionism; and the proliferation of self-conscious groups and schools like the 'Brücke' ('Bridge') in Dresden, the 'Blauer Reiter' ('Blue Rider') in Munich, and the colony of artists that gathered at Worpswede. The shock of the new also made an impact before 1914 in architecture and design. The great icons of the modernist movement, Gropius, Mies van der Rohe and Le Corbusier, had served their apprenticeship with Peter Behrens; Gropius had built his famous Fagus shoe factory in glass; the *Werkbund* exhibition buildings of 1914 in Cologne had prefigured the ideas of the Bauhaus.

Many elements of what we regard as 'Weimar culture' were already in place. And if, in Walter Benjamin's words, Paris was 'the capital of the nineteenth century', Berlin was already preparing to become the capital of the 1920s.[42] The capital was metropolis, world city, and epitome of the modern spirit: it had a vigorous café culture, abundant theatres, journals and publishers, alongside dealers, galleries, and private patrons of avant-garde art, especially among the wealthy Jewish bourgeoisie. Berlin was a magnet for writers and artists before the war: the 'Brücke' group moved there in 1910. But support for antiestablishment or avant-garde culture also existed elsewhere, in the publishing centres of Leipzig and Stuttgart, among the sympathetic museum directors of Cologne and Düsseldorf, from organizations like the Jena Art Association which was unrivalled in its enthusiasm (and practical support) for modernist paintings and graphics. Above all, Munich represented an alternative pole of attraction to the Prussian capital. It was home to a large community of writers and critics, the celebrated *Elf Scharfrichter* (*Eleven Executioners*) political cabaret, some of Germany's most accomplished caricaturists, and three times as many artists in proportion to population as Berlin, including Kandinsky and the rest of the 'Blauer Reiter'. Picasso said in 1897 that if he had a son who wanted to be an artist, he would send him to study in Munich, not Paris.[43]

The cultural avant-garde is often regarded as a politically progressive force, reacting against contemporary society or the stifling convention of official culture. There is some evidence for this view. Cabaret and caricature were explicitly political, and social criticism is not hard to find in modernist literature and art, especially in naturalism. *The Weavers*, Hauptmann's play about the Silesian uprising of 1844, was a political as well as an aesthetic scandal; so was Käthe Kollwitz's series of graphics on the same subject, and her later works on the Peasants War. When a new periodical, *März* (*March*), was founded in Württemberg, its supporters included both the young Hermann Hesse and prominent left-liberal politicians like Conrad Haussmann. Even the title, with its allusion to March 1848 and the springtime of peoples, was a signal that cultural and political aspirations went together. The political distemper within the cultural avant-garde was to be shown in widespread support for the revolution of November 1918. Architects like Gropius and Bruno Taut were among the many who belonged to the 'November group'; Bohemian Munich supported the revolution strongly. The modernist impulse contained a potentially anti-establishment element by its very nature: it was international. The dramatists took their lead from Scandinavia, the painters from France; the architects were influenced by developments in America and moving towards an 'international style'. This was one of the things – the sizable number of their Jewish patrons was another – held against the avant-garde by Kaiser William II. Our sense of the avant-garde as oppositional has undoubtedly been reinforced by the official disapproval it encountered, including outright censorship. The sacking of Hugo von Tschudi as director of the National Gallery in Berlin because of his support for newfangled French painting was a notable example.

Nevertheless, the equation of avant-garde with progressive politics and 'outsider' status is a half-truth. The modernists wanted to subvert aesthetic rules; they did not necessarily want to subvert anything else. Many were profoundly apolitical, or held contemptuous views of democracy and the 'masses'. The poets and painters often saw their ideal public as small and discriminating: revolutionaries in a formal sense, they were élitist by social inclinations, drawn to the 'aristocracy of the spirit'. Many self-consciously advanced cultural groups displayed this disdain, none more so than the 'circle' around the poet Stefan George. There was nothing specifically German about this. It is a commonplace that the modernist embrace of complexity and 'difficulty' was often accompanied by a fastidious social and political conservatism, as figures such as Eliot, Pound and Wyndham Lewis demonstrate. Nor did the internationalism of the modern preclude a chauvinist strain. The painter Lovis Corinth, who mocked the Catholic church in his compositions and admired both Manet and Cézanne, lectured on the need to protect German art from the dangers of contamination by Gallic fashion. He was not alone: the contemporary understanding of 'German' expressionism had many chauvinist undertones. Finally, it is important not to exaggerate the 'outsider' position of the German avant-garde. By 1914, modernists and their viewers, readers, listeners, collectors, impresarios, patrons and critical supporters were a formidable presence across the high-cultural landscape of Imperial Germany. They had established a 'tradition of the new' (Harold Rosenberg) and powerful networks of institutional support.[44] These extended to parts of the official establishment. William II of Württemberg read a socialist daily paper because its coverage of the modern arts was so good. When the Berlin secessionists founded the League of German Artists, their patron was the Duke of Saxe-Weimar, and when Tschudi was fired in Berlin he was promptly hired in Munich.

Yet there was a court-approved, official culture against which the modernists generally defined themselves. It was most conspicuous in the large-scale, public arts like architecture and statuary, and its distinguishing characteristics were pomposity and a firm attachment to pseudo-historical 'tradition'. The monumental yet fussy neoromantic buildings favoured by the Kaiser were characteristic. This style was used not only in the royal castle in Posen, built (at enormous expense) between 1905 and 1910, but in many public buildings. The series of grotesque figures that peopled the Siegesallee in Berlin were the exact equivalent in contemporary official statuary. In painting, the approved style of courts, academies and most official galleries favoured genre works, conventional portraiture and large, historical canvases. At this level, the two most representative artists of the period were Franz von Lenbach, the hugely successful portrait painter, and Anton von Werner, President of the Berlin

Academy and scourge of the modernists, whose celebrated painting of William I's proclamation as Kaiser in 1871 had just the
statuesque, idealizing qualities and abundance of uniforms that
appealed to William II. Werner became William's adviser on
artistic affairs. We should not underestimate the role of the
Kaiser as an arbiter of taste. Given that young men were prepared to grow their moustaches in the royal style and even to
imitate William's rasping voice, it would be surprising if the
All-Highest denunciations of green horses and degenerate prose
had found no echo.

Avant-garde and official culture were both élitist, in their
different ways; but the latter went with the grain of 'common
sense', the conventional taste of the period. Here we have a
third subcategory of contemporary culture. It is best described
as middlebrow, or everyday middle-class, culture. Consider two
statistics. First, by the early twentieth century as many as
100,000 Germans supported themselves from writing, music,
the theatre and related activities, not including white-collar
occupations like box-office staff. The proportion of Kandinskys,
Schoenbergs and Benns – and of serious critics like Julius Meier-
Graefe – was obviously tiny. Secondly, while virtually all Germans could read, it has been estimated that only about 20 per
cent read journals, magazines or literature of any kind, and only
one in five of those – 4 per cent of the adult population – read
'national literature'.[45] Of that smaller group, in turn, we can
safely assume that reading the classics predominated: authors
like Schiller and Goethe, the latter placed squarely in the German literary canon only in the 1870s. It is impossible to go
beyond that and ask how many of those readers used national
literature as a storehouse of quotations, or to shore up their
own sense of respectability – the proportion, in other words,
for whom culture was a 'façade', to use Hermann Glaser's term.[46]
But we do know something about the tastes of the other 16 per
cent of the reading population. Their preferences included the
immensely popular westerns of Karl May, the saccharine
accounts of rural life known as *Heimat* literature, and the sentimental stories serialized in family magazines and newspapers

(16 million copies of daily papers were sold in Germany by 1914). This was the world of the middle- and lower middle-class philistine so derided by the avant-garde, the *Spießer* whose favourite kind of sculpture was the garden gnome.

The Wilhelmine years saw widespread concern among the highly educated that standards of individual cultivation were being eroded. Max Weber called for a renewed, ascetic individualism, the building up of internal 'mastery', to counteract this; Thomas Mann saw the work of the true 'artist' as the best antidote. The sense of cultural malaise was common ground, as it was to numerous intellectuals and educated bourgeois. Within higher education the problem was blamed on the 'mass university'; in society at large it was blamed on 'mass culture'. The targets were numerous. They included the pulp fiction turned out by series like *Romane des Feierabends* (*Novels for Leisure Time*) and *Der Roman für Alle*, (*Novels for Everyone*), together with newer forms of mass entertainment like the vaudeville, variety show and dancehall. Werner Sombart argued that mechanical music had driven out the authentic folk song, part of his passionate lament about the 'desert of modern technical culture'.[47] There was similar dismay over the hurdy-gurdy machines and mechanical rides at fairgrounds, as the former parish fairs became more secularized and commercialized in a new urban setting. As the earlier bioscopes and dioramas gave way to the cinema (of which there were 2500 in Germany by 1914), a parallel concern arose, as it did over the growth of spectator sport, especially soccer and professional cycling. In each case fear was expressed about the creation of passive, regimented consumers.

Avant-garde, official culture, the national literary canon, middlebrow kitsch, commercialized mass entertainment – the jostling together of these very different forms was characteristic of modern societies, as élite culture fragmented and new forms of mechanical reproduction changed the way culture was consumed. It was no longer clear what culture was, a disturbing situation to those, especially the educated middle classes, who thought they knew. The situation was further complicated in

Wilhelmine Germany by the existence of political and religious subcultures, especially those of the Catholics and the labour movement. In the former case we are not talking about the obvious fact that devout Catholics read Bible, prayer-book and devotional literature, but the more striking fact that they had their own playwrights and drama groups, songbooks, literary journals, even their own brand of pulp literature, like the sentimental best-selling novels of Joseph Spillmann. In fact, German Catholic culture contained many of the fault lines evident in the larger culture. There was a small avant-garde of self-conscious Catholic modernists like Karl Muth (a fierce critic of Spillmann's books), an official culture that still looked down on secular literature as the first step to apostasy, a group of middle-class Catholics in the Görres Society who sought to join the broader national culture, and – not least – a general alarm among the educated over mass-produced religious kitsch. Within the milieu of socialist literary, choral and gymnastic groups we also find variations on the cultural debates exercising the larger society. One purpose of the labour movement's separate cultural provision was to prevent workers from being contaminated by 'bourgeois commercialization': the SPD was extremely hostile to penny dreadfuls, just as it condemned soccer as a brutal game. On the other hand, there was widespread scepticism about bourgeois aestheticism ('art for art's sake'), and some looked to advance a specifically 'proletarian literature'. The reality of the socialist subculture was more pragmatic. It was found that workers did follow soccer, just as large numbers borrowed the works of Alexandre Dumas from trade union libraries, and the SPD cultural mission largely boiled down to disseminating classic German literature (although Zola and Gorky were also popular with socialist readers). The Catholic and socialist subcultures were not hermetically sealed: they shared or mimicked many broader developments. The status of Goethe provides an example. Now accepted as part of their own cultural identity by many educated Catholics seeking to enter the mainstream of national life, he was held up by socialists who argued for the worker's right to enjoy the best that 'bourgeois society' had to offer.

There were also many overlaps and points of intersection between avant-garde, official, middlebrow and mass culture more generally. In the first place, technology and market forces operated across the categories. Commercialized mass culture meant lurid pulp fiction and an increasingly debased *Heimat* genre; it also meant that Reclam could offer cheap editions of the classics and Fischer affordable editions of serious contemporary literature. Secondly, the formal distinctions between different kinds of culture became more blurred in this period. The medium that developed into the brash new cinema also lent itself to the mass representation of academicist culture, such as Werner's 'panorama' of the Battle of Sedan. Conversely, modernist intellectuals were already embarking on their twentieth-century love affair with popular culture. Theatrical modernists in Munich borrowed to good effect from vaudeville, circus and popular cabaret. The icons of Americana proved particularly seductive in these circles. The expressionist writer Walter Hasenclever praised the cinema for its specifically American quality; the young Georg Grosz and the writer Rudolf Schlichter were among the many intellectuals captivated by Karl May and cinema westerns.[48] The embrace of American popular culture – jazz, cinema, boxing – by the 1920s avant-garde was anticipated before the war.

Thirdly, the fierce cultural debates of these years led to complex affinities and shifting alliances. Some members of the avant-garde shared with the guardians of official culture a distaste for the vulgarity of mass taste. But there were members of both groups who turned the other way. While intellectuals went to the movies, the Kaiser spoke for a large body of official opinion that appealed to philistine sentiment against un-German experimentation. Socialists and conservatives coincided in their dislike of pulp fiction. But when government ministers, urged on by Catholic morality campaigners, tried to extend the laws against obscenity through the Lex Heinze, Social Democrats joined with liberal politicians and academics, publishers, critics, and leading writers, artists and stage directors to resist the threat of increased censorship. Their efforts were organized in the Goethe League, founded in Munich.[49]

The culture wars of these years had at least one thing in common with the earlier Kulturkampf. Both were conflicts about modernity and its discontents. To draw the comparison, however, is to recognize how much had changed. Modernity and progress were still symbolized in the 1870s by the steam engine and the laboratory. By 1914 Germans lived in a world that contained the electric tram, the automobile, mass advertising, and the velodrome. These were the new emblems of modern times. The broad question of how contemporaries responded to this new mechanical civilization has exercised many German historians – understandably so, given that just a few years later the Nazis were to present themselves as the bitter foes of cultural modernity and demand a return to the simple German virtues. It has often been argued that 'antimodernist' attitudes were exceptionally widespread in Wilhelmine Germany, and to see in this the cultural roots of National Socialism.[50] How does this argument stand up?

The first point that must be made is the continuing fascination of many Germans with their modern world. We have already seen examples of intellectuals who embraced Americana. Berlin, with its frenetic pace, was often likened to an American city, and the comparison was certainly not always negative. Big-city dwellers who threw out the epithet 'provincial' as a taunt expressed an arrogant confidence that they had seen the future, and it worked. The attractions of the modern went well beyond intellectuals and avant-garde. Workers not only went to the movies and watched cycle races; they polished up their factory machines and gave them names. Class-conscious workers commonly subscribed to a sub-Darwinian, vulgar-materialist belief in the march of science. Popular admiration for technology was manifested in countless ways: in the extraordinary cult of the Zeppelin airship, in the crowds that gathered to watch as the underground railway was constructed in Berlin, in the sales of detective stories that extolled the modern forensic techniques of their heroes. Another contemporary genre, science fiction, is also revealing. In 1897, the same year that H. G. Wells' *War of the Worlds* appeared, Kurd Lasswitz published *Auf zwei Planeten (On Two Planets)*. Where Wells' Martian invaders were technological monsters, however, Lasswitz's were benign visitors who brought the hope of an enlightened future. Countless Germans in the early twentieth century were optimistic about the benefits of terrestrial technology, encouraged by the continuing flood of popular scientific literature which now had new marvels to extol, like electricity. Alfred von Urbanitzky's *Electricity in the Service of Humanity* was among the many works advocating 'electro-culture', or 'galvanizing' the soil: radishes and carrots treated this way 'had an exquisite flavour and were very tender and juicy', readers were assured.[51]

That is one side of the story. On the other side were the critics of modernity who preferred their society, like their carrots, 'organic' rather than 'mechanical'. The world was becoming 'more hateful, more artificial, more Americanized every day', lamented Ernst Rudorff, a leading figure in the *Heimat* protection movement.[52] These writers and intellectuals saw the countryside and the traditional small town as the source of the nation's health, the modern city as a threat to it. For Karl Henrici, writing in 1894, the urban landscape was a 'bleak desert' disfigured by 'the levelling influence of crass, calculating materialism, which recognizes no fatherland and takes account only of what can be numerically calculated and recorded'. Karl Scheffler criticized the 'colourless modernity' of the big city; Georg Steinhausen called them 'great boils on the body of the nation'.[53] Berlin was the inevitable symbol of everything these critics deplored – ugliness, uniformity, coldness, lack of true 'creativity' – and it figured prominently in the work of one of the best-known cultural critics of the era, Julius Langbehn, whose *Rembrandt als Erzieher (Rembrandt as Educator)* went through forty-nine printings between 1890 and 1909. For Langbehn, the capital was American in the worst sense, full of restless but senseless activity, spiritually empty. In these and numerous other expressions of hostility, we see what Fritz Stern has called 'vulgar idealism', the by-product of cultural pessimism and mandarin distaste for the surfaces of mass society. This critique of modernity overlapped with hostility towards mass culture, and was often informed by suspicion of the proletariat. It also had its popular counterparts, of which the idealized rusticity in *Heimat* literature is the most obvious. Langbehn argued that 'the provinces should be mobilized and ordered to march against the capital'.[54] He was no organizer; but resentment existed in rural Germany over the changing nature of society, and there were political groups in Wilhelmine Germany willing to appeal to prejudices against the symbols of modern urban society – socialism, 'deviant' sexuality, avant-garde artists, Jews.

These intellectual currents, like the contemporary attraction of the irrational, had their counterparts elsewhere in *fin de siècle* Europe. Antimodernism was probably more pronounced in Germany; but so was the fervent embrace of science and technology. The speed of cultural change generated both fascination and repulsion of an unusual intensity. Twenty years before the Weimar Republic, Germany was already being perceived as a test case of the 'classic modern', a laboratory for modernity and its discontents. The responses to this cannot be neatly pigeonholed in political terms. It was the radical Social Democrat Karl Liebknecht, not Julius Langbehn, who lamented the 'unhealthy concentration of humanity in great deserts of stone', and socialists cycled into the countryside or tilled their allotments as a way of escaping the urban regimentation of their lives, without thereby embracing antimodernism.[55] There was nothing intrinsically reactionary about the attraction of the great outdoors, whether for organized workers, Worpswede painters or the hikers of the Youth Movement. In fact, this impulse had a decidedly emancipatory element. Conversely, the cult of science and technology was not innately liberal. The self-conscious modernity of the eugenics and racial-hygiene movements make that clear enough. Radical nationalists were no less enamoured of machine marvels. The government statistician Rudolf Martin imagined a German empire based on air-power, complete with hospitals for treating tuberculosis suspended 15,000 feet in the air – a perfect fusion of imperialism, technology and welfare. The case of Theodor Fritsch is equally revealing. Anti-Semite, antisocialist, chauvinist, spokesman for the master craftsmen, Fritsch was a reactionary man for all seasons. But in moments left over from denouncing kosher butchers, he also wrote about the planned and zoned 'city of the future' and demanded fast roads for automobiles.[56] Perhaps we should not be surprised that the *Autobahn* could go together with reactionary politics.

Both promodern and antimodern standpoints were ambiguous, capable of being harnessed to very different political positions. This ambiguity runs through the representative movements and individuals of the period. The Garden City Society founded in 1902 was a reformist, even utopian project to devise new ways of urban living, yet it contained an important Pan-German impulse that it took from the League for *Heimat* Protection. Walter Rathenau, head of the electrical combine AEG, was a capitalist of the most dynamic kind, who liked to see himself as a prophet of cultural despair. Educated middle-class critics of modernity were invariably selective in practice, accepting the fruits of technology when it suited and using modern communications to convey their message about the virtues of peasant life. Perhaps the most powerful contemporary intellect to grapple with contradictions like these was Max Weber. More than any other German writer of the period, except for Sigmund Freud, he confronted the balance sheet of modernity, its ambiguities and demands, with a minimum of illusions. A powerful advocate of capitalism and technical rationality, and an admirer of American dynamism which he witnessed at first hand, Weber repeatedly criticized those who sought a lazy-minded return to some imagined Arcadian past. Yet he was troubled by what he saw as the 'disenchantment of the world' (the phrase came from Schiller) and the grey forces of regimentation. The central question was 'not, how we may still further promote and accelerate it, but what we can oppose to this machinery, in order to keep a portion of humanity free from this parcelling out of the soul, from this total dominance of the bureaucratic ideal of life'.[57] Weber's attempt to balance these conflicting positions led to his own hard-won stance of 'heroic pessimism'.

Paul Honigsheim, a member of Weber's prewar Heidelberg circle, later wrote about the 'trend away from the bourgeois way of life, city culture, instrumental rationality, quantification, scientific specialization, and everything else then considered abhorrent phenomena'.[58] This, as we have seen, was a half-truth. It would be more accurate to speak of a widespread cultural revolt in these years, going well beyond the narrow cultural despair on which historians have often concentrated. Psychology, sexology, 'physical culture', holistic medicine, anthroposophy, the paranormal, spiritualism, Buddhism, Tolstoy's visions of rural bliss – these were among the intellectually fashionable concerns of Germans in the early twentieth century, with a potential audience stretching down to the ranks of commercial clerks. Take the utterly obscure Wiesbaden publishing house of J. F. Bergmann, whose staples included military memoirs and travel books. In 1909 its list included *Music and the Nerves, The Subconscious Ego and its Relationship to Health and Upbringing, Marital Bliss*, and *The Emanation of Psychophysical Energy*, an enquiry into 'the direct transmission of thoughts in connection with the question of the radioactivity of the brain'. This was an age of fads, fashions, reform movements and instant utopias. Some, like the advocates of 'electro-culture', handwriting reform and J. H. Schulz's 'autogenic training', were self-consciously modern. Others urged the simple life: the little hut by the lake, vegetarianism, wearing sandals and loose clothing, or no clothing at all. Among the reformers was Isadora Duncan's sister, Elizabeth, who established a girls' school in Berlin-Grunewald where the pupils could 'dance in the open air and listen to the trees rustle'.[59] There is no doubt about it: many Germans with the time and money to spare were trying to get in touch with their inner selves. Weber, like Nietzsche before him, turned a baleful eye on the more manifestly idiotic of these cults, circles and movements. Yet his own insistence on a stern asceticism can be seen as a more serious response to the same sense of suffocation that troubled the hikers, naturalists and barefoot dancers of the Wilhelmine years.

Contemporary cultural revolt was far too rich and various to be fitted into a box labelled 'antimodernism'. It was the mirror image of the materialist, ordered society that Germany had become, a very bourgeois response to the established bourgeois order. The millions touched by one or more of these movements were expressing their sense of unease with that order. In doing so they contributed an important element to the social and cultural ferment of the prewar years.

CHAPTER NINE

The Old Politics and the New

Elites, Parties and Popular Politics

Reporting to London in April 1882, the British ambassador in Berlin referred to the 'German dictator whose power is at its height'. Lord Ampthill's description of Prince Bismarck was echoed by countless contemporaries. By 1882 the German chancellor had already enjoyed two decades as a dominant figure. Unified Germany was an established great power within Europe, and took diplomatic centre-stage when Bismarck acted as 'honest broker' at the Berlin conference of 1885. Domestically, the chancellor had engineered the major realignment of politics in 1878–9, banning the Social Democrats, splitting the liberals, and bringing the Catholic Centre Party in from the cold. Through the 1880s, the decade of colonial acquisitions and social insurance policies, Bismarck apparently held all the strings in his hand. He kept the confidence of the aging king-and-emperor William I, dominated his own colleagues, browbeat opponents, and pushed government business through the national parliament with backing from one or another coalition of parties. In Prussia, by far the most important individual state, Bismarck continued to occupy the decisive post of prime minister. Beyond everyday politics, he enjoyed a prestige often bordering on idolatry. In autumn 1890, Jacob Burckhardt observed that in Germany 'Bismarck was practically the reference point and yardstick for that mysterious thing we call authority'.[1]

Burckhardt used the past tense because in March 1890 the chancellor had been dismissed by Kaiser William II, who came to the throne after the deaths of both William I and his successor

Frederick III in 1888, the 'year of the three emperors'. The many groups that made the pilgrimage to Bismarck's rural seat at Friedrichsruh were now paying homage to an embittered old man with little left to do but disobey his doctor, compose his mendacious memoirs, and cause trouble for his successors, all of which he undertook with relish. Bismarck's dismissal had real as well as symbolic importance: 1890 was a political watershed in the history of Imperial Germany. But we should not automatically interpret this event along the lines of the celebrated *Punch* cartoon that showed the Kaiser 'dropping the pilot' – the seasoned statesman being unwisely jettisoned by a headstrong young ruler. This view was popular with many Germans then and later. It went together with the argument that Bismarck's successors were 'lesser men' who squandered his inheritance. In reality, the first German chancellor left behind a political system with serious problems. Bismarck was already living politically from hand to mouth in the 1880s, often unsure where his Reichstag majorities would come from, less able to confound opponents by producing a rabbit out of the hat. The gamble of universal manhood suffrage, when coupled with repression, led to electoral success for the 'wrong' parties. Bismarck, the sorcerer's apprentice, became the victim of his own cleverness. His departure in 1890 followed defeat of the progovernmental 'cartel' parties (National Liberals and Conservatives) at the polls. Outlawing the socialists had proved as counterproductive as the earlier Kulturkampf, and it was the electoral success of the SPD and other opposition parties in 1890 that made lifting the socialist ban unavoidable. The resulting clash with the Kaiser was the immediate cause of Bismarck's dismissal. The chancellor's use of foreign policy for domestic purposes – banging the colonial drum in 1884, whipping up a war-scare in 1887, attempting the same thing in 1890 – was a further sign of weakness rather than strength, as well as an ominous pointer to the future. Add to these problems the inbuilt tensions between the Empire and Prussia, and it is clear that Bismarck left his successors a troubled system, designed by and for one man, over which even he had lost full control.

The British prime minister Gladstone once remarked that Bismarck made Germany great but the Germans small. Here was a further problem. Bismarck cowed his opponents and treated legitimate opposition as treachery, one result of which was that some talented but independent individuals avoided politics altogether. His attacks drove Catholics, socialists and left-liberals into inflexible positions. At the same time, the political parties were encouraged to become the vehicles of interest groups, trading off votes for favours. Not least, Bismarck's style fostered hero worship of the strong man and an exaggerated respect for nondivisive politics 'above the parties', especially within the German middle classes. None of these problematic developments was the responsibility of one man, but all were a part of the Iron Chancellor's legacy.[2]

Bismarck remained a presence in German politics until his death in 1898, a focal point for disgruntled conservatives and nationalists. But the central figure was now the emperor who gave Wilhelmine Germany its name. Like Frederick William IV half a century earlier, William II started full of promise. He had many gifts – energy, imagination, charm – and projected himself initially as a 'social emperor', expressing paternalist concern for striking coalminers in 1889 and rejecting Bismarck's demand for renewal of the antisocialist law. A thoughtful observer like the socially minded liberal Friedrich Naumann still believed a decade later that William was capable of filling this role. But by then another, more negative side of the emperor had become generally apparent, one familiar to insiders even when he was crown prince. The new Kaiser was petty and narcissistic: he wanted, so the joke ran, to be the bride at every wedding, the stag at every hunt, and the corpse at every funeral. He was also unpredictable, given to cruel practical jokes and personal insults. He slapped King Ferdinand of Bulgaria vigorously on the behind in public, and when the diminutive King of Italy prepared to board the yacht *Hohenzollern*, called out: 'Now watch how the little dwarf climbs up the gangway.' Malevolent bullying was accompanied by wild, ill-considered pronouncements that led many observers to consider him 'not quite sane', like his remark that Bismarck and Moltke the Elder were mere 'pygmies' compared to William I, who would have been canonized in the Middle Ages. To the Kaiser, the Social Democrats were 'monkeys', the conservative nobility 'dogs', the admirals 'old asses'.[3]

Recent writers have devoted much attention to the Kaiser's state of mind. Whether he suffered from arrested development, megalomania or manic-depression, the point is that his personal flaws mattered because he mattered. In 1948, Erich Eyck published a widely-criticized book on William II's 'personal rule'. In the last decade the same case has been advanced with more sophistication and persuasive power by a group of Anglo-American historians.[4] They have shown how the Kaiser exercised an influence on German politics in many different ways. He was a powerful symbolic figure who helped to set the tone of public life and seduced many younger middle-class Germans by acting out the role of 'strong man'. Here William continued the handiwork of Bismarck, although the carefully cultivated pathos of the 'warrior-king' was peculiarly his own. The Kaiser also exercised his prerogatives, as befitted a man who claimed to rule 'by the Grace of the Lord'. He took his power of appointment seriously, and used it – often against the advice of responsible ministers. He absorbed the influence of courtiers and favourites, giving rise to well-founded complaints about 'Byzantine' intrigue. And he interfered in decision-making through personal vetoes, dissenting marginalia on official documents and endless policy pronouncements. At one time or another he antagonized almost every important group in Germany: not just liberals, Catholics, socialists, Jews, and parliamentarians as a group, but the bureaucracy, diplomatic corps, nobility and other German princes.

The Kaiser's governing passion was not exercised in a single direction, not even an autocratic one. William was at once harsh and sentimental, reactionary and 'socially minded', the warrior on horseback who worked at a saddle-topped stool and the modern emperor who liked fast cars and big battleships. His forays into decision-making were equally contradictory and capricious. John Röhl has observed that the chaos within the political machinery of the Empire was not the opposite of personal rule, but 'a consequence of it'.[5] That may be pressing the case a little hard. There were structural constraints that bound all who tried to work the system, especially the problem of reconciling German and Prussian interests that brought down Bismarck's successor, Caprivi, and plagued those who followed him. But the Kaiser both embodied the centrifugal forces in German government, and helped to keep them in place. The problems were felt most intensely by those who tried to fill the dual role of chancellor and Prussian prime minister created by Bismarck (the posts were separated only once, briefly, under Caprivi, a prelude to his fall). Four men undertook this uninviting task in the prewar years: the well-meaning Caprivi, who forfeited the confidence of both William and the Prussian Conservatives; the octogenarian Hohenlohe, a mere caretaker chancellor in the Kaiser's eyes; the egregious Bülow, a pocket-Bismarck who survived longer in the post than anyone after 1890; and the dull, hard-working Bethmann Hollweg, who personified the bureaucrat who 'stuck' to office – Prince Lichnowsky called him the 'leech'.[6] All were initially taken by the Kaiser's charm; all came to suffer his interference and feel his ingratitude, none more than Bülow, who eventually repaid William's disloyalty in kind during the *Daily Telegraph* affair, when (for once) the Kaiser played by the constitutional rules but found himself betrayed by his slippery chancellor. Given the complex and conflicting demands of political management, keeping parliamentary business, moving while acting the part of courtier, each chancellor eventually found himself in the same dilemma. He would be accused by the All-Highest Person of proposing something irresponsible; however indignantly he denied it, his days were then numbered.

The government of Wilhelmine Germany was not inert. The state was, as we have seen, increasingly interventionist, and there was no shortage of foreign policy makers. The problem was a lack of coordination that went beyond the normal compartmentalization of modern government. While ministers dealt with elected politicians, they also had to cope with demands and initiatives that came directly, or indirectly through the Kaiser, from various sources – powerful economic interests, court favourites like Prince Philipp Eulenburg ('Phili', 'Philine' or just 'she' to friends), individual bureaucrats, aides-de-camp and generals. Powerful, quasi-independent centres of influence developed, like the Holstein clique at the Foreign Office, the fiefdom operated by Friedrich Althoff within the Prussian Ministry of Education, which controlled university appointments, and the empire built by Admiral Tirpitz at the Imperial Navy Office. These power-brokers did not just exist in the interstices of the system: they were the system.

Two groups were particularly influential. One was the permanent bureaucracy. This was not, as often said, the bulwark of a 'Junker élite'. It is true that the nobility was still very generously represented in the Prussian field administration, and even more so in the diplomatic corps. But narrow Junker interests did not always prevail within the system – witness the sacking of Prussian Landräte by an irate William, whose desire for a Mittelland canal they had tried to block. Not only did non-nobles and ennobled commoners have their place in the Imperial and Prussian ministerial bureaucracies; officials from old families were not uniformly conservative, certainly not in any atavistic, antimodern sense. They were quite capable of supporting welfare provisions, labour arbitration or technical schooling. The real problem with the bureaucracy was different. Reinforced by a common educational background and the filtering out of politically 'unreliable' men (along with most Catholics and Jews), the senior bureaucracy had a strong collective sense of itself as a representative of the general interest, standing above political conflict. No doubt most senior civil servants are inclined to think this way; they certainly did in contemporary France. In Germany, however, the constitution allowed and even required administration to take the place of government. That is why the political system elevated archetypal career bureaucrats like Hohenlohe and Bethmann.[7]

Secondly, there were the armed forces. Their special position represented the hard kernel of what was authoritarian in the imperial political system. Two issues show what this meant in practice. One was the question of who controlled the military budget. We have to recall that the constitutional conflict in Prussia had arisen over Roon's military bill. The crown won this contest, and the army emerged with greatly heightened prestige, but the new national parliament did not give up its aspirations in this area. After an 'iron budget' that strongly favoured the army had been in effect in the years after 1867, a compromise in 1874 substituted a seven-yearly cycle of military appropriations (the *Septennat*), later changed to a five-yearly cycle, or *Quinquennat*. Appropriations for the navy followed a different pattern: the Reichstag scrutinized, debated and approved consecutive navy bills, beginning in 1898; but the 'self-renewing' element built into the Tirpitz Plan meant that the navy benefited, in effect, from an iron budget such as even the army no longer enjoyed. How did these arrangements work, and what conclusions can we draw from them? On the one hand, parliament *did* scrutinize military appropriations when they came before it. In fact, military bills were among the most fiercely contested in Imperial Germany. Sometimes they could be passed only by extraordinary political efforts, whether conjuring up a war scare (Bismarck, 1887), dissolving the Reichstag and calling new elections (Caprivi, 1893), or treating politicians to the full governmental repertoire of persuasion and propaganda (Tirpitz, especially in 1898). On the other hand, some of the parliamentary victories were Pyrrhic – Bismarck was not unhappy to see the iron budget transformed into a seven-year cycle in 1874, for example, because it increased his own leverage vis-à-vis the army. More important, not one of the army or navy bills placed before the Reichstag was ever defeated. Most important of all, however much parliamentarians might debate the detail of appropriations or army size, they never turned any of these battles into a fundamental issue of parliamentary control. The constitutional conflict was not repeated.

These conclusions throw into sharper relief the most essential aspect of military affairs in Imperial Germany, namely the extensive power of command (*Kommandogewalt*) claimed by the King and Kaiser. This had been jealously asserted by Hohenzollern monarchs since the time of Frederick William IV; it was an article of faith for William I; and William II then stretched this vaguely defined power to its widest possible extreme. Neither the Reichstag, nor the Federal Council as the organ of the other princes, nor the chancellor, was able to challenge this domain of privileged extraconstitutional power. And from it, much else flowed. Soldiers had a vital informal channel to the top through the direct access to the Kaiser that an increasing number of them enjoyed – the Head of the Military Cabinet, the Chief of General Staff, inspectors-general and individual commanding generals. 'Direct access' was the other side of the coin of the gradually weakening position enjoyed by the War Ministry, one of the great achievements of the early nineteenth-century Prussian reformers. Politicians could put the war minister on the spot in parliament; but this only weakened his position at the expense of the permanent military establishment.[8] All of this added up to a formidable series of military redoubts within the political structure. The influence of the army grew after Bismarck's fall, and especially in the last years before 1914, when the homosexual scandal that ruined Philipp Eulenburg and tainted other members of the artistic Liebenberg circle pushed the Kaiser closer to the military members of his entourage. The special place of the army defined what was stubbornly unreformed in Prusso-German politics. One historian has called the power of command the 'core of late-absolutist rule'.[9] Elard von Oldenburg-Januschau may have represented a view that was unusually brutal even by the standards of Junker diehards when he said that the King of Prussia should always be able to detail a lieutenant and ten men and tell them to dissolve parliament. But the idea was in the air of German political life. It can be traced from the political ambitions of General Waldersee at the time of Bismarck's fall, through the later occasions (the late 1890s, 1912–13) when a *Staatsstreich*, or coup against the constitution, seemed possible.

Nevertheless, the authoritarian aspects of Wilhelmine politics should be placed in proper perspective. Waldersee's ambitions failed, after all, like those of his French contemporary General Boulanger. There was to be no coup. Even the possibility of one hardly amounted (as sometimes claimed) to 'a permanent threat' and the evidence suggests that the effect of sabre-rattling was to strengthen rather than weaken the resolve of parliamentary politicians. The system was latently repressive, but it operated much less by intimidation than had been the case in the 1870s and 1880s. Catholic politicians no longer had to defend communities victimized by police or military actions, but fought (with some success) to increase the number of Catholics in the bureaucracy. Attempts after 1890 to obstruct Social Democracy through the press laws cannot be compared with the severity of Bismarck's antisocialist law. The broad trend pointed towards the consolidation and extension of civil rights, including press freedom and the right of strikers to picket. Tough measures were repeatedly brought forward in the 1890s, and repeatedly failed to become law – the 'Revolution Bill', the Lex von der Recke, the 'Hard Labour Bill'. Some restrictions on the right of association were abolished in 1899, prior to implementation of the new German Civil Code, and a new law of association in 1908 was largely liberal, especially with respect to the rights of women. This was important to both sexes, for the presence of women had often served as a pretext to close down the meetings of socialists and others.

There were also changes in the practice of government in Wilhelmine Germany. Historians sometimes refer to German 'sham-constitutionalism', and this is a fair description of a hybrid system – provided we recognize that it was also a 'sham absolutism'.[10] Much of the rhetoric that came from the top was posturing and play-acting. The Kaiser could and did pointedly exclude parliamentarians from court soirées, but this was a back-handed compliment, a spiteful recognition of their ability to frustrate his will. That is why William's chancellors urged him to cultivate Reichstag leaders. While the constitutional powers of the national parliament remained unchanged, its importance grew along with the weight and complexity of the business it transacted. The Federal Council remained the body through which government legislation was introduced, and retained its blocking powers. But parliamentary arithmetic meant that chancellors and state secretaries needed to broker legislation through the Reichstag by striking deals with party leaders and their experts. This was already apparent in Bismarck's last years; it became the norm after 1890. The parties with their blocs of votes had to be treated with respect by the executive. Bülow, the ex-diplomat, was the embodiment of this kind of governmental management, massaging political egos, extracting compromises and building majorities to pass key items of legislation. This was an essential lubricant in a constitutional system with many grey areas: it kept the wheels of government turning. Not for nothing was Bülow called *pomadig*, or oily. State secretaries like Tirpitz and Posadowsky were equally adept at the arts of cajoling.

It is more difficult to gauge the status of representative institutions and their place in public life, but important to try. In addition to the Reichstag, there were parliaments (senates in the Hanseatic cities) across the German political landscape, with rare exceptions like backward Mecklenburg and the directly administered territory of Alsace-Lorraine. The suffrages varied widely. What is striking in the Wilhelmine years, compared to the 1870s and 1880s, is the attention given to suffrage reform. The outcome of the many debates at state level was mixed. In the south – Bavaria, Baden, Württemberg – the suffrage became more democratic through the removal of restrictions or indirect voting. In Prussia, the most important case, the notorious three-class franchise remained despite Social Democratic campaigns to reform it. In Saxony and Hamburg the suffrage was made less democratic as a form of sand-bagging against the 'red flood'. Several points can be made about these apparently ambiguous trends. First, reactionary ruling élites were not confined to spike-helmeted Prussia. They could also be found in 'English' Hamburg; they were certainly present in that 'playground of authoritarianism', the third-largest German state of Saxony.[11] Secondly, what happened in these cases was more complex than it looks at first sight. In Saxony, altering the franchise was regarded by the king as an alternative to a coup against the Reichstag, which he reluctantly accepted as impossible; and the change was carefully dressed up for public opinion, with the move towards a Prussian-type franchise offset by an actual increase in the electorate. In other words, it was important to avoid the appearance of dyed-in-the-wool reaction. A third point follows from this. The outcome of franchise struggles in Baden, Prussia and Saxony was different in each case, conveniently summarizing the political geography of Wilhelmine Germany. But the common denominator was the recognition by governing élites, whether their instincts were conciliatory or the opposite, that parliaments mattered, that thought had to be given to the way things looked – that politics had changed gear.

That was pre-eminently true of the Reichstag. Through the 1880s, critics of Bismarck complained that he wanted a 'neutered' assembly, a 'majority of eunuchs' (Friedrich Kapp).[12] It would be hard to imagine a more damning critique than this, from men who constantly praised manliness as one of the highest virtues. This complaint was heard less in the post-Bismarckian era. The parliamentarians abused by the Kaiser as 'scoundrels' had a more elevated sense of themselves. In the third and fourth decades of its existence the Reichstag enjoyed greater legitimacy as a national institution. Not only did party leaders become more important political players. Members of parliament moved into the imposing and expensive new building designed by Wallot in the 1890s, and received allowances for the first time in 1906. The railways on which they enjoyed the privilege of free travel also carried increasingly bulky mailbags from constituents. There is still much that we need to learn about the culture of parliamentarians – the satisfaction they took in parliamentary conventions and standing orders, and in the passage of 'national' legislation like the Civil Code, or their *esprit de corps*, fostered by seating rituals and the common regime of hotel living and restaurant dining. What can be said is that in a country where people coveted the right to attach the title 'Dr' or 'Commercial Councillor' to their names, the initials MdR – member of the Reichstag – were also a source of pride.[13]

This has to be seen in conjunction with another development: the emergence in Wilhelmine Germany of a remarkably vigorous popular politics. The clearest measure of this is electoral participation. Turnout at Reichstag elections grew from around the 55 per cent mark in the 1870s to 84 per cent in 1912. Given the problems inherent in all electoral registers – voters move, become incapacitated, or die – this was impressively high. It has been estimated that the active abstention rate in national elections was no more than 5 to 7 per cent. Even greater turnouts were sometimes achieved at state and municipal level. In the Württemberg constituency of Rottweil, 93 per cent of the electorate voted in 1895, 94.2 per cent at a 1913 by-election.[14] This is a participation level three times higher than usually found at local elections in present-day Britain. Beyond the numbers, there is eloquent anecdotal testimony to the interest aroused by the political process. Voters made heroic efforts to reach the polling stations through a series of midwinter elections; politicians thumbed their railway timetables and made appearances in the most remote outposts of their constituencies. This interest apparently survived beyond the election-day ritual. The growing correspondence of parliamentarians is one piece of evidence for that, the trade in black-market tickets to the Reichstag gallery another. During the debate over the Moroccan-Congo treaty in 1911, people were allegedly being charged prices rivalling those demanded for a recital by the celebrated Italian opera singer Enrico Caruso.

Several developments made possible this more intense popular identification with politics. Education at all levels was expanding, and the climate of public debate was relatively freer. The press was much more extensive than it had been in the 1870s, when it was still dominated by big-city newspapers – but the rise of the deliberately antipolitical, 'entertaining' mass-circulation newspaper was still in its early stages. Even the small-town press usually provided political coverage, stenographic reports of parliamentary debates appearing next to lists of hop prices and advertisements for corsets. Improved communications allowed politicians to go on the stump. And the suffrage itself was a

The Long Nineteenth Century

factor, of course, for the evidence suggests – unsurprisingly – that turn-out was greatest where voting came closest to being equal, direct and genuinely secret, as it was to the Reichstag. All of this made politics a popular spectacle in a way it had not been when the Empire was founded.

The political drama had new actors as well as spectators. As early as 1880 one prescient Bavarian Conservative noted that 'the masses are coming more into play'.[15] By the 1890s it is no exaggeration to speak of a political ferment at the base of German society. The single most important manifestation of this was the startling rise of the organized labour movement: trade unions, cooperatives, SPD. The antisocialist law of 1878–90 had not only failed to destroy the Social Democratic Party; in many ways it actually had the opposite effect. While changes at the workplace and residential segregation were helping to create a stronger sense of working-class identity, repressive police actions underlined the fact that 'class justice' was more than a slogan. As the Reichstag deputy Wilhelm Hasenclever noted, the antisocialist law had merely created another bond, 'the bond of all the persecuted'.[16] Party newspapers were smuggled in from abroad (see Chapter Five), and local party branches that had been dissolved reappeared as choral societies or workers' benevolent associations. When the antisocialist law was lifted the Social Democratic Party had 100,000 members. By 1907 it had half a million, by 1914 over a million. What this meant is best indicated by comparison. In 1909–10, the SPD had some 720,000 members, which was comfortably more than the major socialist parties of Austria, Belgium, Denmark, France, Italy, the Netherlands, Norway, Sweden, Switzerland and the UK combined.[17]

The core membership remained Protestant male skilled workers, but the party was now making inroads into other groups. It attracted more Catholic workers, especially in the Rhineland and Westphalia (less so in Silesia or the Saarland), who made up 10 per cent of members by 1914. Women also joined: female party members numbered 175,000 by the war. When it came to moving beyond its working-class base, the picture is more mixed. The SPD had little success with peasants or agricultural labourers, and attracted relatively few members of the educated middle class or intelligentsia. In addition to its long-standing strength among journeymen, however, it now found support from many small masters and other petty bourgeois, who constituted as much as 15–20 per cent of members in some cities. The Munich branch in 1912 had no fewer than 369 members who were involved in the drink trade, the so-called 'party publicans' who existed everywhere and provided essential meeting places. They remind us that, even as it grew phenomenally, the SPD was rooted in the everyday life of proletarian neighbourhoods.

The party gave structure to the lives of millions, through its press, meetings, and recreational organizations. It could put hundreds of thousands on the streets at May Day or in support of a suffrage rally. Up to a million people turned out for the funeral of party leader and Reichstag stalwart August Bebel. There was no equivalent anywhere else in the world of the SPD: an independent, class-based, explicitly socialist party of labour with a mass membership. Not least, the SPD was a machine for winning elections. The antisocialist law served to confirm the importance of the ballot box for the party. Despite the harassment of its organization the SPD won around 10 per cent of the national vote in the elections of 1884 and 1887. It doubled that figure in the Reichstag election of 1890, and in 1912 the SPD garnered 4.25 million votes, giving it over a third of all votes cast and making it the largest party in the national parliament. By that time, the SPD was winning three-quarters of the vote in Berlin, three-fifths in industrial Saxony, and a full half in all German communities with a population over 10,000. This success was repeated in state and municipal elections wherever franchise restrictions or chicanery did not obstruct it. The mass mobilization achieved by the SPD was the central fact of popular politics in this period.

It was far from being the only sign of political ferment, however. An astonishing number of new movements sprang up during the 1890s. They were rooted in that broad swathe of German society between ruling élite and working class, and they appeared, literally, left, right and centre. The German Peace Society and the Federation of German Women's Associations gave pacifism and feminism new organizational shape. The National Social Association and the Young Liberal movement sought liberal renewal, while other liberal-reformist groups were founded to address particular issues – housing, education, public health. The last decade of the nineteenth century was a seed time of single-issue groups, from the Evangelical League and the Zionists to organized economic interests. One south German government minister complained about 'the homeopaths, the anti-inoculationists, the pro-cremationists, the agrarians and the publicans'.[18] Finally, the 1890s witnessed the arrival of a cluster of new political groups that were resolutely antisocialist, yet shared with the SPD an antiestablishment tone. Peasants entered the political stage through the Bavarian Peasant League and Otto Böckel's Central German peasant movement. They were joined by the organizations of master craftsmen, shop-keepers, house-owners and white-collar workers that coexisted uneasily under the umbrella of the self-styled Mittelstand move-ment. Both overlapped with new parties espousing political anti-semitism, which first made a national electoral impact in 1893. And this racialist current was also present in turn within radical-nationalist organizations like the Pan-German and Navy Leagues.

There is no single explanation for this explosion of activity. Changes in mass communications certainly provided the oppor-tunity. The motives were varied. The imperative of interest-representation set many of the new movements in motion, as the 'little man' followed the lead of agrarian and industrial élites by organizing behind the rhetoric of 'protecting' or 'saving' his particular group. Interest groups and lobbying also became familiar in other countries at this time, but nowhere else were they so widespread as in Germany. The market control of a highly organized, cartelized capitalism made the political mass market more appealing as a place to redress material grievances. This was true whether you were a worker, a shopkeeper or a barley-grower. Even the least economically powerful could vote. Economic strains were thus displaced into politics, helping to explain the momentum of the SPD, peasant and lower middle-class movements. The fact that the state was historically interventionist and claimed to represent the general interest reinforced this: members of the Mittelstand looked to the state for 'fairness' rather as one would appeal to a benevolent umpire. This was not just a 'dance around the golden calf' (Max Weber).[19] The language of moral outrage ran strongly through the interest organizations. Indeed, the perception that politics was becoming dominated by material concerns provoked its own reaction. Many new groups, with their single-issue fads and patent solutions, can be seen as a backlash against 'materialism', an expression of that 'cultural revolt' examined in Chapter Eight. This was just one example of how popular organizations fed off each other. The same was true of pacifists and radical nationalists, even as both took their cues from the international situation. Lastly, much of the political ferment after 1890 was a reaction to the rise of Social Democracy. Nationalist zealots, advocates of the Mittelstand, bourgeois reformers – all were presenting some kind of alternative to the SPD 'state of the future'.

The new movements had a major impact on the way public life was conducted. This was politics in the age of the typewriter and cheap slide show: organizations assumed greater importance and new kinds of political leader came to the fore. One type was the popular tribune, the parish-pump or community politician. Philipp Köhler, second-in-command and later leader of the Central German Peasants Association, was a classic case. Köhler was *Dorfkönig* or 'king of the village' in his native Langsdorf, where he was mayor, jury foreman, civil registrar, postmaster and founder of the savings bank. The rural mayors of the agrarian movement who stressed their local roots had their counterparts among the craftsmen-politicians of the Mittelstand organizations. A second type of new leader was the man who made a living (or tried to) from politics and penny pamphlets. Hermann Ahlwardt, the headmaster sacked for embezzlement, was one such; Otto Böckel, the former archivist who led the

Hessian peasantry, was another. The Mittelstand and radical nationalist movements contained many similar figures. Some were involved in numerous different groups, like Theodor Fritsch – anti-Semite, anti-Catholic, friend of the shopkeeper, and nationalist at large. Once the only 'agitators' had been Social Democrats; now ministers complained, as Bülow did, about 'beer-bench politics' on the right.[20] These perpetual-motion political adventurers were prototypes of the later Nazi activist: disrespectful and demagogic, hostile to government and élites as well as socialists and Jews, they imparted a new tone to German politics.

The political parties were also transformed by changes in political style and organization. The German party system was already established by the 1870s as a four-party-plus arrangement: liberals (right-wing and left-wing), conservatives, Catholics and socialists, plus minorities. This outward form did not change, although the fortunes of the four main groups varied and the national minority parties of Alsatians, Danes and Poles were joined by new anti-Semitic political parties in the 1890s. But the character of the parties changed fundamentally. The temporary quickening of extraparliamentary politics in the early 1860s had been one of the victims of unification from above. For a quarter of a century, the practice of politics became discreet and gentlemanly, the preserve of 'notables' (*Honoratioren*). It was not just that so many of those elected were related by blood – the parliament of the North German Confederation included eight sets of brothers-in-law, seven sets of brothers, four pairs of cousins, four father-and-son teams. More important, they shared the values of political insiders. Oratory in the chamber was what mattered, and those who spoke for 'out of doors' (like Social Democrats) were censured. Many parliamentarians in the 1870s would have echoed the National Liberal who proclaimed: 'I have not come here for the sake of my constituents'.[21] Election campaigns were correspondingly low-key. All of this was different by the early twentieth century. Parliamentarians worked harder, the orator had been eclipsed by the committee expert, politicians were more professional.

The SPD now served as the model of what a political party should look like – inside parliament, where voting discipline became tighter, and outside, where paid officials, party newspapers, auxiliary organizations and energetic campaigning became the norm. In this way, the parties mimicked the new idiom of extraparliamentary politics. The incorporation of economic interests into local party committees and candidate selection was part of the same process. It is not surprising that early political scientists regarded Germany as a classic home of the new, quasi-military political machine.

Among the nonsocialist parties, the Catholic Centre led the way in abandoning the genteel mode of politics. Its numerous extraparliamentary organizations were headed by the People's Association of German Catholics, founded in 1890 and numbering 850,000 members by 1914. The Conservatives looked to harness the peasant and Mittelstand constituencies, especially through the Agrarian League set up in 1893. They developed a populist, demagogic style which some aristocrats found alien. The liberals were slowest to cast off the old ways, and it is significant that cities with restricted franchises became a great liberal bulwark of the Wilhelmine years. From their different perspectives, SPD, Catholics and Conservatives all levelled the charge of 'liberal élitism'. This squeezing of liberalism between left and right was part of a European-wide trend in the decades before 1900. It should not be overstated, however: there is evidence of renewal around the turn of the century, as National Liberals and left liberals extended their organizations and adapted to new demands. Nor, more generally, should we exaggerate the disappearance of deference towards individual politicians. Bebel on the left and Oldenburg-Januschau on the right both proved that a cult of personality persisted in politics. There were liberals who enjoyed a similar popular respect and affection. What *had* disappeared was the aloof and distant notable politics of the 1870s and 1880s.

Taken together, the political changes in Wilhelmine Germany were striking. They extended from the way government business was done to the arrival of a new kind of popular and party politics. Yet there were limits to these changes. Germany still fell short of being a limited constitutional monarchy. There was no reform of the three-class Prussian franchise, and politics in Prussia stayed out of step with politics at national level. The Reichstag grew in influence but remained ultimately impotent. The aftermath of the Zabern affair (see Chapter Eight) showed that its members could be ignored even when (for once) they expressed strong and unanimous views, if the special place of the army was at stake. There was no move in the direction of genuine parliamentary government; the chancellor did not become a party leader drawn from the majority parties in the Reichstag. The central pillars of the Prusso-German constitutional system remained untouched, including the prerogatives of the Kaiser. Why? This is no idle question, given the changes that did take place, and the fact that effective parliamentary responsibility was established in Bavaria in 1912.

Two structural obstacles to reform have often been noted by historians. First, constituency boundaries for elections to the Reichstag remained unchanged throughout the lifetime of the Empire. They did not reflect population movement into the towns, which was important given the chronic weakness of German urban Conservatism – there was no equivalent of popular Toryism on the London or Lancashire model. Inevitably, it took many more votes to elect a Social Democrat than a Conservative. Here was an inbuilt bias favouring the status quo. Secondly, the executive enjoyed the right to call for a dissolution of parliament. Elections could be timed to benefit progovernmental parties, and fought on issues designed to embarrass the opposition. Neither of these factors was decisive. Unreformed boundaries did not prevent the SPD from becoming the largest party in the Reichstag, or the right-wing Conservatives from dwindling to a rump in the national parliament. Nor did elections fought on terrain chosen by the executive always work. Bismarck failed to repeat his success of 1887 three years later; Bülow failed to damage one of his principal targets – the Catholic Centre Party – in the so-called Hottentot election of 1907, called over the issue of colonial appropriations so that the government could beat the nationalist drum. Two other things may have done as much to impede reform. One was, simply, the practice of cooperation with government in exchange for favours, which the constitution thrust on the parties – a habit that was hard to break. The other was the thorny issue of the monarchy. Critics of the Kaiser were far more numerous than opponents of the institution he represented. But how was it possible to curtail the ravings of the one without appearing to challenge the other? William II, whose own thinking owed little to subtle distinctions, benefited from the ingrained monarchist loyalty of parliamentarians unwilling to throw the baby out with the bathwater. Reluctance to challenge the monarch acted as a brake on politicians from the 'middle parties' essential to any sustained reformist initiative – National Liberals, left liberals, Centre.

Was there any chance of the parties interested in reform bringing joint pressure to bear on the system? Two such possibilities are worth considering. The first was a coalition 'from Bassermann to Bebel' – that is, a centre-left alliance from the National Liberals to the SPD, and including left liberals. These three did become partners in the Grand Coalition created in Baden, and some contemporaries touted the desirability of similar cooperation at national level. The parliamentary arithmetic was against it: even in 1912 these parties had only 197 seats out of 397 in the Reichstag, just short of a majority. But that only pushes the question back a stage, for a comprehensive electoral pact would certainly have given them the seats they needed. There is still a lack of cooperation that needs to be explained. The same is true of another might-have-been: a 'Gladstonian coalition' bringing together organized working class (SPD), Catholic 'Celtic Fringe' (Centre Party) and progressive middle class (left liberals). This potential alliance has often been discussed since Arthur Rosenberg first raised the issue in the 1920s.[22] It is not merely historical hindsight that makes it worth taking seriously. These three parties had a permanent majority of Reichstag seats after 1890; all had been branded as enemies by Bismarck in the past, and it was they who later voted together to pass the Erzberger Peace Resolution (1917) and formed the so-called Weimar Coalition after 1918. It is reasonable to ask why such a coalition failed to become reality before 1914.

War and revolution concentrated the mind wonderfully, of course, requiring political parties to overcome obstacles and sink differences that loomed large in the prewar years. Those obstacles and differences were formidable. The German parties, untrammelled by power, were free to enunciate strong ideological principles. These were buttressed by historical memory. Cooperation between liberals and socialists was soured by the fact that National Liberals had supported the antisocialist law, as well as by differences over social policy and other issues. Catholics were equally unable to forget liberal enthusiasm for the Kulturkampf – just as liberals could barely hide their distaste that the 'clerical' party had acquired a strategic position in German politics after 1890, whether supporting or opposing the government ('the measure of all things', was Friedrich Naumann's gloomy summary of the party).[23] Catholics and socialists developed different, mutually antagonistic, siege mentalities from their earlier experiences of being attacked. The SPD shared the view of the Centre Party as clerical and opportunist; Centre politicians believed that socialism was a threat not only to the denominational school (which was true) but to God and the family as well. In short, the mental barriers between the parties were a serious impediment to cooperation.

The highly developed interest politics pursued by the parties added to the difficulties. Conflicts between town and country, capital and labour, producer and consumer, were built in to party competition. This, it should be said, is normal in modern political systems, and it is also true that conflicting material interests sometimes divided parties internally, rather than dividing them from each other. Both the Centre and National Liberals faced this difficulty. However, the German parties' embrace of interest groups had two very negative effects in the given circumstances. First, the parties had no responsibility for enacting legislation, and often made quite reckless, irresponsible appeals to the various interests. This underlined areas of conflict. Second, and more specifically, the Centre Party was electorally dependent on peasants and small producers. This drove the party – an indispensable part of any reformist bloc – away from potential allies on the left, who represented consumer interests, and into the arms of agrarian Conservatives.

These were authentic divisions between the parties, which imperial governments were not above encouraging on the principle of divide and rule, although none of his successors played this game quite as well as Bismarck had done. The system bequeathed by Bismarck placed yet another obstacle in the way of reform through party cooperation. That was the federal structure, which produced widely varying forms of politics and party constellations in different states. Just as the Baden Grand Coalition was no guide to what might happen in Berlin, so good relations between the parties at national level could be undermined by the course of events in one of the individual states – especially Prussia. What was the point of challenging the imperial government in order to claw an extra increment of power for the Reichstag, if it still mattered decisively what happened within the unreformed Prussian political system? The parties were beset by the difficulty of operating under different conditions from state to state, where their political colouring varied widely. Thus, Social Democrats in southern states tended to be flexible because of the more relaxed political climate. But their counterparts in the Reichstag, faced with the prospect of cooperating with liberals, were likely to remember that liberals in Prussia still resisted franchise reform because it would benefit the SPD, and supported franchise restrictions in Hamburg and Saxony for the same reason.

The single greatest, divide was the one that separated the Social Democrats from the rest – the 'bourgeois parties', as they were known. Fear of the SPD extended well beyond the right. It resulted from what the party stood for as well as its mounting electoral successes. Official SPD policy was to have no truck with bourgeois parties or government budgets. The first, Marxist section of the 1891 Erfurt Programme pronounced the Social Democrats a revolutionary party. Its class-struggle rhetoric was usually uncompromising. In reality, as Max Weber pointed out with habitual sarcasm, the SPD was actually a paper tiger. This was no party of the barricades: its leading intellectual, Karl Kautsky, rightly noted that the SPD was a revolutionary, but not a 'revolution-making', party.[24] It believed rather deterministically that history would deliver the future into its lap. Waiting for revolution, it was caught between accommodation and action, and internally divided. On the right, revisionists led by Eduard Bernstein wanted to modify the Marxist programme, while south German and trade union reformists wanted to emphasize the second half of the party programme, which dealt with support for policies that would ameliorate workers' everyday problems and provided grounds for cooperation with bourgeois parties. On the left, Karl Liebknecht and Rosa Luxemburg, supported by many local branches, called for a more aggressive stance, including use of the general strike as a weapon against the Prussian franchise. The leadership steered a course between left and right, rejecting any formal policy change that would have made the SPD either a genuinely revolutionary party or an explicitly reformist one. Bebel's political skills and Kautsky's nimble dialectical mind held this neither-nor line. Probably the leadership had no choice. Later critics have been harsh in criticizing the party, sometimes for being too tame ('bureaucratic bosses'), sometimes for sticking to the letter of the programme ('Marxist dogma'). But insurrection was a nonstarter given the power of the state (Engels had recognized that), and the party was understandably reluctant to risk what had been built up through great effort on adventurist policies. On the other hand, a fully reformist policy would have alienated workers (in Prussia and Saxony, if not the south) who knew from experience exactly what class struggle and class justice were. The SPD's schizophrenic stance preserved party unity. But the price was to alienate potential bourgeois allies, in so far as such actually existed. Much of propertied Germany (including the lower middle class and peasantry) took SPD rhetoric at face value, believing that this enemy within threatened the social and political order. Their apprehension was reflected in the cold shoulder the bourgeois parties mostly turned towards the SPD, with some short-term, tactical exceptions. Only after the revolution of 1918 did the Social Democrats come to be regarded as a lesser evil.

In a famous Sherlock Holmes story, the significance of the dog was that it failed to bark in the night. Wilhelmine reformers failed to bark, too – or they barked, but failed to bite. The absence of hard, institutional change prior to 1914 points up many negative aspects of Bismarck's political legacy, whether we look at the strong-man mystique, the continuing problems caused by the federal system and especially the position of Prussia, the parties, their divisions and the way they behaved, or the impact of universal manhood suffrage unrestrained by the need to exercise political responsibility. A final point also needs to be made about reform. Limited monarchy, parliamentary government, ministerial responsibility – these were often not the main concerns even of those who saw themselves as reformers. Many liberals were satisfied with the rule of law and creeping constitutionalism, and were mainly concerned to consolidate rights like press freedom. Or their energies went into single-issue concerns – land reform, educational reform, the settlement house and welfare movements. The noisy new mass politics and changing style of parliament undoubtedly encouraged some middle-class liberals to stay on the quieter municipal stage. The widely admired administration of prewar German cities was often presided over by mayors who were a combination of liberal patrician and technocrat. If liberal reformers often by-passed national politics, the new movements of the right that emerged in the 1890s were openly contemptuous of the Reichstag and parliamentarism. Their stance differed from that of old-fashioned conservatives, who disliked parliamentary presumption and looked to king and army as the source of authority. Anti-Semites and radical nationalists were not élitist in this sense. They fostered a populist politics that purportedly sounded the direct voice of the people. They won support by attacks on political horse-trading, deriding parliaments as cumbersome, alien imports that sapped and perverted the national will. The remorseless rise of the SPD in the

Reichstag heightened their fury. The irony is that the allegedly subversive socialists were committed to change through the electoral and parliamentary machinery. It was the nationalist and racialist movements of the right that represented the truly subversive vision of the future, a 'German' future that some believed would be rosier without the Kaiser.

Nationalism, Imperialism, Racism

Prewar national boundaries were porous in many ways. The transatlantic cable, the unprecedented growth in trade and economic interdependence, the growth of middle-class tourism and international sport – all were signs of this. Within Europe, millions crossed borders in search of work; capital crossed borders even more easily. Yet these decades also saw heightened national awareness and nationalist sentiment. The high noon of the European nation-state was an age of navy leagues, patriotic associations and the chauvinist yellow press. All denoted the 'nationalization of the masses' (George Mosse, quoting Adolf Hitler).[25]

The German experience was not unique, and not all forms of German national sentiment were identical, or chauvinist. A certain kind of everyday patriotism was to be found virtually throughout society, fostered by such basic emblems of national identity as currency, flag, and anthem – it was after 1890 that the *Deutschlandlied* ('Deutschland über alles') became widespread. Conscription and the activities of the ex-servicemen's associations, like the universal experience of elementary school with its German history books and German literature, worked in the same direction. So did the decades-long functioning of national institutions like Reichstag, Supreme Court, or post office. Equally important were collective expressions of Germanness like national holidays, parades and public festivities. This generic sense of belonging to a German nation was much stronger by 1914 than it had been in the 1870s. It stretched down into the workaday world, and was perfectly compatible with a strong sense of regional identity, so that the landscape, dialect or cuisine of a particular regional *Heimat* could be – and were – celebrated as both distinctive and part of a larger, national whole. Nationalism in this meat-and-potatoes sense also transcended religious and class barriers – up to a point. There was a growing feeling of German identity among Catholics, especially bourgeois Catholics. Assimilated Jews believed themselves thoroughly German, scorning anti-Semites as uncouth, uncivilized elements who did not represent the 'real' German culture. It was even possible, like the father of sociologist Norbert Elias, to be a liberal Jew yet take pride in your Kaiser moustache. Workers, too, sang both socialist and patriotic songs, hanging pictures of William I on their walls next to portraits of August Bebel. The dilemma that organized workers faced because of their 'double loyalty' was noted in Chapter Five. When the right-wing SPD leader Gustav Noske made his 'Fatherland speech' in 1907 it expressed what was actually a widespread sentiment: that Social Democrats were, or would like the opportunity to be, good Germans, if only a repressive élite would let them. Patriotism came in many forms, therefore, and very few Germans lived wholly beyond its emotional claims – although Poles living within the borders of the Empire almost never felt themselves to be German in the way that most Jews did. In their different ways, Jews, left liberals, Catholics and socialists asserted their Germanness, although not as an exclusive identity. Hermann Hesse was quite exceptional in leaving Germany to settle in Switzerland because of chauvinism at home.

The south German author was escaping something more than simple patriotism, of course. A harsher kind of nationalism became more obvious from the 1880s. It directed itself partly against internal minorities (especially the Poles, as their numbers grew) and against Germans with allegedly divided loyalties – adherents of what nationalists called the gold, red and black internationals: Jews, socialists and Catholics. As militant nationalism began to speak the language of protective tariffs ('protection of national labour'), free-trade liberals also came under

attack, as did other forms of 'cosmopolitanism'. Wilhelmine
nationalists saw the nation as the prime, even exclusive focus of
loyalty at home. And they demanded government support for
Germans excluded from the state established in 1871, especially
the 10 million Germans in Austria-Hungary, as well as those in
the German diaspora elsewhere in eastern Europe. This insistence on the common fate of Germandom had a larger, potentially unlimited scope in the age of imperialism. Growing
nationalist sentiment both encouraged, and in turn fed off, German imperialist ventures, from the first acquisition of colonies
in the 1880s, through the World Policy pursued from the end
of the 1890s and symbolized by that great nationalist cause, the
battle fleet. The more vigorous assertion of German interests,
Continental and global, was accompanied by harsher negative
stereotypes of other European peoples and powers – the arrogant, 'envious' British, the 'decadent', 'archenemy' France, the
'materialist' USA, the 'barbaric' Russians and other Slavs.

What produced this chauvinist bile? A lead was certainly given
by the men at the top. Governments required school books to
adopt a 'German' perspective, built statues and monuments to
German heroes, and asserted national interests with a new intensity. The Protestant clergy added its sanctification, emphasizing
duty and sacrifice to the German cause. Not least, the Kaiser's
limitless enthusiasm for naval building and imperialism was
expressed in immoderate terms: behave like 'Huns', he told the
troops setting off on the China expedition of 1897.[26] Official
nationalism was especially important in initiating the harsh
policy towards the Poles in the Prussian frontier provinces of
Posen and West Prussia. This began with Bismarck's expulsions
in the mid-1880s and continued through Bethmann Hollweg's
willingness to expropriate Polish land shortly before the war, a
pattern of attempted Germanization broken only temporarily
under Caprivi, and centred on the 'struggle for land' and
enforced use of German in schools. But militant nationalist sentiment also had an independent life of its own. Schoolteachers
needed little encouragement to press the German cause: along
with university professors they were at the forefront of beating

the national drum. Nor did princes and governments have a monopoly on national monuments: many were built by subscription, including the Kyffhäuser Memorial (1897) constructed on a mountain in which the medieval emperor Barbarossa was supposedly sleeping until former German glories were restored, the hundreds of Bismarck towers built in the years after the former chancellor's death in 1898, and the centenary memorial to the Battle of Leipzig (1913). There were several reasons for the broad appeal of chauvinism. Partly, it expressed a long-standing German sense of cultural superiority, made harsher by the achievement of nation-statehood and the power that went with it. 'We have turned the Poles into human beings', observed Max Weber in 1896, a view widely shared among German liberals.[27] Like the pathos of the German 'mission' that went with it, this attitude was deeply rooted in the (largely Protestant) educated middle classes. Hardly unknown elsewhere in Europe, it was magnified in Germany by the circumstances of the 'latecomer nation'. Those who came of age with Bismarck's creation tended to treat it as a given and wanted to move on to new challenges, global as well as European. Yet there was fear that Germany was being blocked in the imperial sphere by powers like Britain and France, who had already carved out colonial possessions, while new imperial challengers loomed – the USA, Russia, perhaps Japan.

Chauvinism was an unstable compound of aggression, self-pity and anxiety. This last element should not be underestimated. One historian has noted a 'rhetoric of anxiety' among nationalists, a fear that German virtue was threatened by enemies without and within, the latter including homosexuals and women.[28] The nation, in other words, was a 'manly' cause. This erotically charged aspect of contemporary chauvinism was most evident among the wilder Germanic cults. Whatever their particular brand of lunacy – Baldur, Thor, runic mysticism, sun worship – they shared a tendency to emphasize the all-male group, or *Bund*, as the core of true Germanic identity. But the equating of national cause with hard manliness was more mainstream. It ran through the nationalists' language. The Navy

League had 'placed itself with manliness at the head of the nationalist movement', said one of its leaders. Pan-Germans constantly likened themselves to 'rocks' and 'fortresses' resisting the 'Slav flood'. They were, in their own phrase, 'we men who feel most German'.[29]

The Pan-German League (1891) was the most notorious of the nationalist organizations founded in this period. Others included the Society for Germandom Abroad (1881), the German Language Association (1886), the Colonial Society (1887), the German Society for the Eastern Marches, known as the Hakatisten after its founders, Hansemann, Kennemann and Tiedemann (1894), the National Festival Society (1897), the Navy League (1898), the Imperial League to Combat Social Democracy (1904), the Patriotic Book League (1908) and the Defence League (1912). There was considerable variation of size and function within these groups. Some were small bodies with specific cultural purposes (distributing books to Germans abroad, keeping the German language 'pure'), or concerned with lobbying (like the Colonial Society). The Pan-German League was also modest in size, if in nothing else, and never exceeded 28,000 members. It saw itself as a vanguard organization. Others, however, were mass movements. The Navy League had 330,000 fee-paying members and 770,000 more affiliated through other organizations, the Defence League 350,000 in total, the Hakatisten 220,000. All developed the paraphernalia of modern political life: paid officials, expert speakers, slide shows, posters, newsletters, and – of course – meetings. Recent research has warned us not to exaggerate the intensity of political life even within an active group like the Navy League. Some branches were effectively moribund between annual meetings, as in Weissenfels, where '*nothing* has happened for ten full years apart from the worthless film-shows for the children'.[30] Nevertheless, the mass organizations could pack halls for big occasions – August Keim lectured before 1200 people at Eisenach's Tivoli Hotel in 1912, with 'hundreds more left outside unable to claim a seat' – and reached millions of Germans with their propaganda.[31] They gave focus and institutional shape to nationalist sentiment.

Who joined the nationalist mass organizations? Their support came more from Protestants than Catholics, more from cities and towns than the countryside. Geographically, they were not particularly Prussian in complexion. Their greatest strength was to be found in an L-shaped area that began in Düsseldorf and ended in Dresden, running south from Westphalia and the Rhineland down to Mainz, then eastwards through Hesse and the northern, Franconian part of Bavaria into Thuringia and Saxony. Among the major groups, the Society for the Eastern Marches was the exception that proved every rule: for obvious reasons it was restricted to Prussia, its support stretched down into the estates and small towns, and it picked up Catholic members (mainly in Silesia), who gave their German identity pride of place over solidarity with Polish coreligionists. In social terms, all the organizations enjoyed respectable patrons from the nobility or ruling houses, while serving or retired navy and army officers were prominent (unsurprisingly) in the Navy and Defence Leagues. Business interests also gave support. Heavy industrialists had a leading part in founding the Navy League, and Krupp bailed the Pan-Germans out of a financial crisis. But the driving force behind the nationalist organizations was middle-class Germany – officials, Protestant clergymen, entrepreneurs, professionals, and men engaged in secondary or higher education. The idea of a Navy League was first mooted by an obscure cod liver oil manufacturer, J. E. Stroschein, backed by naval writers and business interests, but the membership soon included many of the great names in German academic life – the 'naval professors'. The Defence League offers a similar cross-section through the bourgeoisie. The two leaders of the Oberhausen branch were typical: the city's chief civil engineer, and the owner of a successful glass factory. The smaller Pan-German League was a distilled version of the same, with the educated middle class to the fore: a quarter of all local leaders possessed doctorates. These men may have harboured anxieties about the German future, but they also had successful careers and brought an ebullient confidence to the national cause. The mass movements also stretched down to the lower-middle class of small businessmen, minor officials and white-collar workers, but they attracted few peasants or proletarians. The main exception was those vulnerable to pressure, like state railway workers. The relationship between these organizations and Germany's rulers is controversial. It used to be argued, comfortingly, that the more outspoken groups – especially the Pan-Germans – were 'extremists', a thorn in the side of responsible statesmen like Bülow and Bethmann. More recently, an exactly opposite view has been advanced by historians such as Hans-Ulrich Wehler and Volker Berghahn, painting these organizations as agencies of mass mobilization from above, designed to rally support behind government policy and head off domestic discontent by encouraging identification with imperialist deeds. Neither interpretation is satisfactory on its own. The truth lies, not in splitting the difference, but in recognizing the dynamic, prickly interaction between 'official' nationalism and the ambitions of the mass organizations.[32] On the face of it, the 'manipulative' approach has much to be said for it. Many smaller organizations enjoyed warm official support, and the aims of the Hakatisten also overlapped with those of the Prussian government – one leading member, Alfred Hugenberg, was an official in the Prussian Settlement Commission during the 1890s. Nor is there any doubt that ministers saw a use for those who espoused a more radical-nationalist agenda. Government was quick to see the potential of the Navy League as a body that might be bent to its own purposes: a Navy Office memorandum referred to the League's 'power to unite the nation'. And Bülow's distaste for the Pan-Germans did not blind him to their value in 'beating the nationalist drum'. During passage of the first navy bill in 1898 the League received funds and pamphlets from the information department of Tirpitz's Navy Office, reserve officers spoke at meetings, rallies were subsidized. As a Foreign Office official later observed: 'If the Pan-German League did not exist, we would have to invent it.'

The Foreign Office had not invented the Pan-German League, however, nor did the aims of radical nationalists and rulers neatly coincide. In the first place, the nationalists demanded more than any government could give them – more ships, more colonies, more German settlements in the east. Whether the issue was the Boer War, 'defence of Germans' in the Habsburg monarchy or Samoa, Pan-German and Navy League militants found the country's leaders wanting in energy and purpose. The official custodians of the nation were accused of betraying the cause out of deference to un-German interests, like the Catholic Centre Party. Many Hakatisten showed real animus towards Junkers who allegedly put their concern for cheap Polish labour ahead of the national interest, and there were frequent allegations about officials and ministers guilty of 'cowardice', 'sabotage' and even 'national betrayal'. The Navy League radical and later Defence League leader, retired general August Keim, did not exempt 'the All-Highest Himself' from these strictures. This was significant. It is a cliché that the nationalist cause completed its migration from left to right in this period, but a soured, populist parody of an older democratic spirit was also evident in the nationalist movements. Heinrich Class, a key figure who led the Pan-Germans after 1904, described how he had learned from an old forty-eighter friend of his father's how one could be 'an enthusiastic son of one's people and yet a determined opponent of one's ruler'. He and others scorned the formal, decorative aspects of nationalism, as defined by princes and ministers. 'Stage pageants and celebrations, parades and the unveiling of statues' only disguised the lack of will in government, argued Class. The journalist Victor Schweinburg observed that the Navy League 'was not founded in order to make a big noise once a year, to send a telegram to the Kaiser, and at the end of the great feast to sing "Lieb Vaterland, magst ruhig sein" through a drunken haze'.

Radical nationalists were violently intemperate; they thought in conspiratorial terms and were forever unveiling plots against the fatherland. But they had a point in claiming that the ruling establishment tried to use them. It is hardly surprising that the Pan-German and Navy Leagues reacted angrily when they were first treated as allies in 1898–1900, only to be denounced afterwards as demagogues. Then, in 1907, Bülow harnessed the radical nationalists behind his so-called Hottentot election campaign, giving a large role to Keim, a man who raged about military unpreparedness and once called an Alsatian member of the Reichstag a scoundrel, a bastard and a traitor. Did the chancellor expect that he could put the genie safely back into the bottle afterwards? He managed only to arouse expectations he could not satisfy and heighten the sense of betrayal. So did Foreign Secretary Kiderlen-Wächter during the second Moroccan crisis in 1911, when he urged Heinrich Class and the Pan-Germans to make extreme demands, so that Kiderlen would be able to say to other governments: 'I am conciliatory, but I have to take public opinion into account.' Kiderlen called this 'letting all the dogs bark'. Once again, the would-be manipulation backfired: the Pan-Germans found the subsequent climb-down over Morocco 'an intolerable humiliation of our fatherland', an opinion that was echoed thoughout the nationalist public. If a shrill 'national opposition' had crystallized by 1914, with the new Defence League at its core, German rulers themselves bore much of the responsibility. They cynically, selectively embraced nationalist demands, and succeeded only in feeding them.

Arguments about Germany's national mission were commonly couched in the language of culture and power. But another category grew in importance during this period: race. Notions of racial difference were a commonplace of European culture. The word race was used much more broadly (and less self-consciously) than it is today, as a synonym for ethnic group. As an anthropological shorthand it did not necessarily imply a classification into superior and inferior. Nevertheless, arguments about race in the discriminatory sense became more common in prewar Europe. This was not a peculiarly German phenomenon, and two of the most widely read race theorists were the Frenchman Arthur Gobineau and the English admiral's son Houston Stewart Chamberlain, who lived in France, Italy and Switzerland before settling in Germany and marrying Eva Wagner, the composer's daughter. Both enjoyed greater influence in Germany than in their native countries, however, Gobineau through disciples in the societies that bore his name and the efforts of the Wagner circle, Chamberlain through his German best-seller presenting a racial interpretation of history, *The Foundations of the Nineteenth Century* (1900). Perhaps more important than either was another Englishman, whose ideas were used – or abused – to lend pseudo-scientific support to racist arguments. We have already seen how Darwin's work was taken up with enthusiasm by German progressive opinion in the 1860s and 1870s, and became an important component of Social Democratic 'materialism'. His arguments were also appropriated for other ends. If the 'struggle for existence' became an apologia for capitalist competition in the USA, the idea of a struggle between nations and races became a familiar part of political discourse in all of the major western powers in the decades before 1914. We find it in England's Lord Milner, France's Théophile Delcassé and America's Theodore Roosevelt, as well as writers and academics in all three countries. But Social Darwinism arguably had a special resonance in Germany, where the biological imperative was seized on as the engine of historical development. The concept of the struggle for existence provided intellectual underpinning, dubious though it was, for the ambitions of a young and vigorous nation supposedly being held back by older, 'declining' powers.

Race was anything but a stable category. Sometimes it was defined culturally in the manner of Gobineau, who associated 'race-mixing' with mediocrity, at other times it was presented as a classification of physical body-types derived from evolutionary theory. The growing number of Germans who spoke the language of race also used various labels to describe their own community of blood – Nordic, Germanic, Teutonic, Aryan. These terms had in common only their intellectual confusion. That is not the arrogance of hindsight: plenty of contemporaries scorned the arguments of the race theorists. Nietzsche, contrary to the image of him spread by his sister Elisabeth, was contemptuous of racism. Max Weber, whose nationalist credentials could hardly be doubted, nevertheless condemned 'zoological nationalism'. The eugenicist Wilhelm Schallmayer dismissed unscholarly terms like Nordic – particularly when stretched to include Dante as a member of the blond master race.[33]

An additional complication is the fact that Germans saw themselves as members of the white race, something they shared with other Europeans at a time when the encounter with non-Europeans became more intensive. Usually that meant an attitude of assumed superiority which made possible a treatment of native peoples then almost unthinkable within Europe itself – even against gypsies. 'The native, to the German, is a baboon and nothing more', in the words of a British Foreign Office observer – a notable case of the pot calling the kettle black, but not for that reason automatically false.[34] Max Weber's brother Alfred, travelling in the Caribbean in 1900, described the Haitians as 'black brutes'.[35] His belief that those with dark skins were naturally indolent was widespread. It was the assumption that led to the virtual forced labour of Africans in the German colonies. And when the subsequent Herrero (1904–7) and East African (1905) uprisings broke out, they were put down with a brutality designed to be exemplary. Although the German colonial administration followed a more liberal course after 1906–7, this was strongly opposed by colonial settlers and plantation owners, as well as many armchair imperialists.

What sort of image did Germans at home have of non-European peoples? It was one that largely underwrote their own sense of superiority. The developing academic discipline of ethnology often became an expression of cultural imperialism, and racism was ingrained in the university. The great American black writer W. E. B. Du Bois, who studied at Berlin in the 1890s and generally compared Germany favourably with the USA, was startled when the historian Treitschke suddenly bellowed out during a lecture: 'Mulattoes are inferior, they feel themselves inferior.'[36] At a more popular level, panoramas depicted the colonial civilizing mission in rosy terms and journalists described 'barbarian' customs, with prurient references to native sexual mores – it was the news of his black concubine, not violence or even murder, that tarnished the image of the imperialist adventurer Carl Peters. The middle-class genre of game hunters' memoirs presented native bearers as simple-minded and backward, while the touring 'people shows' mounted by entrepreneurs like Carl Hagenbeck displayed native peoples like circus animals (which was Hagenbeck's other main business). Somalis, Kalmucks, Labrador Inuit, South Sea Islanders, sub-Saharan Africans – all were put on show as exotics, complete with (often inauthentic) camel races, dancing and snake-charming that reinforced the 'primitive' stereotype. In one exceptionally cruel piece of buffoonery, 'Prince Dido' of the Cameroons was dressed up in top hat and tails, to the huge delight of German audiences. The *Hosennigger* – 'nigger in trousers' – became a popular theme of comic press and burlesque theatre.[37]

There were countervailing tendencies. Cultural fascination with the 'other' sometimes wore a benign face. The painter Emil Nolde, like Paul Gauguin, sought artistic inspiration in the South Seas; Leo Frobenius was an important early writer on what would later be called black identity, or *négritude*. Both were touched by an attraction to the exotic, but that was much less true of the art critic Carl Einstein, whose *Negerplastik* (1915) was a pioneering appreciation of African sculpture that largely transcended the familiar primitive-civilized distinction. There were also German critics of imperialist exploitation, including Social Democrats, left liberals and those animated by Christian conscience. Catholic missionaries were one of the few groups in a position to make their protests on the spot, and many did. The religious defence of native populations had a long history. Despite its own brand of cultural paternalism, it provided moral grounds for respecting non-European lives and dignity against unlimited European pretensions. Within Wilhelmine Germany, however, as within prewar Europe as a whole, these critics were swimming against the current. To see a photograph of the Catholic politician Ludwig Windthorst posing with his black god-children is to be reminded that this was exceptional.[38]

A pervasive sense of white superiority was not peculiar to Germany, and probably contributed less to the forging of national identity than in some other countries. Colonialism was more of an afterthought for the latecomer nation than it was for Britain or France. This made it more frenetic. But the Continent remained the primary focus for nationalists: this was where the German mission was to be played out, one increasingly likely to be couched in racial terms. Intellectuals like Paul de Lagarde and Julius Langbehn, together with nationalist organizations, looked outward to the entire German ethnic community, to a *Volk* united by blood as well as language and culture. (German ethnicity could be generously defined: the Pan-Germans aspired to a political entity that would ultimately include the Habsburg territories, Baltic Russia, Switzerland, Luxemburg, the Netherlands and Belgium.) The other side of the coin was protecting Germandom from alien threats, in the west, but even more in the confrontation with Slav peoples and especially on the Polish 'frontier'. This long-standing issue was increasingly perceived as an issue of racial groups and their survival, an elemental battle of birth rates, population and living space. Hence the 'Slav menace' that the nationalist organizations constantly invoked, and the 'struggle for land' they saw as the solution. Bismarck already showed the traces of Social Darwinist thinking when he argued for anti-Polish measures in the 1880s. Twenty years on, this way of looking at the question had established itself, and a Prussian finance minister could argue for expropriating Polish land because 'national existence' was at stake.[39]

The Poles were only one 'internal enemy'. Others were identified by nationalists concerned about the purity of the racial stock. The criminally insane, alcoholics, 'degenerate' city dwellers – all supposedly sapped German virility and war-readiness. So, of course, did Catholics. A new generation of Evangelical League leaders, influenced by Houston Stewart Chamberlain, turned anti-Catholicism into a more racially charged affair. The Germanic race, or *Stamm*, was held to be Protestant, and experts on cranium measurement were pleased to prove the hereditary stupidity of the papists. Finally, there was another alleged enemy within, for many *the* enemy: the Jew, or 'Semite'. Because of the shadow cast by the attempted extermination of European

Jewry just a few decades later, it is important to be clear about the nature and scope of anti-Semitism in late Imperial Germany. Surveying European society in 1914, it would have taken a great leap of imagination to nominate Germany as the future perpetrator of genocide against the Jews. Tsarist Russia, with its government-encouraged pogroms, the Habsburg lands, even France, might have seemed likelier candidates. There were no pogroms in Wilhelmine Germany, nor any anti-Jewish riots of the kind familiar before and during 1848; there were only events that, in their sheer triviality, seem to mock our own after-knowledge – like students freeing mice in Jewish-owned department stores. On the few occasions that popular violence against Jews was threatened – at Xanten in the Rhineland (1891) and Konitz in West Prussia (1900) – the Prussian authorities swiftly restored order. German Jews were not complacent, but they enjoyed equality before the law, felt themselves to be German, and saw no serious threat to their existence. Emigration to America, or to Palestine, attracted Russian and east European Jews, not their German counterparts, just as the major theorists of Zionism (Leo Pinsker, Ahad Ha'am, Theodor Herzl) came from the Romanov or Habsburg empires, not from Hohenzollern Germany.

Nevertheless, anti-Semitism became more significant in pre-war Germany. That was why Jews set up a defence organization signalling their loyalty, the Central Union of German Citizens of the Jewish Faith. Much of the animus against Jews was familiar in form – aristocratic prejudice, behind-the-hand remarks about 'pushy' Jews, religious hostility towards the 'murderers of Christ'. The incident at Xanten, where a local Jew was accused of ritually slaughtering Christian children, was the sort of thing that had disfigured the history of Catholic Europe. Nor was the racially based anti-Semitism of the period new. As we saw in Chapter Six, it first emerged at the end of the 1870s. But anti-Semitic arguments were elaborated over the following decades, in books and pamphlets put out by right-wing publishing houses such as Diederichs and Lehmann, and through sects and societies dedicated to spreading the creed. The racist individuals and groups already mentioned all included anti-Semitism among their beliefs – Chamberlain, Lagarde, Langbehn, the Gobineau and Wagner circles. So did a host of others, including Friedrich Lange's German Union, Theodor Fritsch's 'Hammer' movement, and Hermann Popert's 'Advanced Guard', dedicated to developing stronger, more beautiful Germans. The Pan-German League became openly, virulently anti-Semitic after 1904, under the leadership of Heinrich Class. (At least one Pan-German used to count Jews on the street.) By 1914, virtually all the modern stereotypes of the Jew – cunning, dishonesty, lasciviousness, disrespect for authority, etc. – were in place. The Jew became the evil figure at the centre of a web of conspiracies supposedly directed against Germany, from international finance capital to socialism, pacifism and feminism. And for the defenders of German racial purity, the Semite represented the archetypal 'mixed race', by contrast with the Aryan.

These were all intellectual coteries or organizations of the middle class, even if the Pan-Germans enjoyed much wider influence. But anti-Semitism also played a part in more popular movements of the period. The politics of organized craftsmen and shopkeepers were heavily tinged by it; the same was also true of their umbrella organization, the Imperial German Mittelstand League. As in the 1870s, the Jewish middleman or department store owner was a scapegoat for the grievances of the small man. The Bavarian Peasant League included Jews in its populist demonology of peasant 'enemies', and anti-Semitism was important in the German-National League of Commercial Employees, the Hamburg-based white-collar organization with its own impressive publishing interests. One of its founders, Friedrich Raab, was a leading officer in the Hamburg Anti-Semitic Electoral League. The disgruntled lower middle class and peasantry provided the mass support for the new anti-Semitic political parties that emerged in the late 1880s and 1890s. The former court chaplain, Adolf Stöcker, had tried to win the workers of Berlin for a populist Christian anti-Semitism earlier in the 1880s. This proved unsuccessful – one of the roles played by Social Democracy was to inoculate workers against the political expression of racism and teach them that anti-Semitism was the 'socialism of fools' (although everyday prejudices certainly persisted). But Stöcker's Christian Social Party had more success with craftsmen, and other parties followed: the Hessen-based Anti-Semitic People's Party (later the German Reform Party), and the German Social Party, with its strength in Saxony and the north. In 1887, the first candidate defining himself as a political anti-Semite was elected to the Reichstag; in 1893 there were sixteen of them, beneficiaries of the agrarian turmoil in the early 1890s.

How important were these parties? We should not overlook their weaknesses. Several of their leaders had financial problems which they tried to solve by dipping their fingers in the till. They were also internally rent by feuding. After a fusion of groups in 1894, renewed splits meant that the eleven anti-Semites in the 1903 Reichstag belonged to no fewer than four different parties. Their electoral strength ebbed, and they never came close to achieving the central point of their formal programmes – to undo Jewish emancipation. But the anti-Semitic parties should not be measured by their legislative performance. Their real significance lay elsewhere, in the links they enjoyed to the Mittelstand and nationalist movements, and in the way their poison spread into mainstream politics. The established parties of the centre-right hijacked anti-Semitic policies and rhetoric. At their 1892 conference Conservatives wrote an anti-Semitic plank into the party programme. As the astute Baron Manteuffel observed: 'We could not avoid the Jewish question unless we wanted to leave the demagogic anti-Semites the full wind of a movement with which they would just have sailed right past us.'[40] The agrarian and Mittelstand agitation was a threat (Böckel's movement was against 'Junkers and Jews'); but it was also an opportunity. For the next twenty years the Conservatives cooperated electorally with the anti-Semites, while incorporating their populist and racist message within the Agrarian League. Some National Liberals also came to terms with anti-Semitism, especially in Hessen and Thuringia, that central belt of Germany where so much of the rapprochement between the old politics and the new worked itself out. The Centre Party made no overt concessions, on principle, and because Catholics were another vulnerable minority. There was no repeat of the Catholic anti-Semitism that arose in the 1870s. But denunciations of 'usurious Jews' and Jewish cultural 'defilement' were commonplace in the party at local level, while leaders gave a nod and a wink to popular prejudice by using coded language. Everyone knew who was being referred to in the phrase 'unfair competition'.

'Respectable' anti-Semitism and other forms of 'mild' racism worked differently from the everyday nationalism described earlier. The first always implied some kind of exclusion, lowering the threshold for the true haters; the second rested on the possibility that patriotism was consistent with other loyalties (Catholic, Jewish, socialist). In Wilhelmine Germany, however, a harsher, integral nationalism grew in importance, along with racially based ideas of what it meant to be German. These views were not confined to a lunatic fringe. They had support among academics and schoolteachers, and entered the language of the political parties, especially the Conservatives (in the case of anti-Semitism) and the National Liberals (in the case of radical nationalism). The same ideas found an echo at the top of the political system, from the Social Darwinism prevalent in the circles around Bethmann Hollweg to the violent anti-Semitic diatribes of the Kaiser. A muted version of them was enshrined in 1913 legislation which severed citizenship from residence and defined it in terms of blood lines, or 'community of descent'.[41] The ethnic definition made it easier for Germans outside the Empire to retain citizenship, while preventing Poles or Jews who lived there from acquiring it – although not stripping citizenship from those who already had it. Ultranationalist and racist ideas, finally, were a binding element in the new right that crystallized in the last years before 1914, stretching from the Conservatives through the Mittelstand movement to the ultranationalists. The new right and its programme were to gain ground during the war.

Germany and the Coming of War

Archduke Francis Ferdinand of Austria was assassinated in Sarajevo on 28 June 1914, triggering events that led to general European war. Its causes have been debated for eighty years, generating a literature so vast that no one could reasonably hope to master it in a lifetime. The problem of interpretation has grown more complex as long-standing issues of diplomacy and high politics have been joined by questions about the role played by economic interests, public opinion, and the domestic calculations of European rulers. From the beginning, however, German actions have been under the microscope. Article 231 of the Versailles Treaty (1919) asserted German 'responsibility' for the war. In the following years many Anglo-Saxon (although not French) writers viewed it as unfair and foolish to impose this burden of guilt. There had, they argued, been deeper underlying causes not exclusive to Germany. Resentful German historians took the same view. The coming of the Second World War altered perspectives. Anglo-Saxon historians were now more ready to see a pattern of German aggression stretching back before 1914, while German historians after 1945 were keen to present Hitler as an aberration within the longer course of German history. Certainly, they argued, Wilhelmine Germany had its annexationist soldiers and Pan-German extremists, but the country's leaders were not bent on aggression and had been forced to fight a defensive war in 1914.

In the last thirty years the kaleidoscope has been shaken again. Arguments about German responsibility have been posed in new ways, and by German scholars. The central figure here was Fritz Fischer, a Hamburg historian who transformed the debate with his 1961 book, *Germany's Grasp for World Power*. He argued that Germany had consistent and aggressive war aims before 1914, that these were shared by 'good' as well as 'bad' Germans, and that Berlin deliberately risked provoking hostilities. A further book in 1969 sharpened the thesis, claiming that the German ruling élite was planning a pre-emptive strike or 'preventive war' from 1912, partly driven by intolerable domestic difficulties.[42]

The Fischer thesis sparked bitter controversy in Germany. Older, established historians attacked his views, rejecting the argument that Germany bore prime responsibility for the war and heatedly denying any parallels or continuity between 1914 and 1939. Many younger scholars followed Fischer, presenting further evidence for the view that German rulers had unleashed the war in order to preserve domestic stability. A generation on, two things are clear. First, while the Fischer controversy is now itself a part of history, the subject of many books and articles, it still provides the framework within which the origins of the war are discussed by both German and non-German historians. Secondly, there is no current consensus. Many adhere to a more or less modified version of the Fischer thesis. Others have found it partial or misleading, although for different reasons. Some, rejecting the so-called 'primacy of domestic policy', have tried to reinstate the decisive importance of international politics for the outbreak of war. In a revival of an older, geopolitical approach, the argument has been made that Germany was subject to the inner logic of its position as 'the power in the middle'. More persuasively, historians have underlined the interdependence of foreign and domestic policy, while political scientists have presented decision-makers as engaged in a 'two-level game' in which each level was relatively autonomous.[43] Even among those who emphasize the role played by domestic considerations, there has been debate over whether Germany really faced internal crisis in 1914 – and whether this was true of Germany alone. Paradoxically, the greatest tribute to Fischer has probably been the emergence of evidence that relativizes his conclusions, as historians of other countries have paid greater attention to the unstable mixture of anxiety and chauvinism so characteristic of prewar Europe. There is still a good case for arguing that Germany bore a major share of responsibility for the war. But any such argument must be grounded in the volatile international situation of the time and set against a realistic analysis of how other powers behaved. It is necessary to compare in order to contrast. The remainder of this chapter therefore examines the forces that undermined peace in Europe, while suggesting what was particularly explosive about the German position and German actions. It concludes by looking at the July crisis.

Europe on the eve of war was divided into two blocs. On one side stood Germany and Austria-Hungary, with Italy as the third, semidetached member of the Triple Alliance. On the other stood the Triple Entente of Russia, France and Britain. Radical critics then and later saw the alliances and accompanying 'secret diplomacy' as major destabilizing forces in their own right, eventually dragging the powers one by one into catastrophe. That is too deterministic. The alliances changed their character over time, and the allies could (and did) hold back their partners as well as urge them on. That, of course, is another way of saying that systems of armed blocs succeed in keeping the peace – until they fail. The alliance system reflected growing international tension and anxiety; it also gave them momentum and an element of rigidity.

What, then, brought the system into existence? The German alliance with Austria dated back to 1879, the more unreliable alliance with Italy to 1882. The Triple Entente came later, the result of agreements between France and Russia (1894), Britain and France (1904), and Britain and Russia (1907). There are two diametrically opposed ways of looking at this diplomatic revolution. From the German perspective, it amounted to 'encirclement'. That is hardly surprising. There were, after all, real differences between Britain and both of its Continental allies, just as republican France and autocratic Russia were strange bedfellows. British and French colonial ambitions clashed in Siam, West Africa and the upper Nile – the last producing, at Fashoda in 1898, an episode that led to talk of war. Britain and Russia also had disputes, notably over Afghanistan and the Indian border. Yet these powers sank their differences and concluded agreements apparently designed to block legitimate German ambitions. Germans pointed to the French thirst for 'revenge' and growing Pan-Slav tendencies in Russia for an explanation; and a growing body of anti-English sentiment saw 'trade envy' of Germany and the selfishness of a declining power as the reason why London acted as it did. Social-Darwinist thinking clearly fed this perception, but the German view was also not wholly false. British opinion *was* nervous of German economic might ('Made in Germany' was a hot issue of the period), and it was Joseph Chamberlain, not Heinrich von Treitschke, who described Britain as a 'weary Titan'.[44] A poem like Kipling's 'Recessional' touched on many of the same themes sounded by German theorists of English 'decline', even if the pathos of Kipling's 'white man's burden' struck Germans as hypocritical. It is not necessary to share the German view of things to recognize that much of the volatility in European diplomacy was injected by a Britain repositioning itself under the impact of global challenges. Faced with rising naval powers like the USA and Japan, confronted with the rivalry of Russia in Asia and France in Africa, aware of being overstretched, Britain sought relief in two ways – by drawing in its horns, and seeking allies. The first was signalled by its withdrawing from defence of the Straits and conceding of primacy in the western hemisphere to the USA, the second by an agreement with Japan in 1902 that marked the formal end of an isolation that was no longer so splendid. All of this had European implications. London's desire to settle outstanding colonial disputes and reduce its commitments drove the search for agreements with France and Russia, the latter concluded after defeat in the Russo-Japanese war of 1905 had brought home to St Petersburg its own vulnerability.

That is one way of looking at what happened, and it is true as far as it goes. But it is not the whole story. The same sequence of events looks different when we recognize that Germany's role was more provocative than passive, more aggressive and less defensive than Berlin liked to believe, or at least admit. The German position was at least as much the outcome of self-exclusion, or *Auskreisung*, as it was of encirclement, or *Einkreisung* – a by-product of German policies and rhetoric. Some of Germany's growing isolation can be attributed to miscalculation. German policy simply exaggerated the degree of alienation between Britain and Russia, and between Britain and France.

The attempt to maintain a 'free hand' as between Russia and Britain also led to the worst of both worlds, a policy of swinging backwards and forwards between one power and the other that clearly reflected divisions between pro-British and pro-Russian elements in the German ruling élite. More than misjudgment was at issue, however: German policy actively antagonized both powers. In the Russian case, an older literature emphasized the nonrenewal of Bismarck's Reinsurance Treaty. This fostered Russian uncertainty, but was not decisive. More recent historians have rightly stressed the role of Germany's aggressive tariff and financial policies in alienating Russia. And everyone agrees that a growing German presence in southeast Europe created friction with the Tsarist Empire. All of this made Russia more susceptible to British overtures. As for Britain, the perceived German threat had several elements. Most familiar is the German challenge to British naval power, plus its disregard for the historic British fear of a dominant Continental power. An active but unpredictable German policy in the Near East proved equally unsettling. Its great symbol, the Baghdad railway, has been described as 'the decisive reason for the fundamental breakdown of Anglo-German relations'.[45] In a more general sense, from the late 1890s at least until the last years before the war, policy in Berlin seemed to be conducted on the basis that Britain would be bound to 'come round' if only the Germans banged the table loudly enough. Just as German racists could never work out whether the British were Nordic cousins or Anglo-Saxon rivals, German statesmen behaved like abusive suitors who alternated between whispering endearments and issuing threats. By 1907 German policy had therefore helped to bring about the very isolation it feared, and subsequent efforts to probe weaknesses in the Triple Entente proved equally counterproductive. During the Second Moroccan crisis of 1911, for example, a reckless and blustering German policy tried to drive a wedge between Britain and France, but instead pushed them closer together.

Morocco was just one instance of a colonial issue coming to the boil. What did imperialist rivalry contribute to the coming of war? The answer should not be taken for granted. Imperialist clashes not only cut across the lines of European alliances. Colonies could potentially serve as a lightning-rod to deflect tension from Europe, as Bismarck had recognized, giving French soldiers the chance to forget their grievances over Alsace-Lorraine as they carved out an empire in sub-Saharan Africa. Moreover, international capitalists could and did cooperate – and move their governments to joint action if western interests were jeopardized, as happened over Egypt and the joint European 'peace-keeping' mission to China after the Boxer Rebellion. There were some things that transcended the differences among white Europeans. Yet imperialism did have destabilizing effects. It became the touchstone of a power's success, creating hopes of material gain or enhanced prestige, fears of being dislodged or left out. And the stakes in what contemporaries saw as a zero-sum game were truly global: declining European colonial powers (Spain, Portugal) and established ones (Britain, France) jockeyed with a Russia expanding to the east, new European nation-states looking to make their mark (Germany, Italy), and the non-European powers of the USA and Japan. The ensuing clashes provided a foretaste of Europe's eclipse in the long term; in the short term they generated conflicts that were carried back into Europe, where they acquired their own momentum. War may not have broken out over Morocco or Samoa, but constant disputes played their part in screwing up the tension and distrust.

Germany, largely by its own actions, was at the heart of the instability created by imperialist rivalry. In the first place, the German pursuit of World Policy from the late 1890s meant that the lightning-rod function of imperialism disappeared. France would hardly have its mind taken off the lost provinces if Germany was also challenging its position in Morocco. Britain was equally allergic to German talk of its 'place in the sun' (Bülow), which was bound to come at some cost to itself. Moreover, Germany's rulers (like others) clearly recognized that conflict on the periphery could not be contained there. Then, there was the problem of German ambitions as a 'latecomer' nation, restless, querulous, demanding a presence whenever imperialist issues arose – down to the pettiness of wanting German leadership of the China expedition. The lack of well-defined German objectives, as well as the threatening tone, created antagonism without substantive rewards. The Kaiser's ill-judged responses during the Boer War were typical. Whether Germany was fomenting British fears of Russia or vice versa, trying to drive a wedge between Britain and the USA, or looking for advantages by playing the 'Japanese peril' card in London and Washington, the results were similar. A meddlesome, hyperactive policy provoked universal distrust. Wagner once said that *adagio* was the true German tempo in music; in German global diplomacy the marking was always *presto*. Finally, Germany's real colonial sphere was central and southeastern Europe, a peripheral zone like Morocco, but one that represented a more serious threat to peace. As the declining Ottoman empire imploded, Britain disengaged from its attempts to keep 'the sick man of Europe' alive, and Russia turned its attention from Asia back to Europe, the Balkans became once more a dangerous flash point. It was not simply its geographical position 'in the middle' that made Germany part of this problem. Berlin was increasingly tied to Vienna, which saw its multinational Habsburg empire threatened by a rising Serbia, backed in turn by Russia. And Germany was actively pursuing its own interests in the region – making a satellite of Romania, seeking military influence in Turkey, looking for economic benefits from a German-dominated *Mitteleuropa*. The German return to a Continental (rather than global) orientation meant, in effect, that its gaze was shifting to a part of Europe that had become the most volatile region in the world, scene of two local wars in 1912 and 1913 – and of a 'Third Balkan War' in 1914.

The alliance system and imperialist tension have to be seen in conjunction with a third factor: the arms build-up of the great powers. This was also a general phenomenon. Military budgets rose everywhere from the 1890s: Krupp benefited in Germany, but so did Schneider-Creusot in France and Vickers in Britain. Nor can it be said that Germany was alone in pouring money into both army and navy: the surrounding land powers of France and Russia also maintained powerful fleets – in fact, Russia's attempt to rebuild its navy after the Japanese defeat of 1905 caused unhappiness in London and Paris, where it was believed that the Russian ally should concentrate on its land forces. Nevertheless, German decisions on armaments and military strategy had especially damaging effects. Germany maintained a powerful army while building a powerful navy. From this, consequences flowed. After the Franco-Russian entente, German army strategy centred on the danger of war on two fronts and produced the Schlieffen Plan, an aggressive solution to the problem that foresaw a quick strike on France before attention was turned to Russia. This entailed a violation of Belgian sovereignty, making it more difficult to keep Britain neutral in the event of Continental war. More fundamentally, army strategy was at odds with naval strategy. Any military planning geared to future war with France and Russia should have been accompanied by a policy designed to win British friendship, or at least neutrality. Yet, from 1898 onwards Germany was constructing a battle fleet that clearly challenged Britain. This self-defeating strategic contradiction can be explained in various ways. We can point to the roles played in German society by the army and navy, the former a 'traditional' institution with a privileged status, the latter striking a more 'modern' chord. We can point to a political system that left General Staff and Admiralty to go their own ways. Or we can point to this strategic incoherence as a reflection of the incoherent German foreign policy already noted, tacking between Russia and Britain and alienating both. The effects, anyway, are clear, especially the effects of the Tirpitz Plan.

German battleship building contributed fundamentally to Anglo-German enmity. It is true, as we have seen, that Germany did not pose the only maritime challenge to Britain in these years. In addition to the rise of the USA and Japan as naval powers, there was continuing concern in London about the French and Russian fleets. Indeed, the 'Dreadnought revolution' which many Germans, then and later, believed to be directed at them, had its origins in the search for a counter to likely French tactics on the open seas, hence the emphasis on speed and long-range gunnery. Sir Reginald Custance of British Naval Intelligence was still worrying in 1906 about combined Franco-Russian naval strength.[46] That said, the size and function of the German fleet caused growing suspicion in London, reaching new levels after 1904. Was the concern justified? The Tirpitz Plan brought together different aims and interests.[47] At the domestic level, the battle fleet was not only dear to the heart of the Kaiser; it appealed to heavy industrialists, nationalists and the middle classes more broadly. It was also unquestionably seen by some as a potential instrument for rallying popular support behind the monarchy. It is not hard to find quotations, from Tirpitz and others, presenting the navy as a 'palliative' against Social Democracy. Finally, as Eckart Kehr noted over sixty years ago, the trade-offs that pushed the naval legislation through the Reichstag even had something for the Catholic Centre Party, which gained recognition of its crucial political position.[48] Naval enthusiasm was also the German version of a contemporary obsession with sea-power, fed by the influential writings of the American Admiral Mahan ('Mahanism'). Widespread German concern with the idea of the 'three world empires' of the future (Britain, Russia, the USA) fuelled the belief that Germany had to have *its* fleet. But the strategic thrust of the battle fleet was directed against Britain in its home waters. The fact that Tirpitz tried to disguise this with talk of the 'risk theory', i.e. deterrence, or the 'alliance value' of the fleet did not reassure the British; it only heightened their suspicion. Britain was to be forced to accept Germany as an equal world power, the North Sea serving as the 'lever' of German strategy. The naval programme thus mimicked German diplomacy towards Britain, conducted with an olive branch in one hand and a large club in the other.

The Tirpitz Plan, like German foreign policy, failed. It was built on miscalculations – that the battleship programme would come though the 'danger zone' without the British noticing, that London would be unable to concentrate enough of the Royal Navy in home waters to counter the German challenge. These assumptions proved false, as some German naval critics had warned. Britain responded, and Germany was faced with an unwinnable naval race. By 1908–9 at the latest the Tirpitz Plan was threadbare. While the admiral himself favoured pursuing the policy with an even faster tempo of ship-building, the German return to a Continental strategy prior to 1914 was effectively a retreat from a failed policy. But the overtures to Britain that accompanied this reorientation came too late to undo the damage.

The interlinked failure of naval strategy and World Policy had two further effects that bore decisively – and dangerously – on German attitudes. First, to the extent that the German desire to cut a figure had become virtually an end in itself, isolation and the failure of the Tirpitz Plan unleashed bitterness. It was directed, of course, at foreigners, but also at German leaders who promised much and delivered little. We find one version of this in the political writings of Max Weber, a liberal critic of the Wilhelmine political system who, as a strong nationalist, blamed that system for a foreign policy of empty posturing. Weber contrasted quiet British successes with the 'noisy intermezzi' and 'theatrical methods' of German diplomacy. More dangerously, radical nationalists levelled mounting criticism of the same kind. Indeed, the belief that German policy was all talk, no action, was rooted in high places. General von Einem and the grey eminence of the Foreign Office, Holstein, both criticized the Kaiser's 'operetta politics'. Frustration led to similar comments by the prewar Chief of General Staff, Moltke the Younger.[49] This was the bitter fruit of German weight being thrown around with little to show for it, which fed the demand for something that went beyond bluff and bluster.

The costs of German policy included the financial costs. Every great power felt the strain of the arms race. It was what led the Tsar to call the first Hague Peace Conference in 1898. The problem was especially acute in Berlin, not because Germany was outspending its rivals, but because it was failing to keep up. Even after major expansion of the army in 1912–13, Germany was spending 3.5 per cent of GNP on defence (and the Austro-Hungarian ally just 2.8 per cent), compared with 4.6 per cent in Russia and 3.9 per cent in France. The figures on defence-plus-debt expenditure show an even larger discrepancy. When it came to central government defence spending, Germany (43 per cent) was significantly outspent by Britain (55 per cent). There were many reasons for this state of affairs. They included a growing public debt, revenue-raising problems caused by the German federal structure and the reluctance of the landed élite to pay its share of taxes, political resistance to military expenditure, and other demands on the public purse – the defence element of public spending actually fell between 1890 and 1913.[50] However 'militaristic' German opinion might have been, and however provocative German strategy and diplomacy, Germany was clearly losing the arms race. A gap opened up between the military capability of the Central Powers and the Triple Alliance in the decade before 1914. Russian and French military reforms already in the pipeline in the prewar years would make the gap larger rather than smaller. This bred a siege mentality in the German ruling élite, and led to talk of a pre-emptive strike while it still held out the possibility of success. The outcome of the First Balkan War in 1912, which strengthened Serbia and weakened the position of the Central Powers, reinforced the thinking of those who looked for a 'military solution'.

This needs to be placed in context. There was a palpable sense of crisis in Europe during these years, fed by the arms race, chauvinist public opinion, 'invasion scare' novels, and mounting fatalism about the inevitability of war. The ingredients in this dangerous cocktail are familiar, and we can understand them. Harder for us to grasp is the widespread contemporary assumption that war, if it came, might prove salutary. Before the carnage of 1914–18, war did not have the associations it has had since. It was, simply, the normal last resort of any self-respecting power. There had, after all, been plenty of small wars in the years before 1914 – in South Africa and the Balkans; between Russia and Japan; and between the USA and Spain, the 1898 hostilities described by US Secretary John Hay as 'this splendid little war'.[51] German reactions, anxious and aggressive, have to be placed against this larger background. It is fair to say that the crisis mood was unusually intense in Germany. There was anger at the arms gap, fear of isolation, and resentment that legitimate German ambitions had been 'misunderstood'. Radical national-ists enjoyed substantial support, as we have seen. And if pacifism was relatively weak in Germany (as research has shown), then its opposite was correspondingly powerful – the belief that war toughened the racial stock, and represented the means of escap-ing endless frustration.[52] These ideas found expression in a book published in spring 1912 by Friedrich von Bernhardi, a former section leader of the General Staff appointed in 1909 as com-manding general of the Seventh Army Corps. *Germany and the Next War* talked of the need to 'push back the Slav barbarians once and for all', defeat France comprehensively, and accept a war on three fronts. Since it was 'inevitable we must fight it, whatever the cost'; the alternative was 'world power or decline'.[53] Bernhardi's book went through nine editions by 1914 and was wildly applauded in Conservative, heavy-industrial and radical nationalist circles. It was one of many signs that a radical right, spearheaded by the Pan-German and Defence Leagues, had crystallized in Germany and wanted war.

To what extent did this thinking find an echo in ruling circles, civilian or military? In December 1912, Chief of General Staff Moltke observed that if there was to be war, then 'the sooner the better'.[54] His remark came during a meeting of senior mili-tary figures called by the Kaiser. In the strong version of the Fischer thesis and the accounts of some later historians, this 'War Council' has come to occupy an important place.[55] It was the moment when the ruling élite supposedly decided in prin-ciple on a preventive war, while recognizing that the country still needed to be prepared for such a step. There are problems with this interpretation. It illustrates well Fischer's somewhat old-fashioned way of piling up quotations and interpreting them literally, rather than contextually, so that they give a misleading impression of fixed intentions. People say what they do, and do what they say; words are never treated as rhetoric, or the product of immediate circumstances. The 'War Council' was convened at least in part so that the Kaiser could discharge his temporary fury over a statement from London. Bethmann was not present; Moltke did not follow his provocative comment with concrete proposals; Tirpitz warned against war; and Chief of Navy Cabinet Müller concluded that the outcome of the meeting was 'pretty well zero'.[56] Similar doubts arise over the importance we attach to German contingency plans. What else are general staffs for, and what else would the great powers be doing at a time of tension? British Foreign Minister Sir Edward Grey, informed in November 1912 that the German government was determined to be ready for war and 'making her preparations accordingly', responded: 'We have made some that would sound alarming if known'.[57] There was no German blueprint for aggression in 1914. Bethmann did not want war; nor did the Kaiser. The chancellor and the German Foreign Office worked hard in 1912–14 to try and mend their fences with London, seeking agreements over the Baghdad railway and the future of Portuguese African colonies (with mixed results), and acting together with Britain to defuse the dangerous tension in the Balkans. This Anglo-German detente placed each power at the head of its respective alliance as a restraining influence.

Several points have to be added, however. First, German 'responsibility' for war should not be restricted to the issue of whether Bethmann, or the German government, or the Kaiser, desired peace in 1912–14 – or, for that matter, earlier. Of course they would have preferred to get what they wanted without war. But German actions going back to the 1890s had done much to create international tension. Bethmann personally was a sensitive, passive, fatalistic man, but he was faced with reaping the whirlwind sown by his predecessors. Others bore more direct responsibility, like Tirpitz, who built a battle fleet aimed at the British and professed his peaceful intentions, or the Foreign Minister Kiderlen, the hawk of 1911 transformed into the dove of 1912. If the hard version of the Fischer thesis interprets responsibility in too tight and mechanical a way, some of his critics interpret it too loosely. Secondly, Berlin was aware that, if war did come, Germany would be at a disadvantage if it came in 1916 or later: there was a window of opportunity. The military men, now in the ascendant, pressed this point. The Anglo-German detente also disguised some harsh realities. The easing of relations proceeded through agreements over peripheral questions; the toughest issues remained unresolved, as the failed Haldane mission of 1912 showed. Berlin rejected a naval agreement; London made it clear that it would not desert its allies in the event of Continental war. The German belief nevertheless persisted that British neutrality could be had, a potentially disastrous self-delusion. Finally, while the meeting of December 1912 was no timetable for war, it did raise the issue of how the government should present its position to domestic opinion if hostilities broke out. And we can see official efforts in 1912–14 to reinforce the public perception that a 'defensive war' might have to be fought against 'backward', 'barbaric' Russia, a line calculated to appeal not just to anti-Slav sentiment but to Social-Democratic dislike of Tsarist autocracy.

Here we come to one of the most contentious issues surrounding the run-up to 1914: the role played by domestic crisis. Did insoluble problems at home drive German rulers to embrace war? They certainly faced a formidable array of problems. To the serious fiscal position and the impossible demands of chauvinist opinion must be added the SPD landslide in the 1912 Reichstag election, which further alienated the right. Some have described the Empire as being in a 'blind alley', to which the response was 'escape forwards' into war.[58] The historians who argue that the clock struck midnight in 1914 are those who generally paint Imperial Germany as existing in a state of 'permanent crisis'. Was the situation really so dire? Bethmann had long pursued his domestic 'politics of the diagonal', tacking between left and right. There is evidence that the domestic situation was actually turning around in 1913, as the 'middle parties' came together and the SPD – for the first time – gave its support to a government finance bill that taxed landed estates. Naturally, this isolated the Conservatives, and there were mutterings about a military coup. But that had happened before, and no coup materialized. Without accepting the rosy view of those who claim that a 'silent parliamentarization' was taking place, it is quite possible to argue that Imperial government was capable of survival and reform on the eve of war.[59] And if it appeared possible finally to woo the Social Democrats, why risk a war that – as Bethmann recognized – would increase the chances of revolutionary change? Overall, the evidence is finely balanced, and it is certainly true that – whether or not the Empire was 'ungovernable' – Germany's rulers were imbued with pessimism, none more than Bethmann. In the domestic as in the international sphere, the soldiers offered energetic solutions, the chancellor weary resignation.

Berlin was not the only capital in which governments had serious domestic problems to cope with during the July crisis. Britain faced strikes, suffragette militancy and an Irish crisis that provoked military disloyalty and raised the spectre of civil war. General Bernhardi was naturally self-interested when he saw 'harsh internal conflicts' in Britain; but King George V himself noted on 21 July 1914 that 'today the cry of civil war is on the lips of the most responsible and sober-minded of my people'.[60] France also faced industrial militancy and political turmoil. There were seven governments and six prime ministers between January 1912 and the outbreak of war. No one has ever seriously maintained that London or Paris went to war because of domestic crisis. The same can be said of Belgrade, even if Serbia was wracked by political upheaval in the summer of 1914. Internal discord probably made war less welcome in Belgrade than it might have been at another time. And Serbia had been a winner in the two Balkan wars: for all the conspiratorial activity of many army officers, there was insufficient resentment and frustration to fuel a powerful war party. That cannot be said of two other European powers intimately involved in the July crisis. Russia had been humiliated in 1905 and backed down in several subsequent international crises, outraging chauvinist opinion and strengthening the hawks at court. The multinational Russian Empire faced discontent among its Muslim subjects; it was in financial disarray; the architect of would-be agrarian reform, Stolypin, had been assassinated; and the concessions that followed the 1905 revolution embittered reactionaries but failed to satisfy liberals. Foreign and domestic politics were as closely intertwined here as they were anywhere, and by every yardstick, including the mood of its rulers, Russia was at least as volatile as Germany in the summer of 1914. That was also true, finally, of Germany's Austro-Hungarian ally. Recent revisionist historians have tried hard to accentuate the positive, but the Dual Monarchy was an unwieldy, potentially unworkable structure in which the Hungarian partner failed to pull its weight and blackmailed Vienna for concessions. Pulled apart by the nationalities question and fearful of Serbia, it was – like Russia, but unlike Germany – a multinational empire whose very existence was threatened by nationalism. Spy scandals and royal sex scandals added to a pervasive sense of decline. The old Habsburg joke ('the situation is desperate, but not serious') had become less amusing by 1914: even more than in Berlin or St Petersburg, the mood in Vienna was one of frustration and fatalism quickened by bellicosity. When Francis Ferdinand was assassinated, many welcomed the opportunity to teach Serbia a lesson.

The stages of the July crisis that followed can be briefly outlined. After discussions in Vienna on how to treat the assassination and putative Serbian involvement, it was decided between 5 and 7 July – after consultations with Berlin – to send a harshly worded ultimatum effectively requiring Serbian humiliation. This note was not sent for more than two weeks: the Hungarians had to be won over to a hard line; difficulties were foreseen in mobilizing the army during harvest time; and it was decided that the ultimatum should not arrive in Belgrade until after a visit of the French president to Russia had ended on 23 July.

The note was delivered that day, and the Serbians – after consulting their Russian ally – accepted most, but not all, of its terms. That initiated the final spasm of the crisis when, despite British efforts to mediate, the momentum for war became unstoppable. The dice were tumbling, in Bethmann's phrase; the powers slithered into war, in Lloyd George's. A chain reaction of partial and full mobilizations was set in train, and the alliance system functioned now to bring the powers one by one into a general European war rather than, as had happened in other crises, to hold them back. The formal declarations of war followed, beginning with Austria-Hungary's against Serbia on 28 July, and ending with the French and British declaration of war on Austria-Hungary on 12 August.

From the point of view of German responsibility for this outcome, three main issues must be addressed. They are the importance of German support for Austria, German attitudes towards possible Russian involvement, and German assumptions about the position Britain would take. On the first of these questions, the central point is the firm German support for the Austrian ally. The Kaiser, whose initial response to the Sarajevo assassination was 'now or never', issued his celebrated 'blank cheque' on 5 July, and this was followed by other German assurances of support.[61] True, Russia issued similar backing to Serbia at the time of the ultimatum; but Vienna and Berlin set the terms of the crisis. Which of them was in the driving seat? It can certainly be argued that Austria was. The Emperor Francis Joseph sought the blank cheque from his German opposite number, after all, and Foreign Minister Berchthold worried that Vienna would be 'left in the lurch' by the Germans.[62] The Austrian Chief of Staff, Conrad, was as keen on a hard line as his German counterpart Moltke, and played a decisive role in the crisis. The Germans not only pushed; they were also being pulled. And yet: Berlin *did* push. When, in the last stages of the crisis, an anxious Bethmann urged Austria to apply the brakes, it was too late. Even Bethmann's belated alarm was directly countered by Moltke's enthusiasm, prompting Berchthold's famous question: 'Who rules in Berlin, Bethmann or Moltke?'[63] Germany not only did not restrain her ally as she had during the crises of 1912–13, but urged Vienna on during the critical period, prompted by a shared perception that the Central Powers had to achieve some kind of victory out of the crisis.

Did that automatically mean war, with Russian involvement? Both Austrian and German military leaders wanted a final settling of accounts with the 'Slav menace'. They saw a long-term Russian threat, but an immediate Russian weakness that gave Austria and Germany their opportunity. Civilian thinking was

different. Bethmann intended the initial German support for
Vienna to have a deterrent effect: a rapid response to the assassination would knock over Serbia before Russia or the other
Entente powers could respond; German diplomacy could then
smooth over a successful *fait accompli*, and domestic nationalist
opinion would be mollified. Austrian delay in issuing the ultimatum destroyed Bethmann's more limited objectives. But
Bethmann's own strategy was highly provocative – a calculated
risk.[64] Russia, facing its own dissatisfied public opinion, had
backed down in the crises of 1908 and 1912–13. Germany was
expecting Russia would back down again, perhaps under French
pressure, and forfeit respect as a great power. This was not only
asking a lot; Bethmann and other German statesmen also *knew*,
from their own recent experiences, that it was asking a lot.
German policy was expressly aimed at forcing a Russian stand-
down, breaking the Entente and risking general European war
in the process. It was, in the light of contemporary realities as
well as hindsight, a huge gamble.

By the last stages of the July crisis it was clear that the gamble
had failed, and German hopes were pinned on achieving British
neutrality, or at least a situation in which Britain did not enter
the war immediately. This position, strongly associated with the
'moderate' Bethmann, was consistent with the thrust of German
diplomacy over the previous two years. And it was, once again,
a high-risk strategy. It is true that Britain had restrained Russia
during the recent Balkan wars, and also that Sir Edward Grey
did make efforts to mediate the present crisis in late July. Does
this entitle us to talk of mixed signals coming from London –
like the signals sent by Britain to Germany in the 1930s? The
analogy is strained, at best. No pre-1914 British diplomats
expressed the sympathetic, pro-German views that later
appeasers did. British commitment to its Continental allies, in
the event of war, had been made clear. The Schlieffen Plan
threatened Belgian neutrality, and thus a fundamental British
interest that was universally recognized. In these circumstances,
to count on British neutrality was another gamble. Bethmann,
Kiderlen and his successor Jagow had failed after 1912 to win

any semblance of a British commitment to neutrality. Why should things be different in July 1914? In fact, Bethmann's information from German diplomats in London indicated clearly that Britain would enter the war, if it came, and the German Foreign Office was full of men – Under-Secretary Zimmermann was one – who accepted this. It is hard to believe that German decision-makers were not ultimately aware of the danger: Bethmann's comment that Germany was taking a 'leap in the dark' encapsulates his sense of anxiety, but also an awareness of the risks that German policy ran.[65] For Moltke, meanwhile, the prospect of British intervention was not regarded with any great dread. For the German military establishment, like their opposite numbers in Vienna, the time had come for a showdown, and the war would be fought – as Bernhardi had urged – whatever the cost. The fatalistic brinkmanship of the civilians and the soldierly zeal for 'preventive war' combined to unleash general European hostilities.

Germany at War, 1914–1918

Thomas Mann set his novel, *The Magic Mountain*, 'in the long ago, in the old days, the days of the world before the Great War'.[1] Contemporaries were agreed that the war was a great watershed. Eighty years later there is no reason to question their judgment. The war touched everything, and some things it changed utterly. Scores of millions were mobilized, 10 million killed, 20 million seriously wounded. They were engaged in a terrible and novel kind of warfare that has played on the European imagination to this day. Nor did 'total war' affect only those who fought. Prolonged hostilities put extraordinary strains on society, altering relations between soldiers and civilians, workers and bourgeois, town and country, men and women. The war permanently reduced the importance of Europe in the world; it toppled four empires, including Hohenzollern Germany; it spawned both revolution and fascism. From the perspective of Germany in the twentieth century, the war certainly represented elements of continuity with the past. But it also marked a break: what happened in Germany after 1918 is unimaginable without the war.

Front and Home Front

The reaction in Germany as war broke out is usually thought to have been enthusiastic. That is a half-truth. The patriotic demonstrations of late July involved relatively small groups, with students and young salesmen prominent. Working-class areas like the Ruhr were quiet. On 28 and 29 July antiwar demonstrations drew 100,000 in Berlin and half a million elsewhere. In the first days of August, as Germany declared war on Russia and France, the mood remained ambiguous. The crowds waiting on the streets for the latest editions of newspapers were tense and serious. There were runs on the banks, food was stockpiled, and rumours spread about spies, poisoned water supplies and bombing raids. Civilian guards in Frankfurt spent an evening shooting at clouds they mistook for French planes. Anxiety was mixed with an unreal, carnival spirit that many attributed to the release of tension: the waiting was over, the worst known. Once hostilities were a fact, antiwar sentiment largely melted away, but it was replaced by a sense of resolve rather than wild chauvinism. The government's presentation of the conflict as a defensive war against autocratic Russia had much to do with the general acceptance of a national duty. Unimpeachably liberal figures like Theodor Heuss, Conrad Haussmann and the homosexual-law reformer Magnus Hirschfeld saw the cause as morally just. So, above all, did the labour movement, and in the Reichstag the SPD voted for war credits on 4 August. The mobilization proceeded smoothly: as in other countries there were fewer absentees than expected. But older observers noted a contrast with the enthusiasm of 1870. The crowds at the stations were often quiet, wives and mothers wept and crossed themselves, children stared blankly. As for the soldiers, Carl Zuckmayer described those who left Mainz, singing, as 'sombrely resolute'.[2] On the other hand, it is clear that something beyond a sense of duty animated many young men in August. War appeared as a form of emancipation, particularly for bourgeois youth reacting against the stifling materialism and conformity of Wilhelmine Germany. This sentiment was shared with their counterparts in other countries. They were, as the British poet Rupert Brooke put it, 'like swimmers into cleanness leaping'. It is harder to say if young lower-class conscripts felt a similar sense of liberation from social disciplines, but many probably did.

The soldiers expected war to be short. The Kaiser told them they would be home, victorious, before the autumn leaves fell.

Germans generally shared this belief. The Schlieffen Plan was designed to win a quick victory over France before the Russian army was fully deployed, and initially things went as planned. In early August more than 500 trains a day carried the German army over the Rhine. It rolled through Belgium and northern France, and three weeks later Paris was threatened. The French government fled to Bordeaux. However, the army was weakened in order to reinforce the eastern front, where the Russians attacked unexpectedly early. Then the French and the British Expeditionary Force held up the German advance at the Battle of the Marne in September, where misjudgments by the German Supreme Command caused Moltke to lose his job to Falkenhayn. The effect was to stabilize the western front by November, after a 'race to the sea' left two forces facing each other from fixed emplacements that stretched from Flanders to Switzerland. The eastern front was more mobile. The Russians won an early success at Gumbinnen, reversed by the German victories of the Masurian Lakes and Tannenberg, which established the mystique of General Hindenburg as the 'German saviour'. An offensive by the Central Powers of Austria and Germany in 1915 was followed, in turn, by the Russians' Brusilov offensive the following year. While the fighting in the east was different from the west, there were common features: offensive successes were enormously costly, and neither side was able to land a knockout blow. The same situation arose on a third front. As Germany increasingly assumed the main burden in the east, Austria turned its attention to Italy, which entered the war on the side of the Entente powers. And in Italy, after a failed Austrian offensive, yet another stalemate arose.

The war of attrition was quite different from what had been anticipated. Cavalry played no role on the western front, although it did in the east. The expected infantry charges, supported by artillery, were mocked by fire power greater and more lethal than predicted, from 'big guns', mortars and machine guns. Fixed and elaborate systems of trenches, first developed by the Germans, were the response. From these sandbagged trenches, topped with barbed wire, the infantry was periodically

The Western Front, 1914–18

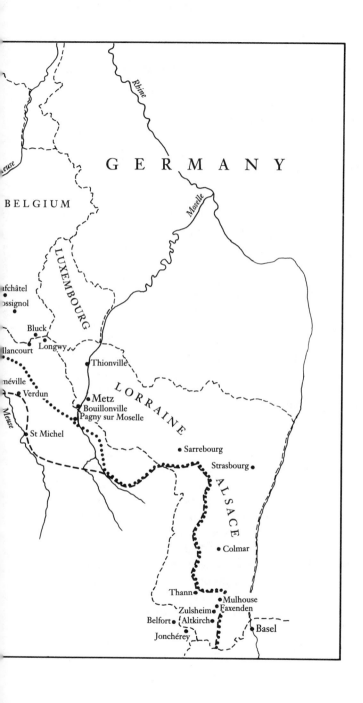

ordered 'over the top' in futile, blood-letting offensives. There
was unprecedented slaughter in the great battles of the western
front – Verdun, the Somme, Ypres, Passchendaele. The use of
modern technology and communications at the command level
had been foreseen by the masters of war. Schlieffen envisaged
the commander in a house 'with roomy offices, where telegraph
and wireless, telephone and signalling instruments are at hand,
while a fleet of automobiles and motorcycles . . . wait for orders'.[3]
Not foreseen was the industrialized carnage. Soldiers went
through the *Wurstmaschine*, or sausage machine, as shells and
mortars killed and dismembered. Corpses filled trenches and
'no-man's land'; others were buried alive. Attempts to break
the stalemate led to new technological weapons of destruction:
flame-throwers, poison gas, phosphorous bombs, tanks, planes.
Brute numbers give a necessary but inadequate measure of this
horror. German casualties alone numbered 1.6 million killed
and 4 million wounded, a third of them seriously. At the end
of 1919 the Reich Insurance Office counted 1.35 million 'war-
wounded': half a million were judged more than 'one-third dis-
abled' by a bureaucracy that had learned to count missing limbs.
In Germany, as elsewhere, the physically maimed and gassed
survivors were a public reminder (when they were seen in public)
of what a generation called the Great War.

The impact of war was also psychological. A connection is
often made between the front-experience and the militarization
of German society in the 1920s, starting with the protofascist
Free Corps of the early postwar years. That is too simple. Germany put 13 million men in uniform; only 400,000 played any
part in the Free Corps. But the war did inject an element of
violence into politics, and it had a larger brutalizing effect. The
most obvious sign of this was the wartime behaviour of soldiers
towards women, children and the elderly. Recent interest in the
'discourse' of atrocities perhaps makes it necessary to state the
obvious: rape and brutality against unarmed civilians were real
and widespread.[4] That was obviously not true only of German
soldiers. But Germany fought the war on foreign soil, where
atrocities were rationalized as reprisals (in Belgium, for

example), and the rounding up of women to serve as army prostitutes was a part of living off the land, like the seizure of hundreds of thousands of supply-horses from France and the Ukraine. It is worth noting the sharply drawn gender lines on the German front. There were no female truck drivers and messengers, as there were in the British army; nor did female doctors serve, as they did in the Austrian forces. German soldiers truly were 'Men without Women' as their counterparts in Hemingway's stories from the Italian front were not. Theirs was, to an unusual degree, an all-male camaraderie, almost a parody of prewar 'masculine' values. It coloured the social and political conflicts of the 1920s.

Yet the war also undermined ideals of male heroism, honour, and chivalry. These may have survived in specific areas of combat, among fighter aces like Richthofen, Boelcke and Immelmann, for example – although, even here, the scope for individual acts of valour has often been exaggerated.[5] For the infantryman the reality was certainly different. After the Battle of the Somme, Ernst Jünger reflected: 'Here chivalry disappeared for ever. Like all noble and personal feelings it had to give way to the new tempo of battle and to the rule of the machine.'[6] If the war dehumanized, it also emasculated. Shock led to panic and hysteria – to weeping and displays of emotion that made men believe, guiltily, that they were behaving 'like women'. The horrors and anxieties could not be explained to wives and mothers at home. Some reacted with aggression, like the later Free Corps members studied by Klaus Theweleit.[7] A more common response was the self-contained silence of Paul, the central character of Erich Maria Remarque's *All Quiet on the Western Front*. This was one form of the 'defensive personality' which developed in the face of intolerable circumstances.[8] Dreams and fantasies, rituals and superstitions – these were the means by which the soldiers coped. Almost all found release in rough humour and songs. The very term *Frontschwein* ('front pig') was, like the French *poilu*, or 'hairy one', a sardonic, anti-heroic label. Most German (and other) soldiers soon felt a sense of distance from the heroic rhetoric intoned by civilians, and the apparent normality that reigned at home.

In fact, the character of the German home front changed as the war went on. Enthusiasm was predictably greatest in the first three months. The victories of August were celebrated, and the intellectual establishment mobilized itself behind the war effort. Public declarations trumpeted the 'ideas of 1914', presenting the German war effort as a defence of culture and idealism against British materialism, French frivolity and Slav barbarism. Thomas Mann's *Reflections of a Nonpolitical Man* was to provide the classic statement of this position, a distillation of views that had long been in circulation but now found unprecedented resonance. Anti-British sentiment was particularly virulent: *Gott strafe England!* – God punish England! – became the slogan. 'The whole of England must burn,' said Count Zeppelin, and – we are told – 'his eyes glittered'.[9] Scientists, historians and writers all took up the ideological offensive. Liberal opinion was well represented. The signatories of an October 'Declaration to the Cultural World!' included architect Peter Behrens and artist Max Liebermann, liberal economist Lujo Brentano, theologian Adolf von Harnack, playwright Gerhart Hauptmann, progressive criminologist Franz von Liszt, and physicist Max Planck.[10] The book trade also went to war. In an October issue of the *Börsenblatt für den deutschen Buchhandel*, Heinrich Lhotzky urged publishers not to 'stint with books', for they would ultimately be more important than armies and navies.[11] Ullstein (later publisher of Remarque's antiwar classic) was one of many houses that obliged with its 'war series'. These books sentimentalized the war for domestic consumption, appealing to an interest in new technological weapons (Richthofen's *Red Fighter Pilot* sold hundreds of thousands) and investing the struggle with heroic idealism. As in other combatant countries, press and cinema also supported the national cause. So did the businesses that produced model Hindenburgs in a variety of sizes and materials, based on the gigantic, three-storey original erected in Berlin's Tiergarten.

Government, army and opinion-formers all echoed the theme of national unity. It had been sounded at the beginning of August when the Kaiser told the Reichstag 'I no longer recognize any parties, I know only Germans', a declaration soon mass-produced on postcards bearing William's photograph. This was the basis of the *Burgfrieden*, or civil truce. It had its counterparts elsewhere, of course, like the French *Union Sacrée*. And in Germany, as in other countries, spontaneous rallying to the nation was stiffened by a government determined to mould popular attitudes as well as foreign opinion, positively (through propaganda) and negatively (through censorship). From the beginning, however, the rhetoric of a national community or *Volksgemeinschaft* covered over the fact that the 'spirit of August' meant different things to different Germans. For organized workers it meant that the strain of their double loyalty, as Germans and socialists, was lifted. They were no longer pariahs: that was how they interpreted the Kaiser's promise that he 'forgave' those who had once criticized him. The government was careful not to disrupt party or trade union meetings in the early months of war, and the socialist newspaper *Vorwärts* (*Forwards*) could now be bought on Prussian railway stations. This was legitimation of a sort: the labour movement acknowledged the need for war credits, and Germany's rulers acknowledged the labour movement. But the truce was conditional on both sides, and the longer the war went on, the more German workers grew disenchanted with it. The same was true of the class that conservatives had always painted as the most loyal, namely the peasantry. It was the propertied and educated middle classes, with professors, students and schoolteachers to the fore, that supported the war longest and most zealously. It was they who purchased war bonds, hammered their contributions into the 'iron nail memorials', and did most to propagate the metaphysical significance of the war effort. But even the bourgeoisie was not immune to rising doubts and falling morale on the home front.

What produced the growing disenchantment? The human cost of the war affected every community. Take, as an example, the village of Marpingen, mentioned in Chapter Six. In 1914 it had 2000 inhabitants: 72 men were killed in the war, leaving 350 bereaved family members. Most of the millions of Germans who suffered these losses left no record of their feelings. One who did was the artist Käthe Kollwitz, in letters and diaries as well as in her work. Her son Peter was killed in October 1914. The diary entries in the following years begin with many subjects – Goethe, her fellow artists, the seasons – but return with a terrible constancy to Peter's death and to fears for her other son. On 17 January 1916 she wrote:[12]

> . . . Where are my children now? what remains for their mother? one boy to the right and one to the left, my right son and my left son, as they used to call themselves. One dead, and one so distant, and I can no longer help him, can give him no more of myself. Everything has changed for ever. Changed, and I am the poorer. My whole life as a mother is behind me. I often have a terrible longing to be back there, to have my children – my boys –, one to the right and one to the left, to dance with them as before, when spring came and Peter brought flowers and we did a spring dance.

Käthe Kollwitz was a socialist whose personal tragedy intensified her hatred of the war. Neither her Protestant faith, nor Goethe, nor German nature provided sufficient reason to be reconciled to her loss. That was no doubt exceptional. The desire to believe that the death of loved ones had meaning and justification was very strong. Both Protestant and Catholic clergy sanctified the spirit of sacrifice in their sermons; the memorialization of the dead drew heavily on the motifs of German nature, culture, and history. The rising death toll could also bind people tighter to the cause.

But as the war continued, still fought on foreign soil, questions arose. What if the aims were more than defensive? And what if the sacrifices were being unevenly borne – if not at the front, then certainly at home? This was the point at which personal tragedies and gradual war-weariness acquired a potentially more negative meaning, when set against the growing privations within Germany. Before 1914 little thought had been given to wartime economic management. German rulers (and economists) shared the universal assumption that no society would be able to handle all-out war for very long, so there were no plans to control labour, output, or the distribution of goods. That changed, as the home front was also 'mobilized'. The process was gradual and piecemeal, involving many different forms of state intervention. They included direct acquisition or sequestration (with compensation) of vital plant, industrial boards to plan output, and the establishment of government agencies such as the War Raw Materials Office and the Imperial Railway Comission. What contemporaries called 'war socialism', or 'Prussian socialism', actually left most of the private economy in private hands. But the framework of state planning and direction became more comprehensive as the war went on, generating numerous points of friction between civilian and military administrators, state and industry. Most important of all, conflicts over production and distribution had an impact on the living standards and morale of every German on the home front, producer and consumer, peasant and worker. The main areas of conflict can be roughly grouped under three headings: the manpower issue, the shortage of civilian goods, and the food-supply problem. All had a crucial effect on the social fabric; the third may well have been decisive in Germany's defeat.

The millions of conscripted men left huge gaps in the labour force, even after Belgian and Polish workers had been brought to Germany. Agriculture lost more than half of its prewar manpower; a third of industrial workers were already in uniform by the end of 1914. Efforts to make good the shortfall were concentrated on industry, which provided the materials for waging war. Government enjoyed some advantages. Agreements with industrialists over conversion to war-production meant that the balance of the industrial workforce was already shifting. The high prices and profits permitted to war-related industries brought relatively high wages in their wake, which attracted labour. And the no-strike pledge by the trade unions made at the beginning of August 1914 held, with few exceptions, through the end of 1915. Nevertheless, problems remained. One response was the gradual development of a system of exemptions and deferments for 'essential labour', especially skilled workers. Another long-term development – probably the most familiar to general readers – was the growing role played by women in the industrial labour force. The significance of this shift should not be over stated. It was a continuation of the prewar trend; and many of the women who now worked in munitions' factories or in public transport had previously been in the paid labour force, in agriculture or domestic service. Nevertheless, between 1913 and 1918 the number of female workers in industrial concerns employing more than ten people rose by a half, while the number of men fell by a quarter. By the end of the war women made up a third of the labour force in these concerns, more than a half in some munitions branches.

This is often seen as a form of emancipation, and in some ways it was. But women were emptied out of the factories again when hostilities ended; and their wartime experiences, however liberating in the abstract, were often desperate. Faced with the double burden of work and raising children in exceptionally difficult conditions (the kernel of truth in later conservative rhetoric about the 'moral crisis' of the family), many opted for night shifts, stinted on sleep and laboured themselves to exhaustion. Yet their very participation in industry aroused long-standing male proletarian anxieties: women were 'usurping' men's jobs, traditional male wage-rates were threatened. This last fear had a basis in fact – male-female wage differentials *were* narrowing. But the hostility, backlash even, was part of a larger anxiety among skilled workers, who also saw their differentials eroded vis-à-vis the unskilled. This was a concern that pitted the middle-aged against the young as well as men against women. The war therefore sharpened old divisions within the working class.

It also generated grievances common to all workers. In the first two years of war, free collective bargaining was being eroded by stealth in favour of state direction. The Auxiliary Labour Law of 1916 then brought a decisive shift. It gave the authorities powers to conscript workers and decide where they should work – in effect, a mobilization· of the labour force aged sixteen to sixty. True, the pill was sweetened with concessions like arbitration boards. From one perspective this trend marked an advance for organized labour: its importance was recognized, and trade union leaders were closely involved in this corporate agreement with government and employers. But there was intense dissatisfaction with the forced-labour element, hardly surprising given the role that job-changing had always played in workers' lives. Discontent was fuelled by two other wartime developments. The pace of work intensified, contributing to an increase in industrial accidents; and the gains in money wages achieved by union leaders were more than wiped out by inflation. In the war years real wages fell by around 20 per cent for workers in war industries, by 40 per cent in other branches. This was the onset of the process that ended in the notorious hyperinflation of 1923. A major reason for it was the inability of the government to cover more than a small part of its expenditure from taxation – a failure to tackle Junker fiscal privileges or tax war profits (they were not taxed at all until June 1916) that belied the rhetoric of national community. The obvious inequality of sacrifice added to popular resentment. At a time when trade union bureaucrats seemed to have been coopted by Germany's political and economic rulers, workers mounted unofficial strikes and a radical shop stewards' movement emerged on the factory floor. The 240 strikes in 1916 represented a resumption of pre-1914 industrial militancy under conditions of growing war-weariness.

Shortages of everyday consumer goods added to the discontent. A War Raw Materials Office was established in 1914 to coordinate industrial production, but as the name suggests priority was given to war needs. Over the course of the conflict, there was a radical shift in resources away from civilian production. Wool and cotton fibres, hence clothing, were in desperately short supply on the home front. Substitutes woven with paper fibre failed to meet with widespread satisfaction, even when fashion models displayed the latest line in paper dresses for illustrated magazines. Basics like matches and kitchen utensils were equally hard to obtain. So, above all, was soap. An Englishwoman living in Berlin noted in her diary during May

1916 that the scarcity of soap had led in some parts of Germany to the enforcement of regulations forbidding white dresses to be worn.[13] The most serious aspect of the difficulty people had in keeping their bodies and their clothes clean was the risk to health, which led in turn to exhortations from governmental agencies about hygiene and the importance of domestic skills. This barrage of advice, the intensification of a prewar trend, was directed mainly at women. It added a psychological burden to what were already problems enough. The supply of services, as well as goods, fell far short of what people had come to expect before 1914. Trams ran irregularly; lights went out when the electricity supply was cut; and the railway system virtually seized up in the winter of 1916–17, one effect of which was a chronic shortage of coal.

Food, or the lack of it, was the third and potentially most explosive aspect of domestic privation and loss of confidence. Some historians have argued that the western Allies won the war and the Germans lost it, because the former were able to maintain supplies of food and provision their cities, the latter were not.[14] The comparison is not accidental. The largest single reason for the German shortage was the Allied blockade. Germany was a net importer of food before 1914. A fifth of all the calories consumed in the Empire came from abroad, a figure that rose to over a quarter for protein and more than two-fifths for fats. While Britain was able to maintain its overseas lines of supply during the war, Royal Navy control of the sea routes to Germany had a devastating effect. When war broke out German vessels sought refuge in neutral ports, many were sunk or captured, and Germany became heavily dependent on neutral shipping. British pressure on neutrals and its elastic definition of war contraband allowed it to exert a stranglehold on the food (and raw materials) reaching Germany. There were some safety valves. As in Napoleonic France a century earlier, necessity proved the mother of invention: the chemical industry provided an *Ersatz*, or substitute, for some goods that domestic agriculture desperately needed, like fertilizer. Germany was also able to circumvent the blockade in part by exploiting its Continental position, bringing in food as well as labour from occupied areas. In 1914 Romania was important as a political and military ally; by 1916 it was wheat that made it decisive. But neither of these expedients made a major dent in the food shortfall, which was worsened by a drop in domestic production approaching 50 per cent as men entered the army and draft animals disappeared from farms.

Food shortages led to rising mortality rates among infants and the elderly, substantial weight losses among the general population, and outright malnutrition, which first registered catastrophically during the 'turnip winter' of 1916–17. Starvation was responsible for 750,000 deaths during the war, a thousand times greater than those resulting from Allied bombing attacks. All Germans felt the impact to some degree. Thomas Mann's children were reduced to eating garden snails ('our hunger got the better of our disgust', wrote Golo Mann in his memoirs).[15] But some suffered more than others. Great efforts were made to keep the soldiers well-fed, the countryside looked after itself, and the same was true to some degree of smaller towns. The working-class population of large cities was the principal victim, for it stood at the end of the queue.

Government controls did less than they might have to improve the situation. Food was rationed from 1915 onwards, beginning with bread and gradually taking in meat and other animal produce. But there were numerous problems. For example, even as the authorities were trying to assure minimal nutritional standards, they were simultaneously taking fats off the market because these were needed for glycerine, an essential base for explosives-manufacture. (By 1918 the ration provided each person with only 7 per cent of prewar fat consumption.) The War Food Office was not established until 1916, and only in the third year of hostilities were procurement and distribution really established on a war footing. They continued to be plagued by lack of central authority and disputes between the different levels of administration. These difficulties affected not only food supply, but morale. Variations in the ration from one town to the next added to the sense of 'unfairness'. That was a key issue. It was not just shortages, inferior products ('K-bread' baked with potato flour, watered milk) and the endless, fatiguing queues for food that made consumers angry, but the perception that sacrifices were being unequally shared. Nothing created bitterness more than the black market, which disposed of somewhere between a fifth and a third of total available food. The black market heightened the resentment between different parts of the population, and created scapegoats: producers, retailers, wealthy middle-class consumers. It also fed a marked increase in anti-Semitic hostility towards supposed 'Jewish speculators'. But the government, which failed in the elementary duty to feed its citizens adequately, was the largest and most inviting target of resentment.

The black market was a by-product of one of the most serious problems faced by German government: its failure to gain the cooperation of the peasantry, especially under a regime of price controls. Price stops on grain led to hoarding or release on to the black market, and animals died through lack of fodder; price stops on animal produce led to the animals being slaughtered and eaten, or passed down unofficial chains of suppliers to a region where prices were more enticing. Regional variations certainly encouraged this response, although it needed little encouragement. Exhortations to the peasantry from government and churches had minimal effect. The Münster diocesan gazette reminded the faithful in 1916 that 'God loves a cheerful giver', but the message fell on stony ground.[16] Primary producers would do anything to avoid giving up their produce at official prices in exchange for funny money. Attempted government controls could not create an adequate food supply to the towns; they succeeded only in alienating rural producers, whose vocal spokesmen painted a picture of plump and cosseted urban consumers that was wildly implausible but readily believed in the countryside. By 1916 there was already widespread peasant as well as working-class discontent.

The social impact of war also had negative effects on middle-class morale. Small businessmen were conspicuous victims of the war economy, as the imperatives of production further tilted the scales in favour of big business. The bitter irony here was that all the prewar flattery about the special state-preserving qualities of the independent sector was exposed as empty rhetoric when a real crisis arose. Official concessions to organized labour made small producers feel even more vulnerable. The petty-bourgeois politics of self-pity now acquired an even sharper edge: one cartoon showed the emaciated Mittelstand being squeezed remorselessly between a fat, cigar-smoking capitalist and an equally bloated worker. The lower middle class of clerks and officials also had reason to see itself as a wartime loser, for the differentials that separated it from workers narrowed appreciably. White-collar workers were socially and politically polarized by war. Hans Fallada's famous novel of white-collar desperation, *Little Man, What Now?*, was set and written in the Weimar Republic; but the insecurity and indignities it described had already become real for many during the war. Finally, the bourgeoisie proper found its way of life altered for the worse by war. It did not suffer the privations of the working class, but the war ended what novelist Stefan Zweig called 'the world of security'.[17] Declining differentials were also a source of resentment here, among grammar school teachers and officials. Meanwhile, the war economy hurt professionals who depended on a robust civilian economy, like architects. All experienced the growing scarcity of servants and the declining value of money. This was especially serious for those dependent on income from annuities or rents, but declining real incomes also affected the salaried. Senior officials earned only half as much in real terms in 1918 as they had four years earlier. The declining value of war bonds rubbed salt in the wound. After the war had been fought on middle-class savings, it was continued by printing money, conjuring up the bourgeois nightmare of inflation. Middle-class insecurity was yet another ingredient in a potent cocktail of domestic tensions. As war continued and mocked the early boasts of quick victory, diverse discontents put growing strain on the social fabric of Germany.

War Aims and Domestic Politics

The rising cost of hostilities was obvious to all the combatants – the cost in human lives, government finances and social stability. Why, then, did the war drag on? One answer is military and strategic. Neither side could land a knockout blow. But we should not confuse cause and effect. The trenches did not determine that the war would continue; political will did that. Faced with deadlock, both sides tried to enlist new allies, which in turn opened up new fronts. So Turkey joined the Central Powers and Italy the Allies, Bulgaria the Central Powers and Romania the Allies. The spread of the war, first within Europe and then beyond (Japan being an early participant on the Allied side), also helped to keep it going by adding new war aims. Both sides employed a further weapon of war: attempting to raise revolts among the subject peoples of their enemies. Germany encouraged Irish rebellion and played on the nationalist sentiment of Russian subjects like the Poles and Ukrainians; it also tried to foment Muslim revolt in India and central Asia against the British Empire (the background to John Buchan's adventure novel, *Greenmantle*). The Allies looked to subvert the multi-national Ottoman Empire by supporting subject peoples (most tragically in the case of the Armenians), and – more half-heartedly – to encourage Czechs and South Slavs within the Habsburg Empire. Sometimes the two sides were making parallel overtures. Germans and Russians both wooed the Poles. Lawrence of Arabia was rivalled by his German counterpart in Persia, Wilhelm Wassmuss. The interaction of great-power calculations with the ambitions of the subject peoples lent the conflict an unpredictable dynamic.

In other ways, too, the war acquired its own momentum. The use of black propaganda to mobilize opinion and the wild rumours that spread about the bestial enemy worked against an old-style diplomatic solution. If (as Germans were told) the French Senegalese were cannibals while British Gurkhas drank the blood of their victims, and if (as some French and Belgians believed) the Kaiser personally tortured children in satanic rituals, then how could anything short of total victory be justified?[18] For governments, the greater the costs of war, the higher the premium on victory. War itself fed annexationist aims: programmes hardened, attitudes became more uncompromising. Both sides snubbed American President Woodrow Wilson's efforts in 1915 and 1916 to arbitrate a 'peace without victors and vanquished', as they did Pope Benedict XV's attempts at mediation in 1917. The air was thick with peace feelers among the combatants in the period between late 1914 and late 1916, but the 'offers' from both sides invariably contained unacceptable conditions. What lay behind these initiatives was the desire to divide the enemy alliance or make a good impression on neutrals; or they were undertaken to reassure domestic opinion that it was the other side that was intransigent.

German war aims must be judged against the background of what other powers coveted. Italy looked to make extensive gains from Austria-Hungary in Dalmatia and elsewhere – that was why Italy entered the war on the Allied side. The three major Allied powers each had designs on the Ottoman Empire – Russia on Constantinople and the Straits, France on Syria, Britain on oil and an Egyptian protectorate. As far as German territory itself was concerned, Britain was committed virtually from the outbreak of hostilities to seizing German colonies in Africa. France aimed to recover Alsace-Lorraine, and there were more ambitious plans to seize the Saar, create satellite states on the left bank of the Rhine, and reorganize German states so that the Bismarckian Empire would be destroyed. Thus, Bavaria and Silesia might be ceded to Austria-Hungary in a separate peace. French aims were less expansionist than those of its allies, but security considerations made it harshly intransigent over the need to weaken Germany territorially and economically. The Treaty of Versailles eventually imposed on Germany by the successful western powers in 1919 allows us to see British and French aims put into practice.

There can be no serious doubt, however, that German ambitions were more extensive than those of other powers. Fritz Fischer demonstrated that the aims laid out in the September programme of 1914, formulated before the German offensive faltered on the Marne, were much broader than had previously been accepted.[19] They included, in the west, German control over Belgium, Luxemburg, the French iron-ore district of Longwy-Briey, and strategic French forts like Belfort. Among the aims in the east were German annexations or the creation of satellite regimes in Poland, Courland, Lithuania, the Ukraine and Finland. Running through this catalogue of aspirations was the need for a German-dominated Central Europe, a *Mitteleuropa* that would effectively have subordinated the Netherlands, Scandinavia and even France in the west, and states like Romania in the east, to German interests. This programme was not only designed to hobble Russia; it also turned Austria-Hungary into a very junior partner of Germany. These ambitions were concerned with more than territorial acquisitions. Eastern Europe was to provide raw materials and land for German colonization. It is not unhistorical to see this as a forerunner of later Nazi schemes, less barbaric certainly, but resting on unmistakable assumptions about the German right to control the destinies of other European peoples. Nor did these aims end in Europe. Turkey and the Berlin-Baghdad railway were to serve as a springboard for German ambitions in the Near and Middle East and into Asia. Other aspirations centred on the Far East and the possibility of turning Latin America away from the United States. But the most elaborate German aims outside Europe concerned Africa, where it was hoped to construct a Central African empire stretching from east coast to west through the acquisition of Portuguese Angola, northern Mozambique, some of French Equatorial Africa, Togo, Dahomey, and parts of Senegal and the Gambia. The German flag would fly in Timbuktu.

Fischer broke new ground by showing the extent of the September programme, and by exhuming from the archives the numerous memoranda, submissions and reports that followed it. His achievement remains the starting point of modern scholarly debate. But questions remain. For example, should every German aspiration be taken at face value or given equal weight? Whatever might be said against older conservative arguments that defended the 'good' Bethmann Hollweg against the 'bad' militarists and Pan-Germans, there is still some point in distinguishing between moderates and extreme annexationists. On the wilder annexationist shores almost nothing was deemed impossible, but not everything they proposed became official policy. There were issues on which Bethmann had misgivings, and it was because he attempted to tack between competing interests and continue his 'policy of the diagonal' that he was repeatedly attacked by military leaders, industrialists and right-wing opinion for alleged softness. That was why he eventually lost his job in 1917. There is a further point: Fischer certainly recognizes that aims were modified in line with the state of the war, but his book sometimes comes close to describing a single, 600-page German shopping list drawn up in 1914. There is irony in this. In the debate over German war aims in 1939–45, it is conservatives who have argued that there was a 'blueprint', liberals who have insisted that wartime circumstances on the ground be given their due. In discussions of the First World War, these roles have been curiously reversed. The dynamics of war mattered, and the high-points of German ambition (the September programme of 1914, the eastern policy of 1918) coincided with the high tides of military success in west and east respectively. What happened in 1918 is indicative. The separate peace with Russia at Brest-Litovsk was harshly punitive: Russia lost virtually all its oil and cotton production, three-quarters of its coal and iron, a third of its railways and agriculture, and a third of its population, including the Ukraine, Finland and the Baltic states. The Treaty of Bucharest imposed similar terms on Romania. It stretches credulity to argue, as Fischer's critic Gerhard Ritter did, that these treaties were merely provisional, or that they did not represent a peace with annexations, or that the economic arrangements were somehow reciprocal. Yet they were not the smooth implementation of the September programme, either. The economic and political rape of eastern Europe in 1918 can only be understood against the background of the opportunities presented by the Bolshevik revolution and unresisted German advance on the one hand, coupled with the growing crisis of food and raw material supplies in Germany. This is not to whitewash, but to contextualize.

In the end, three points deserve emphasis. First, German war aims not only exceeded those of any other combatant: they were aspirations to world power. Secondly, there was a greater consensus over those aims than pre-Fischer historians liked to admit. Annexationist ambitions were not confined to soldiers like Hindenburg and Ludendorff, or to Pan-Germans and other superpatriots. They were shared by civilian ministers, civil servants, Catholic and liberal politicians, liberal intellectuals such as Max Weber and Friedrich Naumann, even by some Social Democrats. This was apparent in discussion of issues like the control of Belgium and Poland, or the belief in some sort of *Mitteleuropa*, whatever disagreements there may have been over detail or tactics. The point is not that there were no differences between extreme annexationists and moderates – there were – but that the moderates were not really so moderate. None of them could conceive of returning to the prewar status quo. Finally, if Versailles put the war aims of the western Allies into practice, Brest-Litovsk showed how far Germany would go if the opportunity arose. When it did, a maximalist programme was pursued. There is little doubt that German success on the western front would have been followed by more of the same.

What Fischer called 'grasping for world power' was an elaboration of prewar *Weltpolitik* (World Policy), with motives that were equally complex. Take the *Drang nach Osten*, or drive to the east. The German claim to dominance in Central Europe was political, racial and cultural; it also rested on arguments that were geographical (this was 'German space') and economic (these were resources a dynamic Germany needed). The same mix fuelled German expansionist ambitions everywhere. Economic lobbyists played an important role. The industrialists made constant demands for annexations that brought iron ore, manganese, oil and phosphates; agrarians were attracted by the promise of cheap labour for their estates. But German war aims also echoed the language of prewar nationalism and imperialism, with their Social Darwinist undertones. War added an extra edge to the view that Germany faced a choice between decline and a struggle for supremacy with the British and Russian empires. That is why German territorial expansion was often cast in defensive terms, like the creation of German-controlled buffer states around Russia as a form of 'security policy'. This amounted to a wartime version of the earlier obsession with encirclement. It derived, in part, from a subjectively genuine German anxiety that not going forwards meant going backwards. There was also an obviously self-serving aspect: trying to persuade neutral opinion that attack was really defence.

Domestic considerations also blocked off the German path to a negotiated settlement. An important element of this was the financial question. The war of 1870–1 had cost Prussia 7 million Marks a day: the cost to Germany of the First World War was 36 million marks a day at the beginning, 146 million Marks a day by early 1918. The fabulous French war indemnity of 1871 would have paid for precisely two days of the later conflict. Total German war expenditure amounted to 150 thousand million Marks. The costs of war were huge and unprecedented for all participants, but the burden was especially heavy on those – like Germany – that were unwilling or unable to expand their domestic tax base. And the 1871 precedent suggested a way out of the dilemma. As State Secretary Karl Helfferich candidly observed: 'We hold fast to the hope of presenting our opponents at the conclusion of peace with the bill for this war that has been forced upon us'.[20] Here was a powerful motive to reject a compromise peace.

The financial issue was one aspect of a larger question: the connection between war aims and domestic politics. The two were always interlinked, but especially so from the turn of 1916–17. On the one side, growing war-weariness and scepticism about German aims fused with criticism of the domestic power structure: demands for a negotiated peace and political reform went together. On the other side, annexationists in the army and civilian élite became more intransigent at home: the uncompromising pursuit of victory and domestic dictatorial powers also went together. Bethmann therefore found himself fighting a war on two fronts at home, as well as abroad. These tensions came to a head in 1917, the decisive year when Germany's strategic position and domestic politics were transformed.

The polarization in German politics that culminated in the July crisis of 1917 can only be understood in relation to the two great external events of that year. The first was the American entry into the war on the Allied side in April. Several things helped to bring this about, beginning with the dilatory and evasive German response to Woodrow Wilson's peace initiative in late 1916, but the decisive move was the German declaration of unrestricted submarine warfare at the end of January 1917. Like Zeppelin attacks, this was regarded in Berlin as a way of bringing Britain to its knees. It was immensely provocative, however. Unrestricted submarine warfare had been waged briefly in 1915, when the previously unenthusiastic Tirpitz suddenly decided that German submarines were a wonder-weapon – all twenty-one of them. But it was ended after US anger at the sinking of the *Lusitania* with loss of American lives. In 1916 Germany retreated a second time from intensified submarine warfare after American warnings. Bethmann saw the risk of precipitating American intervention in 1917, but still bowed to mounting demands for a resumption of unrestricted submarine attacks. Informal requests by Wilson that American ships be spared were snubbed, and Germany compounded the provocation by recklessly encouraging Mexico to declare war on America with the promise of recovering Texas and New Mexico from the Yankees – the celebrated Zimmermann telegram, deciphered by the British and conveyed to Washington. The German decision rested on a two-fold act of faith: that enough shipping could be sunk to knock Britain out of the war before America intervened, if it did; and that American financial and military resources would hardly be decisive anyway. This was another massive gamble, like the gamble on British neutrality in July 1914.

The second decisive external event of 1917 was the Russian revolution of February, that toppled the Tsar. Popular war-weariness was a major cause, and the revolution brought an unstable Provisional Government to power. One possible German response, therefore, was to seek peace with the new regime – a policy that had actually been considered at the highest level earlier, as a means of splitting the Allies and allowing Germany to concentrate on the western front. But in 1917, as before, Berlin was unwilling to offer a genuine compromise peace in the east. Instead, it was decided to extend the policy of internal subversion in Russia by encouraging further revolutionary discontent. Hence the famous sealed train in which the German authorities returned Lenin to Russia to do his worst. (To make it clear he was not a German agent, Lenin insisted on paying his own fare.) Once again, the decision had been taken to go for broke rather than go for peace.

In the long run, these two gambler's decisions had very different outcomes. While the importance of the sealed train should not be exaggerated, Lenin's return contributed to the second, Bolshevik revolution in Russia, which led in turn to Brest-Litovsk. Conversely, American entry into the war can be seen in retrospect as the turning point for the Central Powers, ending their chances of victory in the west. What was decisive in 1917, though, was the failure of either gamble to produce the desired result in the short run. Submarine warfare was very successful through the spring and early summer, causing panic in London; but the British convoy system eventually turned the tide, while American intervention meant that Germany and its allies faced the inexorable prospect of being outmanned, outgunned and outprovisioned. Meanwhile, the Russians fought on despite internal unrest, and Germany faced a fourth winter of war on two fronts.

By July, American and Russian events had created a crisis over war aims. They exacerbated a crisis over domestic reform that was building anyway in 1917. Food shortages, inflation and labour discontent all worsened in the winter of 1916–17, leading to protests and shop-floor radicalism. There were more than 500 strikes involving 1.5 million people in 1917. Official rhetoric about sacrifices rang hollow in the light of domestic inequalities, symbolized by the three-class Prussian franchise. Demands grew for direct and universal suffrage. The twin issues of peace and reform split the SPD in early 1917 and led to the founding of the more left-wing Independent Social Democratic Party (USPD). It contained within it a radical group of 'Spartacists', the embryo of the later Communist Party. Peace and reform also exercised others who had previously supported the government: the majority SPD, the bourgeois parties (other than the Conservatives), and liberal intellectuals like Max Weber. Events in America and Russia sharpened demands for reform by underlining other connections between foreign and domestic politics. The final breach with the United States signified, amongst other things, Woodrow Wilson's preference for democracy over the German political system; and the revolution in Russia was a warning of what might happen in Germany if there was no reform. Bethmann was alive to these pressures. In the spring he drafted proposals for a democratic Prussian franchise, but conservative resistance watered this down into vague promises by the time the Kaiser delivered his Easter message. At the beginning of July, as the prospect of rapid victory receded, the chancellor faced renewed pressure. SPD leaders, aware of the forces to their left, asked Bethmann to dissociate himself from further annexationist demands and introduce political reforms; and the Centre Party's Matthias Erzberger, previously hawkish, announced that he would introduce a Peace Resolution in the Reichstag. This was the two-pronged July crisis.

July 1917 saw the decisive test of wartime political leadership in Germany. It can be compared to the crises weathered by the western Allies, and the comparison is instructive. Lloyd George in Britain and Clemenceau in France emerged as powerful civilian war leaders; so, to a degree, did Orlando in Italy. In the German crisis Bethmann fell, ostensibly because he lost the support of moderate Reichstag parties, actually because he lost the confidence of the élites. It was not the tactical desertion of the Centre Party and SPD that sealed his fate, but the hostility of Crown Prince, Prussian establishment and Supreme Command, who rejected his conversion to suffrage reform and no longer needed his 'diplomatic' virtues now that America was in the war anyway. Bethmann was brought down by the right, not the left, by soldiers, not party leaders. Nothing illustrates that fact better than the identity of his successor, the colourless bureaucrat Georg Michaelis, who was the army's man from the start. The outcome of the July crisis sent a message that the Prussian élite was no more prepared to make domestic political concessions than it was to accept even the relatively modest limitations on German war aims embodied in the Peace Resolution. The latter was duly passed in the Reichstag by the SPD, Progressives and Centre, but as Michaelis wrote to the Crown Prince: 'One can make any peace one likes with this resolution.'[21]

The Supreme Command emerged as the arbiter of German politics after the July crisis, the culmination of a process latent since the beginning of the war. The army played a larger role in nonmilitary matters than its counterparts elsewhere.[22] Under the 'state of war' conditions pronounced as early as 31 July 1914, the army had formal authority over local administration, rights of assembly, and so on. Germany used officers as censors, for example, where Britain used journalists. The army was at the heart of economic and social mobilization, and the War Raw Materials Office set up by industrialist Walter Rathenau was run by the army from 1915 onwards. The Supreme Command called the tune in this sphere after Falkenhayn was dismissed in 1916 and Hindenburg and Ludendorff took over. Ludendorff is credited with coining the term 'total war'. The decisive Auxiliary Labour Law was ultimately Hindenburg's plan, even if the military leadership had to swallow some concessions to trade union leaders and Reichstag parties. The role of officers in implementing the law offers a strong contrast with the operation of the parallel, but civilian, Ministry of Munitions in Britain. From the summer of 1917 the Supreme Command enjoyed an even more powerful position. William II was now a 'shadow Kaiser', supreme warlord in name only, while Michaelis and his successor Hertling were largely figureheads. When Germany's third wartime Foreign Secretary, Kühlmann, pursued a policy towards Russia and Romania that the army considered weak, it spied on him, spread stories about his sybaritic lifestyle, and eventually drove him from office. The moderate parties of the Reichstag, from the SPD across to the National Liberals, had come away from the July crisis of 1917 with next to nothing. The interparty committee they established has sometimes been seen as a forerunner of Weimar parliamentarism, but it had no power. In the last year of war Reichstag politicians possessed less influence than they had before 1914. It was typical of their subordination to the army that only the small USPD voted against Brest-Litovsk (the SPD abstained), and the interparty committee placed itself on ice in order not to disturb the spring offensive of 1918.

The power of the Supreme Command in 1917–18 was such that historians refer to the Ludendorff 'dictatorship'.[23] It was actually a group of officers around Ludendorff who were chiefly concerned with political decisions, but the dominant position of the army is indisputable. It placed its stamp on eastern policy, and the availability of new 'living space' encouraged racial-eugenicist fantasies. Ludendorff had referred as early as 1915 to 'breeding stations' in the east.[24] In 1918 the Supreme Command demanded a ban on contraceptives in Germany and punitive taxation of unmarried men who were failing in their 'natural duties'. The army had the major say in economic mobilization. With the dismissal of General Wilhelm Groener after the July crisis, the one senior soldier who realized that the war could not be won against the German working class, policy towards domestic discontent also became more uncompromising. The state-of-siege laws were widely used, supplemented by constant exhortations from the army's propaganda apparatus. The army was strongly backed by the most inflexible elements in the élite, like Prussian Interior Minister Loebell and senior civil servants, and it worked closely with industrialists and their organizations. Section II of the Supreme Command under Colonel Max Bauer was the most important conduit. The heavy industrial interests of coal, iron and steel enjoyed great influence through figures like Gustav Krupp and Hugo Stinnes, but the electrochemical branches also had close links to the military leadership. Carl Duisberg from the Bayer concern was a frequent visitor at army headquarters. Shippers and bankers were not left out: the company created to exploit Romanian oil was controlled by the four 'D-banks'.

These economic interests were all represented in a mass organization created in September 1917 to provide popular backing for the army's annexationist demands. The Fatherland Party was founded by Tirpitz and Wolfgang Kapp, who later led an unsuccessful coup against the Weimar Republic in 1920. The army put its propaganda apparatus at the disposal of the new organization, and in less than a year it had 1.25 million individual or affiliated members. The Fatherland Party was an umbrella organization for different parts of the prewar right, old and new. It embraced industry, peasant and Mittelstand groups, Pan-Germans and Count Westarp's Conservative Party. Its ultra-hawkish foreign policy was matched by harshly authoritarian domestic prescriptions and violent expressions of racism, including anti-Semitism. The Fatherland Party was a product of the wartime circumstances of 1917–18; it was also a milestone in the forging of a New Right in Germany. One of its members was Anton Drexler, founder of the Nazi Party.

Revolution and Beyond

In an increasingly polarized society, the main opposition to the Supreme Command and its backers came from popular discontent in the streets and factories. The Bolshevik revolution gave the German army vast opportunities in the east, but it also provided a warning – or should have done – about what might happen at home. During the last year of war working-class discontent reached new heights. Half a million went on strike in Berlin in January 1918 and another million elsewhere – in Hamburg, Leipzig, the Ruhr, Cologne, Munich. Strikes and demonstrations over cuts in the ration went on throughout the year, despite attempts at suppression. Women had a prominent part in them. Desperation and war-weariness did not always take organized political form. From Danzig in the east to Koblenz in the west, military commanders reported rising levels of crime committed by a hungry population. Large groups, hundreds strong, made night-time raids into the countryside to strip the crops from the fields. Making due allowance for what soldiers expected in the way of obedience, it is hard not to be struck by reports that refer to a widespread loss of respect for authority. Nor did this apply only to the urban working class. Whatever Mittelstand, white-collar and agrarian spokesmen in the Fatherland Party may have said, the mood in these groups was bitter. Dislike of big-business profits and hostility to the food-requisitioning system created mistrust among the 'little men' and eroded their confidence in authority. Demoralization was also reported among the middle classes.

That was the background to the final German military gamble, the spring offensive that began in March 1918. Like the advance of August-September 1914 and the first months of unrestricted submarine warfare in 1917 it was initially successful. But Germany never had the numerical superiority it would have needed in the west – not least, because of the forces left behind in the east to safeguard the Brest-Litovsk settlement, and the presence of over a million fresh American troops in France. The political decisions taken by German leaders now came home to roost. By June the offensive petered out, in July the Allies counterattacked, and on 8 August they broke through the German lines. This last throw of the dice cost 800,000 German casualties. The Supreme Command now recognized the war was lost, and in a brazen about-turn insisted that there was no alternative but to appeal for peace on Woodrow Wilson's terms. It was a choice between ceasefire and catastrophe, said Ludendorff on 29 September. Soldiers had long muttered about the 'treason' of the home front, and the later 'stab in the back' legend was well established by the summer of 1918. It was clear that the Supreme Command now wanted to saddle the civilian population with the blame and the politicians with the responsibility for military defeat. On the army's initiative the poisoned chalice of the imperial chancellorship was handed to the liberal-minded Crown Prince Max of Baden, whose cabinet was drawn from members of the three parties that had supported the Peace Resolution. Just weeks before the Empire collapsed, Philipp Scheidemann became its first Social-Democratic minister.

On 3 October, the day of his appointment, Prince Max performed the immediate task required of him by the army when he signed a telegram to the Allies sueing for peace. The 'October reforms' followed, measures that had been blocked for decades but suddenly sailed through the system. The Prussian three-class franchise was abolished, the army brought under parliamentary control. These reforms testified to the new-found energy of the political parties, especially the SPD, under conditions of military collapse and popular discontent, but they were made possible only by the temporary abdication of the army. The possibility was real that there might still be a military coup, of the kind attempted by General Kornilov in Russia between the revolutions of February and October. We do not know how the situation might have developed, however, for at the beginning of November a revolution broke out that removed the Hohenzollern Empire.

It began with sailors' mutinies in Kiel and Wilhelmshaven when navy leaders recklessly ordered the fleet to set sail. Except for a brief engagement at Jutland, Germany's costly battleships had sat at anchor throughout the war. In the final revenge of the Tirpitz Plan on its author, they now sparked a revolution. The revolt quickly spread, as workers' and soldiers' councils modelled on the Russian Soviets were established throughout Germany. On 8 November the council in Hamburg named itself the sole authority in the city; the same day a workers', soldiers' and peasants' council pronounced Bavaria a republic. The Kaiser fled Berlin and politicians there found themselves following events in the streets. On 9 November Philipp Scheidemann proclaimed the German Republic to a large crowd in front of the Reichstag; the following day a new government of Peoples' Representatives was set up, led by another Social Democrat, Friedrich Ebert, its members drawn half from the SPD and half from the USPD. Two days later, horrified by the thought of where social unrest might lead, Ebert told a Dutch news agency that the revolution was over.[25] This piece of wishful thinking proved very wide of the mark. Elections were held for a National Assembly in January 1919 and Ebert became President the following month; in August the Weimar constitution was agreed. By then, however, the revolution had assumed more radical form. The USPD left the government even before the elections to the National Assembly, following disagreements with the SPD over social policy, attitudes towards the army, and relations with the council movement. In January there was an abortive uprising by the radical Spartacists, put down by the army with SPD support, in which Rosa Luxemburg and Karl Liebknecht were murdered. Through 1919 there was mounting discontent on the left with the course of the revolution. Support for the USPD rose; in Munich a short-lived Soviet Republic established itself. Revolutionary and counter-revolutionary challenges to the Weimar Republic continued to the end of 1923. In some parts of Germany, such as the Ruhr, there was an undeclared state of civil war between Reds and Whites, with the Social Democrats backing the forces of 'order' (army and Free Corps irregulars) against the radical left.

The SPD has been heavily criticized by historians for what it did and failed to do. The party was, we are told, too ready to come to terms with the army and other elements of the élite, including Junker landowners; it failed to harness popular revolutionary forces or to complete a real transformation of German society. These strictures are perfectly logical coming from critics who would have preferred a Bolshevik Germany, or one organized on the basis of workers' control. They have a more curious ring when levelled by impeccably liberal historians not usually given to enthusiasm for the humbling of army officers or the expropriation of property. It is difficult not to feel some sympathy for the Social Democrats. Accused by the German right of stabbing the monarchy in the back, they are now more likely to be accused of not stabbing it hard enough.

The balance sheet of the SPD's role has entries in both columns. It presided over the formation of Germany's first republic, with parliamentary democracy and genuinely universal suffrage – female as well as male. There was (at least in the short term) no successful counter-revolution in Germany, as there was in Austria or Hungary, and many gains of the revolution were institutionalized under Weimar without the growing dictatorial powers assumed by the Bolsheviks in Russia. These gains included a shorter working day, works councils in heavy industry, and enhanced social welfare provisions. There are also good reasons why the SPD 'failed' to push the revolution further. It was constrained by the politics of peacemaking, notably Woodrow Wilson's preference for a 'moderate' outcome to the revolution. The continuation of the Allied blockade until the Versailles treaty was signed in June 1919, and the terrible food shortages this continued to create in Germany, made it much harder to break up Junker estates – even the USPD did not demand immediate expropriation. The postwar state of German industrial output presented a similar obstacle to wholesale socialization. Coal was a case in point. Virtually no one, including the left, was prepared to embark on a hazardous course of Leninist 'war communism'. Of course, Ebert ('I hate the social revolution like sin'[26]) was not the man to harness the radical forces unlocked by the revolution, even if he had believed it would work. But chiding SPD leaders for being too tame is like accusing a cat of not being a tiger. The party was wedded by its history to legality, order and discipline. There is a further point. It also proved very hard for the USPD – and even for the workers' and soldiers' councils – to harness the real revolutionary forces unleashed in Germany. For the latter, representing a continuation of the shop-floor and grassroots militancy that surfaced in the war, brought previously unorganized groups, especially young workers, on to the political stage. Their actions were spontaneous, their demands utopian, their impulses antipolitical. A body like the Red Army of the Ruhr was on a different wavelength from all the politicians of the left, including USPD leaders like Emil Barth. Rosa Luxemburg herself, never in fact a great favourite with working-class militants, would have found it difficult to divert this radical energy into political channels.

None of this means that criticism of the SPD lacks justification. External pressure from the Allies only reinforced Ebert and his colleagues in doing what they wanted to do anyway, which was to squash the radicalism of the revolution as quickly as possible. The SPD's indecently rapid agreement with the army was a pact with the force that had dragooned workers throughout the war and now wanted socialists (along with Catholics, liberals and Jews) to bear the opprobrium of defeat. Indirectly (and sometimes directly, too) the SPD encouraged the 'stab in the back' legend. Even within the constraints of 1918–19, there was scope for a greater house-cleaning of those in the army, bureaucracy and economic élites who resented the disappearance of the monarchy and never accepted the republic. The persistence of these irreconcilable elements beneath the democratic surface of Weimar was a heavy burden on the republic. It weakened democracy and helped to prepare the way for Hitler. When economic crisis came in 1929, the Nazis were able to mobilize the alienated peasantry, petty bourgeoisie and middle classes, who were too demoralized to resist the revolution in 1918 but never showed much enthusiasm for its outcome. Hitler thus continued what had been begun by the pre-1914 right and carried further by the Fatherland Party. The counter-revolution in Germany came later than it did in Austria or Hungary, but was all the more vicious. The liberal critique of the SPD is not that it failed to carry out revolution red in tooth and claw, but that it did too little to create the underlying conditions for parliamentary democracy. To that indictment might be added the fact that the SPD's actions during the revolution helped to create bitterness and division on the left, with disastrous consequences later.

The causes of the Weimar Republic's collapse and Hitler's rise to power lie beyond the scope of this book. But it is worth concluding with a brief look at what nineteenth-century Germany contributed – and did not contribute – to the coming of the Third Reich. There is a natural desire to believe that large and terrible events have deep-rooted origins. It is therefore important not to underestimate the importance of the short-term, particularly at moments when history seems to have speeded up, as it did between the outbreak of the First World War and Hitler's appointment as German chancellor less than nineteen years later. The war marked a watershed in German history. In countless ways, the years 1914–18 spawned new elements in German political life. Consider, for example, the brutalizing effect of the trenches, the settlement plans for eastern Europe, or the giddy new heights reached by hypernationalism, which was then thwarted by defeat. No less significant was the vicious twist given to anti-Semitism, first by the black-market rumours of 'Jewish speculation', then by the scapegoating of Jews for defeat as part of the stab-in-the-back legend. The list of new elements in the political equation could be extended almost indefinitely. It would include the obvious (resentment over the Versailles treaty), and the far from obvious – such as the fact that the war was responsible both for the former army trucks that transported Hitler's Brownshirts, and for radicalizing many of the small businessmen who made them available. Then, after the war, came a period of revolution and counter-revolution that further helped to poison the politics of the 1920s.

And yet, even burdened with these and many other encumbrances, the Weimar Republic was not doomed. Its most brilliant recent historian has rightly reminded us that the republic did not just have a beginning and an end; its difficulties, and its ultimate failure, deserve to be treated in their own right, not passed over briefly as a prelude to National Socialism – or a postscript to Imperial Germany.[27] Only with the perfect vision of hindsight do we know that it was to be a democratic interlude. The decisions of party politicians, the behaviour of élites, the cumulative effect of crises in different spheres, the impact of the world depression, the ability of the Nazis to exploit popular discontent – all affected the fate of the republic. The Third Reich was emphatically not the 'accident' that many German historians used to favour as an explanation, but contingency was important in bringing it about. One of the criticisms that can be made of more recent German historians who have talked about a German 'special path', or *Sonderweg*, is their over-insistence on a particular, fateful trajectory in modern German history stretching back into the nineteenth century.[28] There is no straight line running from 1848, or Bismarck, to Hitler.

Of course there were genuine continuities that linked the Third Reich to the period of German history considered in this book. Ideologically, the Nazi hodgepodge contained numerous elements that represented a radicalized but recognizable version of pre-1914 sentiments. National Socialism managed to reconcile, at least rhetorically, two powerful and conflicting impulses of the later nineteenth century, and to benefit from each. One was the infatuation with the modern and the technocratic, where there is evident continuity from Wilhelmine Germany to Nazi eugenicists and *Autobahn* builders; the other was the 'cultural revolt' against modernity and machine-civilization, pressed into use by the Nazis as part of their appeal to educated élites and provincial philistines alike. Similar continuities – habits of mind and conscious borrowing – can be found if we turn to more obviously political areas. Starting with German historians writing after 1945, there have always been those who wanted to separate National Socialism from the mainstream of German political tradition. Hence the depiction of Hitler as demonic snake-charmer, seducing the German people with a novel kind of theatrical politics. But such a view disregards important political legacies of nineteenth-century Germany that weakened Weimar and helped National Socialism to succeed: the tendency to think in friend-foe categories, the longing to transcend interest politics, the hankering after a strong man. The role played by extraparliamentary élite groups in helping Hitler to power points to another continuity. Indeed, we can go further. The earlier political methods used by these groups strikingly prefigured Nazi use of the 'big lie'. From the prewar Agrarian League to the Fatherland Party, the German right showed a talent for political dishonesty Goebbels himself might almost have envied. Almost, but not quite: for the point about the conservative élites is that they were ultimately outdemagogued by the greatest demagogues of them all. The movement of former right-wing voters to the Nazis was the revenge of the peasantry and 'little men' on those who had long misled them for political advantage. That was why the élites were forced to come to terms with Hitler, in the belief that they could control him.

These continuities were all real, and it would be wilful to disregard them. But what must be equally insisted on is the danger of foreshortening our perspective, seeing only those things that pointed ahead to 1933. Imperial Germany before the guns of August was no golden age, but the complex tendencies at work in it pointed towards different potential futures: towards reform as well as authoritarianism, social emancipation as well as repression, cultural diversity as well as culture driven into exile. The Nazis emphasized the things they approved of in the German state created in the nineteenth century (order, discipline, national-racial sentiment), while ignoring or denouncing other central characteristics (the rule of law, developing political parties, a largely free press). We should not do the same, or fail to recognize the depth of Nazi loathing for much of what the Kaiser's Germany stood for. The 'National Revolution' inaugurated in 1933 was spurious in countless ways, but it did signal a willed and deliberate break with many values and structures of pre-1914 as well as post-1918 Germany.

NOTES

PREFACE

1. 'The Germans and the French',
   in C. von Clausewitz, *Historical
   and Political Writings*, ed. P. Paret
   and D. Moran (Princeton, NJ,
   1992), pp. 250–62.
2. Quoted in James J. Sheehan,
   'What is German History?
   Reflections on the Role of the
   Nation in German History and
   Historiography', *Journal of
   Modern History*, 53 (1981), p. 1.
3. T. Nipperdey, *Deutsche Geschichte
   1800–1866* (Munich, 1983);
   Deutsche Geschichte 1866–1918, 2
   vols (Munich, 1990, 1992); H.-U.
   Wehler, *Deutsche
   Gesellschaftsgeschichte*, 3 vols
   (Munich, 1987–95).

PROLOGUE: Germany in the
Late Eighteenth Century

1. H. Rebel. 'Why not "Old
   Marie" . . . or someone very
   much like her? A reassessment
   of the question about the
   Grimms' contributors from a
   social historical perspective',
   Social History, 13 (1988), pp. 1–
   24.
2. H. Schelle, *Chronik eines
   Bauernlebens vor zweihundert
   Jahren* (Rosenheim, 1988); C.
   Huerkamp, *Der Aufstieg der
   Ärzte im 19. Jahrhundert*
   (Göttingen, 1985), p. 40; R.
   Schulte, 'Infanticide in Rural
   Bavaria in the Nineteenth
   Century', in H. Medick and
   D. W. Sabean (eds), *Interest and
   Emotion* (Cambridge, 1984), pp.
   91–2.
3. D. W. Sabean, *Property,
   Production, and Family in
   Neckarhausen, 1700–1870*
   (Cambridge, 1990), p. 381.
4. P. Marschalck,
   *Bevölkerungsgeschichte
   Deutschlands im 19. und 20.
   Jahrhundert* (Frankfurt, 1984),
   p. 20; G. Göckenjan,
   'Altersbilder als Konzepte
   sozialer Praxis in deutschen
   Zeitschriften des 18. und 19.
   Jahrhunderts', *Archiv für
   Kulturgeschichte*, 75 (1993), pp.
   395–418.
5. W. Alber and J. Dornheim,
   ' "Die Fackel der Natur
   vorgetragen mit Hintansetzung
   alles Aberglaubens" ', in J. Held
   (ed.), *Kultur zwischen Bürgertum
   und Volk* (Berlin, 1983), p. 178.
6. See W. R. Lee, 'The German
   Family: A Critical Survey of the
   Current State of Historical
   Research', in R. J. Evans and
   W. R. Lee (eds), *The German
   Family* (London, 1981), p. 28.
7. Huerkamp, *Aufstieg der Ärzte*, p.
   22.
8. W. Hagen, 'The Junkers'
   Faithless Servants: Peasant
   Insubordination and the
   Breakdown of Serfdom in
   Brandenburg-Prussia, 1763–
   1811', in R. J. Evans and W. R.
   Lee (eds), *The German Peasantry*
   (London, 1986), pp. 71–101.

Also W. Schulze (ed.), *Aufstände, Revolte und Prozesse* (Stuttgart, 1983); E. Melton, 'Gutsherrschaft in East Elbian Germany and Livonia, 1500–1800: A Critique of the Model', *Central European History*, 21 (1988), pp. 315–49.

9. R. M. Berdahl, *The Politics of the Prussian Nobility* (Princeton, NJ 1988), p. 54.

10. M. Walker, *German Home Towns. Community, State and General Estate 1648–1871* (Ithaca, NY, 1971).

11. W. H. Bruford, *Germany in the Eighteenth Century* (Cambridge, 1965), p. 18; O. Lauffer, 'Ausstattung nach Stand und Rang', in *Wirtschaft und Kultur. Festschrift für Alphons Dopsch* (Leipzig, 1938), pp. 512–34.

12. C. Küther, *Räuber und Gauner in Deutschland* (Göttingen, 1976).

13. E. François, *Koblenz im 18. Jahrhundert* (Göttingen, 1982), p. 35; K. Hoppstädter and H.-W. Herrmann, *Geschichtliche Landeskunde des Saarlandes*, vol. 1 (Saarbrücken, 1960), p. 101.

14. W. Jacobeit, *Schafhaltung und Schäfer in Zentraleuropa* (East Berlin, 1961), pp. 99–111.

15. H. Metzke, 'Die soziale Mobilität der Schäfer und Hirten im nördlichen Sachsen im 17./18. Jahrhundert', *Zeitschrift für Agrargeschichte und Agrarsoziologie*, 41 (1993), pp. 152–3.

16. C. M. Rose, 'Empire and Territories at the End of the Old Reich', in J. A. Vann and S. W. Rowan (eds), *The Old Reich* (Brussels, 1974), pp. 61–76.

17. E. François, *Die unsichtbare Grenze. Protestanten und Katholiken in Augsburg 1648–1806* (Sigmaringen, 1991).

18. See B. Diestelkamp, *Das Reichskammergericht in der deutschen Geschichte* (Cologne and Vienna, 1990).

19. G. Strauss, 'The Holy Roman Empire Revisited', *Central European History*, 11 (1978), pp. 290–301; G. Benecke, *Society and Politics in Germany, 1500–1750* (London, 1974); J. A. Vann, *The Swabian Kreis* (Brussels, 1975).

20. M. Walker, *The Salzburg Transaction* (Ithaca, NY, 1992).

21. T. C. W. Blanning, *Reform and Revolution in Mainz, 1743–1806* (Cambridge, 1974).

22. C. Dipper, *Deutsche Geschichte 1648–1789* (Frankfurt, 1991), pp. 309–10.

23. Cited in J. W. Gerard, *My Four Years in Germany* (London, 1917), p. 44. The remark may be apocryphal.

24. H. Rosenberg, *Bureaucracy, Aristocracy and Autocracy. The Prussian Experience 1660–1815* (Cambridge, Mass., 1958), p. 40.

25. C. Ingrao, 'The Problem of "Enlightened Absolutism" and the German States', and E. Weis, 'Enlightenment and Absolutism in the Holy Roman Empire', both in *Journal of Modern History*, 58 (1986), supplement, pp. 161–97.

26. W. Hagen, 'The Partitions of Poland and the Crisis of the Old Regime in Prussia', *Central European History*, 9 (1976), p. 120, note 16.

27. G. Korff, 'Zwischen Sinnlichkeit und Kindlichkeit. Notizen zum Wandel populärer Frömmigkeit im 18. und 19. Jahrhundert', in Held (ed.), *Kultur zwischen Bürgertum und Volk*, pp. 136–48; C. Ingrao,

'The Smaller German States', in H. M. Scott (ed.), *Enlightened Absolutism* (London, 1990), p. 241.

28. Anonymous author in 1755, probably the later General G. D. von der Groeben: P. Paret, *Yorck and the Era of Prussian Reform 1807–1815* (Princeton, NJ, 1966), p. 18.

29. H. C. Johnson, *Frederick the Great and His Officials* (New Haven, 1973).

30. M. Raeff, *The Well-Ordered Police State. Social and Institutional Change through Law in the Germanies and Russia, 1600–1800* (New Haven, 1983).

31. C. Ingrao, *The Hessian Mercenary State* (Cambridge, 1987).

32. H. Schissler, 'The Junkers: Notes on the Social and Historical Significance of the Agrarian Elite in Prussia', in R. G. Moeller (ed.), *Peasants and Lords in Modern Germany* (London, 1986), pp. 27–8.

33. O. Burkart, 'Die Zusammensetzung des Württembergischen Landtags in der historischen Entwicklung', diss. (Würzburg, 1922), p. 3.

34. The phrase comes from Fernand Braudel. See *Capitalism and Material Life 1400–1800* (London, 1974), pp. 37–54.

35. See E. Boserup, *The Conditions of Agricultural Growth: Economics of Agrarian Change under Population Pressure* (Chicago, 1965).

36. F. Mendels, 'Proto-industrialization: The First Phase of the Industrialization Process', *Journal of Economic History*, 32

(1972); P. Kriedte, H. Medick and J. Schlumbohm, *Industrialization before Industrialization. Rural Industry in the Genesis of Capitalism* (Cambridge, 1981).

37. S. Hochstadt, 'Migration in Preindustrial Germany', *Central European History*, 16 (1983), pp. 223–4.

38. M. Stürmer (ed.), *Herbst des alten Handwerks. Meister, Gesellen und Obrigkeit im 18. Jahrhundert* (Munich, 1986).

39. H. Kellenbenz, *Deutsche Wirtschaftsgeschichte*, vol. 1 (Munich, 1977), p. 331.

40. Walker, *German Home Towns*, pp. 119–33.

41. H.-W. Hahn, *Altständisches Bürgertum zwischen Beharrung und Wandel. Wetzlar 1689–1870* (Munich, 1991).

42. See Blanning, *Reform and Revolution*, on Mainz.

43. J. Gagliardo, *Germany under the Old Regime* (London, 1991), p. 223.

44. D. Hertz, *Jewish High Society in Old Regime Berlin* (New Haven, 1988).

45. R. Kuhnert, *Urbanität auf dem Lande. Badereisen nach Pyrmont im 18. Jahrhundert* (Göttingen, 1984).

46. C. E. McClelland, *State, Society and University in Germany 1700–1914* (Cambridge, 1980), p. 67.

47. H. West, 'Göttingen and Weimar: The Organization of Knowledge and Social Theory in Eighteenth-Century Germany', *Central European History*, 11 (1978), pp. 150–61.

48. See W. Griep and H.-W. Jäger (eds), *Reisen und soziale Realität am Ende des 18. Jahrhunderts* (Heidelberg, 1984); and idem,

*Reisen im 18. Jahrhundert. Neue
Untersuchungen* (Heidelberg,
1986).

49. For an English version, see H.
Reiss (ed.), *Kant's Political
Writings* (Cambridge, 1970).

50. H. Brunschwig, *Enlightenment
and Romanticism in
Eighteenth-century Prussia*
(Chicago, 1974), p. 7.

51. See J. Whaley, 'The Protestant
Enlightenment in Germany', in
R. Porter and M. Teich (eds),
*The Enlightenment in National
Context* (Cambridge, 1981), p.
110.

52. Brunschwig, *Enlightenment and
Romanticism*, p. 187; and on the
larger context, R. Porter,
'Making Faces: Physiognomy
and Fashion in
Eighteenth-Century England',
Études Anglaises, 4 (1985), pp.
385–96.

53. C. B. A. Behrens, *Society,
Government and the
Enlightenment. The Experiences of
Eighteenth-Century France and
Prussia* (New York, 1985), p.
179.

54. J. Melton, *Absolutism and the
Eighteenth-Century Origins of
Compulsory Schooling in Prussia
and Austria* (New York, 1988).

55. N. Elias, *Mozart: Portrait of a
Genius* (Oxford, 1993).

56. R. Engelsing, *Der Bürger als
Leser* (Stuttgart, 1974), pp.
256–67.

57. Cited in R. Szporluk,
*Communism and Nationalism: Karl
Marx versus Friedrich List*
(Oxford, 1988), p. 25.

58. G. Birtsch, 'Freiheit und
Eigentum', in R. Vierhaus (ed.),
Eigentum und Verfassung
(Göttingen, 1972), p. 192.

59. See U. Frevert, 'Tatenarm und

Gedankenvoll? Bürgertum in
Deutschland 1807–1820', in H.
Berding *et al* (eds), *Deutschland
und Frankreich im Zeitalter der
Revolution* (Frankfurt, 1989).

60. H. Dippel, *Germany and the
American Revolution, 1770–1800*
(Chapel Hill, NC, 1977). For a
more positive evaluation of the
German communal-'republican'
tradition, emphasizing 'country'
versus court, people versus
authority, see H. Zückert,
'Republikanismus in der
Reichsstadt des 18.
Jahrhunderts', in G. Birtsch
(ed.), *Patriotismus* (Hamburg,
1991), pp. 53–74; P. Nolte,
'Bürgerideal, Gemeinde und
Republik. "Klassischer
Republikanismus" im frühen
deutschen Liberalismus',
Historische Zeitschrift, 254 (1992),
pp. 609–56.

CHAPTER ONE: In the Shadow
of France

1. W. Kreutz, 'Von der
"deutschen" zur "europäischen"
Perspektive. Neuerscheinungen
zu den Auswirkungen der
Französischen Revolution in
Deutschland und der
Habsburger Monarchie', *Neue
Politische Literatur*, 31 (1986), pp.
415–41.

2. Wehler, *Deutsche
Gesellschaftsgeschichte*, vol. 1, p.
533.

3. Johann Wilhelm Archenholz,
cited in K. Epstein, *The Genesis
of German Conservatism*
(Princeton, NJ, 1966), p. 435.

4. A. Ruiz, 'Deutsche
Reisebeschreibungen über
Frankreich im Zeitalter der
Französischen Revolution

(1789–1799). Ein Überblick', in A. Maczak and J. Teuteberg (eds), *Reiseberichte als Quellen europäischer Kulturgeschichte* (Wolfenbüttel, 1982), pp. 229–51.

5. K. O. von Aretin and K. Härter (eds), *Revolution und Konservatives Beharren. Das Alte Reich und die Französische Revolution* (Mainz, 1990): contributions by Botsch, Lüsebrink, Möllney and Reichardt; H.-J. Lüsebrink and R. Reichardt, *Die 'Bastille'. Zur Symbolgeschichte von Freiheit und Despotismus* (Frankfurt, 1990).

6. R. Paulin, *Ludwig Tieck* (Oxford, 1985), p. 11.

7. Brunschwig, *Enlightenment and Romanticism*, p. 176.

8. Z. Batscha and J. Garber (eds), *Von der ständischen zur bürgerlichen Gesellschaft* (Frankfurt, 1981), pp. 373–90.

9. H. Berding (ed.), *Soziale Unruhen in Deutschland während der Französischen Revolution* (Göttingen, 1988).

10. Epstein, *Genesis of German Conservatism*, pp. 367, 369.

11. C. Ingrao, *The Habsburg Monarchy 1618–1815* (Cambridge, 1994), pp. 220–5, 230–4.

12. C. Ulbrich, 'Traditionale Bindung, revolutionäre Erfahrung und soziokultureller Wandel. Denting 1790–1796', in Aretin and Härter (eds), *Revolution*, pp. 113–30.

13. K. Härter, 'Der Reichstag im Revolutionsjahr 1789', in Aretin and Härter (eds), *Revolution*, p. 171.

14. For a systematic comparison between France and Prussia, see Behrens, *Society, Government and Enlightenment*, esp. Part Three.

15. For a review of the 'German Jacobins' literature, from a prominent sceptic, see T. C. W. Blanning, *The French Revolution in Germany* (Cambridge, 1983), pp. 9–15.

16. See, for example, the works cited in note 5.

17. E. Wangermann, *From Joseph II to the Jacobin Trials. Government Policy and Public Opinion in the Habsburg Dominions in the Period of the French Revolution* (Oxford, 1959).

18. K. O. von Aretin, 'Deutschland und die Französische Revolution', in Aretin and Härter (eds), *Revolution*, p. 17.

19. Paulin, *Tieck*, p. 43.

20. J.-P. Bertaud, cited in Blanning, *French Revolution in Germany*, p. 54, note 118.

21. Nipperdey, *Deutsche Geschichte 1800–1866*, p. 11.

22. V. Press, 'Österreich, das Reich und die Eindämmung der Revolution in Deutschland', in Berding (ed.), *Soziale Unruhen in Deutschland während der Französischen Revolution*, p. 237.

23. T. C. W. Blanning, *The Origins of the French Revolutionary Wars* (London, 1986).

24. C. von Clausewitz, *On War*, ed. M. Howard and P. Paret (Princeton, NJ, 1976), pp. 591–2 (Book 8, Ch. 3).

25. Blanning, *French Revolution in Germany*, p. 87.

26. S. Woolf, 'French Civilization and Ethnicity in the Napoleonic Empire', *Past and Present*, 124 (1989), p. 108.

27. G. Best, *War and Society in Revolutionary Europe* (London, 1982), pp. 113–14; Behrens, *Society, Government and the Enlightenment*, p. 191.

28. J. Walter, *The Diary of a Napoleonic Foot Soldier*, ed. M. Raeff (New York, 1993).

29. R. Dufraisse, 'Französische Zollpolitik, Kontinentalsperre und Kontinentalsystem im Deutschland der napoleonischen Zeit', in H. Berding and H.-P. Ullmann (eds), *Deutschland zwischen Revolution und Restauration* (Düsseldorf, 1981), pp. 328–52.

30. G. Adelman, 'Structural Change in the Rhenish Linen and Cotton Trades at the Outset of Industrialization', in F. Crouzet, W. H. Chaloner and W. M. Stern (eds), *Essays in European Economic History 1789–1914* (London, 1969), p. 87.

31. Summarized in Wehler, *Deutsche Gesellschaftsgeschichte*, vol. 1, pp. 486–505.

32. Rosenberg, *Bureaucracy, Aristocracy and Autocracy*, p. 161.

33. N. Hampson, *The Life and Opinions of Maximilien Robespierre* (London, 1974), p. 100.

34. Blanning, *French Revolution in Germany*, p. 170.

35. G. Rudé, *Revolutionary Europe 1783–1815* (London, 1964), p. 256.

36. H. Berding, *Napoleonische Herrschafts- und Gesellschaftspolitik im Königreich Westfalen 1807–1813* (Göttingen, 1973).

37. P. Nolte, *Staatsbildung als Gesellschaftsreform: Politische Reformen in Preussen und den süddeutschen Staaten 1800–1820* (Frankfurt, 1990).

38. J. A. Vann, 'Habsburg Policy and the War of 1809', *Central European History*, 7 (1974), pp. 294–5.

39. Rosenberg, *Bureaucracy, Aristocracy and Autocracy*, p. 203.

40. See, for example, Wehler, *Deutsche Gesellschaftsgeschichte*, vol. 1, Part Two ('Defensive Modernisierung').

41. Harnisch cited in A. J. LaVopa, *Prussian Schoolteachers: Profession and Office, 1763–1848* (Chapel Hill, NC, 1980), p. 40; Hardenberg in L. Krieger, *The German Idea of Freedom* (Chicago, 1957), p. 158.

42. Paret, *Yorck*, pp. 118–19.

43. Wehler, *Deutsche Gesellschaftsgeschichte*, vol. 1, p. 523.

44. M. Jeismann, *Das Vaterland der Feinde. Studien zum nationalen Feindbegriff und Selbstverständnis in Deutschland und Frankreich, 1792–1918* (Stuttgart, 1992).

45. Walter, *Diary of a Napoleonic Foot Soldier*, p. 105.

CHAPTER TWO: Germany in Transition

1. ... 'Erlöse uns nur/Von jenem Zwitterwesen,/Von jenem Gamaschenrittertum,/Das ekelhaft ein Gemisch ist/Von gotischem Wahn und modernem Lug,/Das weder Fleisch noch Fisch ist.': H. Heine, *Deutschland, ein Wintermärchen*, Kap. XVII.

2. L. J. Baack, *Christian Bernstorff and Prussia: Diplomacy and Reform Conservatism 1818–1832* (New Brunswick, NJ, 1980).

3. A. J. P. Taylor, *The Habsburg Monarchy* (London, 1964), p. 53.

4. M. Müller, *Geschichte der Stadt St Wendel* (St Wendel, 1927), pp. 189–91.

5. T. Mann, *Lotte in Weimar*

(Harmondsworth, Middx., 1968), p. 198.

6. T. Fontane, *Wanderungen durch die Mark Brandenburg*, vol. 1 (Munich, 1987 edn.), pp. 116–18.

7. *Das Caroussel. 1846. Faksimilie-Ausgabe* (Zug and New York, 1985).

8. For this exchange, see D. Barclay, *Frederick William IV and the Prussian Monarchy, 1840–1861* (Oxford, 1995), pp. 49–50.

9. L. J. Flockerzie, 'State-Building and Nation-Building in the "Third Germany": Saxony after the Congress of Vienna', *Central European History*, 24 (1991), pp. 281, 283–4.

10. See H. Rubner, *Forstgeschichte im Zeitalter der industriellen Revolution* (Berlin, 1967). For the motif of the 'northern' forest, see many of the great works of Caspar David Friedrich, or those of his follower, Carl Gustav Carus.

11. E. D. Brose, *The Politics of Technological Change in Prussia* (Princeton, NJ, 1993); W. Fischer, *Der Staat und die Anfänge der Industrialisierung in Baden 1800–1850* (Berlin, 1962).

12. V. Valentin, *Geschichte der deutschen Revolution von 1848–9*, vol. 1 (Berlin, 1930), p. 145.

13. W. Zorn, 'Gesellschaft und Staat im Bayern des Vormärz', in W. Conze (ed.), *Staat und Gesellschaft im deutschen Vormärz 1815–1848* (Stuttgart, 1962), p. 132.

14. H. Henning, *Die deutsche Beamtenschaft im 19. Jahrhundert* (Wiesbaden, 1984), p. 44.

15. J. R. Gillis, *The Prussian Bureaucracy in Crisis* (Stanford, Calif., 1971), pp. 18–66.

16. R. Koselleck, *Preußen zwischen Reform und Revolution* (Stuttgart, 1975).

17. A. Lüdtke, 'The Role of State Violence in the Period of Transition to Industrial Capitalism: The Example of Prussia from 1815 to 1848', *Social History*, 4 (1979), p. 202.

18. Sabean, *Property, Production, and Family*, p. 50.

19. Berdahl, *Politics of the Prussian Nobility*, pp. 180–1.

20. Nipperdey, *Deutsche Geschichte 1800–1866*, p. 148.

21. H. Rosenberg, 'Die Pseudodemokratisierung der Rittergutsbesitzerklasse', in Rosenberg, *Machteliten und Wirtschaftskonjunkturen* (Göttingen, 1978), p. 88.

22. D. Blasius, *Bürgerliche Gesellschaft und Kriminalität: Zur Sozialgeschichte Preußens im Vormärz* (Göttingen, 1976).

23. Handspinners lost an estimated 50 per cent of their income in 1835–50, 75 per cent in eastern Westphalia and Lower Silesia: R. Tilly, *Vom Zollverein zum Industriestaat* (Munich, 1990), p. 11.

24. See W. Abel (ed.), *Handwerksgeschichte in neuer Sicht* (Göttingen, 1978); F. Lenger, *Sozialgeschichte der deutschen Handwerker seit 1800* (Frankfurt, 1988).

25. F.-W. Henning, 'Industrialisierung und dörfliche Einkommensmöglichkeiten', in H. Kellenbenz (ed.), *Agrarisches Nebengewerbe und Formen der Reagrarisierung* (Stuttgart, 1975), p. 159.

26. See R. Szporluk, *Communism and Nationalism: Karl Marx versus*

Friedrich List (Oxford, 1988), pp. 96–151.

27. See M. Riedel, 'Gesellschaft, bürgerliche', in W. Conze *et al* (eds), *Geschichtliche Grundbegriffe*, vol. 2 (Stuttgart, 1975), pp. 719–800.

28. J. J. Sheehan, 'Conflict and Cohesion among German Elites in the Nineteenth Century', in R. Bezucha (ed.), *Modern European Social History* (Lexington, Mass., 1972), p. 4.

29. F. Lenger, *Zwischen Kleinbürgertum und Proletariat* (Göttingen, 1986), pp. 32–4.

30. L. O'Boyle, 'The Problem of an Excess of Educated Men in Western Europe, 1800–1850', *Journal of Modern History*, 42 (1970), pp. 472–95.

31. W. Conze, 'Vom "Pöbel" zum "Proletariat"', in H.-U. Wehler (ed.), *Moderne Deutsche Sozialgeschichte* (Cologne and Berlin, 1966), pp. 111–36; J. Kocka, *Weder Stand noch Klasse* (Bonn, 1990).

32. L. E. Lee, 'Baden between Revolutions: State-Building and Citizenship, 1800–1848', *Central European History*, 24 (1991), p. 255.

33. R. J. Goldstein, *Political Repression in 19th-Century Europe* (London, 1983), p. 70.

34. See F. Ohles, *Germany's Rude Awakening. Censorship in the Land of the Brothers Grimm* (Kent, Ohio, 1992).

35. L. E. Lee, 'The Baden Constitution of 1818', *Central European History*, 8 (1975), p. 109.

36. Zorn, 'Gesellschaft und Staat in Bayern', p. 128.

37. Goldstein, *Political Repression*, pp. 29–31.

38. R. Michaelis-Jena, *The Brothers Grimm* (London, 1970), p. 115.

39. Börne's 'Letters from Paris', cited in H. Brandt, *Parlamentarismus in Württemberg 1819–1870* (Düsseldorf, 1987), p. 203.

40. R. Engelsing, *Analphabetentum und Lektüre* (Stuttgart, 1973), p. 127.

41. H. Bausinger, 'Bürgerlichkeit und Kultur', in J. Kocka (ed.), *Bürger und Bürgerlichkeit im 19. Jahrhundert* (Göttingen, 1987), p. 135.

42. See K. Biedermann, *Mein Leben und ein Stück Zeitgeschichte* (Breslau, 1886), pp. 117–35.

43. H. Rotteck and C. T. Welcker (eds.), *Staats-Lexikon, oder: Encyklopädie der Staatswissenschaften*, 2nd. edn., 12 vols. (Altona, 1845–9), vol. 12, p. 368.

44. J. Diefendorf, *Businessmen and Politics in the Rhineland, 1789–1834* (Princeton, NJ, 1980), pp. 299, 344.

45. See Welcker's letter of 1842, cited in Biedermann, *Mein Leben*, vol. 1, p. 75; on Sallet, see 'Die neue deutsche Lyrik', in *Die Gegenwart*, vol. 8 (Leipzig, 1853), pp. 50–1.

46. R. Wirtz, 'Die Begriffsverwirrung der Bauern im Odenwald', in D. Puls (ed.), *Wahrnehmungsformen und Protestverhalten* (Frankfurt, 1979), pp. 81–104; J. Mooser, 'Religion und Sozialer Protest. Erweckungsbewegung und ländliche Unterschichten im Vormärz am Beispiel Minden-Ravensburg', in H. Volkmann and J. Bergmann (eds), *Sozialer Protest* (Opladen, 1984), pp. 304–24; R. Schenda,

Volk ohne Buch (Frankfurt, 1970),
pp. 430–1.

47. Gailus, 'Rauchen in den
    Straßen', p. 19.

CHAPTER THREE:
The Revolutions of 1848–9

1. H. V. von Unruh, *Erfahrungen
   aus den letzten drei Jahren*
   (Magdeburg, 1851), p. 95.
2. B. A. Boyd, 'Rudolf Virchow:
   The Scientist as Citizen', diss,
   University of N. Carolina,
   Chapel Hill (1981), pp. 21–4.
3. M. Wegmann-Fetsch, *Die
   Revolution von 1848 im
   Grossherzogtum Oldenburg*
   (Oldenburg, 1974), p. 27.
4. Wehler, *Deutsche
   Gesellschaftsgeschichte*, vol. 2, p.
   707.
5. A. Wolff, *Berliner
   Revolutionschronik*, vol. 1 (Berlin,
   1851), p. 298.
6. Hans Christoph von Gagern to
   Heinrich von Gagern,
   Darmstadt, 23 March 1848: H.
   von Gagern, *Das Leben des
   Generals Friedrich von Gagern*,
   vol. 2 (Leipzig and Heidelberg,
   1857), p. 660.
7. W. Schivelbusch, *Disenchanted
   Night: The Industrialization of
   Light in the Nineteenth Century*
   (Berkeley, Calif., 1988), pp. 110–
   14; D. Blackbourn, 'Politics as
   Theatre', in Blackbourn,
   Populists and Patricians (London,
   1987), pp. 246–64.
8. Three examples: W. Kaschuba
   and C. Lipp, *1848 – Provinz und
   Revolution* (Tübingen, 1979); J.
   Sperber, *Rhineland Radicals*
   (Princeton, NJ 1991); P. Nolte,
   *Gemeindebürgertum und
   Liberalismus in Baden 1800–
   1850* (Göttingen, 1994), ch. 5.

9. M. Schubert, 'Lage und
   politisches Handeln Leipziger
   Dienstmädchen während der
   industriellen Revolution',
   *Jahrbuch für Regionalgeschichte
   und Landeskunde*, 18 (1991/2), p.
   115.
10. L. Bamberger, *Erinnerungen*
    (Berlin, 1899), pp. 116, 120,
    reprinting 1848 speeches.
11. C. Elbinger, *Witz und Satire
    Anno 1848* (Vienna, 1948), p. 54.
12. W. Siemann, *Die deutsche
    Revolution von 1848/49*
    (Frankfurt, 1985), p. 126.
13. F. Engels, *Germany: Revolution
    and Counter-Revolution*, in *The
    German Revolutions*, ed. L.
    Krieger (Chicago, 1967), p.
    169.
14. T. Schnurre, *Die
    württembergischen Abgeordneten in
    der konstituierenden deutschen
    Nationalversammlung zu
    Frankfurt am Main* (Stuttgart,
    1912), p. 30.
15. Tilly, *Vom Zollverein*, p. 35.
16. W. Buzengeiger, *Die
    Zusammenhänge zwischen den
    wirtschaftlichen Verhältnissen und
    der politischen Entwicklung in
    Württemberg um die Mitte des 19.
    Jahrhunderts* (Ulm, 1949), p. 49.
17. Nolte, *Gemeindebürgertum*, pp.
    305–90.
18. Elbinger, *Witz und Satire*, p.
    143.
19. G. C. Craig, *The Politics of the
    Prussian Army 1640–1945*
    (Oxford, 1955), p. 107.
20. Fundamental here is M. Gailus,
    Strasse und Brot (Göttingen,
    1990), and in English, 'Food
    Riots in Germany in the late
    1840s', *Past and Present*, 145
    (1994), pp. 157–93.
21. Siemann, *Die deutsche Revolution*,
    p. 194.

22. A. Rapp, 'Württembergische Politiker von 1848 im Kampf um die deutsche Frage', *Württembergische Vierteljahrshefte für Landesgeschichte*, 25 (1916), p. 577.

23. Siemann, *Die deutsche Revolution*, p. 205.

24. Biedermann, *Mein Leben*, vol. 1, p. 385.

25. As Jonathan Sperber does in *Rhineland Radicals*, Part Three: 'Toward a Second Revolution'.

26. C. Kleßmann, 'Zur Sozialgeschichte der Reichsverfassungskampagne von 1849', *Historische Zeitschrift*, 218 (1974), pp. 283–337.

27. Biedermann, *Mein Leben*, vol. 1, p. 225.

28. E. G. Franz, *Das Amerikabild der deutschen Revolution von 1848/49* (Heidelberg, 1958), pp. 98–133.

29. Bamberger, *Erinnerungen*, pp. 140–1; Sperber, *Rhineland Radicals*, pp. 322–4.

30. I. Weber-Kellermann, *Landleben im 19. Jahrhundert* (Munich, 1988), pp. 38–9; R. Muhs, 'Heckermythos und Revolutionsforschung', *Zeitschrift für die Geschichte des Oberrheins*, 134 (1986), pp. 422–41. Blum was a comparable folk hero.

31. M. Agulhon, *The Republic in the Village* (Cambridge, 1982); Engels, *Revolution and Counter-Revolution*, pp. 164–5, 230–4.

32. On communal sentiment, see D. Blackbourn, *Class, Religion and Local Politics* (London and New Haven, 1980), pp. 68–72 (on Württemberg); Nolte, *Gemeindebürgertum* (on Baden).

33. Gagern, *Leben des Generals Friedrich von Gagern*, p. 640.

CHAPTER FOUR: Economy and Society Transformed

1. R. Spree, *Wachstumszyklen der deutschen Wirtschaft von 1840 bis 1880* (Berlin, 1977); R. Tilly, 'The Take-Off in Germany', in E. Angermann and M.-L. Frings (eds), *Oceans Apart? Comparing Germany and the United States* (Stuttgart, 1981), pp. 47–59; Wehler, *Deutsche Gesellschaftsgeschichte*, vol. 2, pp. 589–640.

2. Spree, *Wachstumszyklen*, esp. pp. 320–30.

3. Tilly, *Vom Zollverein*, pp. 50–1.

4. H. Kellenbenz, *Deutsche Wirtschaftsgeschichte*, vol. 2 (Munich, 1981), pp. 45, 105; W. Treue, *Wirtschafts- und Technikgeschichte Preussens* (Berlin and New York, 1984), p. 563.

5. W. Berg, *Wirtschaft und Gesellschaft in Deutschland und Großbritannien im Übergang zum 'organisierten Kapitalismus'.* (Berlin, 1984).

6. R. Berthold et al. (eds), *Produktivkräfte in Deutschland 1800 bis 1870* (Berlin, 1990), pp. 362–70.

7. R. Fremdling, *Eisenbahnen und deutsches Wirtschaftswachstum 1840–1879* (Dortmund, 1975); Fremdling, 'Railroads and German Economic Growth. A Leading Sector Analysis with a Comparison to the United States and Great Britain', *Journal of Economic History*, 37 (1977), pp. 583–604.

8. H. J. Tümmers, *Der Rhein: Ein Europäischer Fluss und seine Geschichte* (Munich, 1994), p. 141; Berthold et al. (eds), *Produktivkräfte*, p. 395.

9. Henning, 'Industrialisierung und dörfliche Einkommensmöglichkeiten', p. 159.

10. S. Pollard (ed.), *Region und Industrialisierung* (Göttingen, 1980); F. Blaich (ed.), *Entwicklungsprobleme einer Region: Das Beispiel Rheinland und Westfalen im 19. Jahrhundert* (Berlin, 1981); H. Kiesewetter and R. Fremdling (eds), *Staat, Region und Industrialisierung* (Ostfildern, 1985).

11. H. Horch, *Der Wandel der Gesellschafts- und Herrschaftsstrukturen in der Saarregion während der Industrialisierung* (St Ingbert, 1985), p. 225.

12. For the classic argument, see H. Rosenberg, *Große Depression und Bismarckzeit* (Berlin, 1967); for criticism, see V. Hentschel, *Wirtschaft und Wirtschaftspolitik im wilhelminischen Deutschland* (Stuttgart, 1980); G. Eley, 'Hans Rosenberg and the Great Depression of 1873–96', in Eley, *From Unification to Nazism* (London, 1986), pp. 23–41.

13. K. N. Conzen, 'German-Americans and the Invention of Ethnicity', in F. Trommler and J. McVeigh (eds), *America and the Germans*, vol. 1 (Philadelphia, 1985), pp. 131–47, and Conzen's *Immigrant Milwaukee* (Cambridge, Mass., 1976); S. Nadel, *Little Germany: Ethnicity, Religion and Class in New York City, 1845–1880* (Urbana and Chicago, 1990).

14. C. Viebig, *Das Weiberdorf. Roman aus der Eifel* (Berlin, 7th edn., 1901).

15. See H. J. Teuteberg (ed.), *Homo Habitans. Zur Sozialgeschichte des* ländlichen und städtischen Wohnens in der Neuzeit (Münster, 1985); C. Wischermann, *Wohnen in Hamburg vor dem ersten Weltkrieg* (Münster, 1983). More 'pessimistic': L. Niethammer and F. Brüggemeier, 'Wie wohnten Arbeiter im Kaiserreich?' *Archiv für Sozialgeschichte*, 16 (1976), pp. 61–134.

16. K. Hoppstädter, ' "Eine halbe Stunde nach der Schicht muß jeder gewaschen sein". Die alten Schlafhäuser und die Ranzenmänner', *Saarbrücker Bergmannskalender* (1963), p. 78.

17. E. Zenz, *Geschichte der Stadt Trier im 19. Jahrhundert*, vol. 2 (Trier, 1980), pp. 225–7.

18. R. J. Evans, *Death in Hamburg. Society and Politics in the Cholera Years* (Oxford, 1987).

19. W. H. Riehl, *Die bürgerliche Gesellschaft*, 2nd revised edn (Stuttgart and Tübingen, 1854), p. 195.

20. C. Applegate, *A Nation of Provincials*, p. 87; C. Zuckmayer, *A Part of Myself* (New York, 1970), pp. 101–3.

21. See H. Siegrist (ed.), *Bürgerliche Berufe* (Göttingen, 1988); and the articles by Michael John (lawyers) and Paul Weindling (doctors) in D. Blackbourn and R. J. Evans (eds), *The German Bourgeoisie* (London, 1991).

22. R. Elkar, *Junges Deutschland in Polemischem Zeitalter* (Düsseldorf, 1979), chs 3–5; F. Zunkel, 'Das Verhältnis des Unternehmertums zum Bildungsbürgertum zwischen Vormärz und Erstem Weltkrieg', in M. R. Lepsius (ed.), *Bildungsbürgertum im 19.*

*Jahrhundert, Teil III:
Lebensführung und ständische
Vergesellschaftung* (Stuttgart,
1992), p. 86.

23. W. Weber, *Priester der Klio*
(Frankfurt 1984), p. 73.

24. Lothar Gall has argued,
however, that businessmen
continued to regard themselves
as more truly independent than
salaried officials or professors:
see Gall, 'Die Bassermanns', in
Lepsius (ed.), *Lebensführung*, p.
110; and at length in Gall's
collective biography, *Bürgertum
in Deutschland* (Berlin, 1989).

25. K. Hausen, 'Family and
Role-Division', in R. J. Evans
and W. R. Lee (eds), *The
German Family* (London, 1981),
pp. 55–6 (Meyer quotation); R.
Virchow, *Über die Erziehung des
Weibes für seinen Beruf* (Berlin,
1865).

26. U. Engelhardt, ' "Geistig in
Fesseln"? Zur normativen
Plazierung der Frau als
"Kulturträgerin" in der
bürgerlichen Gesellschaft
während der Frühzeit der
deutschen Frauenbewegung', in
Lepsius (ed.), *Lebensführung*,
pp. 113–75; U. Frevert, '*Mann
und Weib, und Weib und Mann*'
(Munich, 1995).

27. K. Kaudelka-Hanisch, 'The
Titled Businessman', in
Blackbourn and Evans (eds.),
German Bourgeoisie, Table 3.1, p.
96.

28. R. Gellately, *The Politics of
Economic Despair. Shopkeepers
and German Politics 1890–1914*
(London, 1974), pp. 30–1, 33.

29. D. Blackbourn, 'Between
Resignation and Volatility: the
German Petty Bourgeoisie in
the Nineteenth Century', in

Blackbourn, *Populists and
Patricians*, pp. 84–113; J. Kocka,
*Die Angestellten in der deutschen
Geschichte 1850–1980*
(Göttingen, 1981).

30. U. Branding, *Die Einführung,
der Gewerbefreiheit in Bremen
und ihre Folgen* (Bremen, 1951),
pp. 89–91.

31. H. Schomerus, 'The Family
Life-cycle: A Study of Factory
Workers in Nineteenth-century
Württemberg', in Evans and
Lee (eds), *The German Family*,
p. 179.

32. Cf. the experiences recounted in
A. Kelly (ed.), *The German
Worker: Working-Class
Autobiographies from the Age of
Industrialization* (Berkeley,
Calif., 1987).

33. Lenger, *Zwischen Kleinbürgertum
und Proletariat*, p. 112.

34. J. Kocka *et al* (eds), *Familie und
soziale Plazierung* (Opladen,
1980).

35. H. Zwahr, *Zur Konstituierung des
Proletariats als Klasse* (Berlin,
1978), pp. 165–89.

36. Huerkamp, *Aufstieg der Ärzte*,
pp. 120, 162–4; U. Frevert,
*Krankheit als Politisches Problem
1770–1880* (Göttingen, 1984),
pp. 207–41.

37. U. Engelhardt, 'Zur
Entwicklung der
Streikbewegungen in der ersten
Industrialisierungsphase',
*Internationale Wissenschaftliche
Korrespondenz zur Geschichte der
deutschen Arbeiterbewegung*, 15
(1979), pp. 547–69.

CHAPTER FIVE: From
Reaction to Unification

1. M. Marx-Kruse and E. von
Campe, *Chronik der deutschen*

Jagd (Ebenhausen, 1937), pp. 275, 277–8.

2. Diefendorf, *Businessmen and Politics*, pp. 353–4; W. Gugel, *Die Wahlrechtsfrage in der Geschichte der deutschen liberalen Parteien 1848–1918* (Düsseldorf, 1958), pp. 8–20. cf. H. Rosenberg, *Machteliten*, p. 96, where the three-class franchise is described as a 'bulwark of the aristocratic authoritarian state in Prussia'.

3. E. Gatz, *Rheinische Volksmission im 19. Jahrhundert* (Düsseldorf, 1963).

4. J. Götten, *Christoph Moufang, Theologe und Politiker 1817–1890* (Mainz, 1969), p. 98.

5. See W. Siemann (ed.), *Der 'Polizeiverein' deutscher Staaten* (Tübingen, 1983); and Siemann, *'Deutschlands Ruhe, Sicherheit und Ordnung'. Die Anfänge der politischen Polizei 1806–1866* (Tübingen, 1985).

6. Gillis, *Prussian Bureaucracy in Crisis*, pp. 183–7; A. Funk, *Polizei und Rechtsstaat* (Frankfurt, 1986), pp. 60–70.

7. C. Emsley, *Policing and its Context* (London, 1983), pp. 101–2.

8. G. Grünthal, *Parlamentarismus in Preussen 1848/49–1857/58* (Düsseldorf, 1982) is an important revisionist work on this subject.

9. See T. Parent, 'Die Kölner Abgeordnetenfeste im preu-ßischen Verfassungskonflikt', in D. Düding, P. Friedemann and P. Münch (eds), *Öffentliche Festkultur* (Reinbek, 1988), pp. 259–77; and, more sceptical, T. Offermann, 'Preußischer Liberalismus zwischen

Revolution and Reichsgründung im regionalen Vergleich', in D. Langewiesche (ed.), *Liberalismus im 19. Jahrhundert* (Göttingen, 1988), pp. 109–35.

10. This and other observations in the same vein in M. Gugel, *Industrieller Aufstieg und bürgerliche Herrschaft* (Cologne, 1975), pp. 184–8.

11. U. Frevert, *'Mann und Weib, und Weib und Mann'* (Munich, 1995), pp. 83–132, Sybel quotation p. 117.

12. W. J. Mommsen, *Max Weber and German Politics* (Chicago, 1984), p. 6.

13. Full text in A. Freemantle, *The Papal Encyclicals in their Historical Context* (New York, 1956), pp. 143–52.

14. P. W. Schroeder, *Austria, Great Britain, and the Crimean War* (Ithaca, NY, 1972), esp. pp. 406–7, 418–19.

15. Schiller was variously referred to as a 'prophet' and 'Messiah'. The Schiller monument in Leipzig was dedicated as a 'high altar': R. Noltenius, 'Schiller als Führer und Heiland', in Düding *et al.* (eds), *Öffentliche Festkultur*, pp. 237–58. Schiller quotation from A. Vidler, *The Church in an Age of Revolution* (London, 1974), p. 22.

16. K. H. Börner, *Die Krise der preußischen Monarchie von 1858 bis 1862* (East Berlin, 1976), p. 63.

17. L. Gall, *Der Liberalismus als regierende Partei. Das Grossherzogtum Baden zwischen Restauration und Reichsgründung* (Wiesbaden, 1968).

18. Roon quoted in Nipperdey, *Deutsche Geschichte 1800–1866*, p. 755.

19. Langewiesche, *Liberalismus in Deutschland*, pp. 96–100.

20. Parent, 'Die Kölner Abgeordnetenfeste', p. 271.

21. Report of Lord Loftus, British Ambassador in Berlin, to Foreign Secretary Clarendon, 17 April 1869: V. Valentin, *Bismarcks Reichsgründung im Urteil englischer Diplomaten* (Amsterdam, 1937), pp. 542–3.

22. Sheehan, *German History*; D. Langewiesche, 'Reich, Nation und Staat', *Historische Zeitschrift*, 254 (1992), pp. 341–81; E. Lutz, *Zwischen Habsburg und Preußen. Deutschland 1815–1866* (Berlin, 1985).

23. P. Burg, *Die deutsche Trias in Idee und Wirklichkeit* (Stuttgart, 1989), pp. 355–9.

24. A. Biefang, *Politisches Bürgertum in Deutschland* (Düsseldorf, 1994) is an important new work on this topic, although some of the same material can be found in T. S. Hamerow, *The Social Foundations of German Unification 1858–1871: Ideas and Institutions* (Princeton, NJ, 1969).

25. Langewiesche, *Liberalismus in Deutschland*, p. 103.

26. Langewiesche, 'Reich, Nation und Staat', pp. 369–70; D. Düding, 'Die deutsche Nationalbewegung des 19. Jahrhunderts als Vereinsbewegung', *Geschichte in Wissenschaft und Unterricht*, 10/1991, pp. 620–3.

27. A. Hillgruber, *Otto von Bismarck. Gründer der europäischen Großmacht Deutsches Reich* (Göttingen, Zurich and Frankfurt, 1978), p. 67.

28. L. Gall, *Bismarck, The White Revolutionary*, 2 vols. (London, 1986), vol. 1, p. 28.

29. Ibid, p. 292.

30. H. Kohl (ed.), *Briefe Ottos von Bismarck an Schwester und Schwager* (Leipzig, 1915), p. 3.

31. P. Brandt, 'Reichsgründung', in L. Niethammer *et al.* (eds), *Bürgerliche Gesellschaft in Deutschland* (Frankfurt, 1990), p. 204; Gall, *Bismarck*, vol. 1, p. 128.

32. E. Kolb, *Der Kriegsausbruch 1870. Politische Entscheidungsprozesse und Verantwortlichkeiten in der Julikrise 1870* (Göttingen, 1970).

33. On Bismarck and Bonapartism, see H. -U. Wehler, *The German Empire 1871–1918* (Leamington Spa, 1985), pp. 55–62; M. Stürmer, *Regierung und Reichstag im Bismarckstaat* (Düsseldorf, 1974). Critics include L. Gall. 'Bismarck und der Bonapartismus', *Historische Zeitschrift*, 223 (1976), pp. 618–37, and A. Mitchell, 'Bonapartism as a Model for Bismarckian Politics', *Journal of Modern History*, 49 (1977), with comments in the same issue by O. Pflanze, C. Fohlen and M. Stürmer; O. Pflanze, 'Bismarcks Herrschaftstechnik als Problem der gegenwärtigen Historiographie', *Historische Zeitschrift*, 234 (1982), pp. 562–99.

34. Gall, *Bismarck*, vol. 1, p. 322.

35. R. W. Dill, *Der Parlamentarier Eduard Lasker und die Parlamentarische Stilentwicklung der Jahre 1867–1884* (Erlangen, 1958), pp. 64–5.

36. Report of Ambassador Buchanan to Foreign Secretary Russell, 18 June 1864: Valentin (ed.), *Bismarcks Reichsgründung,*

p. 521; Gall, *Bismarck*, vol. 1, p. 305.

37. W. M. Simon (ed.), *Germany in the Age of Bismarck* (London, 1968), pp. 111–12.

38. T. S. Hamerow, *Social Foundations of German Unification, 1858–1871: Struggles and Accomplishments* (Princeton, NJ, 1972), p. 17.

39. W. Cahn (ed.), *Aus Eduard Laskers Nachlass* (Berlin, 1902), p. 111.

40. E. J. Hobsbawm, *The Age of Capital 1848–1875* (London, 1975), p. 111.

41. G. C. Windell, *The Catholics and German Unity, 1866–71* (Minneapolis, 1954); H. Lacher, 'Das Jahr 1866', *Neue Politische Literatur*, 14 (1969), pp. 83–99, 214–31.

42. J. Bachem, *Erinnerungen eines alten Publizisten und Politikers* (Cologne, 1913), p. 133.

43. D. Fricke, *Bismarcks Prätorianer. Die Berliner Politische Polizei im Kampf gegen die deutsche Arbeiterbewegung (1871–1898)* (East Berlin, 1962), pp. 68–71; K. Frohme, *Politische Polizei und Justiz im monarchischen Deutschland* (Hamburg, 1926).

44. 'What individual warning voices have long predicted, namely that the functions of the Reich would falter and come to a standstill, has now become a commonplace': *Vossische Zeitung*, 20 Jan. 1878.

45. See, for example, the works by Wehler and Stürmer cited in note 33.

46. Rosenberg, *Grosse Depression*, pp. 132–54; H. Böhme, *Prolegomena zu einer Sozial- und Wirtschaftsgeschichte Deutschlands im 19. und 20. Jahrhundert* (Frankfurt, 1969),

pp. 70–81; Sheehan, *German Liberalism*, pp. 181–8. For a summary, see K. D. Barkin, '1878–1879: The Second Founding of the Reich, A Perspective', *German Studies Review*, 10 (1987), pp. 220–35.

47. J. F. Flynn, 'At the Threshold of Dissolution: The National Liberals and Bismarck, 1877/78', *Historical Journal*, 31 (1988), pp. 319–40; Pflanze, *Bismarck and the Development of Germany*, vol. 2, pp. 364–82.

CHAPTER SIX: Progress and its Discontents

1. K. Riha, 'Der deutsche Michel', in K. Herding and G. Otto (eds), *'Nervöse Auffassungsorgane des inneren und äußeren Lebens', Karikaturen* (Gießen, 1980), pp. 186–205; R. Koenig, *The Restless Image* (London, 1973), pp. 32, 136.

2. See H. Kohn, *The Mind of Germany* (London, 1961); G. Mosse, *The Crisis of German Ideology* (London, 1966).

3. R. Engelsing, *Sozial- und Wirtschaftsgeschichte Deutschlands* (Göttingen, 1976), p. 99.

4. M. Riedel, 'Vom Biedermeier zum Maschinenzeitalter: Zur Kulturgeschichte der ersten Eisenbahnen in Deutschland', *Archiv für Kulturgeschichte*, 43 (1961), pp. 106–7.

5. D. Sternberger, *Panorama of the Nineteenth Century* (Oxford, 1977), pp. 20–3.

6. B. Deneke, 'Fragen der Rezeption bürgerlicher Sachkultur bei der ländlichen Bevölkerung', in G. Wiegelmann (ed.), *Kultureller Wandel im 19.*

Jahrhundert (Göttingen, 1973), pp. 55-7.

7. D. F. Weinland, 'Über den Ursprung und die Bedeutung der neueren Zoologischen Gärten', cited N. Rothfels, 'Bring 'em back alive: Carl Hagenbeck and the trade in exotic animals and peoples', Harvard diss., 1994, p. 10; Blackbourn and Eley, *Peculiarities of German History*, pp. 199-201.

8. Nipperdey, *Deutsche Geschichte 1866-1918*, vol. 1: *Arbeitswelt und Bürgergeist* (Munich, 1990), pp. 602-4.

9. D. Footman, *The Primrose Path* (London, 1946), p. 160.

10. E. K. Bramsted, *Aristocracy and the Middle Classes in Germany* (Chicago, 1964), p. 201.

11. H. Schmitt, *Das Vereinsleben der Stadt Weinheim an der Bergstrasse* (Weinheim, 1963), p. 97.

12. T. Thomas, 'Eugen-Anton von Boch', in P. Neumann (ed.), *Saarländische Lebensbilder*, vol. 2 (Saarbrücken, 1984), pp. 185-99.

13. For the aims of the Munich association, see *Thierschutz-Verein in München: Erster Jahresbericht für 1868* (Munich, 1869), pp. 15-14.

14. *Der Zahnarzt: Das Neueste und Wissenswürdigste des In- und Auslandes über Zahnheilkunde*, vol. 1, No. 1, Jan. 1846, p. 1.

15. H. Freudenthal, *Vereine in Hamburg* (Hamburg, 1958); Schmitt, *Vereinsleben der Stadt Weinheim*; O. Dann (ed.), *Vereinswesen und bürgerliche Gesellschaft in Deutschland* (Munich, 1984).

16. L. Beutin, 'Das Bürgertum als Gesellschaftsstand im 19.

Jahrhundert', *Gesammelte Schriften zur Wirtschafts- und Sozialgeschichte*, ed. H. Kellenbenz (Cologne and Graz, 1963), pp. 292 ff.

17. W. Siemann, *Gesellschaft im Aufbruch* (Frankfurt, 1990), p. 90.

18. J. S. Roberts, *Drink, Temperance and the Working Class in Nineteenth-Century Germany* (London, 1984), pp. 58-66.

19. O. Beck, *Land- und volkswirthschaftliche Tagesfragen für den Regierungsbezirk Trier* (Trier, 1866), vi.

20. D. Blackbourn, 'Progress and Piety', in Blackbourn, *Populists and Patricians*, pp. 148-9.

21. A writer in *Im neuen Reich*, cited in J. B. Kissling, *Geschichte des Kulturkampfes im Deutschen Reiche*, vol. 3 (Freiburg, 1916), p. 58.

22. A. Kelly, *The Descent of Darwin: The Popularization of Darwinism in Germany, 1860-1914* (Chapel Hill, NC, 1981), p. 22.

23. Kissling, *Kulturkampf*, vol. 2, p. 295.

24. O. Chadwick, *The Secularization of the European Mind in the Nineteenth Century* (Cambridge, 1975).

25. *The Gay Science (Die fröhliche Wissenschaft)*, paragraph 108.

26. H. McLeod, *Religion and the People of Western Europe 1789-1970* (Oxford, 1981), p. 71.

27. I. Rarisch, *Industrialisierung und Literatur* (Berlin, 1976), pp. 98-105.

28. G. Eisfeld, *Die Entstehung der liberalen Parteien in Deutschland 1858-1870* (Hanover, 1969), p. 91 (on the Centre and Islam): Parent, 'Die Kölner Abgeordnetenfeste', p. 264 (on

Jung); Engelhardt, 'Geistig in Fesseln', p. 184 (on Dohm).

29. W. H. Riehl, *Die Naturgeschichte des Volkes als Grundlage einer deutschen Social-Politik*, vol. 1: *Land und Leute* (Stuttgart, 1854).

30. J. Toury, *Soziale und politische Geschichte der Juden in Deutschland 1847–1871* (Düsseldorf, 1977), pp. 122–3.

31. D. Sorkin, *The Transformation of German Jewry, 1780–1840* (New York, 1987).

32. R. Gay, *The Jews of Germany* (New Haven, 1992), pp. 124, 155; J. J. Petchowski, 'Some Criteria for Modern Jewish Observance', in A. Jospe (ed.), *Tradition and Contemporary Experience* (New York, 1970), pp. 241–2.

33. R. Berman, *Cultural Studies of Modern Germany: History, Representation, and Nationhood* (Madison, Wis., 1993), p. 57.

34. S. M. Lowenstein, 'The Rural Community and the Urbanization of German Jewry', *Central European History*, 13 (1980), pp. 218–36.

35. M. Breuer, *Modernity within Tradition: the Social History of Orthodox Jewry in Imperial Germany* (New York, 1992). On women and tradition, see M. A. Kaplan, *The Making of the Jewish Middle Class. Women, Family, and Identity in Imperial Germany* (New York, 1991), pp. 64–84.

36. *Beyond Good and Evil* (1886), cited McLeod, *Religion and the People*, p. 98.

37. The most recent works on this are G. Hübinger, *Kulturprotestantismus und Politik* (Tübingen, 1994) and H. W. Smith, *German Nationalism and*

38. H. McLeod, 'Protestantism and the Working Class of Imperial Germany', *European Studies Review*, 12 (1982), pp. 323–44.

39. H. Raisch, *Berkheim* (Esslingen, 1982).

40. For a case where a Protestant pastor welcomed a cure from cancer supposedly effected when a craftsman 'threw himself into the arms of the Redeemer', see *Frankfurter Zeitung*, 7 August 1876.

41. The *Allgemeine Kirchen-Zeitung* (Darmstadt) in 1844, cited in R. J. Evans, 'Religion and Society in Modern Germany', in Evans, *Rethinking German History* (London, 1987), p. 143.

42. R. Marbach, *Säkularisierung und sozialer Wandel im 19. Jahrhundert* (Göttingen, 1978), pp. 49–50; Smith, *German Nationalism and Religious Conflict*, pp. 87–9.

43. Kissling, *Kulturkampf*, vol. 2, p. 306.

44. L. Pastor, *August Reichensperger*, vol. 1 (Freiburg, 1899), p. 424.

45. Weber cited in Mommsen, *Max Weber and German Politics*, p. 123 n. 134.

46. J. Sperber, *Popular Catholicism in Nineteenth Century Germany* (Princeton, NJ, 1984), pp. 63–73; G. Korff, 'Formierung der Frömmigkeit', *Geschichte und Gesellschaft*, 3 (1977), pp. 356–7.

47. See D. Blackbourn, *Marpingen. Apparitions of the Virgin Mary in Bismarckian Germany* (Oxford, 1993).

48. H. Reif, *Westfälischer Adel 1770–1860* (Göttingen, 1979), pp. 431–56.

49. See, for example, Rudolf Lill, in

Handbuch der Kirchengeschichte, ed. H. Jedin, vol. 6/1 (Freiburg, 1971), p. 408.

50. J. Rost, *Die wirthschaftliche und kulturelle Lage der deutschen Katholiken* (Cologne, 1911); M. Baumeister, *Parität und katholisches Inferiorität* (Paderborn, 1987).

51. Pastor, *August Reichensperger*, vol. 1, p. 518; Sheehan, *German History*, p. 534; *Frankfurter Zeitung*, 16 January 1878.

52. F. Nietzsche, *The Twilight of the Idols* (1889): 'What the Germans Lack', paragraph 2.

53. P. Paret, *Art as History* (Princeton, NJ, 1988), pp. 133–48.

54. G. Stein (ed.), *Philister – Kleinbürger – Spießer* (Frankfurt, 1985); Pastor, *August Reichensperger*, vol. 1, p. 435.

55. K. P. Harder, *Environmental Factors of Early Railroads* (New York, 1981), p. 293; A. Lüdtke, 'Eisenbahnfahren und Eisenbahnbau', in Niethammer et al. (eds), *Bürgerliche Gesellschaft in Deutschland*, pp. 113–14.

56. Heusinger von Waldegg, cited in W. Schivelbusch, *The Railway Journey* (Leamington Spa, 1986), p. 88.

57. Riehl, *Land und Leute*.

58. H. Bausinger, 'Bürgerlichkeit und Kultur', in J. Kocka (ed.), *Bürger und Bürgerlichkeit im 19. Jahrhundert* (Göttingen, 1987), p. 137.

59. Cited Stern, *Politics of Cultural Despair*, p. 39.

60. J. P. Stern, *Nietzsche* (London, 1978), p. 52.

61. Rosenberg, *Grosse Depression*, p. 109.

62. R. Rürup, *Emanzipation und Antisemitismus* (Göttingen, 1975), esp. pp. 95–114.

63. Continuities are emphasized in R. Erb and W. Bergmann, *Die Nachseite der Judenemanzipation* (Berlin, 1989).

CHAPTER SEVEN: 'Made in Germany': A New Economic Order

1. See E. E. Williams, *Made in Germany* (London, 1896).

2. S. Dillwitz, 'Die Struktur der Bauernschaft von 1871 bis 1914', *Jahrbuch für Geschichte*, 9 (1973), pp. 47–127, esp. pp. 54–5 and table 26, p. 101.

3. K. D. Barkin, *The Debate over German Industrialization 1890–1902* (Chicago, 1970).

4. R. Drill, *Soll Deutschland seinen ganzen Getreidebedarf selbst produzieren?* (Stuttgart, 1895); A. Gerschenkron, *Bread and Democracy in Germany*, new edition (Ithaca, NY, 1989); H. Rosenberg, *Probleme der deutschen Sozialgeschichte* (Frankfurt, 1969).

5. J. C. Hunt, 'Peasants, Grain Tariffs and Meat Quotas', *Central European History*, 7 (1974), pp. 311–31; R. G. Moeller, 'Peasants and Tariffs in the *Kaiserreich*', *Agricultural History*, 55 (1981), pp. 370–84; U. Teichmann, *Die Politik der Agrarpreisstützung* (Cologne, 1955), pp. 463–74.

6. Böhme, *Prolegomena*, p. 93.

7. K. J. Bade, 'Labour, Migration, and the State', in Bade (ed.), *Population, Labour and Migration in 19th- and 20th-Century Germany* (Leamington Spa, 1987), pp. 59–85.

8. G. Hohorst, J. Kocka, G. A.

Ritter (eds), *Sozialgeschichtliches Arbeitsbuch II* (Munich, 1978), pp. 57–8, 66, 88–90.

9. F. Blaich, *Kartell- und Monopolpolitik im Kaiserlichen Deutschland* (Düsseldorf, 1973); Hentschel, *Wirtschaft und Wirtschaftspolitik*.

10. J. Kocka, *Unternehmer in der deutschen Industrialisierung* (Göttingen, 1975), pp. 110–23.

11. Kocka, *Die Angestellten*, p. 79.

12. G. Tietz, *Hermann Tietz: Geschichte einer Familie und ihrer Warenhäuser* (Stuttgart, 1955), pp. 61, 134.

13. W. Fischer, 'Die Rolle des Kleingewerbes im wirtschaftlichen Wachstumsprozess in Deutschland', in F. Lütge (ed.), *Wirtschaftliche und Soziale Probleme der Gewerblichen Entwicklung* (Stuttgart, 1968), pp. 131–41; A. Noll, *Sozio-ökonomischer Strukturwandel in der zweiten Phase der Industrialisierung* (Göttingen, 1975); K. -H. Schmidt, 'Bestimmungsgründe und Formen des Unternehmenswachstums im Handwerk seit der Mitte des 19. Jahrhunderts', in Abel (ed.), *Handwerksgeschichte in neuer Sicht*, pp. 241–84.

14. C. F. Sabel and J. Zeitlin, 'Historical Alternatives to Mass Production', *Past and Present*, 108 (1985), pp. 133–76.

15. K. Wernicke, *Kapitalismus und Mittelstandspolitik* (Jena, 1907), p. 138; S. Volkov, *The Rise of Popular Antimodernism in Germany: The Urban Master Artisans, 1873–1896* (Princeton, NJ, 1978), p. 92.

16. Fischer, 'Rolle des Kleingewerbes', p. 136; Noll, *Sozio-ökonomischer Strukturwandel*, pp. 118–20.

17. R. Boch, *Handwerker-Sozialisten gegen Fabrikgesellschaft* (Göttingen, 1985).

18. Gellately, *The Politics of Economic Despair*, pp. 29–33.

19. K. Scheffler, *Der junge Tobias. Eine Jugend und ihre Umwelt* (Leipzig, 1927), pp. 112–13.

20. H. -G. Haupt, 'Kleinhändler und Arbeiter in Bremen zwischen 1890 und 1914', *Archiv für Sozialgeschichte*, 22 (1982), pp. 108–10; Gellately, *Politics of Economic Despair*, pp. 34–6.

21. E. Heckhorn and H. Wiehr, *München und sein Bier. Vom Brauhandwerk zur Bierindustrie* (Munich, 1989), p. 56.

22. Hohorst, Kocka and Ritter (eds), *Sozialgeschichtliches Arbeitsbuch II*, pp. 85–6.

23. K. J. Bade (ed.), *Imperialismus und Kolonialmission* (Wiesbaden, 1982); H. -U. Wehler, 'Industrial growth and early German imperialism', in R. Owen and B. Sutcliffe (eds), *Studies in the Theory of Imperialism* (London, 1972), pp. 71–92.

24. M. Kitchen, *The Political Economy of Germany 1815–1914* (London, 1978), p. 181.

25. H. -U. Wehler, 'Bismarck's Imperialism 1862–1890', *Past and Present*, 48 (1970), pp. 119–55.

26. J. Iliffe, *Tanganyika under German Rule 1905–1912* (Cambridge, 1969), pp. 23, 77–8, 98–100, 167–9; D. Bald, *Deutsch-Ostafrika 1900–1914* (Munich, 1970), esp. pp. 155–9.

27. D. R. Headrick, *The Tools of*

Empire (Oxford, 1981), p. 195.

28. H. Feis, *Europe the World's Banker* (New York, 1965), p. 74.

29. Kitchen, *Political Economy*, p. 193.

30. H. C. Meyer, *Mitteleuropa in German Thought and Action* (The Hague, 1955).

31. H. A. Winkler (ed.), *Organisierter Kapitalismus* (Göttingen, 1974); U. Nocken, 'Corporatism and Pluralism in Modern German History', in D. Stegmann, B.-J. Wendt and P.-C. Witt (eds), *Industrielle Gesellschaft und Politisches System* (Bonn, 1978), pp. 37–56; G. Eley, 'Capitalism and the Wilhelmine State', in Eley, *From Unification to Nazism* (London, 1986), pp. 42–58.

32. H. J. Varain (ed.), *Interessenverbände in Deutschland*; T. Nipperdey, 'Interessenverbände und Parteien in Deutschland vor dem Ersten Weltkrieg', in H.-U. Wehler (ed.), *Moderne Deutsche Sozialgeschichte* (Cologne, 1966), pp. 369–88; G. A. Ritter, 'Parlament, Parteien und Interessenverbände 1890–1914', in M. Stürmer (ed.), *Das kaiserliche Deutschland* (Düsseldorf, 1970), pp. 340–77.

33. H. Jaeger, *Unternehmer in der deutschen Politik (1890–1913)* (Bonn, 1967), 95, 97.

34. Gugel, *Industrieller Aufstieg und bürgerliche Herrschaft*, p. 171.

35. G. Eley, *Reshaping the German Right* (London, 1980), p. 311.

36. H.-J. Puhle, *Agrarische Interessenpolitik und Preußischer Konservatismus* (Hanover, 1967), pp. 165–84; H. Kaelble, *Industrielle Interessenpolitik in der Wilhelminischen Gesellschaft* (Berlin, 1967), pp. 214–22; D. Stegmann, *Die Erben Bismarcks* (Cologne, 1970) pp. 257–60.

37. The classic statement of this view came in the writings of Eckart Kehr in the 1920s, now available in English as *Battleship Building and Party Politics in Germany 1894–1901*, ed. P. R. Anderson and E. N. Anderson (Chicago, 1973), and *Economic Interest, Militarism, and Foreign Policy*, ed. G. A. Craig (Berkeley, Calif., 1977). Among the important works that took up the argument are Stegmann, *Die Erben Bismarcks*, J. C. G. Röhl, *Germany without Bismarck* (London, 1967) and P.-C. Witt, *Die Finanzpolitik des deutschen Reiches* (Hamburg and Lübeck, 1970).

38. See M. Epkenhans, *Die wilhelminische Flottenrüstung, 1908–1914* (Munich, 1991), Part II. Epkenhans emphasizes, however, that many private shipyards suffered serious economic problems when they overextended to meet navy contracts.

39. G. Eley, '*Sammlungspolitik*, Social Imperialism and the Navy Law of 1898', in Eley, *From Unification to Nazism*, pp. 110–53, quotation p. 122.

40. G. Steinmetz, *Regulating the Social: the Welfare State and Local Politics in Imperial Germany* (Princeton, NJ, 1993), pp. 108–20.

41. N. Ferguson, 'Public Finance and National Security', *Past and Present*, 142 (1994), p. 159. Slightly higher figures are given by Hentschel, *Wirtschaftspolitik*, p. 148.

42. A. Mitchell, *The Divided Path: The German Influence on Social Reform in France after 1870* (Chapel Hill, NC, 1991), pp. 237–40; P. Hennock, *British Social Policy and German Precedents* (Oxford, 1987).

43. Hohorst, Kocka and Ritter (eds), *Sozialgeschichtliches Arbeitsbuch II*, pp. 154–5.

44. See Blackbourn, 'Mittelstandspolitik im deutschen Kaiserreich', in R. Melville *et al.* (eds), *Deutschland und Europa in der Neuzeit* (Stuttgart, 1988), vol. II, pp. 555–73.

CHAPTER EIGHT: Society and Culture

1. L. Andreas-Salomé, *Looking Back* (New York, 1991), p. 118.

2. D. Crew, *Town in the Ruhr* (New York, 1979), pp. 60–2.

3. Spree, *Health and Social Class*, pp. 55–102; A. Peiper, *Chronik der Kinderheilkunde* (Leipzig, 1951), pp. 97–105; C. Huerkamp, 'The History of Smallpox Vaccination in Germany', *Journal of Contemporary History*, 20 (1985), pp. 617–35.

4. Hohorst, Kocka and Ritter (eds), *Sozialgeschichtliches Arbeitsbuch II*, p. 106.

5. F. Beckmann, 'Der Bauer im Zeitalter des Kapitalismus', *Schmollers Jahrbuch*, 51/1 (1927), pp. 47, 58–8; G. Frf. von Schrötter, 'Agrarorganisation und sozialer Wandel (dargestellt am Beispiel Schleswig-Holsteins)', in Rüegg and Neuloh (eds), *Zur soziologischen Theorie und Analyse des 19. Jahrhunderts*, p. 143.

6. F. Jacobs, *Deutsche Bauernführer* (Düsseldorf, 1958), pp. 120–1.

7. Examples in M. Stürzbecher, *Deutsche Ärztebriefe des 19. Jahrhunderts* (Göttingen, 1975).

8. G. Zang (ed.), *Provinzialisierung einer Region* (Frankfurt, 1978); U. Jeggle and J. Schlör, 'Stiefkinder des Fortschritts', in A. Nitschke *et al.* (eds), *Jahrhundertwende: Der Aufbruch in die Moderne*, vol. 1 (Reinbek, 1990), pp. 56–74.

9. Kelly (ed.), *The German Worker*, pp. 188–229.

10. T. Süle, *Preussische Bürokratietradition. Zur Entwicklung von Verwaltung und Beamtenschaft in Deutschland 1871–1918* (Göttingen, 1988).

11. See, for example, the essays in R. J. Evans (ed.), *The German Working Class 1888–1933* (London, 1982).

12. R. J. Evans, *Kneipengespräche im Kaiserreich* (Reinbek, 1989); Kelly (ed.), *German Worker*, p. 33.

13. For the argument, G. Roth, *The Social Democrats in Imperial Germany* (Totowa, 1963); and for criticism, V. L. Lidtke, *The Alternative Culture* (New York, 1985).

14. H. Kaelble, *Historical Research on Social Mobility* (London, 1981), pp. 36–7, 47–54.

15. K. Jarausch, *Students, Society, and Politics in Imperial Germany* (Princeton, NJ, 1982), p. 123; Kocka, *Die Angestellten*, p. 108.

16. W. Benjamin, 'A Berlin Chronicle' [1932], in *One-Way Street* (London, 1979), pp. 293–346.

17. D. L. Augustine, 'Arriving in the Upper Class: the Wealthy Business Elite of Wilhelmine Germany', in Blackbourn and

Evans (eds), *German Bourgeoisie*,
p. 53.

18. See Blackbourn and Eley,
Peculiarities of German History,
pp. 161–3, 228–37.

19. G. A. Ritter and J. Kocka (eds),
Deutsche Sozialgeschichte, vol. 1:
1815–1870 (Munich, 1973), p.
76 (on Wilke); T. Fontane, *Die
Poggenpuhls* [1896], ch. 8; M.
Weber, 'National Character and
the Junkers', in H. H. Gerth and
C. W. Mills (eds), *From Max
Weber* (London, 1974), pp. 386–
95.

20. D. L. Augustine, *Patricians and
Parvenus: Wealth and High
Society in Wilhelmine Germany*
(Oxford and Providence, 1984).

21. H. Berghoff, 'Aristokratisierung
des Bürgertums?',
*Vierteljahresschrift für Sozial- und
Wirtschaftsgeschichte*, 81 1994),
pp. 178–204 (Huldschinsky
remark, p. 192).

22. U. Frevert, 'Bourgeois Honour:
Middle-Class Duellists in
Germany', in Blackbourn and
Evans (eds), *German Bourgeoisie*,
p. 282.

23. H. Bausinger,
'Verbürgerlichung – Folgen
eines Interpretaments', in G.
Wiegelmann (ed.), *Kultureller
Wandel im 19. Jahrhundert*
(Göttingen, 1973), pp. 38–9.

24. M. Funke, *Sind Weiber
Menschen?* (Halle, 1910).

25. L. Machtan and R. Ott,
' "Batzbier!" ', in H. Volkmann
and J. Bergmann (eds), *Sozialer
Protest* (Opladen, 1984), pp.
128–66; R. Schulte, *The Village
in Court* (Cambridge, 1994), pp.
124–7.

26. E. Johnson, 'The Crime Rate',
in R. J. Evans (ed.), *The German
Underworld* (London, 1988), pp.

159–88; M. Grüttner,
'Unterklassenkriminalität und
Arbeiterbewegung:
Güterberaubungen im
Hamburger Hafen 1888–1923',
in H. Reif (ed.), *Räuber, Volk und
Obrigkeit* (Frankfurt, 1984), pp.
153–84; E. G. Spencer, *Police
and the Social Order in German
Cities* (DeKalb, Ill., 1992), pp.
172–3.

27. Johnson, 'The Crime Rate', p.
178.

28. R. J. Evans, 'In Pursuit of the
Untertanengeist', in Evans,
Rethinking German History, pp.
159–61.

29. K.-M. Mallmann, 'Nikolaus
Warken', in P. Neumann (ed.),
Saarländische Lebensbilder, vol. 1
(Saarbrücken, 1982), p. 136.

30. C. Tilly, L. Tilly and R. Tilly,
*The Rebellious Century 1830–
1930* (London, 1975), pp. 191–
238.

31. Eley, *From Unification to Nazism*,
p. 103.

32. E. Thoeny, *Der Leutnant*
(Munich, n.d.), VI: 'Die Juristen'
(cartoon of 1896); M. Kitchen,
*The German Officer Corps 1890–
1914* (Oxford, 1968), p. 123 (on
Fontane).

33. See J. Moncure, *Forging the
King's Sword: Military Education
between Tradition and
Modernization* (New York,
1993).

34. K. von Einem, *Erinnerungen
eines Soldaten* (Leipzig, 1933);
also A. Bucholz, *Moltke,
Schlieffen and Prussian War
Planning* (Oxford, 1991).

35. O. Muser, *Die Agrarfrage*
(Karlsruhe, 1895), p. 30.

36. R. Jessen, *Polizei im
Industrierevier* (Göttingen,
1991), pp. 232–50.

37. W. Ayaß, *Das Arbeitshaus Breitenau* (Kassel, 1992).
38. Spencer, *Police and the Social Order*, pp. 65–6.
39. R. Schulte, *Sperrbezirke* (Frankfurt, 1979), pp. 181–2; O. Mönkemöller, *Korrektionsanstalt und Landarmenhaus* (Leipzig, 1908). I owe the second reference to an unpublished paper delivered by J. Scheffler at a Research Seminar on Modern German History, University of East Anglia, 12–13 July 1985.
40. Wehler, *German Empire*, pp. 101–2; Evans, 'In Pursuit', p. 173; Marianne Weber, *Max Weber, A Biography* (New York, 1975), p. 78.
41. M. Weber, *The Protestant Ethic and the Spirit of Capitalism* (London, 1976 [1904–5]), p. 181; W. J. Mommsen, *The Age of Bureaucracy* (Oxford, 1974), p. 57.
42. 'Paris, Capital of the Nineteenth Century' was the title of the project that Benjamin began in 1927 but had not completed by his death. See Benjamin, *Charles Baudelaire: A Lyric Poet in the Era of High Capitalism* (London, 1973).
43. M. Eksteins, *The Rites of Spring* (New York, 1990), pp. 80–1.
44. H. Rosenberg, *The Tradition of the New* (London, 1962).
45. R. Engelsing, *Analphabetentum und Lektüre* (Stuttgart, 1973), pp. 119–20. The figures are based on Germans and German-speaking Austrians in 1886.
46. H. Glaser, *The Cultural Roots of National Socialism* (London, 1978), pp. 38–96. On quotations, see W. Frühwald,

'Büchmann und die Folgen', in R. Koselleck (ed.), *Bildungsbürgertum im 19. Jahrhundert*, Part II: *Bildungsgüter und Bildungswissen* (Stuttgart, 1990), pp. 197–219.
47. F. Lenger, *Werner Sombart* (Munich, 1994), pp. 136–70, quotation p. 163.
48. P. Jelavich, *Munich and Theatrical Modernism* (Cambridge, Mass., 1985); 'Asphaltcowboys und Stadtindianer', in *Envisioning America*, Busch-Reisinger Museum, Harvard (Cambridge, Mass., 1990), pp. 17–36.
49. R. J. V. Lenman, 'Art, Society and the Law in Wilhelmine Germany: the Lex Heinze', *Oxford German Studies*, 8 (1973–4), pp. 86–113.
50. Prominent examples include Kohn, *Mind of Germany*, Stern, *Politics of Cultural Despair*, K. Bergmann, *Agrarromantik und Großstadtfeindschaft* (Meisenheim am Glan, 1970).
51. Schivelbusch, *Disenchanted Night*, p. 71.
52. R. Sieferle, *Fortschrittsfeinde?* (Munich, 1984), p. 166.
53. Lees, *Cities Perceived*, pp. 182–4.
54. J. Langbehn, *Rembrandt als Erzieher* (Leipzig, 1891), p. 138.
55. K. Liebknecht, 'Die Natur schützen', in *Gesammelte Reden und Schriften*, vol. 5 (Berlin, 1963), p. 481.
56. T. Fritsch, *Die Stadt der Zukunft* (Leipzig, 1912).
57. M. Weber, 'Science as a Vocation', in Gerth and Mills (eds), *From Max Weber*, p. 155; D. Beetham, *Max Weber and the Theory of Modern Politics* (Cambridge, 1985), p. 81.

58. M. Löwy, *Georg Lukács – From Romanticism to Bolshevism* (London, 1979), p. 38.

59. A. Nitschke, 'Der Kult der Bewegung', in Nitschke *et al* (eds), *Jahrhundertwende*, vol. 1, p. 262.

CHAPTER NINE: The Old Politics and the New

1. Quotations: Wehler, *German Empire*, pp. 56, 59.

2. See the section on 'Bismarck's Legacy', in Max Weber, 'Parliament and Government in a Reconstructed Germany', in G. Roth and C. Wittich (eds), *Economy and Society* (New York, 1968), appendix, pp. 1385–92.

3. J. C. G. Röhl, 'The emperor's new clothes: a character sketch of Kaiser Wilhelm II', in Röhl and N. Sombart (eds), *Kaiser Wilhelm II: New Interpretations* (Cambridge, 1982), pp. 23–61.

4. E. Eyck, *Das persönliche Regiment Wilhelms II* (Zurich, 1948); Röhl and Sombart (eds), *Kaiser Wilhelm II*; I. Hull, *The Entourage of Kaiser Wilhelm II* (Cambridge, 1982).

5. Röhl, 'Introduction' to Röhl and Sombart (eds), *Kaiser Wilhelm II*, p. 16.

6. G. Mann, *Reminiscences and Reflections* (New York, 1990), p. 109.

7. See, again, the classic account by Max Weber: 'Parliament and Government', pp. 1393–1416.

8. W. Deist, 'The Kaiser and His Military Entourage', in Röhl and Sombart (eds), *Kaiser Wilhelm II* pp. 169–92.

9. Manfred Messerschmidt, cited in Eley, *From Unification to Nazism*, p. 94.

10. Wehler, *German Empire*, p. 55. Criticism and further references in E. Nolte, 'Deutscher Scheinkonstitutionalismus?', in Nolte, *Was ist bürgerlich?* (Stuttgart, 1979), pp. 179–208.

11. J. Retallack, 'Antisocialism and Electoral Politics in Regional Perspective: The Kingdom of Saxony', in L. E. Jones and J. Retallack (eds), *Elections, Mass Politics, and Social Change in Modern Germany* (Cambridge, 1992), p. 55.

12. Wehler, *German Empire*, p. 56.

13. D. Blackbourn, 'New Legislatures: Germany, 1871–1914', *Historical Research*, 65 (1992), pp. 201–14. See also A. P. Thompson, 'Left Liberals in German State and Society, 1907–1918', University of London Ph. D thesis (1989), to be published shortly by Oxford University Press.

14. S. Suval, *Electoral Politics in Wilhelmine Germany* (Chapel Hill, NC, 1983), p. 21; D. Blackbourn, *Class, Religion and Local Politics* (London, 1980), p. 248.

15. D. Blackbourn, 'The Politics of Demagogy in Imperial Germany', in Blackbourn, *Populists and Patricians* (London, 1987), p. 222.

16. W. L. Guttsman, *The German Social Democratic Party 1875–1933* (London, 1981), p. 61.

17. ibid, table 4.1, p. 131.

18. ibid, p. 223.

19. Beetham, *Max Weber and the Theory of Modern Politics*, p. 222.

20. G. Eley, *Reshaping the German Right* (London, 1980), p. 243.

21. Dill, *Parlamentarische Stilentwicklung*, p. 14.

22. A. Rosenberg, *Imperial Germany* (Boston, 1964), p. 18. First published in Germany in 1929.
23. F. Naumann, *Die politischen Parteien* (Berlin, 1910), p. 39.
24. H. Grebing, *The History of the German Labour Movement* (Leamington Spa, 1985), p. 75.
25. G. Mosse, *The Nationalization of the Masses* (New York, 1975).
26. I. Geiss, *German Foreign Policy 1871–1914* (London, 1976), p. 93.
27. Mommsen, *Max Weber and German Politics*, p. 54.
28. G. Mosse, *Nationalism and Sexuality* (New York, 1985).
29. R. Chickering, *'We Men Who Feel Most German'. A Cultural Study of the Pan-German League* (London, 1984).
30. Eley, *Reshaping*, p. 136.
31. M. S. Coetzee, *The German Army League* (Oxford, 1990), p. 100.
32. For the argument that follows, and references to quotations, see Blackbourn, 'Politics of Demagogy'.
33. Weber, *Max Weber, A Biography*, p. 412; S. F. Weiss, *Race Hygiene and National Efficiency* (Berkeley, 1987), pp. 100–1.
34. V. G. Kiernan, *The Lords of Human Kind* (Harmondsworth, 1972), p. 238.
35. E. Demm, *Ein Liberaler in Kaiserreich und Republik* (Boppard, 1990), pp. 38–9.
36. W. E. B. Du Bois, *The Autobiography of W. E. B. Du Bois* (New York, 1968), p. 165.
37. R. Hücking and E. Launer, *Aus Menschen Neger machen* (Hamburg, 1986), pp. 94–5, 102–3; H. W. Debrunner, *Presence and Prestige: Africans in Europe* (Basel, 1979), pp. 363–4.
38. E. Hüsgen, *Ludwig Windthorst* (Cologne, 1911), p. 296.
39. Hagen, *Germans, Poles, and Jews*, p. 189.
40. P. W. Massing, *Rehearsal for Destruction* (New York, 1949), p. 66.
41. R. Brubaker, *Citizenship and Nationhood in France and Germany* (Cambridge, Mass., 1992), pp. 114–37.
42. F. Fischer, *Griff nach der Weltmacht* (Düsseldorf, 1961), translated as *Germany's Aims in the First World War* (London, 1967); and *Krieg der Illusionen* (Düsseldorf, 1969), translated as *War of Illusions* (London, 1975). It should be noted that the first book was not, in fact, primarily concerned with the *origins* of the war.
43. See, respectively, G. Schöllgen, *Die Macht in der Mitte Europas* (Munich, 1992); P. Kennedy, *The Rise of the Anglo-German Antagonism 1860–1914* (London, 1980); H. Putnam, 'Diplomacy and Domestic Politics: the Logic of Two-Level Games', *International Organization*, 42 (1988), pp. 427–60.
44. A. Friedberg, *The Weary Titan: Britain and the Experience of Relative Decline* (Princeton, NJ, 1988).
45. G. Schöllgen, *Imperialismus und Gleichgewicht* (Munich, 1984), p. 424.
46. Friedberg, *Weary Titan*, p. 160, and pp. 135–208 generally; C. H. Fairbanks, 'The Origins of the *Dreadnought* Revolution', *International History Review*, 13 (1991), pp. 246–72.
47. V. R. Berghahn, *Der Tirpitz-Plan* (Düsseldorf, 1971),

and *Germany and the Approach of War*, pp. 25–42; H. H. Herwig, 'Luxury Fleet': The Imperial German Navy 1888–1918 (London, 1987).

48. E. Kehr, *Battleship Building and Party Politics in Germany, 1894–1901* (Chicago, 1973), first published in Berlin in 1930.

49. D. Blackbourn, 'Politics as Theatre', in *Populists and Patricians*, pp. 250–1.

50. For a recent overview, see N. Ferguson, 'Public Finance and National Security: the Domestic Origins of the First World War Revisited', *Past and Present*, 142 (1994), pp. 141–68.

51. R. Hofstadter, *The American Political Tradition* (London, 1967), p. 211.

52. R. Chickering, *Imperial Germany and a World Without War: the Peace Movement and German Society, 1892–1914* (Princeton, NJ, 1975).

53. Fischer, *War of Illusions*, pp. 38, 242–4.

54. D. Groh, ' "Je eher, desto besser" '. Innenpolitische Faktoren für die Präventivkriegsbereitschaft des Deutschen Reiches 1913/14', *Politische Vierteljahresschrift*, 13 (1972), pp. 501–21.

55. Fischer, *War of Illusions*, pp. 161–4; J. C. G. Röhl, 'Die Generalprobe. Zur Geschichte und Bedeutung des "Kriegsrates" vom 8. Dezember 1912', in D. Stegmann *et al.* (eds), *Industrielle Gesellschaft und Politisches System* (Bonn, 1978), pp. 357–73.

56. Röhl, 'Die Generalprobe', p. 367; Fischer, *War of Illusions*, p. 162.

57. R. J. Crampton, *The Hollow Detente. Anglo-German Relations in the Balkans* (London, 1979), pp. 72–3.

58. V. R. Berghahn, 'Das Kaiserreich in der Sackgasse', *Neue Politische Literatur*, 16 (1971), pp. 494–506; Wehler, *German Empire*, pp. 192–201.

59. G. Schmidt, 'Innenpolitische Blockbildungen am Vorabend des Ersten Weltkrieges', *Das Parlament, Beiheft* 20 (1972), pp. 1–32, and 'Deutschland am Vorabend des Ersten Weltkrieges', in Stürmer (ed), *Das kaiserliche Deutschland*, pp. 397–433. The less convincing case for 'silent parliamentarization' is put by M. Rauh, *Die Parlamentarisierung des Deutschen Reiches* (Düsseldorf, 1977).

60. W. Hünseler, *Das Deutsche Kaiserreich und die Irische Frage 1900–1914* (Frankfurt, 1978), pp. 168, 232.

61. Fischer, *War of Illusions*, pp. 475–8.

62. Berghahn, *Germany and the Approach of War*, p. 188.

63. J. Joll, *The Origins of the First World War* (London, 1984), p. 18.

64. K. H. Jarausch, 'The Illusion of Limited War. Chancellor Bethmann Hollweg's Calculated Risk, July 1914', *Central European History* (1969), pp. 48–76.

65. Berghahn, *Germany and the Approach of War*, p. 191.

EPILOGUE: Germany at War, 1914–1918

1. Foreword to Thomas Mann, *The Magic Mountain* (Harmondsworth, 1960 edn),

first published 1924 as *Der Zauberberg*.

2. Zuckmayer, *A Part of Myself*, p. 146.

3. S. Kern, *The Culture of Time and Space, 1880–1918* (Cambridge, Mass., 1983), p. 300.

4. See J. Horne and A. Kramer, 'German "Atrocities" and Franco-German Opinion, 1914: The Evidence of German Soldiers' Diaries', *Journal of Modern History*, 66 (1994), pp. 1–33.

5. P. Fritzsche, *A Nation of Flyers* (Cambridge, Mass., 1992), pp. 82–101.

6. Eksteins, *The Rites of Spring*, p. 144.

7. K. Theweleit, *Männerphantasien*, 2 vols (Frankfurt, 1977).

8. E. J. Leed, *No Man's Land* (Cambridge, 1979), on the 'defensive personality'.

9. von Einem, *Erinnerungen*, p. 164.

10. 'An die Kulturwelt!', *Das monistische Jahrhundert*, 3, 27/28, 15 October 1914.

11. *Börsenblatt für den deutschen Buchhandel*, 24 October 1914. I owe this and the following references to a paper by Wolfgang Natter given to a conference on Imperial Germany held in Philadelphia in February 1990.

12. Käthe Kollwitz, *Aus meinem Leben* (Munich, 1967 edn), p. 71.

13. Lady Evelyn Blücher, cited in A. Offer, *The First World War: An Agrarian Interpretation* (Oxford, 1989), p. 27.

14. This is the central thesis of Offer, *The First World War*. See also J. Winter, 'Some Paradoxes of the First World War', in R. Wall and J. Winter (eds), *the Upheaval of War* (Cambridge, 1988), pp. 35–41.

15. G. Mann, *Reminiscences and Reflections* (New York, 1990), p. 33.

16. R. G. Moeller, *German Peasants and Conservative Agrarian Politics, 1914–1924* (Chapel Hill, NC, 1985), p. 51.

17. Cited in W. Conze, *The Shaping of the German Nation* (London, 1979), p. 63.

18. Eksteins, *The Rites of Spring*, pp. 234–6.

19. Fischer, *Germany's Aims in the First World War*.

20. J. G. Williamson, *Karl Helfferich 1872–1924: Economist, Financier, Politician* (Princeton, NJ, 1971), p. 126.

21. Fischer, *Germany's Aims in the First World War*, p. 404.

22. That is the decisive point, for even in Britain Lloyd George's war leadership sometimes deferred excessively to 'expert' military opinion over *strategic* issues. See J. Turner, *British Politics and the Great War: Coalition and Conflict, 1915–1918* (London and New Haven, 1992).

23. See M. Kitchen, *The Silent Dictatorship* (London, 1976).

24. Wehler, *German Empire*, p. 213.

25. A. J. Ryder, *The German Revolution of 1918* (Cambridge, 1967), p. 159.

26. Ryder, *German Revolution*, p. 169. For a contextualizing of Ebert's famous remark (to Prince Max of Baden) that is more sympathetic than many commentators, see P.-C. Witt, *Friedrich Ebert* (Bonn, 1988), p. 88.

27. D. Peukert, *The Weimar Republic*
     (London, 1991).
28. That is a central theme of Blackbourn and Eley, *Peculiarities of German History*.

SELECT BIBLIOGRAPHY
OF ENGLISH-LANGUAGE WORKS

The first section contains general books. The second lists essay collections, interpretative and thematic books that cover all, or much, of the period. The remaining sections are organized according to the chronological divisions within the book. A few works are listed in more than one section. The bibliography contains articles as well as books. Many English-language journals either specialize in German history, or regularly carry articles on it. Those well worth consulting include *Central European History*, *European History Quarterly*, *German History*, *German Studies Review*, *Historical Journal*, *Journal of Modern History*, *Past and Present*, and *Social History*.

GENERAL WORKS

V. R. Berghahn, *Imperial Germany 1871–1914* (Oxford, 1994).

W. Carr, *A History of Germany, 1815–1945* (London, 3rd edn, 1987).

G. A. Craig, *The Germans* (Harmondsworth, 1978).

G. A. Craig, *Germany 1866–1945* (Oxford, 1981).

C. A. Macartney, *The Habsburg Empire 1790–1918* (London, 1968).

G. Mann, *The History of Germany since 1789* (London, 1968).

D. Orlow, *A History of Modern Germany 1871 to the Present* (Englewood Cliffs, NJ, 1987).

A. Ramm, *Germany 1789–1919: A Political History* (London, 1968).

J. J. Sheehan, *German History 1770–1866* (Oxford, 1989).

A. Sked, *The Decline and Fall of the Habsburg Empire 1815–1918* (London, 1989).

H.-U. Wehler, *The German Empire 1871–1918* (Leamington Spa, 1985).

INTERPRETATIONS AND THEMATIC WORKS COVERING MORE THAN ONE PERIOD

A. T. Allen, *Feminism and Motherhood in Germany, 1800–1914* (New Brunswick, NJ, 1991).

C. Applegate, *A Nation of Provincials. The German Idea of Heimat* (Berkeley, 1990).

K. J. Bade (ed.), *Population, Labour and Migration in 19th and 20th Century Germany* (Oxford and Providence, RI, 1987).

R. Berman, *Cultural Studies of Modern Germany: History, Representation and Nationhood* (Madison, Wis., 1993).

D. Blackbourn, *Populists and Patricians* (London, 1987).

D. Blackbourn and G. Eley, *The Peculiarities of German History* (Oxford, 1984).

D. Blackbourn and R. J. Evans (eds), *The German Bourgeoisie* (London, 1991).

K. Borchardt, 'The Industrial Revolution in Germany, 1700–1914', in C. Cipolla (ed.), *The Fontana Economic History of Europe*, 4/1 (Glasgow, 1973), pp. 76–160.

J. Campbell, *Joy in Work, German Work: The National Debate, 1800–1945* (Princeton, NJ, 1989).

J. Cocks and K. H. Jarausch (eds), *The German Professions, 1800–1950* (Oxford, 1990).

G. A. Craig, *The Politics of the Prussian Army 1640–1945* (Oxford, 1955).

R. Dahrendorf, *Society and Democracy in Germany* (London, 1968).

G. Eley, *From Unification to Nazism* (London, 1986).

R. J. Evans (ed.), *The German Working Class* (London, 1982).

R. J. Evans, *Rethinking German History* (London, 1987).

R. J. Evans (ed.), *The German Underworld* (London, 1988).

R. J. Evans and W. R. Lee (eds), *The German Family* (London, 1980).

R. J. Evans and W. R. Lee (eds), *The German Peasantry* (London, 1986).

J. C. Fout (ed.), *German Women in the Nineteenth Century* (New York, 1984).

U. Frevert, *Women in German History* (Oxford and Providence, RI, 1990).

R. Gay, *The Jews of Germany* (New Haven, 1992).

D. Good, *The Economic Rise of the Habsburg Empire, 1750–1914* (Berkeley, 1984).

H. Grebing, *The History of the German Labour Movement* (Leamington Spa, 1985).

W. Hagen, *Germans, Poles and Jews: The Nationality Conflict in the Prussian East, 1772–1914* (Chicago, 1980).

M. Hughes, *Nationalism and Society: Germany 1800–1945* (London, 1988).

G. Iggers, *The German Conception of History* (Middletown, Conn., 1983).

G. Iggers (ed.), *The Social History of Politics* (Leamington Spa, 1985).

R. E. B. Joeres, and M. J. Maynes (eds), *German Women in the Eighteenth and Nineteenth Centuries* (Bloomington, Ind., 1986).

P. J. Katzenstein, *Disjointed Partners: Austria and Germany since 1815* (Berkeley, 1976).

M. Kitchen, *The Political Economy of Germany, 1815–1914* (London, 1978).

L. Krieger, *The German Idea of Freedom* (Boston, 1957).

C. McClelland, *State, Society, and University in Germany, 1700–1914* (Cambridge, 1980).

R. G. Moeller (ed.), *Peasants and Lords in Modern Germany* (London, 1986).

G. Mosse, *The Nationalization of the Masses* (New York, 1975).

W. Mosse, *Jews in the German Economy* (Oxford, 1987).

E. Sagarra, *A Social History of Germany, 1648–1914* (London, 1977).

K. Schleunes, *Schooling and Society* (New York, 1989).

J. J. Sheehan, *German Liberalism in the Nineteenth Century* (Chicago, 1978).

J. J. Sheehan, 'What is German History? Reflections on the Role of the *Nation* in German History and Historiography', *Journal of Modern History*, 53 (1981), pp. 1–23.

F. B. Tipton, *Regional Variations in the Economic Development of Germany during the Nineteenth Century* (Middletown, Conn., 1976).

P.-C. Witt, *Wealth and Taxation in Central Europe* (New York, 1987).

THE LATE EIGHTEENTH CENTURY

C. B. A. Behrens, *Society, Government and the Enlightenment. The Experiences of Eighteenth-Century France and Prussia* (New York, 1990).

P. Bernard, *The Limits of Enlightenment: Joseph II and the Law* (Urbana, Ill., 1979).

P. Bernard, *From the Enlightenment to the Police State* (Urbana, Ill., 1991).

E. Blackall, *The Emergence of German as a Literary Language, 1700–1775* (Cambridge, 1959).

T. C. W. Blanning, *Joseph II and Enlightened Absolutism* (London, 1970).

T. C. W. Blanning, *Reform and Revolution in Mainz, 1743–1803* (Cambridge, 1974).

T. C. W. Blanning, 'The Enlightenment in Catholic Germany', in R. Porter and M. Teich (eds), *The Enlightenment in National Context* (Cambridge, 1981), pp. 118–26.

W. H. Bruford, *Germany in the Eighteenth Century* (Cambridge, 1965).

H. Brunschwig, *Enlightenment and Romanticism in Eighteenth-Century Prussia* (Chicago, 1974).

F. L. Carsten, *Princes and Parliaments in Germany from the Fifteenth to the Eighteenth Century* (Oxford, 1959).

H. Dippel, *Germany and the American Revolution, 1770–1800* (Chapel Hill, NC, 1977).

C. Duffy, *The Army of Frederick the Great* (London, 1974).

N. Elias, *Mozart: Portrait of a Genius* (Oxford, 1993).

J. Gagliardo, *Reich and Nation: The Holy Roman Empire as Idea and Reality, 1763–1806* (Bloomington, Ind., 1980).

J. Gagliardo, *Germany Under the Old Regime, 1600–1790* (London, 1991).

P. Gay, *The Enlightenment*, 2 vols (New York, 1966–9).

W. Hagen, 'The Junkers' Faithless Servants: Peasant Insubordination and the Breakdown of Serfdom in Brandenburg-Prussia, 1763–1811', in Evans and Lee (eds), *The German Peasantry*, pp. 71–101.

D. Hertz, *Jewish High Society in Old Regime Berlin* (New Haven, 1988).

O. Hintze, *The Historical Essays*, ed. F. Gilbert (New York, 1975).

S. Hochstadt, 'Migration in Preindustrial Germany', *Central European History*, 16 (1983), pp. 195–224.

M. Hughes, *Law and Politics in Eighteenth-Century Germany* (Woodbridge, Suffolk, 1988).

C. Ingrao, *The Hessian Mercenary State* (Cambridge, 1987).

C. Ingrao, *The Habsburg Monarchy 1618–1815* (Cambridge, 1994).

H. C. Johnson, *Frederick the Great and his Officials* (London, 1975).

J. Knudsen, *Justus Möser and the German Enlightenment* (Cambridge, 1986).

P. Kriedte, H. Medick and J. Schlumbohm, *Industrialization before Industrialization* (Cambridge, 1981).

V. Lange, *The Classical Age of German Literature, 1740–1815* (New York, 1982).

E. Melton, '*Gutsherrschaft* in East Elbian Germany and Livonia,

1500–1800: A Critique of the Model', *Central European History*, 21 (1988), pp. 315–49.

J. Van H. Melton, *Absolutism and the Eighteenth-Century Origins of Compulsory Schooling in Prussia and Austria* (Cambridge, 1988).

F. Mendels, 'Proto-Industrialization: The First Phase of the Industrialization Process', *Journal of Economic History*, 32 (1971), pp. 241–61.

A. Menhennet, *Order and Freedom: Literature and Society in Germany from 1720 to 1805* (London, 1973).

G. Pestelli, *The Age of Mozart and Beethoven* (Cambridge, 1984).

M. Raeff, *The Well-Ordered Police State* (New Haven, 1983).

G. Ritter, *Frederick the Great* (Berkeley, 1968).

H. Rosenberg, *Bureaucracy, Aristocracy, and Autocracy. The Prussian Experience, 1660–1815* (Cambridge, Mass., 1958).

H. M. Scott (ed.), *Enlightened Absolutism* (London, 1990).

G. Strauss, 'The Holy Roman Empire Revisited', *Central European History*, 11 (1978), pp. 290–301.

K. Tribe, 'Cameralism and the Science of Government', *Journal of Modern History*, 56 (1984), pp. 163–84.

J. A. Vann, *The Making of a State: Württemberg, 1593–1793* (Ithaca, NY, 1984).

J. A. Vann and S. W. Rowan (eds), *The Old Reich* (Brussels, 1974).

M. Walker, *German Home Towns: Community, State, and General Estate, 1648–1871* (Ithaca, NY, 1971).

M. Walker, *The Salzburg Transaction* (Ithaca, NY, 1992).

E. Wangermann, *The Austrian Achievement 1700–1800* (London, 1973).

A. Ward, *Book Production, Fiction and the German Reading Public, 1740–1800* (Oxford, 1974).

J. Whaley, *Religious Toleration and Social Change in Hamburg (1529–1819)* (Cambridge, 1986).

THE AGE OF REVOLUTIONS 1789–1849

B. C. Anderson, 'State-Building and Bureaucracy in Early-Nineteenth-Century Nassau', *Central European History*, 24 (1991), pp. 222–47.

L. J. Baack, *Christian Bernstorff and Prussia: Diplomacy and Reform Conservatism 1818–1832* (New Brunswick, NJ, 1980).

D. Barclay, *Frederick William IV and the Prussian Monarchy, 1840–1861* (Oxford, 1995).

R. M. Berdahl, *The Politics of the Prussian Nobility: The Development of a Conservative Ideology, 1770–1848* (Princeton, NJ, 1988).

G. Best, *War and Society in Revolutionary Europe, 1770–1870* (London, 1982).

R. M. Bigler, *The Politics of German Protestantism: The Rise of the Protestant Church Elite in Prussia, 1815–1848* (Berkeley, 1972).

T. C. W. Blanning, *The French Revolution in Germany* (Cambridge, 1983).

T. C. W. Blanning, *The Origins of the French Revolutionary Wars* (London, 1986).

J. Blum, *The End of the Old Order in Rural Europe* (Princeton, NJ, 1978).

K. Brauer and W. Wright (eds), *Austria in the Age of the French Revolution* (Minneapolis, Minn., 1991).

E. D. Brose, *The Politics of Technological Change in Prussia* (Princeton, NJ, 1993).

C. von Clausewitz, *On War*, ed. M. Howard and P. Paret (Princeton, NJ, 1976).

C. von Clausewitz, *Historical and Political Writings*, ed. D. Moran and P. Paret (Princeton, NJ, 1992).

W. Conze, 'From "Pöbel" to "Proletariat"', in Iggers (ed.), *Social History of Politics*, pp. 49–80.

L. Dickey, *Hegel, Religion, Economics, and the Politics of Spirit, 1770–1807* (Cambridge, 1987).

J. Diefendorf, *Businessmen and Politics in the Rhineland, 1789–1834* (Princeton, NJ, 1980).

F. Engels, *Germany: Revolution and Counter-Revolution*, in *The German Revolutions*, ed. L. Krieger (Chicago, 1967).

K. Epstein, *The Genesis of German Conservatism* (Princeton, NJ, 1966).

F. Eyck, *The Frankfurt Parliament 1848–1849* (London, 1968).

F. Eyck, *Loyal Rebels: Andreas Hofer and the Tyrolean Uprising of 1809* (Lanham, MD., 1986).

J. Gagliardo, *From Pariah to Patriot: The Changing Image of the German Peasant, 1770–1840* (Lexington, KY, 1969).

M. Gailus, 'Food Riots in Germany in the late 1840s', *Past and Present*, 145 (1994), pp. 157–93.

J. R. Gillis, *The Prussian Bureaucracy in Crisis, 1840–1860* (Stanford, Calif., 1971).

M. Gray, *Prussia in Transition: Society and Politics under the Stein Reform Ministry of 1808* (Philadelphia, 1986).

T. S. Hamerow, *Restoration, Revolution, Reaction: Economics and Politics in Central Europe, 1815–1871* (Princeton, NJ, 1958).

J. Kocka, 'The Entrepreneur, the Family and Capitalism: Some Examples from the Early Phase of Industrialization in Germany', *German Yearbook on Business History* (1981), pp. 53–82.

E. E. Kraehe, *Metternich's German Policy*, 2 vols (Princeton, NJ, 1963–84).

A. LaVopa, *Prussian Schoolteachers: Profession and Office, 1763–1848* (Chapel Hill, NC, 1980).

L. E. Lee, *The Politics of Harmony: Civil Service, Liberalism, and Social Reform in Baden, 1800–1850* (Newark, NJ, 1980).

L. E. Lee, 'Baden between Revolutions: State-Building and Citizenship, 1800–1848', *Central European History*, 24 (1991), pp. 248–67.

W. R. Lee, *Population Growth, Economic Development, and Social Change in Bavaria, 1750–1850* (New York, 1977).

M. Lindemann, *Patriots and Paupers, Hamburg, 1712–1830* (Oxford, 1990).

D. McLellan, *Karl Marx* (New York, 1973).

F. Marquardt, 'A Working Class in Berlin in the 1840s?', in H.-U. Wehler (ed.), *Sozialgeschichte Heute* (Göttingen, 1974), pp. 191–210.

P. H. Noyes, *Organization and Revolution: Working-Class Associations in the German Revolutions of 1848–49* (Princeton, NJ, 1966).

L. O'Boyle, 'The Problem of an Excess of Educated Men in Western Europe, 1800–1850', *Journal of Modern History*, 42 (1970), pp. 472–95.

F. Ohles, *Germany's Rude Awakening, Censorship in the Land of the Brothers Grimm* (Kent, Ohio, 1992).

P. Paret, *Yorck and the Era of Prussian Reform, 1807–1815* (Princeton, NJ, 1966).

P. Paret, *Clausewitz and the State* (London, 1976).

G. Pedlow, *The Survival of the Hessian Nobility, 1770–1870* (Princeton, NJ, 1988).

R. J. Rath, *The Viennese Revolution of 1848* (Austin, TX, 1957).

K. Roider, *Baron Thugut and Austria's Response to the French Revolution* (Princeton, NJ, 1987).

H. Rosenberg, *Bureaucracy, Aristocracy, and Autocracy. The Prussian Experience, 1660–1815* (Cambridge, Mass., 1958).

D. W. Sabean, *Property, Production and Family in Neckarhausen, 1700–1870* (Cambridge, 1990).

J. Sammons, *Heinrich Heine* (Princeton, NJ, 1979).

W. Schieder, 'Church and Revolution: Aspects of the Social History of the Trier Pilgrimage of 1844', in C. Emsley (ed.), *Conflict and Stability in Europe* (London, 1979), pp. 65–95.

H. Schmitt, 'Germany without Prussia: A Closer Look at the Confederation of the Rhine', *German Studies Review*, 6 (1983), pp. 9–39.

J. J. Sheehan, 'Liberalism and Society in Germany, 1815–1848', *Journal of Modern History*, 45 (1973), pp. 583–604.

W. M. Simon, *The Failure of the Prussian Reform Movement, 1807–1819* (Ithaca, NY, 1955).

A. Sked, *The Survival of the Habsburg Empire: Radetzky, the Imperial Army, and the Class War, 1848* (London, 1979).

A. Sorel, *Europe and the French Revolution* (London, 1969).

D. Sorkin, *The Transformation of German Jewry, 1780–1840* (New York, 1987).

J. Sperber, *Rhineland Radicals: The Democratic Movement and the Revolution of 1848–1849* (Princeton, NJ, 1991).

R. Stadelmann, *Social and Political History of the Revolution of 1848/49* (Athens, Ohio, 1975).

J. E. Toews, *Hegelianism: The Path toward Dialectical Humanism 1805–1841* (Cambridge, 1980).

V. Valentin, *1848: Chapters of German History* (London, 1940).

J. A. Vann, 'Habsburg Policy and the War of 1809', *Central European History*, 7 (1974), pp. 291–310.

W. Vaughan, *German Romantic Painting* (London, 1980).

M. Walker, *German Home Towns: Community, State, and General Estate, 1648–1871* (Ithaca, NY, 1971).

J. Walter, *The Diary of a Napoleonic Foot Soldier*, ed. M. Raeff (New York, 1993).

E. Wangermann, *From Joseph II to the Jacobin Trials* (Oxford, 1959).

K. Wegert, 'The Genesis of Youthful Radicalism: Hesse-Nassau, 1806–19', *Central European History*, 10 (1977), pp. 185–205.

THE AGE OF PROGRESS, 1849–80

E. Ackerknecht, *Rudolf Virchow: Doctor, Statesman, Anthropologist*
(Madison, Wis., 1953).

E. N. Anderson, *The Social and Political Conflict in Prussia 1858–1864*
(Lincoln, Neb., 1954).

M. L. Anderson, *Windthorst: A Political Biography* (Oxford, 1981).

M. L. Anderson, 'The Kulturkampf and the Course of German
History', *Central European History*, 19 (1986), pp. 82–115.

W. Arndt, *The Genius of Wilhelm Busch* (Berkeley, 1982).

R. Austensen, 'Austria and the "Struggle of Supremacy in Germany",
1848–1864', *Journal of Modern History*, 52 (1980), pp. 195–225.

D. Blackbourn, *Marpingen: Apparitions of the Virgin Mary in
Bismarckian Germany* (Oxford, 1993; New York, 1994).

H. Böhme (ed.), *The Foundations of the German Empire* (Oxford, 1971).

E. K. Bramsted, *Aristocracy and the Middle Classes in Germany* (Chicago,
1964).

J. Breuilly, *Labour and Liberalism in Nineteenth-Century Europe: Essays
in Comparative History* (Manchester, 1992).

N. Bullock and J. Read, *The Movement for Housing Reform in Germany
and France, 1840–1914* (Cambridge, 1984).

W. Carr, *The Wars of German Unification* (London, 1991).

O. Chadwick, *The Secularisation of the European Mind in the Nineteenth
Century* (Cambridge, 1975).

G. A. Craig, *The Battle of Königgrätz: Prussia's Victory over Austria,
1866* (Philadelphia and New York, 1964).

R. H. Dominick, *Wilhelm Liebknecht and the Founding of the German
Social Democratic Party* (Chapel Hill, NC, 1982).

A. Dorpalen, *Heinrich von Treitschke* (New Haven, 1957).

R. Fremdling, 'Railroads and German Economic Growth', *Journal of
Economic History*, 37 (1977), pp. 583–604.

L. Gall, *Bismarck, The White Revolutionary*, 2 vols (London, 1985).

F. Gregory, *Scientific Materialism in Nineteenth-Century Germany*
(Boston, 1977).

T. S. Hamerow, *The Social Foundations of German Unification, 1858–
1871*, 2 vols (Princeton, NJ, 1969–72).

J. F. Harris, 'Eduard Lasker and Compromise Liberalism', *Journal of
Modern History*, 42 (1970), pp. 342–60.

K. Hausen, 'Technical Progress and Women's Labour in the

Nineteenth Century. The Social History of the Sewing Machine', in Iggers (ed.), *Social History of Politics*, pp. 259–81.

R. Hayman, *Nietzsche* (New York, 1980).

W. Hoffmann, 'The Take-Off in Germany', in W. W. Rostow (ed.), *The Economics of Take-Off into Sustained Growth* (New York, 1963), pp. 95–118.

N. M. Hope, *The Alternative to German Unification. The Anti-Prussian Party: Frankfurt, Nassau and the Two Hessen 1859–1867* (Wiesbaden, 1973).

M. Howard, *The Franco-Prussian War* (London, 1961).

J. H. Jackson, *Migration and Urbanization in the Ruhr Valley, 1850–1900* (San Diego, Calif., 1980).

M. John, 'Liberalism and Society in Germany, 1850–1880: The Case of Hanover', *English Historical Review*, 102 (1987), pp. 579–98.

J. Katz, *Out of the Ghetto: The Social Background of Jewish Emancipation, 1770–1870* (Cambridge, Mass., 1973).

A. Kelly, *The Descent of Darwin: The Popularization of Darwinism in Germany, 1860–1914* (Chapel Hill, NC, 1981).

J. Komlos, *The Habsburg Monarchy as a Customs Union* (Princeton, NJ, 1983).

I. N. Lambi, *Free Trade and Protection in Germany, 1868–1879* (Wiesbaden, 1963).

D. C. Large and W. Weber (eds), *Wagnerism in European Culture* (Ithaca, NY, 1984).

A. Lees, *Revolution and Reflection: Intellectual Change in Germany during the 1850s* (The Hague, 1974).

A. Lees, *Cities Perceived* (New York, 1985).

S. M. Lowenstein, 'The Rural Community and the Urbanization of German Jewry', *Central European History*, 13 (1980), pp. 218–36.

C. McClelland, *The German Historians and England* (Cambridge, 1971).

A. Mitchell, *Bismarck and the French Nation 1848–1870* (New York, 1971).

A. Mitchell, 'Bonapartism as a Model for Bismarckian Politics', *Journal of Modern History*, 49 (1977), pp. 181–99.

G. R. Mork, 'Bismarck and the "Capitulation" of German Liberalism', *Journal of Modern History*, 43 (1971), pp. 59–75.

W. E. Mosse, *The European Powers and the German Question, 1848–71* (Cambridge, 1958).

L. O'Boyle, 'Learning for its Own Sake: The German University as

Nineteenth-Century Model', *Comparative Studies in Society and History*, 21 (1983), pp. 3–25.

P. Paret, *Art as History* (Princeton, NJ, 1988).

A. Perkins, 'The Agricultural Revolution in Germany, 1850–1914', *Journal of European Economic History*, 10 (1981), pp. 71–118.

O. Pflanze, *Bismarck and the Development of Germany*, 3 vols (Princeton, NJ, 1990).

Y. Reinharz, *The Jewish Response to German Culture* (Hanover, NH, 1985).

E. Sagarra, *Tradition and Revolution. German Literature and Society, 1830–1890* (New York, 1971).

W. Schivelbusch, *The Railway Journey* (New York, 1979).

P. W. Schroeder, *Austria, Great Britain and the Crimean War: The Destruction of the European Concert* (Ithaca, NY, 1972).

J. J. Sheehan, *German Liberalism in the Nineteenth Century* (Chicago, 1978).

D. E. Showalter, *Railroads and Rifles: Soldiers, Technology, and the Unification of Germany* (Shoestring, 1975).

W. M. Simon (ed.), *Germany in the Age of Bismarck* (London, 1968).

J. Sperber, *Popular Catholicism in Nineteenth-Century Germany* (Princeton, NJ, 1984).

F. Stern, *Gold and Iron: Bismarck, Bleichröder, and the Building of the German Empire* (London, 1977).

J. P. Stern, *Reinterpretations: Seven Studies in Nineteenth-Century German Literature* (London, 1964).

J. P. Stern, *Nietzsche* (London, 1978).

D. Sternberger, *Panorama of the Nineteenth Century* (Oxford, 1977).

R. Tilly, *Financial Institutions and Industrialization in the Rhineland, 1815–1870* (Madison, Wis., 1966).

R. Tilly, 'The Take-Off in Germany', in E. Angermann and M. L. Frings (eds), *Oceans Apart? Comparing Germany and the United States* (Stuttgart, 1981), pp. 47–59.

M. Walker, *Germany and the Emigration, 1816–1885* (Cambridge, Mass., 1964).

G. C. Windell, *The Catholics and German Unity, 1866–1871* (Minneapolis, MN, 1954).

S. Zucker, *Ludwig Bamberger* (Pittsburgh, Penn., 1975).

THE AGE OF MODERNITY, 1880–1914

L. Abrams, *Workers' Culture in Imperial Germany* (London, 1991).

C. E. Adams, *Women Clerks in Wilhelmine Germany* (Cambridge, 1988).

J. C. Albisetti, *Secondary School Reform in Wilhelmine Germany* (Princeton, NJ, 1983).

J. C. Albisetti, *Schooling German Girls and Women* (Princeton, NJ, 1988).

A. T. Allen, *Satire and Society in Wilhelmine Germany* (Louisville, KY, 1985).

L. Andreas-Salomé, *Looking Back* (New York, 1991).

D. L. Augustine, *Patricians and Parvenus: Wealth and High Society in Wilhelmine Germany* (Oxford, 1984).

M. Balfour, *The Kaiser and His Times* (London, 1964).

K. D. Barkin, *The Controversy over German Industrialization 1890–1902* (Chicago, 1970).

D. Beetham, *Max Weber and the Theory of Modern Politics* (London, 1974).

W. Benjamin, 'A Berlin Chronicle' [1932], in *One-Way Street* (London, 1979), pp. 293–346.

V. R. Berghahn, *Germany and the Approach of War in 1914* (London, 1973).

R. Berman, *The Rise of the Modern German Novel* (Cambridge, Mass., 1986).

D. Blackbourn, 'The *Mittelstand* in German Society and Politics, 1871–1914', *Social History*, 4 (1977), pp. 409–33.

D. Blackbourn, *Class, Religion and Local Politics in Wilhelmine Germany* (London, 1980).

D. Blackbourn, 'The Politics of Demagogy in Imperial Germany', in Blackbourn, *Populists and Patricians*, pp. 217–45.

R. Blanke, *Prussian Poland in the German Empire, 1871–1914* (Boulder, Colo., 1981).

W. K. Blessing, 'The Cult of Monarchy. Political Loyalty and the Workers' Movement in Imperial Germany', *Journal of Contemporary History*, 13 (1978), pp. 357–75.

G. Bonham, *Ideology and Interests in the German State* (Hamden, Conn., 1991).

M. Breuer, *Modernity within Tradition: the Social History of Orthodox Jewry in Imperial Germany* (New York, 1992).

E. D. Brose, *Christian Labor and the Politics of Frustration in Imperial Germany* (Washington, DC, 1985).

R. Brubaker, *Citizenship and Nationhood in France and Germany* (Cambridge, Mass., 1992).

A. Bucholz, *Moltke, Schlieffen and Prussian War Planning* (Oxford, 1991).

D. Calleo, *The German Problem Reconsidered* (Cambridge, 1980).

J. Campbell, *The German Werkbund* (Princeton, NJ, 1978).

L. Cecil, *The German Diplomatic Service, 1871–1914* (Princeton, NJ, 1979).

G. Chapple and H. Schulte (eds), *The Turn of the Century: German Literature and Art, 1890–1915* (Bonn, 1981).

R. Chickering, *Imperial Germany and a World without War* (Princeton, NJ, 1975).

R. Chickering, 'We Men Who Feel Most German'. *A Cultural Study of the Pan-German League* (London, 1984).

M. S. Coetzee, *The German Army League* (Oxford, 1990).

J. E. Craig, *Scholarship and Nation-Building* (Chicago, 1982).

R. J. Crampton, *The Hollow Detente. Anglo-German Relations in the Balkans* (London, 1979).

D. Crew, *Town in the Ruhr: A Social History of Bochum, 1860–1914* (New York, 1979).

A. V. Desai, *Real Wages in Germany, 1871–1914* (Oxford, 1968).

K. Doerner, *Madmen and the Bourgeoisie: A Social History of Insanity and Psychiatry* (Oxford, 1981).

J. R. Dukes and J. Remak (eds), *Another Germany* (Boulder, Colo., 1988).

G. Eley, *Reshaping the German Right* (London, 1980).

R. J. Evans, *The Feminist Movement in Germany, 1894–1933* (London, 1976).

R. J. Evans, 'Prostitution, State and Society in Imperial Germany', *Past and Present*, 70 (1976), pp. 106–29.

R. J. Evans (ed.), *Society and Politics in Wilhelmine Germany* (London, 1978).

R. J. Evans, *Death in Hamburg: Society and Politics in the Cholera Years, 1830–1910* (Oxford, 1987).

N. Ferguson, 'Public Finance and National Security: the Domestic Origins of the First World War Revisited', *Past and Present*, 142 (1994), pp. 141–68.

F. Fischer, *War of Illusions: German Policies from 1911 to 1914* (London, 1975).

R. Fletcher, *Revisionism and Empire* (London, 1984).

B. Franzoi, *At the Very Least She Pays the Rent. Women and German Industrialization* (Westport, Conn., 1985).

U. Frevert, 'Professional Medicine and the Working Classes in Imperial Germany', *Journal of Contemporary History*, 20 (1985), pp. 637–58.

U. Frevert, 'Bourgeois Honour: Middle-Class Duellists in Germany', in Blackbourn and Evans (eds), *The German Bourgeoisie*, pp. 255–92.

P. Gay, *Freud, Jews, and Other Germans* (Oxford, 1978).

D. Geary, 'The German Labour Movement, 1848–1919', *European Studies Review*, 6 (1976), pp. 297–330.

I. Geiss, *German Foreign Policy, 1871–1914* (London, 1976).

R. Gellately, *The Politics of Economic Despair: Shopkeepers and German Politics 1890–1914* (London, 1974).

A. Gerschenkron, *Bread and Democracy in Germany* (Ithaca, NY, 1989 edn).

H. H. Gerth and C. W. Mills, *From Max Weber* (London, 1974).

G. Golde, *Catholics and Protestants. Agricultural Modernization in Two German Villages* (London, 1975).

M. Gordon, 'Domestic Conflict and the Origins of the First World War', *Journal of Modern History*, 46 (1974), pp. 191–226.

W. Guttsman, *The German Social Democratic Party 1875–1933* (London, 1981).

A. Hackett, *The Politics of Feminism in Wilhelmine Germany, 1890–1918* (New York, 1979).

A. Hall, *Scandal, Sensation, and Social Democracy* (Cambridge, 1977).

N. Hamilton, *The Brothers Mann* (London, 1978).

B. Heckart, *From Bassermann to Bebel* (New Haven, 1974).

P. Hennock, *British Social Policy and German Precedents* (Oxford, 1987).

H. H. Herwig, *The German Naval Officer Corps* (Oxford, 1973).

H. H. Herwig, *'Luxury Fleet': The Imperial German Navy 1888–1918* (London, 1980).

S. Hickey, *Workers in Imperial Germany: Miners in the Ruhr* (Oxford, 1985).

D. J. Hughes, *The King's Finest. A Social and Bureaucratic Profile of Prussia's General Officers, 1871–1914* (New York, 1987).

I. Hull, *The Entourage of Kaiser Wilhelm II* (Cambridge, 1982).

J. C. Hunt, 'Peasants, Grain Tariffs and Meat Quotas', *Central European History*, 7 (1974), pp. 311–31.

J. Iliffe, *Tanganyika under German Rule 1905–1912* (Cambridge, 1969).

H. Jacob, *German Administration since Bismarck* (New Haven, 1963).

K. H. Jarausch, ' "The Illusion of Limited War". Chancellor Bethmann Hollweg's calculated risk, July 1914', *Central European History*, 2 (1969), pp. 48–76.

K. H. Jarausch, *The Enigmatic Chancellor. Bethmann Hollweg and the Hubris of Imperial Germany* (New Haven, 1973).

K. H. Jarausch, *Students, Society and Politics in Imperial Germany* (Princeton, NJ, 1982).

P. Jelavich, *Munich and Theatrical Modernism* (Cambridge, Mass., 1985).

M. John, *Politics and the Law in Late Nineteenth-Century Germany* (Oxford, 1989).

J. Joll, *The Origins of the First World War* (London, 1984).

L. E. Jones and J. Retallack (eds), *Elections, Mass Politics, and Social Change in Modern Germany* (Cambridge, 1992).

D. Kaiser, 'Germany and the Origins of the First World War', *Journal of Modern History*, 55 (1983), pp. 442–74.

M. A. Kaplan, *The Making of the Jewish Middle Class. Women, Family, and Identity in Imperial Germany* (New York, 1991).

E. Kehr, *Battleship Building and Party Politics in Germany, 1894–1901*, ed. P. R. and E. N. Anderson (Chicago, 1973).

E. Kehr, *Economic Interest, Militarism and Foreign Policy*, ed. G. A. Craig (Berkeley, 1977).

A. Kelly (ed.), *The German Worker* (Berkeley, 1987).

P. M. Kennedy, *The Rise of the Anglo-German Antagonism, 1860–1914* (London, 1980).

P. M. Kennedy and A. J. Nicholls (eds), *Nationalist and Racialist Movements in Britain and Germany before 1914* (London, 1981).

P. M. Kennedy (ed.), *The War Plans of the Great Powers, 1880–1914* (London, 1979).

M. Kitchen, *The German Officer Corps, 1890–1914* (Oxford, 1968).

J. Kocka, 'White-Collar Employees and Industrial Society in Imperial Germany', in Iggers (ed.), *Social History of Politics*, pp. 113–36.

R. Koshar, *Social Life, Local Politics and Nazism. Marburg, 1880–1935* (Chapel Hill, NC, 1985).

B. Ladd, *Urban Planning and Civic Order in Germany, 1860–1914* (Cambridge, Mass., 1990).

M. Lamberti, *State, Society and the Elementary School in Imperial Germany* (Oxford, 1989).

I. N. Lambi, *The Navy and German Power Politics* (London, 1984).

W. Laqueur, *Young Germany* (London, 1962).

A. Lees, *Cities Perceived* (New York, 1985).

R. J. V. Lenman, 'Art, Society and the Law in Wilhelmine Germany: the Lex Heinze', *Oxford German Studies*, 8 (1973–74), pp. 86–113.

K. A. Lerman, *The Chancellor as Courtier. Bernhard von Bülow and the Governance of Germany, 1900–1909* (Cambridge, 1990).

R. S. Levy, *The Downfall of the Anti-Semitic Political Parties in Imperial Germany* (New Haven, 1975).

H. H. Liang, *The Social Background of the Berlin Working-Class Movement* (Ann Arbor, Mich., 1980).

V. L. Lidtke, *The Outlawed Party* (Princeton, NJ, 1966).

V. L. Lidtke, 'Social Class and Secularization in Imperial Germany', in *Leo Baeck Institute Yearbook* (1982), pp. 21–40.

V. L. Lidtke, *The Alternative Culture* (Oxford, 1985).

D. S. Linton, *'Who Has the Youth, Has the Future'* (Cambridge, 1991).

H. McLeod, 'Protestantism and the Working Class of Imperial Germany', *European Studies Review*, 12 (1982), pp. 323–44.

G. Masur, *Imperial Berlin* (London, 1971).

H. C. Meyer, *Mitteleuropa in German Thought and Action* (The Hague, 1955).

R. G. Moeller, 'Peasants and Tariffs in the *Kaiserreich*', *Agricultural History*, 55 (1981), pp. 370–84.

W. J. Mommsen, 'Domestic Factors in German Foreign Policy before 1914', *Central European History*, 6 (1973), pp. 11–43.

W. J. Mommsen, *Max Weber and German Politics* (Chicago, 1984).

J. Moncure, *Forging the King's Sword: Military Education between Tradition and Modernization* (New York, 1993).

J. A. Moses, *The Politics of Illusion* (London, 1975).

J. A. Moses, *German Trade Unionism from Bismarck to Hitler*, vol. 1 (London, 1982).

G. Mosse, *The Crisis of German Ideology* (London, 1966).

R. Murphy, *Guestworkers in the Ruhr* (Boulder, Colo., 1983).

J. P. Nettl, *Rosa Luxemburg*, 2 vols (Oxford, 1966).

J. P. Nettl, 'The German Social Democrats 1890–1914 as a Political Model', *Past and Present*, 30 (1965), pp. 65–95.

H. Neuburger, *German Banks and German Economic Growth, 1871–1914* (New York, 1977).

J. Neufeld, *The Skilled Metalworkers of Nuremberg* (New Brunswick, NJ, 1989).

J. A. Nichols, *Germany after Bismarck: The Caprivi Era, 1890–1894* (Cambridge, Mass., 1958).

M. Nolan, *Social Democracy and Society* (Cambridge, 1981).

P. Paret, *The Berlin Secession* (Cambridge, Mass., 1980).

R. Pascal, *From Naturalism to Expressionism. German Literature and Society 1880–1918* (London, 1973).

P. G. J. Pulzer, *The Rise of Political Anti-Semitism in Germany and Austria* (New York, 1964).

J. Quataert, *Reluctant Feminists in German Social Democracy, 1885–1917* (Princeton, NJ, 1979).

J. Remak, *The Gentle Critic* (Syracuse, NY, 1964).

J. N. Retallack, *Notables of the Right* (London, 1988).

F. Ringer, *The Decline of the German Mandarins* (Cambridge, Mass., 1969).

G. Ritter, *The Schlieffen Plan* (London, 1958).

J. S. Roberts, *Drink, Temperance and the Working Class in Nineteenth-Century Germany* (London, 1984).

J. C. G. Röhl, *Germany without Bismarck* (London, 1967).

J. C. G. Röhl, *1914: Delusions or Design* (London, 1973).

J. C. G. Röhl and N. Sombart (eds), *Kaiser Wilhelm II: New Interpretations* (Cambridge, 1982).

K. Roper, *German Encounters with Modernity. Novels of Imperial Berlin* (Atlantic Highlands, NJ, 1991).

A. Rosenberg, *Imperial Germany* (Boston, 1964).

H. Rosenberg, 'The Pseudo-Democratisation of the Junker Class', in Iggers, *Social History of Politics*, pp. 81–112.

R. J. Ross, *Beleaguered Tower. The Dilemma of Political Catholicism in Wilhelmine Germany* (Notre Dame, Ind., 1976).

G. Roth, *The Social Democrats in Imperial Germany* (Totowa, NJ, 1963).

R. E. Sackett, *Popular Entertainment, Class, and Politics in Munich, 1900–1923* (Cambridge, Mass., 1982).

D. Schoenbaum, *Zabern 1913. Consensus Politics in Imperial Germany* (London, 1982).

L. Schofer, *The Formation of a Modern Labour Force. Upper Silesia, 1865–1914* (Berkeley, 1975).

G. Schöllgen (ed.), *Escape into War?* (Oxford, 1990).

C. E. Schorske, *German Social Democracy 1905–1917* (Cambridge, Mass., 1955).

R. Schulte, *The Village in Court* (Cambridge, 1994).

J. J. Sheehan, *The Career of Lujo Brentano* (Chicago, 1966).

J. J. Sheehan, 'Liberalism and the City in Nineteenth-Century Germany', *Past and Present*, 51 (1971), pp. 116–37.

J. J. Sheehan (ed.), *Imperial Germany* (New York, 1976).

D. Silverman, *Reluctant Ally* (Philadelphia, 1972).

H. W. Smith, *German Nationalism and Religious Conflict* (Princeton, NJ, 1995).

W. D. Smith, *The German Colonial Empire* (Chapel Hill, NC, 1978).

E. G. Spencer, *Police and the Social Order in German Cities* (DeKalb, Ill., 1992).

R. Spree, *Health and Social Class in Imperial Germany* (New York, 1987).

P. D. Stachura, *The German Youth Movement, 1900–1945* (London, 1981).

G. D. Stark, *Entrepreneurs of Ideology* (Chapel Hill, NC, 1981).

G. Steinmetz, *Regulating the Social: the Welfare State and Local Politics in Imperial Germany* (Princeton, NJ, 1993).

F. Stern, *The Politics of Cultural Despair* (Berkeley, 1961).

W. Struve, *Elites against Democracy* (Princeton, NJ, 1973).

S. Suval, *Electoral Politics in Wilhelmine Germany* (Chapel Hill, NC, 1985).

U. Tal, *Christians and Jews in Germany, 1870–1914* (Ithaca, NY, 1974).

R. H. Thomas, *Nietzsche in German Politics and Society, 1890–1918* (Manchester, 1983).

S. R. Tirrell, *German Agrarian Politics after Bismarck's Fall* (New York, 1971).

T. Veblen, *Imperial Germany and the Industrial Revolution* (London, 1915).

S. Volkov, *The Rise of Popular Antimodernism in Germany: The Urban Master Artisans 1873–1896* (Princeton, NJ, 1978).

M. Weber, 'Parliament and Government in a Reconstructed Germany', in G. Roth and C. Wittich (eds), *Economy and Society* (New York, 1968), appendix, pp. 1381–1462.

M. Weber, *Max Weber, A Biography* (New York, 1975).

H.-U. Wehler, 'Bismarck's Imperialism 1862–1890', *Past and Present*, 48 (1970), pp. 119–55.

P. J. Weindling, *Health, Race and German Politics between National Unification and Nazism* (Cambridge, 1989).

S. F. Weiss, *Race Hygiene and National Efficiency* (Berkeley, 1987).

D. Welch, 'Cinema and Society in Imperial Germany, 1905–1918', *German History*, 8 (1990), pp. 28–45.

D. S. White, *The Splintered Party: National Liberalism in Hessen and the Reich, 1867–1918* (Cambridge, Mass., 1976).

J. Woycke, *Birth Control in Germany, 1871–1933* (London, 1988).

J. K. Zeender, *The German Center Party, 1890–1906* (Philadelphia, 1976).

WAR AND REVOLUTION, 1914–1918

W. T. Angress, *Stillborn Revolution* (Princeton, NJ, 1963).

J. Ashworth, *Trench Warfare, 1914–1918* (New York, 1980).

C. L. Bertrand (ed.), *Revolutionary Situations in Europe, 1917–1922* (Montreal, 1977).

K. Birnbaum, *Peace Moves and U-Boat Warfare* (Hamden, Conn., 1970).

C. B. Burdick and R. H. Lutz (eds), *Political Institutions of the German Revolution, 1918–1919* (Stanford, Calif., 1966).

D. K. Buse, 'Friedrich Ebert and the German Crisis, 1917–1920', *Central European History*, 5 (1972), pp. 234–55.

F. L. Carsten, *Revolution in Central Europe, 1918–1919* (London, 1972).

F. L. Carsten, *War Against War: British and German Radical Movements in the First World War* (Berkeley, 1982).

R. A. Comfort, *Revolutionary Hamburg* (Stanford, Calif., 1966).

U. Daniel, 'Women's Work in Industry and Family: Germany 1914–1918', in R. Wall and J. Winter (eds), *The Upheaval of War* (Cambridge, 1988), pp. 267–96.

M. Eksteins, *The Rites of Spring* (New York, 1990).

K. Epstein, *Matthias Erzberger and the Dilemma of German Democracy* (Princeton, NJ, 1959).

L. Farrar, *The Short War Illusion* (Santa Barbara, Calif., 1973).

G. D. Feldman, *Army, Industry, and Labor in Germany, 1914–1918* (Princeton, NJ, 1966).

M. Ferro, *The Great War 1914–1918* (London, 1973).

F. Fischer, *Germany's Aims in the First World War* (London, 1967).

S. Freud, 'Thoughts on War and Death', *The Standard Edition of the Complete Psychological Works*, vol. 14 (London, 1957).

P. Fritzsche, *A Nation of Flyers* (Cambridge, Mass., 1992).

H. Gatzke, *Germany's Drive to the West* (Baltimore, Md., 1950).

D. Geary, 'Radicalism and the Worker: Metalworkers and Revolution 1914–23', in Evans (ed.), *Society and Politics in Wilhelmine Germany*, pp. 267–86.

C. Genno and H. Wetzel (eds), *The First World War in German Narrative Prose* (Toronto, 1980).

K. W. Hardach, *The First World War* (Berkeley, 1977).

K. Hausen, 'The German Nation's Obligation to the Heroes' Widows of World War I', in M. R. Higonnet *et al.* (eds), *Behind the Lines* (New Haven, 1987), pp. 126–40.

D. Horn, *The German Naval Mutinies of World War I* (New Brunswick, NJ, 1969).

J. Horne and A. Kramer, 'German "Atrocities" and Franco-German Opinion, 1914: The Evidence of German Soldiers' Diaries', *Journal of Modern History*, 66 (1994), pp. 1–33.

S. Kern, *The Culture of Time and Space, 1880–1918* (Cambridge, Mass., 1983).

M. Kitchen, *The Silent Dictatorship* (London, 1976).

J. Kocka, *Facing Total War. German Society 1914–1918* (Leamington Spa, 1984).

A. Kunz, *Civil Servants and the Politics of Inflation in Germany, 1914–1924* (Berlin, 1986).

E. J. Leed, *No Man's Land: Combat and Identity in World War I* (Cambridge, 1979).

T. Mann, *Reflections of a Nonpolitical Man* [1918] (New York, 1983).

A. J. Mayer, *The Politics and Diplomacy of Peacemaking* (London, 1968).

A. Mitchell, *Revolution in Bavaria* (Princeton, NJ, 1965).

R. G. Moeller, *German Peasants and Conservative Agrarian Politics, 1914–1924* (Chapel Hill, NC, 1985).

W. J. Mommsen, 'The German Revolution 1918–20', in R. Bessel and E. J. Feuchtwanger (eds), *Social Change and Political Development in Weimar Germany* (London, 1981), pp. 21–54.

D. W. Morgan, *The Socialist Left and the German Revolution* (Ithaca, NY, 1975).

G. Mosse, 'War and the Appropriation of Nature', in V. R. Berghahn and M. Kitchen (eds), *Germany in the Age of Total War* (London, 1981), pp. 102–22.

A. Offer, *The First World War: An Agrarian Interpretation* (Oxford, 1989).

E. M. Remarque, *All Quiet on the Western Front* (various edns).

L. J. Rupp, *Mobilizing Women for War* (Princeton, NJ, 1978).

A. J. Ryder, *The German Revolution of 1918* (Cambridge, 1967).

G. Silberstein, *The Troubled Alliance: German-Austrian Relations 1914–1916* (Lexington, KY., 1970).

D. Stevenson, *French War Aims Against Germany, 1914–1919* (Oxford, 1982).

J. Tampke, *The Ruhr and Revolution* (London, 1979).

C. P. Vincent, *The Politics of Hunger: The Allied Blockade of Germany, 1915–1919* (Athens, OH, 1985).

R. M. Watt, *The Kings Depart* (London, 1969).

R. W. Whalen, *Bitter Wounds. German Victims of the Great War, 1914–1939* (Ithaca, NY, 1984).

J. G. Williamson, *Karl Helfferich, 1872–1924: Economist, Financier, Politician* (Princeton, NJ, 1971).

R. Wohl, *The Generation of 1914* (Cambridge, Mass., 1979).

C. Zuckmayer, *A Part of Myself* (New York, 1970).

INDEX